The New Class Society

The New Class Society

Goodbye American Dream?

Third Edition

Robert Perrucci and Earl Wysong

ROWMAN & LITTLEFIELD PUBLISHERS, INC.
Lanham • Boulder • New York • Toronto • Plymouth, UK

ROWMAN & LITTLEFIELD PUBLISHERS, INC.

Published in the United States of America
by Rowman & Littlefield Publishers, Inc.
A wholly owned subsidiary of The Rowman & Littlefield Publishing Group, Inc.
4501 Forbes Boulevard, Suite 200, Lanham, Maryland 20706
www.rowmanlittlefield.com

Estover Road
Plymouth PL6 7PY
United Kingdom

British Library Cataloguing in Publication Information Available

Library of Congress Cataloging-in-Publication Data
Perrucci, Robert.
  The new class society : goodbye American dream? / Robert Perrucci & Earl Wysong.
— 3rd ed.
    p. cm.
  Includes bibliographical references and index.
  ISBN-13: 978-0-7425-4553-3 (cloth : alk. paper)
  ISBN-10: 0-7425-4553-9 (cloth : alk. paper)
  ISBN-13: 978-0-7425-4554-0 (pbk. : alk. paper)
  ISBN-10: 0-7425-4554-7 (pbk. : alk. paper)
  1. Social classes—United States. 2. United States—Social conditions—1980–
I. Wysong, Earl, 1944– II. Title.
  HN90.S6P47 2008
  305.50973—dc22   2007011493

Printed in the United States of America

∞™ The paper used in this publication meets the minimum requirements of
American National Standard for Information Sciences—Permanence of Paper
for Printed Library Materials, ANSI/NISO Z39.48-1992.

Contents

Tables and Figures

TABLES

FIGURES

Preface

More than thirty-five years ago, soon-to-be U.S. Supreme Court Justice Lewis F. Powell Jr. warned, in a memo to the U.S. Chamber of Commerce, that the free enterprise system was under attack by antibusiness forces. He called on the business community "to take direct political action" in support of its shared interests. Powell's memo was part of the beginning of what we describe in chapter 2 as the "political dimension of the class war." Powell and many wealthy Americans in the business community were concerned with declining corporate profits and with what they saw as an alarming expansion of the U.S. welfare state in the 1960s and 1970s. To reverse these developments would require a coordinated, well-funded, and multifaceted response by wealthy elites in the business community. We view the response that emerged in the 1970s and that has continued to the present as a one-sided class war waged on many fronts against the political and economic interests of the working class by large segments of the wealthiest American class. This class, which includes the owners and senior executives of major U.S. corporations, has, with the assistance of many affluent Americans who are part of what we call the privileged class, achieved a multidecade record of stunning victories over working-class interests. Profits are up, unions are down, and the shares of national income and wealth received and held by the wealthiest Americans are at or near historic record highs. The thirty-year track record of economic and political successes achieved by and for wealthy Americans has been mirrored by thirty years of stagnating wages and declining economic prospects for working-class Americans.

When we began writing the first edition of this book more than a decade ago, the features we viewed as central to the "new class" society included the melding of organizational structures, resources, and class interests—most notably among affluent Americans, a one-sided class war against workers, and the growing polarization of classes. At the time, there was not much scholarly or public attention paid to these features and others we explored in the first edition. But in recent years our exploration of the causes, contours, and consequences of the "new class" society has become a less lonely enterprise. The last few years have witnessed the emergence of a kind of "cottage industry" of inequality studies. Several authors have produced books, articles, and reports on various aspects of economic and/or class inequalities. This edition will likely be competing for readers and shelf space with other books focused on inequality issues. Even so, we think our book provides readers with a unique and compelling framework for understanding the organizational foundations of the U.S. class structure, the ongoing class war, the causes and consequences of class inequalities, and the prospects for reducing class inequalities and redeeming the American Dream.

When we wrote the preface to the second edition of our book, September 11 had just occurred. We used the occasion of that traumatic terrorist attack on the World Trade Center as a point of departure for discussing the multiple links that tie the concentration of economic and corporate power together in American society. As we write this preface to the third edition of our book, we think it is useful to discuss the links between an event of political significance in 2006, the midterm elections, and issues concerning the U.S. class structure and class inequalities.

On November 7, 2006, American voters shifted control of Congress from the Republican Party to the Democratic Party. In the 110th Congress, Democrats assumed control of all congressional committees responsible for shaping legislation. What can we realistically expect from the new Congress? The 2006 elections, many pundits claimed, produced a new political landscape, but is this the case where class inequalities are concerned? Is the 2007–2008 Democrat-controlled Congress likely to enact legislation that would seriously address the increasing polarization of American society into a secure, privileged class and an ever-more insecure new working class?

An old U.S. folk phrase suggests a partial answer to the questions posed above: "he who pays the piper calls the tune." This bit of wisdom may be doubly true in politics, where political campaigns continue to be funded by individual and corporate donors with "deep pockets." There is another folk saying from Latin America: "Political revolutions are like playing the violin. You pick it up with your left hand, and play it with your right." The combination of these two aphorisms, if we accept them as reflecting a modicum of political "truth," suggests we may have good reasons to be skeptical about the ability or willingness of the new Congress to enact legislation that will significantly reverse the declining educational and occupational opportunities for working-class Americans.

While still basking in the glow of their victory, Democratic congressional leaders identified a number of high-priority legislative items, including increasing the minimum wage, providing college students with tuition tax credits, reforming congressional ethics, and making prescription drugs more affordable. Each of these ideas seems worthy of consideration, but none of them addresses the widening income-wealth gap between the privileged class and the working class. If the political power shift to the Democrats is to make a difference for working-class Americans, it would need to produce new federal tax and spend policies that would *redistribute* economic resources from the privileged class to the working class. Such legislation would be a signal that the legislative branch of the federal government had become an advocate of working-class interests in the class war. But with congressional political campaigns largely financed by wealthy Americans, it is difficult to imagine such a scenario.

If the redistribution of class-based economic resources from the wealthy to the workers is not likely to be a high priority for members of Congress from either party, what can we expect? Very likely we will hear many members trumpeting the cause of "middle-class Americans." This tired cliché means nothing where the class interests of workers are concerned. It allows politicians to appear as *if* they support the interests of a broad group of working Americans (the "middle class"), while not actually supporting workers' interests in any meaningful fashion. As progressives know, this is the "middle-class scam."

After more than three decades of a class war that has shifted more and more of America's wealth from the working class to the privileged class, many believe it is time for the pendulum to swing in the other direction. But the pendulum will need a strong push, and it will have to come from millions of working-class Americans who support progressive social movement organizations that represent their interests. Only then will Congress act.

Acknowledgments

The publication of this third installment of our "New Class Project" was facilitated by the efforts and contributions of many people. We are grateful to executive editor Alan McClare for his strong and consistent support of our interest in developing a third edition that would not only update the content of earlier editions but also include provocative new features. With Alan's support, we crafted a volume that extends our fresh approach to class analysis, continues our attention to the intersection of class, gender, and racial inequalities, and incorporates a new series of "class issues in the media" features at the end of each chapter to further engage readers' awareness and understanding of class issues and inequalities. We appreciate the assistance of several individuals associated with Rowman & Littlefield who helped move the third edition to completion. We are especially indebted to Lynn Weber for her close reading of the manuscript, her editing prowess, and her attention to many details, which resulted in changes that added clarity and precision to the third edition. However, the authors are responsible for any and all errors or mistakes that may remain in the book.

We would also like to express our appreciation to several contributors who provided materials that made possible many of the distinctive features of the book. Tony Faiola prepared the fine graphics found throughout the book. Artists Lloyd Dangle, Ted Rall, and Tom Tomorrow (aka Dan Perkins) created the cartoons "with attitude" that are woven into the chapters. Comedian Dave Lippman wrote the analysis of late-night television comedy shows found at the end of chapter 7. Dr. David W. Wright, Wichita State University, shared with us many of his original research materials—including data on U.S. workers' incomes as well as findings on occupational patterns and trends. Selected features of his work were incorporated into the book at various points, referenced by footnotes, and noted in the bibliography.

Finally, we would like to thank the many readers, supporters, and instructors who found the earlier editions of the book to be informative and useful (as well as critical readers who took the time to write and explain their reactions to us). We are grateful to past readers and we hope that they, along with many new readers, will find the third edition "strikes sparks" that illuminate—in new and useful ways—the study of class analysis and inequalities.

1

Class in America

My momma always said that life is like a box of chocolates. You never know what you're gonna get.

—*Forrest Gump*, 1994

The lead character of the popular film *Forrest Gump* illustrates that despite limitations of intellect, his pure heart, guileless character, sincerity, hard work, and positive mental attitude enable him to prevail over life's hardships. Gump's disarming qualities defrost the cynicism of a heartless world and open the path to material success, social respect, and personal fulfillment. His achievements appear to affirm his momma's homily, reinforce belief in the American Dream, and give testimony to the pervasive ideological belief that all men are created equal.

However, movie ideals often clash with social realities. Is life really like a box of chocolates—unpredictable and capricious in detail but essentially rewarding to the pure of heart? Consider the contrast between the fictional experience of Forrest Gump and the real-life experiences of Jim Farley.

Jim Farley's fellow workers at Federal Mogul Corporation's roller bearing plant on the east side of Detroit called him Big Jim—not so much because of the size of his body, they said, as because of the size of his heart.

They liked the soft-spoken yet tough manner in which he represented them as a union committeeman. And they liked his willingness to sit down over a shot and a beer at the nearby Office Lounge and listen to the problems they had with their jobs, their wives, or their bowling scores.

Jim Farley had come North from eastern Kentucky, because mechanization of the mines and slumping demand for coal made finding work there impossible. The idea of leaving behind the mountains where he had grown up for the punch-in,

1

punch-out factory life in a big city like Detroit didn't appeal to him much—but nei-ther did the thought of living on relief, like so many unemployed miners in his hol-low and most others in Pike County. . . .

Federal Mogul announced that it would be phasing out its Detroit operations by early 1974 and moving bearing production to a new plant in Alabama. Farley, say those who knew him, became a different man almost overnight—tense, moody, withdrawn. A month after the announcement he suffered a heart attack. Physically, he recovered rapidly. Mentally, things got worse. His family and friends called it "nerves." . . .

With close to 20 years at Federal Mogul, the thought of starting all over again—in an unfamiliar job, with no seniority and little hope for a decent pension—was not pleasant. But Farley had little choice. Three times he found work, and three times he failed the physical because of his heart problem. The work itself posed no difficulty, but none of the companies wanted to risk high workers' compensa-tion and health insurance premiums when there were plenty of young, strong workers looking for jobs.

As Farley's layoff date approached, he grew more and more apprehensive. He was 41 years old: what would happen if he couldn't find another job? His wife had gone to work at the Hall Lamp Company, so the family would have some in-come. But Farley's friends were being laid off, too, and most of them hadn't been able to find work yet either—a fact that worsened his outlook.

Farley was awake when Nancy left for work at 6:15 A.M. on January 29, but he decided to stay home. His nerves were so bad, he said, that he feared an ac-cident at work. His sister-in-law Shirley stopped by late that morning and found him despondent. Shortly before noon he walked from the kitchen into his bed-room and closed the door. Shirley Farley recalls hearing a single click, the sound of a small-bore pistol. She rushed to the bedroom and pounded on the door. There was no response.

Almost 20 years to the day after Jim Farley left the hills of eastern Kentucky, his dream of a secure life for his family was dead. And so was he.[1]

Most people would see Jim Farley's death as an unnecessary personal tragedy. Here was a man with severe psychological problems who simply could not cope with the stress of job loss. "Millions of people lose a job in this lifetime, but they don't commit suicide" might be the typical response. There is a strong tendency to see unemployment as individual failure and the in-ability to "bounce back" as further evidence of that failure.

But there is another way to look at Jim Farley's death, one that recognizes a long chain of life experiences that produce patterns of predictable hardship and limited opportunities. Farley's chances in life are powerfully shaped by his social-class location, which constrains opportunities. His life is like that of millions of others who barely finish high school and move through half a dozen different jobs hoping to find one that will provide a decent wage and long-term security. Yet, just as the class structure constrains the lives of people like Jim Farley, it confers numerous advantages and opportunities on others. The same class structure that shapes laws denying workers a right to a job gives companies like Federal Mogul the right to do what they wish with their property. They can close a plant with little or no consideration of their workers or the community. In fact, tax laws may provide incentives for closing plants and building new ones in countries with lower-wage workers. The conditions leading to Jim Farley's death some twenty-five years ago have now spread across the land. Millions of workers in stable, high-wage jobs in America's basic industries have been told they are no longer needed. Thousands of plants are closed and sit empty in steel towns along the rivers of the Monongahela Valley in Pennsylvania. They were among the first to go in the dramatic reshaping of America's class structure that eliminated the middle-class worker, and they were soon followed by similar dislocations in the auto, textiles, glass, and electronics industries.

After the flight of manufacturing to foreign shores, corporate America's appetite for profits began to turn to its white-collar labor force. Suddenly, the giant corporations like IBM, AT&T, and GM discovered "downsizing" or "rightsizing" or "restructuring," in which the use of new technology and new work organization resulted in a 10 to 20 percent reduction in employees. The 1990s brought the global economy, and it became the corporate "bogeyman," disciplining workers with the constant threat of further shutdowns and layoffs to allow American firms to compete with other firms and other workers across the globe.

What are we to make of America's love affair with Forrest Gump? Why the attraction to the Gump myth in the face of the harsh realities? Maybe believing that life is like a box of chocolates leads to an expectation of sweet (but mixed) outcomes and makes predictable class-based disappointments and hardships easier to bear. After all, during the Great Depression of the 1930s, Hollywood produced some of its most upbeat and fanciful films.

To make sense of Jim Farley's death (and maybe even the popularity of Forrest Gump), we need to recognize that the American class structure in the past thirty years has been dramatically altered. What we are seeing is not a temporary aberration that will be soon put right but a fundamental shift in the distribution of economic and political power that constitutes the class structure. To understand the declining fortunes of millions of Jim Farleys and the corporate decisions of thousands of Federal Moguls, it is necessary to examine the workings of class structure and how it shapes the lives of workers, the decisions of politicians, and the actions of corporations.

INEQUALITY

The real news is that the median wage—the take-home pay of the worker smack in the middle of the earnings ladder—is still less than it was before the last recession. At the same time the upper reaches of America have never had it so good.

—Robert B. Reich, *Nation*, February 16, 1998

Most Americans have a keen sense of the presence of inequality. We learn about it in many ways on a daily basis from our observations of people, homes, cars, neighborhoods, and news accounts of the "rich and famous." There is good evidence that we start to learn about inequality at a very early age and accumulate additional knowledge throughout our lives.[2]

If we were to talk with a group of "average" Americans about their awareness of social differences among people in our society, we might hear something like the following:

> It's those ballplayers and movie stars that make all the money. Millions of dollars a year for playing a game or acting like a jerk in front of a camera. Then there's the rock stars getting rich off the videos they sell to kids.
>
> The middle class is getting a screwing. The honest, hard-working slob who pays taxes, tries to raise a family, and has a helluva time making ends meet. It used to be that hard work would pay off with a steady job, a house of your own, and a decent car. But you can forget about that happening today.
>
> There are lots of people in this country who are called poor, because their income is below some official poverty line. Some of these people are probably in bad shape through no fault of their own. But there's a lot who just don't want to work, who would rather get a government check and food stamps. I would rather take a minimum-wage job than lose my self-respect by taking handouts.

Most Americans are aware of different forms of inequality. They know about income inequality and the patterns of discrimination against women and racial and ethnic groups. This awareness can be traced to stories in the mass media or what they may have learned in courses in high school or college. Knowledge of inequality is often conveyed in stories about the gender gap in salary, or the homeless, or the number of children or older Americans living below the poverty line. But what about the social arrangements that produce inequality and are responsible for its persistence? A pervasive form of inequality cuts across age, race, ethnicity, and gender to confer privilege on a minority of Americans while relegating the rest to varying degrees of insecurity, need, or despair. This is class inequality, a structured system of unequal rewards that provides enormous advantages to a small percentage of people in the United States at the expense of the overwhelming majority. Inequality is contained within a class system that resembles a game of monopoly that is "rigged" so that only certain players have a chance to own Park Place, and a great many others go directly to jail.

The discussion of class in America is a taboo subject because of the national reluctance to examine how the class system of the United States operates on a day-to-day basis. We do not learn from our schools or media how a privileged but organized minority of Americans is able to amass a disproportionate share of our national wealth and to transmit that privilege across generations to create a permanent economic, political, and social elite class. This structured class inequality is both the cause and the consequence of the ability to control important resources such as money, education, votes, or information. And for this system to work, the majority of disadvantaged Americans must be persuaded to believe that the way things work out for people is fair. This is done by distracting attention from class inequality and focusing the national spotlight on conflict between blacks and whites, women and men, gays and straights, pro-choice and antiabortion partisans. Evidence that class is a taboo topic comes from Project Censored, a Sonoma State University study of the mainstream media's coverage of important news stories.[3] A panel of over one hundred faculty and community judges identified the most important news stories of 2004 and the coverage given to these stories in the media. The top-ranked story in importance that was poorly covered in the mainstream media was "Wealth Inequality in the Twenty-First Century Threatens Economy and Democracy."

American society is complex. It contains a diverse population of people of different races, ethnic origins, and religions. The people are divided across a complicated and shifting political spectrum spanning liberalism, the radical Right, the religious Right, conservativism, libertarianism, and democratic socialism. Politics are played out across a dizzying array of interest groups concerned about the environment, abortion, flag burning, animal rights, prayer in schools, gun ownership, sexual harassment, and sexual lifestyles and hundreds of other groups that are for or against something. Some of these interest groups confront each other over their different ideas on rights, justice, and freedom—or what we might call the "pursuit of happiness." However, most of the interest groups try to use the powers of government to aid them by changing tax law, funding health care, or reducing air pollution. This means that to be successful, interest groups have to lobby members of Congress. And government, with its millions of employees and thousands of agencies and departments, oversees the use of a $2.6 trillion budget, a task that entails taking money from most people and giving some of it to other people.

The day-to-day operation of this society is made possible by the 140 million Americans who are in the labor force. The work they do is described in the ten thousand occupations listed in the *Dictionary of Occupational Titles*. The economy, often described as if it were separate from the rest of society, is made up of thousands of establishments where people make a living, from the multinational General Motors with 324,000 employees worldwide (in 2005) to the family-owned Korean grocery in Brooklyn.

Many of those Americans who are still socially alert and concerned about how our society works read newspapers and magazines, watch news programs on television, or belong to an interest group. But the socially aware are probably also overwhelmed by this entity we call society (a nineteenth-century French sociologist called it "the Great Being"). The complexity, the contradictions, the madness of modern life lead the average American to alternate between anger, involvement, and frustration and often finally to withdraw into some safe haven or escapist activity.

Everyday life has become so complicated that we have created a host of new occupations for people whose job it is to keep us informed about the workings of "the Great Being." These jobs are found in what is humorously referred to as the "hot-air sector" of our economy, where "experts," "pundits," and "advocates" give us an hour-by-hour, blow-by-blow account of the number of jobs created or lost, the strength or weakness of long-term bonds, the creeping or waning of inflation, and the international crisis of the week involving famines, floods, and "ethnic conflicts" (although the Russian bear has been caged, the world is still portrayed as a dangerous place). We get some relief from the hot-air sector by tuning in on "drop your pants in public" talk shows like the *Jerry Springer Show* or the fantasy/reality shows that promote voyeurism and dream makeovers of homes, bodies, and families. The daily accounts of murder and mayhem (especially gang violence and drive-by shootings) are presented as if they are happening in our own city or on our own block. This image of complexity is intimidating and keeps millions of Americans from taking an active interest in civic life.

Amid all this complexity and contradiction and conflict, is it any wonder that most Americans have lost confidence in their elected officials, corporations, schools, or unions? Is it any wonder that fewer than four in ten citizens vote in presidential elections? Americans seem to be constantly off balance, unsure about what to believe, suspicious of every leader who promises a "better way," and ultimately cynical about the possibilities for change. Escape may be the only way out, or so it seems. If we have the money or credit cards, we can escape into consumerism. If not, there is television, booze, or drugs.

But there is another way to look at American society; it is a view that is rarely presented in newspapers, discussed on television, or taught to our school children. This view says that it is possible to understand how society works and how the pursuit of happiness becomes available to some but not to others; that amid all the complexity, one can find stable and enduring patterns in our collective lives. The stable and enduring pattern that is the focus of this book is the new class system.

MAPPING THE CLASS STRUCTURE: PAST TRADITIONS AND NEW REALITIES

Mapping the U.S. social-class structure and defining what class means in America have always been difficult and slippery tasks. Academic sociologists, journalists, and pundits have applied a variety of contrasting images and approaches to these topics. The use of such varied approaches has contributed to confusion and inconsistencies in academic and public arenas concerning the nature of the American class structure and how class can best be defined. Even so, poll data indicate that most Americans recognize the existence of a clearly identifiable, patterned U.S. class structure, as well as the reality and importance of class inequalities. Survey findings suggest that Americans tend to view class structure in terms of a cakelike image, with groups of people organized into layers and stacked in a ranking system that ranges from low to high across gradual and shaded degrees of class differences. Such a view implies that the people grouped together within each layer are part of a specific social class and that class location is based on the possession of similar shares of important resources. This image appears to include the notion that class is partly a function of economic factors as well as cultural and lifestyle differences among people.

Sociological models of class structure and definitions of social class have sought to achieve greater precision and clarity than public views and images. But whereas some academic maps and definitions are similar to public perceptions, others are strikingly different. Although past sociological efforts to map the class structure and define class have not been uniform, they have tended to be organized around one of two distinct traditions or approaches—the production model and the functionalist model.

The production model is a kind of single-factor approach in which people's positions in the production process (and their possession of economic wealth) occupy center stage. It views class structure as organized on the basis of the relationship people have with the means of production: people tend to be either owners of productive wealth, like factories, offices, malls, airlines, rental properties, and small businesses, or nonowners—workers.

This approach is grounded in the work of Karl Marx, who focused on owner (bourgeoisie) and nonowner (proletariat) classes. But some contemporary sociologists (neo-Marxists) have refined and extended the original two-class model to reflect the reality that the production and corresponding occupational structures are much more complex today than they were in the 1880s.[4] Recent sociological variations of this approach move beyond the two-class model to produce a multilevel image of class structure with a relatively short list of levels or classes. However, unlike the public image of classes shading into one another because of gradually shifting economic and lifestyle differences, Marxian production models view the class structure as more sharply divided by inequalities that reflect people's positions in the production process. In these models, classes are typically based on occupational categories, such as owners, managers, small employers, semiautonomous employees, and hourly wage workers. In each instance, class position is based on a person's location in the production process—which also closely corresponds to the possession of income and wealth and to the occupational roles people perform. Owners (big and small) set policy and control the production process; managers assist owners and act as "order givers," who oversee the production process and often accumulate portions of productive wealth themselves; workers are "order takers" and typically do not share in the ownership of productive wealth (or at most own only very small portions); the poor are excluded from both ownership and most forms of desirable work. (But according to this model, some segments of the poor may be used by owners and managers from time to time as a force to pressure workers into accepting lower wages or less desirable working conditions.)

The functionalist model was partly inspired by Max Weber's view that social stratification is a complex, multidimensional phenomenon and cannot be understood on the basis of a single factor. Unlike the Marxian production model, in which ownership and control (or the lack of it) are critical to producing the class structure (and defining class), the functionalist approach provides a cake-like image of the class structure and views the layers (classes) as organized according to variations in the levels of prestige. Prestige levels are viewed as reflecting a combination of several qualities individuals possess. These include the level of importance attached by cultural values to different occupational categories individuals occupy, educational levels they attain, and variations in their incomes. Although money does matter somewhat in some functionalist models, prestige—especially occupational prestige, not wealth per se—is the critical factor shaping the class structure and locating people within it. According to functionalist models, occupations requiring advanced formal education such as teaching and social work confer high levels of prestige on people who work at them, even though their income levels may be lower than some factory or business occupations requiring less education.

As noted, functionalist models encourage a layer-cake view of the class structure. In contrast to production-model views of sharp class divisions based on production positions and economic wealth, functionalist models envision a multilayer class structure with shaded degrees of prestige and income dividing the social classes. Thus, functionalist models are somewhat similar to the public image of class structure. But functionalist models often completely omit references to class and substitute the term *socioeconomic strata* as a way of describing the layered rankings of people possessing similar levels of prestige and economic resources. The strata that make up the class structure are typically arranged by functionalist models into descriptive class categories that are further subdivided. For example, the highest class is often divided into upper-upper-class and lower-upper-class groupings with the same "upper" and "lower" prefix designations applied to the middle and lower classes as well. Approached in this way, class structure takes on a kind of shaded, layer-cake image with classes more akin to statistical categories than groupings of real people.[5]

BEYOND TRADITION: NEW CLASS REALITIES
AND THE DISTRIBUTIONAL MODEL

If calling America a middle-class nation means anything, it means that we are a society in which most people live more or less the same kind of life. In 1970 we were that kind of society. Today we are not, and we become less like one each passing year.

—Paul Krugman, *Mother Jones*, November–December 1996

The production and functionalist models differ in many respects, but both emphasize the importance of occupation as a key factor in determining class location—although for different reasons. As we have seen, the production model emphasizes the links between occupation, production position, and class, whereas the functionalist model emphasizes the links between occupation, prestige, and socioeconomic position. Although both models have made useful contributions in analyzing class inequalities in the past, their exclusive focus on the occupationally linked factors of production and prestige is inadequate to the tasks of both describing and understanding the emerging realities and complex dimensions of the new American class system.

To more fully understand the origins, nature, and dynamics of the new class system, in this book we develop and apply a new model of class analysis. Our model retains the focus on occupations that is central to production models and incorporates consideration of organizations and the distributional processes (e.g., income, pensions, taxes) they control. We argue that a combination of location in the occupational structure (production model) and organizational membership (distribution model) can be used to identify class membership, describe our map of the stratification system, and consider the consequences of class inequalities. We refer to our approach as the distributional model of class analysis, and it includes at least four major features that distinguish it from previous models of class analysis.

The first distinctive feature of our model is our view that the emerging new class system is organizationally based. This means that the class structure is viewed as increasingly organized around and through large, organizational structures and processes that control the distribution of several forms of valuable economic and social resources. We maintain that large organizations—through various levels and groups of "gatekeepers" within them—direct, channel, and legitimate the distribution of these resources to individuals and groups. Occupations are still important in our approach, not simply because of their role in production but because of the organizations in which their work is conducted. Lawyers are not important as lawyers; they are important because of the firms in which and for which they do their work. This view is directly linked to the second important feature of our approach: We define classes as collectivities of individuals and families with comparable total resources over time. The condition "over time" is used to emphasize that variations in the levels of resources distributed to and held by individuals and families tends to persist over time (i.e., within and between generations) and that their impact on the life chances and experiences of people occupying different classes is substantial and enduring. Class location reflects the extent to which people possess combinations of four forms of generative economic and social resources: investment, consumption, skill, and social capital (discussed later). People possess variations in these forms of capital in large measure owing to the nature and extent of the links they have to upper-level authority positions within corporate, government, and cultural structures. Thus, we view the class structure as being largely shaped by the distribution of organizationally controlled forms of capital that, held in greater or lesser amounts, determine the class locations of individuals and groups.

A third major feature of our approach concerns the idea that large organizations are centrally involved in legitimating the distributional processes, as well as the class inequalities that arise from them. As we will see in later chapters, this means that large organizations are key sources for generating various forms and kinds of idea systems and explanations that justify the distribution of the four forms of capital to various individuals and groups as fair and legitimate. The fourth and final major feature of our approach rests on our assertion that the U.S. class structure is increasingly polarized by class inequalities into two broad class divisions. This leads us to argue that the new class system more closely approximates a double-diamond image of class structure than the cakelike, stacked-layer images evoked by earlier models of class analysis.

Our distributional model takes into account the reality that large organizations dominate the economic, political, and cultural landscapes today and through complex distributional structures and processes shape the nature and details of the new American class system. In this system, social classes consist of collections of real people (not statistical categories) who hold similar levels of, and have similar access to, the four forms of generative capital. These forms of capital are distributed to class members through organizationally based structures and processes that, as we will see, are dominated by privileged groups who themselves possess high levels of all four forms of capital.

GENERATIVE CAPITAL AND CLASS STRUCTURE

Our image of a double-diamond class structure is based on the way that vital life-sustaining resources are distributed and the availability of these resources over time. In some societies the most important resource is land because it allows one to grow food to eat and to exchange the surplus food for housing, health care, and seeds to grow more food. Peasant farmers in Central America are permanently impoverished because most land is held in large estates. These estates produce coffee or cotton for export; that is, they produce for foreign exchange or money. Peasants, without land, face the choice of starvation, working for the owner of a large landholding, or moving to the city in search of work.

In American society today, capital is the main resource used in exchange for what we need and want, and it is found in four forms: consumption capital, investment capital, skill capital, and social capital. We call these resources generative capital because they can produce more of the same resource when invested, or they can contribute to the production of another resource (e.g., social capital can produce investment capital).

Consumption Capital

Consumption capital is usually thought of as income—what we get in our wages and salary, unemployment checks, Social Security, or welfare checks. The lucky people have enough of it to buy food and clothing, pay the rent or mortgage, and make payments on the furniture or car. The really lucky people have a little money left over. But for most people, there is plenty of month left over when the money runs out.

When thinking about how much consumption capital families have and how they spend it, we immediately recognize that food can mean lobster or macaroni and cheese; clothing can mean second-hand from the thrift shop or name brands and fashionable labels. People vary in their weekly or monthly consumption capital, and two families with the same monthly income may choose to spend it in very different ways.

Figure 1.1 describes the distribution of income among families in the United States in 2002. Almost 18 percent of the families had incomes above

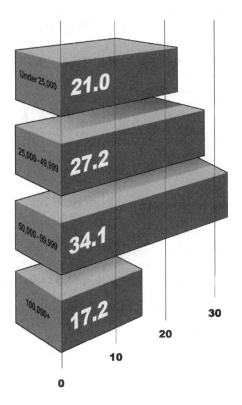

Figure 1.1. Money Income of Families, 2002

Source: Mishel, Bernstein, and Allegretto 2005.

$100,000 per year. At the other extreme, 21 percent of families had annual incomes below $25,000. The general pattern of the distribution of family income over the last thirty years reveals an increase in the proportion of families with upper levels of income and a decrease in the families with middle-level income. In 1969, about 4 percent of families had incomes of $100,000 or more. This percentage increased to 8 percent in 1989 and to over 18 percent in 2000. Across this same time period, middle-level incomes ($25,000 to $50,000) declined from 41 percent of families in 1969, to 33 percent in 1979, to 30 percent in 1989, and finally to 27.5 percent in 2000. About one-quarter of all families across the four time periods had incomes below $25,000, putting many Americans in the category of "working poor."[6]

Consumption capital is closely linked to position in the system of production, or occupation. Some jobs pay a lot more than others, but there is also large variation in the incomes of people with the same occupation. Salaries of lawyers, professors, or engineers may vary from upper six figures at the high end to incomes barely above the national average for wage and salaried workers. (In 2003, the median household income for wage and salaried workers was $43,318.) Thus, position in the system of production is important, but it does not tell us the full story when considering the question of income. Attempts to map the class structure by using only occupational categories or occupational prestige rankings will invariably combine persons who are getting vastly different returns on their educational assets. The salaries of lawyers, professors, or engineers will be due partly to their occupation and partly to the particular organizations in which they do their work (in addition to other resources discussed later).

Investment Capital

Investment capital is what people use to create more capital. If you have a surplus of consumption capital (the money left over when the month runs out), you can save it and earn interest each month. You can buy a house, pay off the mortgage over twenty to twenty-five years, and wait for the rising market value of homes to build equity, which you can recover if and when you sell the house. Or you can create a 401(k) account at work, or an independent retirement account (IRA), and invest in stocks or bonds to earn dividends and capital gains. You can buy an old house, a "fixer-upper," renovate it, divide it into apartments, and collect rent. If your annual rent receipts exceed the combined cost of mortgage payments, property taxes, insurance, and maintenance costs, you will earn a profit.

Most Americans have very little investment capital. Home ownership is a major source for the accumulation of family wealth. Many families depend on the rising market value of their homes as their source of retirement income. A very rosy scenario says that if you bought a house for $50,000 and sold it twenty-five years later for $150,000, that would be the main source of your retirement income. But not many Americans own homes with that kind of appreciation in value. What about retirement accounts? William Greider (*Nation*, June 27, 2005) estimates that there are forty-eight million families that have 401(k) accounts, but the median value of these accounts is $27,000. If the value of your 401(k) doubled and reached $55,000 at your retirement, you might be able to buy an annuity that would provide $398 per month and keep you at the poverty level. However, the reality of private investment accounts like the 401(k) or IRA is that only the most affluent Americans have enough surplus income to amass savings in such accounts. At one time, employers provided their workers with defined-benefit pension plans, but they are becoming a thing of the past, leaving most Americans with only their Social Security when they stop working.

If you have a great deal of investment capital, you can live off returns on investments in stocks or investments in a business. If you own a business, it probably means that you will employ others and will have to decide how much to pay workers and whether or not to provide them with health insurance or retirement plans. The less you need to pay them, the more you will have for yourself.

The are many ways to use investment capital to produce wealth, which provides power and independence and is a major source of well-being for families. Wealth is determined by the total current value of financial assets (bank accounts, stocks, bonds, life insurance, pensions) plus durable assets such as houses or cars, minus all liabilities such as mortgages and consumer debt. Thus, we can describe a family's wealth in terms of total net worth (financial assets plus durable assets minus liabilities) or total financial wealth (only financial assets). The distinction is important because financial assets can generate income (interest, dividends) but durable assets like homes or cars are "lived in" or are for "driving around."

The level of wealth inequality in the United States is much greater than the level of income inequality. Much less is known about wealth than about income distribution in the United States, but wealth is probably a more significant indicator of inequality because of its role in transmitting privilege across generations. Some sociologists have described wealth inequality as "the buried fault line of the American social system."[7] Figure 1.2 presents the shares of total net worth and total financial wealth in 1983, 1989, 1992, and 2001 for the top 1 percent, the middle 19 percent, and the bottom 80 percent of households. It is clear that there is enormous disparity in wealth controlled by the top 20 percent of the population compared with that of the bottom 80 percent. The privileged classes in 2001 controlled 84.4 percent of total net wealth and 92.8 percent of financial wealth—both figures represent increases over 1983. Wealth provides security, well-being, independence, and power to a privileged minority in American society, who can use that wealth to advance their privileged-class interests. The members of this privileged class have accumulated wealth while in positions that are at the intersection of an occupation

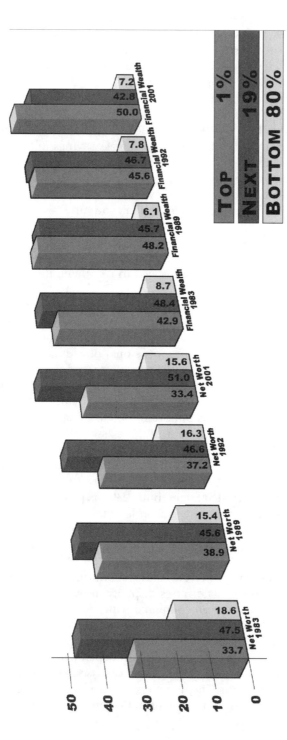

Figure 1.2. Percentage Shares of Total Net Worth and Total Financial Wealth, 1983–2001

Source: Edward N. Wolff 2004, 67; Mishel et al. 2005, 282, 287.

and an organizational position. Consider the case of a new Ph.D. in business from the University of Chicago who received a starting salary of at least $100,000 at Columbia University, while another Ph.D. recipient from an obscure business school may receive $50,000 for a starting salary at a less prestigious university.[8] This same new Ph.D. from the University of Chicago received comparable offers from Harvard, Duke, and the University of North Carolina. This is clearly a case of elite universities preparing their graduates for positions in elite universities and paying salaries that serve to enhance the salaries of everyone else at those elite universities.

Those with significant wealth are likely to be the corporate elite, top managers, doctors and corporate lawyers, members of Congress, White House staff, cabinet officials, professors at elite universities, media elite, "talking heads" on television, and assorted cultural elites. They are Democrats and Republicans, conservatives and liberals, Christians and Jews, pro-choice and antiabortion supporters, radical feminists and Promise Keepers. They have a common commitment to keeping 80 percent of the population "bamboozled" while pretending to represent their interests. They have a common bond, which is high income, job security, and wealth, and they will rig the rules of the game in order to preserve and extend their privilege.

Skill Capital

Skill capital is the specialized knowledge that people accumulate through their work experience, training, or education. Skilled plumbers learn their craft through apprenticeship programs and years of on-the-job experience. Skilled doctors learn their craft primarily in medical schools, but their skills are developed further through work experience.

Skill capital is exchanged in a labor market, just as investment capital is used in connection with a financial market. Both plumbers and doctors try to get the highest return for their skill in the form of wages or fees, and they do this through collective associations like labor unions (United Automobile Workers) or medical societies (American Medical Association). When skill capital is organized in the form of collective associations, there is greater likelihood of job security or high wages. Workers with unorganized skills (i.e., nonunion) or with low levels of skill are more vulnerable when dealing with employers or clients.

The most important source of skill capital in today's society is located in the elite universities that provide the credentials for the privileged class. For example, the path into corporate law with six-figure salaries and million-dollar partnerships is provided by about two dozen elite law schools where the children of the privileged class enroll. Similar patterns exist for medical school graduates, research scientists, and those holding professional degrees in management and business. After the credentialed skill is provided by elite universities, the market value of that skill (and its income- and wealth-producing capability) is protected by powerful corporations and professional associations. People in high income- and wealth-producing professions will seek to protect their market value not only for themselves but also for their children, who will enter similar fields.

Social Capital

Social capital is the network of social ties that people have to family, friends, and acquaintances. These ties can provide emotional support, financial assistance, and information about jobs. Social capital is used by immigrants in deciding which communities they will settle in when they come to the United States. These same immigrants use social capital to get settled and to find jobs. Social ties are also used by doctors, lawyers, and other professionals to facilitate their affiliations with more or less prestigious organizations where they will begin to "practice" their work.

The basis of social ties can be found in school ties and in kinship, religious, and political affiliations. For example, graduates of elite universities often become the new recruits at national law firms, major corporations, foundations, and government agencies. A study by the Office of Management and Budget reports that 40 percent of foreign service professionals in the State Department come from eight Ivy League colleges. Another example is found in a story in the *New York Times* (November 10, 1995) about some of the appointments made of new lawyers to join the staff of New York State's new attorney general. One new employee is the daughter of the best friend of the state's U.S. senator; she is paid $75,000 a year. Another employee just admitted to the bar is the daughter of another lawyer who served on the attorney general's election committee; she is paid $60,000 a year.[9] But social capital is used for more than just getting high-paid secure jobs. It is also used to solidify class interests by making sure that people marry within their corporate or professional class. For example, consider the type of "personal ad" that appears in many upscale magazines for the young urban professional:

> Join the Ivy League of Dating. Graduates and faculty of the Ivies, Seven Sisters, Johns Hopkins, M.I.T., Stanford, U. of Chicago, CAL Tech, Duke, U.C. Berkeley, Northwestern, meet alumni and academics. The Right Stuff! Call XXX–XXX–XXXX.

One has to wonder what the "right stuff" is. These ads may appeal to people who are simply trying to meet someone on their intellectual level, but they could instead join MENSA, an association of people with high IQ. More likely it is an effort to match same-class individuals with credentialed skills. This is the way to get dual-earner-household doctors, attorneys, and corporate elites or the "mixed marriages" of doctors and fashion designers or artists who become the "darlings" of *People* magazine fare.

Although everyone has at least a minimal level of social capital, it should be clear that access to different forms of social capital (like consumption, investment, and skill capital) is distributed very unequally. Having a family member able to loan you $100 or a friend who works in a retail store and can tell you about a job opening is not the same as being a member of a fraternity or sorority at an elite university. Social capital refers to current memberships people hold in social networks that are linked to varying levels of organizational power, prestige, and opportunities. Individuals can be connected by strong ties (e.g., family members) or weak ties (e.g., acquaintances) to formal and informal social networks that are associated with varying levels of organizational resources and power. A person's position in these social networks provides access to information and opportunities that can be converted into important financial and social benefits. For example, the extent of investment capital owned or controlled can be the result of holding high positions in large organizations; paid and unpaid leadership positions in economic, political, or cultural organizations can be used to advance personal careers or provide opportunities for relatives and friends. Thus, social capital must be viewed as a class-linked resource that both protects and advances privilege and provides a barrier for those "upstarts" seeking to expand their generative capital.

GENERATIVE CAPITAL AND POWER

The residents of one zip code—10021—on New York City's Upper East Side contributed more money to Congress during the 1994 elections than did all the residents of 24 states.

—Ellen Miller and Randy Kehler, *Dollars and Sense*, July–August 1996

The distribution of these scarce and valued resources—consumption capital, investment capital, skill capital, and social capital—is the basis for class inequality among individuals and families in America. This inequality is revealed when resources are converted into economic power, political power, and social power. Economic power is based on the resource of money (consumption capital and investment capital), and it usually is used to provide food, shelter, and clothing. People who have more economic power can buy more things and better things and thereby make their lives more comfortable and enjoyable. Money can be converted into other valued things like health care, which enables those with more money to live longer and healthier lives. Money can protect people when unfortunate or unforeseen events occur, like an earthquake, tornado, or flood. Recovering from these natural disasters and from human disasters like unemployment or illness is possible when you have economic power. Money also has the special quality of being transferable to others and can be used to transmit advantage.

Consumption capital can be used to procure social capital. For example, families with money can use it to help secure the futures of their children by purchasing special experiences through travel, tennis lessons, scuba diving, dance, and the creative arts in the hope that such experiences will foster or strengthen social relationships with others having similar experiences. It is also done by buying entry into prestigious educational institutions that provide their students with lifelong advantages. Families who buy elite educational degrees for their children are using their consumption capital to develop both social capital and skill capital. Graduates of elite universities have a special advantage in converting their credentialed skill capital into better jobs. They establish the social contacts that can be used later in life to solidify or enhance their social position. Many families, recognizing the payoff that comes with a degree from an elite college, prepare their children with Scholastic Aptitude Test prep courses in the eighth grade and private school education. In 2000 to 2001, Harvard University received 19,009 applications for 1,650 places in the entering class. In 2004, Harvard admitted 2,029 students from among a pool of 20,000 applicants. Those lucky enough to be selected can expect annual costs of about $40,000 for tuition, fees, room and board, and personal expenses. The median family income of a Harvard student is $150,000, indicating that these families are using their consumption capital to invest in the education of their children.

Three out of four families in the United States have very little economic power. Even so-called middle-class families on the "brink of comfort" (as they

Table 1.1.   Monthly Budget for Family of Four (1998 and 2006)

	1998	2006
Housing	$793	$942
Utilities	247	293
Furnishings	109	129
House operations	73	86
Food	555	659
Auto	558	663
Clothing	137	163
Health care	165	196
Entertainment	207	246
Other	64	76

are sometimes described—see *New York Times* story by Charisse Jones, February 18, 1995) find themselves in a constant struggle to make ends meet. There are thousands of anecdotal stories about how people struggle to meet family expenses, but the most systematic evidence is provided by the U.S. Department of Labor in its preparation of a consumption budget for an average married couple with two children (see table 1.1).[10]

This monthly budget totals $2,908, or $34,896 annually in 1998. If the 1998 figures are adjusted for inflation, or the cost of buying the same goods and services in 2006, the monthly budget is $3,453, or $41,436 annually. Although the cost of living has increased between 1998 and 2006, wages of the average worker have not kept pace with inflation. In order to have $3,453 to spend each month, the household's gross annual income (before taxes) would have to be well over $41,436, because workers must pay a payroll tax, and state and federal income taxes from their monthly pay checks. Workers pay a payroll tax for social security of .0765%, or $255 a month ($3,060 annually) on a $40,000 salary. They also pay state and federal taxes of at least 10 percent of income, for another $400 a month. Thus, in order to have a monthly disposable income of $3,453 (or $41,436 annually), while paying all taxes ($255 + $400), one would need a monthly income of $4,108 or $49,296 annually. As we know from the income distribution reported in figure 1.1, about 48 percent of families in the United States earn less than $49,999 annually.

Moreover, this budget assumes one wage earner, because a number of monthly expenditures would increase with two wage earners. Less than one-half of American families earn enough money to live by the U.S. Department of Labor budget, and when they do, they are often two-earner families. Two people working full-time, each earning about $10 per hour, will have a combined gross income of about $41,000. If two people with children are working to make this income, then you will have to add child care to the consumption budget, which can be from $100 to $300 a week. This middle-class budget for a family on the "brink of comfort" will produce nothing for savings, and little for retirement beyond social security taxes. If one or both of the wage earners in this family should experience unemployment for a month or longer, the family would be in serious difficulty.

If the hypothetical family just described is on the brink of comfort, what must things be like in a female-headed household with one or two children where the mother brings home about $1,000 a month from a $7.00-an-hour job as a retail clerk? This family is sitting on the official poverty line, or maybe one paycheck above or below it. Clearly, a household budget for three or four persons of $1,000 a month generates no economic power.

The problem facing three of every four families in the United States is not simply that they are just making ends meet—whether on $30,000 a year or $12,000 a year—but that their consumption capital is limited, unstable, and unpredictable. They cannot count on these resources over time in any predictable way, and if they should experience any period of joblessness, they will face a serious crisis. Possession of stable and secure resources over time is the key to economic power. The predictability of resources allows people to plan and save in order to provide for the future. They can think about buying a home, sending a child to college, saving for retirement, or starting a business. Most American workers have very unstable incomes, even if they are sometimes earning what seems like a "high" salary. For example, take the case of the United Auto worker employed in a General Motors assembly plant. During periods of peak production and heavy overtime, a worker might earn $5,000 per month. This is a $60,000-a-year job, assuming that the monthly salary continues all year. But that's the rub. When overtime disappears and production schedules are cut back because of overproduction, that $60,000 may be quickly cut to $40,000, or layoffs might reduce that income even more; at worst, the plant may be shut down and production moved to a lower-wage area in the United States or some other country—which is exactly what happened to hundreds of thousands of high-wage blue-collar workers in the 1970s, 1980s, and 1990s.

Political power is the result of collective actions to shape or determine decisions that limit or enhance peoples' opportunities. The tenants of a housing project can combine their time to collect signatures on a petition calling on the housing director to provide better services. Corporations in a particular sector of the economy can combine their money (economic power) to hire lobbyists who will seek to influence members of Congress to support or oppose legislation that will affect those corporations. Individuals and organizations with more economic power have a different set of opportunities for exercising political power than groups without economic power.

The clearest examples of how collective economic power can be converted into political power are in the area of corporate welfare—the practice of congressional action that provides billions of dollars in federal loans and subsidies to specific industries. More than $100 million a year goes to corporations like McDonald's, Pillsbury, and Sunkist to help them advertise their products in foreign countries. The Pentagon provides another $100 million a year to a group of semiconductor firms to help them compete internationally. This money goes not to small, struggling firms but to giants like Intel and National Semiconductor Corporation.[11] The total annual corporate welfare bill just from business tax preferences from the federal government was estimated at $195 billion in fiscal 2000.[12] In addition to special tax breaks for corporations, in 2002 the federal government spent $93 billion on programs that subsidize private business activities (Cato Institute Handbook for the 108th Congress). Groups with little economic power usually try to exercise political power through mass mobilization of persons with grievances. Bringing together hundreds or thousands of persons for a march on city hall conveys a visible sense of a perceived problem and an implied threat of disruption. The capacity to disrupt may be the only organized weapon available to those without economic resources. Such actions usually get the attention of political leaders, although this does not always produce the results desired by aggrieved groups.

Social power involves access to public services and the interpersonal networks that can be used to solve many of the day-to-day problems that confront most families. Public services like police, fire protection, and public transportation can provide people with the security to use public space for living, leisure, and getting to and from work, stores, and day-care facilities. Interpersonal networks consist of the informal groups and formal associations that are available in a community for persons with certain interests and concerns. The availability of community groups concerned about the presence of toxic-waste dumps, the spread of crime, and the quality of the schools in their communities provides opportunities for people to learn about many things in addition to toxic waste, police protection, and education. Such groups often provide links to information about jobs, or how to approach a local banker for a loan, or how to obtain information about financial aid for college students.

Opportunities to develop social power vary widely across groups. People who have jobs that provide little flexibility in their work schedules or are physically demanding may have little time or inclination for participating in community groups at the end of a hard day. Similarly, some jobs offer more opportunities than others to develop the interpersonal networks that can be drawn upon to help a family member find a job or to help in finding good and affordable legal assistance.

There is considerable evidence from social research that Americans with greater economic resources and those holding upper managerial positions in organizations are more likely to actively participate in a variety of community affairs.[13] These active participants accumulate information about community affairs and social contacts that can be used to advance or solidify the interests of one's social group. Some of the key players in this process of accumulating social power have been identified as women from professional families who are out of the labor force and have the discretionary time for civic affairs.[14] An interesting example of how social power operates among the privileged classes is provided by the case of the Morrison Knudsen Corporation.[15] It happened that the chairman's spouse started a private charity organization to provide young women with alternatives to abortion. The spouse served as unpaid executive director of the charity and was apparently successful in obtaining donors to support its activities. The success of the charity could perhaps be traced to the fact that five of the charity's directors are the spouses of directors of Morrison Knudsen, and three of the directors of the charity are senior executives of the corporation. Thus, the spouse of the board chairman of Morrison Knudsen was able to use her social power to put together a charity organization capable of drawing upon the political and economic power of directors from the privileged elite. Such opportunities would certainly not be available to a community organization trying to oppose the location of toxic-waste sites in their area or one trying to get the local police to be more responsive to the concerns of local citizens.

CLASS STRUCTURE AND CLASS SEGMENTS

The combination of capital and power can be used to describe the class structure of American society. One popular way of describing the class structure of a society is with a physical or geometric shape or image. The shape or image conveys the relative proportions of people in a society who have some valued thing, like money or education. The pyramid (figure 1.3), for example, illustrates a class structure in which a small percentage of a society (10 percent) has a great deal of the commodity, another 30 percent has a little less, and the majority (60 percent) has the least amount of the valued commodity.

Another frequently used image is the diamond (figure 1.4), which provides a different picture of the way valued things are distributed. The diamond image says that a small percentage (10 percent) of a society has a lot of something, another small percentage (10 percent) has very little of something, and most of the people (80 percent) are in the middle, with moderate amounts of the valued commodity.

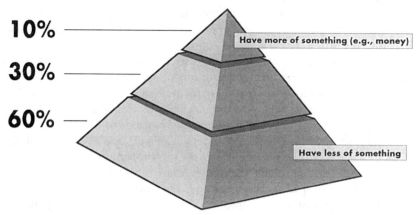

Figure 1.3.   Pyramid Diagram of Class Structure

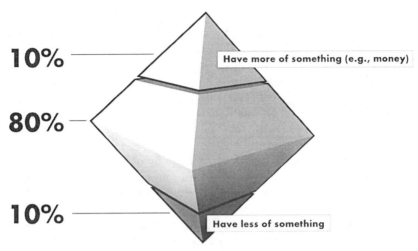

Figure 1.4.   Diamond Diagram of Class Structure

In each of these class structures, the class positions of people can be simply designated as upper class, middle class, or lower class. Thus, the pyramid image represents a society in which most persons are lower class, and the diamond image represents a middle-class society. If asked to choose between the two societies depicted here, most people would probably choose the society represented by the diamond image because most of the people are in the middle class. If you chose to live in the pyramid society, you would have a 60 percent chance of being in the lower class.

However, before choosing one of these societies in which to live, you might want a little more information. You might want to know about the particular attribute or characteristic that puts people in each class. Is it something they are born with, like skin color or physical size, or is it some characteristic they learn or acquire, like being a good hunter or a skilled craft worker? You might also want to know something about how people in each class live in terms of basic necessities, material comforts, physical security, and freedom. Finally, it might be important to know if it is possible for people to change their class position within a lifetime or across generations, or if there are opportunities for their children to rise above the class into which they were born.

Thus, the image of a society as pyramidal or diamond shaped provides an overall view of how people in that society are distributed on some valued characteristic or attribute. But it does not tell about the society's "rules" for determining or changing class position.

Let us try to make all this a little more concrete by examining American society. Most efforts to portray the American class structure have focused on occupations as the main determinant of the class structure and of people's positions in that structure. Occupations have been classified according to the public's opinion of the social standing or prestige associated with being a public school teacher, or a dentist, or a mechanic, or a machine operator. When large numbers of Americans are asked to rate occupations on a scale ranging from "excellent" to "poor" in social standing, they consistently place U.S. Supreme Court justice, physician, and corporate manager at the top of the list; at the bottom are garbage collector, filling station attendant, and janitor. The prestige hierarchy of occupations has remained pretty stable in studies done over several decades and in different countries.[16] This has led some analysts to see occupational prestige as the basis of class structure in American society. They also assert that the term *class* is not meaningful because prestige is determined according to a continuous system of rankings of occupations, without any sharp boundaries or divisions between occupations.

However, if you look behind these prestige rankings to ask what it is that people are actually ranking, you will find that what is being evaluated is not simply the prestige of an occupation but also its income and power. In our society, the occupational structure embedded in organizations is the key to understanding the class structure, and a person's occupation is one aspect of class position. But how do the hundreds of different occupations combine to create a structure of distinct classes with different amounts of economic, political, and social power? What aspects of occupations determine their position in the class structure?

People often speak of their occupation or their job as what they do for a living. An occupation or job describes how a person is related to the economy in a society or what one does in the process of the production of goods and services. An occupation or job provides people with the means to sustain life (to make a living), and the sum total of the work done by people in their occupations or jobs is the wealth generated by the economic system. In one sense, there is a parallel or symmetric relation between the availability of jobs and the amount of wealth that is generated. The more people in a society that are working at making a living, the better the economic health of the total society. But there is also a sense in which there is an asymmetric relationship between the well-being of working people (how much of a living they make) and the total wealth that is generated. Some people contribute more to the total wealth than they receive for their work, as in the case of some workers whose wages are a fraction of the value of their products when they are sold. And some people may receive ten or twenty times more in income for their work than that received by others. So, although there may be 130 million Americans involved in occupations and jobs for which they are compensated, their amount of compensation varies widely according to how they are related to the production process. There are a variety of ways in which people are related to the production process in today's economy.

The Privileged Class

The activity of some people in the system of production is focused on their role as owners of investment capital. Such a person may be referred to colloquially as the "boss" or, in more respectful circles, as a "captain of industry," an "entrepreneur," or a "creator of wealth," but in the language of class analysis, they are all owner-employers. The owner may actually be the sole proprietor of the XYZ Corporation and be involved in the day-to-day decisions of running that corporation. But ownership may also consist of the possession of a large number of shares of stock in one or several corporations in which many other persons may also own stock. However, the ownership of stock is socially and economically meaningful only when (1) the value of shares owned is sufficient to constitute "making a living," or (2) the percentage of shares of stock owned relative to all shares is large enough to permit the owner of said shares to have some say in how the company is run. Members of this group (along with the managers and professionals) control most of the wealth in America. The point of this discussion is to distinguish owners of investment capital from the millions of Americans who own shares of stock in companies, who own mutual funds, or whose pension funds are invested in the stock market. The typical American stock owner does not make a living from that ownership and has nothing to say about the activities of the companies he or she "owns."

On the lower rungs of the owner-employer group are the proprietors of small, but growing, high-tech firms that bring together investment capital and specialized knowledge in areas involving biomedical products or services and computer software firms. These are "small" businesses only in Department of Commerce classifications (less than $500,000 in sales), for they bear no resemblance to the Korean grocery, the Mexican restaurant, or the African American hair salon found in many American cities. They are more typically spin-off firms created by technical specialists who have accumulated some capital from years of employment in an industrial lab or a university and have obtained other investment capital from friends, family, or private investors.

A second activity in the system of production is that of the manager, the person who makes the day-to-day decisions involved in running a corporation, a firm, a division of a corporation, or a section within a company. Increasingly, managers have educational credentials and degrees in business, management, economics, or finance. Managers make decisions about how to use the millions of dollars of investment capital made available to them by the owners of investment capital.

The upper levels of the managerial group include the top management of the largest manufacturing, financial, and commercial firms in the United States. These managers receive substantial salaries and bonuses, along with additional opportunities to accumulate wealth. Table 1.2 presents a typical pattern of "modest" compensation for the officers of a large firm in 2003. We refer to this compensation as "modest" because it is far below the multi-million-dollar packages of compensation for CEOs at IBM, AT&T, Disney, or Coca-Cola (which range from $20 million to $50 million). But such distinctions are probably pointless because we are describing executives whose wealth is enormous in comparison with others not in their class. For example, the top CEO in the group just listed also owns one hundred thousand

Table 1.2. Compensation for Corporate Executives (2003)

Position	Annual Compensation	Bonus	Stock Awards
President and CEO	$745,385	$450,000	$2,028,125
Executive vice pres.	299,897	119,000	745,000
Executive vice pres.	273,846	120,000	558,750
Senior vice pres. and General Counsel	242,885	34,000	447,000
Senior vice pres. and CFO	275,192	128,000	558,750
Vice president	342,029	174,760	—
Executive vice pres.	322,400	5,000	—

Source: Based on data from the Annual Report and Proxy Statements, Great Lakes Chemical Corporation, 2003, Indianapolis, Ind.

shares of stock and has options for another hundred thousand shares in the corporation he heads. The value of these shares fluctuates with the market value of the stock, which in the summer of 2001 was $31 a share, or about $3 million for the one hundred thousand shares.

The lower levels of the managerial group carry out the important function of supervising the work done by millions of workers who produce goods and services in the economy. The success of this group, and the level of its rewards, is determined by its ability to get workers to be more productive, which means to produce more at a lower cost.

Professionals carry out a third activity in the economic system. This group's power is based on the possession of credentialed knowledge or skill, such as an engineering degree, a teaching degree, or a degree in public relations. Some may work as "independent professionals," providing service for a fee, such as declining numbers of doctors, dentists, and lawyers. But most professionals work for corporations, providing their specialized knowledge to enhance the profit-making potential of their firm or of firms that buy their services. The professional group is made up of university graduates with degrees in the professional schools of medicine, law, business, and engineering and in a variety of newly emerging fields (e.g., computer sciences) that serve the corporate sector. The possession of credentialed knowledge unifies an otherwise diverse group, which includes doctors who may earn $500,000 a year and computer specialists who may earn $60,000 a year.

The potential to accumulate wealth is very great among certain segments of professionals. The mean net salary in 2005 for all physicians surveyed in one report was $180,000. There were great differences between the incomes of family practice physicians, who averaged $168,110 in 2005, and specialty physicians, such as radiologists and oncologists, who averaged $316,620.[17] Unfortunately, these averages hide the salaries of graduates from elite medical schools and those affiliated with the most prestigious hospitals. Also absent is information about doctor's entrepreneurial activities, such as ownership of nursing homes or pharmaceutical firms.

Similar opportunities for high income exist among lawyers, where partners at the nation's elite law firms average $335,000 and associates average $80,000 (1998). Even law professors at prestigious law schools have a chance to amass a small fortune while teaching and practicing law or consulting. A recent *New York Times* story reported that a professor at Harvard Law School gave the school a bequest of $5 million.[18] The *Times* reported that the professor is "not one of the school's prominent moonlighters" and is "unlike Prof. Alan M. Dershowitz, the courtroom deity who has defended Leona Helmsley and Mike Tyson and is on the O. J. Simpson defense team." So how did the professor do it? By "writing and consulting."

Professors at elite universities who are in selected fields like law, medicine, business, biomedical engineering, or electrical engineering have opportunities to start high-tech firms and to consult for industry in ways that can significantly enhance income. Even "modest" activities, like becoming an outside director for a bank or industrial firm, can be very rewarding. Most major U.S. corporations have nonemployee directors, who are paid an annual retainer of about $20,000 and who receive about $2000 to $3000 for each board or committee meeting they attend, thereby producing an annual compensation of anywhere from $50,000 to $80,000. A colleague in a business school at a Big Ten university who is a professor of management has been on the board of directors of a chemical corporation for twenty years. His annual retainer is $26,000. He gets an additional $1,000 a day for attending meetings of the board or committee meetings and $500 a day for participating in telephone conference meetings (the board meets six times a year, and committees convene from one to six times a year). Each nonemployee director gets a $50,000 term life insurance policy and a $200,000 accidental death and dismemberment insurance policy. After serving on the board for a minimum of five years, directors are eligible for retirement benefits equal to the amount of the annual retainer at the time of retirement. Retirement benefits begin at the time of the director's retirement from the board and continue for life.

Why does the president of this university or its board of trustees allow a professor to engage in such lucrative "outside activities"? Maybe it's because the president, whose annual salary is $200,000, holds four director positions that give him more than $100,000 a year in additional income.

Professionals in elite settings not only make six-figure salaries, but they have enough "discretionary time" to pursue a second line of activity that may double or triple their basic salaries. Not a bad deal for the professional class.

However, not everyone with a credentialed skill is in the privileged professional class. We exclude from this group workers like teachers, social workers, and nurses, who despite their professional training and dedication fail to get the material rewards accorded to other professionals. Moreover, they are usually labeled as "semiprofessionals," implying that they somehow fall short of the full professionals. This may be due to the fact that most of these "semiprofessionals" are women and that their services do not provide direct benefits to the privileged class. They deal with people in nonproductive roles, such as students, patients, or human-service clients, and they deal mostly with people without much in the way of consumption or investment capital. We also exclude university professors at nonelite schools. They are excluded because of the large number of faculty at hundreds of nonelite colleges and universities who make modest salaries; many of them are not even employed in tenure-track positions. We also exclude the thousands of attorneys working for legal-services agencies and franchise law firms and in public defender positions. Professionals in these positions are excluded because of limited job security, modest levels of income, and little investment capital. Thus, we distinguish between elite and marginalized professional groups, with only the former being in the privileged class.

The New Working Class

Finally, there is the large majority of Americans—employees who sell their capacity to work to an employer in return for wages. Members of this group typically carry out their daily work activities under the supervision of the managerial group. They have limited skills and limited job security. Such workers can see their jobs terminated with virtually no notice. The exception to this rule is the approximately 13 percent of workers who are unionized, but even union members are vulnerable to having their jobs eliminated by new technology, restructuring and downsizing, or the movement of production to overseas firms.

This working group also consists of the many thousands of very small businesses that include self-employed persons and family stores based on little more than "sweat equity." Many of these people have been "driven" to try self-employment as a protection against limited opportunities in the general labor market. But many are attracted to the idea of owning their own business, an idea that has a special place in the American value system: it means freedom from the insecurity and subservience of being an employee. For the wage worker, the opportunities for starting a business are severely limited by the absence of capital. Aspirations may be directed at a family business in a neighborhood where one has lived, such as a dry cleaning store, a beauty shop, a gas station, or a convenience store. Prospects for such businesses may depend upon an ethnic "niche," where the service, the customer, and the entrepreneur are tied together in a common cultural system relating to food or some personal service. The failure rate of these small businesses is very high, making self-employment a vulnerable, high-risk activity.

Another sizable segment of wage earners, perhaps 10 to 15 percent, has very weak links to the labor market. For these workers, working for wages takes place between long stretches of unemployment, when there may be shifts to welfare benefits or unemployment compensation. This latter group typically falls well below official poverty levels and should not be considered as part of the "working poor." The working poor consists of persons who are working full-time at low wages, with earnings of about $12,000 a year—what you get for working full-time at $6.00 an hour.

Table 1.3.   Class Structure in America

Class Position	Class Characteristics	Percentage of Population
Privileged Class		
Superclass	Owners and employers. Make a living from investments or business ownership; incomes at six- to seven-figure level, yielding sizable consumption and investment capital.	1–2%
Credentialed Class		
Managers	Mid- and upper-level managers and CEOs of corporations and public organizations. Incomes for upper-level CEOs in seven-figure range, others six figures.	13–15%
Professionals	Possess credentialed skill in form of college and professional degrees. Use of social capital and organizational ties to advance interests. Incomes from 100K to upper-six figures.	4–5%
New Working Class		
Comfort class	Nurses, teachers, civil servants, very-small-business owners, and skilled and union carpenters, machinists, or electricians. Incomes in the $35–50K range but little investment capital.	10%
Contingent Class		
Wage earners	Work for wages in clerical and sales jobs, personal services, and transportation and as skilled craft workers, machine operators, and assemblers. Members of this group are often college graduates. Incomes at $30K and lower.	50%
Self-employed	Usually self-employed with no employees, or family workers. Very modest incomes, with high potential for failure.	3–4%
Excluded class	In and out of the labor force in a variety of unskilled, temporary jobs.	10–15%

Table 1.3 summarizes these major segments of Americans with different standing in the current economy. The groups are distinguished as (1) those who own capital and businesses, (2) those who control corporations and the workers in those corporations, (3) those who possess credentialed knowledge that provides a protected place in the labor market, (4) the self-employed small-business owners who operate as solo entrepreneurs with limited capital, and (5) those with varying skills who have little to offer in the labor market beyond their capacity to work.

These segments of the class structure are defined by their access to essential life-sustaining resources and the stability of those resources over time. As discussed earlier, these resources include consumption capital, investment capital, skill

capital, and social capital. The class segments differ in their access to stable resources over time, and they represent what is, for all practical purposes, a two-
class structure, represented by a double diamond (see figure 1.5). The top diamond represents the privileged class, composed of those who have stable and
secure resources that they can expect will be available to them over time. This privileged class can be subdivided into the superclass of owners, employers, and

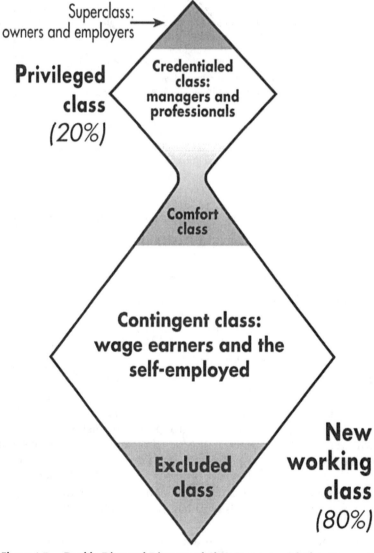

Figure 1.5.   Double-Diamond Diagram of Class Structure and Class Segments

CEOs, who directly or indirectly control enormous economic resources, and the credentialed class of managers and professionals with the knowledge and expertise that is essential to major industrial, financial, commercial, and media corporations and key agencies of government. The bottom diamond is the new working class, composed of those who have unstable and insecure resources over time. One segment of this class has a level of consumption capital that provides income sufficient for home ownership and for consumption patterns that suggest they are "comfortable." Thus, we label this segment the "comfort class," representing school teachers, civil servants, social workers, nurses, some small-business owners, and skilled, unionized carpenters, machinists, or electricians. Despite their relatively "high" incomes ($35,000 to $60,000), the comfort class is vulnerable to major economic downturns or unforeseen crises (e.g., health problems) and has limited investment capital to buffer such crises (see figure 1.5).

The largest segment of the new working class is composed of the wage earners with modest skills and unpredictable job security. This group includes, for example, machine operators in manufacturing plants, bank clerks, and the supervisors who could be displaced by new production technology, computerized information systems, or other "smart" machines. Their job insecurity is similar to that of the growing segment of temporary and part-time workers, thereby making them the "contingent class."

At the bottom of the new working class are those without marketable skills who move in and out of the labor force in temporary jobs or in seasonal employment. They are the "excluded class," who are treated as "waste" because they are no longer needed as either cheap labor or consumers or who fill the most undesirable jobs in restaurant kitchens or as nighttime cleaners of downtown buildings.

It is important to keep in mind that a person's location in the double-diamond class structure is related to his or her occupation but not determined by that occupation (as is the case in the production and functionalist models of class, discussed earlier in this chapter). Some lawyers are in the top diamond, and some, in the bottom. Some engineers, scientists, and professors are in the privileged class, and some, in the new working class. It is not occupation that determines class position but access to generative capital—stable, secure resources over time.

ORGANIZATIONS AND INEQUALITY: CLASS, GENDER, RACE

As powerful as race and racism are in determining the life chances to African Americans, the politics of inequality will play a more significant and central role, both inside the black community, and in its relations with other groups. In short, class matters, and the battle for economic fairness will in many respects be the most fundamental factor in the future of African-American politics.

—Manning Marable, *The Black World Today*, February 22, 2000

While our primary concern is with examining the nature and consequences of the new class structure in the United States, we also recognize that inequality has many faces. It is our view that a wide array of class, as well as gender- and race-based, forms of inequalities exist in American society and that they are grounded in and linked to large organizations, especially corporations, and the resources they control.

As we noted earlier, social-class membership reflects people's possession of four forms of generative capital. We also pointed out that access to and possession of various levels of all types of generative capital depend on the nature, level, and type of organizational affiliations that individuals hold. For example, an individual might hold an upper-level executive or managerial position with a corporation. The dollar value of this affiliation is expressed through the consumption capital (i.e., salary) and investment capital (e.g., stock options) held by that individual. Organizational affiliations that generate high levels of consumption and investment capital would also be likely to produce high levels of social capital through informal and formal social and business ties to other individuals with similar types and levels of organizational affiliations.

But class inequality, with its oppositional groupings of privileged and working classes, is not the only structure of dominance found in contemporary American society. There is also gender inequality and racial/ethnic inequality, which establishes oppositions between women and men and between persons of color and whites. Sometimes gender and racial/ethnic inequalities are expressions of class inequality in that poor women and poor African Americans and poor Hispanics are denied access to opportunities for a good education and good jobs. In these cases, gender and racial/ethnic inequalities reinforce class inequality by placing women, blacks, and Hispanics with low incomes, limited educational credentials, and no influential social connections in subordinate positions in the economic, political, and cultural sectors. However, sometimes gender and racial/ethnic inequalities affect the lives of women and nonwhites for reasons other than class inequality. When women or African Americans with educational credentials or work experience are denied good jobs or promotion opportunities, it may be simply because of discrimination based on gender or race.

It is our view that understanding the structures and processes that undergird the origins and reproduction of class, as well as gender- and race-/ethnicity-based, forms of inequality must begin with a focus on organizations. To clarify and illustrate how organizationally based factors underlie and are critical to all three forms of inequality, we begin by considering this question: what factors facilitate or impede people's access to organizational affiliations with stable, resource-rich organizations at the levels and types of links (e.g., occupation) that yield the high levels of all (or most) forms of generative capital associated with privileged-class membership? The short answer to our question involves organizational policies and practices that structure the processes by which people gain access to organizational affiliations at various levels and of various types. Organizational policies and practices that shape and guide the affiliation process (especially where employment decisions are concerned) are routinely claimed by policy-making and policy-executing organizational representatives to operate according to the principles of meritocracy. However, substantial evidence documents that such policies actually function as class-, gender-, and race-biased gatekeeping mechanisms.[19]

We view organizational policies and practices governing affiliation processes as comprising two "inequality scripts," one formal, the other informal. At the formal level, these scripts identify the organizational roles (e.g., career positions) and specify the formal credentials necessary to access the roles (e.g., educational level or experience). The informal level represents the covert dimension of affiliation decisions made by organizational gatekeepers. At this level, informal qualifications, including class background, gender, and racial/ethnic membership, enter into affiliation decisions. In most organizations, we are likely to find not one, but several, inequality scripts. Hiring practices for positions at the non-privileged-class level are likely to be handled by middle-level managers in personnel or human resources departments. Filling positions at the privileged-class level, such as hiring/promoting senior executives, are typically directed by senior, privileged-class members of the organization.

Upper-level positions, or positions on career ladders to the top, are typically filled via inequality scripts that selectively advantage the children, friends, and associates of current members of the privileged class. High-level positions are compensated by high incomes, are linked to long career ladders within the organization, and typically require elite educational credentials. Persons from privileged-class backgrounds are most likely to successfully negotiate the organizational affiliation process and "fit" into these organizational roles that demand and yield high levels of generative capital. This is the case because they benefit indirectly from various forms of family "sponsorships" and "investments" that frequently result in elite educational credentials.

Abundant evidence exists that women and blacks especially have been negatively affected by organizationally based inequality scripts in at least three ways. First, working-class women and blacks have historically been more likely than working-class white males to be employed in smaller and less capitalized organizations, resulting in lower wages, fewer benefits, and greater job insecurity.[20] Second, even when working-class women and blacks have been able to get jobs with resource-rich organizations, they are often employed in gender and racially segregated jobs. There is substantial evidence that the American workplace is segregated by gender and race. Women comprise 95 percent of nurses, but only 22 percent of doctors; 98 percent of dental assistants, but only 10 percent of dentists; 98 percent of secretaries; 86 percent of elementary school teachers; 97 percent of receptionists; and 78 percent of cashiers.[21] The top occupations for black and Hispanic men are truck driver, janitor, security guard, assembler, construction laborer, farm worker, cook, and gardener. The occupations with the highest levels of gender and racial segregation are also those with the lowest incomes.[22]

Third, when women or people of color rise to privileged-class positions, the promotion process often includes an invisible "glass ceiling" and/or tokenism. These features are evident in studies that have documented the disproportionate representation of white males versus women and blacks in accessing organizational affiliations at privileged-class levels.[23] Women in management positions are often viewed as having dual commitments to work and family, thus as less suitable for fast-track careers. Some have suggested that women in upper management often forgo high-demand, high-reward positions, selecting instead mommy-track options that permit them to get less demanding work assignments (less travel, no night or weekend assignments) in return for more time outside of work.[24] However, even if these decisions are viewed as "choices," they are made by women who know that if they want to have a career, they will still have to work the "second shift" at home. African Americans who have benefited from affirmative action policies to attain upper-management positions in corporations are often placed in racialized positions involved with black consumer markets or dealing with politically based community issues.[25]

In everyday life, gender- and race-based forms of inequality are more often reported in the mainstream media—and are often more visible and more readily identifiable at personal levels—than class-based inequality. The persistence of tradition-based, informal social scripts organized around social identity hierarchies based on gender and race help sensitize and reinforce individual and collective attention to inequalities in these areas. Traditionally, these informal scripts have "assigned" white males to positions of dominance vis-à-vis women and blacks. The informal evidence that appears to support these scripts and the male privileges written into them help create resentment and divisions among working-class men, women, and people of color.

The gender- and race-based inequalities and grievances experienced in everyday life make it more difficult for working-class men, women, and people of color to recognize their common class interests as members of the working class. Also, the immediate and personalized experiences of gender- and race-based inequalities tend to distract most members of the working class from the organizationally based sources of critical class-, gender-, and race-based inequalities and grievances. Most people fail to recognize that such inequalities are grounded in, and linked much more closely to, the organizationally based inequality scripts that create and perpetuate class divisions rather than informal, microlevel social scripts. Even though we view class-, gender-, and race-based inequalities as organizationally based and driven, we also view class inequalities as qualitatively different from gender and racial grievances. This is the case because we believe class inequalities transcend gender- and race-based grievances and have the potential to unite all members of the new working class in efforts to promote changes that will reduce all three forms of inequality.

In our view, a focus on social class is central to understanding major features and trends in our society today. Gender and racial inequalities are real and far from unimportant as features and experiences. But returning to class provides us with a unifying image of structured inequality.

THE NEW AMERICAN CLASS STRUCTURE DEFINED

The gap between the haves and have-nots is greater now than at any time since 1929.

—Edward N. Wolff, *Top Heavy: The Increasing Inequality of Wealth in America and What Can Be Done about It*, 1996

Figure 1.5 provides a picture of the new American class structure as a "double diamond," divided between the privileged and those lacking the privileges that come with money, elite credentials, and social connections. This two-class structure is composed of approximately 20 percent privileged Americans and 80 percent nonprivileged Americans. Members of the employer, managerial, and professional classes have a stable income flow, employment stability, savings, pensions, and insurance. Their positions in the economy enable them to use their resources to accumulate more resources and to ensure their stability over time. The new working class has little in the way of secure resources. Their jobs are unstable as they can be eliminated by labor-replacing technology or corporate moves to offshore production. Only marginal professionals and craft workers possess some skills that provide short-term security, but even their skills are being eroded by new technology, the reorganization of work, and the decline of union power.[26]

This image of class structure in American society is based on three important principles that define the new American class structure and how it works in practice.

Class Structure Is Intergenerationally Permanent

One of the most significant aspects of class structures is their persistence over time. The inequality that a person experiences today provides the conditions that determine the future. This aspect of class structure is rarely discussed by the media or even by scholars devoted to the layer-cake image of inequality. In fact, most discussion of class structure views that structure, and one's place in it, as temporary and ever changing. The belief in equality of opportunity states that regardless of where a person starts out in life, it is possible to move up through hard work, motivation, and education. Similarly, the overall structure is viewed as changing, as revealed in statistics on the median income, the expanding middle class, or the declining percentage of the population living below the poverty line. In short, the popular image of class differences is that they are temporary and constantly changing. But in fact, nothing could be further from the truth when it comes to the new class system in the United States.

The rules of the game that shape the class structure are designed to reproduce that structure. Let's consider a few of those rules and how they work. First, our legal system gives corporations the right to close down a plant and move the operation overseas, but it does not give workers a right to their jobs. Owners and employers have property rights that permit wide latitude in making decisions that impact on workers and communities. But workers' jobs are not viewed as a property right under the law. The protected right to a secure job would provide workers with a stable resource over time and modify their vulnerable situation in the class system.

Second, people in privileged classes have unrestricted opportunities to accumulate wealth (i.e., extensive consumption capital and investment capital). The accumulation process is based on tax laws that favor the rich, a variety of loopholes to avoid taxes, and an investment climate that enables the rich to get richer. The share of net worth and financial wealth going to the top 20 percent of the population is staggering (see figure 1.2). One out of five Americans owns almost everything, while the other four are on the outside looking in.[27]

This extraordinary disparity in wealth not only provides a clear picture of the polarized two-class structure; it also provides the basis for the persistence of that structure. Because inheritance and estate laws make it possible to do so, wealth is transmitted across generations, and privilege is thereby transmitted to each succeeding generation. At the end of May 2001, the U.S. Congress passed a new tax bill that included the elimination of the federal estate tax, thereby enabling the privileged class to transmit its wealth without a tax penalty. This was part of President George W. Bush's tax-reform proposal, which provided significant tax reduction for people with six-figure earnings, but only modest reductions for middle- and low-income families. Moreover, there were no reductions in payroll taxes, including those supporting Social Security and Medicare, which account for a much higher percentage tax on lower-income families than on those in upper-income brackets.

Another feature of the American class structure that contributes to its permanence is the sheer size of the privileged class. It consists of approximately twenty million households, or between forty million and fifty million people. A class of this numerical size, with its associated wealth, is able to fill all the top positions across the institutional spectrum. Moreover, it is able to fill vacant positions or newly created positions from among its own members. Thus, recruitment of talented women and men from the nonprivileged class will become increasingly rare.

Third, the so-called equality of opportunity in America is supposed to be provided by its system of public education. Yet everyone who has looked at the quality of education at the primary and secondary levels knows that it is linked to the class position of parents. Spending per pupil in public schools is tied to property taxes, therefore the incomes of people in school districts. Schools in poor districts have the poorest physical facilities, libraries, laboratories, academic programs, and teachers.[28] Some of the children who survive this class-based public education are able to think about some sort of postsecondary education. But even here the game is stacked against them.

Going to college is based on the ability to pay the costs of tuition and, unless students live at home, room and board. Even at low-cost city colleges or state universities, the expenses exceed what many working-class families can afford. On the other hand, even if college attendance were not tied to ability to pay, it is not likely that many youngsters from low-income families would think of college as a realistic goal, given the low quality of their educational experience in the primary and secondary grades.

Thus, the rules of the game that are the foundation for the class structure are designed primarily to transmit advantage and disadvantage across generations. This persistence of structure exists even when there are instances of upward social mobility—the sons and daughters of working-class families who move into the professional classes. This upward mobility occurs in a very selective way and without changing the rules of the game. For example, when the birthrates among the privileged-class children cease to fill all the high-level, organizationally based, professional positions for doctors, lawyers, engineers, computer specialists, and managers, it may become necessary to recruit the most talented young men and women from the working class. The most talented are identified through special testing programs and curriculum tracking and are encouraged to consider advanced education. "Elite" colleges and universities develop special financial and academic programs for talented working-class students, and a variety of fellowship programs support those with financial need. Upward mobility is made possible not by changing the rules of the game but by "creaming" the most talented members of the working class. The creaming process has the dual effect of siphoning off potential leaders from the working class and supporting the belief in equality of opportunity and upward mobility.

The overall effect that the rules of the game have on the class structure is that the rate of upward mobility of persons from low- and middle-income social backgrounds is small and declining. This conclusion is based on our research that compared the socioeconomic positions (based on occupation, education, and earnings) of a sample of fathers in 1979 with the positions held by their adult sons in 1998 (the adult sons were then aged thirty-three to forty). The results of this intergenerational father-son mobility study indicated that the likelihood of upward intergenerational mobility from the lower ranks to the top or near-top ranks declined from the 1990s as compared with the 1970s. We also found that compared with the 1970s, a greater proportion of the upper ranks of the class structure in the 1990s appear to be occupied by children from advantaged class backgrounds. In short, the U.S. class structure today appears to have increasingly hardened across generational lines.[29]

There Is No Middle Class

The functionalist view of class structure, as noted earlier, presents a "layer-cake" image of class differences. There are six or eight classes made up of groups of occupations that differ in prestige, education level, or income. These differences between classes are not sharp and discontinuous; rather, there are gradual shadings of difference between one class and another. The layer-cake image encourages a belief in a "center" or a "middle class" that is large and stands between the upper and lower classes. The different groups in the middle may think of themselves as being "better off" than those below them and may see opportunities to move up the "ladder" by improving education, job skills, or income.

This image of class structure is stabilizing in that it encourages the acceptance of enormous material inequality in American society because of the belief that anyone can improve his or her situation and become one of the "rich and famous." It also encourages greater attention to the small differences between groups and tends to ignore the large differences. For example, many Americans are hardworking men and women who often work two jobs to make ends meet but are limited by these low-wage and no-benefit jobs. These people are often most hostile to the welfare benefits provided for people who are just below them in income. A working poor person gets $12,000 a year for full-time work, whereas a welfare family may get the same amount in total benefits without working. However, these same working poor rarely have their hostility shaped and directed toward the rich, who may be more responsible for the low wages, limited benefits, and inadequate pensions of the working poor.

The belief in a middle class also allows politicians to proclaim their support for tax breaks for what they call the middle class while debating whether the middle class includes those with incomes up to $250,000 a year or only those earning $100,000.

In our conception of class structure, there can be no middle class. Either you have stable, secure resources over time, or you do not. Either you have a stable job and income, or you do not. Either you have secure health insurance and pensions that provide adequate income, or you do not.

Classes Have Conflicting Interests

In the functionalist layer-cake theory of class structure, each class is viewed as having more or less of some valued quality or commodity, such as education, occupational skill, or income. Members of each class may aspire to become members of the classes above them, and they may harbor negative opinions of and prejudices toward those in classes below them. But classes, in this theory, are not fundamentally opposed to one another. Of course, there is often discussion of why members of certain classes might support or oppose particular political candidates because of their social or economic policies. But these alliances or oppositional views are seen as linked to shifting issues and are not tied to class interests.

Our view is more closely aligned with the central ideas of Marxist class analysis, which stresses the role of exploitation and dominance in class relations. We see in the United States today the two large classes of privileged- and working-class Americans having fundamentally different and opposed objective interests so that when one class improves its situation the other class loses. The advantages of the privileged class, expressed in its consumption capital, investment capital, skill capital, and social capital, are enjoyed at the expense of the working class. Any action to make the resources of the working class more stable—by improving job security or increasing wages and pensions, for example—would result in some loss of capital or advantage for the privileged.

Given the existence of oppositional interests, it is expected that members of the privileged class will work to advance their interests. As employers, they will seek to minimize worker wages and benefits and to fight efforts by workers to organize. As media owners, filmmakers, and writers they will produce cultural products and information that undermine efforts by the working class or African Americans to organize and advance their interests. Think, for example, about how the media and opinion makers are quick to cry "class warfare" whenever a social critic such as Ralph Nader points to the wealth of the privileged. Think also about how the opinion makers react to African Americans like Al Sharpton when they seek to occupy positions of leadership or to social critics like Noam Chomsky when they criticize U.S. policies. They are usually ignored or marginalized by media and opinion makers.

These three principles—class structure has intergenerational permanence, there is no middle class, and classes have conflicting interests—provide a basis for understanding the central defining features of the American class structure. We have, in effect, tried to answer the question, what is class inequality? In the next chapter, we address the question, how does class inequality work?

CLASS ISSUES IN THE MEDIA: ELECTIONS AND NEWS

One of the arguments presented in this chapter is that in public discussion, social class in America is a taboo topic. Although public officials and mainstream media often discuss issues of poverty, homelessness, or income inequality, the average American is rarely presented with a sustained discussion of America's social-class structure, which is the reason for poverty, inequality, and homelessness. The 2004 presidential election

(continued)

appeared to provide an opportunity to challenge the taboo on discussion of class in America. The Democratic candidate for vice president of the United States, Senator John Edwards, made "two Americas" a central theme in many of his campaign speeches. When he accepted the nomination of his party at the Democratic Convention in Boston on July 28, 2004, Edwards stated,

> We still live in two different Americas, one for people who live the American Dream and don't have to worry, and another for most Americans who work hard and still struggle to make ends meet. We can build one America where we no longer have two health care systems. One for people who get the best health care money can buy and then one for everybody else. . . . We shouldn't have two different economies in America, one for people who are set for life and then one for most Americans who live paycheck to paycheck.[30]

That's pretty strong stuff for a national presidential campaign, and it almost sounds like John Edwards read our book describing the "double-diamond" class structure. The "two Americas" theme was picked up by many mainstream media. For example, a LexisNexis search of New York newspapers for June to November 2004 found 125 hits for "two Americas" or "class warfare." Another search of the *New York Times* for the same period found over two hundred hits for "middle class," where the term had been included in a political speech or in an article published in the *Times*.

Was the taboo on discussion of class broken during the 2004 election campaign? Unfortunately, that is not the case. Closer inspection of the news items that discussed the "two Americas" or "class warfare" revealed very little support for Edwards's claim. About 60 percent of all the printed reactions were critical of the idea of an America that is divided along class lines, often charging Edwards with being a demagogue and a hypocrite (because he's a millionaire) for trying to foment class warfare. Another 20 percent of the news items examined data on income and wealth inequality, often concluding that top-earning households in the United States are unfairly attacked in class-warfare rhetoric. Why? Because they are the best educated and most productive workers, pay the most taxes, and make the greatest investment in job creation and economic growth. Here is the conclusion to one of these analyses: "In one sense, John Edwards is correct: There is one America that works a lot and pays a lot in taxes, and there is another America that works less and pays little. However, the reality is the opposite of what Edwards suggests. It is the higher-income families who work a lot and pay nearly all the taxes. Raising taxes even higher on hard-working families would be unfair and, by reducing future investments, would reduce economic growth, harming all Americans in the long run."[31] How's that for reverse class warfare?

The other feature of many news stories about class in America is the very inadequate discussion of the class structure and class segments. The powerful and dominant upper class is ignored, while the favored middle class gets all the attention. One article about the "shrinking middle class" defines the middle class as households with income between $25,000 and $75,000 in 2003.[32] That is a pretty wide range of incomes, and a family earning $25,000 a year is hardly living the American Dream. Another article discussing the decline of middle-class jobs describes "decent-paying jobs" as those paying $12 to $13 an hour.[33] Once again, the middle class starts at about $25,000.

The inadequacy of class analysis in news stories about the 2004 election campaign is revealed in the remedies that are often proposed to deal with the problems of income inequality. One favorite remedy is enhancing the opportunities for higher education by providing more financial aid to low-income students. A popular plan among the politicos is providing a tax credit that would allow families paying college tuition to reduce their taxes up to $4,000 a year. This proposal would be a boon to the families earning $100,000 or more who send their children to the elite colleges and universities, but will it really help a poor kid from a family earning $25,000 to go to college? This is not a serious proposal to help people in the bottom part of the double-diamond class structure.

A second example of class issues "breaking out" in the public media occurred in 2005, when the *New York Times*, on Sunday, May 15, 2005, began a series of articles on "Class Matters." The first article on that Sunday, "Class in America: Shadowy Lines That Still Divide," provides a good account of the level of income inequality in the United States, along with evidence on the declining opportunities for upward mobility. Moreover, the article provides a good understanding of the idea of class structure as an enduring pattern of inequality transmitted over time. Subsequent articles are more anecdotal and topical. For example, the second article on health care ("Class Is a Matter of Life and Death") provides examples of how people with different levels of income deal with health-related issues. Another article deals with cross-class marriages, examining how social relationships are shaped by income and education.

The *Times* series also has a tendency to slip into partisan politics by pointing out how the Bush administration's tax cuts increased income inequality between the haves and have-nots, or how the administration's policies on inheritance taxes would solidify the wealth and power of the rich in America. While the above may be true, what the *Times* fails to point out is that current patterns of class inequality are the product of decades of public policies that have favored the privileged class. And during these decades of class-biased public policies on taxes, jobs, health care, and education, both Democrats and Republicans have been in control of the White House and Congress. In short, the class structure is a product of the privileged class using its economic and political power to protect and transmit its privileges, and the *New York Times* doesn't tell you how that is done.

NOTES

1. Don Stillman, "The Devastating Impact of Plant Relocations," *Working Papers* (July–August 1978): 42–53.

2. Cecelia Burns Stendler, *Children of Brasstown: Their Awareness of the Symbols of Social Class* (Urbana: University of Illinois Press, 1949); Robert G. Simmons and Morris Rosenberg, "Functions of Children's Perceptions of the Stratification System," *American Sociological Review* 36 (1971): 235–49; Scott Cummings and Del Taebel, "The Economic Socialization of Children: A Neo-Marxist Analysis," *Social Problems* 26 (December 1978): 198–210; Anthony M. Orum and Roberta S. Cohen, "The Development of Political Orientations among Black and White Children," *American Sociological Review* 38 (1973): 62–74; Jeannette F. Tudor, "The Development of Class Awareness in Children," *Social Forces* 49 (1971): 470–76.

3. Peter Phillips and Project Censored, *Censored 2005: The Top 25 Censored Stories* (New York: Seven Stories Press, 2004).

4. For an orthodox Marxian view, see Charles H. Anderson, *The Political Economy of Social Class* (Englewood Cliffs, NJ: Prentice Hall, 1974). For a sophisticated neo-Marxian analysis, see Erik O. Wright, *Classes* (London: Verso, 1985), and *Interrogating Inequality* (London: Verso, 1994). Wright's early analysis emphasizes ownership and control of the means of production and control of labor as the defining conditions for determining class location; his more recent work adds control of organizational assets and ownership of skill assets.

5. For a good example of the functionalist multidimensional model of class, see Dennis Gilbert and Joseph A. Kahl, *The American Class Structure* (Chicago: Dorsey Press, 1987). For an approach that emphasizes the status or prestige of occupations, see Peter M. Blau and Otis D. Duncan, *The American Occupational Structure* (New York: Wiley, 1967).

6. Data not shown. See Lawrence Mishel, Jared Bernstein, and Sylvia Allegretto, *The State of Working America, 2004/2005* (Ithaca, NY: Cornell University Press, 2005), 88.

7. Melvin Oliver, Thomas M. Shapiro, and Julie E. Press, "'Them That's Got Shall Get': Inheritance and Achievement in Wealth Accumulation," in *Research in Politics and Society*, ed. Richard E. Ratliffe, Melvin Oliver, and Thomas M. Shapiro, vol. 15 (Greenwich, CT: JAI Press, 1995).

8. Katherine S. Mangan, "A Shortage of Business Professors Leads to 6-Figure Salaries for New Ph.D.'s," *Chronicle of Higher Education* 47 (May 4, 2001): A12–A13.

9. Clifford J. Levy, "New York Attorney General Remakes Staff by Patronage," *New York Times*, November 10, 1995.

10. David S. Johnson, John M. Rogers, and Lucilla Tan, "A Century of Family Budgets in the United States," *Monthly Labor Review* (May 2001): 28–45.

11. This estimate was provided by the Cato Institute and reported in Stephen Moore, "How to Slash Corporate Welfare," *New York Times*, April 5, 1995.

12. U.S. Congress, House Committee on the Budget, *Unnecessary Business Subsidies*, 106th Cong., 1st sess., Serial 106–5 (Washington, DC: U.S. Government Printing Office, 1999).

13. See Alan Neustadtl and Dan Clawson, "Corporate Political Groupings: Does Ideology Unify Business Political Behavior?" *American Sociological Review* 53 (1988): 172–90; Robert Perrucci and Marc Pilisuk, "Leaders and Ruling Elites: The Interorganizational Bases of Community Power," *American Sociological Review* 35 (December 1970): 1040–57; Robert Perrucci and Bonnie L. Lewis, "Interorganizational Relations and Community Influence Structure," *Sociological Quarterly* 30 (1989): 205–23; and David Knoke, *Organized for Action: Commitment in Voluntary Associations* (New Brunswick, NJ: Rutgers University Press, 1981).

14. Arlene Kaplan Daniels, *Invisible Careers: Women Civic Leaders from the Volunteer World* (Chicago: University of Chicago Press, 1988).

15. Diana B. Henriques, "Ties That Bind: His Directors, Her Charity," *New York Times*, March 21, 1995.

16. Robert W. Hodge, Paul M. Siegel, and Peter H. Rossi, "Occupational Prestige in the United States: 1925–1962," in *Class, Status, and Power*, ed. Reinhard Bendix and Seymour M. Lipset (New York: Free Press, 1966); Robert W. Hodge, Donald J. Treiman, and Peter H. Rossi, "A Comparative Study of Occupational Prestige," in Bendix and Lipset, *Class, Status, and Power*.

17. David N. Gans, "Physicians: Working Harder and Enjoying It Less," *MGMA Connexions*, November/December 2006: 22-23.

18. David Herzenhorn, "The Story behind the Generous Gift to Harvard Law School," *New York Times*, April 7, 1995.

19. Richard L. Zweigenhaft and G. William Domhoff, *Diversity in the Power Elite: Have Women and Minorities Reached the Top?* (New Haven, CT: Yale University Press, 1998).

20. Barbara Reskin and Irene Padavic, *Women and Men at Work* (Thousand Oaks, CA: Pine Forge Press, 1994), ch. 4; Donald Tomaskovic-Devey, *Gender and Racial Inequality at Work* (Ithaca, NY: ILR Press, 1993), ch. 4.

21. Randy Hodson and Teresa A. Sullivan, *The Social Organization of Work*, 2nd ed. (Belmont, CA: Wadsworth, 1995), appendix, table 1.

22. Reskin and Padavic, *Women and Men at Work*, 120.

23. Reskin and Padavic, *Women and Men at Work*, ch. 5.

24. Felice N. Schwartz, "Management Women and the New Facts of Life," in *Working in America*, ed. Amy S. Wharton (Mountain View, CA: Mayfield Publishing, 1998), 415–21; Arlie Hochschild and Anne Machung, "The Second Shift: Working Parents and the Revolution at Home," in Wharton, *Working in America*, 376–90.

25. Sharon M. Collins, "The Marginalization of Black Executives," *Social Problems* 36 (October, 1989): 317–31.

26. Harley Shaiken, *Work Transformed: Automation and Labor in the Computer Age* (New York: Holt, Rinehart and Winston, 1985); David F. Noble, *Forces of Production: A Social History of Industrial Automation* (New York: Knopf, 1984); Robert Perrucci and Carolyn C. Perrucci (Eds.), The Transformation of Work in the New Economy (Los Angeles: Roxbury, 2007).

27. Edward N. Wolff, *Top Heavy: The Increasing Inequality of Wealth in America and What Can Be Done about It* (New York: Twentieth Century Fund, 1996).

28. Jonathan Kozol, *Savage Inequalities: Children in America's Schools* (New York: Harper, 1991).

29. Earl Wysong, Robert Perrucci, and David W. Wright, "A New Approach to Class Analysis: The Distributional Model, Social Closure, and Class Polarization" (paper presented at the 2002 meetings of the American Sociological Association, Chicago, Illinois).

30. David Reinhard, "The Democratic Convention: In Search of Two Americas," *Oregonian*, July 29, 2004, B13.

31. Robert Rector and Rea S. Hederman Jr., "Two Americas: One Rich, One Poor? Understanding Income Inequality in the United States," *Heritage Foundation Reports*, August 24, 2004.

32. Timothy Egan, "Economic Squeeze Plaguing Middle-Class Families," *New York Times*, August 28, 2004, A12.

33. Louis Uchitelle, "Blacks Lose Better Jobs Faster as Middle-Class Work Drops," *New York Times*, July 12, 2003, A1.

2

Separate Realities:
The Dream and the Iceberg

To the C students I say, You, too, can be President of the United States.

—George W. Bush, Yale University
Commencement Address, cited in *Nation*, June 11, 2001

That's why they call it the American dream; you have to be asleep to believe it.

—George Carlin, *Sacramento Bee*, December 2, 2005

"The fruit doesn't fall far from the tree." Prior to the first three decades of the post–World War II period, this aphorism linking children, parents, and social class stood at the intersection of commonsense observations and social science research.[1] From wealthy elites to white trash, personal experiences, popular culture, and sociological data supported the widely shared consensus that social class tends to "run in families." But following World War II, real wages (adjusted for inflation) for working-class Americans began trending in an upward direction. At the same time, the postwar period witnessed improving opportunities for advancement from the working class into more prestigious occupations.[2] For members of the newly forming blue- and white-collar middle-income groups of the 1950s and 1960s, these patterns provided a reassuring vision of a comfortable and secure future for themselves and their children. Improving living standards, combined with traditional beliefs in the open-ended economic and social opportunities in America, contributed to an enthusiastic, shared embrace of the American Dream as a cultural ideal among members of virtually all social classes.[3] The *American Dream*, a term coined by historian James Adams during the Great Depression, is predicated on the belief that humble class origins are not destiny.[4] It is grounded in the widely shared belief that American society offers equal and unlimited opportunities

45

for upward mobility for those who embrace a strong work ethic, regardless of class origins.[5] Although the details of the dream vary, Americans typically envision it as including freedom, happiness, family, economic security (an above-average and secure income), higher educational levels (for themselves and their children), personal fulfillment (a rewarding job), home ownership, and financial success.[6]

Somewhat paradoxically, the dream runs both parallel with and counter to the general trend whereby children tend to replicate the class ranking of their parents. For privileged-class families, the dream offers a reassuring sense of continuity: the advantaged positions of parents can and will be passed on to, and extended by, their children. For working-class families, the dream represents a possible future of reward, fulfillment, and affluence, especially for their children. To some extent, the early post–World War II period seemed to provide middle-income families with evidence that the dream was within reach. Thus, among members of the nonprivileged classes, the dream has resonated powerfully as a mythic cultural ideal and, at least for a time, as an attainable reality. Today, however, there is growing evidence that opportunities for realizing the American Dream, especially for those in the new working class, are being shredded by powerful economic, political, and cultural forces that are part of the emerging, iceberglike new class society.

The purpose of this chapter is threefold. First, we clarify our iceberg metaphor and consider the taboo nature of class analysis. Second, we identify three important "above the waterline" trends associated with the new class system that are at odds with the ideals of the American Dream. Third, we consider two dynamic dimensions of the new class system (discussed in detail in later chapters) that we view as submerged "beneath the waterline" of conventional social analysis: conflicting class interests and the structures and processes that maintain and legitimate the class system. Bridging and blending elements of critical sociology, trend analysis, and popular culture, this chapter explores the social geography and dynamic forces at the heart of the new class society. It previews themes of power, greed, betrayal, deception, heartbreak, resistance, and hope that are central to the story of social class in America. As we will see, it is a twisted tale previewing a long, strange trip intended for travelers, not tourists.

THE THREE-THOUSAND-MILE ICEBERG

The first lesson of sociology . . . [is] the importance of class consciousness.

—Charles H. Anderson, *Toward a New Sociology*, 1974

Like a huge iceberg stretching coast to coast across the American social horizon, the new class society combines a dramatic profile of sharply defined and disturbing visible features with a submerged and hidden mass of potentially society-wrecking forces and consequences. Compared with the social structure of the recent past, the new structure is sharply leaner in the middle, larger and much meaner at the bottom, and increasingly "secessionistic" among the privileged few at the top. In the terms of figure 1.5, it is a structure that combines privilege, security, and affluence for those in the upper diamond with increasing peril, insecurity, and eroding incomes for those in the lower diamond.

Recent political developments, public-opinion trends, and media reports suggest many Americans are interested in class inequality issues and are increasingly aware of some of the most visible features of the class iceberg. The trail of evidence supporting this view includes, for example, widespread public support for progressive, pro-working-class politicians elected in 2006, such as U.S. Senators Sherrod Brown (D-OH) and Bernie Sanders (I-VT), U.S. Representatives Jerry McNerney (D-CA) and John Yarmuth (D-KY), and many other such candidates at the state and local levels.[7] It continues in the form of growing public support for the protection of working-class interests in areas such as trade policy, Social Security, and taxes. In these areas we also find widespread public opposition to expanding so-called free trade agreements, Social Security privatization schemes—such as those promoted by President Bush—and tax cuts for the rich.[8] Recent national poll results indicate growing public disenchantment with the rich, and large corporations represent yet another aspect of public concern with increasing class inequalities.[9] Further evidence is apparent in grassroots interest in and support for progressive political challenges to the expansion of global capitalism as manifested by organized citizen action efforts throughout the first decade of the twenty-first century.[10] Indeed, in the mid-2000s, even the mainstream media (large commercial media firms) began to reflect growing public interest in class issues as the *Economist*, the *Los Angeles Times*, the *New York Times*, the *Wall Street Journal*, and the *Washington Post* all published high-profile reports on various aspects of social-class inequalities.[11] (We explore the content of these reports in the box at the end of chapter 5, "Class Issues in the Media: Spinning Inequality.")

Coexisting with public interest in class inequalities are contrarian social trends and developments that suggest many Americans are confused, divided, and distracted where such issues are concerned. These tendencies are considered in detail in chapter 7, but high levels of public interest in escapist forms of popular culture, especially those promoted by the mass media, illustrate this point. Mushrooming TV-driven celebrity lifestyle reports, "reality" programming, *WWE SmackDown!*, *World Poker Tour* competitions, and 24/7 sports coverage involve working-class audiences in a kind of parallel universe of entertainment where fantasies are realized and the grim realities of class inequalities recede from view. Other forms of evidence indicative of confusion about, or distraction from, class inequality issues can be found in high levels of public involvement in escapist or passive forms of consumer-oriented activities, including recreational shopping, religious fundamentalism, websurfing, gambling, and diversionary films.

The existence of mixed forms of evidence where interest in class inequalities is concerned suggests that Americans generally lack a consistent focus on, or clear understanding of, the submerged dimensions of the class iceberg, including conflicting class interests, the structures and processes that legitimate the class system, and the possibilities for changing it.[12] We think the paradoxical trends of interest/concern and confusion/distraction stem, at least in part, from the taboo nature of social class in America.

SOCIAL CLASS: THE LAST TABOO

> Class is the last great taboo. These days it's more socially acceptable to talk about sex than it is about . . . class.
>
> —Felice Yeskel, "Class Action in the News," April 1, 2006

Mainstream American social institutions today openly address a wide range of issues that until recently have been considered taboo as topics for public discussion. Despite the expanding inventory of previously censored cultural and lifestyle issues (e.g., sexual orientation, abortion, rape, family violence, race and gender inequalities), social-class *analysis* remains the last taboo. This is especially the case for analyses involving the nature and consequences of social-class structures, interests, and power inequalities. Examples of topics excluded from consideration by conventional social institutions under the taboo include inquiries into the one-sided class war waged by the superclass against the working class, interpretations of working-class economic and political interests as legitimate, the merits of a labor party, and the need for new redistribution policies developed by and for the new working class that would shift substantial privileged-class economic and political resources to workers. Where these and other features of class analysis are concerned, a virtual blackout exists among mainstream social institutions. Few public forums exist for wide-ranging discussions of these topics, and they have been consistently marginalized and ignored by the schools, the mass media, and most political leaders. Despite occasional media attention to *some* class-related lifestyle issues and economic inequalities—as discussed later in this section, in the box at the end of this chapter ("Class Issues in the Media: The American Dream"), and in chapter 5—the taboo against social-class *analysis* remains firmly in place.

Class analyses involving the issues noted above are not curricular themes covered in schools at the primary or secondary level and are seldom included in university-level courses.[13] In the mainstream media, we find attention to working-class interests to be virtually nonexistent. In the print media, newspaper editors have little interest in, or sympathy for, working-class interests or issues. Majorities ranging from 54 percent to 60 percent of editors report that they side with business in labor disputes and also in business-worker conflicts involving issues such as minimum-wage increases and plant-closing legislation.[14] Every major U.S. daily newspaper includes a separate business section, but none includes a separate "class" or even "labor" section, and none of the 1,457 daily U.S. newspapers includes a regular commentary column written by a socialist or social democrat.[15] A similar situation exists in the electronic media, as illustrated by a study of the three network television evening news programs, which found the networks devote only 2 percent of total airtime to workers' issues.[16] Television news interview programs mirror this pattern. A study of the major TV networks' Sunday morning talk shows covering nineteen months identified only 2 representatives of organized labor out of 364 guests. More recent studies found "no labor guests" have ever appeared on NBC's Sunday morning *Chris Matthews Show* since its debut in 2002, while Matthews's cable show, *Hardball* (MSNBC), interviewed labor leaders only six times in a fifteen month period spanning 2004 and 2005.[17]

Politicians typically avoid class-based rhetoric, especially the use of language and policy labels that might openly emphasize or reveal the conflicting economic and political interests of working-class versus privileged-class members. This is the case because political candidates, especially presidential candidates, who violate what amounts to an unwritten rule against framing class inequalities as legitimate public policy issues risk being accused of promoting divisive and disruptive "class warfare" by privileged-class-based mainstream media pundits and their class cousins, "responsible" public officials, politicians, and business leaders.[18] Candidates who violate this rule are likely to be pressured by mainstream pundits to conform; if that fails and candidates persist, they are likely to be marginalized, ignored, or ridiculed by mainstream media pundits and political leaders. The end result may be political stigma and a failed campaign. But not always. For example, in 2006 a number of congressional candidates advocating pro-working-class policies won their elections.[19] This topic is considered in more detail at the end of chapter 4 in the box, "Class Issues in the Media: U.S. Elections and the Class Taboo."

Only two exceptions exist to the taboo on public discussions of class issues. First, it is acceptable to discuss the "middle class" and problems faced by this class.[20] Because large numbers of Americans identify themselves as middle class, references to this group actually serve to disguise and mute class differences because the term is so inclusive—it includes nearly everyone. When the mainstream media profile middle-class concerns, as was the case in the mid-2000s (as noted earlier), such reports increase public interest in, and the market for, such reporting. The 2005 *New York Times* "Class Matters" series (later published as a book) illustrates the mainstream media approach to class inequalities. The *Times* series, like a few other high-profile mid-2000s media reports on growing economic inequalities and middle-class concerns (discussed at the end of chapter 5), did not address conflicting class interests or class power inequalities. Instead, the *Times* series focused mainly on class-based lifestyle differences, social experiences, and income inequalities. On the latter issue, the *Times* acknowledged that in recent years U.S. income inequality has increased substantially while "social mobility" from lower and middle incomes to higher-income ranks "seems to have stagnated."[21] The series also noted that the advantages of privileged-class-based family membership—more so than merit alone—now have become (much more so than in the past) centrally important in ensuring the continued distribution of high levels of economic rewards to privileged-class members. Despite these trends, the series reassured middle-class readers that mobility is still possible by including profiles of individuals who have "moved up."

Following the series, the *Times* published an editorial that assured concerned middle-class readers that the paper was on their side. This piece argued in favor of "a truly merit-based society where class finally fades from importance."[22] While the *Times*'s editorial sentiment may be laudable, in the absence of structural changes that would reduce privileged-class advantages, members of the working and middle classes are left in the same powerless and disadvantaged position as was the case when the *Times* profiled their plight nine years earlier in its "Downsizing of America" series. Then, as now, in the final analysis, the central focus of each series was not on class-based policy reforms but on individual effort. In the mid-1990s, "The lesson, heard again and again, [was] that while government and business can do some things, in the end workers have little to fall back on but themselves."[23] In the mid-2000s, the "lesson" was get an education! While the *Times* editorial favored some programs facilitating greater access to college for low-income groups, the *unstated* message (lesson) was that in the meantime, working- or middle-class individuals interested in improving their lot in life should find ways to advance their education.[24]

The second exception to avoidance of class issues includes mass media glimpses into the lives of the privileged class, as well as tours of the excluded class.[25] Television programs often take viewers to both destinations. The glamour of life at the top is routinely showcased on both conventional and tabloid-style TV newsmagazines (e.g., *60 Minutes, 20/20, Entertainment Tonight, Inside Edition*); such programs frequently broadcast profiles of wealthy entertainment and sports figures, along with occasional reports on charismatic corporate elites. The grim realities of life-at-the-bottom experiences turn up most often on occasional PBS or cable TV documentaries concerning poverty, homelessness, welfare, and related issues.

Sometimes the plight of the poor becomes the focus of mainstream media attention—as in the aftermath of Hurricane Katrina, which stuck New Orleans and the U.S. Gulf coast on August 29, 2005. In this instance, dramatic television and print media coverage of rescues and government relief miscues focused public attention on the widespread and intense suffering of the poor.[26] But the attention was short-lived. Despite occasional media reports in the following weeks encouraging the allocation of more public resources to deal with the problems of poverty, by October the plight of the poor, as laid bare by Katrina, had begun to fade from media, government, and public attention as the war in Iraq and new stories on a wide range of other issues recaptured national headlines.[27] Less than a year after Katrina, it was clear that "the promised national debate about urban poverty never took place; instead, New Orleans . . . drifted helplessly in the currents of White House hypocrisy and conservative contempt."[28] In the end, when TV and other mainstream media report on the economic top or bottom, the accounts do not involve class analysis. Instead, they serve as models or morality tales, the first to aspire to and the other to avoid. The two models are never presented as causally related: one is not rich because the other is poor.[29]

The taboo nature of class is a product of institutional biases that discourage and deflect media and public discussions of class issues, especially conflicting class interests. These biases are grounded in privileged-class interests in encouraging public silence on, or even confusion about, class issues. Members of the superclass have an especially strong interest in not having public attention called to their class-based advantages or to broader class inequalities because a close examination of the origins of and basis for these inequalities—including the wealth, power, and privileges of this class—might call the entire class system into question.[30]

Superclass preferences for avoiding public discussions of class inequalities are paralleled by the interests of credentialed-class members in maintaining their own positions of comfort and security. Allied with and following the lead of their superclass sponsors, many credentialed-class members are rewarded for helping to keep class analysis out of the arena of public discourse. In their roles as government officials, organizational managers, media producers, and community leaders, credentialed-class professionals often pursue organizational policies and practices that have the effect of deflecting public attention away from class inequalities and class-based analysis of social issues and problems.[31]

Individuals and groups proposing higher taxes on the wealthy are attacked by many credentialed-class political leaders and media editors as advocating destructive and divisive "class warfare."[32] Whether the topic is taxes, income, educational opportunities, or other class-based inequalities, privileged-class advantages and working-class disadvantages are mostly topics to be avoided, not discussed.[33] Social inequalities (when they are considered) are most often framed by credentialed-class journalists, pundits, and political leaders as problems of gender, race, or other cultural-ethnic divisions (i.e., recent immigrants)—or perhaps as the result of personal or genetic flaws (e.g., a lack of intelligence or a "predisposition" to problems limiting achievement, such as alcoholism, drug use, or mental illness).[34] Class analysis of social inequalities is typically out of the picture—as it is framed by mainstream media coverage or political leaders' views.

Although privileged-class interests are major factors underlying the class taboo, we do not see a "class conspiracy" driving the neglect of class issues in public discourse. Rather, we see the superclass and its credentialed-class allies as bound by shared cultural assumptions, values, experiences, worldviews, and organizational memberships.[35] These shared qualities lead to strong, common commitments to maintaining the economic, political, and cultural status quo.[36] Such views lead members of these two classes (and most Americans) to explain material and social success (or failure) on the basis of factors other than class-based resources.[37]

Despite the taboo driving public neglect of class analysis, it has become virtually impossible for workers and their families, politicians, reporters, and even privileged-class members to ignore several class-related trends that are transforming the nature of social geography and social experiences in the United States today. Although these trends are increasingly obvious and growing in significance as subjects of public commentary and even political discourse, they are only the most visible and obvious features of the social-class iceberg today.

ABOVE THE WATERLINE: NEW CLASS SOCIETY TRENDS

I agree that rising inequality is a concern. The strength of the economy itself requires a belief of the broad American public that they are beneficiaries of a rising economy.

—Ben Bernanke, Federal Reserve chairman,
BusinessWeek.com, February 16, 2006

While American society has always been divided by substantial class inequalities, recent developments in the economic, political, and cultural arenas have produced major changes in the U.S. class system. Three important class-related trends fall above the waterline of the class iceberg in the sense of being increasingly visible and obvious sources of growing public concern and commentary: (1) class polarization, (2) downward mobility, and (3) class secession.

Class Polarization

We're becoming a society increasingly divided between haves and have-nots. The rich are getting richer, the poor are getting poorer, and the middle class is one layoff or illness away from bankruptcy.

—Henry Cook, Responsible Wealth member, *Too Much*, April 18, 2005

Class polarization refers to the growing division of the United States into two main classes: the privileged class and the new working class. This trend is the result of four convergent developments that have become increasingly evident since the early 1970s. First, a pattern of growing income inequality has placed increasing numbers of persons and families in the upper- and lower-income ranges, with declining numbers in the middle. Second, a corresponding pattern of stagnating or falling real wages for many working Americans has eroded living standards for all but those in the highest income groups. Third, a pattern of shrinking fringe benefits for more and more workers has emerged, particularly in the areas of health care and pensions, resulting in ever higher levels of economic insecurity among middle- and low-income groups. Finally, the increasing use of contingent, contract, temporary, and part-time workers by a wide range of employers has contributed to a growing "contingency work-force" characterized not only by low pay and prestige but also by vanishing-point levels of job security.

Once upon a time—and not too long ago—the material realities of life for middle-income Americans were such that references to this group by social scientists and journalists as the "middle class" were understandable, if overstated. Of course, as is often the case with class issues, the precise meaning of this concept was (and is) somewhat elusive and subject to debate. Even so, since the end of World War II, for most mainstream academic researchers, as well as for the American public, middle-class status has typically been associated with an identifiable core of economic and social resources. These include "respectable" jobs (mid-level prestige or higher); stable, mid-level (or higher) incomes; security benefits (health care, pensions); and participation in conventional social institutions such as churches, schools, community groups, and other voluntary organizations.[38]

For the first three decades of the post–World War II period, most academic definitions and popular perceptions of an American middle class were grounded in an economic reality whereby a majority of middle-income individuals and families possessed stable jobs and experienced gradually rising real incomes.[39] The reinforcement of these core features among middle-income groups by additional material resources anchored middle-class status (e.g., expanding levels of employer-provided benefits, including health care, life and disability insurance, vacation time, and pensions).[40] This stable resource base made it possible for many middle-income families, over time, to increase their stock of investment capital (by homeownership and investment savings), skill capital (by additional education and by sending children to college), and social capital (using more free time to participate in various social groups and organizations). The material and social resources of middle-income Americans, combined with widespread egalitarian cultural beliefs of America as a middle-class nation, were reflected in subjective class-identification studies that from the 1940s through the 1980s consistently found majorities of Americans identifying themselves as members of the middle class or upper middle class.[41]

In short, the middle-income/middle-class linkage was predicated on workers' access to organizational resources that went beyond income alone. In post–World War II America, job stability and rising real wages, combined with other economic and social resources available to middle-income households, produced a large group that could readily realize a modest version of the

American Dream. The resource base of middle-income Americans at this time could even provide a platform for upward mobility, especially for their children. However, "sometime around 1973, the American dream stopped working. That's the year that the real hourly wage (inflation-adjusted) for non-supervisory workers—almost three-quarters of the workforce—peaked. Since then, it's fallen."[42] As real wages fell, other major structural changes in this period transformed the national economy in ways that produced a "crisis of the American Dream."[43]

Although not causes in and of themselves, as the most visible features of the class polarization process, the four convergent developments cited earlier in this section offer a starting point for understanding the extent to which the material realities of the U.S. middle-income group have been transformed. An examination of these developments, in conjunction with the evidence concerning the distribution of consumption capital (income) and related material resources in the last thirty years, supports our view that a polarized new class system has emerged—minus a middle class. (A portion of what has been called the middle class is best understood as part of the comfort-class segment in our model.) To many who considered themselves part of the middle-class, the period since the early 1970s brought the "end of the world"—as they knew it.

Declining Middle Incomes and Wages

Although all U.S. national income studies include middle ranges, middle-income levels do not necessarily translate into "middle-class status." In fact, recent income and wage studies indicate many average wage workers and their families have experienced reduced living standards since 1973. Our chapter 1 summary of annual U.S. family income trends over the past thirty years revealed that the percentage of middle-income Americans declined sharply, while the percentages in the top and bottom income groups increased. Studies using more expansive definitions of middle income than those cited in chapter 1 have reported similar patterns for this same period. For example, one study, defining "middle income" very broadly, found that the proportion of U.S. families earning between $25,000 and $100,000 (in 2004 dollars) fell from 70.9 percent of all families in 1969 to 59.7 percent in 2004.[44] Almost all of the decline in this large range of middle-income families occurred for those earning between $25,000 and $50,000 (in 2004 dollars), which declined from 39.5 percent of all families in 1969 to 25.7 percent in 2004. By contrast, families earning over $100,000 (in 2004 dollars) increased from 5 percent of all families in 1969 to 20.1 percent in 2004.[45] Underscoring the shift toward greater income inequality over the last thirty years, the U.S. family income Gini ratio (a measure of income inequality whereby zero equals total equality and one equals total inequality) increased from 0.356 in 1973 to 0.444 in 2003.[46]

The last thirty years witnessed not only declining proportions of middle-income families but also reductions in real earnings for many Americans. Average per-hour real wages (in 2005 dollars) declined for production and nonsupervisory workers (about 80 percent of the workforce) from $17.13 in 1973 to $16.11 in 2005. Thus, in 2005 the average weekly earnings of production and nonsupervisory workers amounted to $644.40 (forty hours at $16.11 per hour). If a worker earned this amount for fifty-two weeks, his or her 2005 income would have been $33,509. This amount was $2,121 less in real income (adjusted for inflation) than the $35,630 annual income a worker in the same classification would have earned in 1973 (at $17.13 per hour in 2005 dollars).[47]

While many workers' real wages have declined since 1973, *within* the new working class we find important variations along the lines of gender and race/ethnicity. For example, the median hourly real wage for men declined in the 1973–2005 period from (in 2005 dollars) $15.76 (1973) to $15.64 (2003), but it rose for *women* from $9.95 to $12.82.[48] Throughout the 2000s, women's real hourly wages (average and median) remained lower than men's, but the trend line for female wages tracked up, not down during the past thirty years. This was not the case for black and Hispanic male workers, who, like male workers generally, experienced declining wages. For example, in 1973, 51.7 percent of black males and 48.6 percent of Hispanic males earned (in 2005 dollars) modest-to-high wages of between $12.00 to $28.79 per hour; however, by 2005, the proportions of minority males with earnings in this range had declined to 43.5 percent for blacks and 36.4 percent for Hispanics. During this same period, the proportions of low-wage black and Hispanic males increased. In 1973, 45.3 percent of black and 48.4 percent of Hispanic male workers earned wages (in 2005 dollars) at or only slightly above the poverty level (between $7.20 [or less] to $12.00 per hour), but in 2005, 48.2 percent of black and 56.9 percent of Hispanic male workers had earnings in this range.[49] These trends reflect the fact that since 1973, most male minority workers experienced sharper wage declines than was the case for male wage earners generally in this period.

As the wage trends cited above suggest, within the new working class, workers of color are likely to experience the greatest income inequalities. This pattern is also evident in median family income trends throughout the 1973–2004 period. White median family income (in 2004 dollars) rose from $46,384 in 1973 to $56,700 in 2004. Black median family income also increased from $26,770 in 1973 to $35,158 in 2004, but obviously remained far below white income. Compared to increases in white and black family incomes, Hispanic median family income rose only slightly, increasing from $32,095 in 1973 to $35,401 in 2004.[50] The seeming paradox of *increasing* median family incomes (for all three racial/ethnic groups) during a period of *declining real wages* for many workers is really not a paradox at all. The increases recorded in family incomes, especially for lower- and middle-income families with children, occurred primarily *because wives sharply increased their annual hours of work.* For example, wives between the ages of twenty-five and fifty-four with children in the middle-income quintile increased their annual hours of paid employment from 849 in 1979 to 1,327 in 2004.[51]

The evidence concerning income trends supports the conclusion that there has been a growing polarization of income in the United States. Using Census Bureau information, the Economic Policy Institute (EPI) provides a useful way of illustrating the extent of inequality concerning income redistribution in the United States. The EPI reports the shares of aggregate (total) national income received by U.S. families divided into five quintile groups, arrayed by income levels from the lowest 20 percent to the highest 20 percent (all amounts in 2004 dollars).

Drawing upon EPI and Census Bureau data, figure 2.1 summarizes several aspects of family income levels and redistribution trends in recent years. First, it illustrates, using side-by-side comparisons, the shares of national income received by families in each quintile group for 1974 and 2004. Second, the first line at the bottom of the figure reports the percentage changes in family income shares from 1974 to 2004 for each quintile group. Finally, the last line at the bottom of the figure provides a summary of 2004 family income ranges for each quintile.[52]

During the 1974–2004 period, each quintile group experienced changes in the percentage of aggregate income received, ranging from highly positive to highly negative. The top 20 percent experienced an 18 percent increase in its share of national income (from 40.6 percent in 1974 to 47.9 percent in 2004), whereas the other four quintiles all experienced decreases in their shares of national income. These ranged from a modest loss of 3 percent for the fourth quintile (dropping from 24.1 percent to 23.0 percent) to a whopping 26 percent loss for the bottom quintile (dropping from 5.7 to 4.0 percent). The changes in income shares for these five groups reflect the reality that income was redistributed over the 1974–2004 period in an upward direction.

The income ranges reported as the last line of figure 2.1 provide a context for considering the impact of upward income redistribution. The income range for the bottom quintile in 2004 included all families with incomes up to $24,780 (in 2004 dollars). This means not only that families in this group have the lowest incomes, but also that they will be most affected by income losses because they have the fewest resources to begin with. Yet this group suffered the greatest loss in income share during the 1974–2004 period. The income ranges for the second quintile ($24,781 to $43,400), the middle quintile ($43,401 to $65,832), and the fourth quintile ($65,833 to $100,000) provided these groups with greater cushions (compared with the bottom quintile) to absorb income losses. Of course, the top quintile, with an income range of $100,001 and up, needed no cushion; it increased its income share by 18 percent.

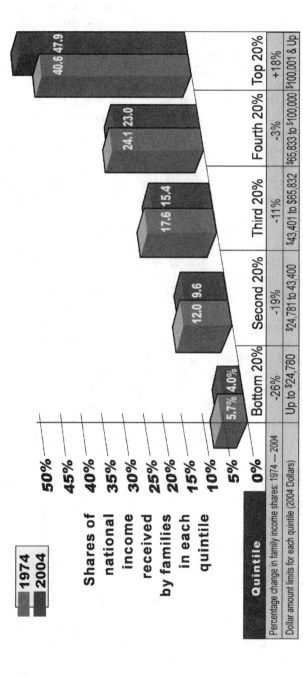

Quintile	Bottom 20%	Second 20%	Third 20%	Fourth 20%	Top 20%
Percentage change in family income shares: 1974 — 2004	-26%	-19%	-11%	-3%	+18%
Dollar amount limits for each quintile (2004 Dollars)	Up to $24,780	$24,781 to 43,400	$43,401 to $65,832	$65,833 to $100,000	$100,001 & Up

Figure 2.1. Family Income Shares and Changes, by Quintile Group, 1974-2004.

Source: Economic Policy Institute, "Family Income Limits by Quintile, 1974–2004; Share of Aggregate Family Income by Quintile," 1–2.

The growing gap between top and bottom income groups is even more evident when we compare changes in the shares of income *after federal taxes* for different income groups. According to a 2005 Congressional Budget Office (CBO) study, in 1981 the after-tax income share received by the top 10 percent of U.S. households was 27.9 percent, while the bottom 40 percent received only 18.9 percent.[53] Another 2005 CBO study found that in 2003 (the most recent year available), the after-tax income share of the top 10 percent group ($190,400 average after-tax annual income, 2003 dollars) had grown to 33.9 percent, but the bottom 40 percent share had shrunk to 15.3 percent ($22,450 average after-tax annual income, 2003 dollars).[54] The CBO also projected federal tax rates under current law from 2001 to 2014. These projections indicate the effective federal tax rates on income received by the top 10 percent would decrease through 2014 (increasing in this group's income share) and that tax rates for the bottom 40 percent would increase (further decreasing this group's income share).[55]

Top-earning groups have far outdistanced average wage earners over the past two decades, but the very highest paid groups, such as the chief executive officers (CEOs) of major U.S. firms, have done the best. During the 1980–2005 period, average total compensation for CEOs at large U.S. firms increased about 800 percent. In 1980 average total annual CEO compensation was forty-two times what average workers earned. But like the Energizer Bunny, the CEO group kept going and going. In 1990, the CEO-to-average worker pay ratio grew to 107:1 and then jumped to 269:1 in 1996. In 2000, it reached a peak of 525:1, declined to 281:1 in 2002, climbed to 301:1 in 2003, and rose to 411:1 in 2005.[56] In 2005, average total compensation for CEOs at two hundred of the largest U.S. corporations was $11.3 million, but median total compensation was $17.9 million for CEOs at the one hundred largest U.S. firms.[57] By comparison, average CEO pay at large U.S. firms was $9.8 million in 2003, $3.4 million in 1990, and $1.4 million in 1980 (all amounts in 2005 dollars).[58]

While CEO pay increased dramatically, the average annual incomes of production workers in the same period *decreased* slightly from $33,758 in 1980 to $33,509 in 2005 (in 2005 dollars, forty hours per week for fifty-two weeks).[59] Minimum-wage workers did even worse. They experienced a 30 percent *decrease* in their real average annual incomes, dropping from about $14,460 in 1979 to $10,300 in 2005 (both amounts in 2005 dollars for two thousand annual working hours).[60] If production and minimum-wage workers had received 800 percent pay increases (like CEOs) since 1980, in 2005 their annual incomes would have been about $261,000 and $47,000, respectively.

Few minority members or women become CEOs. One study found that minorities make up only about 1 percent of Fortune 500 top executives.[61] While women make up almost half of the U.S. workforce, in 2005 only two Fortune 500 firms had women CEOs or presidents and ninety of those five hundred firms didn't have any women corporate officers.[62] When women do become senior corporate managers, they earn less than men: "Female managers' earnings now average 72 percent of their male colleagues' [earnings]."[63] Females were also totally absent from the one hundred fifty highest paid CEOs in the 1990–2004 period and only one nonwhite male made the list—"Charles Wang, founder and former CEO of Computer Associates."[64]

Losses in Benefits

Although executives are doing well, members of the new working class, as we have seen, generally find their incomes shrinking. In recent years, the falling incomes of many workers have been matched by reductions or stagnation where fringe benefits are concerned. During the 1979–1989 period, the "annual growth in hourly benefits" (including employer-provided health insurance, pension plans, and payroll taxes) amounted to just $0.04 per year.[65] In the 1987–2005 period, fringe benefits for private-sector hourly wage earners as a percentage of workers' total compensation remained nearly flat at 19.4 percent in 1987 and 19.7 percent in 2005.[66] ("Fringe benefits" include employer-paid pension plans, insurance [health and life], and payroll taxes [the employer portion of Social Security and unemployment taxes].)

Reductions in pension and health-care coverage over the past several years illustrate the extent to which workers' benefits have fallen. The proportion of all private-sector workers covered by all types of employer-provided pension plans declined from 50.6 percent in 1979 to 45.5 percent in 2004. White workers in the private sector saw pension coverage (of all types) fall from 52.2 percent (1979) to 50.6 percent (2004). Minority members fared less well than whites as pension coverage for blacks fell from 45.8 percent in 1979 to 42.2 percent in 2004; for Hispanics it fell from 38.2 percent in 1979 to 25.0 percent in 2004. By contrast, the percentage of women workers covered by employer-provided pensions in the private sector rose slightly from 41.3 percent in 1979 to 44.3 percent in 2004.[67]

Not only has the proportion of workers covered by employer-provided pensions declined, but so has the quality of such plans, which tend to fall into two categories. First, defined-benefit plans "are generally considered the best plans from a workers' perspective because they guarantee a worker a fixed payment in retirement based on pre-retirement wages and years of service regardless of stock market performance." Second, defined-contribution plans provide for employer contributions to an individual worker's retirement account (to which workers often can add).[68] Under these plans, retirement income depends upon the investment options provided by employers and upon investment decisions workers make over time. Because of these conditions associated with defined contribution plans, workers are often presented with substantial limitations and uncertainties that can make retirement income problematic and unpredictable.[69]

The proportion of full-time private-sector workers in medium and large firms (one hundred workers or more) covered by defined-benefit pension plans fell from 84 percent in 1980 to 50 percent in 1997. For workers in small firms, such coverage declined from 20 percent in 1990 to 15 percent in 1996.[70] In 1995 the proportion of workers covered by defined-contribution pension plans exceeded the proportion covered by defined-benefit plans. Since then, the proportion of workers covered by defined-benefit plans has continued to decline, while the proportion covered by defined-contribution plans has continued to increase.[71] In 2005 about 21 percent of all private-sector workers had access to, and were participating in, defined-benefit pension plans; by contrast, 53 percent of private-sector workers had access to defined-contribution pension plans, but only 42 percent were participating in such plans.[72] Given the important differences between the two types of pension plans, it is clear that "the shift from traditional defined-benefit plans to defined-contribution plans represents an erosion of pension quality."[73]

Regarding health care, the share of private-sector wage and salary workers covered by employer-provided health-care plans, where employers pay amounts ranging from partial to full premiums, declined from 69 percent of private-sector workers in 1979 to 55.9 percent in 2004. This trend affects workers in all gender and racial categories. From 1979 to 2004, health-care coverage fell for male workers from 75.4 to 58.7 percent and from 59.4 to 52.5 percent for female workers. During the same period, coverage for whites fell from 70.3 to 59.8 percent; black health-care coverage dropped from 63.1 to 54.1 percent, and coverage for Hispanics fell from 60.4 to 39.7 percent.[74]

In parallel with declining health-care coverage were increased premium costs for workers, and increased percentages of workers were required by employers to help fund their health-care plans. The increase in health-care premiums paid by workers for family-coverage medical care rose (in 2006 dollars) from an average of $155 per month in 1996 to $172 per month in 1999 to $226 in 2006.[75] The proportion of full-time private-sector workers required to make contributions for single medical coverage increased from 26 percent in 1980 to 69 percent in 1997 to 76 percent in 2004; for family medical coverage, the percentage of workers required to make contributions increased from 46 percent in 1980 to 80 percent in 1997 to 89 percent in 2004.[76]

Growing Contingent Work

Workers' wages and benefits fell in part due to the growing use by employers of more non-full-time workers to reduce labor costs. The alternatives to full-time employment include a number of work arrangements variously referred to by researchers and journalists as "contingent" or "nonstandard" work.[77] Despite the lack of comprehensive trend data on contingent work, different forms of information suggest that employers are employing more workers outside of full-time work arrangements.[78] Today, "over a quarter of all workers [are] now working at jobs that are contingent or nonstandard."[79] This category includes regular part-time workers, independent contractors, and all other types of nonstandard workers (temps, on-call workers, contract firms).

The distribution of contingent work follows familiar patterns of gender- and minority-based inequalities. In 2005, women made up 54.7 percent of all nonstandard workers. Moreover, female, black, and Hispanic workers, along with workers with less than a high school degree, were overrepresented in the lowest-paid forms of nonstandard arrangements: temp and on-call work.[80] As we might expect, contingent workers "generally earn less and receive fewer fringe benefits than workers with similar skills in regular full-time jobs."[81] Wages average about 10 to 20 percent less (per hour) for women and men working part-time or as temps compared with similar workers in full-time jobs. Regarding benefits, in 2005 only 20.8 percent of all nonstandard workers received employer-provided health insurance (of any type), and only 22.8 percent were participating in employer-offered pension plans (of any type).[82]

The trend toward increasing contingent work has been paralleled (and fueled) by declining levels of unionization among U.S. workers. The share of U.S. wage and salary workers who are union members fell from 24 percent in 1973 to 12.0 percent in 2006.[83] (U.S. unionization rates in 2006 were 7.4 percent for private-sector workers and 36.2 percent for government workers.) The falling rate of unionization directly lowers wages and fringe benefits for many workers as unionized jobs disappear. Also, as union rates decline, "there is less pressure on non-union employers to raise wages (a 'spillover' or 'threat effect' of unionism)."[84]

Increasing contingent work and falling unionization rates have been paralleled by declines in both job stability and quality throughout the 1979-to-mid-2000s period.[85] One recent study reported that now only one-quarter of working Americans have a "good job," defined as a job that pays at least $16 per hour (or about $32,000 per year before taxes) and includes employer-paid health insurance and a pension.[86] Unfortunately, the number of good jobs available to American workers is likely to decline further in the future as the income, benefit, contingent work, unionization, and job-security trends noted above intensify class polarization and increasingly divide the United States into a society of haves and have-nots.

Downward Mobility

> I may look middle class . . . but I'm not. My boat is sinking fast.
>
> —Mark McClellen, unemployed manager
> due to plant closing, *Class Matters*, 2005

Downward mobility is one type of vertical movement possible in class-stratified societies. Vertical social mobility refers to movements by individuals or groups up or down across class boundaries and often involves generational comparisons. Intergenerational vertical mobility occurs when an individual rises above or falls below the class ranking of his or her parents (e.g., an individual with working-class parents rises as an adult to membership in the superclass). Intragenerational vertical mobility occurs when an individual rises above or falls below the class ranking he or she held at an earlier point in adult life without reference to his or her parents' class ranking (e.g., a physician who, for whatever reasons, falls to a position as a laborer). Social mobility also can be horizontal, as might occur when an adult worker moves from one occupation of average prestige and pay to another with similar prestige and pay levels.[87]

When sociologists track vertical social mobility, those using functionalist models typically utilize a combination of income, job prestige, and educational attainment as indicators of class. Production model advocates are more likely to focus on an individual's role in the production process (laborer, manager, owner) as a guide to class rank. Functionalist model studies of vertical social mobility in the United States in the 1960s and 1970s, using occupational prestige rankings as indicators of class position, found substantial occupational mobility occurring mainly in an upward direction. By contrast, production model studies focusing on capitalist property ownership as an indicator of class found little evidence of intergenerational mobility into the "capitalist property ownership class" in the 1980s and 1990s.[88] More recent research (based largely on functionalist and income-based approaches) indicates upward intergenerational mobility rates in the United States were lower in the 1990s and early 2000s than in the 1970s.[89]

Downward mobility refers to the experience of falling in terms of social-class membership. The concept has been used as a way of summarizing the economic, social, and psychological losses many middle-income (or above) workers have experienced due to job losses and other forms of economic restructuring in the United States. The label spotlights the "falling from grace" experience of middle-income workers displaced from their jobs and often discovering they cannot find new work that will replace the income, health, pension, and job security benefits of their former jobs. For many workers, the results of job loss include sharp, permanently impaired living standards, diminished long-term economic security, anger, self-doubt, depression, guilt, and dislocated personal relationships.[90]

The term *downward mobility* was initially applied by researchers to the job displacement experiences of blue-collar workers who lost jobs due to plant closings, automation, or layoffs. More recently, the term has also been applied to diverse types of workers, including managerial and professional white-collar employees who have lost their jobs due to corporate practices such as "restructuring," "outsourcing," and "downsizing." As a result of social science research and media coverage of factory closings and related job losses dating from the 1980s to the present, downward mobility entered the public lexicon as a label for what came to be a high-profile, savage, and persistent social trend.[91]

The personal effects and extent of downward mobility have figured prominently in mass media reports on this topic. Examples from the middle and latter 2000s included "page one" media reports on plans by Ford, General Motors, and Chrysler to eliminate 140,000 U.S. white- and blue-collar auto worker jobs by 2012 and on Ford's offer of early retirement buyouts to all 75,000 of its United Automobile Workers union–represented workers.[92] These gloomy reports were preceded and followed by other well-publicized reports on the outsourcing of U.S. high-tech jobs to offshore venues, corporate bankruptcy filings, and pension defaults by U.S. steel and airline firms.[93] One notable corporate drama with downward mobility implications for thousands of workers that received high-profile media coverage involved the Delphi Corporation, a large General Motors auto supplier firm. Delphi's senior executives declared bankruptcy in late 2005 for the U.S. division, and CEO Steve Miller asked the federal judge supervising the bankruptcy proceedings to void the collective bargaining agreements covering Delphi's unionized workers. As a result, twenty-four thousand unionized U.S. Delphi workers represented by the United Automobile Workers union faced a potential wage cut from about $50,000 per year in 2006 to about $24,000 in 2007 and 2008.[94]

In the mid- and latter 2000s, the drama of large-scale job cuts and falling wages affecting thousands of workers generated compelling first-person media reports and underscored the fact that downward mobility was continuing as a highly visible social trend. Research findings using various methodological approaches support the conclusion that downward mobility is a common experience for large numbers of American workers and their families today—just as it was in the 1980s and 1990s.[95] The reality and fear of downward mobility have served, and continue to serve, as major sources of anxiety, grief, dislocation, and frustration for millions of American workers and their families.

While our approach to class analysis differs from functionalist and production models, our general conceptualization of downward mobility is similar to how this phenomena is viewed by other models. In the language of our model, downward mobility occurs when substantial, job-related losses by workers and their families involving income (consumption capital), insurance benefits, and other economic resources (e.g., job security, pension resources) shift workers and their families deeper into the depths of the contingent or excluded class segments of the new working class. Despite the fact that our distributional model does not include a middle class, we agree that downward mobility is an important and persistent social trend that has negatively affected many workers and families in both middle-income and more affluent groups, including new-working-class members located in what we term the *comfort-class* segment.[96]

The *sources* of downward mobility are viewed differently by various authors, depending on whether their focus is on underlying structural factors, such as the nature of capitalism, or on more immediate factors, such as company-level practices involving job displacement, downsizing, and outsourcing. Regardless of the sources, three related developments increase the intensity and extent of the downward mobility experience for workers and their families: massive job losses, income reductions, and downward intergenerational drift among young adults from middle-income (or upper-middle-income) families who cannot find jobs that will allow them to replicate their parents' income levels or living standards.

Down by Work: Lost Jobs

One study estimated as many as one-fifth to one-third of all workers experienced downward mobility in the 1980s due to job displacement.[97] Such estimates are not surprising given that from 1979 to the mid-1990s, more than forty-three million jobs were eliminated in the United States due to displacement and downsizing.[98] And despite the fact that more new jobs have been created than have been eliminated since 1979, most new jobs (over 70 percent) involve work in low-paying industries, and these industries are also projected to provide the largest share of all new U.S. jobs through 2014.[99] In the manufacturing sector, which is highly unionized, 2.5 million jobs were lost between 1979 and 1999, and 700,000 more jobs in that sector disappeared in the period from July 2000 to May 2001.[100] After the U.S. economy entered a recession in March 2001, more jobs were lost. Job losses accelerated following the September 11 terrorist attacks, and by August 2003, a total of 2.4 million nonfarm U.S. jobs had been lost due to the recession and the "jobless recovery" that followed. "In June 2004 . . . the economy was still down 1.2 million jobs from the March 2001 peak—an unparalleled occurrence this far into a recovery."[101] In the mid- and latter 2000s, the number of jobs created in the United States each month was often below the one hundred fifty thousand new jobs needed each month "just to absorb the labor market's natural population growth."[102]

Down by Money: Lost Income

The income consequences of job displacement are typically disastrous for what were formerly middle-income wage earners. Workers displaced from the auto, steel, meatpacking, and aerospace industries in the mid-1980s reported income losses of about 44 percent compared with their previous earnings in the first two years after being laid off.[103] In the mid-1990s, of 2.2 million full-time workers laid off in 1993 and 1994, only two-thirds had found full-time work by 1996. More than one-half of this group was earning less than what their previous jobs paid, and more than one-third experienced pay cuts of 20 percent or more. The average weekly median earnings for this group declined about 14 percent, but older full-time workers (in their late fifties and early sixties) who found new jobs experienced pay decreases averaging 37 percent.[104]

During the 1999–2000 period, two million workers permanently lost jobs they had held for three or more years due to plant closings and other forms of job displacement. A study of this group found that by early 2002, of the 92 percent who had lost full-time jobs, only 62 percent were again working in full-time wage and salary jobs. Of this group, half reported earning less than what they had previously earned, and 25 percent reported earnings on their new jobs that "were 20 percent or more below those on the job they had lost."[105] As was the case in earlier studies, displaced older workers (forty-five to sixty-four) experienced the greatest losses in earnings.[106] A study by Koeber and Wright found a similar pattern of older age/greater income loss. Their research involving 2,424 displaced workers revealed that for males over fifty, average weekly earnings declined by $98, from $743 (past job) to $644 (current job); for females over fifty, average weekly earnings declined by $44, from $419 (past job) to $375 (current job).[107]

In addition to income losses related to job displacement, the thirty-year pattern of falling real per-hour and weekly wages (adjusted for inflation) for average workers further reinforces the downward mobility drift experienced by many workers. As noted earlier, average real hourly wages fell from $17.13 per hour in 1973 to $16.11 per hour in 2005 (in 2005 dollars). As real hourly wages declined, so did average weekly real wages, which fell from $685.20 in 1973 to $644.40 in 2005. Assuming workers were employed fifty-two weeks in each of the two baseline years, this means workers' real incomes, apart from any income losses associated with job displacement, declined by $2,121, dropping from $35,630 in 1973 to $33,509 in 2005.[108]

Down by Age: Lost Living Standards

The extent of recent downward intergenerational mobility is difficult to determine, in part because of definitional issues concerning the meanings of the terms *class, generations,* and *downward mobility.* Despite these issues, recent income-based research findings, as well as studies of occupational trends, indicate that young workers today are finding it difficult to match the living standards achieved by older workers in the previous generation.

Two intergenerational income studies from the late 1990s produced similar findings: young U.S. adult workers in the 1990s earned substantially lower real incomes (on average) than those of comparable young workers in the recent past.[109] More recent intergenerational income studies have reported similar results.[110] A more complex 2007 intergenerational study compared the income, educational, and occupational levels achieved by over 4,700 fathers in 1979 with the levels of these three resources achieved by their adult sons (2,554) and daughters (2,212) in 2004. Among other results, this study found that compared to similar studies in the 1960s and 1970s, there was substantially more downward mobility among young adults in the mid-2000s.[111] These findings, as well as those from income studies, are reinforced by comparisons of "entry-level" wages for high school–educated workers, which indicate sharp income drops have occurred across generational lines. For example, the real entry-level hourly wage received by male high school graduates (ages nineteen to twenty-five) declined from $13.39 in 1973 to $10.93 in 2005 (wages for both years computed in 2005 dollars); female high school graduates' entry-level hourly wage fell from $9.81 in 1973 to $9.08 in 2005.[112] While some young workers (e.g., college educated) experienced modest wage gains in the 1973–2005 period, the fact remains "that entry level wages for men and women high school graduates in 2005 were still below their levels of 1979 or 1973."[113]

Research findings showing lower wages for young U.S. workers today than was the case a generation ago should not be surprising given the massive shifts that have occurred in the U.S. occupational and wage structures over the past thirty years. For young workers, finding a "good job" is increasingly problematic, as illustrated by a recent study which found only 50 percent of young workers (ages eighteen to thirty-four) without college degrees (73 percent of all young workers) held full-time, permanent jobs.[114] Given the kinds of jobs young workers hold, wage trends among young workers, and the fact that most U.S. job growth through 2014 is projected to occur in low-wage occupations, it appears that downward intergenerational mobility is, and will continue to be, a relatively common experience among young adults today and in the future.[115]

Class Secession

America's top tier has grown infinitely richer and more removed over the past 25 years. It is not unfair to say that they are literally living in a different country. Few among them send their children to our public schools.

—Senator James Webb (D-VA), *Wall Street Journal*, November 14, 2006

As class polarization and downward mobility intensify and contribute to growing community tensions and social problems, the privileged class is increasingly distancing itself from public institutions in ways that suggest not simply more suburbanization but a kind of class secession. Of course, the very wealthy have always separated themselves from the nonwealthy through exclusive neighborhoods, clubs, and schools. However, what Robert Reich once termed the "secession of the successful" now combines traditional forms of physical and social separation and increasing numbers of privately provided services with the ideology of neoliberalism, an idea system of free market fundamentalism that encourages and legitimates hostility to public institutions.[116] In short, class secession today involves both a separatist social identity and a conscious secessionistic mentality.

One measure of the increasing physical separation of the privileged class from the working class is the growing number of home-owner associations, which typically govern details of home and property maintenance in neighborhoods and communities that are physically separate and sometimes walled off from surrounding lower-income areas. The Community Associations Institute (CAI) estimated that in 1990 U.S. association-governed communities numbered 130,000, including 11.6 million housing units and 29.6 million residents. By 2005 these numbers had grown to 274,000 communities with 22.1 million housing units and 54.6 million residents.[117] Such organizations are typically initiated by developers to supervise upscale housing developments. Membership is usually mandatory for home owners. An association board of directors (appointed first by the developer and later elected by home owners) enforces developer-designed codes, covenants, and restrictions regarding property use, maintenance, and services; all home buyers must sign a contract in which they agree to abide by the association's rules. Association-provided services are financed by membership fees and may range from basics like trash collection to maintenance of parks, recreation sites, private security guards, and even lobbying activities. The latter service logically follows the reality that associations are private concerns representing groups with narrow, private interests.[118] As the CAI points out, "community associations have become increasingly popular because they help protect home values and help meet increased demand for privatization of services . . . that were once provided by government."[119] Associations also lobby state and local governments on various issues such as zoning decisions and tax relief for services they already provide, like garbage collection.[120]

Of all community associations, those that govern physically walled and gated upscale residential developments are among the fastest growing. In 1987 there were an estimated twelve thousand U.S. gated communities; by 1998, the number had grown to thirty thousand with a total population of eight million Americans.[121] In the mid-2000s, about twenty million Americans lived in seven million households located in developments where "community access is secured with walls or fences."[122] In large cities, developers estimate eight of ten new urban projects are gated.[123] In the suburbs, regional data suggest gated suburban communities are growing rapidly. For example, "about 40 percent of new homes in California are behind walls . . . [and] most subdivisions approved by Palm Beach, Fla., in the past five years are gated."[124]

The combination of high income, physical isolation, and privately provided services in gated communities is both supported and encouraged by neoliberalism in the form of what political scientist Evan McKenzie refers to as an "ideology of privatism—an ideology that overlays and reinforces sentiments favoring exclusiveness, exclusion, and isolation." In his study of home-owners' associations, McKenzie maintains that this ideology, when combined with the physical isolation that "privatization for the few" produces, can lead to "an attenuated sense of loyalty and commitment to public communities." As a result, he believes there could be "a gradual secession from the city . . . [with the city becoming] financially untenable for the many and socially unnecessary for the few. Certainly this steady secession would make the lives of those who remained in the city increasingly difficult."[125]

In the contemporary period, idea systems such as neoliberalism and privatism have been vigorously promoted by U.S. superclass elites as part of a large-scale, privileged-class-led attack on publicly supported institutions, such as schools and most forms of government-funded services. Mass media dissemination of ideas asserting that government-based services are inefficient or ineffective or both helps facilitate and legitimate public hostility to public institutions.[126] Policies based on these ideas, such as reducing government services (except for the police and military) and government regulations, serve elites' economic interests. In fact, many top executives of American firms now openly accept the view that "their job is to maximize shareholder returns, not to advance public goals."[127] Today, idea systems

Copyright © Lloyd Dangle. Reprinted with permission.

based on privatization help "normalize," facilitate, and legitimate the growth of class-segregated communities and contribute to the erosion of privileged-class support for mixed-class public institutions, such as nongated neighborhoods, municipal services, public schools, and community hospitals.

The mainstream media occasionally report on growing class segregation and secession issues (though the latter term is seldom used). In the mid-2000s, the *New York Times* reported "that researchers are finding . . . increasing economic segregation."[128] A *Newsweek* cover story offered this view of class secession: "Increasingly the [privileged class] is choosing to live in ways that minimize its mixing with . . . [other classes]. . . . Sometimes it just moves farther out into the suburbs, or higher up the high rise. But increasingly often it chooses to live in a walled and gated community guarded by private security forces."[129] This observation intersects with research that suggests the attraction of gated community life is linked, in part, to residents' interests in the security, safety, and protection they believe such communities provide.[130] While members of all classes presumably share interests in safety and security, members of the privileged class more often have the resources to pursue these interests in ways that involve physical forms of class secession. These would include not only gated communities but also, for example, "the rise of the Hummer lifestyle," meaning the popularity of large sport utility vehicles (SUVs) among privileged-class consumers because of the militarylike security such vehicles appear to provide drivers and passengers.[131]

Above the Waterline Trends: Social Consequences and Popular Culture

The consequences of class polarization, downward mobility, and class secession for millions of new-working-class members and their families over the past three decades include a growing sense of insecurity and pessimism. These trends are reflected in public attitudes, lifestyle choices, and even the popular music of today's youth. Two national public-opinion surveys in the mid-2000s reported similar findings: nearly two-thirds of Americans believe the American Dream is becoming harder to achieve.[132] For example, in one study, "62 percent of Americans say that the American Dream is harder to achieve today compared to their parents' generation . . . and 64 percent say that the American Dream is harder to achieve today compared to 10 years ago."[133] Moreover, only 15 percent say that all or most Americans will be able to achieve the American Dream, and 42 percent do not think that they will be able to achieve the American Dream in their lifetime. Also, majorities of respondents in one poll said the American Dream is harder to achieve today in part because the "current society favors the rich" and because "wages for workers are too low."[134] A 2006 survey of U.S. adults found only one-third expected children would grow up to be better off than people today, while half expected children would be worse off.[135] The latter finding was reinforced by another 2006 survey of adult workers, which found a majority believed the next generation would be worse off than the current generation.[136] These results are in contrast to those reported in a 1999 national survey, which found 55 percent of respondents expected children would be better off as adults than their parents.[137]

Perhaps consistent with many American workers' pessimistic views regarding their prospects for achieving the American Dream, marriage rates and traditional family lifestyles have declined. In 1970, married couples with a child (or children under age eighteen) accounted for 50 percent of all U.S. families and 40 percent of all U.S. households. But in 2004, the proportion of traditional families (married couples with children under eighteen) had declined to 34 percent of all families and to 23 percent of all households. During the same period, nonfamily households as a share of all households increased from 19 percent in 1970 to 32 percent in 2004.[138] While shifts in the age structure of the U.S. population may partially explain these trends, they may also be due, at least in part, to many workers' shrinking income and benefit levels. For many, it is increasingly apparent that the financial security central to the American Dream and the economic resources necessary to support traditional family lifestyles are drifting out of reach today.

"The world is a vampire—set to drain [you]," sang Smashing Pumpkins, a popular alternative rock band more than a decade ago. In the mid-2000s, the singer Pink asked on her *I'm Not Dead* album how the president could sleep "while the rest of us cry?" Despite being a decade apart, these two grim takes on the life chances of youth were not isolated musical messages. In fact, themes of pessimism and cynicism were, and are, often woven into the lyrics of U.S. popular music. The content of many songs makes it clear that the bands—and their youthful audiences—know they're being used, and they don't like it. In the mid-2000s, some youthful audiences began to show their objection to their generally gloomy life chances (and to the Iraq war) by supporting (with their dollars) sales of "new protest" music aimed largely at the Bush administration. Musicians from divergent genres, including Pink, Pearl Jam, Merle Haggard, Neil Young, Eminem, Green Day, Bruce Springsteen, and Madonna, produced anti-Bush songs in the mid-2000s.[139] While popular support for a new wave of political protest songs is an interesting development, attacking—or even defeating—Bush the political leader doesn't address or even begin to change the privileged-class-based policies that have produced and perpetuate the conditions that concern some youthful audiences. The reality is that few contemporary *and popular*, youth-oriented songwriters/bands offer emancipatory visions or alternatives to youthful working-class audiences regarding how they can counter, in meaningful ways, the sense that their future life chances are compromised by an increasingly unequal social order they neither control nor understand.

With some exceptions, much contemporary popular music conjures up for today's youth a bleak, iron-cage imagery of their world. Many young people appear to feel trapped in a predictable, downsized, dead-end society composed of institutions that ensnare rather than liberate them, including school, work, the pop culture industry (which rationalizes and markets "cool" to kids and young adults), religion, and prison. But they also appear unsure of what to do about their situation, other than to shop, consume, and posture. For many youth, rebellion and authenticity are displayed and achieved by embracing the subculture of cool: consuming "alternative" music, clothes, styles, "rebel" attitudes (e.g., post-punk, thug, gangsta), and violent video games, often promoted by clever "liberation marketing" styles of hip corporations.[140] Youthful "rebellion" is sometimes expressed through the consumption of music and music videos that contain defiant ("politically incorrect") lyrics and images embracing "thuglike" attitudes, styles, and gestures, as in some forms of rage rock, hip-hop, and rap.

Of course, musical content also reflects the complex class-based inequalities of the society; these inequalities help energize protest songs (as noted above), and more complex music messages or themes encouraging resistance to, or liberation from, the forces driving downward mobility do appear in some youth music.[141] However, the content more typically reflects rather narrow, self-absorbed concerns and frustrations of youthful angst, as well as frequent references to a staple pop music theme: the achievement of personal salvation (or fulfillment) through the transformative power of redemptive love. In short, the children of post–World War II middle-income Americans appear trapped in a subcultural zeitgeist that reflects their feelings of increasing anxiety and frustration about a downward-trending class system they were born into and are trapped by, but that does not provide them with the experiences or knowledge necessary to understand, influence, or reshape it.

BENEATH THE WATERLINE: CONFLICTING CLASS INTERESTS

Capitalists have long believed that workers *as a class* need to be strictly disciplined and controlled.

—Michael Zweig, *What's Class Got to Do with It?* 2004

Although the class iceberg thrusts some obvious features of the system into view, with the right kind of conceptual sonar gear, we can also peer beneath the waterline. There we can glimpse some hidden features of the new class society. To begin, we view the preceding three trends as closely related to, and reflective of, conflicting class interests. Contrary to the "win-win" language and imagery so prevalent in media accounts of business and labor relationships, we see superclass corporate owners and their credentialed-class allies as having interests that are fundamentally opposed to those of working-class Americans. It is our view that privileged-class interests trend in the direction of preserving and extending class-based economic, political, and cultural inequalities. Such interests translate into a privileged-class agenda centered on maintaining and enhancing the wealth, power, privilege, and security of the superclass and of its credentialed-class allies. This agenda is pursued through privileged-class dominance of the major economic, political, and cultural organizations of society.[142]

Protecting Privilege

Large corporations and corporate-generated wealth are at the heart of conflicting class interests and privileged-class power. The economic resources controlled by major U.S. corporations are staggering. Although the total U.S. "corporate population" consists of 5.2 million firms with total annual receipts of over $20 trillion, a relatively small number of huge companies dominate the U.S. economy as well as all major sectors of American business.[143]

The five hundred largest firms (the Fortune 500) represent only 0.0001 percent (one-thousandth of 1 percent) of all U.S. corporations. Even so, this select group received $9.1 trillion in revenues in 2005, an amount that represents over 40 percent of all annual U.S. corporate revenues.[144] Within specific business sectors, the economic dominance of large firms is readily apparent. In manufacturing, for example, only 280 U.S. corporations out of 280,000 active firms have assets exceeding $2.5 billion, but the combined assets of these firms represent 76 percent of the total assets held by all U.S. manufacturing companies ($8.2 trillion). The net income received by these 280 firms represents 85 percent of all net income received by all U.S. manufacturing corporations.[145]

Corporate concentration is even more pronounced in banking and insurance. While the United States has about seventy-six hundred banks, the top eighteen commercial banks (by revenues received) held $6.4 trillion in assets in 2005, about 63 percent of all banking assets.[146] The 10 largest U.S. insurance companies (mutual and stock firms by revenues received) held $1.9 trillion in assets in 2005, about 52 percent of total assets held by all 1,123 U.S. insurance firms.[147] It is important to note that large U.S. firms not only dominate the national economy today but also play increasingly dominant roles in the global economy since many are multinational companies with subsidiaries scattered around the globe.[148]

Most giant U.S. corporations are largely owned and controlled by a small number of superclass elites who are assisted by their credentialed-class allies. In general, the superclass includes the top wealth-owning and income-receiving groups in the United States, including the four hundred U.S. billionaires in 2006.[149] (In 2005 there were 793 billionaires in the world.[150]) Superclass members also hold virtually all of the seats on the boards of directors of the largest U.S. firms, which in 2005 included approximately 5,350 director positions in S&P 500 firms.[151] The wealthiest 1 percent of U.S. households is the core of the superclass. Today, this group owns about 40 percent of all common stock (excluding pension funds). The slightly-less-wealthy own smaller shares. Below the top 1 percent, the next wealthiest 4 percent owns about 29 percent, the next 5 percent owns 13 percent, the next 10 percent owns 11 percent, but the bottom 80 percent owns only 7.9 percent.[152] The smaller levels of stock ownership held by groups in the 19 percent of wealthy Americans below the top 1 percent suggest that as wealth ownership shares shrink, the superclass gradually merges into the upper and middle ranks of the affluent credentialed class.

Where income is concerned, the superclass occupies the top 1 percent category (as is the case with wealth). According to a 2005 CBO study (cited earlier in this chapter), in 2003 (the latest year available) this group included 1.1 million households with *average after-tax* incomes (in 2003 dollars) of $701,500 ($1,022,400 average pretax incomes).[153] Below the superclass, the top earning members of the credentialed class are found in those households that make up the top 10 percent income category; lower-earning credentialed-class members are found in millions of households in the highest income quintile. The CBO study noted that the top 10 percent income group included 11.5 million households with 2003 *average after-tax* incomes of $190,400 ($269,000 average pretax incomes); the highest quintile group included 22.8 million households with 2003 *average after-tax* incomes of $138,500 ($184,500 average pretax incomes).[154]

Members of the superclass who are actively involved in organizational governance occupy top positions of power and authority in the largest and most powerful economic, political, and cultural organizations in the society. Such superclass executives, along with their credentialed-class subordinates, are considered by social science researchers to form the heart of an American "power elite." Members of this group play active corporate officer and board member roles and occupy public-policy-influencing positions in public and private organizations—and have been the focus of research documenting this group's membership, power, and self-conscious and cohesive nature.[155]

Various forms of data concerning income levels and sources illustrate that the higher the income, the lower the percentage derived from salaries and wages and the greater the percentage derived from wealth, most often in the form of dividends, interest, and other forms of corporate-based compensation. To illustrate, 80 percent of American households (the bottom four income quintiles combined) receive about 70 percent of all income from wages and salaries; only 7 percent comes from business income and all types of investment capital income (over 22 percent comes from other sources, mainly Social Security and unemployment compensation). In contrast, for the top 1 percent of American households (by income), business income and investment capital income sources account for 53 percent of all income this group receives; only 35 percent of the income for this group is derived from wages and salaries.[156] Underscoring the latter point, data from executive compensation studies reveal that salaries plus bonuses represent only a small portion of CEOs' total annual incomes. For example, according to *USA Today*, a survey of

240 large U.S. firms found CEO median income to be $17.9 million in 2005, but the salary plus bonus incomes for the ten highest compensated CEOs in the survey averaged "only" $5.9 million. This was the case because in addition to their salary and bonus incomes, the top ten CEOs collectively received a total of $877.6 million in "option gains" income (an average of $87.8 million each).[157] These figures illustrate that for the ten top-paid CEOs in the 2006 *USA Today* survey, the average salary and bonus income for each CEO amounted to only about 7 percent of the average *total* compensation received by each member of this group.

The incomes of credentialed-class managers and white-collar professionals who assist superclass elites in sustaining the corporate project are nowhere near those of superclass members, but they are still substantial. In Washington, D.C., the salary received by members of Congress has often been viewed as the top of the middle class and, thus, as the floor of the upper middle class.[158] In 2007, that floor was $168,500.[159] This figure represents an approximate baseline minimum for privileged-class managers and professionals, especially in large private-sector firms. Senior corporate office holders, such as chief financial officers (CFOs), in midsized firms illustrate salary "upgrades" (above congressional salaries) routinely paid to privileged-class members. In the mid-2000s, the annual median income for CFOs in firms with sales between $100 and $500 million was $198,855. Income levels of CFOs in larger firms are much higher (typically seven figures) than for CFOs in midsized firms. Only in smaller firms (annual sales between $10 and $25 million) do we find CFO incomes below congressional salaries, but even there CFO median pay was still a respectable $103,762.[160]

From newly rich corporate officers to the oldest American family fortunes, skybox-level incomes and wealth are clearly linked to the ongoing production of corporate profits. Privileged-class corporate officers understand this connection. Therefore, superclass members actively involved in corporate governance, along with a select group of upwardly mobile credentialed-class members groomed by superclass sponsors, work diligently to ensure the continued financial health, power, and survival of the corporate enterprise. At the highest levels of wealth, the corporate basis of immense personal wealth is clearly illustrated by CEO fortunes linked to specific firms. Examples include Bill Gates's $50 billion Microsoft-based fortune, Warren E. Buffett's $42 billion Berkshire-based empire, and Philip H. Knight's $7.3 billion Nike-based holdings.[161] Large corporations are clearly the engines that generate the income and wealth of the superclass and also of its credentialed-class allies.

As a result of privileged-class ownership and control of large firms, the class interests of this group are served in three ways. First, much of the value of the goods and services produced by workers is distributed through corporate-based channels and practices to superclass corporate owners and to their credentialed-class allies. The heart of this process is simple and increasingly transparent today. It begins with corporations' paying workers far less (in wages and benefits) than the market value of what they produce. The difference between wages paid and the market value of what workers produce is retained as profits. The process concludes with the retained profits' being distributed to CEOs and managers as salaries, bonuses, and stock options and to stockholders as dividends. When the U.S. fast-food industry pays most of its workers at or near minimum-wage rates and provides virtually no paid fringe benefits, it is not surprising that McDonald's could easily afford a $3.4 million compensation package in 2005 for CEO James A. Skinner.[162] Similarly, when Nike pays El Salvadoran workers 29 cents per garment to make Nike jerseys that retail for $140 each in U.S. markets, it's no surprise that Nike chairman Phil Knight was paid $3.5 million in 2005 and is a billionaire.[163]

Second, the corporate-derived income and wealth of the privileged class are used as class-based resources for penetrating and controlling government to develop and reinforce a body of law and public policies that legitimate privileged-class dominance and institutionalize class inequalities. Such arrangements make class-based social inequities and biases in the economic and political order favoring the privileged class appear to be "normal" or even "natural." Also, control of government allows the privileged class to actively pursue public policies that serve its immediate interests, such as tax cuts (primarily benefiting higher-income groups), reduction in the size of government (fewer business regulations means more profits), and welfare cuts (creating a larger pool of low-wage workers, using the poor as scapegoats). Third, privileged-class control of public-opinion-shaping institutions such as the state, the mass media, and the educational system is used to ignore, conceal, marginalize, contest, disguise, or misrepresent issues and information that would expose class-based inequalities and legitimate class-based grievances of workers.

We believe the interests of the new working class, in contrast with privileged-class interests, trend in the direction of reducing existing class-based economic, political, and cultural inequalities. This means, first, that workers have economic interests in receiving a larger share of the value of the goods and services they produce in the form of higher wages as well as more extensive and secure fringe benefits. Such outcomes would occur at the expense of superclass owners of productive property and their credentialed-class allies by reducing profit margins. Second, workers also have political interests in contesting privileged-class control of government in order to use law and public policies on behalf of the working class as instruments for reducing economic and political class inequalities. For example, workers' opportunities and economic security would be enhanced by an expansion of social spending for education, a national health-care system, and additional protections for the environment. Third, at the cultural level, workers also have interests in using the mass media and schools to expose class-based inequalities and to legitimate the class-based grievances of workers.

Our view of the existence of conflicting class interests does not mean that we see the privileged and working classes as equally aware of or equally well organized to work toward the active realization of their interests. To the contrary, as the later chapters illustrate, we see privileged-class members as much more conscious of their collective class interests, more cohesive in pursuing them, and in possession of much greater (and more unified) organizational resources than the working class. The net result is that, compared with the working class, the privileged class is much more aware of, and able to effectively pursue and realize, its common class interests.

Class War in America

> The war that nobody talks about—the overwhelmingly one-sided class war—is being waged all across America. Guess who's winning.
>
> —Bob Herbert, *New York Times*, June 6, 2005

Nowhere is the reality of conflicting class interests, privileged-class consciousness, and the overwhelming power of superclass-dominated organizational resources more apparent than in the story behind the transformation of the American class system in the period from the 1970s to the present. The trends of class polarization, downward mobility, and class secession are the direct result of policy decisions made and sponsored by superclass-controlled organizations over the past thirty years that collectively represent nothing less than total class war. Although varying explanations exist for the current configuration of the American class system, none approaches the explanatory power of a class-war analysis. Although the details of the story are complex, the main actors, events, and policies underlying it are stunningly simple. They are fundamentally grounded in conflicting class interests and linked to the dynamics of an almost totally one-sided class war sponsored and directed by the superclass and driven by corporate resources.

The story behind today's new class society begins in the late 1960s and early 1970s. Several progressive political and social movements supported by organized labor, consumer and environmental organizations, and other reform-minded groups during this period led to an expansion of New Deal–based national policies that effectively increased opportunities for—as well as the economic, occupational, and physical well-being of—working-class Americans. Such policies included numerous Great Society programs such as Medicare and Medicaid, as well as several new federal regulatory acts in six major areas, including consumer products, discrimination in employment, traffic safety, consumer finance, job safety, and the environment.[164] Among these acts were groundbreaking measures such as the 1966 Coal Mine Safety Act, the 1969 National Environmental Policy Act, and the 1970 Occupational Health and Safety Act. For workers, the net effect of the progressive legislation enacted in the 1960s and early 1970s was a welcome expansion of the U.S. welfare state.

Members of the superclass viewed pro-worker policy developments with fear and loathing: "The expansion of the welfare state in the 1960s and 1970s created panic among the U.S. capitalist class."[165] This reaction was undoubtedly magnified by the parallel trend of declining corporate profits during this period.[166] The superclass response was a concerted, large-scale mobilization for total class war: "The leadership of the capitalist class tended to reject political moderation and, through their inner circle connections, came to share a belief in the need for a right-wing offensive."[167] At the heart of this effort was the conscious creation of a two-pronged political and economic strategy for the purpose of waging class war on a scale unprecedented in American history. The following sections introduce two key dimensions of this class war, both of which are explored in more detail in later chapters.

The Political Dimension of the Class War

In the political and public policy arenas, the superclass dramatically expanded the organizational and resource base undergirding its political lobbying and policy-influencing capacity. Developments of this sort were precisely what Lewis F. Powell Jr. envisioned in a 1971 memorandum to the U.S. Chamber of Commerce just two months before his nomination to the U.S. Supreme Court by President Richard Nixon. In his memo, Powell warned that the free enterprise system was under attack by antibusiness forces. He called on the business community to take "direct political action" in support of its shared interests and added "that political power . . . must be used aggressively and with determination."[168] One researcher summarized Powell's message on the need for collective political mobilization and action by the corporate community: "To truly succeed in resetting the terms of American politics, corporations needed to systematize their approach, creating new institutions and giving those institutions sustained support."[169]

The list of heavyweight, superclass-promoted, political lobbying developments that emerged following Powell's memo begins with the Business Roundtable. Organized in 1972 by John Harper, head of Alcoa Aluminum, and Fred Borch, the CEO of General Electric, it included two hundred CEOs from the largest banks and corporations, and it remains one of the most formidable corporate lobbying and policy-setting organizations today.[170] In that same year, to further beef up superclass political pressure on Congress, the National Association of Manufacturers moved to Washington, D.C. Also, the number of corporations represented by registered lobbyists grew dramatically, from 175 in 1971 to 650 in 1979, and membership in the U.S. Chamber of Commerce more than doubled, from 36,000 in 1967 to 80,000 in 1974.[171] By the mid-2000s, Washington, D.C., lobbying organizations numbered 3,257 (with most representing privileged-class interests) and employed over 37,000 registered federal lobbyists.[172] The combined annual expenditures of all Washington lobbying organizations in the mid-2000s ($2.2

billion) were about double the amount of money contributed to the campaigns of all congressional candidates in the 2004 elections (of course, many campaign donations are from the same superclass-controlled firms that hire Washington lobbyists).[173]

The 1970s and 1980s also witnessed the development and growth of an extensive corporate-funded network of conservative "think tanks" aimed at influencing public policy with conservative ideas and policies, such as "supply-side" economics and "welfare reform."[174] From the 1970s through the 2000s, this network produced (and continues to produce) books, policy papers, and press releases providing the ideological rationale ("free market") and the "empirical evidence" justifying political efforts to "reform" (typically via privatization schemes) various public programs and institutions such as welfare, Social Security, Medicare, Medicaid, and all levels of public education.[175]

To help fund the political campaigns of candidates favorable to privileged-class business interests, the number of corporate political action committees (PACs) grew from 89 in 1974 to 1,206 in 1980.[176] Business mobilization of PACs continued to grow, and in 2005 corporate and related trade association PACs totaled 2,621.[177] In the 2004 election cycle, corporate-organized and -dominated PACs accounted for 73 percent of the $289 million contributed by all PACs to congressional candidates.[178] In addition to the expansion of corporate PACs, the amounts of money from business-based political contributions of all types also increased dramatically as election expenditures for all congressional candidates spiraled up from $342.4 million in 1981 and 1982, to $765.3 million in 1995 and 1996, to a record, at the time, of $1.16 billion in 2003 and 2004.[179]

The 2004 and 2006 federal elections witnessed record spending by candidates compared to previous comparable election cycles. In 2004 (a presidential election year), spending by and on behalf of all candidates for federal offices (i.e., presidential, congressional) totaled $4.2 billion compared with $3 billion in 2000. In 2006 (a midterm election), the total was $2.8 billion compared with $2.2 billion in 2002.[180] As we will see in chapter 4, the increasing cost of political campaigns has led to an ever greater dependence, especially at the national level, by both Republicans and Democrats on direct high-dollar contributions from wealthy individuals and corporate PACs and from extensive, but indirect, support from so-called 527 committees (mostly funded by superclass sources). These committees, named for the section of the federal tax code that governs them, became increasingly important in the 2004 election as a result of the 2002 Bipartisan Campaign Reform Act (BCRA), which banned "soft money" (e.g., indirect) contributions to federal candidates.[181] In the 2004 elections, "hard money" contributions (regulated by BCRA limits but coming primarily from wealthy individuals and corporate PACs) to both major parties and federal candidates totaled about $3 billion, split roughly 54 percent for Republicans and 46 percent for Democrats.[182] The tilting effect of privileged-class dominance of national election funding in favor of candidates from both major parties supporting the interests of this class is evident in comparisons of total PAC and individual donations to federal candidates and parties from business sources versus labor sources over the past decade. The ratio was 11:1 in 1996, 15:1 in 2000, 24:1 in 2004 ($1.5 billion from business versus $61.6 million from labor), and at least 20:1 in 2006.[183]

The political mobilization of superclass-funded organizations hit the jackpot with the election of the Ronald Reagan and George H. W. Bush administrations. Their record of strong support for superclass-based corporate interests and hostility to welfare-state programs is well known. As David Stockman, the architect of Reagan's economic policies, put it, "The Reagan Revolution required a frontal assault on the American welfare state."[184] Superclass interests received further boosts in the 1994 and 1996 congressional elections as Republicans captured and then retained control over both houses of Congress. Led by then House speaker Newt Gingrich, conservative Republicans openly pledged to dismantle the New Deal and Great Society social legislation. The process began in earnest with the highly publicized "Contract with America" and achieved notable success with the passage of welfare "reform" legislation in 1996—with support from many Democrats and President Bill Clinton.[185]

The superclass scored big again in 2000 with the couplike selection of President George W. Bush as a result of the 5–4 Supreme Court ruling on the Florida election results and with the installation of a Republican-dominated Congress.[186] The rising superclass political tide reached a new high in 2004 as Bush was reelected along with Republican majorities in both houses of Congress. The 2000 and 2004 superclass electoral successes led directly to the initiation or expansion of several federal policies supporting privileged-class interests and especially the interests of the superclass. Examples of these policies will be considered in detail in chapter 4. In the next section, we limit our consideration to a summary of developments in one area of federal policy of special interest to the privileged class—tax cuts.

At the time of this writing, it remains to be seen if the Democratic takeover of Congress in 2007 will produce any rollbacks of the 2001–2006 federal tax cuts for the privileged class. Since about two-thirds of the money spent by congressional candidates of both parties in the 2006 elections came from 129,731 wealthy donors who contributed $2,000 or more each, a rollback of the 2001–2006 tax cuts, even by a Democrat-controlled Congress, appears unlikely.[187] The "new" 110th Congress (2007–2008) is much like the "old" 109th Congress (2005–2006) in one very important respect: its members' campaigns were largely funded (as usual) by wealthy members of the privileged class, the group with the strongest interest in retaining the tax cuts. Reflecting these realities, Mark Dudzic, Labor Party national organizer, was not optimistic that the 110th Congress would enact pro-working-class legislation: "Past experience should tell us that the new Congress will do nothing to confront the impact of the growing concentration of corporate power on the lives and aspirations of working people. Refreshing as the election results may seem, working people will soon be reminded that the Democratic Party, as well as the Republican, remains dominated by corporate interests."[188]

Federal Tax Cuts: 2001 to 2006   During the first five years of his administration, President Bush signed into law five major tax cuts (excluding the Katrina Emergency Tax Relief Act of 2005). Three substantially reduced federal taxes for privileged-class individuals and families (or extended reductions) and two reduced federal taxes for corporations (which also benefited the privileged class, but a bit more indirectly). By the midpoint of Bush's second term, his administration had enacted tax cuts totaling $1.65 trillion, plus another $1.6 trillion by 2016 if all tax cuts were made permanent.[189] The following paragraphs briefly describe the five major tax cuts and summarize their effects.

In 2001, the Economic Growth and Tax Relief Reconciliation Act of 2001 was passed by Congress with Republican and Democratic support; this law reduced federal taxes on individuals and families by $1.35 trillion (over nine years), with most of the reductions going to the top 20 percent and top 1 percent income groups.[190] On May 28, 2003, President Bush signed the Jobs and Growth Tax Relief and Reconciliation Act of 2003. This act "lowered the top tax rate on corporate stock dividends from 35 percent to 15 percent, and reduced the top capital gains tax rate from 20 percent to 15 percent."[191] A 2006 analysis revealed that 71 percent of the economic benefits of this act went to individuals with annual incomes over $200,000 and nearly 43 percent of the capital gains and dividend tax cuts went to tax filers with incomes over $1 million.[192] On May 17, 2006, Bush signed the Tax Increase Prevention and Reconciliation Act of 2005. This third tax cut extended the 2003 capital gains and stock dividend tax cuts through 2010.[193]

Corporate taxes were reduced by the Job Creation and Worker Assistance Act of 2002 and the American Job Creation Act of 2004. Both acts favored privileged-class interests. The 2002 act provided workers with additional unemployment insurance benefits totaling $14 billion, but U.S. corporations were the biggest winners receiving $114 billion in tax cuts.[194] The 2004 act was supported by 428 major U.S. corporations and trade associations.[195] It provided $137 billion in tax cuts to large segments of the business community, including manufacturers and multinational companies.[196]

The Political Dimension of the Class War: Many Fronts   The political dimension of the class war goes far beyond tax cuts favoring the privileged class. As we will see in later chapters, this dimension of the class war is fought on many fronts. Republican officeholders are typically the most openly enthusiastic supporters of privileged-class interests. But the enactment of many features of the anti-working-class social, labor, and trade policies of the Bush administration via recent congressional votes on a wide range of issues (e.g., see chapter 4: workplace safety, bankruptcy "reform," class action litigation "reform," Central American trade policy) illustrate the political reality that many Democrats routinely support privileged-class-favored policies. This was also true in the previous administration; for example, President Clinton worked diligently to ensure the passage of anti-working-class legislation such as the North American Free Trade Agreement in 1993 and the so-called 1996 welfare reform act.

While some Democrats sometimes support the interests of the new working class, too often this is not the case. The U.S. *Labor Party News* made this point in a mid-2000s comment on job losses and government hostility to labor unions: "Neither Republicans nor Democrats . . . seriously address [the loss of U.S. manufacturing jobs or] other issues vital to workers and their families and many Democrats actively aid and abet the anti-worker assault."[197] Journalist Alexander Cockburn sees little difference between the two major U.S. political parties; he views both as largely serving the interests of the privileged class: "The central political issue in the first decade of the 21st century is the decay of the American political system and of the two prime parties that share the spoils. . . . The Democrats have produced no laws, indeed have campaigned against laws that would make [it easier for workers to establish and join unions]."[198] As we document in later chapters, the consequences of intensified, business-driven political lobbying, along with increased privileged-class funding of both major political parties, include the increasingly transparent conversion of large segments of the Democratic Party into a political force reflecting the hegemonic power of superclass-based corporate interests. One result, as Ralph Nader notes, is that "now we have a two-party convergence—one might call it a collaboration or a conspiracy—against the broader political wishes of the American people."[199]

The Economic Dimension of the Class War

In the economic arena, superclass corporate elites dictate policies aimed at increasing profits by waging war on workers' wages. Domestically, this has involved the use of government to establish and maintain a hard line against workers' rights and wage demands. Reagan's 1981 firing of striking air-traffic controllers established a tough, anti-labor policy trend that continued with his appointments of anti-labor members to the National Labor Relations Board and with other actions, such as his threat to veto the high-risk bill of 1986–1987, which would have mandated government protection for high-risk workers' health.[200]

The pro-business, anti-labor policies of the Reagan administration that benefited the economic and political interests of the privileged class were continued and extended by the Bush I, Clinton, and Bush II presidencies. In each administration, we find evidence of strong support for policies aimed at reducing worker and union rights, social spending, governmental regulations on businesses, and taxes on corporations and wealthy individuals; we also find each administration supporting a growing list of so-called free trade agreements.[201]

Internationally, the "globalization strategy" of U.S. firms is another feature of the economic dimension of the class war. It involves the use of technological innovations to facilitate the transfer of manufacturing jobs to Third

World nations. Over the past thirty years, credentialed-class corporate managers and professionals have combined new technologies, such as satellite communication, computers, standardized production procedures, and containerized shipping, into technical systems that have facilitated (and continue to facilitate) the globalization of production.[202] These developments have accelerated the "capital flight" transfer of production facilities from the United States to nations such as China, Mexico, and Indonesia and have made the use of cheap Third World labor ever more feasible and profitable. Numerous U.S. firms, including General Motors, Ford, Zenith, and Converse, continue to locate more and more of their production facilities in Third World nations, and some, such as Nike (headquartered in Beaverton, Oregon), produce virtually all of their products in Third World nations. In the mid-2000s, U.S.-headquartered multinational firms and foreign affiliates controlled by U.S. firms employed over twenty-two million workers, many of them in Third World nations.[203]

The transformation of the manufacturing sector by corporate globalization strategies has accelerated the development of a postindustrial, service-based economy—and hastened the drift toward class polarization. Over the past thirty years, the proportion of U.S. workers engaged in manufacturing fell from 33.1 percent in 1970 to a projected 8.2 percent in 2014. This decline has been paralleled by a sharp increase in service-sector employment, rising from 62.5 percent of all workers in 1970 to a projected 78.5 percent in 2014.[204] The service economy trend intensifies class divisions because of the corporate-generated, two-tiered labor market that is especially evident in the service sector. This system consists of firms utilizing a small group of high-paid "core" workers, such as managers, professionals, computer programmers, and other information analysts, and a very large group of moderate- to low-paid "peripheral" workers, viewed as less central to organizational needs and goals.

The differences in pay and benefits for the two groups are closely linked to differences in levels of skill and social capital. Variations in these resources tend to reflect the prestige of the educational credentials workers possess, as well as their social ties to organizational leaders (social capital). Thus, workers' possession of these class-based capital resources influence their proximity to corporate and organizational power and their access to the limited number of well-paid positions. Peripheral workers occupy a spectrum of jobs ranging from modestly paid occupations, such as teachers and police officers, to much lower-paid positions, such as cashiers, guards, nursing aides, orderlies and attendants, and janitors, which are projected to be among the occupations with the largest job growth in the 2004–2014 period.[205] However, even modestly paid service workers find themselves continuously subject to wage and benefit pressures as private and public employers increase contingent-labor staffing policies.[206] At the bottom, as we noted earlier, the lowest-paid service workers are increasingly linked to large organizations through temporary agencies as contract or contingent laborers.[207]

With superclass interests as a dominant force in the national government, significant features of the welfare state benefiting the new working class have been, and are currently being, dismantled. The minimal levels of economic security that national social policies afforded workers and the poor in the past are increasingly disappearing. At the same time, the combination of superclass-sponsored government-corporate attacks on unions, the growing "privatization" of government jobs, and the globalization process has led to a continuous erosion of workers' wages, benefits, and rights. These developments have been accompanied by corporate layoff and downsizing policies that have led to the disappearance of many blue- and white-collar, middle-income positions. The end result of these class-war-driven policies and practices has been the emergence of an increasingly economically polarized and hardened new class society. In this new order, even the so-called middle class is now recognized by many mainstream contemporary authors as experiencing the corro-

sive effects of class war, including substantially diminished opportunities for realizing the American Dream and growing levels of risk and hardship.[208]

BENEATH THE WATERLINE: CLASS MAINTENANCE AND LEGITIMATION

To maintain their power and privilege, elites have learned to . . . exploit nonelites without their realizing they are being exploited.

—Harold R. Kerbo, *Social Stratification and Inequality*, 2006

The second hidden dimension of the class iceberg involves the structures and processes that maintain and legitimate the new class society. Of course, elite classes in stratified societies have always devoted a portion of their considerable resources to legitimating and reinforcing the class system, thereby ensuring their continued possession of disproportionate levels of wealth, power, and privilege. However, the problems of maintaining and legitimating the emerging new class society have been rendered more complex by the extreme inequalities of the system and the tension between these class realities and the relentless, media-driven promotion of the American Dream as a cultural ideal (see the box at the end of this chapter, "Class Issues in the Media: The American Dream"). Thus, the current class-maintenance and -legitimation strategies, structures, and policies combine sophisticated extensions of approaches used in the past with emerging, innovative forms of control and distraction.

The Class-Power-Network Model

Our perspective on how the new class system is maintained and legitimated is based on an organizational model of class interests and power. It views large firms as repositories of superclass resources and also as dominant sources of power in virtually all sectors of society. According to this approach, privileged-class leaders use corporate-based resources to create, fund, and control extensive, overlapping organizational networks within the economic, political, and cultural social arenas. These networks consist of organizations linked by various connections, such as interlocked board members, shared public policy interests, and common goals, including the maintenance and legitimation of concentrated privileged-class power and wealth.

In the economic arena, network examples include superclass-controlled trade associations and peak corporate groups, such as the Business Roundtable. Superclass-funded public policy "think tanks," lobbying organizations, and PACs are examples of organizational networks within the political arena. In the cultural arena, network examples include superclass-funded foundations, civic and cultural organizations, and elite university boards of trustees. We view these interlocked organizational networks as directed by privileged-class leaders who use them to pursue strategies and objectives that reinforce the shared economic, political, and cultural interests of their class. These include legitimating corporate autonomy, power, and profit maximization, as well as maintaining the organizational structure of the new class system so as to perpetuate the advantaged positions, interests, and privileges of the superclass and its credentialed-class allies. However, we also believe the organizations within these networks typically present public facades that disguise or deemphasize their privileged-class biases and the ways in which they function as surrogate actors for privileged-class interests.

Although the class-power model views superclass leaders as participating in conscious and deliberate activities to protect privileged-class interests, it is not based on a conspiracy theory of power. We do not view superclass leaders as a group that secretly conspires to promote its interests and maintain class inequalities. Rather, following G. William Domhoff, we view the coordinated, interest-supporting activities of superclass leaders and their credentialed-class allies as grounded in a complex structural system that is populated by a relatively homogeneous group that is similar in many important respects. Privileged-class leaders tend to have similar elite educational backgrounds, to be officers of large, interlocked firms, and to be members of a small number of elite social and cultural organizations. The class-based, shared family, business, and social experiences of this group lead to shared common values, worldviews, and commitments to maintaining the status quo.[209] From where privileged-class leaders stand, life is good, and the system works. The shared culture of the superclass leads not to conspiracy but rather to an authentic boosterism for the corporate model and the "magic of the market." There's no need for a conspiracy when the most common question among privileged-class leaders is, why change what works (for us!)?

Dominant Class-Power Networks

Figure 2.2 illustrates the main features of our class-power-network model. At the top, the model views the dominant class-power base as grounded in the organizationally active superclass members and their credentialed-class allies (the power elite). This group is centrally involved in directing and coordinating the three overlapping corporate-based dominant power networks. Strategies for class maintenance and legitimation extend downward through four basic social institutions: the national economy, the state, media and culture, and the educational system. The following five chapters consider in detail how the maintenance and legitimation strategies identified by the model are linked to organizational policies and practices directed by privileged-class leadership. And they illustrate how these strategies and related policies serve privileged-class interests, especially by helping to perpetuate and legitimate structured inequalities within the new class society.

By focusing on the top half of the model, we can begin to see how the abstract notion of superclass dominance is channeled through real organizations that collectively merge into powerful networks. From the top down, the dominant

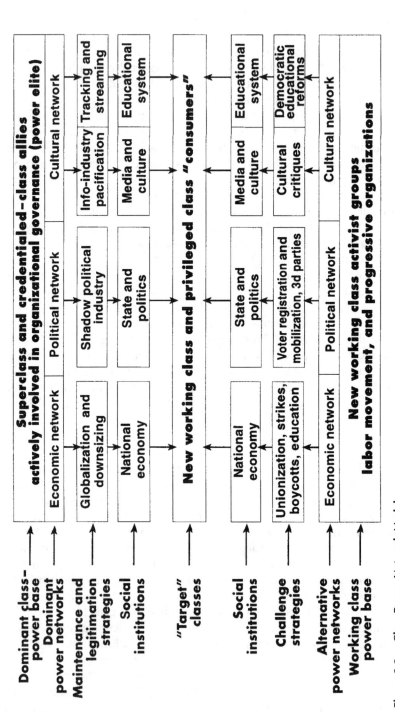

Figure 2.2.   Class-Power Network Model

power networks pursue superclass interests through corporate-based activities penetrating the four routine institutional structures of society. As we will see, the corporate practices and public policies that emerge from these structural linkages weave legitimation, co-optation, distraction, and coercion into a dense organizational web that sustains the new class system's inequalities.

Members of the new working class find themselves targets of the dominant power networks depicted by the model. Specific public policies, programs, business practices, and cultural ideas maintaining and legitimating superclass interests, the corporate empire, and class inequalities in the new class system are routinely and repeatedly directed at working-class members (and privileged-class consumers) through the four basic social institutions shown in the model.

For members of the working class, the cumulative effects of lives lived under superclass-dominated social institutions encourage public acceptance of class hierarchies, extensive corporate power, and the inequalities associated with these arrangements. Oligopolistic corporate control of the economy (e.g., aerospace, auto, electrical, media industries), corporate-funded bashing of big government (Rush Limbaugh), and corporate-media sponsored celebrations of the free enterprise system (e.g., Fox News Channel) produce patterns of ideas and experiences that constantly remind the working class that private businesses are "good" and public enterprises are "bad" (or at best inefficient).[210] In short, working-class behaviors and attitudes are shaped in ways that promote public acceptance (ideological legitimation) of class inequalities. Such outcomes ensure that the distribution of capital resources in the new class society remains relatively unchallenged and unchanged—with a small number of highly rewarded positions reserved for members of the privileged-class top diamond and those in the new-working-class bottom diamond restricted to positions with much lower rewards.

Alternative Class-Power Networks

Of course, the top portion of figure 2.2 is only part of the story. At the bottom of the figure we find an alternative class-power base grounded in new-working-class activist groups. The labor movement, along with other progressive groups, such as many women's rights, civil rights, environmental, and gay rights organizations, form the heart of three overlapping alternative power networks. These alternative networks challenge, with varying degrees of vigor and with limited resources, the strategies, policies, and messages of the dominant power networks within the economy, the state, the media, and the schools. The alternative-network dimension of our model underscores the point that we do not equate superclass dominance in the economic, political, and cultural arenas with total control. On one hand, inequalities embedded in the new class society are largely maintained and legitimated by the actions, policies, and ideas orchestrated by superclass-sponsored and credentialed-class-managed organizations within the dominant power networks. But on the other hand, these activities and ideas are subject to challenges by alternative-power-network actors in the economic, political, and cultural arenas, with labor unions serving as the core alternative organizational force.

Our inclusion of trade unions as a key feature of the alternative power networks does not mean that we view unions as speaking with a single voice for workers or that we view all unions as consistent advocates for workers' common class interests. We recognize the labor movement includes diverse and sometimes contradictory trends and actions. Even so, among organizational alternatives to corporate power, trade unions possess the greatest concentration of human and economic resources and represent the most significant alternative organizational force countering corporate dominance. But this recognition does not diminish the importance of other organizations in the alternative power networks, some of which are linked to leaders and funding sources associated with privileged-class backgrounds. Some of these individuals and groups might, in some sense, be considered "class traitors" by more conventional privileged-class members. Such organizations include women's rights groups (e.g., National Organization for Women), civil rights groups (e.g., National Association for the Advancement of Colored People), public interest groups (e.g., Ralph Nader's numerous organizations), alternative, pro-new-working-class national circulation magazines (e.g., *Nation, Progressive, Mother Jones, In These Times*), progressive research and policy groups (e.g., Economic Policy Institute), and some religious organizations. These groups, often in conjunction with trade unions, are frequently involved in challenging the strategies, objectives, and policies of the dominant power networks.

Inequality and Inequity

The efforts of alternative-power-network groups to promote economic, political, and social policy changes that will reduce class-, gender-, and race-/ethnicity-based inequalities call attention to the distinction between inequality and inequity. *Inequality* refers to the objective reality (factually verifiable) that various distinct and identifiable groups (e.g., class, gender, racial/ethnic groups) receive unequal shares of various forms of scarce and valued resources distributed within the society. For example, much of the evidence presented thus far concerning differences in the distribution of consumption and investment capital illustrates that the highly unequal economic and political outcomes people experience in the United States are often based on their membership in class, gender, and race-/ethnicity-based groups.

Inequity refers to a subjective judgment that the unequal access to scarce and valued resources experienced by groups distinguished by class, gender, and/or racial/ethnic membership is unfair and unjust. This concept interprets the organizationally based policies and practices used as the bases for unequally distributing scarce and valued resources as fundamentally flawed in the sense that they arbitrarily privilege some groups over others and thereby violate basic standards of fairness in the distributional process. Thus, people who observe class and other group-based forms of inequality through the lens of inequity view organizational policies and practices that produce highly unequal resource outcomes for such groups as requiring substantial revision and change.[211] From an inequity perspective, class, gender, and racial inequalities in areas such as the distribution of income, wealth, health care, economic security, and educational and occupational opportunities are not viewed simply as reflections of merit-based distributional processes; rather, they tend to be viewed as evidence of fundamental biases and flaws embedded in a variety of distributional processes that perpetuate unfair economic, political, and cultural advantages of existing privileged-class groups at the expense of non-privileged-class groups.

Almost by definition, a worldview of class (and other) inequalities based on an inequity interpretation necessitates and legitimates changes in the economic, political, and cultural arenas aimed at substantially narrowing the current range of inequalities. This is the orientation and approach taken by most individuals and groups that are part of the alternative power networks. While most participants in these networks are unlikely to envision total equality as a realistic goal, the pursuit of *equity*, the distribution of scarce and valued resource in a fair and just manner, does appear to be a widely shared objective among the members of these networks.

Of course, it is possible to argue that substantial inequalities are legitimate and justified. For example, contemporary justifications of class inequalities are often grounded in Herbert Spencer's late-nineteenth-century ideology of social Darwinism. Spencer celebrated the supposed superiority of the wealthy, viewed the poor as inferior and deserving of their fate, and justified class inequalities on the basis of a pseudoscience of "survival of the fittest."[212] Echoes of Spencer's views still resonate in the United States today, especially among the privileged class. For example, research evidence indicates that individuals with higher-class backgrounds are more likely than those with lower-class backgrounds to view people with higher-level occupations and educations as deserving greater incomes than people with lower-level occupations and educations.[213]

BACK TO THE FUTURE:
THE ICEBERG, THE DREAM, AND THE DETAILS

> Titanic came around the curve, into the Great Iceberg. Fare thee, Titanic, Fare thee well.
>
> —Leadbelly (H. Ledbetter), "Fare Thee Well, Titanic," 1912

As the Titanic disaster reminds us, icebergs can be treacherous, especially the huge, frozen mass below the waterline. Our exploration of the hidden portion of the class iceberg is also fraught with danger, though not of the physical sort. Because of the taboo nature of class, few people venture below the waterline of conventional social analysis. Down there, visibility is limited. The images are murky. The dangers abound with miscommunication, misunderstanding, and charges from "respectable quarters" that it is unproductive or even un-American to make the trip: better to stick with the dream than explore the iceberg. Even so, we'll take our chances. We think the potential rewards are worth the risks, and we invite you to join us.

The remainder of this book represents a tour of territory that for most Americans is familiar and yet, in many ways, unknown. Our class-power-network model serves as the basic map for exploring the hidden features of the new class society. As we will see, the dominant power networks are not abstract, ivory-tower inventions but real organizational webs of power that we encounter daily. By tracking the interests, strategies, and activities of privileged-class-dominated organizations, the model helps us understand how this class dominates organizations, public policies, programs, ideas, and social behavior in the economic, political, and cultural arenas.

Like a magnifying glass, the model serves as a lens, bringing into focus the details of the ways in which the dominant power networks have created, and work to maintain and legitimate, the new class society. Using this lens, we will discover how the web of power spun by the dominant power networks attempts to control the production and enforcement of ideas about, debates over, attention to, and enactment of class-relevant laws and public policies, as well as the production and distribution of values and beliefs related to personal fulfillment, the mass consumption of goods and services, and the uses of work and leisure time. The cultural dimension of the dominant power networks has become increasingly important to the legitimation process. This is the case because the cultural network includes potent organizations (e.g., the media and schools) that disseminate ideas, information, and images that help legitimate the new class system and serve as vehicles for distracting public attention away from the many inequalities of the system (as we will see in chapters 5, 6, and 7).

The class-power-network model will also help us see and better understand another important dimension of the class iceberg—the "underdogs" of class conflict. The alternative-power-networks portion of the model provides us with a map for understanding how dominant-power-network strategies, policies, programs, and ideas favoring privileged-class interests are contested and challenged in specific terms by real organizations and real people. These challenges are grounded in an agenda emphasizing fair play, an end to arbitrary class inequalities, and greater opportunities for all Americans to actually achieve the American Dream and thereby bring about a class-iceberg meltdown.

CLASS ISSUES IN THE MEDIA: THE AMERICAN DREAM

In 2006, an episode of *The Oprah Winfrey Show* was titled "What Class Are You? Inside America's Taboo Topic." In some respects, it was a rare television event in that social class *was* the focal point of a mass-market TV program. However, as is often the case when class issues are considered in the mainstream media, the "class taboo" actually remained firmly in place. (On Oprah's website, this episode was linked to the *New York Times* "Class Matters" series.) There were no discussions of class interests, power inequalities, or the privileged-class dominance of U.S. political and economic institutions. Instead, the program focused largely on class-based lifestyle differences and the American Dream. In one key segment, Oprah interviewed moviemaker Jamie Johnson, "an heir to the Johnson & Johnson pharmaceutical fortune," about *The One Percent*, his documentary film focused on the very wealthy, including his own family. Another key segment featured results from a poll taken for the show "How Do You Feel about Class?" The first four questions on the eight-item poll dealt with respondents' views on the American Dream.[1]

Oprah's focus on class (especially the rich) and the American Dream was similar to how these topics are often linked and presented in the media. The U.S. mainstream media generate a steady stream of articles and reports on the American Dream. In the first half of the 2000–2010 decade, U.S. newspapers published an average of about thirteen hundred "American Dream" headline articles per year, with "success stories" (of the rags-to-riches variety) making up a large portion of these reports.[2] One of the most common themes threaded through such articles (even those that acknowledge the dream may be more difficult to attain today than in the past) is that the American Dream remains alive, well, and within reach in this "unique land where past and parentage put no limits on opportunity."[3] Although many cautionary economic, political, and social developments in the mid- and latter 2000s (e.g., fewer "living-wage" jobs, war, rising energy prices, declining class mobility) contributed to a tempering of earlier (i.e., late 1990s) exuberant storylines proclaiming the dream-as-within-everyone's-reach-right-now, mainstream media promotion of the dream as alive and well continues in many forms.

Promotion of the dream is evident in both mainstream media reports showcasing American Dream success stories and in the proliferation of "reality" television programs where "ordinary people" are elevated to exceptional material success by displaying some combination of talent, stamina, determination, luck, or deceit (depending on the program). Showcase stories often focus on entertainment celebrities and sports figures from modest origins who overcame long odds but still achieved spectacular success, such as Oprah, two-time Oscar winner Hilary Swank, and cyclist Lance Armstrong. Such celebrities serve as exemplars—proof that the American Dream is alive and within reach. The lesson they convey is clear: the road to success is still wide open in America to those willing to dream big and make the most of the opportunities to succeed—opportunities available to everyone! This is one lesson laid-off white-collar job seekers are encouraged to embrace by "transition industry" hucksters in Barbara Ehrenreich's recent book on the "futile pursuit" of the American Dream.[4]

(*continued*)

CLASS ISSUES IN THE MEDIA: THE AMERICAN DREAM (*continued*)

Reality-based television programming offers a different, but no less compelling, kind of "proof" that the American Dream is alive and available to ordinary people. Popular TV reality programs in the latter 2000s, such as *American Idol, Survivor,* and *The Apprentice,* elevate "winners" into Cinderella-like celebrities who appear to attain (at least for awhile) levels of economic success associated with the American Dream. In some respects, celebrity showcase reports, as well as reality TV programs, can be viewed as contemporary versions (with better production values and with real, rather than fictional, characters) of Horatio Alger Jr.'s popular "rags-to-riches" novels of the late nineteenth and early twentieth centuries (before the term *American Dream* was coined).[5] Today, as in the past, the U.S. popular media message is twofold: first, the American Dream is widely attainable; second, those who have achieved the dream—at spectacular levels—deserve not only their success, but also fawning media attention, public applause, and popular fascination.

Partly as a result of the mainstream media's framing of the American Dream as a reality that can readily lead to riches, this view appears to be firmly embedded in U.S. culture.[6] The media-driven popular faith in the dream-wealth linkage leads many Americans (especially the young) to view themselves not as part of the working class or even the middle class but as members of what might be called the "prerich class." To illustrate, a recent poll found that nearly 25 percent of U.S. teenagers believe they will have $1 million in assets by age forty, and 15 percent think they will earn more than $1 million annually.[7] For believers encouraged by "rags-to-riches" media reports, the American Dream means they are certain to make the transition to the "actually rich class" in the not-too-distant future. With such a mind-set, it is not difficult to imagine that believers in the dream may also entertain the fantasy that when they succeed, perhaps Oprah will ask them to appear on her show and share their success stories with her (and her audience).

NOTES

1. *The Oprah Winfrey Show*, "What Class Are You? Inside America's Taboo Topic," http://www.oprah.com/tows/pastshows/200604/tows_past_20060421.jhtml (visited May 13, 2006).

2. The figure cited refers to the average annual number of U.S. newspaper articles with "American Dream" found in headline titles and lead paragraphs in the 2000–2006 period. It is based on the authors' analysis, using appropriate search parameters, of U.S. newspapers indexed in the Lexis-Nexis data base and published during this period.

3. Wessel, "As Rich-Poor Gap Widens in the U.S., Class Mobility Stalls."

4. Barbara Ehrenreich, *Bait and Switch: The (Futile) Pursuit of the American Dream* (New York: Metropolitan, 2005).

5. Richard L. Zweigenhaft, "Making Rags out of Riches," *Extra!* (January–February 2004): 27–28; Zweigenhaft and Domhoff, *Diversity in the Power Elite,* 3.

6. National League of Cities, "The American Dream in 2004"; Center for a New American Dream, "New American Dream Survey Report," New York Times, *Class Matters,* 6.

7. Mark Maier, "High-School Economics: Corporate Sponsorship and Pro-Market Bias," *Dollars and Sense* (May–June 2002): 15.

NOTES

1. See, for example, Seymour M. Lipset and Reinhard Bendix, *Social Mobility in Industrial Society* (Berkeley: University of California Press, 1959); Harry J. Crockett Jr., "The Achievement Motive and Differential Occupational Mobility in the United States," *American Sociological Review* 27 (1962): 191–204; Reinhard Bendix and Frank W. Howton, "Social Mobility and the American Business Elite—II," *British Journal of Sociology* 9 (1958): 1–14.

2. Peter Blau and Otis D. Duncan, *The American Occupational Structure* (New York: Wiley, 1967); David L. Featherman and Robert M. Hauser, *Opportunity and Change* (New York: Academic Press, 1978).

3. Joan Huber and William H. Form, *Income and Ideology: An Analysis of the American Political Formula* (New York: Free Press, 1973); James R. Kluegel and Eliot R. Smith, *Beliefs about Inequality: Americans' Views of What Is and What Ought to Be* (New York: Aldine De Gruyter, 1986); Beth A. Rubin, *Shifts in the Social Contract* (Thousand Oaks, CA: Pine Forge Press, 1996), 7–8.

4. James Truslow Adams, *The Epic of America* (Boston: Little, Brown and Company, 1933). In his best selling book, Adams wrote, "The American Dream [is] that dream of a land in which life should be better and richer and fuller for everyman, with opportunity for each according to his ability or achievement. . . . It is . . . a dream of a social order in which each man and each woman shall be able to attain to the fullest stature of which they are innately capable . . . regardless of the fortuitous circumstances of birth or position" (415).

5. Janny Scott and David Leonhardt, "Class in America: Shadowy Lines That Still Divide," *New York Times*, May 15, 2005, 16.

6. John E. Farley, "What's in the American Dream," in *Sociology* (Englewood Cliffs, NJ: Prentice Hall, 1990), 99; Center for a New American Dream, "New American Dream Survey Report," September 2004, 4–5, on the Internet at http://www.newdream.org/about/new.php (visited August 27, 2005); Change to Win, "The American Dream Survey 2006," August 28, 2006, on the Internet at http://www.changetowin.org/features/the-american-dream-survey.html (visited October 18, 2006); National League of Cities, "The American Dream in 2004: A Survey of the American People," September 2004, on the Internet at http://www.nlc.org (visited November 5, 2005).

7. Alexander Cockburn and Jeffrey St. Clair, "Count Your Blessings: NeoCons and NeoLibs Take a Big Hit as Voters Say No to Bush, War and Free Trade," *CounterPunch* (November 8, 2006), on the Internet at http://www.counterpunch.org/cockburn11082006.html (visited November 8, 2006); William Greider, "Watershed," *Nation* (December 4, 2006): 14–18; Jim Hightower and Phillip Frazer, "It Was a 'Throw the Bums Out' and a 'Change America's Direction' Election," *Lowdown* (December 2006): 1–4; John Nichols, "What Can Sherrod Brown Do for the Democrats?" *Nation* (October 2, 2006): 11–14; John Nichols, "Being Like Bernie," *Nation* (August 15–22, 2005): 15–18.

8. Roger Bybee, "NAFTA's Hung Jury," *Extra!* (May–June 2004): 14–15. CBS News/*New York Times* poll, "Foreign Trade and the U.S. Economy," January 31, 2006, 2; "Little Support for Bush's Social Security Agenda," *American Teacher* (September 2005): 17; David Sirota, "A Primary Concern: Free Trade Could Be Key for Democrats in '08," *In These Times* (April 2006): 28–29; David Sirota, "Debunking 'Centrism,'" *Nation* (January 3, 2005): 18–19.

9. Steve Rendall and Anna Kosseff, "Are Progressive Views Unpopular?" *Extra!* (September–October 2004): 19. David Sirota, "Embracing Populism," *In These Times* (December 2006): 4.

10. Business Roundtable, "Business Roundtable Deeply Disappointed by Doha Talks Suspension" (press release, July 24, 2006); Dana R. Fisher, Kevin Stanley, David Berman, and Gina Neff, "How Do Organizations Matter? Mobilization and Support for Participants at Five Globalization Protests," *Social Problems* 52 (2005): 102–21; "Shifting the Trade Debate, CAFTA and Beyond," *Public Citizen News, 2005 Annual Report*, March–April 2006, 7; "Unions Join Protests over the Next Step in Free Trade, the FTAA," *Labor Notes* (January 2004): 8–9; Timothy A. Wise, "World Trade Talks Collapse," *Dollars and Sense* (September–October 2006): 44–45.

11. "A Rising Tide?" *Washington Post*, March 12, 2006, B6; "Ever Higher Society, Ever Harder to Ascend," *Economist* (January 1, 2005): 22–24; Peter G. Gosselin, "If America Is Richer, Why Are Its Families So Much Less Secure?" *Los Angeles Times*, October 10, 2004, A1; Scott and Leonhardt, "Class in America"; David Wessel, "As Rich-Poor Gap Widens in the U.S., Class Mobility Stalls," *Wall Street Journal*, May 13, 2005, A1.

12. Jeff Faux, "The Party of Davos," *Nation* (February 13, 2006): 18–22; David Moberg, "Class Consciousness Matters," *In These Times* (July 11, 2005): 28–29.

13. Charles E. Hurst, *Social Inequality* (Boston: Allyn and Bacon, 1995), 308–10.

14. David Elsila, Michael Funke, and Sam Kirkland, "Blaming the Victim: The Propaganda War against Workers," *UAW Solidarity* (April 1992): 11–17.

15. John W. Wright, ed., *The New York Times Almanac 2006* (New York: Penguin, 2005), 392; Robert W. McChesney, *Rich Media, Poor Democracy* (Chicago: University of Illinois Press, 1999), 298; Scott Sherman, "An Appeal to Reason," *Nation* (March 10, 1997): 15–19.

16. Jonathan Tasini, "Lost in the Margins: Labor and the Media," *Extra!* (Summer 1990): 2–5.

17. Peter Hart, "Why Is Labor off TV?" *Extra!Update* (August 2005): 3.

18. Lewis F. Powell Jr. writes, "This setting of the 'rich' against the 'poor,' of business against the people, is the cheapest and most dangerous kind of politics" ("Attack on American Free Enterprise System," August 23, 1971, 5, on the Internet at http://www.historyisaweapon.com/defcon1/powellmemo.html, visited July 18, 2006); Steve Rendall, "Media See the Poor as Aggressors in 'Class War,'" *Extra!* (January–February 2001): 10; Norman Solomon, "Media Fire Shots across Edwards' Bow," *Extra!Update* (August 2004): 1.

19. Greider, "Watershed," 14–18; Hightower and Frazer, "It Was a 'Throw the Bums Out' and a 'Change America's Direction' Election"; John Nichols, "The 'Seattle Senators,'" *Nation* (December 18, 2006): 8–10; Sirota, "Embracing Populism"; Louis Uchitelle, "Here Come the Economic Populists," *New York Times*, November 26, 2006, 4.1.

20. Diana Kendall, *Framing Class: Media Representations of Wealth and Poverty in America* (Lanham, MD: Rowman & Littlefield, 2005), 183–228.

21. Scott and Leonhardt, "Class in America," 16.

22. "Class and the American Dream," *New York Times*, May 30, 2005, 14.

23. Janine Jackson, "We Feel Your Pain," *Extra!* (May–June 1996): 11–12.

24. "Class and the American Dream," *New York Times*.

25. Kendall, *Framing Class*, 21–58, 93–136.

26. Evan Thomas, "The Lost City: After Katrina," *Newsweek* (September 12, 2005): 43–52.

27. Jerry Adler, "The Fight against the Flu," *Newsweek* (October 31, 2005): 39–45; Ari Kelman, "In the Shadow of Disaster," *Nation* (January 6, 2006): 13–15; Leonard Pitts, "Images of Poor Will Fade Away," *Indianapolis Star*, September 24, 2005, A12.

28. Mike Davis, "Who Is Killing New Orleans?" *Nation* (April 10, 2006): 12. Also see Neil deMause, "Katrina's Vanishing Victims," *Extra!* (July–August 2006): 17–23; Paul Street, "The Personal and the Structural in New Orleans: Media Lessons from Katrina," *Dollars and Sense* (November–December 2005): 10–11; Michael Tisserand, "The Katrina Factor," *Nation* (January 1, 2007): 18–19.

29. Gregory Mantsios, "Class in America: Myths and Realities," in *Race, Class, and Gender in the United States*, ed. Paula S. Rothenberg (New York: St. Martin's Press, 1995).

30. Ronald Aronson, "The Left Needs More Socialism," *Nation* (April 17, 2006): 28–30; Robert W. McChesney, "Journalism, Democracy, and Class Struggle," *Monthly Review* (November 2000): 1–15; Robert W. McChesney and John Bellamy Foster, "The 'Left-Wing' Media?" *Monthly Review* (June 2003): 1–16; Jim Naureckas, "From the Top: What Are the Politics of Network Bosses?" *Extra!* (July–August 1998): 21–22; Jim Naureckas, "Where's the Power: Newsroom or Boardroom?" *Extra!* (July–August 1998): 23.

31. Julie Holler, Janine Jackson, and Hilary Goldstein, "Outside (and Inside) Influence on the News: Fear and Favor 2005," *Extra!* (March–April 2006): 15–20; Gregory Mantsios, "Media Magic: Making Class Disappear," in Rothenberg, *Race, Class, and Gender in the United States*; Martin N. Marger, *Social Inequality*, 3rd ed. (Boston: McGraw-Hill, 2005), 363–80.

32. See, for example, David Bacon, "Class Warfare," *Nation* (January 12–19, 2004): 17–20; Donald L. Barletta and James B. Steele, *America: Who Really Pays the Taxes?* (New York: Touchstone, 1994), 93–94; Michelle Cottle, "The Real Class War," *Washington Monthly* (July–August 1997): 12–16; Jeff Faux, *The Global Class War: How America's Bipartisan Elite Lost Our Future—and What It Will Take to Win It Back* (New York: Wiley, 2006); Everett Carl Ladd and Karlyn H. Bowman, "The Nation Says No to Class Warfare," *USA Today,* May 1999, 24–26; Irwin M. Stelzer, "Death and Taxes: The House Votes to Eliminate the Inheritance Tax," *Weekly Standard* (May 9, 2005): 1; Rendall, "Media See the Poor as Aggressors in 'Class War.'"

33. Janine Jackson, "Good News! The Rich Get Richer," *Extra!* (March–April 2006): 6–7; Steve Rendall and Anna Kosseff, "I'm Not a Leftist, but I Play One on TV: Progressives Excluded as Right Battles Center," *Extra!* (September–October 2004): 17–23; David Croteau, "Challenging the 'Liberal Media' Claim," *Extra!* (July–August 1998): 4–9.

34. See, for example, Hurst, *Social Inequality,* 305–12; Harold R. Kerbo, *Social Stratification and Inequality,* 5th ed. (New York: McGraw-Hill, 2006), 254–64; Margo Pepper, "No Corporation Left Behind," *Monthly Review* (November 2006): 39–41; Adolph L. Reed Jr., "The Real Divide," *Progressive* (November 2005): 27–32.

35. G. William Domhoff, *Who Rules America? Power, Politics, and Social Change,* 5th ed. (Boston: McGraw-Hill, 2006), 49–75.

36. Thomas Dye, *Who's Running America? The Bush Restoration,* 7th ed. (Upper Saddle River, NJ: Prentice Hall, 2002), 137–39.

37. Hurst, *Social Inequality,* 300; Marger, *Social Inequality,* 356–69.

38. Richard D. Coleman and Lee Rainwater, *Social Standing in America* (New York: Basic Books, 1978); Marger, *Social Inequality,* 109–19; U.S. Bureau of the Census, "Income Inequality (Middle Class)—Narrative," 2005, on the Internet at http://www.census.gov/hhes/income/midclass/midclasn.html (visited November 11, 2005).

39. Lawrence Mishel, Jared Bernstein, and Sylvia Allegretto, *The State of Working America, 2006–2007* (Ithaca, NY: IRL Press, 2007), 43–58; Hurst, *Social Inequality,* 23.

40. Randy Hodson and Teresa A. Sullivan, *The Social Organization of Work,* 2nd ed. (Belmont, CA: Wadsworth-Thomson, 2002), 157–61.

41. George Gallup and S. F. Rae, *The Pulse of Democracy* (New York: Simon and Schuster, 1940), 169; Robert W. Hodge and Donald J. Treiman, "Class Identification in the United States," *American Journal of Sociology* 73 (March 1968): 535–47; Mary R. Jackman and Robert W. Jackman, *Class Awareness in the United States* (Berkeley: University of California Press, 1982), 18; Reeve Vanneman and Lynn Weber Cannon, *The American Perception of Class* (Philadelphia: Temple University Press, 1987).

42. Doug Henwood, "American Dream: It's Not Working," *Christianity and Crisis* (June 8, 1992): 195–97.

43. Bennett Harrison and Barry Bluestone, "The Crisis of the American Dream," in *Great Divides,* ed. Thomas A. Shapiro (Mountain View, CA: Mayfield, 1998), 179–91.

44. Mishel, Bernstein, and Allegretto, *The State of Working America, 2006–2007,* 74.

45. Mishel, Bernstein, and Allegretto, *The State of Working America, 2006–2007,* 74.

46. Mishel, Bernstein, and Allegretto, *The State of Working America, 2006–2007,* 59.

47. David W. Wright, "Changes in Hourly Earnings and Weekly Earnings, 1947–2005," *Work Series* (Wichita State University), November 2006, A19–A20.

48. Mishel, Bernstein, and Allegretto, *The State of Working America, 2006–2007,* 162.

49. Mishel, Bernstein, and Allegretto, *The State of Working America, 2006–2007,* 128–29.

50. Mishel, Bernstein, and Allegretto, *The State of Working America, 2006–2007,* 49.

51. Mishel, Bernstein, and Allegretto, *The State of Working America, 2006–2007,* 89.

52. Economic Policy Institute, "Data Zone: Family Income Limits by Quintile, 1947–2004, Share of Aggregate Family Income by Quintile," 1–2, on the Internet at http://www.epinet.org (visited October 26, 2006).

53. Congressional Budget Office, "Historical Effective Federal Tax Rates: 1979 to 2002," March 2005, 2, table 1C, on the Internet at http://www.cbo.gov (visited November 7, 2005).

54. Congressional Budget Office, "Historical Effective Federal Tax Rates: 1979 to 2003," December 2005, 4–5, summary tables 1 and 2, on the Internet at http://www.cbo.gov (visited November 13, 2006).

55. Congressional Budget Office, "Effective Federal Tax Rates under Current Law, 2001 to 2014," August 2004, on the Internet at http://www.cbo.gov (visited November 13, 2006).

56. Sarah Anderson, John Cavanagh, Chuck Collins, Eric Benjamin, and Sam Pizzigati, "Executive Excess 2006: 13th Annual CEO Compensation Survey" (Washington, DC, and Boston: Institute for Policy Studies and United for a Fair Economy, August 30, 2006), 30.

57. Eric Dash, "Off to the Races Again, Leaving Many Behind," *New York Times*, April 9, 2006, B1, B7 (average CEO income). Gary Strauss and Barbara Hansen, "CEO Pay Soars in 2005 as a Select Group Break the $100 Million Mark," *USA Today*, April 11, 2006 (median CEO income), on the Internet at http://www.usatoday.com/money/companies/management/2006-04-07-ceo-alpha.htm (visited April 17, 2006).

58. Amounts are based on the authors' analysis of data reported by and cited in Anderson et al., "Executive Excess 2006," 30–32, 54.

59. Wright, "Changes in Hourly Earnings and Weekly Earnings, 1947–2005."

60. Mishel, Bernstein, and Allegretto, *The State of Working America, 2006–2007*, 189.

61. John J. Macionis, "Diversity in the New Century: Changes in the Workplace," in *Sociology* (Upper Saddle River, NJ: Prentice Hall, 2001), 424.

62. John Gettings and David Johnson, "Wonder Women," *Infoplease Daily Almanac*, November 20, 2005, 1, on the Internet at http://www.infoplease.com/spot/womenceo1.html (visited November 20, 2005).

63. "The Conundrum of the Glass Ceiling," *Economist* (July 27, 2005): 63.

64. Sarah Anderson, John Cavanagh, Scott Klinger, and Liz Stanton, "Executive Excess 2005: 12th Annual CEO Compensation Survey" (Washington, DC, and Boston: Institute for Policy Studies and United for a Fair Economy, August 30, 2005), 21.

65. Lawrence Mishel, Jared Bernstein, and Sylvia Allegretto, *The State of Working America, 2004–2005* (Ithaca, NY: IRL Press, 2005), 135.

66. Mishel, Bernstein, and Allegretto, *The State of Working America, 2006–2007*, 115.

67. Mishel, Bernstein, and Allegretto, *The State of Working America, 2006–2007*, 136.

68. Mishel, Bernstein, and Allegretto, *The State of Working America, 2004–2005*, 141.

69. James H. Moore, Jr., "Projected Pension Income: Equality or Disparity?" *Monthly Labor Review* (March 2006): 58–67.

70. "Current Labor Statistics, Tables 34 and 35," *Monthly Labor Review* (July 2005): 126–27.

71. Mishel, Bernstein, and Allegretto, *The State of Working America, 2006–2007*, 137; Mary Williams Walsh, "More Companies Ending Promises for Retirement," *New York Times*, January 9, 2006, A1.

72. Stephanie L. Costo, "Trends in Retirement Plan Coverage over the Last Decade," *Monthly Labor Review* (February 2006): 58–64.

73. Mishel, Bernstein, and Allegretto, *The State of Working America, 2004–2005*, 141.

74. Mishel, Bernstein, and Allegretto, *The State of Working America, 2006–2007*, 133.

75. John E. Buckley and Robert W. Van Giezen, "Federal Statistics on Healthcare Benefits and Cost Trends: An Overview," *Monthly Labor Review* (November 2004): 45; Ida Hellander, "A Review of Data on the U.S. Health Sector," *International Journal of Health Services* 36 (2006): 792; Ida Hellander, "A Review of Data on the Health Care Sector of the United States," *International Journal of Health Services* 31 (2001): 38; Nicholas Skala and Ida Hellander, "A Review of Data on the U.S. Health Sector," *International Journal of Health Services* 36 (2006): 159.

76. Buckley and Van Giezen, "Federal Statistics on Healthcare Benefits and Cost Trends: An Overview"; "Current Labor Statistics: Table 25," *Monthly Labor Review* (May 2001): 90.

77. See, for example, Anne E. Polivka, "Contingent and Alternative Work Arrangements, Defined," *Monthly Labor Review* (October 1996): 3–9; Steve Hipple, "Contingent Work in the Late-1990s," *Monthly Labor Review* (March 2001): 3–27; Mishel, Bernstein, and Allegretto, *The State of Working America, 2006–2007*, 236; "Contingent Workers," *Monthly Labor Review* (August 2005): 2.

78. Mishel, Bernstein, and Allegretto, *The State of Working America, 2006–2007*, 237–38; Fred Magdoff and Harry Magdoff, "Disposable Workers: Today's Reserve Army of Labor," *Monthly Review* (April 2004): 18–35.

79. Magdoff and Magdoff, "Disposable Workers," 28.

80. Mishel, Bernstein, and Allegretto, *The State of Working America, 2006–2007*, 239; Mishel, Bernstein, and Allegretto, *The State of Working America, 2004–2005*, 258–59.

81. Mishel, Bernstein, and Allegretto, *The State of Working America, 2004–2005*, 260.

82. Mishel, Bernstein, and Allegretto, *The State of Working America, 2006–2007*, 242–43.

83. U.S. Department of Labor, Bureau of Labor Statistics, "Union Members in 2006" (press release, January 25, 2007), 1. Also see Mishel, Bernstein, and Allegretto, *The State of Working America, 2006–2007*, 180.

84. Mishel, Bernstein, and Allegretto, *The State of Working America, 2004–2005*, 189.

85. Mishel, Bernstein, and Allegretto, *The State of Working America, 2006–2007*, 216–18, 224–28; Robert Pollin, *Contours of Descent: U.S. Economic Fractures and the Landscape of Global Austerity* (New York: Verso, 2005), 205.

86. John Schmitt, "How Good Is the Economy at Creating Good Jobs?" (Washington, DC: Center for Economic and Policy Research, October 2005), 3–6.

87. Richard T. Schaefer, *Sociology*, 10th ed. (New York: McGraw-Hill, 2007), 197–98.

88. Kerbo, *Social Stratification and Inequality*, 372–77.

89. Annette Bernhardt, Martuna Morris, Marck S. Handcock, and Marc A. Scott, *Divergent Paths: Economic Mobility in the New American Labor Market* (New York: Russell Sage Foundation, 2001); Greg J. Duncan and Wei-Jun J. Yeung, "Extent and Consequences of Welfare Dependence among America's Children," *Children and Youth Services Review* 17 (1995): 157–82; Earl Wysong and David W. Wright, "Is Social Mobility a Social Problem? Recent Intergenerational Mobility Trends, the American Dream, and the Media" (paper presented at the North Central Sociological Association Annual Meeting, Indianapolis, Indiana, March 25, 2006).

90. David Dooley, JoAnn Prause, and Kathleen A. Ham-Rowbottom, "Underemployment and Depression: Longitudinal Relationships," *Journal of Health and Social Behavior* 41 (December 2000): 421–36. Also see Robert A. Rothman, *Working: Sociological Perspectives*, 2nd ed. (Upper Saddle River, NJ: Prentice Hall, 1998), 183–88; Robert A. Rothman, *Inequality and Stratification: Race, Class, and Gender*, 5th ed. (Upper Saddle River, NJ: Pearson–Prentice Hall, 2005), 238.

91. See, for example, Aaron Bernstein, "Back on the Edge," *Business Week* (April 23, 2001): 42–43; Barry Bluestone and Bennett Harrison, *The Deindustrialization of America* (New York: Basic Books, 1982); Barbara Ehrenreich, *Fear of Falling* (New York: Harper, 1989); Ryan Helwig, "Worker Displacement in 1999–2000," *Monthly Labor Review* (June 2004): 54–68; Katherine S. Newman, *Falling from Grace: The Experience of Downward Mobility in the American Middle Class* (New York: Free Press, 1988) and *Declining Fortunes* (New York: Basic Books, 1993); New York Times, *Downsizing of America* (New York: Random House, 1996); Carolyn C. Perrucci, Robert Perrucci, Dena B. Targ, and Harry Targ, *Plant Closings: International Context and Social Costs* (Hawthorne, NY: Aldine de Gruyter, 1988); Louis Uchitelle, *The Disposable American: Layoffs and Their Consequences* (New York: Knopf, 2006).

92. General Motors, "GM North America to Undergo Major Capacity Reduction" (press release, November 21, 2005), 1–3; Sven Gustafson, "38,000 at Ford Taking Buyouts," *Indianapolis Star*, November 30, 2006, C1; Roger Kerson, "Buyouts Offer Options to Ford Workers," *UAW Solidarity* (November–December 2006): 6–7; Micheline Maynard, "Ford Eliminating up to 30,000 Jobs and 14 Factories," *New York Times*, January 24, 2006, A1; "News Watch," *Labor Notes* (November 2006): 4.

93. New York Times, *Downsizing of America*; Daniel McGinn and Keith Naughton, "How Safe Is Your Job?" *Newsweek* (February 5, 2001): 34–43; Adam Cohen, "This Time It's Different," *Time* (January 8, 2001): 18–22; Sharon P. Brown and Lewis B. Siegel, "Mass Layoff Data Indicate Outsourcing and Offshoring Work," *Monthly Labor Review* (August 2005): 3–10; Teresa Ghilarducci, "The End of Retirement," *Monthly Review* (May 2006): 12–27; Pete Engardio, "The Future of Outsourcing," *Business Week* (January 30, 2006): 50–58; Michael Ellis, "Ford to Cut 10% of White-Collar Jobs," *Indianapolis Star*, November 22, 2005, C4.

94. Dee-Ann Durbin, "Specter of Delphi Deal Leads to GM Upgrade," *Indianapolis Star*, May 13, 2006, C1; Ted Evanoff, "Battle for Prosperity," *Indianapolis Star*, November 13, 2005, D1, D8; Tiffany Ten Eyck, "Rank and File Auto Workers Reflect on Past Actions, Plan for Future," *Labor Notes*, December 2006, 6–7; David Moberg, "Delphi Dodges Union Contract," *In These Times* (June 2006): 30–31; Tiffany Ten Eyck, "As Auto Workers Meet, Concessions Continue and Union Remains Silent," *Labor Notes* (July 2006): 1, 14.

95. Stanley Aronowitz, *The Last Good Job in America* (Lanham, MD: Rowman & Littlefield, 2001); Bernhardt et al., *Divergent Paths*; Wysong and Wright, "Is Social Mobility a Social Problem?"; Earl Wysong and David W. Wright, "What's Happening to the American Dream? Sons, Daughters, and Intergenerational Mobility Today" (paper presented at the Midwest Sociological Society Annual Meeting, Chicago, Illinois, April 4–7, 2007).

96. Theoretically, downward mobility from the privileged class into the new working class could occur in our model, but we believe it is rare, and the topic would require separate attention. Therefore, we do not address it here.

97. Newman, *Falling from Grace*.

98. New York Times, *Downsizing of America*, 50.

99. Lawrence Mishel, Jared Bernstein, and John Schmitt, *The State of Working America, 2000–2001* (Ithaca, NY: Cornell University Press, 2001), 169; Mishel, Bernstein, and Allegretto, *The State of Working America, 2006–2007*, 166–68; U.S. Department of Labor, Bureau of Labor Statistics, *Occupational Projections and Training Data, 2006–2007 Edition*, Washington, DC, February 2006.

100. Mishel, Bernstein, and Schmitt, *Working America 2000–2001*, 169; John Miller, "When Is the Economy in a Recession?" *Dollars and Sense* (July–August 2001): 32.

101. Mishel, Bernstein, and Allegretto, *The State of Working America, 2004–2005*, 9.

102. Dena Libner, "Unequal Recovery," *Dollars and Sense* (May–June 2005): 30; also see Jeannine Aversa, "Upbeat Jobs News Precedes Election," *Indianapolis Star*, November 4, 2006, C1— "the economy added 92,000 jobs in October [2006]."

103. Jeffrey R. Lustig, "The Politics of Shutdown," *Journal of Economic Issues* 19 (1985): 123–59.

104. Gene Koretz, "Downsizing's Painful Effects," *Business Week* (April 13, 1998): 23.

105. Helwig, "Worker Displacement in 1999–2000," 66.

106. Helwig, "Worker Displacement in 1999–2000," 66.

107. Charles Koeber and David W. Wright, "W/Age Bias in Worker Displacement: How Industrial Structure Shapes the Job Loss and Earnings Decline of Older American Workers," *Journal of Socio-Economics* 30 (2001): 343–52.

108. Wright, "Changes in Hourly Earnings and Weekly Earnings, 1947–2005," A19–A20.

109. Geoffrey Paulin and Brian Riordon, "Making It on Their Own: The Baby Boom Meets Generation X," *Monthly Labor Review* (February 1998): 10–21; Kurt Schrammel, "Comparing the Labor Market Success of Young Adults from Two Generations," *Monthly Labor Review* (February 1998): 3–9.

110. Wysong and Wright, "Is Social Mobility a Social Problem?"

111. Wysong and Wright, "What's Happening to the American Dream?"

112. Mishel, Bernstein, and Allegretto, *The State of Working America, 2006–2007*, 153.

113. Mishel, Bernstein, and Allegretto, *The State of Working America, 2006–2007*, 152.

114. AFL-CIO, "Young Workers without College Degrees Are the 'Forgotten Majority,'" in *High Hopes, Little Trust: A Study of Young Workers and Their Ups and Downs in the New Economy* (Washington, DC: AFL-CIO, 1999), 1.

115. Daniel E. Hecker, "Occupational Employment Projections to 2014," *Monthly Labor Review* (November 2005): 70–81; also see Tamara Draut, *Strapped: Why America's 20- and 30-Somethings Can't Get Ahead* (New York: Doubleday, 2005).

116. Robert B. Reich, "Secession of the Successful," *New York Times Magazine*, January 20, 1991, 42; David Harvey, *A Brief History of Neoliberalism* (New York: Oxford University Press, 2005).

117. Community Associations Institute, "Data on U.S. Community Associations," on the Internet at http://www.caionline.org/about/facts.cfm (visited May 15, 2006).

118. Tim Vanderpool, "Secession of the Successful," *Utne Reader* (November–December 1995): 32–34.

119. Community Associations Institute, "Data on U.S. Community Associations."

120. Vanderpool, "Secession of the Successful."

121. Edward J. Blakely and Mary Gail Snyder, *Fortress America: Gated Communities in the United States* (Washington, DC: Brookings Institution Press, 1997), 7–8; Chuck Collins and Felice Yeskel, *Economic Apartheid in America* (New York: The New Press, 2000), 37.

122. U.S. Bureau of the Census, Current Housing Reports, Series H150/03, *American Housing Survey for the United States: 2003* (Washington, DC: U.S. Government Printing Office, 2004), 60.

123. Blakely and Snyder, *Fortress America: Gated Communities in the United States*, 180.

124. Haya El Nasser, "Gated Communities More Popular, and Not Just for the Rich," *USA Today*, December 16, 2002, 1A.

125. Evan McKenzie, *Privatopia* (New Haven, CT: Yale University Press, 1994), 105, 186.

126. Harvey, *A Brief History of Neoliberalism.*

127. Robert B. Reich, *The Work of Nations: Preparing Ourselves for the Twenty-first Century* (New York: Knopf, 1991), 140. Also see Byron L. Dorgan, *Take This Job and Ship It* (New York: Thomas Dunne Books, 2006), 16–17, 85–87.

128. New York Times, *Class Matters* (New York: Times Books, 2005), 150.

129. Jerry Adler, "The Rise of the Overclass," *Newsweek* (July 31, 1995): 45–46.

130. Blakely and Snyder, *Fortress America*; Setha Low, *Behind the Gates: Life, Security, and the Pursuit of Happiness in Fortress America* (New York: Routledge, 2003).

131. Andrew Ross, "Duct Tape Nation: Land Use, the Fear Factor, and the New Unilateralism," *Harvard Design Magazine* (Spring–Summer 2004): 1–5.

132. Center for a New American Dream, "New American Dream Survey Report"; National League of Cities, "The American Dream in 2004."

133. Center for a New American Dream, "New American Dream Survey Report."

134. Center for a New American Dream, "New American Dream Survey Report."

135. Pew Research Center, "Once Again, the Future Ain't What It Used to Be," May 2, 2006, on the Internet at http://www.pewresearch.org (visited July 12, 2006).

136. Change to Win, "The American Dream Survey 2006."

137. Pew Research Center, "Once Again, the Future Ain't What It Used to Be."

138. U.S. Department of Commerce, *Statistical Abstract of the United States: 2000* (Washington, DC: U.S. Government Printing Office, 2000), 54; U.S. Department of Commerce, *Statistical Abstract of the United States: 2006* (Washington, DC: U.S. Government Printing Office, 2005), 51.

139. Lorraine Ali, "Sounding Off on Bush," *Newsweek* (May 15, 2006): 13; also see Stephan Smith-Said, "Why Neil Young Is Wrong," *Progressive* (July 2006): 32–33.

140. Tom Frank, "Let Them Eat Lifestyle," *Utne Reader* (November–December 1997): 43–47; Thomas Frank, *The Conquest of Cool* (Chicago: University of Chicago Press, 1997); Thomas Frank, *One Market under God* (New York: Doubleday, 2000).

141. See Theresa A. Martinez, "Popular Culture as Oppositional Culture: Rap as Resistance," *Sociological Perspectives* 40 (1997): 265–86; Keith Goetzman, "Righteous Babe: Interview with Ani DiFranco," *Utne Reader* (July–August 2001): 94–96; Katherine Turman, "Interview: Chris Martin," *Mother Jones* (January–February 2004): 78–79; Antonino D'Ambrosio, "Progressive Interview: Chuck D," *Progressive* (August 2005): 37–41; Greg Tate, "The Color of Money," *Nation* (February 23, 2006): 23–26.

142. See, for example, Ben H. Bagdikian, *The New Media Monopoly* (Boston: Beacon Press, 2004); Domhoff, *Who Rules America?*; Dye, *Who's Running America?*

143. The "over $20 trillion" figure is projected for the mid-2000s based on information for 2002 reported in the U.S. Department of Commerce, *Statistical Abstract of the United States: 2006*, 503; Kerbo, *Social Stratification and Inequality*, 179–82.

144. Ellen McGirt, "A Banner Year," *Fortune* (April 17, 2006): 192–94.

145. The number of manufacturing firms, as well as the assets and net income for firms in this sector, was derived from data reported by the United States Department of the Treasury, Internal

Revenue Service, "2002 Returns of Active Corporations, Table 4," "SOI Tax Stats—Corporation Data by Sector or Industry," on the Internet at http://www.irs.gov/taxstats/bustaxstats (visited December 5, 2005).

146. Banking assets computed from data reported in "Fortune 500 Largest U.S. Corporations" and "The Fortune 1000 Ranked within Industries," *Fortune* (April 17, 2006): F1–F19, F47; U.S. Department of Commerce, *Statistical Abstract of the United States: 2006,* 762.

147. Insurance assets computed from data reported in *Fortune* ("Fortune 500 Largest U.S. Corporations" and "The Fortune 1000 Ranked within Industries") and U.S. Department of Commerce, *Statistical Abstract of the United States: 2006,* 761.

148. U.S. Department of Commerce, *Statistical Abstract of the United States: 2006,* 529.

149. Matthew Miller and Tatiana Serafin, eds., "The Forbes 400," *Forbes* (October 9, 2006): 294, 296–304.

150. Luisa Kroll and Lea Goldman, eds., "Billionaire Bacchanalia," *Forbes* (March 27, 2006): 111–78; Matthew Miller and Peter Newcomb, "The Forbes 400," *Forbes* (October 10, 2005): 89.

151. Jeffrey Marshall and Ellen M. Heffes, "Recruiter's Study Finds Change, and Progress," *Financial Executive* (November 2005): 10.

152. Mishel, Bernstein, and Allegretto, *The State of Working America, 2006–2007,* 258.

153. Congressional Budget Office, "Historical Effective Federal Tax Rates: 1979 to 2003," 4.

154. Congressional Budget Office, "Historical Effective Federal Tax Rates: 1979 to 2003," 4.

155. For examples, see G. William Domhoff, *State Autonomy or Class Dominance?* (New York: Aldine de Gruyter, 1996); Domhoff, *Who Rules America?*; Michael Useem, *The Inner Circle* (New York: Oxford University Press, 1984); Dye, *Who's Running America?*

156. Mishel, Bernstein, and Allegretto, *The State of Working America, 2006–2007,* 77.

157. Strauss and Hansen, "CEO Pay Soars in 2005 as a Select Group Break the $100 Million Mark."

158. Donald L. Barlett and James B. Steele, *America: What Went Wrong?* (Kansas City, MO: Andrews and McMeel, 1992), xiii.

159. Paul E. Dwyer, "Salaries of Congress: A List of Payable Rates and Effective Dates, 1789–2006," *CRS Report for Congress,* Congressional Research Service, April 18, 2006, 1.

160. "Benchmarking Data Available by Industry," *Financial Executive* (December 2004): 12.

161. Kroll and Goldman, "Billionaire Bacchanalia," 174–78.

162. McDonald's Corporation, "Notice of 2006 Annual Shareholders Meeting and Proxy Statement," April 7, 2006, 17.

163. Charles Bowden, "Keeper of the Fire," *Mother Jones* (July–August 2003): 70; Nike Corporation, "Notice of Annual Meeting of Stockholders and Proxy Statement," August 12, 2005, 13.

164. Murray L. Wiedenbaum, *Business, Government, and the Public* (Englewood Cliffs, NJ: Prentice Hall, 1977), 5–8.

165. Vicente Navarro, "Production and the Welfare State: The Political Context of Reforms," *International Journal of Health Services* 21 (1991): 606.

166. Robert J. Samuelson, "Great Expectations," *Newsweek* (January 8, 1996): 31; also see Mishel, Bernstein, and Allegretto, *The State of Working America, 2004–2005,* 96.

167. Val Burris, "The Two Faces of Capital: Corporations and Individual Capitalists as Political Actors," *American Sociological Review* 66 (2001): 376.

168. Powell, "Attack on American Free Enterprise System," 14.

169. Ted Nace, *Gangs of America: The Rise of Corporate Power and the Disabling of Democracy* (San Francisco, CA: Berrett-Koehler, 2003), 168. Also see Diana B. Henriques, "Putting the Corporation in the Dock," *New York Times,* September 14, 2003, 3.

170. Business Roundtable, "About Us: Business Roundtable History," on the Internet at http://www.businessroundtable.org//aboutUs/history.aspx (visited July 23, 2006); Lee Drutman and Charlie Cray, "The People's Business," *In These Times* (March 14, 2005): 17; John B. Judis, "The Most Powerful Lobby," *In These Times* (February 21, 1994): 22–23.

171. Navarro, "Production and the Welfare State," 606.

172. Political Money Line, "Federal Lobby Directory: Individual Lobbyists," on the Internet at http://www.fecinfo.com (visited January 15, 2006).

173. Alex Knott, "Industry of Influence Nets More Than $10 Billion," Center for Public Integrity, on the Internet at http://www.publicintegrity.org/lobby/report.aspx?aid=675 (visited May 21, 2006).

174. Michael Patrick Allen, "Elite Social Movement Organizations and the State: The Rise of the Conservative Policy-Planning Network," in *Research in Politics and Society*, vol. 4, *The Political Consequences of Social Networks*, ed. Gwen Moore and J. Allen Whitt (Greenwich, CT: JAI Press, 1992), 87–109; Drutman and Cray, "The People's Business," 17.

175. Drutman and Cray, "The People's Business," 17. Also see Michael Dolny, "Right, Center Think Tanks Still Most Quoted," *Extra!* (June 2005): 28–29.

176. Federal Election Commission, "FEC Releases New PAC Count" (press release, July 28, 1989).

177. FEC, "Semi-Annual PAC Count—2000–2005," *Record* (March 2005): 9.

178. The PAC contribution amount reported is based on FEC data: FEC, "PAC Activity Increases for 2004 Election" (press release, April 13, 2005); the PAC percentage listed is based on the authors' analysis of information reported in various FEC documents. See notes 39 and 69 in chapter 4 for details concerning how the percentage was computed.

179. FEC, "Congressional Candidates Spend $1.16 Billion during 2003–2004" (press release, June 9, 2005), 1.

180. Center for Responsive Politics, "Summary," in *Influence, Inc.*, (Washington, DC: Center for Responsive Politics, 2000), 1–5; Center for Responsive Politics, "Nov. 6 Update," November 8, 2006, on the Internet at http://www.opensecrets.org/press releases/2006/PreElection.10.25.asp (visited November 8, 2006); Julia Malone, "Campaign Was the Most Costly: Near $4 billion," *Indianapolis Star*, November 7, 2004, A17.

181. Center for Public Integrity, "527s in 2004 Shatter Previous Records for Political Fundraising," December 16, 2004, on the Internet at http://www.publicintegrity.org/527 (visited April 6, 2005). Center for Responsive Politics, "Federal Campaign Finance Law: Contribution Limits," November 6, 2002, 1–2, on the Internet at http://www.opensecrets.org/basics (visited December 18, 2005).

182. These percentages were based on the authors' calculations using several FEC documents and tables listing contributions from individuals and PACs; these documents are referenced in, or attached to, FEC press releases dated February 3, 2005, April 1, 2005, and June 9, 2005.

183. Center for Responsive Politics, "2006 Election Overview: Business-Labor-Ideology Split in PAC and Individual Donations to Candidates and Parties," November 7, 2006, 1, on the Internet at http://www.opensecrets.org/overview/blio.asp?cycle=2006 (visited November 15, 2006). The 2006 ratio of "at least 20 to 1" was based on our estimate that business donations totaled $969 million versus labor donations of $49 million. Our $969 million figure includes $849 million from business sources as noted by the Center for Responsive Politics. It also includes our estimate that at least $40 million of the $53 million donated by "ideological" sources and $80 million of the $119 million donated by "other" sources were from business interests. Center for Responsive Politics, "2004 Election Overview: Business-Labor-Ideology Split in PAC and Individual Donations to Candidates and Parties," March 28, 2005, 1, on the Internet at http://www.opensecrets.org/overview (visited December 18, 2005); Center for Responsive Politics, "Business, Labor, and Ideological Donors," *Who's Paying for This Election?* (Washington, DC: Center for Responsive Politics, 2000), 1.

184. Quoted in Navarro, "Production and the Welfare State," 607.

185. Robert Perrucci and Earl Wysong, *The New Class Society* (Lanham, MD: Rowman & Littlefield, 1999), 133–34.

186. Alexander Cockburn and Jeffrey St. Clair, "It Really Was a Coup," *CounterPunch* (December 2000): 2.

187. Sam Pizzigati, "The New Congress: Why Deep Pockets Can Relax," *Too Much* (November 13, 2006): 3; Center for Responsive Politics, "2006 Election Overview: Donor Demographics," November 7, 2006, 1, on the Internet at http://www.opensecrets.org/overview/DonorDemo graphics.asp?cycle=2006 (visited November 15, 2006).

188. Mark Dudzic, "The Midterm Elections: A Return to Politics as Usual," *Party Builder*, November 2006, on the Internet at http://www.thelaborparty.org/a_06elec.html (visited November 17, 2006).

189. Anna Bernasek, "'Temporary' Tax Cuts Have a Way of Becoming Permanent," *New York Times*, May 14, 2006, C3.

190. Congressional Budget Office, "Historical Effective Federal Tax Rates: 1979 to 2002," March 2005, 1; Ellen Frank, "Reaganomics Redux: What to Expect from a Bush Presidency," *Dollars and Sense* (July–August 2001): 7; Pollin, *Contours of Descent*, 94–97.

191. Citizens for Tax Justice, "Tax Cuts on Capital Gains and Dividends Doubled Bush Income Tax Cuts for the Wealthiest in 2003" (press release, April 5, 2006), 1.

192. Citizens for Tax Justice, "Tax Cuts on Capital Gains and Dividends Doubled Bush Income Tax Cuts for the Wealthiest in 2003," 1.

193. Edmund L. Andrews, "House Passes a $2.7 Trillion Spending Plan," *New York Times*, May 18, 2006, A1.

194. Pollin, *Contours of Descent*, 98.

195. U.S. House of Representatives, Committee on Ways and Means, "428 Major Companies and Organizations Support the American Jobs Creation Act" (press release, July 8, 2004).

196. Michael Scherer, "Make Your Taxes Disappear!" *Mother Jones* (March–April 2005): 72.

197. "Labor Party to Seek Ballot Access in South Carolina," *Labor Party News* (December 2005): 3.

198. Alexander Cockburn, "Presidential Elections: Not as Big a Deal as They Say," *CounterPunch* (June 16–30, 2004): 3.

199. Quoted in Wesley J. Smith, "Nobody's Nader," *Mother Jones* (July–August 1996): 61.

200. Earl Wysong, *High Risk and High Stakes: Health Professionals, Politics, and Policy* (Westport, CT: Greenwood Press, 1992).

201. See, for example, Eliza Brinkmeyer, "Vote for CAFTA, Pay the Price," *Public Citizen News* (November–December 2005): 1, 12; Perrucci and Wysong, *The New Class Society*, 126–35; Pollin, *Contours of Descent*, 21–47, 77–124; Sam D. Sieber, *Second Rate Nation: From the American Dream to the American Myth* (Boulder, CO: Paradigm, 2005); Frederick R. Strobel and Wallace C. Peterson, *The Coming Class War and How to Avoid It* (Armonk, NY: M. E. Sharpe, 1999), 55–61.

202. Peter Dicken, "Technology: The 'Great Growling Engine of Change,'" in *The Transformation of Work in the New Economy*, ed. Robert Perrucci and Carolyn Perrucci (Los Angeles, CA: Roxbury, 2007), 116–27.

203. U.S. Department of Commerce, *Statistical Abstract of the United States: 2006*, 529.

204. Hodson and Sullivan, *The Social Organization of Work*, 258; Jay M. Berman, "Industry Output and Employment Projections to 2014," *Monthly Labor Review* (November 2005): 45–69.

205. Hecker, "Occupational Employment Projections to 2014."

206. Mishel, Bernstein, and Allegretto, *The State of Working America, 2006–2007*, 238.

207. Mishel, Bernstein, and Allegretto, *The State of Working America, 2006–2007*, 239–40.

208. For examples, see Jared Bernstein, *All Together Now: Common Sense for a Fair Economy* (San Francisco, CA: Berrett-Koehler, 2006); Lou Dobbs, *War on the Middle Class: How the Government, Big Business, and Special Interest Groups Are Waging War on the American Dream and How to Fight Back* (New York: Viking, 2006); Faux, *The Global Class War*; Norton Garfinkle, *The American Dream vs. the Gospel of Wealth: The Fight for a Productive Middle-Class Economy* (New Haven, CT: Yale University Press, 2006); Jacob B. Hacker, *The Great Risk Shift: The Assault on American Jobs, Families, Health Care, and Retirement and How You Can Fight Back* (New York: Oxford University Press, 2006); Thom Hartman, *Screwed: The Undeclared War against the Middle Class—and What We Can Do about It* (San Francisco, CA: Berrett-Koehler, 2006).

209. Domhoff, *Who Rules America?* 49–75; Richard L. Zweigenhaft and G. William Domhoff, *Diversity in the Power Elite: Have Women and Minorities Reached the Top?* (New Haven, CT: Yale University Press, 1998), 192–94.

210. Seth Ackerman, "The Most Biased Name in News," *Extra!* (July–August 2001): 10–12; Adolph Reed, "The 'Public Is Bad; Private Is Better' Scam," *Labor Party News* (October 2005): 1–2.

211. For a discussion of equity and liberty, see Marger, *Social Inequality*, 207.

212. Charles Derber, *The Wilding of America* (New York: St. Martin's Press, 1996), 141–42.

213. Wayne Alves and Peter Rossi, "Who Should Get What? Fairness Judgments of Distribution of Earnings," *American Journal of Sociology* 84 (1978): 541–64.

3

The Global Economy
and the Privileged Class

Allowing the defenders of privilege to monopolize the term "globalization" for their own vision too easily allows them to portray themselves as agents of an impersonal process and to paint advocates of global justice as narrow specialists or naïve opponents of technological progress.

—Salih Booker and William Minter, *Nation*, July 9, 2001

In March 2004, a Gallup poll reported that 61 percent of Americans say they are concerned that they might lose a job because the employer is moving that job to a foreign country. One source of that job-loss anxiety can probably be traced to a number of high-profile pieces in the *New York Times*, the *Wall Street Journal*, and *USA Today* about the remarks of senior IBM officials calling on IBM to move high-technology jobs in computer programming and software design to foreign workers in India and China. This practice came to be labeled "outsourcing" in the mainstream media, and it extended beyond computer professionals to include customer-service call-center, data-entry, and claims-processing jobs. Another reason for the 61 percent of Americans with job-loss anxiety may have been linked to the fact that be-tween 2000 and 2003, manufacturing employment dropped by 2.8 million.[1] Maybe some of the 61 percent of Americans with job-loss anxiety could re-call the fact that, after World War II, manufacturing, as a share of total U.S. jobs, was at a peak of 40 percent, and slipped to 27 percent in 1981, and slipped further to 12 percent in 2005. Or maybe they remembered 2001, when record layoffs led to the worst U.S. job market since the recession of 1990 and 1991. In the period from January to June 2001, U.S. companies announced 652,510 layoffs. From manufacturing to high-tech, workers lost jobs at the fastest rate in years. Although the 2001–2004 job cuts were dra-matic, they were merely the latest chapter in what has been a long story for

U.S. workers. Twenty-five years earlier, we documented the experiences of eight hundred fifty workers who lost jobs due to a plant closing. Little did we know at the time that it was the beginning of what has since become an all-too-familiar pattern of job loss for millions of workers.

On December 1, 1982, an RCA television cabinet factory in Monticello, Indiana, closed its doors and shut down production. Monticello, a town of five thousand people in White County (population twenty-three thousand), had been the home of RCA since 1946. The closing displaced eight hundred fifty workers, who were members of Local 3154 of the United Brotherhood of Carpenters and Joiners. Officials at RCA cited the high manufacturing costs and foreign competition as key factors leading to the closing.

Reactions of displaced workers from RCA were varied, with most expressing either a general sense of despair or a feeling of confidence that they would survive. One worker was hopeful, stating, "Losing one's job is a serious jolt to your attitude of security, preservation, and well-being. However, I feel strongly that we must look forward to hope and faith in our country and its people. Deep inside I want to believe that tough times won't last, but tough people do. This will mean a lot of sacrifice, determination, and change in those people affected by losing one's job." Less hopeful views are revealed in the following remarks:

> We are down to rock bottom and will probably have to sell the house to live or exist until I find a job here or somewhere else. I have been everywhere looking in Cass, White, and Carroll counties. We have had no help except when the electric company was going to shut off the utilities in March and the Trustee [County Welfare] paid that $141. My sister-in-law helps us sometimes with money she's saved back or with food she canned last summer. The factories have the young. I've been to all the factories. (Personal interviews with RCA workers.)

Whether the personal response to the closing was faith, fear, or anger, the common objective experience of the displaced workers was that they had been "dumped" from the "middle class." These displaced factory workers viewed themselves as middle class because of their wages and their lifestyles (home ownership, cars, vacations). Most had worked at RCA for two decades or more. They had good wages, health-care benefits, and a pension program. They owned their homes (with mortgages), cars, recreational vehicles, boats, and all the household appliances associated with middle-class membership. All the trappings of the American Dream were threatened as their seemingly stable jobs and secure incomes disappeared. In the space of a few months, these workers and their families joined the growing new working class—the 80 percent of Americans without stable resources for living.

The severity of this jolt to their sense of well-being and their "downward slide" is also revealed in the bleak picture displaced workers have of their future and the futures of their children: "I'm afraid it will be years before I get up the courage to buy a car, appliance, or anything on a long-term note, regardless of how good the pay is in a new job"; "I have a National Honor Society daughter with one more year of high school. If she can't get aid there's no way she can go to college" (personal interviews with RCA workers).

The experiences of the eight hundred fifty RCA workers from Monticello, Indiana, were part of a national wave of plant closings that swept across the land two decades ago. According to a study commissioned by the U.S. Congress, between the late 1970s and mid-1980s, more than eleven million workers lost jobs because of plant shutdowns, relocation of facilities to other countries, or layoffs. Most of these displaced workers were in manufacturing. Subsequent displaced worker surveys commissioned by the Bureau of Labor Statistics estimated that between 1986 and 1991 another 12 million workers were displaced, but now they were predominantly from the service sector (about 7.9 million).[2] When these displaced workers found new jobs, it was often in industry sectors where wages were significantly lower than what they had earned, and jobs were often part-time and lacked health insurance and other benefits.

Beginning in the mid-1970s and continuing to the present, the American class structure was being reshaped from the layer-cake-like "middle-class" society into the double-diamond structure described in figure 1.5. The first step in this reshaping was a privileged-class-led attack on higher-wage unionized workers, eliminating their jobs in the auto industries, steel mills, rubber plants, and textile mills. The reshaping continued through the late 1980s to the mid-1990s, when the strategy was expanded to include not only plant closings and relocations but "restructuring and downsizing" strategies as well, often directed at eliminating white-collar jobs. In 2003 and 2004, the corporate strategy of "outsourcing" became the latest approach to eliminating American jobs. Outsourcing involves using the capabilities of the Internet and new telecommunications technology to hire workers in other countries to take over jobs filled formerly by American workers. For example, workers in India or China may be hired by a U.S. computer company to work in its customer-service department. So, when a customer in Kansas or Indiana calls the computer company for help in solving a user problem, they may be talking to a service representative in Calcutta or Beijing. More highly educated engineers or computer specialists may also be hired to work in software development while remaining in their home countries and being paid a small fraction of what would be paid to an American professional.[3]

The rush to downsize in some of America's largest and most prestigious corporations became so widespread in the 1990s that a new occupation was needed to handle the casualties. The "outplacement professional" was created to put the best corporate face on a decision to downsize, that is, to terminate large numbers of employees, as many as ten thousand. The job of these new public relations types is to get the general public to accept downsizing as the normal way of life for corporations that have to survive in the competitive global economy. Their job is also to assist the downsized middle managers in managing their anger and getting on with their lives.

The *Human Resources Development Handbook* of the American Management Association provides the operating philosophy for the outplacement professional: "Unnecessary personnel must be separated from the company if the organization is to continue as a viable business entity. To do otherwise in today's globally competitive world would be totally unjustified and might well be a threat to the company's future survival."[4]

The privileged 20 percent of the population are hard at work telling the other 80 percent about the harsh realities of the changing global economy. "Lifetime employment" is out. The goal is "lifetime employability," which workers try to attain by accumulating skills and being dedicated and committed employees. Even Japan's highly touted commitment to lifetime employment (in some firms) is apparently unraveling, as reported in a prominent feature article in the *New York Times*.[5] It should be no surprise that an elite media organization like the *Times*, whose upper-level employees belong to the privileged class, should join in disseminating the myth of the global economy as the "hidden hand" behind the downsizing of America. The casualties of plant closings and downsizings are encouraged to see their plight as part of the "natural law" of economics.

This enormous transformation of the U.S. economy over a thirty-year period has been described by political leaders and media as the inevitable and therefore normal working of the emerging global economy. Some, like former president Ronald Reagan, have even applauded the changes as a historic opportunity to revitalize the economy. In a 1985 report to Congress, Reagan stated, "The progression of an economy such as America's from the agricultural to manufacturing to services is a natural change. The move from an industrial society toward a postindustrial service economy has been one of the greatest changes to affect the developed world since the Industrial Revolution."[6]

A contrasting view posits that the transformation of the U.S. economy is not the result of natural economic laws or the "hidden hand" of global economic markets but, rather, of calculated actions by multinational corporations to expand their profits and power. When corporations decide to close plants and move them overseas where they can find cheap labor and fewer government regulations, they do so to enhance profits and not simply as a response to the demands of global competition. In many cases, the U.S. multinationals themselves are the global competition that puts pressure on other U.S. workers to work harder, faster, and for lower wages and fewer benefits. Only rarely do mainstream media and mainstream economic analysts reveal that the "hidden hand" is made up of multinational firms that export high-wage jobs to low-wage countries by either building factories overseas, starting joint ventures with foreign companies, or outsourcing jobs.

THE GLOBAL ECONOMY AND CLASS STRUCTURE

> Markets, which in mainstream ideology are as natural as gravity, have frequently been created and deepened through coercive state action—ranging from enclosures (the privatization of common lands) in Britain hundreds of years ago to NAFTA's eviction of Mexican peasants from their land today.

—Doug Henwood, *In These Times*, September 30, 1996

Discussion about the new global economy by mainstream media reporters and business leaders generally focuses on three topics. First is the appearance of many new producers of quality goods in parts of the world that are normally viewed as less developed. Advances in computer-based production systems have allowed many countries in Southeast Asia and Latin America to produce goods that compete with those of more advanced industrial economies in Western Europe and North America. Second is the development of telecommunications systems that permit rapid economic transactions around the globe and the coordination of economic activities in locations separated by thousands of miles. The combination of advances in computer-based production and telecommunications makes it possible for large firms, especially multinationals, to decentralize their production and locate facilities around the globe. Third is the existence of an international division of labor that makes it possible for corporations to employ engineers, technicians, or production workers from anywhere in the world. This gives corporations great flexibility when negotiating with their domestic workforce over wages and benefits. These changes in how we produce things and who produces them have resulted in expanded imports and exports and an enlarged role for trade in the world economy. Leading this expansion has been increased foreign investments around the world by the richer nations. It is estimated that two-thirds of international financial transactions have taken place within and between Europe, the United States, and Japan.[7]

The changes just noted are often used as evidence of a "new global economy" *out there* constraining the actions of all corporations to be competitive if they hope to survive. One concrete indicator of this global economy *out there* is the rising level of international trade between the United States and other nations. In the 1960s, the United States was the dominant exporter of goods and services, while imports of foreign products played a small part in the U.S. economy. Throughout the 1970s, foreign imports claimed an increasing share, and by 1981 the United States "was importing almost 26 percent of its cars, 25 percent of its steel, 60 percent of its televisions, tape recorders, radios, and phonographs, 43 percent of its calculators, 27 percent of its metal-forming machine tools, 35 percent of its textile machinery, and 53 percent of its numerically controlled machine tools."[8] Imports from developing nations went from $3.6 billion in 1970 to $30 billion in 1980.

Throughout the 1980s, the United States became a debtor nation in terms of the balance between what we exported to the rest of the world and what we imported. By 2004, the U.S. trade deficit indicated that the import of goods and services exceeded exports by a record high of $617.7 billion. This is the largest deficit since the previous high in 2000 of $370 billion, or the previous record high in 1987 of $153.4 billion. The gap between what we buy from other countries and what we sell to them is called the trade deficit, and it has been growing for thirty years. But what do these trade figures tell us? On the surface, they appear to be a function of the operation of the global economy because the figures indicate that in 2004 we had a $75.2 billion deficit with Japan, $162 billion with China, $45.1 billion with Mexico, $68.5 billion with Canada, and $110 billion with the European Union.[9] It appears that Japanese, Chinese, and Mexican companies are doing a better job of producing goods than U.S. companies, and thus we import products rather than producing them ourselves. But is this the correct conclusion? The answer lies in how you count imports and exports.

Trade deficit figures are based on balance-of-payment statistics, which tally the dollar value of U.S. exports to other countries and the dollar value of foreign exports to the United States; if the dollar value of Chinese exports to the United States exceeds the dollar value of U.S. exports to China, the United States has a trade deficit with China. This would appear to mean that Chinese companies are producing the goods being exported to the United States. But that is not necessarily the case. According to the procedures followed in calculating trade deficits, "the U.S. balance of payments statistics are intended to capture the total amount of transactions between U.S. *residents* and *residents* of the rest of the world."[10] If "resident" simply identifies the geographical location of the source of an import, then some unknown portion of the $49.7 billion U.S. trade deficit with China could be from U.S.-owned firms that are producing goods in China and exporting them to the United States. Those U.S. firms are residents of China, and their exports are counted as Chinese exports to the United States. For example, Nike Corporation has seven hundred plants scattered around Southeast Asia and elsewhere, and the products they export to the United States contribute to our trade deficit even though a U.S. company is behind the trade.

Thus, the global economy that is *out there* forcing U.S. firms to keep wages low so we can be more competitive might actually be made up of U.S. firms that have located production plants in countries other than in the United States. Such actions may be of great benefit to the U.S. multinational firms that produce goods around the world and export them to the U.S. market. Such actions may also benefit U.S. consumers, who pay less for goods produced in low-wage areas. But what about the U.S. worker in a manufacturing plant whose wages have not increased in twenty years because of the need to compete with "foreign companies"? What about the worker who may never get a job in manufacturing because U.S. firms have been opening plants in other countries rather than in the United States? As the comic strip character Pogo put it, "We have met the enemy, and it is us."

American multinational corporations' foreign investments have changed the emphasis in the economy from manufacturing to service. This shift has changed the occupational structure by eliminating high-wage manufacturing jobs and creating a two-tiered system of service jobs. There have been big winners and big losers in this social and economic transformation. The losers have been the three out of four Americans who work for wages—wages that have been declining since 1973. These American workers constitute the new working class (see chapter 1). The big winners have been the privileged classes, for whom jobs and incomes have expanded. Corporate executives, managers, scientists, engineers, doctors, corporate lawyers, accountants, computer programmers, financial consultants, health-care professionals, and media professionals have all registered substantial gains in income and wealth in the last thirty years. And the changes that have produced the "big losers" and "big winners" have been facilitated by the legislative actions of the federal government and elected officials of both political parties, whose incomes, pensions, health care, and associated "perks" have also grown handsomely in the past two decades.

This chapter demonstrates that the privileged classes have benefited at the expense of the working classes. The profits of corporations and stockholders have expanded because fewer workers produce more goods and services for lower wages. The profits of corporations are distributed to executives, managers, and professionals in higher salaries and benefits because they are able either to extract more work from workers while paying them less, or to justify inequality by providing distracting entertainment for the less fortunate, or to control them if necessary. The privileged class is able to maintain its position of advantage because its members control the jobs and incomes of other Americans. They also occupy upper executive positions that provide control of the mass media and education, which are the instruments of ideological domination. If all of this is not enough, they also control the means of violence (military, national guard, police, and the investigative and security apparatus) that are used to deal with large-scale dissent.

CREATING THE GLOBAL ECONOMY:
THE PATH TO CORPORATE PROFITS

We have entered the era of Empire, a "supranational" center consisting of networks of transnational corporations and advanced capitalist nations led by the one remaining superpower, the United States.

—Michael Hardt and Antonio Negri, *Empire*, 2000

When World War II ended in 1945, all but one of the industrial nations involved had experienced widespread destruction of their industrial systems and the infrastructure that is necessary for a healthy economy to provide sufficient food, shelter, and clothing for its people. Although all nations that partici- pated in the war suffered terrible human losses, the United States alone emerged with its economic system stronger than it was at the start of the war.

For nearly thirty years following World War II, the United States dominated the world economy through its control of three-fourths of the world's invested capital and two-thirds of its industrial capacity. At the close of the war, there was concern in the United States that the high levels of production, profits, and employment stimulated by war mobilization could not be sustained. The specter of a return to the stagnation and unemployment experienced only a decade earlier during the Great Depression led to the search for a new eco- nomic and political system that would maintain the economic, military, and political dominance of the United States.

The postwar geopolitical-economic policy of the United States was designed to provide extensive foreign assistance to stimulate the recovery of Western Eu- rope. This policy would stimulate U.S. investment in Europe and provide the capital for countries to buy U.S. agricultural and industrial products. The pol- icy was also designed to "fight" the creation of socialist governments and so- cialist policies in Western Europe, governments that might not be sympathetic to U.S. capital, trade, and influence. The foreign assistance policy known as the Marshall Plan was instituted to provide $22 billion in aid over a four-year pe- riod and to bring together European nations into a global economic system dominated by the United States.[11]

This system was the basis for U.S. growth and prosperity during the 1950s, the 1960s, and the early 1970s. By the mid-1970s, steady improvements in the war-torn economies of Western Europe and Asia had produced impor- tant shifts in the balance of economic power among industrialized nations. The U.S. gross national product was now less than twice that of the Soviet Union (in 1950 it was more than three times), less than four times that of Germany (down from nine times in 1950), and less than three times that of Japan (it was twelve times in 1950). With many nations joining the United States in the production of the world's goods, the U.S. rate of growth slowed. As England, France, Germany, and Japan produced goods for domestic con- sumption, there was less need to import agricultural and industrial products from the United States.

The profits of U.S. corporations from the domestic economy were in a steady decline through the late 1960s and into the 1970s. In the early 1960s, the annual rate of return on investment was 15.5 percent. In the late 1960s, it was 12.7 percent. In the early 1970s, it was 10 percent, and after 1975 it slipped below 10 percent, where it remained.

The privileged classes in the United States were concerned about declining profits. This affected their accumulation of wealth from stocks, bonds, divi- dends, and other investments. It affected corporate, managerial, and profes- sional salaries indirectly, through the high rate of inflation that eroded the purchasing power of consumption capital (i.e., salaries) and the real value of investment capital (i.e., value of stocks, bonds, etc.). To account for the U.S. decline, business leaders and the national media listed the usual suspects.

The leading "explanation" was that U.S. products could not compete in the global economy because of the power of organized labor. This power was reflected in the high labor costs that made products less competitive and in cost-of-living adjustments that increased wages at the rate of inflation (which was sometimes at double digits). Union control of work rules also made it difficult for management to adopt innovations to increase productivity and reduce dependence on labor.

Next on the list was the American worker, who was claimed to have embraced a declining work ethic, resulting in products of lower quality and higher cost. U.S. workers were portrayed as too content and secure and thus unwilling to compete with the ambitious workers of the rapidly developing economies.

The third suspect was the wide array of new regulations on business that had been adopted by the federal government to protect workers and the environment. Corporate executives complained about the increased cost of doing business that came from meeting the workplace standards of the Occupational Safety and Health Administration or the air and water pollution standards of the Environmental Protection Agency.

The explanations business leaders put forth for declining profits, selfish unions, lazy workers, and government regulations were said to make American products less competitive in the global economy. They provided the rationale for an attack on unions and on workers' wages and helped to justify massive plant closings and capital flight to low-wage areas. They also served to put the government on the defensive for its failure to be sensitive to the "excessive" costs that federal regulations impose on business.

What was rarely discussed in the business pages of the *New York Times* or the *Wall Street Journal* was the failure of corporate management in major U.S. firms to respond to the increasing competition to the once U.S.-dominated production of autos, steel, textiles, and electronics. In the early 1960s, imports of foreign products played a small part in the American economy, but by 1980, things had changed. In the early 1960s, imports accounted for less than 10 percent of the U.S. market, but by 1980 more than 70 percent of all the goods produced in the United States were actively competing with foreign-made goods.[12]

American corporations failed to follow the well-established management approach to the loss of market share, competitive advantage, and profits. Instead of pursuing long-term solutions, like investing in more efficient technology, new plants, research and development, and new markets, corporate executives chose to follow short-term strategies that would make the bottom line of profits the primary goal. The way was open for increased foreign investment, mergers, plant closings, downsizing, and outsourcing.

WHEN YOUR DOG BITES YOU

With industrial jobs shrinking in the United States, and so much of what we
buy, from clothing to electronics to automobiles, now made abroad, a common perception is that "globalized" production is a primary cause of falling
living standards for American workers.

—Richard B. DuBoff, *Dollars and Sense*, September–October 1997

While corporate profits from the domestic U.S. economy were declining
steadily from the mid-1970s, investment by U.S. corporations abroad showed
continued growth. The share of corporate profits from direct foreign investment increased through the 1970s, as did the amount of U.S. direct investment abroad. In 1970, direct investment by U.S. firms abroad was $75 billion,
and it rose to $167 billion in 1978. In the 1980–1985 period, it remained be-
low $400 billion, but thereafter increased gradually each year, reaching $716
billion in 1994. The one hundred largest U.S. multinational corporations reported foreign revenue in 1994 that ranged from 30 to 70 percent of their total revenue: IBM had 62 percent of total revenue from foreign sources; Eastman Kodak, 52 percent; Colgate-Palmolive, 68 percent; and Johnson &
Johnson, Coca-Cola, Pepsi, and Procter & Gamble each, 50 percent.[13]

American multinational corporations sought to maintain their profit margins by increasing investments in affiliates abroad. This strategy may have kept
stockholders happy and maintained the price of corporate stocks on Wall
Street, but it would result in deindustrialization—the use of corporate capital
for foreign investment, mergers, and acquisitions rather than for investment in
domestic operations.[14] Instead of investing in the U.S. auto, steel, and textile
industries, companies were closing plants at an unprecedented rate and using
the capital to open production facilities in other countries. By 1994, U.S. companies employed 5.4 million people abroad, more than 4 million of whom
worked in manufacturing.[15] Thus, millions of U.S. manufacturing workers
who were displaced in the 1980s by plant closings saw their jobs shifted to foreign production facilities. Although most criticism of U.S. investment abroad
is reserved for low-wage countries like Mexico and Thailand, the biggest share
of manufacturing investment abroad is in Germany and Japan—hardly low-
wage countries. The United States has large trade deficits with Japan and Western Europe, where the hourly wages in manufacturing are 15 to 25 percent
higher than in the United States.[16] This fact challenges the argument made by
multinational corporations that if they did not shift production abroad, they
would probably lose the sale of that product.

The movement of U.S. production facilities to foreign countries in the 1980s
and 1990s was not simply the result of a search for another home where they
could once again be productive and competitive. It appeared as if RCA closed
its plant in Monticello, Indiana, because its high-wage workers made it impossible to compete with televisions being produced in Southeast Asia. Sad-

dened by having to leave its home in Indiana of thirty-five years, RCA would have to search for another home where, it was hoped, the company could stay at least another thirty-five years, if not longer. Not likely: plants did not close in the 1980s to find other homes; the closures were the first step in the creation of the homeless and stateless multinational corporation, an entity without ties to place or allegiances to people, communities, or nations.

Thus, the rash of plant closings in the 1970s and 1980s began as apparent responses to economic crises of declining profits and increased global competition. As such, they appeared to be rational management decisions to protect stockholder investments and the future of individual firms. Although things may have started in this way, it soon became apparent that what was being created was the *spatially decentered firm*, a company that could produce a product with components manufactured in a half-dozen different plants around the globe and then assembled at a single location for distribution and sale. Although spatially decentered, the new transnational firm was also centralized in its decision making, allowing it to coordinate decisions about international investment. The new firm and its global production system were made possible by significant advances in computer-assisted design and manufacturing that made it unnecessary to produce a product at a single location. They were also made possible by advances in telecommunications that enabled management at corporate headquarters to coordinate research, development, design, manufacturing, and sales decisions at various sites scattered around the world.

The homeless and stateless multinational firm is able to move its product as quickly as it can spot a competitive advantage associated with low wages, cheaper raw materials, advantageous monetary exchange rates, more sympathetic governments, or proximity to markets. This encourages foreign investment because it expands the options of corporations in their choice of where to locate, and it makes them less vulnerable to pressure from workers regarding wages and benefits.

The advantages of the multinational firm and foreign investments are also a product of the U.S. tax code. In addition to providing the largest firms with numerous ways to delay, defer, and avoid taxes, corporate profits made on overseas investments are taxed at a much lower rate than profits from domestic operations. Thus, as foreign investments by U.S. firms increased over the last two decades, the share of total taxes paid by corporations declined. In the 1960s, corporations in the United States paid about 25 percent of all federal income taxes, and in 1991 it was down to 9.2 percent. A 1993 study by the General Accounting Office reported that more than 40 percent of corporations with assets of more than $250 million either paid no income tax or paid less than $100,000.[17] Another study of two hundred fifty of the nation's largest corporations reported that in 1998 twenty-four of the corporations received tax rebates totaling $1.3 billion, despite reporting U.S. profits before taxes of $12.0 billion. A total of forty-one corporations paid less than zero federal income tax in at least one year from 1996 to 1998, despite reporting a total of $25.8 billion in pretax profits.[18] In testimony before the Committee on the Budget of the U.S. House of Representatives, Ralph Nader reported that in fiscal year 1999 corporations received $76 billion in tax exclusions, exemptions, deductions, credits, and so forth, and that the estimates for the years 2000 to 2004 would reach $394 billion in corporate tax subsidies.[19]

Nader's estimate of corporate money hidden from taxation was well below the reported $500 billion in foreign profits that have been generated by multinationals. One reason that large multinational firms pay such low tax rates is that their foreign profits are not brought back into the United States and thus remain protected from taxes. Recognizing the growing size of the pool of untaxed foreign profits, in early 2005 the Bush administration proposed a one-time tax break for companies to bring their foreign profits back home. For example, Hewlett-Packard has $14 billion in untaxed foreign profits, and pharmaceutical giants like Merck and Johnson & Johnson have, respectively, $15 billion and $12.3 billion. The new legislation states that foreign profits would be taxed at a rate of 5.25 percent instead of the standard corporate tax rate of 35 percent.[20] This kind of "sweet deal" for multinationals will only mo-

Copyright © Tom Tomorrow. Reprinted with permission.

tivate them to continue to invest their money abroad. If the president and Congress were really concerned about protecting the jobs of American workers, they could curb the use of offshore contractors by limiting the tax deductions for payroll costs of jobs sent to other countries.

CREATING THE NEW WORKING CLASS

They call this "global competitiveness," but that's globaloney. Call it by its real name: Class War.

—Jim Hightower, *Dollars and Sense*, November–December 1997

We do not stay in America to optimize employment; we stay to improve our productivity.

—Intel executive, *New York Times*, May 11, 2004

When the large multinational firm closes its U.S. facilities and invests in other firms abroad or opens new facilities abroad, the major losers are the production workers who have been displaced and the communities with lower tax revenues and increased costs stemming from expanded efforts to attract new businesses. But this does not mean that the firms are losers, for they are growing and expanding operations elsewhere. This growth creates the need for new employees in finance, management, computer operations, information systems, and clerical work. The total picture is one of shrinking production plants and expanding corporate headquarters, shrinking blue-collar employee rolls and two-tiered expansion of high-wage professional-managerial and low-wage clerical positions.

Having been extraordinarily successful in closing U.S. plants, shifting investment and production abroad, and cutting both labor and labor costs (both the number of production workers and their wage-benefit packages), major corporations now turned their attention to saving money by cutting white-collar employees. In the 1990s, there were no longer headlines about "plant closings," "capital flight," or "deindustrialization." The new strategy was "downsizing," "rightsizing," "reengineering," or how to get the same amount of work done with fewer middle managers and clerical workers.

When Sears, Roebuck and Company announced that it could cut fifty thousand jobs in the 1990s (while still employing three hundred thousand people), its stock climbed 4 percent on the New York Stock Exchange. The day Xerox announced a planned cut of ten thousand employees, its stock climbed 7 percent. Eliminating jobs was suddenly linked with cutting corporate waste and increasing profits. Hardly a month could pass without an announcement by a major corporation of its downsizing plan. Tenneco Incorporated would cut eleven thousand of its twenty-nine thousand employees. Delta Airlines would eliminate 18,800 jobs, Eastman Kodak would keep pace by eliminating

16,800 employees, and AT&T announced 40,000 downsized jobs, bringing its total of job cuts since 1986 to 125,000. Not to be outdone, IBM cut 180,000 jobs between 1987 and 1994. The practice continues into the new century; as reported in the *New York Times* (July 13, 2001), Motorola, Inc., announced on July 12, 2001, that it would cut thirty thousand jobs in 2001. On that same day, although it reported an operating loss in the second quarter of 11 cents per share, Motorola stock rose by 16 percent.

Even the upscale, more prestigious banking industry joined in the rush to become "lean and mean." A total of ten bank mergers announced in 1995 would result in 32,400 jobs lost because of the new "efficiencies" that come with mergers. Even banks that were already successful in introducing "efficiencies" were not immune to continued pressure for more. Between 1985 and 1995, Chase Manhattan's assets grew by 38 percent (from $87.7 billion to $121.2 billion), and its workforce was reduced 28 percent, from 44,450 to 33,500 employees. Yet when Chase was "swallowed" by Chemical Banking Corporation in a merger, both banks announced further reductions totaling twelve thousand people.

Job loss in the last decade appeared to hit hardest those who were better educated (some college or more) and better paid ($40,000 or more). Job loss aimed at production workers in the 1980s was "explained" by the pressures of global competition and the opportunities to produce in areas with lower-wage workers. The "explanation" for the 1990s downsizing was either new technology or redesign of the organization. Some middle managers and supervisors were replaced by new computer systems that provide surveillance of clerical workers and data-entry jobs. These same computer systems also eliminate the need for many middle managers responsible for collecting, processing, and analyzing data used by upper-level decision makers.

Many companies used advances in production technology to increase productivity without adding more employees. For example, an Intel factory with the same five thousand workers has been able to more than double the number of chips it produces because of upgraded technology that both increases the size of the silicon wafers from which chips are cut and reduces the size of the computer chips themselves. Thus, the same five thousand workers produced larger wafers from which more than twice as many chips can be cut.[21]

Redesign of organizations was achieved by eliminating middle levels within an organization and shifting work both upward and downward. The downward shift of work is often accompanied by new corporate plans to "empower" lower-level workers with new forms of participation and opportunities for career development. All of this redesign reduced administrative costs and increased the workload for continuing employees.

Investors, who may have been tentative about the potential of profiting from the deindustrialization of the 1980s because it eroded the country's role as a manufacturing power, were apparently delighted by downsizing. During the 1990s and continuing beyond 2000, the stock market skyrocketed from below 3,000 points on the Dow Jones Industrial Average to 10,458 in April 2005, an increase of almost 250 percent. The big institutional investors apparently anticipated that increasing profits would follow the broadly based actions of cutting the workforce.

Downsizing is often viewed by corporations as a rational response to the demands of competition and thereby as a way to better serve their investors and ultimately their own employees. Alan Downs, in his book *Corporate Executions*, challenges four prevailing myths that justify the publicly announced layoffs of millions of workers.[22] First, downsized firms do not necessarily wind up with smaller workforces. Often, downsizing is followed by the hiring of new workers. Second, Downs questions the belief that downsized workers are often the least productive because their expertise is obsolete: According to his findings, increased productivity does not necessarily follow downsizing. Third, jobs lost to downsizing are not replaced with higher-skill, better-paying jobs. Fourth, the claim that companies become more profitable after downsizing and that workers therefore benefit is only half true. Many companies that downsize do report higher corporate profits and, as discussed earlier, often achieve higher valuations of their corporate stock. But there is no evidence that these profits are being passed along to employees in the form of higher wages and benefits.

After challenging these four myths, Downs concludes that the "ugly truth" of downsizing is that it is an expression of corporate self-interest to lower wages and increase profits. This view is shared by David Gordon, who documents the growth of executive, administrative, and managerial positions and compensation during the period when "downsizing" was at its highest.[23] Gordon describes bureaucratic "bloat" as part of a corporate strategy to reduce the wages of production workers and increase and intensify the level of managerial supervision. Slow wage growth for production workers and top-heavy corporate bureaucracies reinforce each other, and the combination produces a massive shift of money out of wages and into executive compensation and profits. This "wage squeeze" occurred not only in manufacturing (because of global competition) but also in mining, construction, transportation, and retail trade.[24] Although it is to be expected that foreign competition will have an impact on wages in manufacturing, it should not affect the nontrade sector to the same extent. Thus, the "wage squeeze" since the mid-1970s that increased income and wealth inequality in the United States is probably the result of a general assault on workers' wages and benefits rather than a response to global competition.

The impact of these corporate decisions on the working class was hidden from public view by the steady growth of new jobs in the latter part of the 1990s and by the relatively low rate of unemployment. In his second term in office, President Bill Clinton made frequent mention of the high rate of job creation (without mentioning that they were primarily low-wage service jobs) and the historically low unemployment rate. Unfortunately, the official rate of unemployment can hide the real facts about the nation's economic health. For example, an unemployment rate of 4.2 percent in 1999 excludes part-time workers who want full-time work and discouraged workers who have given up looking. If these workers are added to the unemployed, we have an "under-employment rate" of 7.5 percent, or about 10.5 million workers. The official unemployment rate also hides the fact that unemployment for black Americans was 8.0 percent in 1999 and that in urban areas there were pockets of unemployment that approached 25 percent.[25]

Thus, the result of more than two decades of plant closings and shifting investment abroad, as well as a decade of outsourcing jobs and downsizing America's largest corporations, has been the creation of a protected privileged class and a new working class, each with very different conditions of employment and job security. The three major segments of the new working class are core workers, temporary workers, and contingent workers.

Core Workers

Core workers are employees possessing the skills, knowledge, or experience that are essential to the operation of the firm. Their income levels place them in the "comfort class" described in chapter 1. They are essential for the firm, regardless of how well it might be doing from the standpoint of profits and growth; they are simply needed for the firm's continuity. Being in the core is not the same as being in a particular occupational group. A firm may employ many engineers and scientists, only some of whom might be considered to be in the core. Skilled blue-collar workers may also be in the core. Core employees have the greatest job security with their employing organizations; they also have skills and experiences that can be "traded" in the external labor market if their firm should experience an unforeseen financial crisis. Finally, core employees enjoy their protected positions precisely because there are other employees just like them who are considered temporary.

Temporary Workers

The employment of temporary workers is linked to the economic ups and downs that a firm faces. When sales are increasing, product demand is high, and profits match those of comparable firms, then the employment of temporary workers is secure. When inventories increase or sales decline sharply, production is cut back, and temporary employees are laid off or fired. The temporary workers' relationship to the firm is a day-to-day matter. There is no tacit commitment to these employees about job security and no sense that they "belong to the family."

A good example of the role of temporary workers is revealed by the so-called transplants, the Japanese auto firms like Toyota, Nissan, and Honda that have located assembly plants in Kentucky, Ohio, Michigan, Illinois, Indiana, and Tennessee. Each of these firms employs between two thousand and three thousand American workers in their plants, and they have made explicit no-layoff commitments to workers in return for high work expectations (also as a way to discourage unionization). However, in a typical plant employing two thousand production workers, the no-layoff commitment was made to twelve hundred hires at start-up time; the other eight hundred hires were classified as temporary. Thus, when there is a need to cut production because of weak sales or excessive inventory, the layoffs come from the pool of temporary workers rather than from the core workers. Sometimes these temporary workers are not even directly employed by the firm but are hired through temporary help agencies like Manpower. Employment through temporary help agencies doubled between 1982 and 1989 and more than doubled again between 1989 and 2000, approaching almost four million workers employed through temporary help agencies. After the stock bubble burst in 2001, temporary employment fell throughout the recession and gradually increased again through 2003 and 2004.[26] These temporary workers are actually contingent workers.

Contingent Workers

Workers in nonstandard employment arrangements (part-time workers, temporary workers, independent contractors) are often described as contingent workers. Some of these workers, as noted earlier, are employees of an agency that contract with a firm for their services. As we pointed out in chapter 2, about one in four persons in the labor force is a contingent worker, that is, a temporary or part-time worker.[27] These workers can be clerk-typists, secretaries, engineers, computer specialists, lawyers, or managers. They are paid by the temp agency and do not have access to a company's benefit package of retirement or insurance programs. Many of the professionals and specialists who work for large firms via temp firms are often the same persons who were downsized by those same companies. The following experience of a downsized worker is an ironic example of how the contingent workforce is created:

> John Kelley, 48, had worked for Pacific Telesis for 23 years when the company fired him in a downsizing last December. Two weeks later, a company that contracts out engineers to PacTel offered him a freelance job.
> "Who would I work for?" Kelley asked.
> "Edna Rogers," answered the caller.
> Kelley burst out laughing. Rogers was the supervisor who had just fired him. "That was my job," he explained. "You're trying to replace me with myself."[28]

These three groups of workers fit into the bottom part of the double-diamond class structure described in chapter 1, and it is only the core workers who have even the slightest chance to make it into the privileged class. Core workers with potential to move up generally have the credentials, skills, or social capital to have long-term job security or to start their own business, and therefore the possibility of having substantial consumption capital (a good salary) and capital for investment purposes. Let us now consider how the privileged class holds on to its advantaged position in the double-diamond class structure.

CARE AND FEEDING OF THE PRIVILEGED CLASS

The federal government of 1997 is a very different creature from that of, say, 1977—more egregiously corrupt and sycophantic toward wealth, more glaringly repressive, and even less responsive to the needs of low- and middle-income people.

—Barbara Ehrenreich, *Nation*, November 17, 1997

Most people who are in the privileged class are born there, as the sons, daughters, and relatives of highly paid executives, professionals, and business owners. Of course, they do not view their "achievements" that way. As one TV comedian once said of former President George H. W. Bush, "He woke up on second base and thought he'd hit a double." But some members of the privileged class have earned their places, whether by means of exceptional talent, academic distinctions, or years of hard work in transforming a small business into a major corporation. Regardless of how much effort was needed to get where they are, however, members of the privileged class work very hard to stay where they are. Holding on to their wealth, power, and privilege requires an organized effort by businessmen, doctors, lawyers, engineers, scientists, and assorted political officials. This effort is often cited to convince the nonprivileged 80 percent of Americans that the privileged are deserving of their "rewards" and that, in general, what people get out of life is in direct proportion to what they put in. This effort is also used to dominate the political process so that governmental policies, and the rules for making policy, will protect and advance the interests of the privileged class.

However, before examining the organized effort of the privileged class to protect its privilege, it is first necessary to examine how members of the privileged class convince one another that they are deserving. Even sons and daughters from the wealthiest families need to develop biographical "accounts" or "stories" indicating that they are deserving. This may involve accounts of how they worked their way up the ladder in the family business, starting as a clerk but quickly revealing a grasp of the complexities of the business and obtaining recognition from others of their exceptional talent.

Even without the biographical accounts used by the privileged class to justify exceptional rewards, justification for high income is built into the structure of the organizations they join. In every organization—whether an industrial firm, bank, university, movie studio, law firm, or hospital—there are multiple and distinct "ladders" that locate one's position in the organization. New employees get on one of these ladders based on their educational credentials and work experience. There are ladders for unskilled employees, for skilled work-

ers, and for professional and technical people with specialized knowledge. Each ladder has its own distinct "floor" and "ceiling" in terms of what can be expected regarding salary, benefits, and associated perks. In every organization, there is typically only one ladder that can put you in the privileged class, and this usually involves an advanced technical or administrative career line. This career line can start at entry levels of $70,000 to $80,000 annual compensation, with no upper limit beyond what the traffic will bear. These are the career ladders leading to upper executive positions providing high levels of consumption capital and opportunities for investment capital.

Claiming Turf

Many young attorneys, business school graduates, scientists, engineers, doctors, economists, and other professionals would like to get entry-level positions on these upper-level career ladders. In fact, there are probably many people who are qualified for entry positions in terms of their educational credentials and work experiences. So, how are people selected from among the large number of qualified applicants for such desirable career opportunities? The answer is simple: once credential qualifications and experience are used to define the pool of eligible applicants, the choice of who gets the job depends on the applicants' social capital. In chapter 1, we defined *social capital* as the social ties that people have with members of their college, fraternity or sorority, ethnic group, or religious group. People get jobs through their social networks, which provide them with information about job openings and with references valuable to those doing the hiring.[29] These social networks are usually composed of persons with similar social backgrounds. A recent study examined the social backgrounds of persons in the highest positions in corporations, the executive branch of the federal government, and the military. Although there is increased diversity among leaders today compared with 1950 with respect to gender, ethnicity, and race, the "core group continues to be wealthy white Christian males, most of whom are still from the upper third of the social ladder. They have been filtered through a handful of elite schools of law, business, public policy, and international relations."[30]

A good illustration of how social capital works is found in a study of 545 top position holders in powerful organizations in the United States.[31] Ten institutional sectors were studied, including Fortune 500 industrial corporations, Fortune 300 nonindustrial corporations, labor unions, political parties, voluntary organizations, mass media, Congress, political appointees in the federal government, and federal civil servants. Within each sector, fifty top position holders were interviewed—persons who may be considered "elites in the institutional sectors that have broad impact on policy making and political processes in the U.S."[32] Although we have no information on the incomes and wealth of the 545 elites, it is very likely they would fit our definition as members of the privileged class.

Table 3.1 provides some of the findings from this study, which identify the ethnic-religious composition of elites and their distribution across different institutional sectors. As can be seen from the first line of the table, 43 percent of all the elites in the study were WASPs (Protestants with ancestry from the British Isles), 19.5 percent were Protestants from elsewhere in Europe, 8.5 percent were Irish Catholics, 8.7 percent were Catholics from elsewhere in Europe, 11.3 percent were Jews, and 3.9 percent were minorities (nonwhites and Hispanics). The second line indicates the percentage of the national population of men born before 1932 from different ethnic-religious backgrounds. The third line indicates the percentage of the national population of college-educated men born before 1932 of each ethnic background. A comparison of line (1) with lines (2) and (3) shows the extent to which each ethnic-religious group may be overrepresented or underrepresented among the elites. Thus, WASPs and Jews are overrepresented among elites relative to their composition in the general population; the elite representation of other Protestants and

Table 3.1. Ethnic-Religious Representation among Elites

	WASPs	Other Protestants	Irish Catholics	Other Catholics	Jews	Minorities	Probably WASPs
1. Overall elite	43.0	19.5	8.5	8.7	11.3	3.9	5.0
2. Men born before 1932	22.9	22.5	4.2	17.2	2.9	14.4	13.4
3. College-educated men born before 1932	31.0	19.8	6.0	15.5	8.9	5.2	10.3
4. Institutional sectors							
Business	57.3	22.1	5.3	6.1	6.9	0.0	2.3
Labor	23.9	15.2	37.0	13.0	4.3	2.2	4.3
Political parties	44.0	18.0	14.0	4.0	8.0	4.0	8.0
Voluntary organizations	32.7	13.5	1.9	7.7	17.3	19.2	7.7
Mass media	37.1	11.3	4.8	9.7	25.8	0.0	11.3
Congress	53.4	19.0	6.9	8.6	3.4	3.4	5.2
Political appointments	39.4	28.8	1.5	13.6	10.6	3.0	3.0
Civil service	35.8	22.6	9.4	9.4	15.1	3.8	3.8

Source: Alba and Moore (1982), table 1.

Irish Catholics is comparable to their representation in the national population; and other Catholics and minorities are underrepresented among elites.

More interesting for our purposes are the overrepresentation and underrepresentation of elites in different institutional sectors. Overrepresentation would suggest the operation of social ties operating to get positions for persons with the same ethnic-religious background. White Anglo-Saxon Protestants are greatly overrepresented in business and in Congress. Irish Catholics are very overrepresented in labor and politics. Jews are sharply overrepresented in mass media, voluntary organizations, and federal civil service. This ethnic-religious overrepresentation indicates that social capital may be used to get access to career ladders leading to the privileged class. Moreover, there appears to be ethnic-religious specialization in the institutional sectors "colonized." People help to get jobs for relatives and friends, whether the job is for a Mexican immigrant in a Los Angeles sweat shop or a young Ivy League graduate in a Wall Street law firm. Parents invest their capital in an Ivy League education for a son or daughter, who then uses the social capital of family or school ties to enter a career path into the privileged class.

Securing Turf

After obtaining positions on career ladders that will make them members of the privileged class, our entry-level managers, attorneys, and faculty become aware of the very high incomes enjoyed by their senior colleagues. One response to these high salaries is to feel that they are unjustified and to exclaim, "Why should the president of the university make $300,000 a year when some of our professors with twenty years experience are making $60,000?" A second response is to recognize that the president's salary is used to justify the $230,000 salaries of the executive vice presidents, which in turn justify the $150,000 salaries of the deans, which in turn justify the $120,000 salaries of senior professors in selected fields. People in positions of power in organizations work together to justify their high salaries by creating beliefs about the need to be competitive in the market or to risk losing valuable people.

The second response is the typical one for people involved in career ladders that promise access to the privileged class. This response might be called symbiotic greed, where the parties are locked together in a mutually beneficial relationship. As the salary of the president rises, so do the salaries of all the others who are on the privileged-class career ladder. The rub is that only a small proportion of all the managers, attorneys, or faculty are on that career ladder, even though they may share the same educational credentials and work experience. This is a form of misguided self-interest, wherein low-level employees support the high salaries of their superiors because of the belief that they may one day also have such a high salary.

Although it may seem surprising, members of the privileged class often feel that their incomes are far below what they deserve or they feel relatively deprived in comparison to those above them in the income hierarchy. A recent story in the *New York Times* ("Well-Off but Still Pressed, Doctor Could Use Tax Cut")[33] provided thinly veiled support for President Bush's tax cut, along with a sympathetic story of a surgeon earning $300,000 a year who says he does not feel rich. The good doctor, who lives in a $667,000, four-bedroom house with a pool, frets about his retirement, college tuition, and the anticipated cost of future weddings for his five daughters. Moreover, he is pained by the appearance of the new high-tech millionaires driving around in Porsches. The good doctor's wife exclaims, "We don't have the luxuries that you would think in this bracket," as she describes shopping at cheaper grocery stores and clipping coupons. The message of the article is that there are rich people and super-rich people, and both would benefit from a tax cut. In short, you can never have too much money!

Now to the organized effort by businessmen, doctors, lawyers, and the like to protect the interests of the privileged class. This effort is revealed in three ways: (1) Members of the privileged class hold upper-level positions in all the major institutions of American society. These institutions control enormous resources that can be used to shape public awareness, the political process, and the nation's policy agenda. (2) The organizations to which the privileged class belong form associations in order to hire lobbyists, contribute to political campaigns, and shape legislation in their interests. (3) The members of the privileged class who are in professional occupations, like medicine and law, are represented by powerful professional associations that protect their members against any efforts by other groups to encroach on their "turf." Thus, the American Medical Association (AMA) makes sure that state legislatures continue to give doctors a monopoly over what they do by preventing nurses, or pharmacists, or chiropractors, or holistic practitioners from providing certain types of care to clients. Similarly, the American Bar Association acts to prevent paralegals from competing with lawyers in handling wills, estates, or certain types of litigation.

Not every segment of the privileged class is unified on all issues. Doctors are not pleased with the actions of attorneys when they vigorously pursue malpractice suits against doctors and hospitals. The AMA has urged Congress to pass legislation limiting the dollar amount of damages that might be awarded in malpractice claims. Lawyers resist such efforts because they make their living from obtaining 30 percent of the damage awards made to persons suing doctors or hospitals. Similarly, the banking industry and the large industrial corporations may differ on whether they would like to see the Federal Reserve Board raise or lower interest rates. Some sectors of the business community may support giving China special trade concessions, while others may be opposed. In 2005, Congress passed, and the president signed, a "tort reform" bill that would have the effect of reducing damage awards in malpractice suits. This legislation pleased doctors and hospitals and displeased lawyers.

Despite the differences and disagreements over specific policies by members of the privileged class, they are unified in their support for the rules of the game as they are currently played: The privileged class is unified in its view of how the political process should operate. Individuals and organizations should be free to lobby members of Congress on matters of interest to them. Individuals and organizations should be free to contribute money to political action committees and to political parties. And above all else, privileged-class members agree that business should be able to operate in a free and unregulated environment and that the country runs just fine with a two-party system.

Then, there are the really big policy issues, where the "payoffs" are substantial to almost all segments of the privileged class. The North American Free Trade Agreement (NAFTA) and the General Agreement on Tariffs and Trade (GATT) were supported by Presidents Reagan, Bush, and Clinton and by a bipartisan majority of both houses of Congress. When President George W. Bush took office in 2001, he proceeded to promote the so-called Free Trade Area for the Americas (FTAA), which would extend NAFTA throughout the Western Hemisphere. Taken together, NAFTA and FTAA represent the effort of the international privileged class to have countries in the Americas adopt economic policies to attract foreign investment, encourage "free trade," and restrict government efforts to protect the rights of workers. These agreements promise to advance the global economy and the continued pursuit of profits across the globe by multinational corporations.

The privileged class in the United States achieved major victories in the 1980s through their efforts to reduce government spending on a variety of social programs that benefit the working class. Using the scare tactics of budget deficits and the national debt, the privileged class supported a balanced-budget agreement that required the president and Congress to reduce spending on welfare, education, Medicare, and Medicaid. In the 1990s, the privileged class turned its attention to the global economy by devising ways to protect opportunities for investment and profit around the globe. The main way to achieve this was to make it easy for large corporations to circle the globe in search of the best opportunities and thereby threaten workers everywhere so as to keep their wages and benefit demands at low levels. Facing the oft-repeated threat that there are "other" workers willing to do the same work for less money, the American working class has lived with declining earnings and disappearing health benefits and employer-provided pensions. And all this occurred during an eight-year economic recovery and a booming stock market!

Recent research on the effects of globalization has focused on the question of whether the increase in global competition and investment has led to the emergence of a transnational business community or transnational capitalist class. Multinational corporations, through their interlocking relationships, have the potential to act in concert and to exert their influence on nation states in which they operate and on international regulatory bodies. The research evidence is mixed. One study of interlocking directorates among the 176 largest corporations in the world economy in 1976 and 1996 reports that there is little evidence that interlocks among corporations have shifted from ties within national boundaries to a transnational pattern.[34] A second study of interlocking directorates among the *Fortune* Global 500 (largest firms by revenues, irrespective of sector or activity) in 1983 and 1998 reports "a significant increase in both the total number of interlocks and an even greater growth in transnational ties."[35] A third view of a transnational capitalist class looks beyond the interlocks that may tie together multinational industrial corporations and international banks. The focus here is on the ideology of consumerism that is allegedly shared by corporate executives and promoted by them to advance the common interests of a transnational corporate and capitalist class.[36]

During the 1990s, major U.S. and foreign corporations joined forces to lobby Washington policy makers to relax federal policies on international trade. This included granting most-favored-nation trading status to China (with whom we have a high trade deficit) and passing NAFTA, which eliminated trade barriers between the United States, Canada, and Mexico. Before the passage of NAFTA, the United States had a $1 billion trade surplus with Mexico, but in the year following NAFTA, that surplus became a $16.2 billion deficit, and today it is a $45.1 billion deficit.[37]

To garner public support for free trade, President Clinton frequently pointed out that for every $1 billion in goods and services we export to other countries, we create twenty thousand jobs at home. This may be true, but the problem is that it also works in reverse: for every $1 billion of goods that we import, we lose twenty thousand jobs. And, as indicated earlier in this chapter, in 2000 the United States had a trade deficit of $370 billion with other countries.

Despite claims by officials in Canada, Mexico, and the United States that NAFTA has been a success, an analysis of the impact of NAFTA seven years after its adoption indicates that 766,000 actual and potential jobs were eliminated in the United States "between 1994 and 2000 because of the rapid growth in the U.S. export deficit with Mexico and Canada."[38] Thus, we lose many more jobs than we create with our free-trade policies. But free trade is not about jobs; it is about profits for corporations and the privileged class.

Defending Turf

In February 1998, the *New York Times* published a two-page open letter to the Congress of the United States entitled "A Time for American Leadership on Key Global Issues."[39] The letter expresses concern about "a dangerous drift toward disengagement from the responsibilities of global leadership." Congress is asked to approve new fast-track negotiating authority, which would extend NAFTA-like agreements to other countries in Latin America and around the globe, and to support the International Monetary Fund bailout of failed banks in Southeast Asia (although it failed to mention the benefit to U.S. banks and financial institutions that are heavily invested in those economies).

Signatories to this letter include two former presidents (Jimmy Carter and Gerald Ford), forty-two former public officials (secretaries of defense, treasury, commerce, and state; CIA directors; national security advisers; U.S. senators), and eighty-eight corporate presidents and CEOs (AT&T, Boeing, Amoco, Chase Manhattan Bank, IBM, Time Warner, Bank America, etc.). Many of the former public officials now work as lobbyists for the U.S. and foreign multinationals that "feed at the public trough" via tax loopholes and federal subsidies.

Why would these 132 members of the privileged class spend $100,000 for this two-page ad in the *Times*? Surely not to influence members of Congress. Corporations and the privileged class have more effective ways of doing that, such as the $3 million in campaign contributions by Philip Morris or the $2.5 million that Chiquita Brands CEO Carl Linder gave to both political parties from 1993 to 1996. Perhaps the ad was designed to convince the working class to support fast-track legislation. Probably not. The circulation of the *New York Times* is about 1.6 million, and very few of those readers are from the working class. The most likely targets of the ad were the nationally scattered members of the privileged class that the elite leaders wanted to mobilize at the grass roots. The ad was designed to get the millions of privileged doctors, lawyers, journalists, managers, scientists, stock brokers, and media executives to mobilize public opinion through the hundreds of professional and business associations that represent their interests. The privileged class constitutes 20 percent of the population (about fourteen million families), and when mobilized, it can represent a potent political force.

Opposition to the privileged-class agenda on the global economy is fragmented and operates with limited resources. Critics of NAFTA and the GATT, like Ralph Nader and Jesse Jackson, can hardly stand up to the National Association of Manufacturers or the U.S. Chamber of Commerce. The opposition to NAFTA and the GATT voiced by reactionary populists Ross Perot and Pat Buchanan, who appeared to be "traitors" to the interests of the privileged class, was dealt with swiftly and sharply by the major media. Perot was given the persona of a quirky, eccentric millionaire who was trying to buy the presidency because he had nothing better to do with his time and money. Buchanan was vilified as a cryptoracist, anti-Semite, and general all-around loose cannon.

The attacks on Perot and Buchanan by academics and political commentators on media talk shows should not be surprising. Elite universities and the major media are controlled by the wealthy and corporate elite who are at the top of the privileged class. The major networks of ABC, CBS, NBC, CNN, Fox, and Turner Broadcasting determine what the overwhelming majority of Americans will receive as news and entertainment. Two of the major networks are owned by major multinational firms, and institutional investors control substantial percentages of stock in the networks.

Is it any wonder, therefore, that efforts to attack the status quo are immediately marginalized or co-opted? An example of this process was revealed during the Republican presidential primary in early 1996. Pat Buchanan was making his usual bombastic attacks on immigration, NAFTA, and the GATT, when he suddenly started lobbing some grenades at the corporate elite while yelling about "corporate greed." Here are a few samples from speeches made in February of 1996: "When AT&T lops off 40,000 jobs, the executioner that does it, he's a big hero on the cover of one of these magazines, and AT&T stock soars"; "Mr. Dole put the interest of the big banks—Citibank, Chase Manhattan, Goldman Sachs—ahead of the American People."[40]

When it appeared that Buchanan's reactionary populist attack on the corporate elite was striking a responsive chord among people on the campaign trail, the *New York Times* decided to take the extraordinary step of publishing a seven-part series called "The Downsizing of America," which ran from March 3 through March 9, 1996. Some might call this a major public service by the *Times*, designed to inform Americans about an important issue. Others might say it was a clever effort to take the issue out of Buchanan's hands and to shape it and frame it in ways that would deflect the criticisms and attacks on the corporate elite. The *Times* series did not point an accusing finger at corporate America for the loss of millions of jobs. If anything, the series made the reader either feel sorry for everyone, including the "guilt-ridden" managers who had to fire workers ("Guilt of the Firing Squads"), or blame everyone, including downsized workers. In an extraordinary example of blaming the victim, consider the following "explanation" for downsizing: "The conundrum is that what companies do to make themselves secure is precisely what makes their workers feel insecure. And because workers are heavily represented among the 38 million Americans who own mutual funds, they unwittingly contribute to the very pressure from Wall Street that could take away their salaries even as it improves their investment income."[41]

The *New York Times* series did not help its readers to understand who benefits from downsizing, but it did help to defuse the issue and to take it out of the hands of those who might be critical of corporate America. It is an example of the pacification of everyday life (discussed more fully in chapter 7).

Resistance to the Global Economy

> The rules created by NAFTA are imbalanced; they encourage capital mobility by extending trinational protection to investors while protections for workers and the environment are left to national governments. . . . One result has been a rise in inequality and insecurity among working people.
>
> —Jeff Faux, *Nation*, May 28, 2001

In this chapter we have tried to provide a glimpse of the meaning of the bogeyman global economy. The term has been used to threaten workers and unions and to convince everyone that they must work harder if they want to keep their jobs. The global economy is presented as if it is *out there* and beyond the control of the corporations, which must continually change corporate strategies in order to survive in the fiercely competitive global economy. It is probably more accurate to view the current global economy as an accelerated version of what U.S. financial and industrial corporations have been doing since the end of World War II—roaming the globe in search of profits. The big change is that since the 1980s, U.S. firms have found it easier to invest overseas. They have used this new opportunity to create new international agreements like NAFTA and FTAA that attack organized labor and threaten workers to keep their wage demands to a minimum. In this view, the global economy is composed primarily of U.S. companies investing abroad and exporting their products to the United States (as the largest consumer market in the world) and other countries. These multinational corporations have an interest in creating the fiction that the global economy is some abstract social development driven by "natural laws" of economics, when it is actually the product of the deliberate actions of one hundred or so major corporations.

There has been growing popular opposition to the international accords that are creating the new global economy. In December 1999, the so-called Battle in Seattle signaled the growing resistance to globalization. Tens of thousands protested against the World Trade Organization's (WTO) "free trade" agenda, which would threaten U.S. workers' jobs and wages and provide little protection against environmental damage. Protesters were confronted by police using pepper spray and tear gas to prevent disruption of the WTO meeting.[42] On April 20 to 22, 2001, the Third Summit Meeting of the Americas took place in Quebec City, Canada. Heads of state from thirty-four countries in the Americas (Cuba was excluded) assembled for negotiations on the so-called Free Trade Area for the Americas. Once again, tens of thousands demonstrated against this new effort to make it easier for international finance capital and multinational corporations to control the global economy.[43]

The resistance that took place in Seattle and Quebec City (as well as in Washington, D.C., and Davos, Switzerland) reveals the operation of the alternative power networks described in chapter 2. Groups representing labor, environmentalists, antisweatshop campaigns, and human rights activists came together to challenge the international agreements that provide few protections for working people throughout the Americas. They are calling for trade agreements that protect the rights of workers to a living wage, regulations on the behavior of multinational corporations and international finance capital, and consideration of environmental protections consistent with economic and social development.[44]

The problem posed by the global economy is that it has increased the influence of large corporations over the daily lives of most Americans. This influence is revealed in corporate control over job growth and job loss, media control of information, and the role of big money in the world of national politics. At the same time that this growing influence is revealed on a daily basis, it has become increasingly clear that the major corporations have abandoned any sense of allegiance to, or special responsibilities toward, American workers and their communities.

This volatile mix of increasing influence and decreasing responsibility has produced the double-diamond class structure, where one in five Americans is doing very well indeed, enjoying the protection that comes with high income, wealth, and social contacts. Meanwhile, the remaining four out of five Americans are exploited and excluded.

CLASS ISSUES IN THE MEDIA: REALITY TV?

Who Wants a Job?

The television monitor brightens, and the screen is filled with the image of a soaring eagle holding a globe of the world in its talons. A booming disembodied voice pours out of the screen over the image of the soaring eagle: "N-N-N, the News from Nowhere Network is proud to present the host of our show, the incomparable Regal Menace." The applause is prolonged and deafening as the audience dutifully responds to the blinking "Applause" sign.

"Welcome ladies and gentlemen, and to all Americans, to the world's most watched television show, *Who Wants to Have a Job?* Tonight's show is brought to you by the most famous and loved man in Arkansas, known to his friends as the Chicken Hawk, because he has stuffed more birds than anyone else in the world. No, it's not Bill Clinton, but none other than Harry Pardoo and his world renown Cyberbird Chicken Farm, a totally automated, robotized production system for the world's most tender, juiciest birds. Harry's motto is, When someone flips you the bird, say thank you, as long as it's a Pardoo bird. Now let's meet some of Harry's happy birds."

Accompanied by bump-and-grind music, a chorus line of Disney-like chickens with human legs in mesh stockings and voluptuous, very human breasts dance around a barnyard that looks like it's from the infamous chicken ranch in Las Vegas. After plugging the virtues of the Pardoo birds, the screen scrolls the same phrase repeated in several languages.

"A Pardoo chicken in every pot."
"Un poulet perdue dans chaque poile."
"Una pollito dentro de todos barrigon."
"Tutti bisogna pollo biondo con grande fenditura."

The list of phrases cause some consternation and amusement to viewers around the world, as the production call-in board is lit up like a Christmas tree. Apparently, the commercial potential of the Internet exceeds the capacity of the producers to translate words free of local meanings. The first phrase is clear enough—everyone should buy a Pardoo chicken. The second phrase in French says there is a lost chicken in every pot. In Spanish we have a chick in every potbelly. And the incorrigible Italians are asked to believe that everyone should have a blond chicken with great cleavage.

The camera is back on Regal.

"Okay folks, you know how our game is played. Each week we bring to our stage two contestants from different communities who are going to try and convince you,

(*continued*)

the audience, and our panel of judges that they deserve to get the new company that is looking for a new place to roost. There are three rounds of questions for our contestants. After each round, the judges will rate our contestants' performance, and you, the audience, can register your choice through the applause sensometer. Now let's meet our contestants."

A booming disembodied voice fills the screen as a spotlight follows a tiny figure from offstage to the podium near center stage and close to the audience. "Meet Hector Rodriguez Tomar, from Ciudad Pollo, Mexico."

Regal meets the contestant at his podium. "Welcome, Hector, *bienvenido*. May I call you Rod?" Hector smiles at Regal's pronunciation, and although initially puzzled by the question, he recovers quickly. "Yes, Rodriguez is my mother's family name. It is our custom to use both parents' family names."

"A great custom, Rod. And now for our second contestant. Ladies and Gentlemen, meet Charlie W. Trash from Flint, Michigan, in the good old U. S. of A."

Regal moves in again. "Welcome, Charlie. And what do you do in Flint, Michigan?"

"Well, right now, I ain't doing much of anything. That's why I'm on the show."

"Right, Charlie. But isn't Flint an automobile town?" asks Regal somewhat tentatively, not being sure what this guy will say next. He is wondering if the producers screened him.

"Yeah, it used to be. I had a great job at the Olds plant. We made some great cars back then. Why, I had a '76 Cutlass with over one hundred fifty thousand miles on it, and it could still hum along at ninety."

Regal asks the next question with a touch of gravitas. "Well what happened to change all that, Charlie?"

"It started with those candy-ass Japanese cars. Small, no power, no chrome, and everyone worrying about the A-rabs raising gasoline prices. I still think we could have beat the Japs head to head, because we had a better product. But then GM started to outsource our work wherever they could find cheap labor. That was the beginning of the end."

"You sound a little angry, Charlie," says Regal, hoping to put him on the defensive. "Don't you think the workers in Flint bear some responsibility for the shutdown of their plants?"

"Oh, sure. They probably cut some corners, took off too many Mondays to go fishing and hunting. But we did our job, and you can't compete when the playing field ain't level. When NAFTA came in, we didn't have a prayer. Jobs went south big time."

Putting on his best Mike Wallace voice, Regal clarifies. "NAFTA, that's the North American Free Trade Agreement, correct?"

"Au contraire," Charlie shoots back to a slightly stunned Regal. "It's called free trade, but free trade ain't the same as fair trade. People need to understand the kind of capital flows that exist between countries. Some capital is for investment, and some is for speculation. The politicians don't talk straight on this issue, all the time trying to blow smoke up our ass. The union people voted for Bill Clinton, and his thank you was NAFTA."

Regal is flustered, and he tries to move on. "You may have a point there, Charlie. Let's see if our other contestant agrees with you. Well, Rod, what do you do in Ciudad Pollo?"

"Right now, not too much. We haven't seen any of those jobs that Charlie thinks came from NAFTA. I used to work at Pollo Dios Mio!—that means heavenly chicken—one of Mexico's largest chicken farms and processing plants. It was a great job."

Again with the gravitas, Regal asks, "What happened, Rod. How did you go from chicken heaven to chicken down below? Or should I say chicken *diablo*?" Regal breaks into chuckles, drawing audience laughter.

"*Si, pollo inferno.* It has been hell for the people of our town. The plant was moved to Thailand. The company said they could use special growth hormones on the chickens in Thailand, cutting by half the time from birth to chicken parts. We couldn't do that in Mexico because of NAFTA's environmental regulations."

"That's quite a story, Rod," says Regal with a broad smile. "You and Charlie have really interesting stories to tell. But now it's time to play *Who Wants to Have a Job?*" he shouts, waving his arms to the audience. The audience rises to its feet waving arms with a mixture of thumbs-up and thumbs-down gestures. "One of you, Rod or Charlie, is going to win a chicken farm and processing plant for your home town. There will be hundreds of new jobs and all the good things that come with that."

A giant screen behind Regal shows pictures of a prosperous community with smiling people walking in parks, eating in restaurants, and shopping at the mall.

"That's what life can be like again in Ciudad Pollo or Flint, Michigan," shouts Regal. "Now, let the games begin. Charlie won the coin toss, so he gets the choice of going first or second."

"I guess I'll go first," says Charlie, rocking side to side as if he's dancing and trying to look enthusiastic.

"Good choice, Charlie," blasts Regal. "Now, to the first question. And remember, Charlie, you can ask for help from someone in your support group. The question: Some experts say that towns are like people—they either have to grow or they die. How do you respond to that statement?"

Charlie looks puzzled. "Grow or die, that's the question? Seems like it's better to grow than die, but why do you have to die if you don't grow? Can't you grow too much and die? My Aunt Bertha on my mother's side weighed about three hundred pounds, and she died before she was forty. Loved that fast food, and it got her. But I'm not sure I understand the question. Flint grew in the sixties and seventies, and it still died. Well, it's not really dead, but folks talk about it like it's dead. Why can't you just have a decent job without bringing all this other stuff in?"

Regal jumps in to pump some life into the contestant. "Why don't you ask someone from your support group if they want to help. Who is the guy waving his arms and jumping up and down?"

"That's Wayne Babbit from Flint. He's with the Chamber or the Development Council, one of those business groups."

Regal waves his arm toward the end of the stage. "Come on up here, Wayne." He arrives at the podium with a broad grin and bouncing with energy. "Tell us who you are and what you do in Flint."

"I'm Wayne Babbitt, and I'm president of the Flint Chamber of Commerce and a member of the Economic Development Commission of Southeastern Michigan."

"It's great to have you on the show, Wayne," says Regal. "What do think about the question of whether a town has to grow or die?"

(*continued*)

CLASS ISSUES IN THE MEDIA: REALITY TV? (*continued*)

"That's a no-brainer, Regal. You don't have to be a rocket scientist to know that without growth, a town stagnates. It loses pride in itself. It turns inward. Mom-and-pop stores are quaint, but that's not where it's at. Wal-Mart gives you more choice and better price. To survive in the global economy a town has to sell itself to attract new business. And you sell yourself with a positive, can-do attitude and attractive options. It's just like in the animal kingdom. Those who survive have learned to dress up their act with fancy feathers, mating dances, and overpowering smells. The guys and gals that survive have put together the best show to get somebody's attention."

Regal feels oddly stimulated by Wayne's passionate remarks, unable to tell if it's spiritual or an erotic feeling. "Well you have sold me, Wayne. But what is Flint going to do to attract the new Pardoo chicken plant?"

"That's easy," Wayne shoots back. "We have tax abatements that will help Pardoo avoid property taxes for at least ten years and maybe longer. We will use state and local development funds to help prepare the work site, bring in utilities, widen roads, and anything else to get the plant up and running. And if we need to train the Pardoo workers, we can pay their salaries for up to six months, with federal funds set aside to help workers displaced from jobs because of foreign competition."

"That sounds like a great deal for Pardoo," beams Regal. "The good people of Flint look like they're willing to go balls-out, I mean all-out, for Pardoo." The audience is screaming with laughter at Regal's locker room expression. "It's an innocent expression, folks," chuckles Regal, enjoying the good spirits of the audience. "I think we use it to motivate people at church fund-raisers."

"I like that expression, Regal. It captures what we're all about," says Wayne amid continuing laughter. "I'm going to use that expression at my next Chamber meeting—a great motivational phrase."

Regal takes control again. "Speaking of motivation, what is the work force like in Flint? What can the Pardoo people expect from their workers?"

Wayne seemed to be waiting for this soft ball question. "We've got the finest workers that money can buy. There are thousands of laid-off auto workers just begging for work. Now, I know they are ex-union, and that will scare some employers. But they have learned their lesson. Unions can't protect them from companies that move their plants overseas."

"Suppose that Pardoo won't hire ex-union workers," says Regal, hoping to generate some heated discussion. "I've heard that happens."

Wayne is beaming once again. "You want foreign workers, we will give you foreign workers. We can get all the Mexicans you need, legal or illegal. You want temporary workers, we have a large Manpower office in Flint that provides all the temps you need. Low wages, no benefits, no problems. They work for Manpower and not for Pardoo. The company gets all the workers they need without the headache of having employees."

There is a low groan from the audience, and Regal feels the need to introduce some fairness into the discussion. "Now, wait a minute, Wayne. How can you talk about hiring illegals? Isn't that illegal?"

"You have to get out more, Regal," says Wayne with a smirk. "The INS has almost stopped raiding businesses that hire illegals. There is a shortage of workers and the

Immigration and Naturalization folks have started looking the other way at border crossings. The illegals help to keep wages down and inflation under control. I'll bet even Alan Greenspan hires illegals to do his cooking and gardening."

The audience is hooting and cheering. Regaining his composure, Regal turns to the audience. "Okay, enough fun and games. Let's turn to our second contestant, Rod Tomar, and see how he reacts to the idea that towns must grow or die. The ball is in your court, Rod. What say you?"

Hector Rodriguez Tomar had intended to speak on this question, but after seeing the performance of Wayne Babbit from Flint, he decides to call upon the mayor of his city. "I am going to ask the *alcalde*, the mayor, of Cuidad Pollo to answer that question. Alcalde Angel Jesus Alquiladizo."

Regal didn't have a clue that this was coming, so he is not prepared to deal with the very complicated pronunciation task in front of him. "Mr. Mayor, please come to the podium." There is great applause, whistling, and shouts of "*jefe, jefe, jefe*" from the crowd. The audience seems to be stacked with residents from Cuidad Pollo. "We are honored, sir, to have you on our program. What do you have to say about the grow or die question?"

"As mayor of the great city of Cuidad Pollo, I can assure the Pardoo chickens that their last days in our city will be among the happiest of their short lives. Everyone in the world knows that in our city, the chickens come first. Chickens are in our hearts, our history, our culture. This also means that the companies that work with chickens also come first, and they are also in our hearts, our history, our culture. I believe that we have some of the most chicken-hearted companies in the world in our city."

"Great, Mr. Mayor," says Regal, wondering how long he can continue to avoid calling this guy by one of his names. "But how will you counter the offer of tax abatements by the people of Flint, Michigan?" There is a sputter of applause and some shouts of "Go, Wolverines" from the back rows.

"*No problema,* Mr. Regal. *Primero,* first, you don't have to worry about getting approval for tax abatements. In Flint, you might get them, but then again you might not, especially if some citizens' group starts making noise about tax abatements. The Pardoo plant in Cuidad Pollo will be located in an EPZ. Do you know what that is?"

"What is an EPZ, Mr. Mayor?" replies Regal dutifully, but also with some interest in furthering his knowledge.

"An EPZ is an export processing zone. It is an area of land that has been designated by the government of Mexico for foreign companies to locate their production plants. Everything that is produced in the zone is free of any taxes as long as it is for export out of Mexico."

Charlie Trash blurts out, "You mean to tell me that none of those chickens processed in a plant in your city can be sold to the people who live there? What the hell is the point?"

"Please, Mr. Trash, you had your turn," says Regal in his most official manner. "You will get a chance to speak again." The crowd is hooting and shouting a mixture of "Regal, Regal" and "gringo, gringo." Regal tries to quiet the crowd with his upraised arms. "Please continue, Mr. Mayor."

"*Gracias.* Thank you. So, first, no taxes, ever! And next, no environmental regulations. That's another advantage of being in an EPZ. In Flint, you're going to have to

(continued)

CLASS ISSUES IN THE MEDIA: REALITY TV? (*continued*)

get rid of the waste that goes with a chicken operation. That means you will either have to build a waste processing plant or contract out to someone else to haul your waste."

Regal suddenly feels that Flint is not getting a fair hearing, and maybe the crowd will start pulling for the underdog. "But tell me, Mr. Mayor, how will waste be handled in Cuidad Pollo?"

"*Bueno.* I will tell you. First, we dig a huge ditch from the plant toward the river about two miles away. It's a nice downhill slope that will carry the waste washed along by the water from the city's wells."

"Won't that be an awful lot of smelly waste laying around until it reaches the river?" asks Regal, turning up his nose and holding it. A segment of the crowd hoots.

"Not so," replies the mayor. "The beauty of our operation is that we use nature to care for nature. Our region has more turkey vultures than any other place in Mexico. And once that waste starts down the ditch toward the river, there will be more vultures in that ditch than you can imagine. I wouldn't be surprised to learn that no waste ever reached the river. We are going to have the best-fed vultures of anyplace in the world."

The Mexicans in the audience are on their feet cheering and screaming, "*Buitres, buitres, vosotros todos buitres.*"

Regal turns to his cameraman, who happens to be an illegal from Mexico. "What are they yelling?"

"Vultures, vultures, you are all vultures."

The big TV screen cuts to commercial, as Regal tells the audience that a panel of judges will decide which city deserves to get the chicken plant. Regal shouts at his assistant, Sally, "Call Jack and see if he agrees that it's a no-brainer. Hector gets it hands down. Just like the swallows went back to Capistrano, the chickens are going back to Mexico."

Sally replies gleefully, "You're out of the loop again. Jack's gone. His job has been outsourced to India. Your new producer is Ramkrishna Neerasai."

NOTES

1. Brink Lindsey, "Job Loss and Trade: A Reality Check," Trade Briefing Paper 19, Cato Institute, March 17, 2004.

2. Office of Technology Assessment, *Technology and Structural Unemployment* (Washington, DC: Congress of the United States, 1986); Thomas S. Moore, *The Disposable Work Force* (New York: Aldine de Gruyter, 1996).

3. Steve Lohr, "Offshore Jobs in Technology: Opportunity or a Threat ?" *New York Times*, December 22, 2003; Steve Lohr, "Debate over Exporting Jobs Raises Questions on Policies," *New York Times*, February 23, 2004; Alan Reynolds, "Offshoring Which Jobs?" *Washington Times*, June 6, 2004.

4. Joel Bleifuss, "The Terminators," *In These Times* (March 4, 1996): 12–13.

5. Sheryl Wu Dunn, "When Lifetime Jobs Die Prematurely: Downsizing Comes to Japan, Fraying Old Workplace Ties," *New York Times*, June 12, 1996.

6. John Miller and Ramon Castellblanch, "Does Manufacturing Matter?" *Dollars and Sense* (October 1988).

7. Noam Chomsky, *The Common Good* (Monroe, ME: Common Courage Press, 2000).

8. Robert B. Reich, *The Next American Frontier* (New York: Times Books, 1983).

9. Commerce Department, U.S. Bureau of the Census, Foreign Trade Division, Washington, D.C., 2005.

10. John Pomery, "Running Deficits with the Rest of the World—Part I," *Focus on Economic Issues*, Purdue University (Fall 1987) (emphasis added).

11. For an extended discussion, see Michael Stohl and Harry R. Targ, *Global Political Economy in the 1980s* (Cambridge, MA: Schenkman, 1982).

12. Reich, *Next American Frontier*.

13. "The 100 Largest U.S. Multinationals," *Forbes* (July 17, 1995): 274–76.

14. Barry Bluestone and Bennett Harrison, *The Deindustrialization of America* (New York: Basic Books, 1982).

15. Louis Uchitelle, "U.S. Corporations Expanding Abroad at a Quicker Pace," *New York Times*, July 25, 1998.

16. David M. Gordon, *Fat and Mean: The Corporate Squeeze of Working Americans and the Myth of Managerial Downsizing* (New York: Free Press, 1996).

17. Richard J. Barnet and John Cavanagh, *Global Dreams: Imperial Corporations and the New World Order* (New York: Simon and Schuster, 1994).

18. Robert S. McIntyre, "Testimony on Corporate Welfare," U.S. House of Representatives Committee on the Budget, June 30, 1999. On the Internet at http://www.ctj.org/html/corpwelf.htm (visited June 25, 2001).

19. Ralph Nader, "Testimony on Corporate Welfare," U.S. House of Representatives Committee on the Budget, June 30, 1999, on the Internet at www.nader.org/releases/63099.html (visited June 25, 2001).

20. Edmund L. Andrews, "Foreign-Profit Tax Break Outlined," *New York Times*, January 14, 2005.

21. See Gordon, *Fat and Mean*, ch. 2.

22. Alan Downs, *Corporate Executions* (New York: AMACOM, 1995).

23. Gordon, *Fat and Mean*, 191.

24. Louis Uchitelle, "Surge in Jobs Mostly Bypass the Factory Floor," *New York Times*, May 11, 2004.

25. Lawrence Mishel, Jared Bernstein, and John Schmitt, *The State of Working America, 2000–2001* (Ithaca, NY: Cornell University Press, 2001), 220; Marc Breslow, "Job Stats: Too Good to Be True," *Dollars and Sense* (September–October 1996): 51.

26. Lawrence Mishel, Jared Bernstein, and Sylvia Allegretto, *The State of Working America, 2004–2005* (Ithaca, NY: Cornell University Press, 2005), 269–73.

27. Chris Tilly, *Half a Job: Bad and Good Part-Time Jobs in a Changing Labor Market* (Philadelphia: Temple University Press, 1996); Kevin D. Henson, *Just a Temp* (Philadelphia: Temple University Press, 1996).

28. Ann Monroe, "Getting Rid of the Gray," *Mother Jones* (July–August 1996): 29.

29. Mark Granovetter, *Getting a Job: A Study of Contacts and Careers* (Cambridge, MA: Harvard University Press, 1974).

30. Richard L. Zweigenhaft and G. William Domhoff, *Diversity in the Power Elite: Have Women and Minorities Reached the Top?* (New Haven, CT: Yale University Press, 1998), 6.

31. Richard D. Alba and Gwen Moore, "Ethnicity in the American Elite," *American Sociological Review* 47 (June 1982): 373–83.

32. Alba and Moore, "Ethnicity in the American Elite," 374.

33. Jim Yardley, "Well-Off but Still Pressed, Doctor Could Use Tax Cut," *New York Times*, April 7, 2001, A1, A8.

34. William K. Carroll and Meindert Fennema, "Is There a Transnational Business Community?" *International Sociology* 17 (September 2002): 393–419.

35. Jeffrey Kentor and Yong Suk Jang, "Yes, There Is a (Growing) Transnational Business Community: A Study of Global Interlocking Directorates 1983–98," *International Sociology* 19 (September 2004): 355–68.

36. Leslie Sklar, *The Transnational Capitalist Class* (Oxford: Blackwell, 2001).

37. Richard W. Stevenson, "U.S. to Report to Congress NAFTA Benefits Are Modest," *New York Times*, July 11, 1997.

38. Robert E. Scott, "NAFTA'S Hidden Costs," Economic Policy Institute, Washington, D.C., May 21, 2001.

39. "A Time for American Leadership on Key Global Issues," *New York Times*, February 11, 1998.

40. Francis X. Clines, "Fueled by Success, Buchanan Revels in Rapid-Fire Oratory," *New York Times*, February 15, 1996.

41. Louis Uchitelle and N. R. Kleinfield, "On Battlefield of Business, Millions of Casualties," *New York Times*, March 3, 1996.

42. Jim Phillips, "What Happens after Seattle?" *Dollars and Sense* (January–February 2000): 15–16, 31–32.

43. David Moberg, "Tear Down the Walls: The Movement Is Becoming More Global," *In These Times* (May 28, 2000): 11–14.

44. Hermann Maiba, "Grassroots Transnational Social Movement Activism: The Case of People's Global Action," *Sociological Focus* 38 (February 2005): 41–63.

4

The Invisible Class Empire

The way our ruling class keeps out of sight is one of the greatest stunts in the political history of any country.

—Gore Vidal, *Progressive*, September 1986

"Push the Button. Don't push the button . . ." This cryptic line from the popular ABC television series *Lost* supposedly offers a clue to the elusive truth about Oceanic Airlines flight 815. The survivors (and the viewers) think they might be able to figure what's going on, but mysterious events—sometimes linked to what appear to be paranormal phenomena and at other times tied to shadowy and sinister human interventions—keep the truth just out of reach.

Like the *Lost* survivors and viewers, we also believe it's possible to unravel elusive truths about what's *really* going on. But unlike the *Lost* cast and fans, our focus is on the reality of economic and political inequalities rather than events on a fictional island. More specifically, our concern in this chapter is with superclass political power and evidence that reveals the "truth" about this highly charged issue. As Gore Vidal suggests, ruling-class political dominance is a long-standing, but typically unacknowledged and unexplored, feature of American society. Occasionally, it has been candidly recognized—sometimes by writers of elite origins such as Vidal, as well as by players at the top of the political game. President Woodrow Wilson once observed that "the masters of the government of the United States are the combined capitalists and manufacturers of the U.S."[1] However, such public candor is rare and may entail negative personal and professional consequences. Vidal, for example, maintains that his public musings on ruling-class political power have earned him undying elite enmity as a class traitor and that, as a result, both he and his work have been marginalized and demonized by the privileged-class-controlled mass media.[2]

Superclass elites have long recognized that publicly acknowledged, front-page, robber-baron plutocracy is inconsistent with American cultural ideals of democracy and political equality—and dangerous to their interests. Up-front publicity revealing the nature and extent of superclass political dominance would magnify the tensions between democratic ideals and concentrated class-power realities by calling into question the institutional legitimacy of American politics and public policy. For these reasons, superclass leaders prefer to keep the existence of, and details about, the extent of their class-based power out of sight.

THE INVISIBLE EMPIRE AND THE GOLDEN TRIANGLE

It is the interaction of class and organizational imperatives at the top of all American organizations . . . that leads to [upper] class dominance in the United States.

—G. William Domhoff, *Who Rules America?*
Power, Politics and Social Change, 2006

We believe the superclass preference is for Americans to know less, not more, about "the truth that is out there" concerning the invisible class empire that dominates our national political system. The term *invisible class empire* refers to the hidden structures and processes through which superclass leaders, along with their credentialed-class allies, penetrate and dominate the American political system. It also refers to the processes used to disguise this reality and the concealed political, economic, and cultural dimensions of superclass power.

It is an empire in the sense that the privileged-class leadership has crafted a far-flung and widely dispersed collection of resources, organizations, and processes into a coherent political force that ensures the perpetuation of its interests. It is invisible in the sense that the class-based dimensions of the resources and control processes that undergird the empire are largely excluded from American public attention. In the political arena, the silence of incumbents, wannabes, and pundits promotes public inattention. In the cultural arena, public inattention grows out of an almost total mass media blackout of reporting on the empire, combined with a nearly total neglect of the subject by the U.S. educational system—at all levels.

As noted in chapter 2, the privileged-class leaders who guide and direct this empire are sometimes referred to as the power elite.[3] At the top, this group consists of superclass members who are active in organizational governance (corporate and political). It shades downward to include a second tier (with respect to class) of semiautonomous managers and assistants. This junior-partner portion of the power elite includes upwardly mobile corporate officers, attorneys, major political office holders, national lobbyists, and other specialists drawn largely from the credentialed class. These groups directly assist the su-

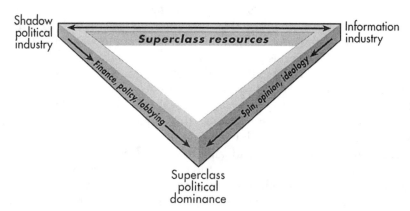

Figure 4.1. The Golden Triangle of Class Power

perclass elite or indirectly serve their interests. All of these groups together, with superclass leadership at the center, form a kind of directorate that charts and oversees general economic and political policies, as well as routine institutional practices necessary to maintain the class empire.

This chapter begins the process of peeling back the cloak of invisibility that shields the empire by exposing the organizational foundations of what we call the golden triangle of class power. As figure 4.1 illustrates, superclass resources, grounded in the investment capital that members of this class personally hold or control as corporate officers, serve as the basis for financing and controlling two major "industries." The shadow political industry (explored in this chapter) and the information industry (examined in chapter 5) both drive and conceal superclass power. The convergence of these twin structures leads to *superclass political dominance*. This term refers to the ways in which the routine operation of the two industries promotes superclass domination over major class-relevant public policy outcomes concerning economic and political issues. And it reflects the reality that superclass media ownership provides this class with substantial cultural influence (e.g., shaping popular cultural content), which also has important political and class-power implications and consequences.

The shadow political industry extends downward as the left flank of the triangle. It consists of several real-life organizations that provide the political muscle underlying the class empire. This industry parallels, or shadows, the national political and public policy-making processes. Largely created, funded, and dominated by the superclass, this industry consists of four specialized, interrelated organizational groups devoted to (1) federal lobbying—Washington, D.C.–area lobbying organizations funded largely by superclass-class-based resources to influence policy-making processes in Congress and federal agencies; (2) political finance—corporate-based individual wealth, political action committees

(PACs), and 527 committees; (3) policy planning—think tanks, research institutes, policy discussion groups, and foundations; and (4) classwide lobbying—peak corporate groups and corporate-professional group coalitions. The primary "product" of this industry is control—of politics and government. Its goal is to monitor and intervene in the political arena in ways that protect and promote superclass economic and political interests.

The information industry anchors the right flank of the triangle. Grounded in the largest mass media corporations, this industry serves privileged-class leaders' political and economic interests in two ways. First, much of the "news" and editorial commentary disseminated by firms at the heart of this industry help legitimate or conceal the nature and extent of superclass power. Second, large portions of the megaprofits generated through the operations of large media firms are channeled back to superclass owners, with smaller profit shares flowing to credentialed-class, second-tier media executives and managers.[4] This industry operates via three interrelated control processes generating the information, ideas, images, and economic, political, and social commentary that reinforce superclass interests. Considered in detail in chapter 5, these are (1) the mainstream ideology process, (2) the public-opinion process, and (3) the spin-control process.

The structures and processes of both industries converge at the bottom of the triangle into *superclass political dominance*. As noted earlier, this term refers to the domination of superclass interests over class-relevant political and economic public policy outcomes, as well as their potent influence in shaping cultural content. As we will see, public policy and cultural-content outcomes reflect and reinforce superclass dominance by legitimating or disguising (or both) the nature, extent, and consequences of privileged-class power generally. In the political and economic arenas, superclass leaders, along with their credentialed-class allies, are viewed as directing and controlling most major class-relevant national public policy outcomes. Examples of superclass-dominated policy outcomes are considered later in this chapter, especially as the results of classwide lobbying. The concept of superclass political dominance also includes the idea that privileged-class leaders, especially through the information industry, influence the dissemination of news and commentary, as well as the entertainment content of popular culture, in ways that reinforce superclass interests. These topics are considered at length in chapters 5 and 7.

The triangle model develops selected features of the more general class-power-network model introduced in chapter 2. It does not attempt to address all dimensions or features of superclass power. Even so, it provides a powerful tool for conceptualizing the core of privileged-class economic, political, and cultural power in the United States. By locating superclass power and dominance in organizationally based resources, structures, and processes driven by class interests and unified by a class-based ideology, this concept avoids conspiracy-based theories as the basis for understanding superclass cohesion and power.

Superclass holders of wealth, power, and privilege, as well as their credentialed-class allies, have individual and collective interests in maintaining their advantaged positions. The triangle model (figure 4.1) zeroes in on the two "industries" that support and sustain privileged-class-based advantages. It also calls attention to the reality that superclass leaders frequently know and interact with one another because they occupy interlocked top positions in large organizations, they control high levels of investment capital, and they participate in overlapping corporate, political, and social arenas. These circumstances, combined with high levels of social, consumption, and skill capital held by superclass members and their credentialed-class allies, serve as the foundation for a widely shared superclass worldview, or political-economy ideology. This idea system blends assumptions grounded in privileged-class interests concerning how the political and economic systems should be organized and function together. In general, it tends to view the economic and political status quo as reasonable, legitimate, and just.[5] The model views the common bonds of economic resources, interests, social identity, and ideology as foundations upon which superclass leaders create, maintain, and justify the linked structures and processes that drive the triangle.

Acting on the basis of a shared worldview and through routine organizational structures and processes, superclass leaders and their credentialed-class allies orchestrate political strategies and media policies aimed at preserving and extending their wealth, power, and privilege. The model views those at the top as holding a strong, shared sense that the "system" works and as pursuing concerted, but nonconspiratorial, strategies and tactics that preserve it. Their mantra is, why change what works for us?[6]

THE SHADOW POLITICAL INDUSTRY

The growing concentration of . . . wealth gave rise to a parallel concentration of political power, to the benefit of corporations and other large donors.

—Kevin Phillips, *American Dynasty*, 2004

Although the shadow political industry is not a totally new development, in the new class society this flank of the triangle has expanded to unprecedented levels of size, complexity, and sophistication. Compared with the recent past, this industry has also become a much more widely shared, class-collaborative project linking superclass leaders with growing numbers of credentialed-class professionals who work, either directly or indirectly, on behalf of superclass interests. These political, legal, and policy-oriented professionals possess specialized lobbying, legal, research, and communication skills, plus political contacts that are critical to the maintenance of superclass interests and power. High-profile media reports on congressional lobbying scandals in the mid-2000s (e.g., Abramhoff, DeLay) increased public awareness of influence peddling in Washington, but apparently the public was not particularly shocked by such reports.[7] A *New York Times* poll found that 77 percent of Americans believed that lobbyists' bribing of members of Congress "is the way things work in Congress."[8] It appears most Americans *are* aware of how some features of the shadow political industry operate, but public cynicism doesn't provide meaningful insights into the details of this industry. We think that to more fully understand the shadow political industry, it is necessary to examine the class-based organizational structures that undergird it rather than to focus on individual lobbying scandals or public cynicism.

FEDERAL LOBBYING: FUNDING PRIVILEGED-CLASS INFLUENCE IN WASHINGTON

> Special interests routinely spend far more on lobbying each election cycle than they do contributing to politicians and political parties.
>
> —Center for Public Integrity,
> "Industry of Influence Nets . . . $10 Billion," 2006

Class collaboration in the shadow industry is particularly evident in the growing numbers of credentialed-class professionals who work for the numerous organizations that are part of this industry—including those employed by numerous lobbying firms located in the Washington, D.C., area. Most of these firms represent superclass-controlled organizations and actively lobby both the Congress and federal agencies on behalf of their interests. To accommodate superclass-connected clients, Washington lobbying firms employ a small army of individual lobbyists and spend billions of dollars annually. Attorneys figure prominently in the Washington lobbying community because, as a group, they often possess the knowledge, skills, and political contacts essential to effectively influence congressional and agency policy-making processes. While not all D.C.-area attorneys are lobbyists, some D.C. lawyers own well-known lobbying firms, and many others either work directly for lobbying firms or perform contract work for such firms.[9] In recent years, there has been a substantial increase in the number of D.C. attorneys, which has paralleled the growth of the Washington lobbying community. For example, in the mid-2000s, more than 80,000 attorneys were members of the District of Columbia Bar, compared with 73,000 in 2001 (up from 10,925 in 1972).[10] Based on data reported per the federal Lobbying Disclosure Act (LDA) of 1995, the number of registered federal lobbyists in Washington grew from 11,043 in 1998 to 37,332 in 2005.[11] Although the registered lobby group is large, the LDA definition of a lobbyist is very narrow and does not cover many professionals involved in lobbying activities, such as "'strategic advisors' and consultants who devise lobbying strategies" (e.g., former members of Congress).[12] Using more expansive definitions of lobbyists (than set forth by the LDA) and also recognizing that some lobbyists fail to register, the total Washington-area lobbying community is estimated by some analysts to include at least eighty thousand and maybe more than one hundred thousand lobbyists (plus support staff).[13]

Focusing only on the conservative LDA reporting requirements, we can see that lobbying is a big business within the shadow industry. According to LDA reports, total lobbying expenditures reached $2.2 billion in 2005, up from $1.26 billion in 1997. As a result of continued increases in the numbers of lobbyists and lobby spending, in the mid-2000s there were about seventy active lobbyists and $4.1 million in annual lobbying expenditures *for each member of Congress* (compared to twenty-two active lobbyists and $2.7 million in annual lobbying expenditures per congressional member in 1999).[14] As noted in chapter 2, the annual expenditures of all Washington lobbying firms (about $2.2 billion) are about double the total political campaign contributions to all congressional candidates in the 2004 elections (about $1.1 billion).[15] Lobbyists are likely to have favorable access to members of Congress and federal agencies not only because of the resources at their command but also because of personal connections many have with current members of Congress and federal agency heads. For example, in the mid-2000s, among registered federal lobbyists were 240 former members of Congress and agency heads and more than 2,200 individuals who had worked for the federal government in some capacity (43 percent of congressional members who left office since 1998 have registered to lobby).[16]

Most members of the Washington, D.C., lobbying community are employed (directly or indirectly) by large corporate clients or trade associations representing corporate interests because these groups have the most money to spend.[17] This is especially evident when we consider that the one thousand largest industrial, financial, and service firms control 75 percent of the sales, assets, and profits in these areas.[18] The links tying D.C.-area lobbyists—and many other credentialed-class professionals—to superclass-controlled corporate clients form a dense, reciprocal web, weaving together superclass corporate interests, credentialed-class professional skills, and political contacts. These links are cemented by steep-green contracts and annual salaries ranging from $300,000 for veteran Capitol Hill staffers to $2 million and more for "well-regarded top officials," such as retired members of Congress.[19] Such bonding occurs in part because superclass-controlled organizations represent the main market for the highly paid, specialized lobbying, legal, research, and communication skills possessed by political and policy-oriented professionals. By their sheer size—corporate-based trade associations and other research and lobbying groups funded by the superclass make up 72 percent of the Washington lobby community—these organizations are the major employers of high-paid professional talent.[20]

The web of superclass corporate influence in the D.C. lobbying community is also illustrated in part by the fact that several Washington lobbying firms are subsidiaries of huge public relations and advertising corporations. For example, the lobbying firm BKSH & Associates is part of Burson-Marsteller, the largest public relations firm in the United States, which in the late 1990s was owned by the giant Young & Rubicam advertising company.[21] In October 2000, a corporate merger expanded the BKSH lobbying and corporate parent connection into the international arena: "Young & Rubicam [parent company of Burson-Marsteller] became a member of the WPP Group plc, the world's most comprehensive communications services group."[22] The client base of WPP (an English firm) includes "more than 300 of the *Fortune* Global 500; over one-half of the NASDAQ 100 and over 30 of the *Fortune* e-50. . . . Collectively, the Group has 92,000 people working in over 2,000 offices in 106 countries."[23]

Superclass Dominance of Shadow Industry Professionals

The group that generally supervises and controls the shadow industry and drives the market for credentialed-class professionals' lobbying, political finance, and policy-planning services consists largely of the top twenty thousand officers and directors located in the one thousand largest U.S. industrial, financial, and service firms.[24] These top corporate office holders form the privileged-class heart of the institutional power elite, and their firms represent the core of the superclass organizational power base. This group exercises control over enormous levels of investment capital and tends to intersect or overlap with the wealthiest 1 percent of all Americans.[25] The members of this group also either possess or are hardwired into the highest levels of social capital and command extremely high levels of consumption capital. Many members of this group—at least a third—occupy their positions due to inherited wealth from family fortunes.

Studies of what we term *superclass leaders* indicate that about 30 percent come from very wealthy families. The largest group (about 59 percent) comes from families in the top 20 percent income group (the privileged class by our definition), about 3 percent comes from families located in the bottom 80 percent income group (the new working class), and the remaining 8 percent could not be classified.[26] Some superclass leaders, such as Steve Case (former CEO of AOL-Time Warner) and Bill Gates (Microsoft), are "newly rich" as a result of entrepreneurial ventures. While often described in the media as having "middle-class" origins, many superclass entrepreneurs, such as Case and Gates, actually come from wealthy family backgrounds.[27] Some current superclass leaders have in fact "moved up" in major corporate hierarchies to elite positions, but in almost every case, these rising executives are from credentialed-class family origins.[28] This route typically involves assistance from superclass "sponsors." Such individuals act as gatekeepers in identifying and grooming a few rising executives and political operatives from nonsuperclass backgrounds for membership in the power elite—typically, first as junior members and later as full partners. Nonelites who are sponsored in this fashion are usually selected and assisted on the basis of their acquisition of critical social capital (e.g., elite educational credentials) and relevant personal qualities, such as allegiance to superclass ideology, organizational effectiveness, talent, and charm.[29]

Despite commanding huge resources, great power, and high status, the superclass is still a relatively small group. Its leadership base is too small to attend to the detailed activities necessary to translate general superclass policy preferences into specific public policy outcomes favoring its interests and perpetuating its political dominance. Superclass leaders need junior partners to help ensure that their interests are protected and served in the political and economic arenas. Thus, through their presence on policy-making boards of corporate, cultural, civic, and other organizations, the most organizationally active superclass leaders (the senior power elite) recruit, cultivate, utilize, and generously reward the expertise and assistance of a wide range of professionals who serve superclass interests in the shadow industry. These are the individuals who direct the industry's daily activities. They include high-profile political operatives like Karl Rove (President George W. Bush's chief political advisor), along with thousands of lesser-known professionals located in the various superclass-funded lobbying, political finance, and policy-planning organizations that are at the core of the shadow industry.[30]

Largely faceless and unknown to the American public, the shadow industry's professional cadre, along with the staff members they supervise, have an increasingly routine presence in the political life of our society. Their careers are closely linked to the success of the superclass project of controlling U.S. politics and the state. A recent example would be the "Hamilton Project"—what author William Grieder called a sophisticated "deep lobby" group crafting trade and economic policies for the 2008 Democratic presidential campaign. Organized in early 2006 by Robert Rubin, executive cochair of Citigroup and former Treasury secretary in the Clinton administration, the project consisted of economists and financiers supposedly "developing ameliorative measures to aid the threatened [U.S.] workforce."[31] But the elite origins and composition of the group made it highly unlikely that it would advocate policies that challenge the basic features of the existing global trading system. Professionals like the Hamilton Project participants are the shock troops for, and key political allies of, the class empire, and they are active participants in the federal lobbying, political-finance, policy-planning, and classwide lobbying organizations that are central to superclass power and dominance in the United States.

POLITICAL FINANCE: IT'S MONEY THAT MATTERS

To a very significant degree, big money interests control Washington. . . . [Politicians] are terrified of standing up to big money because they'll be punished.

—Congressman Bernie Sanders, *In These Times*, June 20, 2005

The story of superclass domination of politics and the state through the shadow political industry continues with the financing of political campaigns. Money has always been an important factor in politics, but the increasing use of expensive, high-tech production, communication, and marketing technologies in political campaigns has shifted it to center stage. The effects of these changes on the costs of political campaigns have been dramatic. In 2004, the cash required to mount *winning* political campaigns complete with paid staff, computers, polling, consultants, phone banks, direct mailing, websites, and media advertising topped out at $367 million for the presidency (not counting indirect party funding or expenditures by 527 committees), $7.3 million for a Senate seat, and $1.14 million for a House seat.[32] By comparison, Bill Clinton's 1996 presidential campaign cost $113 million, and winning Senate and House candidates in that year spent an average of $4.7 million and $673,000, respectively, on their campaigns.[33]

The 2006 elections represented a continuation of the trend of rapidly escalating campaign costs, especially for congressional candidates. To meet these costs, in the 2005–2006 election cycle through October 18, 2006, "Congressional candidates . . . raised $1.14 billion . . . an increase of 30% . . . over the comparable period in 2004." Candidates for the thirty-three Senate campaigns raised $457.4 million (up 39 percent from 2004) and candidates for House campaigns raised $546.2 million (up 25 percent from 2004).[34] Virtually all of the money raised by congressional candidates came from wealthy individuals, corporations, and trade associations, but wealthy individuals were especially important. This latter group contributed 61 percent of all campaign funds received by congressional candidates in 2006.[35] The total cost of the 2006 midterm elections, including all forms of spending by and for congressional candidates, was estimated at $2.8 billion (divided about equally between Republican and Democratic candidates and their supporters). This amount represented a 27 percent increase in spending over the $2.2 billion spent in 2002 (the most recent comparable *midterm* congressional election).[36]

As the dollar figures rise higher for each new election cycle, it is important to recall that campaign expenditures are not one-time costs. Each new campaign requires new money. To pay for future campaigns in the *next election cycle*, representatives and senators will need to raise *at least* about $11,000 and $23,000, respectively, *every week* of their current terms in office. Being a serious candidate today requires serious money. Our review of campaign-funding issues covered in the following sections centers primarily on the 2004 federal elections. This is the case because presidential election years generate not only more public interest but higher and more complex levels of funding and detailed forms of reporting than is the case with midterm elections.

The winner-take-all nature of the American political system helps drive up the cost of campaigns. Politicians clearly understand the sentiment expressed in Vince Lombardi's well-known sports aphorism: "Winning isn't everything. It's the only thing." To increase their odds of winning elections, candidates typically try to raise and spend more campaign dollars than their opponents. In contested races, all candidates understand the realities of the winner-take-all system and that improving their odds of winning requires mountains of money. In 2004, the mountain was $4.2 billion high—the total amount raised and spent by candidates, parties, and candidates' supporters in campaigns for all federal offices that year ($1.2 billion more than in 2000).[37] While candidates with the most money are not guaranteed political victories, they nearly always win. In the 2004 congressional elections, the candidates who raised the most money won 96 percent of the 435 House and 34 Senate seats up for grabs in the Congress.[38] Despite these grim realities, it is important to note that election losses by privileged-class candidates *do not* typically produce for them great financial hardships or the loss of their class location. When privileged-class members (the largest source of political candidates) lose elections, they simply turn their attention back, in most cases, to professional or upper-level corporate employment (perhaps as lobbyists) or to running their own businesses; sometimes wealthy losing candidates immediately begin planning and even self-funding their candidacies for the next election cycle.

So, where does the cash candidates spend on campaigns come from? The answer is the same for both Democrats and Republicans: primarily from wealthy individuals and from corporate-organized and dominated PACs. In the 2004 House campaigns, contributions of more than $200 from individuals and donations from business-related PACs to candidates made up 70 percent of Republicans' total receipts and 63 percent of Democrats' total receipts.[39] In the 2004 Senate races, candidates from both major parties raised a total of $323.7 million from individual contributors, with 77 percent of that amount coming from individuals donating more than $200.[40] All congressional candidates (from both parties) raised a total of $720.8 million in the 2004 elections from individual contributors (up 34 percent from 2002), and of that amount, 78 percent came from individuals donating more than $200.[41]

A Primer on Federal Campaign Finance Law: Past and Present

Most information regarding financial contributions to candidates and political parties involved in elections for federal offices comes from public records compiled by the Federal Election Commission (FEC) as mandated by federal laws, amendments to existing laws (e.g., 1971, 1974, 2002), and specific rules and regulations published in the *Federal Register*.[42] Additional information regarding funds contributed to and spent by tax-exempt nonprofit organizations on federal election-related activities comes from public records compiled by the Internal Revenue Service (IRS) as mandated by various sections of the Internal Revenue Code.[43]

Under federal law and FEC rules, in federal elections, individuals, PACs, political parties, and political committees (classified into various legal categories) may legally make what are referred to by the FEC as "hard money" contributions to federal candidates and national political parties. These same constituencies may also legally make what the FEC refers to as "soft money" contributions to organizations involved in federal elections that are outside the domain of federal campaign finance laws and FEC regulations. The terms *hard money* and *federal funds* are used interchangeably by the FEC and refer to political contributions subject to federal campaign finance laws and regulations, which limit the allowable amounts that can be raised, prescribe how these funds can be raised and spent, and mandate public reporting of such funds. The terms *soft money* and *nonfederal funds* are also used interchangeably by the FEC and refer to political contributions "raised outside the limits and prohibitions of federal campaign finance law for activity affecting federal elections."[44]

From the inception of modern campaign finance reform in 1974 until 2002, when funds to be used for political purposes in federal elections were contributed *to party committees and not directly to candidates*, the FEC considered such donations as soft money. There were virtually no limits on how such funds were raised, the amounts raised, donor sources, or spending practices, and public reporting requirements were minimal.[45] Until the enactment of reform legislation in 2002, soft money contributions (often donated in amounts of $100,000 or more) to political party committees were typically used by state and national parties to finance party-building activities and to assist individual candidates for federal offices in various ways.[46] As noted in chapter 2, the 2002 Bipartisan Campaign Reform Act (BCRA) outlawed soft money contributions to political party committees for use in federal elections, and it modified federal campaign finance rules regarding hard money. However, the law *did not* forbid the use of other forms of what are still called "soft money" in federal elections. While the BCRA was enacted in part to curtail perceived abuses in how federal political campaigns were financed, the new law did not significantly curtail the influence of wealthy individuals and PAC donors on the political process.

The BCRA *increased* limits on hard money contributions to federal candidates from individual donors and indexed maximum contribution amounts for inflation (so contribution limits will rise in future elections as inflation increases). For example, in the 2006 election cycle, one person could contribute $2,100 for each candidate he or she chose to support (up to a $40,000 total for all candidates supported) and $61,400 to all national party committees and PACs (but no more than $40,000 of the $61,400 total to PACs). PACs were essentially unaffected by the BCRA both in terms of the sources and amounts of PAC receipts and PAC contributions to candidates. Under the new law, as in the past, individuals are limited to contributions of no more than $5,000 to any PAC or political committee (up to a total of $40,000 for all PAC contributions per election cycle). Each PAC may contribute up to $5,000 per election (primary and general election) to any candidate for federal office; consistent with previous federal regulations, the new law places no limits on the number of PACs that may support a given candidate. Also, as in the past, the BCRA limits multicandidate committees and other political committees to $5,000 in contributions to each PAC supported per election cycle; there are no limits on the total amount that can be contributed by these kinds of organizations in each election cycle to all PACs—the same as previous federal regulations.[47]

The BCRA appears to have unintentionally facilitated the rapid growth of substantial contributions from wealthy donors of soft money in forms not regulated by the FEC or the new law. This is especially evident in the recent expansion of the so-called 527 committees—so-named because of the section of the Internal Revenue Code that grants tax-exempt status to political committees. Since the BCRA outlawed one major form of soft money, party committee contributions, much of the money that formerly flowed into these soft money channels appears to have been redirected by the new law into 527s. This trend is illustrated by IRS records, which reveal that 527 committees raised $534 million in the 2004 election cycle, which was nearly five times more than the $114 million raised in 2000.[48] These committees were not regulated in the past by the FEC, and the BCRA did not change this situation. (In the 2006 election cycle, 527 committees raised about $151 million for use in federal elections.[49])

Today (despite calls for reform), there are no limits on contribution amounts, on contributors (foreign governments may contribute), or on the total amount of money 527s may raise or spend. Only three federal rules apply to 527 committees: (1) each committee must file a statement of organization with the IRS, (2) each committee must file regular reports listing contributions and expenditures with the IRS, and (3) committees cannot contribute money to federal candidates, coordinate activities with federal candidates' campaigns, or expressly advocate for the election or defeat of a specific federal candidate.[50] The first two rules are simply record-keeping requirements and in no way limit the scope of committee activities or the funding of the organizations. The third rule limits the use of specific language in communications paid for by 527s, but as the 2004 election illustrated, this rule has little practical effect in terms of inhibiting the political content of 527-sponsored mass media–disseminated messages.

Despite the existence of federal laws and regulations that limit hard money political contributions and that require IRS reporting of legal soft money political donations, most of the funds contributed in either form to candidates, parties, and other politically linked organizations come from the same sources: wealthy individuals and resource-rich PACs (especially corporate PACs). Moreover, as we will see, both major political parties and most federal candidates they field today are primarily financed—through various organizations that channel money to federal candidates, political parties, and 527 committees—by funds from the superclass. New campaign finance regulations imposed by the BCRA have not diminished the staggering amounts of money raised for federal elections, and only the superclass has access to the amounts of money needed by candidates today. As noted earlier, a total of $4.2 billion was raised and spent by all federal candidates and organizations supporting the candidates in the 2004 elections (up from $3 billion in 2000). Of the 2004 total, about $3 billion came from hard money contributions—in all forms permitted by both pre- and post-BCRA federal laws and regulations.[51]

Individual Contributions: Top of the Class

Although PACs often receive media attention as important sources of campaign dollars, the primary sources of campaign funding for candidates in the 2004 House and Senate elections (as in the past) were individual contributions, most often in amounts of more than $200.[52] Contributions from individuals to congressional candidates totaled $720.8 million in 2004. Senate candidates received a total of $324 million from individuals, of which $250.1 million was in amounts of $200 or more and $193.3 million was from donations of $750 or more. House candidates received $396.7 million from individuals, of which $311.4 million was in amounts of more than $200.[53]

Individual contributions of more than $200 made up the single largest source of funding for Republican and Democratic candidates in the 2004 congressional races, averaging 47 percent of all contributions.[54] Sometimes the candidates and the wealthy contributors were the same people because, in several congressional races, wealthy candidates legally financed their own campaigns. In 2004, congressional candidates contributed or loaned $132.2 million to their campaigns, up 21 percent from the $109.1 million reported in the 2002 election cycle. In the 2004 election, Senate candidates donated or loaned their campaigns $77.7 million (from their personal resources), while for House candidates, these self-funding sources totaled $54.6 million.[55]

Aside from personally wealthy politicians, who are the people making large political donations? The short answer is, a tiny minority of Americans—mainly privileged-class members, and especially those in the superclass. Few people make political contributions, and the ones who do, especially those who contribute more than $200, are almost entirely upper-income members of the privileged class. Of the donors who contribute over $200 to political campaigns or parties, over 80 percent have annual incomes of $100,000 or more.[56] By contrast, in the United States, only 12 percent of all U.S. households and only 4 percent of individuals (with income) have annual incomes of $100,00 or more.[57] During the 2004 election cycle, only about one-half of 1 percent of the U.S. adult population gave contributions of $200 or more to federal candidates, parties, and PACs totaling $1.9 billion. An even smaller group composed of just over one-tenth of 1 percent of the U.S. adult population made contributions of $2,000 or more and collectively donated a total of $1.4 billion, or 74 percent of all federal candidate, party, and PAC contributions in the 2004 elections.[58] Business executives dominate the individual donor group and in recent federal elections have "out-contributed labor leaders and staff by a factor of 1000:1."[59]

People with family incomes above $75,000 are more than one hundred times more likely to contribute to candidates than those with family incomes below $15,000.[60] But even $75,000 incomes are far below the amounts earned by the 256,861 Americans who, in amounts of $2,000 or more, gave $1.4 billion to federal candidates, parties, and PACs in the 2004 election cycle.[61] Among all political donors, "one out of five makes $500,000 a year and another three out of five make over $100,000."[62] Wealthy donors reside almost exclusively in large cities: individual contributions in amounts of $200 or more from the most generous zip codes in just three metropolitan urban areas— Washington, D.C., New York City, and Los Angeles—totaled $163.4 million in donations to federal candidates, parties, and PACs in the 2004 election cycle.[63]

A study of the one hundred top individual political contributors found that this group donated nearly $26.5 million to federal candidates in the 2004 election cycle.[64] All of the top one hundred contributors were corporate executives, investors, business owners, or attorneys. Of the total group, eighty-one contributed "Solidly Republican" and only nineteen contributed "Solidly Democratic." The top-ranked contributor (Davis S. and Katherine A. Phillips of Phillips Industries, High Point, NC) donated $459,907 (100 percent Republican), while the lowest-ranked contributor (David V. and Leigh Anne Dorris of Dorris Law Firm, Leroy, IL) donated $211,850 (100 percent Democratic).[65]

An earlier study of the top four hundred political contributors found that half of the donors were either corporate heads or lawyers, and many appeared on the *Forbes* magazine list of America's wealthiest individuals. "The majority are bankers, lawyers, investors, or other businessmen with a big financial stake in the outcome of [federal] legislation."[66] In short, from the perspective of our class model, the top one hundred and the top four hundred appear, almost without exception, to be superclass members, superclass wannabes, or credentialed-class agents largely representing superclass clients. In each case, the strategy is the same—the top one hundred or top four hundred invest in politics to protect privileged-class interests. For privileged-class political donors, "underwriting campaigns has become part of the cost of doing business, an investment that pays dividends in access to policymakers with the power to reduce taxes, ward off regulations, award contracts, and dole out subsidies."[67]

Corporate PACs: Another Class Act

In the 2004 congressional races for the general election, PACs donated $162 million to Republicans and $127 million to Democrats; this made PACs the second largest source of congressional candidate funding, averaging 24 percent of all contributions (after individual contributions at 60 percent).[68] However, the overall average masks the relative importance of PAC funding in House and Senate races. In 2004, PAC contributions accounted for just 20 percent of the funds raised by *winning* Senate candidates; but among *winning* House candidates, PAC contributions made up 39.4 percent of their total receipts.[69]

Corporate PACs plus corporate-dominated trade, membership associations, and health PACs, combined with corporate domination of what we estimate to be at least one-half of what the FEC terms *nonconnected* PACs, are of special importance in reinforcing superclass political dominance—for four reasons. First, these PACs collect, control, and disburse a majority of all PAC money. Second, they are almost exclusively organized and administered by committees of upper-level corporate managers from large corporations who share a common business-based worldview that reflects superclass interests. Third, corporate and corporate-dominated PACs consistently reflect classwide business unity growing out of shared interests and the effects of federal limits on PAC donations. Fourth, although PAC funding accounts for only about one-fourth of all congressional campaign receipts, business PAC dollars tend to parallel the contribution patterns and political preferences of most wealthy individual donors from the privileged class. While it is true that *some* wealthy individual donors make contributions to candidates that appear to favor policies that would constrain the interests of large resource-rich firms and their PACs, for the most part most wealthy individual donors, most corporate PACs, and most corporate-dominated PACs support conservative, pro-business candidates. Regarding the fourth point, the author of one PAC study observed, "On this point, at least, the behavior of individual capitalists and of corporate PACs are more alike than different."[70] These four factors lead to contribution patterns whereby most corporate and corporate-dominated PAC contributions flow to politicians who endorse policies that protect and extend the wealth and power of large corporations and the superclass elites who control them.

In the 2003–2004 election cycle, a total of 4,867 PACs raised $915.7 million and spent $842.9 million. In the 2004 elections, PACs donated $289 million to all congressional candidates and $21 million to presidential candidates; PACs also spent $48.6 million on behalf of, and $8.7 million against, various candidates and reported spending a total of $144.5 million in nonfederal funds (soft money). The 1,622 corporate PACs plus all other PACs representing corporate interests (about 1,600) contributed $211 million to congressional candidates—73 percent of total PAC donations to this group in 2004.[71]

Despite the huge sums they control today, corporate PACs as campaign-funding vehicles are relatively new. Following the Watergate-related revelations of secret corporate political donations to the Nixon campaign, it first appeared that corporate campaign contributions would be severely limited. However, in 1975 the FEC (established by federal law in 1971) ruled, by a vote of four to three, that the Sun Oil Corporation PAC could solicit funds from both stockholders and employees. After the so-called SUN-PAC decision, the number of corporate PACs increased from 89 in 1974 to 433 in 1976 and has continued to increase since that time.[72]

The political power of the more than thirty-two hundred corporate and corporate-dominated PACs (by our estimate in 2005) rests in the hands of PAC committees that are almost exclusively composed of privileged-class corporate managers and officers.[73] These committees bring together superclass members and upwardly mobile credentialed-class corporate professionals.[74] The two groups are closely linked through their shared involvement with, and concern for, shaping corporate policies that favor superclass and corporate interests and through a shared political worldview. The political unity, consensus, and cohesion typically found among corporate PAC managers is based on "a set of underlying material relations—loans from the same banks, sales and purchases from each other, interlocking boards of directors, common interests in accumulating capital and avoiding government regulations that might restrict their power."[75] These material and social relations reinforce PAC managers' interpretations of, and decisions and actions on, both politics and business— in favor of superclass interests. Thus, the millions of dollars that corporate PACs raise, control, and disburse tend to be directed by PAC committees to those candidates most favorable to shared, superclass-based business interests.

Although corporate PAC contributions are sometimes disbursed in ways that appear to reflect efforts by competing firms or economic sectors to promote their narrow interests at the expense of other firms or sectors, such patterns are not the norm. More often, corporate PAC contributions tend to be mutually supportive. Convergent patterns of corporate PAC giving indicate classwide business unity on a wide range of regulatory and labor policy issues—rather than hardball competition. Superclass unity is especially evident in cases of policies affecting corporate control over labor markets, including issues such as working conditions and unionization campaigns.[76]

Corporate PAC contribution patterns of classwide unity also reflect the influence of federal law, which, as noted earlier, limits each PAC to a maximum $5,000 donation per candidate per election. Under this rule, superclass leaders recognize that only by acting together can the corporate community have a major impact on funding the political process in ways that protect and serve their common class interests. The $5,000 PAC limit means that individual competing PACs would have very limited power because several small, cross-purpose PAC contributions would cancel out one another's influence. By contrast, a classwide strategy of mutually supportive, convergent patterns of campaign funding magnifies corporate PAC power over the political process. This strategy serves the interests of the superclass power elite who occupy and control the top positions in corporate America. Thus, the legal incentives for PAC collaboration, combined with corporate PAC officers' experiences with their peers, results in a shared network of contacts, information, and reciprocal patterns of gift giving to those candidates most supportive of shared superclass and corporate interests.[77]

Studies of corporate PAC contributions consistently document the pattern of classwide business unity, rather than competition or conflict in the political

Copyright © Tom Tomorrow. Reprinted with permission.

arena, as the dominant reality. Although a few examples of competing business PACs can be found, "opposed to this [behavior] are literally dozens of examples of companies that 'hate each other,' are 'suing each other all of the time,' and are each other's major competitors but that nonetheless work well together in Washington. They cooperate in promoting the same policies, sponsoring joint fundraisers [for candidates], and in general behaving as a unified bloc." One study of corporate PAC donations found business to be unified in three out of four political races, giving, on average, nine times more money to one candidate than to the other. Moreover, "PAC officers may disagree with their counterparts at other corporations, but the unstated rules forbid public disputes, and only reluctantly will one business directly oppose another."[78] The superclass leadership of the corporate community recognizes that only by acting together can business PACs use their combined resources to exert substantial, sustained power over the campaign-funding dimension of the political process.

Connecting the Dots

As we have seen, corporate PACs are not the only players in the campaign-funding game, but compared with their most obvious competitors, such as organized labor and public citizen groups, they are by far the largest and best-funded PACs. The importance of corporate PACs in funding the political process, the superclass bias of PACs, and corporate PAC links to both major parties are key features of the political finance process. Consider the following "dots":

- Corporate, trade, membership, health PACs, 2,522; labor PACs, 306. In 2005, corporate-linked PACs outnumbered labor PACs by nearly eight to one.[79]
- Business contributions, 24; labor contributions, 1. Combining PAC and large individual contributions for the 2004 elections, business contributed twenty-four times more than labor to federal candidates.[80]
- PAC contributions (2003 to 2004) to Democratic candidates for federal offices, $133.7 million; PAC contributions to Republican candidates for federal offices, $173.5 million.[81]
- PAC contributions (2003 to 2004) to incumbent candidates for federal offices, $246.8 million; PAC contributions to challenger candidates, $22.3 million.[82]

If we connect the corporate-PAC- and wealthy-individual-funding "dots," we begin to see a pattern. Superclass-driven campaign funding represents more than just the pooled resources of another interest group. Corporate PAC dollars combine with wealthy-donor contributions to create a powerful political force field dominating both major political parties and the entire political process. Although the Republican Party has long been perceived as the party of superclass and business interests in American politics, these same groups also have a long record of channeling substantial funds to the Democratic Party and Democratic candidates.

Over the past two decades, superclass support for the Democratic Party and Democratic candidates generally, especially for national offices, has increased dramatically. In the 1990s, it became increasingly clear that both major parties were receiving similar levels of superclass-based funding. For example, from 1991 through 1994, the Republican Party raised $95 million in soft money, with more than 90 percent of the large donations, more than $20,000 each, coming from business interests, including corporations, executives, trade associations, and lobbying firms. During the same period, the Democratic Party raised $75 million in soft money with more than 70 percent coming from corporate donors.[83] In the 2003–2004 and 2005–2006 election cycles, about 75 percent of individual and PAC donations to federal candidates and to the Democratic and Republican parties came from business interests.[84]

Since the late 1970s, the traditional superclass dominance of the Republican Party has been complemented by its increasing "colonization" of the Democratic Party. This process was facilitated by the takeover of the Democratic Party by the corporate-linked Democratic Leadership Council (DLC). Founded in the mid-1980s, the DLC is directly and indirectly linked (via the New Democrat Network) with dozens of corporate contributors from the Fortune 500, such as Bank One, Dow, DuPont, Merrill Lynch, Microsoft, Morgan Stanley, and Raytheon.[85] In the mid-1990s, one researcher summarized the effects of the increasing penetration of the Democratic Party by superclass interests through its political funding practices in these terms: "Fifteen years ago when the Democrats became more adept in attracting corporate money, a *Wall Street Journal* article stated that 'Business already owns one party and now has a lease, with an option to buy, on the other.' The disregard for labor by centrist Democrats has less to do with ideology, analysis, or changing demographics. It's simply a reflection of Democrat dependence on corporate money."[86] By the mid-2000s, despite some stirrings by dissatisfied progressives within the party and the emergence of Web-based fund-raising in the 2004 elections, little had changed.[87] The Democratic Party leadership and most Democratic candidates for federal offices remained largely dependent on funding from wealthy privileged-class donors (usually linked to business interests) and on corporate-dominated PACs.[88] Reflecting on these realities, Mark Dudzic, Labor Party national organizer (cited in chapter 2) observed, "Democrats . . . are chained to the corporate interests that control the money and media that define American politics. For more than a generation these interests have been waging a one-sided class war against American workers. And even though polls consistently show that putting up a real fight would resonate broadly with the American people, the Democratic establishment has aggressively blocked any attempt to run a campaign against corporate domination."[89]

The combination of wealthy contributors and corporate PAC money tilts the political playing field into a perpendicular configuration with the high end accessible only to elite players with steep-green chips. As we have shown, the political campaign dimension of the class empire rests on a dense web of financial connections whereby funds donated and controlled by the superclass become the dominant financial resource that underwrites the political process—for both major political parties. Moreover, wealthy campaign donors are not disinterested citizens acting on the basis of some civic obligation to fund the democratic process. For example, one survey of donors in a recent presidential election "revealed that 76 percent said 'influencing policy/government' was a 'very important' reason why they gave money."[90] We believe the evidence supporting our contention that the mountain of superclass-controlled cash distributed in each election cycle helps ensure that the superclass retains an iron grip over U.S. politics is more than circumstantial. "Judge for yourself. The evidence . . . [is] enough to convict our political system of serving the interests of the wealthy. Whether the subject is health care reform, environmental regulation, farm subsidies, weapons production, or trade policy, it is difficult to even get a hearing in Washington without spreading around a lot of dough."[91]

POLICY PLANNING: THE BIG PICTURE

> The policy-planning network is . . . the programmatic political party for the upper class and the corporate community.
>
> —G. William Domhoff, *State Autonomy or Class Dominance?* 1996

Is big government the source of many national problems today? Are vampirelike "greedy geezers" sucking the financial lifeblood of the younger generation—pushing Social Security and Medicare toward bankruptcy? Do we need to slash and burn the funding of social programs to reduce taxes, promote economic growth, and increase defense spending? Are welfare, drugs, crime, and homosexuality eroding America's moral fabric? Does the threat of terrorism require the curtailing of traditional privacy rights and personal freedoms? The short answer to these questions is yes—at least according to many organizations that are part of the superclass-funded national policy-planning network.[92]

The Policy-Planning Network

The policy-planning network consists of several superclass-dominated organizations, including think tanks, research institutes, policy discussion groups, and foundations.[93] Grounded in superclass resources and institutions, this network is dedicated to setting the national policy agenda, establishing policy priorities, and shaping public policy outcomes. It is based on a superclass worldview, shared by credentialed-class professionals who implement routine network functions, that sees the existing economic and political reward, opportunity, and power structures as the most legitimate and the preferred national organizational arrangement (especially compared with more egalitarian alternatives).[94] The network functions through a variety of organizations and processes that collectively promote superclass interests by sustaining the economic and political status quo—or slight variations thereof.

The links between this network and superclass political dominance are tied to the reality that "policy planning in the United States takes place largely outside of government, in private policy-planning organizations funded by private corporations and foundations."[95] This means that the organizations in the superclass-funded policy-planning network generate most of the research, ideas, and policy discussions that dominate and shape the national policy agenda, priorities, debates, and most legislative or regulatory "solutions." The multifaceted input from this network into the national government is clearly tilted in favor of policies that support and extend existing class-based wealth, income, and power inequalities and thereby reinforce superclass economic and political interests. It should be noted that despite the shared economic and political interests of the superclass, divisions do exist within this class on some policies and issues (e.g., see the estate tax discussion in the next section and our comments on Responsible Wealth in note 6). Even so, more often than not, there is a consensus within the superclass in favor of policies that support "economic growth, a stable business cycle, incentives for investment, economy and efficiency in government, a stable two-party system, and maintaining popular support for political institutions."[96]

Network Members: Naming Names

Think tanks and research institutes are typically nonprofit organizations that provide settings where experts from academic disciplines and former public office holders discuss a wide range of contemporary social problems and consider alternative policies for dealing with them.[97] Although the classification of specific organizations as think tanks or research institutes is contested terrain in the social sciences, researchers generally agree that the policy-planning network core consists of a very short list of five superclass-connected and politically influential "centrist" organizations. The Business Roundtable, the Brookings Institution, and the RAND Corporation are key players in the formation of U.S. domestic policies, and the Council on Foreign Relations (CFR) and the Trilateral Commission play similar, central roles in the establishment of American foreign policies.[98] In addition to the five core players, five other major centrist groups also play important roles in the policy-planning network: the Business Council, the U.S. Chamber of Commerce, the Committee for Economic Development (CED), the Conference Board, and the National Association of Manufacturers (NAM).[99]

Parallel with the major centrist organizations is an increasingly influential cluster of conservative think tanks. Prominent organizations in this group include the Hoover Institution, American Enterprise Institute (AEI), Heritage Foundation, the Center for Strategic and International Studies, the Manhattan Institute, and the Institute for Research on the Economics of Taxation.[100] Over the past thirty years, these organizations have emerged as important contributors to the policy-formation process. "In the mid- to late 1970s, business began its own [political] countermobilization. . . . Money was shifted out of liberal and moderate think tanks and policy organizations (the Brookings

Institution, Council on Foreign Relations, and Committee for Economic Development) to newly founded or reinvigorated conservative equivalents (the American Enterprise Institute, Hoover Institution, and Heritage Foundation). . . . [By] 1980 the conservative organizations spent substantially more than the moderate ones."[101] A study by the National Committee for Responsive Philanthropy (NCRP) found that in the 1990s "center-right and far-right think tanks [continued] to grow rapidly suggesting the 1990s [extended the process of] continued institution building by political conservatives." Over the 1990–2000 period, the NCRP estimated that spending by the top twenty conservative think tanks exceeded $1 billion.[102] Based on recent annual budgets of twenty-four large conservative think tanks, this group's spending again surpassed $1 billion, but in half the time—between 2001 and 2006.[103]

In the mid-2000s, some wealthy liberals took steps to fund an expanded network of progressive think tanks as part of a new "Democracy Alliance" initiative affiliated with the Democratic Party. The goal was to raise $200 million over five years to expand the progressive think tank structure, which numbered nineteen in 2003 (e.g., Economic Policy Institute, Center for Public Integrity, Center on Budget and Policy Priorities) with total annual spending estimated at about $75 million.[104] Presumably a larger network of progressive think tanks would be able to compete more effectively with right-wing think tanks in developing policy positions and publications aimed at influencing government and corporate policy making and public opinion. Also, such a network might help balance the current pattern of right-wing think tanks' being far more frequently cited as sources by mainstream media reporters than progressive think tanks.[105]

This is an interesting development, but whether this initiative will alter the current centrist-right-wing think tank hegemony over policy development remains to be seen. It is clear that the superclass is not totally unified on all corporate and public policy issues. This is illustrated, for example, by positions taken by organized groups representing wealthy Americans regarding efforts by some members of Congress to end the federal estate tax on multi-million-dollar estates. While most organized groups representing wealthy Americans favor ending the federal estate tax (or the "death tax," as it is called by those who want to end it), one organization representing a group of wealthy individuals known as Responsible Wealth has publicly advocated retaining the estate tax and has actively lobbied for it in Congress.[106] Thus, while most superclass members are likely to continue to support centrist and right-wing think tanks, one segment of this class may be willing to help underwrite an expanded progressive think tank structure. Conceivably, such a structure could facilitate the development of public and corporate policy positions that would appeal to large segments of the working class and, if implemented, would perhaps even require minor sacrifices where the economic and political interests of the superclass are concerned. However, developments of this sort would not fundamentally alter the class structure;

rather, such outcomes would actually enhance the legitimacy of the institutional structures that support superclass interests.

Policy discussion groups are often affiliated with think tanks and research institutes, but these groups have somewhat different goals and function in ways that are distinct from think tanks. They serve as important meeting grounds where superclass corporate elites and their professional allies from various venues come together. The purpose of these informal weekly or monthly meetings is partly to share ideas but also to allow superclass leaders opportunities to identify, recruit, and groom talented individuals from the professional ranks for top leadership positions within government and other key organizations in the policy-planning network. The meetings also help to legitimate the organizations and their activities by portraying both in altruistic terms and by emphasizing the nonprofit, "independent" status of the organizations. The key organizations that serve as policy discussion groups (or facilitate such activities) often overlap with think tank organizations and include NAM, the U.S. Chamber of Commerce, the Conference Board, the CFR, the CED, the American Assembly, and the Brookings Institution.[107]

Foundations and Board Interlocks

As we saw earlier, federal lobbying and campaign funding are two central features of superclass influence where public policy making and the political process are concerned. The same principle of superclass dominance also applies to policy planning, but instead of wealthy lobbyists and political donors, superclass-dominated foundations serve as the major financial engines providing much of the funding for the policy-planning network.[108] These tax-exempt, nonprofit organizations are often the creations of corporate entrepreneurs and wealthy families who founded them in part to reduce their own taxes, as well as to use them as vehicles for encouraging policies favorable to their class interests.[109]

The resources controlled by foundations are staggering. The Foundation Center identified a total of 66,398 foundations in the United States in the mid-2000s. At this time, the top one hundred U.S. foundations (by asset size) held combined assets of $202.4 billion, which accounted for 42 percent of all assets held by all U.S. foundations ($476.7 billion). The top one hundred U.S. foundations (by total giving—nearly identical to the top one hundred by asset size) awarded grants in the mid-2000s that totaled more than $11.2 billion annually; this amount accounted for 37 percent of all foundation giving annually in the mid-2000s (about $30 billion). In the mid-2000s, the top fifteen U.S. foundations (by asset size) held over $114.1 billion in combined assets, which accounted for 24 percent of all assets held by all U.S. foundations. The top five foundations are all linked to large, well-known corporate firms and fortunes. In the mid-2000s, they included the Bill and Melinda Gates Foundation (Microsoft, no. 1, $28.7 billion), the Ford Foundation (Ford Motors, no. 2, $10.7 billion), the J. Paul Getty Trust (Getty Oil, no. 3, $9.6 billion), the Robert Wood Johnson Foundation (Johnson & Johnson, no. 4, $8.9 billion), and the Lilly Endowment (Lilly Pharmaceuticals, no. 5, $8.5 billion).[110]

Foundations are managed by boards of directors or trustees composed primarily of members from the superclass and closely allied members of the credentialed class. One study of large foundations found that over 34 percent of the top foundation leaders were members of exclusive upper-class social clubs. The top fifty foundation boards include a total of 402 director positions that are filled mainly by men (85 percent) who attended Ivy League or other prestigious universities. Moreover, many Rockefellers, Mellons, Lillys, Danforths, and members of other wealthy families (such as the Waltons of Wal-Mart fame) sit on the boards of directors of their family foundations and also often serve on corporate boards of several other firms.[111] For example, recent Rockefeller Foundation trustees have included John D. Rockefeller III; Richard H. Jenrette, chairman of Equitable Life Insurance; Arthur Levitt, chairman of the American Stock Exchange; Frank G. Wells, former CEO of Walt Disney; and Harold Brown, a director of AMAX, CBS, and IBM and former U.S. secretary of defense.[112]

Foundations' budgets come mainly from dividends received through their ownership of large blocks of corporate stock. These organizations spend their annual budgets on a variety of activities, but support of policy-planning network organizations is a consistent funding priority. For example, the Brookings Institution, a mainstream, centrist think tank with a staff of 340, an annual budget of $49 million, and $231 million in investment resources,[113] received a total of $28.7 million in grants and contracts in 2005, including a minimum of $4.5 million from eight large foundations.[114] Over the years, Brookings has benefited from both foundation and corporate funding, attracting in 2005, for example, forty-one foundation donors (gifts over $25,000) and sixty-two corporate donors (gifts over $5,000). Donors to Brookings of cash gifts in 2005 at the level of "$500,000 and Above" included the U.S. Chamber of Commerce, as well as seven large foundations such as the John D. and Catherine T. MacArthur Foundation.[115]

Top foundations have historically provided substantial support to a variety of large, politically centrist policy-planning organizations like the Brookings Institution. The Ford Foundation, for example, has been a continuing financial supporter of Brookings.[116] Another example of a mainstream policy-planning group benefiting from financial support by top foundations is the Council on Foreign Relations. Over the years, it has received substantial funding from the Ford, Lilly, Mellon, and Rockefeller foundations.[117]

Conservative policy-planning think tanks have also benefited substantially from foundation support. Between 1977 and 1986, twelve foundations (including Pew Memorial, Coors, Lilly, and nine other smaller foundations) provided more than $63 million of the $88 million in grant funds received by the top ten conservative think tanks.[118] More recently, conservative foundations have increased their involvement in funding conservative think tanks, university programs, media groups, and other organizations linked to the policy-planning network.[119] Their goal is to promote a more conservative policy agenda extolling the virtues of the free market and the dangers of government regulations.

A 1997 National Center for Responsive Philanthropy study found that from 1992 to 1994, twelve core conservative foundations (Lynde and Harry Bradley, Sarah Scaife, John M. Olin, and nine others) donated $210 million to promote conservative activities. More than $80 million went to conservative think tanks and other organizations that advocated unregulated free markets, such as the Heritage Foundation ($8.9 million), the American Enterprise Institute ($6.9 million), the Cato Institute ($3.9 million), the Hudson Institution ($3.3 million), and the Manhattan Institute ($2.1 million). Large portions of the remaining $130 million went to academic centers, legal groups, and media outlets that promote the free market cause.[120]

In a follow-up report to the 1997 study, the NCRP found that conservative foundations have continued to serve as important sources of support for conservative think tanks. Over a third of the estimated $1 billion spent by the top twenty conservative think tanks over the 1990–2000 period came from conservative foundations. Contributions from scores of large corporations and several wealthy individuals accounted for most of the rest of conservative think tank funds expended over the past decade.[121] More recently, as noted earlier, twenty-four conservative think tanks spent over $1 billion between 2001 and 2006, and, as was the case in the 1990–2000 period, conservative foundations served as important sources of this support.[122]

In addition to foundation funding, superclass members influence policy planning by serving as directors on think tank boards. Mainstream policy-planning organizations' boards of directors are especially likely to reflect close ties with the superclass.[123] For example, the Business Roundtable, with an annual budget of over $22 million, has 160 corporate members, including many of the largest U.S. financial and industrial firms, such as Citigroup, General Motors, and ExxonMobil.[124] The organization's directors are extensively interlocked within the corporate community. In the late 1990s, Roundtable directors held 207 directorships with 134 corporations, including 32 that were in the top 50 in size. Many Roundtable directors have also served as directors or trustees for policy-planning organizations, such as the Business Council, the Council on Foreign Relations, and the Brookings Institution.[125] The trustees of the Brookings Institution and the CFR average four corporate directorships each, and only 6 percent of the trustees for these two organizations were not members of corporate boards. Moreover, more than two-thirds of the directors of the CFR, the Business Roundtable, and the Brookings Institution graduated from just twelve prestigious universities.[126]

CLASSWIDE LOBBYING: INVESTING IN PRIVILEGE

We espouse democratic principles and we go through the motions, but we've become a de facto plutocracy, a government controlled by the wealthy. When this happens in other countries, we call it corruption. Here, it's called lobbying.

—Bill O'Brien, *DallasNews.com*, 2006

In American politics, lobbying has two faces: special-interest competition and classwide practices. The former is familiar and widely reported, but the latter, consistent with the class taboo, is seldom the topic of media attention or public discussion. Lobbying's special-interest face has been the subject of increased media attention since the passage of the 1995 Lobbying Disclosure Act.[127] As noted earlier, LDA records reveal special-interest lobbying groups (primarily large corporations) spent $2.2 billion in 2005 on efforts to influence federal laws and policies (up from $1.26 billion in 1997).[128] This means that publicly disclosed lobby expenditures, through registered agents at the national level, now average about $183 million per month. But even this staggering sum is only part of the story. An earlier study of all forms of lobbying estimated that "$8.4 billion is spent each year in Washington to lobby the federal government."[129] Lobbying groups also spend another $1 billion annually at the state level.[130]

Mainstream media reports on lobbying typically emphasize that although lobbying is a big business, it is also a highly competitive enterprise involving intense rivalries among powerful forces and organizations contending with one another to promote their own narrow agendas and interests. A study by the Center for Responsive Politics in the late 1990s illustrates this storyline. The study identified the American Medical Association (AMA) and Philip Morris as among the top-spending lobbyists in the first half of 1997, reporting expenditures of $8.5 and $5.9 million, respectively.[131] A related report distributed via the Associated Press (AP) to many mainstream newspapers identified Philip Morris as a firm that "wants to limit its legal liability on cigarettes," and the AMA was said to be interested in health-care issues such as "urging caution on reform of the Food and Drug Administration."[132] It is easy to infer from the context of the report that Philip Morris was lobbying to *prevent* tighter controls on tobacco products and the AMA was working, in part, to *promote* the strength of a federal agency (the FDA) that may play a major role if tobacco is regulated as a drug. While this example is from the late 1990s, by the mid-2000s little had changed. In 2005, the annual lobbying expenditures of the AMA ($19 million) and Philip Morris ($13 million) placed both groups in the top ten list of organizations spending the most on lobbying for all of 2005.[133] And the AMA and the tobacco industry were still being presented in mass media reports as lobbying adversaries on health-related policy issues.[134]

Mainstream media accounts of lobbying tend to leave readers and viewers with the impression that although lobbying is not necessarily fair to poorly funded groups, the high-stakes, special-interest competition among "heavy hitters" leads to a rough balance of power. In fact, such stories often imply that competition among the "big boys," combined with the spotlight of media attention, act as a kind of checks-and-balances system limiting the most egregious excesses of undue government influence among well-heeled lobby groups. Although we would agree that special-interest competitive lobbying is an important feature of our political system, we contend it is of secondary importance compared with the political-influence dealing and policy-shaping power of lobbying's other face.

Classwide lobbying is very different from the competitive, special-interest face of political lobbying most often presented in the media. It is supported by a wide array of superclass-dominated organizations acting in concert to promote legislative and regulatory policies supportive of superclass interests. Also, this form of lobbying nearly always pits highly unified corporate-based coalitions against coalitions of organized-labor, consumer, and citizen's groups in policy contests. The next five sections describe and illustrate classwide lobbying. First, we provide a brief overview of the classwide lobbying community. Second, we discuss how classwide coalitions produced recent policy outcomes favoring superclass interests at the federal level in four areas: ergonomic regulations, free trade, bankruptcy law, and class action lawsuits. Third, we examine a recent policy contest involving Social Security "reform" to illustrate that classwide political domination does not equal total control of policy making. In the final two sections, we summarize how privileged-class-crafted national taxation and spending policies benefit this class at the expense of the working class.

We could have chosen many examples to illustrate the nature, extent, and consequences of classwide lobbying, but we believe our choices exemplify how superclass unity and political dominance are reflected in classwide lobbying campaigns and policies. The examples illustrate that classwide campaigns organized and funded by the superclass typically dominate public policy making and produce policy outcomes that serve the economic and political interests of this class (at the expense of the working class). Even so, groups within the alternative power networks do challenge and contest superclass dominance—and sometimes they win.

The Classwide Lobby Community

The classwide lobby community comprises a core of peak business groups, which are mainly nonprofit trade associations consisting of several individual corporate members with shared views and policy objectives. Depending on the issues, peak groups can and do participate in both classwide and special-interest lobbying, and some also serve as members of the policy-planning network. Peak groups tend to be organized around groups of top corporate leaders from large firms (e.g., CEOs) and specific industries (e.g., oil, electronics), as well as general, shared business interests (e.g., commerce and trade). Historically, peak groups have formed the organizational core of classwide lobbying efforts. On several issues that have reached congressional legislative or regulatory reform policy contests, a small number of peak groups have consistently been at the center of lobbying activities representing the interests of the business community as a whole, as well as the class interests of wealthy elites.

Among the most influential classwide lobbying groups are the CEO-dominated organizations, including the Business Roundtable, the Committee for Economic Development, and the Conference Board.[135] Specific, industry-wide peak groups that frequently play leadership roles in promoting, coordinating, and supporting classwide lobbying campaigns include the National Association of Manufacturers, the Chemical Manufacturers' Association, the American Petroleum Institute, the American Mining Congress, the Health Insurance Association of America, the Pharmaceutical Research and Manufacturers Association, and many others. More general, shared business interests are represented by peak groups such as the U.S. Chamber of Commerce and, for smaller firms, the National Federation of Independent Business (NFIB).

Classwide Coalitions and Policy Outcomes

Industrywide and CEO-headed peak groups have historically taken the lead in creating ad hoc coalitions to promote classwide business unity and to spearhead lobbying campaigns aimed at influencing legislative outcomes on policies where shared superclass and broad corporate interests are at stake. Four recent federal policy contests illustrate the potency of classwide lobbying efforts.[136] First, in early 2001, NAM served as the nerve center for a coalition of business groups known as the National Coalition on Ergonomics, which favored overturning workplace rules to prevent repetitive motion injuries that were issued in the closing days of the Clinton administration. With NAM at the point, joined by the U.S. Chamber of Commerce, NFIB, and other groups, the coalition orchestrated an intense lobbying campaign that led to votes in both houses of Congress in favor of legislation repealing the rules despite strong opposition from organized labor.[137]

Second, the Bankruptcy Abuse Prevention and Consumer Protection Act of 2005 was pushed through Congress in April 2005 by a corporate coalition led by the finance, insurance, and real estate industries. This same group also accounted for "more than $306 million in individual and political action contributions during the 2004 election cycle" to federal candidates (with 59 percent of that amount going to Republican candidates).[138] Similar bills had been introduced in every Congress since 1998 but had failed. However, the

combination of intense classwide lobbying efforts, large superclass-based political contributions, and the political composition of Congress produced a
superclass victory over labor and consumer groups opposed to the legislation.
Signed into law by President Bush on April 20, 2005, the new law (which
took effect in October 2005) made it more difficult for middle-income families "to use Chapter 7 of the bankruptcy code, which provides an immediate
fresh start." Instead, most debtors will be forced into a Chapter 13 bankruptcy, "which requires a court-supervised payment plan that can last up to
five years." Interestingly, the new law includes a "millionaire's loophole" that
permits wealthy individuals to set up "asset protection trusts" (not available
to average income families) to shield substantial assets from creditors.[139]

Third, the Business Roundtable organized a classwide corporate coalition
that helped secure passage (by a 217–215 vote in the House) in mid-2005 of
the controversial Central America Free Trade Agreement (CAFTA), which was
strongly opposed by labor and consumer groups.[140] Critics said CAFTA du-
plicated "most elements of the North American Free Trade Agreement
(NAFTA)" and extended "the corporate-led globalization model of NAFTA to
five Central American countries and the Dominican Republic."[141] In a follow-
up to the CAFTA congressional vote, a study by Public Citizen's Global Trade
Watch division reported that thirty members of the U.S. House (from both
parties), whose votes were crucial to the trade bill's passage, "have since received $2.8 million in corporate campaign cash" from pro-CAFTA corpora-
tions.[142] The Global Trade Watch director said the study "shows how desperate pro-CAFTA corporations were able to pass an expansion of NAFTA over
the objections of the public."[143]

Finally, the U.S. Chamber of Commerce, joined by the Business Roundtable
and one hundred other major corporations and trade associations, witnessed
the success of a six-year corporate campaign involving at least 475 lobbyists
and the expenditure of millions of dollars of campaign contributions, lobbying, and advertising expenses as Congress passed the Class-Action Fairness Act
of 2005.[144] This act, which President Bush signed into law on February 18,
2006, requires that most large class action lawsuits, often involving consumer
and worker grievances against large firms, be shifted to federal courts, which
are considered to be "less friendly to plantiffs."[145] The enactment of this law
was a major victory for the superclass, but it was only one of "a series of measures aimed at curbing lawsuits" sought by the superclass. Other "tort reform"
efforts sponsored by the superclass that corporate lobby coalitions hope to
pass in the future "take aim at medical malpractice judgments and asbestos exposure claims."[146]

Challenging Classwide Lobbying and Superclass Dominance

In the mid-2000s, a classwide lobbying campaign to "reform" Social Security organized and funded by superclass sponsors was defeated by a labor-

led alternative-power-network coalition. Under the plan proposed by President Bush in early 2005, "reform" meant Social Security would be transformed from an old-age and disability pension program funded by individual and employer contributions and administered by the federal government into a system that would divert a significant share of Social Security contributions into private individual investment accounts administered by for-profit financial firms.[147]

President Bush made Social Security privatization the centerpiece of his second-term agenda, and he focused squarely on this issue in his 2005 State of the Union Address.[148] However, by the end of 2005, Bush's plan to privatize Social Security was dead, despite his own substantial efforts to persuade the public and Congress of the need to "reform" the program and despite massive expenditures of over $200 million in 2005 by corporate-backed groups on public relations and lobbying campaigns in support of Bush's privatization initiative.[149] So, what went wrong? Why did the superclass privatization scheme fail to drive a stake through the heart of Social Security? The short answer is that the dominant power networks controlled by the superclass (described in chapter 2) are not all-powerful, and in this instance, the alternative power networks, energized by organized labor, were able to mobilize enough resources and allies to defeat a major superclass policy initiative. The following paragraphs provide a more detailed answer.

The Social Security system of federally administered pensions for the aged and disabled grew out of policies developed by think tank–like groups funded by the Rockefeller family in the 1920s and early 1930s (the Industrial Relations Counselors and the Social Science Research Council). As envisioned by these groups, a federal pension system would provide a mechanism for making labor markets more efficient (by removing older and disabled workers), motivating workers (through pension guarantees), and reducing the likelihood of social unrest (retirees and disabled workers with pensions would not become destitute or desperate).[150] The Social Security Act of 1935 contained most of the original features envisioned by the policy discussion groups funded by the Rockefeller family, but it was publicly justified (in the act's preamble) as contributing to the "general welfare" of the nation (and not to labor market efficiencies and social control).[151] Despite the fact that Social Security originated with superclass support, this support was divided as both NAM and the U.S. Chamber of Commerce opposed its 1935 passage in Congress.[152] Reflecting the views of superclass opponents, Alf Landon, the 1936 Republican presidential candidate, said that taxes paid into Social Security were "wasted" and the promised benefits were a "hoax"—themes repeated by conservative politicians since that time, such as Barry Goldwater in the 1960s and President Ronald Reagan in the 1980s.[153]

In the seven decades since Social Security was implemented, the program has enjoyed widespread popular support (with public approval ratings of 90 percent).[154] But conservative superclass members opposed to Social Security began a campaign in the 1980s to undermine the program and to recruit a wider spectrum of superclass allies to their cause. In 1983, the Cato Institute, a conservative think tank, prepared a document outlining a political strategy for privatizing Social Security. It included a media campaign of constant criticism "to undermine public confidence in the soundness of the program," the development of "a network of influential supporters of private accounts, including Wall Street brokers who would profit from them," and "a privatization plan waiting [for the opportune political moment]."[155]

The Cato Institute and Heritage Foundation developed blueprints for privatizing Social Security in the 1980s and 1990s. With massive corporate support, these organizations (and others) aggressively sought wider superclass support for privatization. They also cultivated sympathetic media coverage, appealed to the privileged class for support, and attempted to recruit the working class to the "privatization cause."[156] By the mid-2000s, it was apparent that the plan to eliminate Social Security via privatization was supported by large segments of the superclass. The plan was attractive to superclass interests at three levels: economic, political, and ideological. At the economic level, superclass-owned brokerage firms would profit from as much as $118 billion per year that could, under the Bush plan, be diverted from Social Security into private accounts. (The Merrill Lynch brokerage firm more conservatively estimated the amount at $70 billion annually.[157]) If the Bush plan passed, other superclass-owned firms would have access to the funds diverted from Social Security to finance a variety of corporate ventures. At the political level, elimination of federally guaranteed pensions would reduce the "social wage," material benefits provided by the state to citizens as a "right." Such a reduction would increase the economic insecurity of the working class and strengthen the political and economic power of the superclass. At the ideological level, eliminating Social Security resonated with superclass elites who dislike even the *idea* of government programs that benefit workers. Grover Norquist, a long-time Washington-based lobbyist and antigovernment advocate, illustrated this view when he reportedly said Social Security should be privatized "not because the system is going broke, but because it's a lousy program."[158]

In the late 1990s and early 2000s, a network of superclass-controlled coalitions was created by corporate and political supporters to lobby for privatization both in Congress and in the court of public opinion.[159] Three organizations were central to these activities. First, the Alliance for Worker Retirement Security (AWRS) was created by NAM in 1998 with forty members, including the American Bankers Association, the Business Roundtable, the U.S. Chamber of Commerce, the Securities Industry Association, and many individual financial firms and banks.[160] Second, the Coalition for the Modernization and Protection of America's Social Security was created by AWRS and funded by major U.S. corporations "to run an outside-the-beltway PR campaign to juice up public support for privatization."[161] Third, the United Seniors Association (USA), initially created in 1991 by direct-mail, conservative fund-raiser

Richard Viguerie as an organization supposedly advocating for seniors' interests, changed its name in February 2005 to USA Next. Reportedly funded with some $28 million in corporate contributions, the role of USA Next in the privatization campaign would be to attack groups opposed to the president's plan, such as the American Association of Retired Persons (AARP), the fifty-five-million-member organization for people over fifty.[162] In addition to these core coalitions, a fourth network of more than twenty "front groups" was created by Wall Street firms to support privatization. These groups had innocuous-sounding names, such as "For Our Grandchildren," "Progress for America," "Freedom Works," and "Alliance for Retirement Prosperity."[163]

The 2004 elections created what the supporters of Social Security privatization viewed as the ideal political context for legislative action. President Bush strongly supported privatizing the program, and conservative Republican majorities controlled both houses of Congress. But it didn't happen. Instead, despite Bush's "Social Security spring offensive," his sixty-day, thirty-five-state tour to promote his privatization plan, the public reacted with suspicion, and organizations opposed to Bush's plan successfully created a unified coalition of more than two hundred groups "under the banner of Americans United to Protect Social Security" (AUPSS).[164] The coalition was anchored by unions, especially the AFL-CIO and the American Federation of State, County, and Municipal Employees (AFSCME). It also included the Campaign for America's Future, MoveOn.org, USAction, and the AARP. At every stop in Bush's tour, AUPSS was there challenging every speech and every statement. At the same time, Democrats in Congress united in opposition to the president's plan.[165]

As a result of AUPSS's activities and Democratic congressional leaders' opposition to Bush's plan (and *despite* favorable media coverage of it), public support for Bush's plan never materialized.[166] A series of CNN/*USA Today*/Gallup polls revealed substantial public opposition to privatization. In February 2005, the polls found 75 percent of "poor and middle class workers opposed Bush's plan," and in June the same polls found 64 percent of all Americans surveyed "disapproved of President Bush's handling of Social Security."[167] Republican congressional support for Bush's plan began to unravel in the summer as constituents voiced their opposition to the plan and as some local and regional newspapers published editorials opposing the plan.[168] Before Hurricane Katrina hit, Senator Lindsay Graham (R-SC), a strong supporter of Bush's plan, realized the problem for Republican members of Congress when he said that Bush "ran on it, we didn't. He's not up for election again. We are."[169] Events such as Katrina, the indictment and resignation of Rep. Tom Delay (R-TX) from his post as U.S. House majority leader, and growing public opposition to the Iraq war drove the final nails into the privatization coffin, but the battle was really won by "an organized progressive mobilization that inform[ed] citizens and arous[ed] their oppostion."[170]

This Social Security campaign illustrates that superclass political dominance does not equal absolute control over all class-relevant policy contests.[171] Even so, this was not a stake-through-the-heart loss for the superclass. Despite a setback in this battle, the superclass war against workers continues on many issues, including free trade and the political balance of class power. The historical record reveals that when superclass economic and political interests are at stake, the organizations representing this class are persistent, resourceful, and often victorious—even after sustaining initial defeats.[172] The historical record also makes it clear that superclass policy losses almost never equal capitulation, especially where classwide superclass and corporate interests are at stake. The recent Social Security defeat is likely to represent only a temporary setback for superclass interests. The policy-making process is still in motion on this issue, and the jury of history is still out. Superclass policy preferences on core economic issues, including government-administered "entitlement" programs, labor law, trade, and taxes, are akin to the qualities of characters in classic science fiction films, such as *Dawn of the Dead* and *The Terminator*. Like undead zombies, superclass-promoted policies are continually reanimated, and like futuristic cyborgs, *they never stop*!

Classwide Lobbying: Federal Taxation and Spending Policies

The jury is not out on the issue of superclass dominance over federal tax and spending policies. However, these are two areas where classwide and special-interest lobbying sometimes intersect and overlap, thereby at times obscuring classwide campaigns and superclass dominance. Journalists often focus on special-interest lobbying and point out that the political contributions of individual firms or industry PACs often appear to lead to specialized tax breaks or federal subsidies for specific firms or industries. Although such policy outcomes are often both obvious and outrageous, they are actually of secondary importance to classwide lobbying. The cumulative effects of classwide campaigns dating from the 1960s aimed at shaping federal (as well as state and local) tax and spending policies to further advantage privileged-class interests are evident in current federal, state, and local laws. Classwide tax-cut campaigns in 1985–1986, 1996–1997, 2001, and 2002–2006 illustrate how unified superclass efforts (under three different presidents) produced major changes in federal tax rates benefiting the wealthy and corporations.

Classwide Campaigns and Tax Reform: 1986

The list of companies and trade associations that lobbied Congress as key committees considered and crafted the Tax Reform Act of 1986, the 1997 Budget Reconciliation Act, and the 2001 Tax Relief Act, and four major tax cuts enacted in the 2002–2006 period included the "usual suspects" involved in classwide lobbying campaigns—plus some new groups. The record of the 1985 House tax-reform hearings fills nine volumes (over nine thousand pages), and the vast majority of the nearly one thousand witnesses who appeared represented corporate interests. Although many corporate representatives sought specialized benefits for individual firms or industries, some of the most potent corporate players advocated preserving and extending tax breaks that would promote the classwide advantages and interests of wealthy corporate owners and officers. This message was evident in testimony from witnesses representing the Business Roundtable, NAM, the U.S. Chamber of Commerce, NFIB, and many others.[173]

House hearings held in 1990 on the impact, effectiveness, and fairness of the Tax Reform Act of 1986 generated seventy-six statements for the record. Of this number, forty-nine came from corporations or trade associations, with most praising various features of the 1986 act. Many of these statements were submitted by the same classwide organizational advocates that had supported the legislation in 1985. The few critics submitting statements in 1990, such as the AFL-CIO and AFSCME, pointed to problems that the 1986 tax law had created as a result of reducing tax rates for corporations and very wealthy individuals. The testimony of these witnesses called attention to the classwide benefits embedded in the 1986 act—extensive financial benefits for superclass and many credentialed-class members—and to the substantial costs that were passed along to the entire working class.[174]

Classwide Campaigns and Tax Reform: 1997

In 1997 the "same old gang" lobbied for more reductions in federal corporate taxes, capital gains taxes, and inheritance taxes. In the context of an expanding economy, political pressures to balance the budget, Republican control of the Congress, and a compliant president (Clinton), the issue was not whether taxes would be cut—that was a foregone conclusion. The real issues involved which taxes would be cut and how the cuts would be distributed.

The tax cuts mandated by the Budget Reconciliation Act of 1997 (BRA) primarily benefited members of the superclass and their wealth-producing machines called corporations. As the details of the tax bill were being crafted, members of Congress again, as in 1986, listened closely to lobbyists from NAM, the U.S. Chamber of Commerce, and NFIB, who coordinated their efforts to win business tax cuts—ostensibly to improve fairness, investment, and productivity (and not just to juice profits).[175] This corporate-focused lobbying effort to reduce taxes was reinforced by classwide coalitions seeking cuts in the capital gains and estate taxes. In all three instances, the lobbying campaigns were aimed at tax cuts that would primarily produce classwide benefits for wealthy Americans.

The lobbying effort to reduce the capital gains tax was led by a coalition of conservative groups that publicly focused attention on the need for Congress to use "tax revenue windfalls" created by a rapidly growing economy "for tax cuts for all Americans." The coalition included several groups fronted by well-known conservative political and business leaders that long favored cuts in capital gains taxes: Jack Kemp of Empower America; Lewis K. Uhler of the National Tax Limitation Committee; David Keating of the National Taxpayers Union; Steve Forbes of Americans for Hope, Growth, and Opportunity; Matt Kibbe of Citizens for a Sound Economy; and Harrison Fox of Citizens for Budget Reform.[176]

The estate-tax-reduction campaign was led by a coalition of 105 lobbying groups backed by privileged-class members with financial interests in passing family fortunes intact (tax free) to the next generation.[177] And federal estate tax rates are not a trivial issue for the rich. Prior to the 1997 tax law, estates were taxed at federal rates of 18 percent on the first $10,000, 37 percent for assets of more than $500,000, and 55 percent for estates valued in excess of $3 million. Although the estate-tax cut was claimed by its supporters to benefit all Americans, few parents amassed estates above the pre-1997 $600,000 federal exemption ($1.2 million for married couples) to pass

Copyright © Lloyd Dangle. Reprinted with permission.

along to their heirs. In 1996, a total of 69,772 estates with assets in excess of $600,000 filed forms with the Internal Revenue Service, but after allowable deductions and exemptions, only 31,918 estates paid federal estate taxes—just 1.2 percent of all estates.[178]

The 1997 classwide tax-reduction campaigns paid off for the privileged class. The BRA cut capital gains taxes from 28 to 20 percent. The minimum corporate tax was eliminated, and the federal estate (inheritance) tax exemption was raised from $600,000 to $1 million ($1.3 million for family farms and businesses).[179] The 1997 act distributed three-fourths of individual tax cuts to people with annual incomes of more than $100,000. Over one-third of all tax breaks went to the wealthiest 1 percent, who ended up with more tax relief than the bottom 80 percent. At the same time, "changes in the Alternative Minimum Tax (AMT) . . . lowered the tax burden for corporations by $18.3 billion over 10 years."[180] The richest 5 percent of American families got 83 percent of the benefits from cuts in the capital gains tax, the elimination of the minimum corporate tax, and the near doubling of the estate-tax exemption. Families in the top 20 percent income group scored annual tax breaks of more than $1,000, but those in the top 1 percent received tax breaks averaging "$16,157 per year." This amount included average tax cuts of $7,939 in capital gains, $6,313 in estate taxes, and $2,353 in corporate taxes, minus small increases ($451 on average) in excise taxes. Families in the middle 20 percent income group received a tax break of only $153 per year, and families in the lowest and second-lowest income groups saw either no tax cuts or slight tax increases.[181]

Classwide Campaigns and Tax Reform: 2001

During the 2000 presidential campaign, candidate Bush proposed a tax-cut plan to be phased in over ten years.[182] On February 8, 2001, Treasury Secretary Paul O'Neill presented President Bush's plan, known then as the "Agenda for Tax Relief," to Congress.[183] It was marketed to the public and Congress on the grounds of fairness and as a recession-fighting measure.[184] Four months later, on June 7, President Bush signed the Economic Growth and Tax Relief Reconciliation Act of 2001 into law at an estimated cost to the Treasury of $1.35 trillion in lost revenue over the next ten years.[185] It was "the largest income tax rollback in two decades."[186]

Nearly 71 percent of the tax cuts in 2001 went to individuals in the top 20 percent income group.[187] But some tax reductions primarily benefited only the richest 1 percent. For example, the 2001 law increased the estate tax exemption for a married couple to $4 million in 2006 with further reductions scheduled through 2009; also, the estate tax would be totally repealed (at least temporarily) in 2010.[188] As a result of these changes, only one in two hundred estates (one-half of 1 percent) will owe any federal estate taxes.[189] By contrast, the law left marginal tax rates unchanged for Americans with taxable incomes of less than $27,050 (singles) or $45,200 (married couples).[190] Most of the law's benefits for wealthy taxpayers were phased in beginning with 2002 and will continue to grow through 2010. For example, the average annual tax cut for an individual in the top 1 percent income group was $2,991 in 2001, but this amount rose to $42,075 in 2007 and will rise to $69,042 in 2010.[191] In short, "after 2001, the richest 20 percent get 84.1 percent of the overall benefits and the top 1 percent alone [get] more than half of the overall benefits."[192]

The most pernicious effects of the 2001 tax law and of the other tax cuts enacted in 2002 to 2006 will be to "starve" federal programs that benefit working-class Americans in the future. According to the United Automobile Workers union, "the new law will effectively crowd out the ability of the federal government to provide funds to strengthen Social Security and Medicare. . . . In addition, it will preclude the federal government from making major investments in education, health care, and many other important areas."[193] Some observers view such long-term effects as part of a deliberate strategy by the privileged class.[194] As writer Ruth Conniff noted, "Make no mistake. We are being set up for the repeal of the last of the hard-earned New Deal antipoverty and health care programs for the elderly and poor Americans."[195]

So, why did the lopsided tax law loaded with benefits for the highest income groups and laden with many long-term negatives for working-class Americans pass so quickly? We know it wasn't because of a grassroots clamor by average-income Americans. Polls showed little public support. Although a majority of Americans in a national survey favored the *concept* of reducing federal income tax rates "across the board," only 16 percent thought the Bush plan would "do 'a lot' to improve their own financial situation."[196] In one poll of registered voters, only 7 percent of respondents ranked taxes as the "most important issue facing the country."[197] Moreover, a substantial coalition of groups representing middle-income workers' interests, known as Fair Taxes for All, opposed the Bush plan (e.g., AFL-CIO, AFSCME, National Association for the Advancement of Colored People, National Women's Law Center, People for the American Way).[198]

The real reason the tax-cut legislation moved so expeditiously through Congress was because of unified, active support provided by a group of several powerful organizations representing the material, political, and ideological interests of the privileged class. This group, known as the Tax Relief Coalition, was organized in February; its founding members included the U.S. Chamber of Commerce, NAM, the National Association of Wholesalers-Distributors, and NFIB. Another two hundred fifty business and taxpayer groups were invited to join the coalition and were asked to pay $5,000 each in dues, primarily to pay for advertising "in Capitol Hill publications."[199]

The coalition members set aside individual organizational interests for specialized forms of tax cuts in favor of a unified, classwide approach in support of Bush's plan. Jerry Jasinowski, president of NAM, pointed out that "loading up the bill with too many [special] provisions could doom it." He emphasized the need for business unity and said, "We need to be very judicious and forego trying to add a lot of things to this bill because it will just be seen as a corporate Christmas tree."[200] The coalition's objective was simply to get the Bush plan through Congress. As Dirk Van Dongen, president of the National Association of Wholesalers-Distributors, said, "Our goal is to mobilize grass roots on behalf of the package. We welcome into membership in the coalition any organization or corporation that will take the pledge [to support Bush's package]." Other corporate trade groups that were considering lobbying efforts to add specialized tax cuts to the bill, which might have complicated congressional support for it, were waved off by the coalition.[201] Based on the end results and the final form of the law, it is clear the coalition was a major political force behind the successful classwide campaign in favor of the 2001 act.

Classwide Campaigns and Tax Reform: 2002 to 2006

As was the case with the 2001 tax reductions, superclass interests prevailed as additional federal tax cuts were enacted in the 2002–2006 period. Our focus here is on four major tax laws enacted during this period that cut taxes for individuals and corporations. Each of these four major tax cuts rewarded the classwide lobbying efforts and campaign finance contributions of the superclass.[202] The two tax cuts for individuals were the Jobs and Growth Tax Relief and Reconciliation Act of 2003 (JGTRRA) and the Tax Increase Prevention and Reconciliation Act of 2005 (TIPRA—signed by President Bush on May 17, 2006).[203] The JGTRRA was "the third largest [tax cut] in U.S. history" and largely benefited wealthy taxpayers.[204] It cut the top tax rate to 15 percent on both capital gains (from 20 percent) and stock dividends (from 35 percent) and "accelerated the 2001 rate cut for top income brackets."[205] A 2006 analysis of the JGTRRA revealed that 71 percent of the economic benefits of this law went to individuals with annual incomes over $200,000, and nearly 43 percent of the capital gains and dividend cuts went to tax filers with incomes over $1 million.[206] The TIPRA extended the capital gains and stock dividend tax cuts enacted in 2003 by the JGTRRA through 2010.[207]

The two corporate tax-cut laws were the Job Creation and Worker Assistance Act of 2002 (JCWAA) and the 2004 American Jobs Creation Act (AJCA); both clearly favored superclass interests. Although the 2002 law provided workers with additional unemployment insurance benefits totaling $14 billion, U.S. corporations were the biggest winners, receiving $114 billion in tax cuts.[208] The 2004 AJCA was a follow-on to the 2002 JCWAA. It was supported by 428 major U.S. corporations and trade associations (including the Business Roundtable, NAM, and the U.S. Chamber of Commerce).[209] The AJCA provided "$137 billion in new tax breaks for corporate America."[210] The classwide nature of this corporate tax cut (like the 2002 act) was evident in that "almost every industry in America received special favors."[211]

As we noted, the extraordinary economic benefits of the tax cuts in 2001, 2003, and 2006 for individual taxpayers went almost entirely to members of the superclass and to a lesser extent to those in the credentialed class. At the same time, the economic benefits of the 2002 and 2004 corporate tax cuts benefited, almost exclusively, superclass members who own and control most corporate stock and receive most forms of corporate-distributed income.[212] By the midpoint of Bush's second term, his administration had facilitated the enactment of tax cuts that will total at least $1.65 trillion by 2010 plus another $1.6 trillion by 2016 if the tax cuts are made permanent.[213] As we have seen, virtually all of these enormous tax breaks have been, and will be, provided to wealthy taxpayers either directly, through reductions in superclass members' personal taxes, or indirectly, through reductions in corporate taxes, which increase funds available to corporate boards and officers for distribution to company executives and wealthy shareholders.[214] Final tax-savings score for the 1986–2006 period: privileged class, trillions of dollars; new working class, chump change.

Taxploitation and Spendsploitation

As we noted earlier, the new working class comprises some 80 percent of Americans with limited capital resources and with a share of total economic output that is small and declining. As the history of federal tax and spending policies illustrates, not only does this group have little influence in the shaping of national policies, it is increasingly exploited by policies governing how taxes are collected from individuals and corporations and by the ways in which government spends tax revenues.

Of course, the policies directing how government taxes and spends do not have to be exploitative. For example, tax rates could be used to remedy the high levels of income and wealth inequalities in the United States today by levying higher tax rates on corporations and wealthy individuals. The money raised by such policies could be spent on public goods that improve opportunities for, and the economic well-being of, the nonprivileged. Better schools, national health insurance, government-financed higher education, reconstruction of public infrastructure facilities, and job creation, training, and placement are all examples of public goods that could be financed by funds raised through higher taxes on the privileged class. As it now stands, goods that potentially could be publicly funded, such as health care and higher education, must be purchased by most Americans from their earnings, but most of the nonprivileged can barely afford these goods. Thus, tax and spending policies in the United States do not function to redistribute wealth and income but rather extend their misdistribution and concentration.

In the United States today, national (as well as state and local) tax laws and spending policies are dictated by the wealthy and powerful through both class-wide and interest-group lobbying. As we have seen, these lobbying efforts are very effective because they are driven by the same groups that are centrally involved in the financing of most political campaigns. Thus, the ways that tax dollars are collected and distributed are not only not redistributive, but they collect an increasing share of taxes from the nonprivileged and spend the money in ways that disproportionately benefit the privileged. We should think of superclass-dominated national tax and spending policies as examples of *taxploitation* and *spendsploitation*, two types of exploitation that compound the more general levels of wealth and income inequality.

We illustrate these forms of exploitation with three figures depicting "American pies." The basic idea of the "Wealth Pie" shown in figure 4.2 was introduced in our chapter 1 discussion of wealth inequalities in the United States. It shows that in 2004, the richest 20 percent of Americans controlled about 91 percent of the financial wealth of the country, meaning ownership of stocks, bonds, and commercial real estate. The other 80 percent of Americans held the remaining 9 percent of total wealth.[215] This means that about 120 million workers (80 percent of the total U.S. labor force in 2007) work every day throughout their entire adult lives producing wealth that goes largely to others, while they receive a few "crumbs" from the pie themselves. The extraordinary extent of wealth inequality in the United States could be reduced if the wealthy were required to pay higher tax rates on their incomes and assets and if they were prevented from transferring their wealth to their children. But as we have seen, that is not the way U.S. tax and inheritance laws have been written.

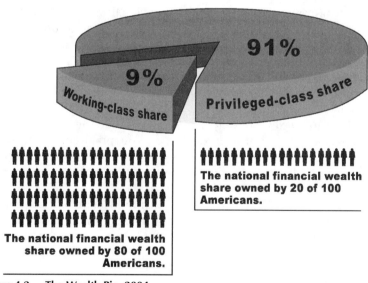

Figure 4.2.   The Wealth Pie, 2004
Source: Kennickell 2006, 29; Wolff 2004, 30.

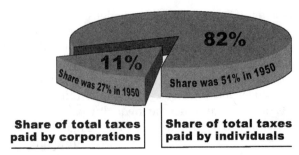

Figure 4.3.   The Tax Pie, 2007

Note: The amounts shown in the diagram do not total 100 percent because other forms of taxes were collected. However, these other forms include taxes (such as excise) that are typically paid by individuals.
Thus, the individual share shown in the diagram is lower than the actual shares paid by individuals.

Source: Office of Management and Budget 2007.

The "Tax Pie" (figure 4.3) illustrates the share of total taxes paid by individuals and corporations. In 2007, the share of total federal tax revenues paid by
U.S. corporations through corporate income taxes was estimated to be 11 percent. This figure is down sharply from the 27 percent share corporations paid
in 1950. By contrast, in 2007 the taxes paid by individuals (individual income
taxes plus Social Security and Medicare taxes) made up an estimated 82 percent of federal tax revenues. This figure is up sharply from the 51 percent share
paid by individuals in 1950.[216]

But as we have already noted, not all individual taxpayers get the same
breaks from federal tax policies. Take the case of Social Security. In 2007,
nearly all American workers paid about 7.7 percent of the first $97,500 in an-
nual earnings to the Social Security fund.[217] However, in 2007, more than 90
percent of American workers earned less than $97,500 annually, so they paid
Social Security taxes on 100 percent of their earned incomes.[218] In contrast,
privileged-class Americans who earned $200,000 or $2 million in 2007 also
paid Social Security taxes, but only on $97,500 of their income. So, the non-
privileged pay taxes on all of their income, and the privileged pay taxes on a
small percentage of their income. But at payout time, the rich still collect their
full Social Security checks, even though they are likely to still have incomes in
the range of hundreds of thousands of dollars.

The U.S. Tax Code is filled with ways for rich individuals and corporations
to reduce their taxes (often to less than zero), while working-class Americans
make up for these lost taxes.[219] The reason for this is simple: the tax code is
written by the privileged class and for the privileged class, who justify their advantaged status with the widely shared ideological aphorism "when the rich
do well, everyone does well." Why would this be the case? Because, as the rest
of the story goes, the rich invest their money, which in turn creates more jobs

and more wealth shared by all Americans. This fairy tale, akin to the former divine right of kings myth, was invented by the superclass, seconded by the credentialed class, widely believed by the working class, and turned into law by Congress. Congress is receptive to this tale because most of its members are either already among the rich or are on the make, and the superclass provides them with huge political campaign contributions and lobby gifts to influence their votes on taxes.

The crash-and-burn reality of this fairy tale propagated by the privileged class is evident every year at tax time, when thousands of corporations and wealthy individuals escape taxes. For 2003 (the most recent year available), of the 2,536,439 income tax returns for filers with adjusted gross incomes (AGIs) of $200,000 or more, there were 2,824 "returns without U.S. income tax." In 2003, 152,324 tax returns in the highest income bracket (AGIs $200,000 or more) had an "effective tax rate" of less than 15 percent. Most taxpayers with AGIs over $200,000 paid tax rates between 15 and 25 percent in 2003.[220] These levels were not much above the rates paid by average wage earners. For example, households in the middle-income fifth (average pretax incomes of $51,900) were taxed at an effective federal tax rate of 13.6 percent in 2003 (income taxes, Medicare, and Social Security).[221] Such tax inequalities exist because the rich enjoy a variety of special exemptions, deductions, and other favored rules written into the tax code by our generous and understanding legislators.

Figure 4.4 presents two "redistribution pies," which provide vivid illustrations of how the largely privileged-class members of Congress choose to spend the tax dollars that are collected. However, before we look at figure 4.4, we should note that large chunks of federal spending are legally mandated and are not subject to annual congressional review. For example, Social Security payments to retired Americans (now under attack) and interest payments on the national debt (never under attack) are forms of entitlement spending that cannot be avoided. But in recent years, discretionary spending on "welfare programs," such as Aid to Families with Dependent Children (AFDC) and food stamps, has come under attack by both Democrats and Republicans.

In the mid-1990s, a majority of both parties in both houses of Congress voted to "end welfare as we know it," and in August 1996 President Clinton signed the Personal Responsibility and Work Opportunity Act. The new law ended the AFDC program and replaced it with the Temporary Assistance to Needy Families (TANF) program. Among other things, the 1996 law ended the federal guarantee of cash assistance to poor families, set time limits on how long families can receive assistance from TANF funds (sixty months), mandated 22 percent cuts in food stamps and Supplemental Security Income over the first six years, and instituted penalties to states that do not force substantial portions of their adult TANF recipients into narrowly defined work programs.[222]

Figure 4.4.   The Redistribution Pie, 2007

Note: Temporary Assistance to Needy Families (TANF) is the current federal program providing cash assistance to poor families. In 1997 it replaced the previous Aid to Families with Dependent Children (AFDC) federal program.

Source: Office of Management and Budget 2007.

Although AFDC was the primary federal "welfare program" of last resort providing cash assistance to the poorest of poor American families, it accounted for less than 1 percent of annual federal expenditures. The TANF program that replaced AFDC cost taxpayers about $17.5 billion in 2007, which amounted to less than 1 percent of the total $2.7 trillion federal budget for that fiscal year.[223] It is instructive to compare the political attacks on, and the media attention devoted to, "welfare dependency" to almost exactly opposite reactions where the total 2007 U.S. defense budget of $527 billion is concerned (up from $348 billion in 2002).[224] In fact, total annual federal defense spending is actually much higher than the 2007 budget estimate. This is the case because in 2006 Congress passed supplemental spending bills totaling $120 billion to fund the wars in Iraq and Afghanistan, and more "supplemental spending" is likely in 2007 and beyond.[225]

Figure 4.4 illustrates the relative size of federal "wealthfare" spending (the defense budget) versus federal welfare (TANF) appropriations for 2007. Of course, some portion of defense spending is legitimate on the grounds of protecting U.S. national security (though how much is open to debate). But large chunks of defense spending exist primarily to juice the profits of military contractor firms and to feed the hundreds of thousands of highly paid scientists, engineers, and civilian employees who work in government, industry, and university research and administration units throughout the "national security state."[226] In short, the superclass and their credentialed-class allies are the principal beneficiaries of much defense spending. Consequently, we do not see political attacks on, or hear media complaints about, the "dependency" induced by defense spending.

There is no national debate over the defense "wealthfare" for the privileged class (or other forms of wealthfare), because this group has strong lobbies in Washington, and its members control the major media and educational institutions. But no one lobbies for the poor. As Bob Dole (Republican candidate for president in 1996) once said, "poor people don't have a PAC." All they do is irritate the rich by their presence—and sometimes serve as a convenient scapegoat to blame for the fading fortunes of the working class. But poor people do not vote and they have no political clout, so their programs are cut while defense spending continues to grow—even in a post–Cold War world.

It is clear that classwide lobbying helps juice federal spending in ways that ensure the privileged class gets large shares of the American pie. True, as Ringo Starr once sang, "You know it don't come easy." Keeping the federal cash spigot open requires that the superclass funnel millions of dollars to prime the congressional pump. Classwide political-campaign financing and classwide lobbying practices are expensive. But for the superclass and its credentialed-class allies, the tax and spending payoffs are huge.

SUPERCLASS INTERESTS, POLITICAL POWER, AND LEGITIMACY

> The upper class . . . is a dominant class . . . because the cumulative effect of its various distributive powers leads to a situation where its policies are generally accepted by most Americans.
>
> —G. William Domhoff, *Who Rules America? Power, Politics and Social Change*, 2006

The superclass has always had critical interests in controlling politics and government. These political interests are logical extensions of its economic interests. Superclass control over great wealth has historically provided this group with a critical resource for influencing the selection and election of political candidates, the electoral process, and policy formation, implementation, and enforcement. As we have seen, superclass funding of candidates leads to powerful influence over elected lawmakers and helps ensure superclass dominance over the formation and implementation of laws and public policies as well as major appointments to the state bureaucratic apparatus. Under this system, the state becomes a vehicle for legitimating existing class-power relationships and the production and distribution of wealth. Laws governing incorporation, corporate rights, taxes, and the regulation of labor markets ensure the dominance and legitimacy of large corporate enterprises in the economy. The stamp of state legitimacy, combined with ancillary laws and regulations, affords corporations effective control over workers' terms of employment and control over the production and distribution of wealth for elite owners. Completing the circle of power, corporate-generated wealth provides superclass members with the economic resources they need to access and dominate the political process and the state.

Although economic wealth and the shadow political industry provide the superclass with the structural foundation facilitating its domination of politics and government, this arrangement is inconsistent with American democratic ideals. Superclass domination of the political and economic arenas is contradicted by widely shared democratic values and equal-opportunity ideals. Left unaddressed, these contradictions could lead working-class members to call into question the legitimacy of the U.S. political and economic systems. However, superclass-owned organizations that make up the information industry have developed control processes that help obscure, and thereby reduce, the tensions generated by the clash between economic and political realities and cultural ideals. These control processes help minimize the prospects of a "crisis of legitimacy" for superclass-controlled economic and political institutions. The next chapter explores the role played by the information industry in maintaining the legitimacy of superclass power.

CLASS ISSUES IN THE MEDIA:
U.S. ELECTIONS AND THE CLASS TABOO

As we noted in chapter 2, U.S. politicians typically avoid class-based rhetoric, and few openly express support for redistributive public policies (such as tax law changes) that would advance the collective interests of the working class at the expense of the privileged class. National political candidates are encouraged to be silent on class-based policies that would favor workers by privileged-class media pundits, business leaders, and most wealthy political contributors. These groups encourage candidates, especially Democrats, to support policies that will benefit the affluent and large corporations (e.g., "free trade" and tax cuts for elites) and to present them in their campaigns as if they promote the interests of all Americans.[1] Since candidates are expected to appeal to all Americans, groups that enforce the "no class rule" in the media and in politics are often willing to tolerate a "middle-class" exception to the taboo, as we noted in chapter 2. This means some discussion and debate of very broadly defined "middle-class" issues and interests is permitted in political campaigns within the boundaries of the political "center."

Candidates are pressured to be "centrist" unifiers rather than divisive "pro–working class warriors." This was certainly the case in the 2006 midterm elections. The magazine *Extra!* (published by the media watchdog group FAIR) pointed out that "centrism [was] the dominant message of national political pundits and journalists—at least for Democrats. . . . Many of the most prominent political journalists in the country have made it their business to press the Democrats to move the party rightward."[2] Pressures on candidates to move to the center also came from within the Democratic Party. Following the 2006 elections, the *Washington Post* reported "top Democrats told their members they cannot allow the party's liberal wing to dominate the agenda next year."[3] The "move to the center" message is important because such a shift increases political support for, and reduces opposition to, superclass-favored policies.

Many Democrats running for national offices in the 2006 elections observed the class taboo and ran on centrist economic policy positions. Even so, by one estimate, "100 or more [Democratic] candidates ran aggressively on liberal or populist economic issues—against unregulated free trade and the offshoring of American jobs, against special interests, corporate excesses, and social issues."[4] Does this mean that the 2006 elections witnessed a major breakdown of the class taboo? Perhaps not. Most Democratic candidates who campaigned in support of populist-style economic policies framed their message, like winning Senate candidate Sherrod Brown in Ohio, as "fighting for the middle class."[5] However, even candidates sympathetic to working-class interests like Brown, Senator-elect Bernie Sanders (I-VT), and others kept low profiles when it came to television ads and conflicting class interests. As one reporter observed, "not a single candidate . . . appears to have run a TV ad that features a commitment to confronting America's top-heavy distribution of wealth and income."[6]

The Democrats won control of both houses of Congress in the 2006 elections in large part because of public concerns with, and dissatisfaction over, both the Iraq war and the lackluster performance of the U.S. economy where "middle-class" interests were concerned.[7] Regarding the latter issue, one postelection report observed that "the hidden story of the election was the appeal of economic populism in a country whose middle class is increasingly feeling the squeeze."[8] While many Democratic candidates in 2006 ran on populist-style pledges of support for the "middle class,"[9] few campaigned openly for policies that would *redistribute* substantial economic resources to the working class at the expense of the privileged class. From this perspective, it appears the class taboo remained largely intact in the 2006 elections.

In the 2004 presidential campaign, the major candidates stuck, for the most part, to the "no class warfare" script. While the election was rich with possibilities for the development of class-based political messages, President Bush and his supporters successfully focused the campaign primarily on noneconomic issues: presidential leadership, the "war on terror," patriotism (support for U.S. troops in Iraq and Afghanistan), and the so-called moral issues—"God, guns, and gays."[10] Much of the campaign centered around which candidate would be the better "manager"—of the war on terror, the insurgency in Iraq, U.S. morality, and, last but not least, the so-called economic recovery. As one critic of both John Kerry and President Bush put it, "Kerry offer[ed] himself mainly as a more competent manager of the Bush agenda."[11]

With economic concerns reduced largely to management issues, only relatively minor exceptions to the class taboo were apparent in the campaign. One example occurred after Democratic presidential nominee John Kerry selected John Edwards as his vice presidential running mate. Edwards was viewed by many mainstream media

(*continued*)

pundits as too sympathetic to working-class interests, and following his selection by Kerry, "powerful newspapers fired warning shots across the bow of the Kerry-Edwards campaign."[12] A *Washington Post* editorial criticized Edwards's support for protectionist trade policies and cautioned against "veering into class warfare."[13] The *New York Times* described Edwards as "the happy class warrior, the smoothest divisive force in politics today."[14] Edwards's media treatment led FAIR to comment, "In the media world view, economic populism is like a dog that must be housebroken and kept on a leash. Sometimes, to maintain discipline, it needs to be whacked on the nose with a newspaper."[15]

Kerry, the ultimate centrist candidate, easily avoided running afoul of the no class rule. He was reminded during the primary campaigns that significant political risks are associated with even minor violations of the unwritten class rule as many mainstream media pundits encouraged him to "move to the right, abandon progressive stances and occupy the political center."[16] For the most part, he followed this advice. While Kerry and Edwards did make occasional populistlike rhetorical references in some of their speeches (e.g., Edwards's use of the "two Americas" theme), these were exceptions, and such references were overshadowed by the centrist themes and policy references that dominated their political messages during the campaign.[17]

Independent presidential candidate Ralph Nader, who campaigned in 2004 on a variety of policies supportive of working-class interests, found his policy views, and indeed his entire campaign, marginalized by the mainstream media. However, in contrast to the 2000 campaign, when pundits often condemned Nader's class-based policy positions, in 2004 most of the mainstream media simply ignored his policy positions. When Nader's views were reported, they were often treated as pronouncements from a predictable crank and grump—not to be confused with the views of "legitimate candidates." A *New York Times* "postmortem" of Nader's candidacy reflected how the mainstream media reported on his campaign. First, the reporter noted, "His platform never drew much attention, in part because of the distraction of some Democrats' fight to keep Mr. Nader off the ballot in key states."[18] Second, consistent with media portrayals of Nader's views as out of touch with those of most Americans, the reporter emphasized Nader's "diminishing relevance": "At . . . less than one-sixth of his 2000 vote total . . . [t]he returns seemed to repudiate Mr. Nader's argument that many Americans are looking for a progressive alternative to the two major parties. . . . His increasingly lonely, almost quixotic stance brings to mind . . . the image of Old Testament Prophets."[19]

Examples of consequences for presidential candidates who violate the no class rule were perhaps more readily apparent in the two races that preceded 2004, viz, the 1996 reactionary populist presidential campaign of Pat Buchanan, the 2000 progressive populist campaign of Nader, and to a lesser extent Al Gore's 2000 campaign (see chapter 8).[20] But regardless of the election year, the lesson is the same: candidates who call attention to class-based inequalities and/or propose remedies that would transfer resources from the privileged class to the working class become predictable lightning rods for attacks from privileged-class members in the media, political, and business arenas.

A final illustration of privileged-class-based efforts to steer political candidates away from violating the class taboo concerns the 2008 presidential election. Two years before the 2008 election, the mainstream media began reminding Democratic contenders that centrism was the only viable position for a presidential bid. The "only a centrist Democratic candidate has any chance to win in 2008" message was repeated by reporters and pundits such as Andrea Mitchell (NBC), Howard Fineman (*Newsweek*), David Broder (*Washington Post*), and the editors of the *Tampa Tribune*.[21] This was the case *despite* the popularity of populist economic policies among many voters as revealed by public-opinion polls and by election victories in 2006 by candidates who campaigned on such policies.[22] It is clear that media elites and other credentialed-class supporters of superclass interests can be counted on in 2008—and beyond—to enforce the class taboo and pressure presidential candidates to avoid running as advocates for the economic interests of the working class.

NOTES

1. Peter Hart and Steve Rendall, "Move Over—Over and Over," *Extra!* (July–August 2006): 12.

2. Hart and Rendall, "Move Over—Over and Over," 12.

3. Peter Baker and Jim VandeHei, "A Voter Rebuke for Bush, the War and the Right," *Washington Post*, November 8, 2006, A1.

4. William Greider, "Watershed," *Nation* (December 4, 2006): 16.

5. Christopher Hayes, "The New Democratic Populism," *Nation* (December 4, 2006): 13.

6. Sam Pizzigati, "Campaign 2006: A Glaringly Missing Issue," *Too Much* (November 3, 2006): 3.

7. David Corn, "And Now, Iraq," *Nation* (November 27, 2006): 5; Christopher Hayes, "The New Democratic Populism," 11; Jane Bryant Quinn, "The Economic Perception Gap," *Newsweek* (November 20, 2006): 59.

8. Hayes, "The New Democratic Populism," 11.

9. William Greider, "Watershed," *Nation* (December 4, 2006): 14–18; Jim Hightower and Jim Frazer, "It Was a 'Throw the Bums Out' and a 'Change America's Direction' Election," *Lowdown* (December 2006): 1–4; John Nichols, "The 'Seattle Senators,'" *Nation* (December 18, 2006): 8–10; Louis Uchitelle, "Here Come the Economic Populists," *New York Times*, November 26, 2006, 1.4.

10. Robert L. Borosage and Katrina vanden Heuvel, "Progressives: Get Ready to Fight," *Nation* (November 29, 2004): 13.

11. Alexander Cockburn, "Presidential Elections: Not as Big a Deal as They Say," *CounterPunch* (June 16–30, 2004): 5.

12. Norman Solomon, "Media Fires Shots across Edwards' Bow," *Extra!Update* (August 2004): 1.

13. "Mr. Kerry's Choice," *Washington Post*, July 7, 2004, A18.

14. William Safire, "The Body Politic Will Reject a 'Charisma Transplant,'" *New York Times*, July 7, 2004, 21.

15. Solomon, "Media Fires Shots across Edwards' Bow."

16. Peter Hart, "Move to the Right! Pundits' Advice for Kerry Has a Familiar Ring," *Extra!Update* (June 2004): 1.

17. David Moberg, "Election Reflection," *In These Times* (December 13, 2004): 23, 37.

18. Scott Shane, "Nader Is Left with Fewer Votes, and Friends, after '04 Race," *New York Times*, November 4, 2004, A13.

19. Shane, "Nader Is Left with Fewer Votes, and Friends, after '04 Race," A13.

20. Robert Perrucci and Earl Wysong, *The New Class Society: Goodbye American Dream?* 2nd ed. (Lanham, MD: Rowman & Littlefield, 2003), 45–46.

21. Hart and Rendall, "Move Over—Over and Over," 16.

22. Hart and Rendall, "Move Over—Over and Over," 16.

NOTES

1. Quoted in Vicente Navarro, "Medical History as Justification Rather Than Explanation: A Critique of Starr's *The Social Transformation of American Medicine,*" *International Journal of Health Services* 14 (1984): 516.

2. Gore Vidal, "The End of History," *Nation* (September 30, 1996): 11–18.

3. G. William Domhoff, *State Autonomy or Class Dominance?* (New York: Aldine de Gruyter, 1996), 25; G. William Domhoff, *Who Rules America? Power, Politics and Social Change,* 5th ed. (Boston: McGraw-Hill, 2006), 103–107.

4. Ben H. Bagdikian, *The New Media Monopoly* (Boston: Beacon Press, 2004), 27–54; Doug Donovan and Peter Kafka, "Hosts with the Most," *Forbes* (March 19, 2001): 164–66; Julie Hollar, Janine Jackson, and Hilary Goldstein, "Outside (and Inside) Influence on the News: Fear and Favor 2005," *Extra!* (March–April 2006): 15–20; Mark Lloyd, "Lessons for Realistic Radicals in the Information Age," in *The Future of Media: Resistance and Reform in the 21st Century,* ed. Robert McChesney, Russell Newman, and Ben Scott (New York: Seven Stories Press, 2005), 73–95; Robert W. McChesney, *Rich Media, Poor Democracy* (Chicago: University of Illinois Press, 1999), 48–62.

5. Val Burris, "The Myth of Old Money Liberalism: The Politics of the *Forbes* 400 Richest Americans," *Social Problems* 47 (2000): 360–78; Domhoff, *Who Rules America?* 49–75; Michael C. Dreiling, "The Class Embeddedness of Corporate Political Action: Leadership in Defense of the NAFTA," *Social Problems* 47 (2000): 21–48; Jeff Faux, *The Global Class War: How America's Bipartisan Elite Lost Our Future—and What It Will Take to Win It Back* (New York: Wiley, 2006); David Harvey, *A Brief History of Neoliberalism* (New York: Oxford University Press, 2005); Alan Neustadtl and Dan Clawson, "Corporate Political Groupings: Does Ideology Unify Business Political Behavior?" *American Sociological Review* 53 (1988): 172–90; Maynard S. Seider, "American Big Business Ideology: A Content Analysis of Executive Speeches," *American Sociological Review* 39 (1974): 802–15; Richard L. Zweigenhaft and G. William Domhoff, *Diversity in the Power Elite: Have Women and Minorities Reached the Top?* (New Haven, CT: Yale University Press, 1998), 192–94.

6. It should be noted that not all superclass and credentialed-class members share the view that the economic and political status quo is fair and just. For example, members of the organization known as Responsible Wealth explicitly disavow such views. "Responsible Wealth is a national network of business people, investors and affluent Americans who are concerned about the deepening wealth divide in America and who advocate widespread prosperity." United for a Fair Economy, "Wealthy Say, 'No, Thanks' to Tax Cuts" (press release, April 6, 2005), on the Internet at http://www.faireconomy.org/press/2005/ResponsibleTax Pledgepr.html (visited May 15, 2006).

7. David Hammer, "Pressured, Ohio's Ney Resigns from Congress," *Indianapolis Star,* November 4, 2006, A4; Craig Holman, "For Real Lobbying Reform, Stop the Flow of Money," *Public Citizen News* (March–April 2006): 1, 4; Michael Isikoff, "On DeLay's Trail: The E-mail Factor," *Newsweek* (April 10, 2006); Michael Isikoff, Holly Bailey, and Evan Thomas, "A Washington Tidal Wave," *Newsweek* (January 16, 2006): 40–43; Conor Kenny, "Capital Crimes," *In These Times* (August 2006): 20–25; "Disgraced Republicans," *Nation* (October 23, 2006): 3.

8. CBS News/*New York Times* poll, January 20–25, 2006, 29.

9. Source Watch, "Lobbying," on the Internet at http://www.sourcewatch.org/index.php?title=Lobbying (visited May 21, 2006).

10. District of Columbia Bar, "2004–2005 Annual Report," on the Internet at http://www.dcbar.org/inside_the_bar/structure (visited May 21, 2006); District of Columbia Bar, "Attorney Resources," on the Internet at http://www.dcbar.org/attorney_resources/index.html (visited July 8, 2001).

11. The number of lobbyists in 1998 is from Center for Responsive Politics, "Summary," in *Influence, Inc.* (Washington, DC: Center for Responsive Politics, 2000), 1, 3; the number of lobbyists in 2005 is from Political Money Line, "Federal Lobby Directory: Individual Lobbyists," on the Internet at http://www.fecinfo.com (visited January 15, 2006).

12. Center for Responsive Politics, "Summary," 1, 3.

13. Jeffrey H. Birnbaum, *The Lobbyists* (New York: Times Books, 1992); Alex Knott, "Industry of Influence Nets More Than $10 Billion," 3, on the Internet at http://www.publicintegrity.org/lobby/report.aspx?aid=675 (visited May 21, 2006); Kevin Phillips, "Fat City," *Time* (September 26, 1994): 51.

14. Lobby expenditures (1990s) are from Center for Responsive Politics, "Summary," 1; lobby expenditures (2005) are from Political Money Line, "Money in Politics Databases: Overall Spending for Federal Lobbying," on the Internet at http://www.fecinfo.com (visited January 15, 2006).

15. Knott, "Industry of Influence Nets More Than $10 Billion."

16. Knott, "Industry of Influence Nets More Than $10 Billion"; Source Watch, "Lobbying."

17. Jeffrey H. Birnbaum, "The Road to Riches Is Called K Street," *Washington Post*, June 22, 2005, A1; Allan Shuldiner and Tony Raymond, *Who's in the Lobby? A Profile of Washington's Influence Industry* (Washington, DC: Center for Responsive Politics, 1998), 7–19.

18. Dan Clawson, Alan Neustadtl, and Denise Scott, *Money Talks* (New York: Basic Books, 1992), 182; "The Fortune 1000 Ranked within Industries," *Fortune* (April 17, 2006): F44–F67.

19. Birnbaum, "The Road to Riches Is Called K Street," A1; also see Domhoff, *Who Rules America?* 153–54, 167–71; Phillips, "Fat City," 52.

20. Center for Responsive Politics, *Influence, Inc.; National Trade and Professional Associations of the United States* (Washington, DC: Columbia Books, 2006); Kay L. Schlozman and John T. Tierney, *Organized Interests and American Democracy* (New York: Harper and Row, 1986), 77.

21. Domhoff, *Who Rules America?* 114, 174; also see BKSH, "United States—The Company" and "Our Perspective," 2006, on the Internet at http://www.bksh.com (visited November 27, 2006).

22. Burson-Marsteller, "About Us—Family of Companies," 2006, on the Internet at http://www.burson-marsteller.com/pages/about/companies (visited November 27, 2006).

23. WWP, "Annual Report and Accounts 2005," 2, on the Internet at http://www.wwp.com (visited November 27, 2006).

24. Clawson, Neustadtl, and Scott, *Money Talks*, 182; Domhoff, *Who Rules America?* 18–30.

25. Domhoff, *Who Rules America?* 74–75; also see Arthur B. Kennickell, "Currents and Undercurrents: Changes in the Distribution of Wealth, 1989–2004," U.S. Federal Reserve System, January 30, 2006, 23, on the Internet at http://www.federalreserve.gov/pubs/oss/oss2/scfindex.html (visited May 16, 2006); Chuck Collins, "Horatio Alger Where Are You?" *Dollars and Sense* (January–February 1997), 9; S. M. Miller, "Born on Third Base: The Sources of Wealth of the 1996 *Forbes* 400," United for a Fair Economy, February 1997, 5–6.

26. Domhoff, *Who Rules America?* 72.

27. G. William Domhoff, *Who Rules America? Power and Politics*, 4th ed. (Boston: McGraw-Hill, 2002), 27, 58, 63; also see Richard L. Zweigenhaft, "Making Rags out of Riches," *Extra!* (January–February 2004): 27–28.

28. Thomas Dye, *Who's Running America? The Clinton Years* (Englewood Cliffs, NJ: Prentice Hall, 1995), 175; Domhoff, *Who Rules America?*, 5th ed., 72–74.

29. Domhoff, *State Autonomy or Class Dominance*, 1996, 25; Domhoff, *Who Rules America?*, 5th ed., 63–65; Harold R. Kerbo, *Social Stratification and Inequality*, 6th ed. (New York: McGraw-Hill, 2006), 392.

30. Birnbaum, "The Road to Riches Is Called K Street"; Louis Dubose, "Bush's Hitman," *Nation* (March 5, 2001): 11–15; Michael Isikoff and Evan Thomas, "Back on the Stand," *Newsweek* (May 8, 2006): 30–31.

31. William Greider, "Born-Again Rubinomics," *Nation* (July 31–August 7, 2006): 20–23.

32. Bush's 2004 receipts are based on Federal Election Commission (FEC) records as reported by the Center for Responsive Politics, "2004 Presidential Election," on the Internet at http://www.opensecrets.org/presidential/index.asp (visited December 12, 2005). Dollar amounts for 2004 winning congressional candidates are reported by the FEC, "Congressional Candidates Spend $1.16 Billion during 2003–2004" (press release, June 9, 2005).

33. Dollar amounts for winning 1996 presidential and congressional candidates: Larry Makinson, *The Big Picture: Money Follows Power Shift on Capitol Hill* (Washington, DC: Center for

Responsive Politics, 1997), 5–6. By comparison, George W. Bush's 2000 presidential campaign cost $193 million, and winning Senate and House candidates in 2000 spent an average of $7.2 million and $837,083 on their campaigns. *Source:* Center for Responsive Politics, "2000 Election Overview, Stats at a Glance: Congressional Races," "2000 Presidential Race: Total Raised and Spent," on the Internet at http://www.opensecrets.org/2000elect/index/AllCands.htm (visited July 29, 2001).

34. FEC, "Congressional Campaigns Spend $966 Million through Mid October" (press release, November 2, 2006), 1.

35. FEC, "Congressional Campaigns Spend $966 Million through Mid October," 1.

36. Center for Responsive Politics, "Nov. 6 Update," November 8, 2006, and Center for Responsive Politics, "2006 Election Analysis," November 9, 2006, both on the Internet at http://www.opensecrets.org/pressreleases/2006/PreElection/PostElection (visited November 15, 2006).

37. Center for Responsive Politics, "Nov. 6 Update"; Center for Responsive Politics, "2006 Election Analysis"; Julia Malone, "Campaign Was the Most Costly: Near $4 Billion," *Indianapolis Star,* November 7, 2004, A17. For amount spent in 2000, see Eric Bates, "Campaign Inflation," *Mother Jones* (March–April 2001): 48.

38. The 96 percent win rate by the highest fund-raising candidates for the 435 U.S. House and 34 U.S. Senate races in 2004 is based on the authors' analysis of candidates' receipts reported by the FEC, "Summary of General Election Congressional Campaigns 2003–2004," tables "House General Election" and "Six Year Financial Summary for Senate Campaigns through December 31, 2004" (press release, June 9, 2005).

39. The percentages reported for Republican and Democratic candidates in 2004 House campaigns are based on the authors' analysis of candidates' receipts reported in FEC documents: "Congressional Candidates Spend $1.16 Billion during 2003–2004," table "Contributions from Individuals by Size of the Contribution, 2002 and 2004" (press release, June 9, 2005); "PAC Activity Increases for 2004 Elections," table "PAC Contributions to Candidates, 1996 through 2004 Election Cycles" (press release, April 13, 2005). In calculating the percentages, we conservatively estimated that one-half (50 percent) of all 2004 PAC contributions to candidates from PACs the FEC classified as "nonconnected" came from wealthy individuals and/or business interests. This estimate was based on our review of FEC documents regarding the criteria used to classify "Nonconnected Committees" and on our analysis of income sources for a sample of "nonconnected" PACs drawn from 2004 FEC PAC records (see note 73). *Sources:* FEC, *Campaign Guide for Nonconnected Committees* (Washington, D.C., October 2005); FEC, "Advisory Opinions: Non-Affiliations of SSFs," *Record* (February 2005): 4–7; FEC, "2004 PAC Stats" (press release, June 30, 2004).

40. FEC, "Contributions from Individuals by Size of the Contribution, 2002 and 2004."

41. FEC, "Contributions from Individuals by Size of the Contribution, 2002 and 2004."

42. FEC, "FEC History and Mission," 3, on the Internet at http://www.fec.gov/mission.shtml (visited January 23, 2006); "Federal Election Commission, Political Party Committees Donating Funds to Certain Tax-Exempt Organizations and Political Organizations," *Federal Register* (March 16, 2005): 12787–90.

43. FEC, "Campaign Finance Law Quick Reference for Reporters," on the Internet at http://www.fec.gov/press/bkgnd/bcra-overview.shtml (visited May 1, 2006); Center for Public Integrity, "527s in 2004 Shatter Previous Records for Political Fundraising," on the Internet at http://www.publicintegrity.org/527/report.aspx?aid=435 (visited May 21, 2006). U.S. Department of the Treasury, Internal Revenue Service, "Section 527 Political Organizations Revised Tax Filing Requirements" (press release, November 2002); IRS, "IRS Acts to Enforce Reporting and Disclosure by Section 527 Political Groups" (press release, August 19, 2004).

44. FEC, "Campaign Finance Law Quick Reference for Reporters," 1.

45. Derek Willis, "Debating McCain-Feingold," *Congressional Quarterly* (March 10, 2001): 524–27.

46. Clawson, Neustadtl, and Scott, *Money Talks,* 11; Public Campaign, *Hard Facts on Hard Money* (Washington, DC: Public Campaign, 2001), 4.

47. This summary of features included in the 2002 BCRA is based on information from several sources, including FEC, "Campaign Finance Law Quick Reference for Reporters"; Center for Responsive Politics, "Federal Campaign Finance Law: Contribution Limits," on the Internet at http://www.opensecrets.org/basics/law/index.asp (visited May 16, 2006); Jan Witold Baran and Carol A. Lanham, "Corporations and PACS: More Important Than Ever," *Metropolitan Corporate Counsel* (July 2004): 1–2.

48. Center for Public Integrity, "527s in 2004 Shatter Previous Records for Political Fundraising."

49. Center for Responsive Politics, "Nov. 6 Update," 5.

50. This summary regarding 527 committees is based on information from IRS, "Filing Requirements for Section 527 Organizations," on the Internet at http://www.irs.gov/charities/political (visited May 16, 2006); The Center for Public Integrity, "527 Frequently Asked Questions" and "527s in 2004 Shatter Previous Records for Political Fundraising."

51. FEC, "2004 Presidential Campaign Finance Activity," *Record* (March 2005): 9–11; FEC, "Congressional Candidates Spend $1.16 Billion during 2003–2004" (press release, June 9, 2005); FEC, "PAC Activity Increases for 2004 Elections" (press release, April 13, 2005); FEC, "Party Financial Activity Summarized for the 2004 Election Cycle" (press release, March 2, 2005); Malone, "Campaign Was the Most Costly."

52. FEC, "Contributions from Individuals by Size of the Contribution, 2002 and 2004"; Center for Responsive Politics, "Campaign Contributions, 2003–2004," on the Internet at http://www.opensecrets.org/overview/DonorDemographics.asp?cycle=2004 (visited May 16, 2006).

53. Dollar amounts listed are based on the authors' calculations using information reported by the FEC, "Contributions from Individuals by Size of the Contribution, 2002 and 2004."

54. FEC, "Contributions from Individuals by Size of the Contribution, 2002 and 2004."

55. Dollar amounts and percentages are based on the authors' calculations using information reported by the FEC, "Financial Activity of All Congressional Candidates—1992–2004."

56. Spencer Overton, "The Donor Class: Campaign Finance, Democracy, and Participation," *University of Pennsylvania Law Review* 153 (2004): 76.

57. U.S. Department of Commerce, *Statistical Abstract of the United States: 2006* (Washington, DC: U.S. Government Printing Office, 2005), 459, 467.

58. Center for Responsive Politics, "Campaign Contributions, 2003–2004: Donors," on the Internet at http://www.opensecrets.org/overview/DonorDemographics.asp?cycle=2004 (visited May 16, 2006).

59. Public Campaign, *Hard Facts on Hard Money*, 1.

60. Ellen Miller and Randy Kehler, "Mischievous Myths about Money in Politics," *Dollars and Sense* (July–August 1996): 23.

61. Center for Responsive Politics, "Campaign Contributions, 2003–2004: Donors."

62. Micah L. Sifry and Nancy Watzman, *Is That a Politician in Your Pocket? Washington on $2 Million a Day* (Hoboken, NJ: John Wiley and Sons, 2004), 13.

63. Center for Responsive Politics, "2004 Election Overview: Top Zip Codes," on the Internet at http://www.opensecrets.org/overview/topzips.asp?cycle=2004 (visited May 16, 2006).

64. Center for Responsive Politics, "2004 Election Overview: Top Individual Contributors," on the Internet at http://www.opensecrets.org/overview/topindivs.asp?cycle=2004 (visited May 16, 2006).

65. Center for Responsive Politics, "2004 Election Overview: Top Individual Contributors."

66. Ted Gup, "The Mother Jones 400," *Mother Jones* (March–April, 1996): 43.

67. "The 400 Home Page, Campaign Inflation," *Mother Jones* (2001): 3, on the Internet at http://www.Motherjones.com/news/special_reports/mojo_400 (visited January 22, 2006).

68. Dollar amounts and percentages are based on the authors' calculations using information reported by the FEC, "Financial Activity of All Congressional Candidates—1992–2004."

69. Percentages listed are based on the authors' calculations using information reported by the FEC, "Congressional Candidates Spend $1.16 Billion during 2003–2004."

70. Val Burris, "The Two Faces of Capital: Corporations and Individual Capitalists as Political Actors," *American Sociological Review* 66 (2001): 378.

71. FEC, "PAC Activity Increases for 2004 Elections," table "PAC Contributions to Candidates, 1996 through 2004 Election Cycles" (press release, April 13, 2005); the percentage is based on the authors' calculations of PAC contributions to congressional candidates as reported in FEC documents and using assumptions described in note 39.

72. Clawson, Neustadtl, and Scott, *Money Talks*, 32–33.

73. Our estimate of more than 3,200 "corporate-dominated PACs" is based on an FEC report that lists 4,184 PACs divided into six categories and on our analysis of the extent to which PACs are governed and funded by privileged-class business owners-managers affiliated with corporate interests. Our estimate of corporate-dominated PACs includes all 1,622 "Corporate" PACs, all 900 "Trade/Member/Health" PACs, all 99 "Corporation w/o Capital Stock" PACs, and at least one-half of all 1,223 "Nonconnected" PACs. *Source:* FEC, *Record*, March 2005, 9.

74. Burris, "The Two Faces of Capital," 369; Domhoff, *Who Rules America?*, 5th ed., 148.

75. Clawson, Neustadtl, and Scott, *Money Talks*, 161.

76. Clawson, Neustadtl, and Scott, *Money Talks*, 140–41.

77. Clawson, Neustadtl, and Scott, *Money Talks*, 181.

78. Clawson, Neustadtl, and Scott, *Money Talks*, 176, 160.

79. FEC, *Record*, March 2005, 9. (Note: This comparison *only* includes corporate-linked PACs identified by FEC categories. If we use our 3,200 corporate-dominated total, labor PACs are outnumbered by business PACs by a 10:1 ratio.)

80. Center for Responsive Politics, "2004 Election Overview: Business-Labor-Ideology Split in PAC and Individual Donations to Candidates and Parties," March 28, 2005, 1, on the Internet at http://www.opensecrets.org/overview (visited December 18, 2005).

81. FEC, "PAC Activity Increases for 2004 Elections," 2.

82. FEC, "PAC Activity Increases for 2004 Elections," 2.

83. Charles Lewis, "The Buying of the President," *Dollars and Sense* (July–August 1996): 28, 41.

84. Center for Responsive Politics, "2004 Election Overview: Business-Labor-Ideology Split in PAC and Individual Donations to Candidates and Parties"; Center for Responsive Politics, "2006 Election Overview: Business-Labor-Ideology Split in PAC and Individual Donations to Candidates and Parties," November, 7, 2006, on the Internet at http://www.opensecrets.org/overview/blio.asp ?cycle=2006 (visited November 18, 2005).

85. John Nichols, "Behind the DLC Takeover," *Progressive* (October 2000): 29.

86. Marty Jezer, "Soft Money, Hard Choices," *Dollars and Sense* (July–August 1996): 30.

87. Alexander Cockburn, "Dems and Dives," *Counterpunch* (March 1–15, 2005): 1–2; Alexander Cockburn and Jeffrey St. Clair, "How Go the Dems?" *Counterpunch* (February 1–15, 2005): 1–2; William Greider, "Rebels," *Nation* (January 9–16, 2006): 16–18; Robin Toner, "Optimistic, Democrats Debate the Party's Vision," *New York Times*, May 9, 2006, A1.

88. Center for Responsive Politics, "Campaign Contributions, 2003–2004: Donors"; Center for Responsive Politics, "2004 Election Overview: Business-Labor-Ideology Split in PAC and Individual Donations to Candidates and Parties"; David Sirota, *Hostile Takeover: How Big Money and Corruption Conquered Our Government—and How We Can Take It Back* (New York: Crown Publishers, 2006).

89. Mark Dudzic, "Time to Abandon Illusions about Democrats," *Labor Party Press* (January–February 2005): 8.

90. Public Campaign, *Hard Facts on Hard Money*, 9.

91. Marc Breslow, "Government of, by, and for the Wealthy," *Dollars and Sense* (July–August 1996): 23–24.

92. Seth Ackerman, "The Most Biased Name in News," *Extra!* (July–August 2001): 10–18; Seth Ackerman, "Selling the Social Security Scare," *Extra!* (January–February 2005): 6; Dean Baker, "Generation Excess," *Extra!* (March–April 1996): 12–13; Charles Derber, *The Wilding of America*, 3rd ed. (New York: Worth, 2004), 92–98; Mike Males, "The Myth of the Grade-School Murderer," *Extra!* (May–June 2001): 30; James Wollman and James McBride, "Medicare Part D Gets an 'F,'" *Dollars and Sense* (January–February 2006): 29–30.

93. Domhoff, *Who Rules America?*, 4th ed., 69–98.

94. Dye, *Who's Running America?* 215; also see Michael Dolny, "What's in a Label?" *Extra!* (May–June 1998): 9–10; David Croteau, "Challenging the 'Liberal Media' Claim," *Extra!* (July–

August 1998): 4–9; David Harvey, *A Brief History of Neoliberalism* (New York: Oxford University Press, 2005).

95. Thomas R. Dye, "Organizing Power for Policy-Planning: The View from the Brookings Institution," in *Power Elites and Organizations*, ed. G. William Domhoff and Thomas R. Dye (Newbury Park, CA: Sage, 1987), 185–86.

96. Dye, "Organizing Power for Policy-Planning," 188.

97. Domhoff, *Who Rules America?*, 4th ed., 78–80.

98. Dye, *Who's Running America?* 222–27.

99. Val Burris, "Elite Policy-Planning Networks in the United States," in *Research in Politics and Society*, vol. 4, *The Political Consequences of Social Networks*, ed. Gwen Moore and J. Allen Whitt (Greenwich, CT: JAI Press, 1992), 115–20.

100. Michael Patrick Allen, "Elite Social Movement Organizations and the State: The Rise of the Conservative Policy-Planning Network," in *Research in Politics and Society*, vol. 4, *The Political Consequences of Social Networks*, ed. Gwen Moore and J. Allen Whitt (Greenwich, CT: JAI Press, 1992), 95.

101. Clawson, Neustadtl, and Scott, *Money Talks*, 139.

102. National Committee for Responsive Philanthropy, "$1 Billion for Ideas: Conservative Think Tanks in the 1990s" (press release, March 12, 1999), 2.

103. The $1 billion–plus spending estimate by twenty-four large conservative think tanks in the 2001–2006 period is based on the authors' calculations using information from multiple sources. These included (1) Thomas B. Edsall, "Rich Liberals Vow to Fund Think Tanks; Aim Is to Compete with Conservatives," *Washington Post*, August 7, 2005, A1, and (2) Annual Reports and Federal Form 990 Income Tax Returns for the twenty-four think tanks.

104. Edsall, "Rich Liberals Vow to Fund Think Tanks." Also see Ari Berman, "Big $$ for Progressive Politics," *Nation* (October 16, 2006): 18–24.

105. Michael Dolny, "Think Tank Survey: Right, Center Think Tanks Still Most Quoted," *Extra!* (May–June 2005): 28–29; Michael Dolny, "Think Tank Survey: Study Finds First Drop in Think Tank Cites," *Extra!* (May–June 2006): 24–25.

106. Responsible Wealth, "Who We Are," July, 7, 2006, on the Internet at http://www.reponsible wealth.org (visited July 22, 2006); United for a Fair Economy, "Victory on Estate Tax," July 6, 2005, on the Internet at http://www.faireconomy.org/press/senate_hr_8.html (visited July 22, 2006). Public Citizen and United for a Fair Economy identified several "super-wealthy families," business organizations, and trade associations involved in a "massive coalition" dedicated to repealing the estate tax. See Robert Yule, "Super-Wealthy Families Try to Repeal Estate Tax," *Public Citizen News* (May–June, 2006): 1, 11; United for a Fair Economy, "Ten Super-Wealthy Anti-Estate Tax Families Listed on Forbes 400" (press release, September 27, 2006).

107. Domhoff, *State Autonomy or Class Dominance?* 34, 38.

108. Domhoff, *State Autonomy or Class Dominance?* 29–32.

109. Kerbo, *Social Stratification and Inequality*, 170–71; also see Domhoff, *Who Rules America?*, 4th ed., 73–78.

110. The Foundation Center, "Top 100 U.S. Foundations by Asset Size," "Top 100 U.S. Foundations by Total Giving," and "Aggregate Fiscal Data by Foundation Type, 2003," on the Internet at http://www.fdncenter.org (visited January 18, 2006).

111. Dye, *Who's Running America?* 11, 135, 171, 192.

112. Kerbo, *Social Stratification and Inequality* ,170; also see Dye, *Who's Running America?* 135.

113. Brookings Institution, "About Brookings," on the Internet at http://www.Brookings.edu/index/about.htm (visited July 12, 2006); also see Brookings Institution, *Annual Report 2005* (Washington, D.C.), 42–43.

114. Brookings Institution, *Annual Report 2005*, 36, 42.

115. Brookings Institution, *Annual Report 2005*, 36–37.

116. Dye, "Organizing Power for Policy-Planning," 183.

117. Dye, *Who's Running America?* 225.

118. Allen, "Elite Social Movement Organizations and the State," 96–97.

119. Edsall, "Rich Liberals Vow to Fund Think Tanks."

120. Robert Parry, "Who Buys the Right?" *Nation* (November 18, 1996): 5–6.

121. National Committee for Responsive Philanthropy, "$1 Billion for Ideas," 1–2. Also see Sam Husseini, "Checkbook Analysis," *Extra!* (May–June 2000): 23–24.

122. Based on the authors' analysis of donations to conservative think tanks by conservative foundations; also see Domhoff, *Who Rules America?* 92.

123. Domhoff, *Who Rules America?*, 5th ed., 93.

124. Business Roundtable, "About Us," on the Internet at http://www.businessroundtable.org//aboutUs/history.aspx (visited July 12, 2006); annual budget figure from U.S. Department of Treasury, Internal Revenue Service, "Return of Organization Exempt from Income Tax—Form 990, the Business Roundtable," 23-7236607 (Washington, D.C., 2005); also see Lee Drutman and Charlie Cray, "The People's Business," *In These Times* (March 14, 2005): 17; John B. Judis, "The Most Powerful Lobby," *In These Times* (February 21, 1994): 22–23.

125. Domhoff, *Who Rules America?*, 4th ed., 92–94.

126. Dye, *Who's Running America?* 236–37.

127. Peter Nye, "Lobbying and Gift Reform Shines Sunlight on Influence Peddling," *Public Citizen* (January–February 1996): 1, 3.

128. See note 14 for lobby expenditure sources in 1997 and 2005.

129. Office of Congressman Dick Armey, "Washington's Lobbying Industry: A Case for Tax Reform—Executive Summary," June 19, 1996, 1–4, 1.

130. Center for Public Integrity, "State Lobbyists Near the $1 Billion Mark," on the Internet at http://www.publicintegrity.org/hired guns/report.aspx?aid=728 (visited January 1, 2006).

131. Shuldiner and Raymond, *Who's in the Lobby?* 7.

132. Jim Drinkard, "Lobbying Costs Hit $100 Million a Month," *Indianapolis Star,* March 7, 1998, A1–A2.

133. Political Money Line, "2005 Lobbying Reports Covering 1/1/05–6/30/05" and "2005 Lobbying Reports Covering 7/1/05–12/31/05," on the Internet at http://politicalmoneyline.com/cgi-win/lp_sector.exe?DoFn=ye&Year=05 (visited May 21, 2006).

134. Kathleen Fackelmann, "Fired Up over Film Smoking," *USA Today,* May 18, 2005, 10D.

135. Domhoff, *Who Rules America?*, 4th ed., 84–94. Also see Clawson, Neustadtl, and Scott, *Money Talks,* 180.

136. Although the four policy contests considered here occurred during a period when the Republican Party controlled the presidency and both house of Congress (2001 to 2006), political support for classwide policies is bipartisan in nature. The four measures discussed would not have passed Congress without Democratic support. Moreover, legislative proposals supporting super-class interests have passed Congress and been signed into law as the result of classwide lobbying in periods when the Democratic Party controlled the presidency and both houses of Congress. For example, the North American Free Trade Agreement (NAFTA, 1993) and the Welfare "Reform" Act of 1996 were enacted into law with strong support from then president Bill Clinton and Democrats holding leadership positions in Congress.

137. Rebecca Adams, "GOP-Business Alliance Yields Swift Reversal of Ergonomics Rule," *Congressional Quarterly Weekly* (March 10, 2001): 535–39.

138. Bob Guldin, "Flawed Bankruptcy Law Rewards Finance Industry, While Families Beset by Health Costs Lose Protection," *Public Citizen News* (May–June 2005): 11.

139. Guldin, "Flawed Bankruptcy Law Rewards Finance Industry," 11.

140. U.S. Labor Education in the Americas Project, "A Union Activist's Guide to CAFTA," *Labor Notes* (June 2005): 8–9.

141. "2005: Year in Review," *Labor Party News* (January 2006): 3; "Shifting the Trade Debate, CAFTA and Beyond," *Public Citizen News, 2005 Annual Report,* March–April 2006, 7.

142. Eliza Brinkmeyer, "Handful of Pro-CAFTA Reps. Have Received $2.8 Million in Corporate Campaign Cash," *Public Citizen News* (May–June 2006): 13.

143. Brinkmeyer, "Handful of Pro-CAFTA Reps. Have Received $2.8 Million in Corporate Campaign Cash," 13.

144. Public Citizen, *Unfairness Incorporated: The Corporate Campaign against Consumer Class Actions* (Public Citizen's Congress Watch, June 2003); Seth Stern, "Republicans Win on Class Action," *Congressional Quarterly Weekly* (February 21, 2005): 460.

145. Seth Stern, "2005 Legislative Summary: Class Action Lawsuits," *Congressional Quarterly Weekly* (January 2, 2006): 46.

146. Keith Perine, "Class Action Lawsuit Measure Advances amid Heavy Lobbying, Concern over State Law," *Congressional Quarterly Weekly* (April 12, 2003): 882.

147. Doug Orr, "Social Security Q&A," *Dollars and Sense* (May–June 2005): 15–20.

148. Joel Bleifuss, "R.I.P. FDR?" *In These Times* (February 28, 2005): 3.

149. Jim Hightower and Phillip Frazer, "Naming the Names behind the Grab for Social Security," *Lowdown* (April 2005): 1–8.

150. Domhoff, *Who Rules America?*, 4th ed., 164–65.

151. Domhoff, *Who Rules America?*, 4th ed., 167.

152. Domhoff, *Who Rules America?*, 4th ed., 168.

153. Hightower and Frazer, "Naming the Names behind the Grab for Social Security," 1.

154. Jim Hightower and Phillip Frazer, "Social Security Ain't Broke, So Don't Fix It, Tweak It," *Lowdown* (March 2005): 2.

155. Hightower and Frazer, "Naming the Names behind the Grab for Social Security," 3.

156. Doug Henwood, "TV on Social Security: It's Broke, Fix It," *Extra!* (May–June 1999): 8–12.

157. Hightower and Frazer, "Naming the Names behind the Grab for Social Security," 4.

158. Hightower and Frazer, "Naming the Names behind the Grab for Social Security," 3.

159. AFL-CIO, "Front Groups for the Attack on Retirement Security," 2006, 1–14, on the Internet at http://www.aflcio.org/issues/retirementsecurity/socialsecurity (visited May 28, 2006).

160. Hightower and Frazer, "Naming the Names behind the Grab for Social Security," 4.

161. Hightower and Frazer, "Naming the Names behind the Grab for Social Security," 4.

162. Hightower and Frazer, "Naming the Names behind the Grab for Social Security," 4.

163. Hightower and Frazer, "Naming the Names behind the Grab for Social Security," 4.

164. "Anatomy of a Victory," *Nation* (December 19, 2005): 3–4; also see Orr, "Social Security Q&A," 15.

165. "Anatomy of a Victory," *Nation*, 3–4.

166. Seth Ackerman, "Selling the Social Security Scare," *Extra!* (January–February 2005): 6.

167. Geov Parrish, "Wrecking Social Security," *Populist Progressive* (March 15, 2005): 13; also see "Little Support for Bush's Social Security Agenda," *American Teacher* (September 2005): 17.

168. "Anatomy of a Victory," *Nation*, 3–4.

169. "Anatomy of a Victory," *Nation*, 4.

170. "Anatomy of a Victory," *Nation*, 4.

171. Other examples illustrating that labor-based coalitions can defeat superclass policy initiatives occurred in the late 1990s. The corporate campaign to give President Clinton "fast-track" authority to negotiate foreign trade agreements was defeated in 1997; in 1998, corporate efforts to reduce union funding of pro-labor political candidates (through so-called pay check protection legislative proposals) were defeated in Congress and in the California state legislature. Both issues are discussed at length in the second edition of *The New Class Society*.

172. Domhoff, *Who Rules America?*, 4th ed., 175; G. William Domhoff, *Who Rules America? Power and Politics in the Year 2000* (Mountain View, CA: Mayfield Press, 1998), 266–81.

173. U.S. Congress, House of Representatives, *Comprehensive Tax Reform*, Committee on Ways and Means, 99th Cong., 1st sess., Serial 99–41 (Washington, DC: U.S. Government Printing Office, 1985).

174. U.S. House Committee on Ways and Means, *Impact, Effectiveness, and Fairness of the Tax Reform Act of 1986*, 101st Cong., 2nd sess., Serial 101–92 (Washington, DC: U.S. Government Printing Office, 1990).

175. "Alternative Minimum Tax Reform Act: Chamber of Commerce of the United States of America," and "Alternative Minimum Tax Reform Act: Statement of National Association of Manufacturers," *Congressional Record* (May 8, 1997): S4236–38; "The Small Business Capital Gains Enhancement Act of 1997," *Congressional Record* (May 15, 1997): S4588–91; "Amendment No. 519," *Congressional Record* (June 26, 1997): S6449–51.

176. "Pro-Taxpayer Groups Urge Congress to Act Now on Future Tax Cuts," *Congressional Record* (June 27, 1997): S6678–79.

177. Michelle Cottle, "The Real Class War," *Washington Monthly* (July–August 1997): 15.

178. John Miller, "More Wealth for the Wealthy: The Estate Tax Giveaway and What to Do about It," *Dollars and Sense* (November–December 1997): 26–27.

179. John Miller, "Tax Cuts: Clinton and Congress Feed the Wealthy," *Dollars and Sense* (November–December 1997): 43; Miller, "More Wealth for the Wealthy," 26.

180. "The Rich Get a Good Return on Their Campaign Investments," *Sanders Scoop* (Winter 1998): 1.

181. Miller, "Tax Cuts," 43.

182. Daniel J. Parks, "Bush May Test Capitol Hill Clout Early with Expedited Tax-Cut Proposal," *Congressional Quarterly Weekly* (January 6, 2001): 42.

183. Lori Nitschke, "Tax Plan Destined for Revision," *Congressional Quarterly Weekly* (February 10, 2001): 318–21.

184. Howard Fineman and Rich Thomas, "Snip! Snip! Snip!" *Newsweek* (February 19, 2001): 18–22.

185. Daniel J. Parks, "Under Tight Spending Ceilings, Democrats Lower Their Sights," *Congressional Quarterly Weekly* (June 9, 2001): 1364.

186. Adria Scharf, "Tax Cut Time Bomb," *Dollars and Sense* (March–April 2004): 39.

187. Citizens for Tax Justice, "Final Version of Bush Tax Plan Keeps High-End Tax Cuts, Adds to Long-Term Cost," on the Internet at http://www.inequality.org/bushtaxplan2.html (visited August 8, 2001). Also see John Miller, "Getting Back More Than They Give," *Dollars and Sense* (September–October 2001): 60–62.

188. Citizens for Tax Justice, "Phase in Dates for the Bush Tax Cuts, Including 2003 Legislation (Calendar Years)" (press release, April 13, 2004), 1–3.

189. Sam Pizzigati, "Stat of the Week: Estate Tax Odds," *Too Much* (June 5, 2006): 4.

190. Jane Bryant Quinn, "Tax Cuts: Who Will Get What," *Newsweek* (June 11, 2001): 30.

191. Citizens for Tax Justice, "CBO Projects $8.5 Trillion in Borrowing over Next Decade under Bush Policies," subtopic "Effects of the Bush Tax Cuts Enacted through 2004 (with Sunsets) by Income Group (Calendar Years)" (press release, January 26, 2006), 1–3.

192. Robert Pollin, *Contours of Descent* (New York: Verso, 2005), 97.

193. "Bush Tax Plan Will Squeeze Medicare, Education," *UAW Solidarity* (July–August 2001): 4.

194. William Greider, "Stockman Returneth," *Nation* (April 2, 2001): 4–6.

195. Ruth Conniff, "The Budget Surrender," *Progressive* (June 2001): 13.

196. Fineman and Thomas, "Snip! Snip! Snip!" 20.

197. Lori Nitschke, "Tax-Cut Bipartisanship Down to One Chamber," *Congressional Quarterly Weekly* (March 10, 2001): 532 (529–32).

198. Lori Nitschke, "Coalitions Make a Comeback," *Congressional Quarterly Weekly* (March 3, 2001): 474.

199. Nitschke, "Coalitions Make a Comeback," 470, 474.

200. Nitschke, "Tax Plan Destined for Revision," 321.

201. Nitschke, "Coalitions Make a Comeback," 474.

202. Michael Scherer, "Make Your Taxes Disappear!" *Mother Jones* (March–April 2005): 74; Public Citizen, *Unfairness Incorporated*.

203. The White House, "Fact Sheet—Extending the President's Tax Relief: A Victory for American Taxpayers" (press release, May 17, 2006).

204. Scharf, "Tax Cut Time Bomb," 39.

205. Scharf, "Tax Cut Time Bomb," 39.

206. Citizens for Tax Justice, "Tax Cuts on Capital Gains and Dividends Doubled Bush Income Tax Cuts for the Wealthiest in 2003" (press release, April 5, 2006), 1.

207. Edmund L. Andrews, "House Passes a $2.7 Trillion Spending Plan," *New York Times*, May 18, 2006, A1.

208. Pollin, *Contours of Descent*, 97–99.

209. U.S. House of Representatives, Committee on Ways and Means, "428 Major Companies and Organizations Support the American Jobs Creation Act" (press release, July 8, 2004).

210. Scherer, "Make Your Taxes Disappear!" 72.

211. Scherer, "Make Your Taxes Disappear!" 74.

212. Lawrence Mishel, Jared Bernstein, and Sylvia Allegretto, *The State of Working America, 2006–2007* (Ithaca, NY: IRL Press, 2007), 77, 258.

213. Anna Bernasek, "'Temporary' Tax Cuts Have a Way of Becoming Permanent," *New York Times*, May 14, 2006, C3.

214. Citizens for Tax Justice, "Bush Policies Drive Surge in Corporate Tax Freeloading: 82 Big U.S. Corporations Paid No Tax in One or More Bush Years" (press release, September 22, 2004), 1–6; Citizens for Tax Justice, "Effects of the Bush Tax Cuts Enacted through 2004 (with Sunsets) by Income Group (Calendar Years)," 1.

215. The "wealth pie" percentages presented in figure 4.2 are the authors' estimates based on information from two sources: (1) Arthur B. Kennickell, "Currents and Undercurrents: Changes in the Distribution of Wealth, 1989–2004," Federal Reserve Board, January 30, 2006, 29, on the Internet at http://www.federalreserve.gov/pubs/oss/oss2/scfindex.html (visited April 25, 2006), and (2) Edward N. Wolff, "Changes in Household Wealth in the 1980s and 1990s in the U.S." (Working Paper No. 407, Levy Economics Institute and New York University, May 2004), 30.

216. Office of Management and Budget, "Historical Tables," in *Budget of the United States Government: Fiscal Year 2007* (Washington, DC: U.S. Government Printing Office, 2006), 22, 29.

217. Social Security Administration, "Maximum Taxable Earnings," on the Internet at http://www.ssa.gov/cgi-bin/ssa.cfg/php/enduser/std (visited November 13, 2006).

218. Our estimate that over 90 percent of individuals have incomes less than $97,500 is an estimate based on information from the following IRS source, which reported that in 2004 only 9.5 percent of individual income tax returns had adjusted gross incomes of $100,000 or more: U.S. Department of the Treasury, Internal Revenue Service, "Individual Income Tax Returns, Preliminary Data, 2004," *The Statistics of Income (SOI) Bulletin* (Winter 2005–2006): 14.

219. David Cay Johnston, *Perfectly Legal: The Covert Campaign to Rig Our Tax System to Benefit the Super Rich—and Cheat Everybody Else* (New York: Portfolio, 2003).

220. Brian Balkovic, "High Income Tax Returns for 2003," *The Statistics of Income (SOI) Bulletin* (Spring 2006): 54.

221. Congressional Budget Office, "Historical Effective Federal Tax Rates: 1979–2003," December 2005, Table 1, 4, on the Internet at http://www.cbo.gov (visited November 18, 2006).

222. Randy Albelda, "Farewell to Welfare but Not to Poverty," *Dollars and Sense* (November–December 1996): 17; Randy Albelda, "Welfare Reform, Ten Years Later," *Dollars and Sense* (January–February 2006): 6–7, 27; Neil deMause, "The Smell of Success," *Extra!* (November–December 2006): 6–7; Hank Hoffman, "Time Is Tight," *In These Times* (November 12, 2001): 7–8.

223. Office of Management and Budget, "Appendix: Department of Health and Human Services, 'Administration for Children and Families, TANF,'" in *Budget of the United States Government: Fiscal Year 2007* (Washington, DC: U.S. Government Printing Office, 2006), 452.

224. Office of Management and Budget, "Analytical Perspectives, Supplemental Materials: 27. Detailed Function Table," in *Budget of the United States Government: Fiscal Year 2007* (Washington, DC: U.S. Government Printing Office, 2006), 2, 16; Office of Management and Budget, "Historical Tables," 53.

225. David Rogers, "U.S. Annual War Spending Grows," *Wall Street Journal*, March 8, 2006, A4; The White House, "Fact Sheet: President Signs Emergency Funding Bill" (press release, June 15, 2006).

226. Joel Bleifuss, "Warfare or Welfare," *In These Times* (December 9, 1996): 12–14; "Explosive Job Growth," *Mother Jones* (May–June 2006): 17; Huck Gutman, "Soldiers for Hire," *Monthly Review* (June 2004): 11–18.

5

The Information Industry

> In the United States, the media system is set up to maximize profit for a handful of large companies. The system works well for them, but it is a disaster for the communication needs of a healthy and self-governing society.
>
> —Robert W. McChesney, *The Future of Media*, 2005

"All the news that's fit to print." This quote published daily as part of the *New York Times* masthead suggests the ideal of news reporting in the U.S. media: diverse, impartial, balanced, and complete. But this ideal is far from reality. As we will see, there is substantial evidence that subtle and insidious forms of censorship are pervasive throughout virtually all print and electronic news media outlets owned and operated by large corporations in the United States (the mainstream media). Media censorship in the United States doesn't involve overt, heavy-handed, formal rules of reporting or the killing of new stories by government censors. "Instead, it comes stealthily under the heading of Missed Opportunities. . . . [It is] a subtle system of information suppression in the name of corporate profit and self interest."[1]

For the past thirty years, Project Censored, a nonprofit media watchdog group, has been identifying and researching "important censored . . . news stories that the corporate media has failed to cover." The organization's publications make it clear that such forms of censorship in the United States today grow largely out of the routine structures and operations of the mega-merged corporations that own and control the U.S. news media. Project Censored's annual list of the "Top 25 Censored Stories" covers several categories spanning (and often linking) U.S. domestic and international issues. For example, the top story in 2005 focused on how "Wealth Inequality in [the] Twenty-First Century Threatens Economy and Democracy." It emphasized the links between and the consequences of both domestic and international trends towards greater concentrations of wealth ownership. In 2006, the top story, more domestically focused, considered how the Bush administration had tried to eliminate open government. The common thread binding all twenty-five stories together each year is their neglect or marginalization by the mainstream media. They are, as judged by the Project Censored panel, "the 25 most important censored news stories that the corporate media has failed to cover."[2]

Project Censored's annual list of censored news stories reveals two important features of the relationship between superclass-based corporate power and the media. First, contrary to what some conservatives imagine to be the case, mass media reports that are critical of superclass corporate power or of corporate and public policies that promote superclass interests are extremely rare.[3] Mainstream media accounts of corporate activities that promote superclass interests rarely include the kind of in-depth, critical, investigative reporting found in the censored stories. Second, the censored stories illustrate that media reports critical of superclass-based corporate power, corporate policies, or instances of corporate-government collusion against public or workers' interests are almost always "broken" by small, alternative media sources. For the past thirty years, most of the reports covered in Project Censored's annual listing of censored stories were first published by a variety of alternative news magazines, such as the *Nation*, *In These Times*, the *Progressive*, *Multinational Monitor*, and *Mother Jones*.

An important aspect of corporate media censorship not explicitly addressed by Project Censored is the use by well-heeled corporations and trade associations of "strategic action lawsuits against public participation" (SLAPP suits). Such lawsuits provide deep-pocket corporations with a potent weapon for suppressing media reports and activities by citizens' groups, which corporate owners and managers may view as unflattering, embarrassing, or threatening to their interests. As Public Citizen President Joan Claybrook has said, "libel suits, such as the meat industry's [1998] case against talk show host Oprah Winfrey, that are basically frivolous . . . can bankrupt citizen organizations that criticize corporate behavior."[4] Small media outlets can also be targets. For example, in the 1990s the Briggs and Stratton corporation filed a $30 million libel and invasion-of-privacy lawsuit against the *National Catholic Reporter* (*NCR*) in response to a story critical of the company's plans to downsize its Milwaukee-area operations.[5]

SLAPP suits make it clear that when the agents of superclass power are stung by media critiques, they have enormous resources at their disposal to punish offenders. These suits serve as chilling reminders to all potential critics of the risks they face if they challenge superclass corporate power or policies. While the exact number of SLAPP suits filed each year in the United States is difficult to know, the California Anti-SLAPP Project estimates that thousands of such cases occur annually.[6]

Even if SLAPP suits are ultimately decided in favor of critics, they are expensive, time-consuming, and energy-draining challenges to organizations with typically limited resources. The threat of SLAPP suits is likely to induce caution and even self-censorship as social justice activists or editors for small media outlets consider whether to publish reports critical of powerful corporations. Consider the Briggs and Stratton suit. Although the case was eventually dismissed by a federal judge in 1998, the *NCR* editorial announcing the decision noted, "Such suits have lately grown more common and are designed to make individuals or seemingly more vulnerable media think twice before criticizing big corporations or interests. It is, in other words, a bullying tactic rather than a search for justice, never mind a search for truth."[7]

This chapter explores how organizationally based structures and processes produce what Project Censored describes as "information suppression." It focuses on the links between class interests, mega–media firms, and powerful media-driven processes that shape public views on economic, political, and cultural issues. In short, we consider how the mainstream media shape, censor, manage, and disseminate ideas, information, and news in ways that protect and promote the interests of the privileged-class, especially those of the superclass, while ignoring or marginalizing working-class interests. As we will see, information-industry owners and managers have a preference for media content that will maximize profits and promote superclass interests. Their message is keep it light, keep it bright, and keep it moving.

THE MAINSTREAM CORPORATE MEDIA

The media conglomerates are not the only industry whose owners have become monopolistic in the American economy. But media products are unique in one vital respect. They do not manufacture nuts and bolts: they manufacture a social and political world.

—Ben H. Bagdikian, *The New Media Monopoly*, 2004

The information industry consists of giant interlocked electronic- and print-media corporations that are largely owned by superclass members and managed by a small number of superclass leaders in conjunction with credentialed-class junior partners.[8] These firms disseminate information, ideas, and images about, and interpretations of, national and global economic, political, and social news and issues to national and international audiences. The industry can be viewed as part of an even larger enterprise that some critics have termed "Big Media," the "culture industry," or the "national entertainment state."[9] Such labels suggest that in addition to generating news and commentary largely consonant with superclass interests, the industry also serves as a major conduit for disseminating most forms of mass entertainment, corporate public relations (PR) propaganda, product ads, promotional campaigns, and paid political advertising.

The content of the news and information delivered by the electronic- and print-media arms of the information industry is not neutral in terms of viewpoints conveyed or class interests served. But the news media are also not liberal in the sense of being critical of mainstream economic and political institutions or policies, as many conservative pundits, such as radio talk show host Rush Limbaugh and Fox News Channel's Bill O'Reilly, claim. Studies of media content do reveal consistent biases—but of a pro-business, pro-privileged-class sort. News story lines and accompanying images typically begin with pro-business sources, such as superclass-funded think tanks.[10] And the commercial media most often "favor style and substance that [are] consonant with their corporate [economic] interests."[11] In fact, "major advertisers have insisted that [messages consistent with their products and interests] . . . be expressed not in the ads, but in the ostensibly 'independent' news reporting . . . of newspapers, magazines, radio, and television."[12] The information industry consistently delivers news and information that effectively reinforce superclass and corporate interests—at the expense of working-class interests in an informed citizenry and participatory democracy. "It is a disaster for anything but the most superficial notion of democracy—a democracy where, to paraphrase John Jay's maxim, those who own the world ought to govern it."[13]

Polls suggest deep public skepticism exists concerning news media credibility.[14] Even so, the information industry dominates national attention regarding current affairs, with most Americans getting most of their news about such events from mainstream media outlets. According to recent national surveys, 55 to 60 percent of Americans report they get most of their news from television. Newspapers are a distant second news source (25 to 30 percent) followed by radio (10 percent), Internet or online services (5 to 10 percent), and magazines (1 percent).[15] These percentages have been stable since 1996 and indicate that despite claims about the importance of the Internet as a source of information, TV and newspapers remain the major news sources for 80 to 90 percent of the public. This means the five major television news networks (ABC, CBS, CNN, FOX, NBC) are the primary sources of information in the United States today. It also means the 1,457 daily U.S. newspapers rank as the second most important source of news for Americans.[16] However, it should be noted that "ninety-eight percent of all cities have only one daily newspaper and these are increasingly controlled by huge chains like Gannett and Knight-Ridder."[17] To illustrate, in 2005, Gannett and Knight-Ridder reported annual revenues of $7.7 and $3 billion, respectively, and ranked 296 and 614 on the Fortune 1000 list.[18] In 2006, Knight-Ridder was acquired by the McClatchy Company. Following this move, McClatchy management announced plans to sell twelve of the thirty-two Knight-Ridder newspapers it acquired. Even after divesting itself of all twelve newspapers (in 2006), McClatchy was the second-largest newspaper publisher in the United States "measured by daily circulation (approximately 3.2 million), with 32 daily newspapers and 50 non-dailies."[19]

In the latter 2000s, the core of the information industry consisted of a small number of large, interlocked news media firms with both electronic and print divisions. However, large news media firms are themselves owned by even larger corporate conglomerates. Today, four large firms, General Electric (GE), Time Warner (TW), Disney, and the News Corporation (NC), own as subsidiaries the largest electronic media firms that run major U.S. television news operations. A fifth firm, CBS Corporation (spun off as a separate company from Viacom in 2005), derives most of its income from a variety of television holdings, including a major television news operation (CBS News); in addition to television, CBS also has major holdings in radio, outdoor advertising, and publishing businesses.[20]

All five companies listed above are U.S.-based firms. (The News Corporation, headed by CEO Rupert Murdoch, relocated its corporate headquarters from Australia to Delaware in November 2004.[21]) In addition to operating news operations, these five large firms own or control several other media and entertainment corporations, including cable television networks, radio stations, newspapers, magazines, book publishing companies, and film studios.[22] The following listing includes (1) the total 2005 corporate revenues for each firm; (2) the major television networks and news operations owned by each firm; (3) the 2005 revenues generated by television networks, cable, and other media operations for each firm; and (4) a partial listing of other media companies owned or jointly operated by each parent firm through various subsidiaries.[23]

- *General Electric.* In 2005, GE's total corporate revenues were $149.7 billion. GE owns NBC and NBC News. In 2004, GE acquired Vivendi Universal Entertainment, a French media firm, and merged it with NBC to create a comprehensive media subsidiary, NBC Universal. The 2005 revenues for NBC Universal totaled $14.7 billion. GE, through NBC Universal, owned, in 2005, thirty television stations and had two hundred affiliates; NBC Universal owned or had equity investments in fourteen cable TV properties, including Bravo, CNBC, CNBC World, MSNBC, the A&E Network, the History Channel, mun2, National Geographic International, the USA Network, the SCI FI Channel, and the Sundance Channel. Feature films for theaters are produced and distributed through three units: Universal Pictures (e.g., *United 93, American Dreamz, Inside Man*), Focus Features, and Rogue Pictures. Universal Studios Home Entertainment markets DVD products for home viewing. The company also has interests in Paxson Communications and owns Universal Parks and Resorts.
- *Time Warner.* In 2005, TW's total corporate revenues were $43.6 billion. TW owns Turner Broadcasting and CNN News, and in 2005, its TV network and cable revenues totaled $19.1 billion. (TW revenues also included $8.2

billion from its AOL subsidiary.) TW TV ownership and joint cable ventures, in 2005, included TBS, TNT, Home Box Office, the WB Network, the Cartoon Network, Court TV, Time Warner Cable, and Comcast. Other holdings include Time, Inc., which, in 2005, published over 150 magazines (45 in the United States and 105 in other countries), including *Time, Sports Illustrated, People,* and *Fortune.* The Time Warner Book Group (TWBG) included Little, Brown and Warner Books. (TWBG was sold to Hachette in 2006 for $538 million.) Warner Brothers and New Line Cinema released, in 2005, a total of thirty-six feature films for theaters (e.g., *Harry Potter and the Goblet of Fire, Batman Begins, Good Night and Good Luck, Wedding Crashers*). Warner Brothers Television Production, Inc., and Warner Home Video, Inc., produce television shows and other programming for broadcast and for home entertainment. TW also owns smaller media properties, such as D. C. Comics and E. C. Publications, Inc., the publisher of *Mad Magazine.*

- *The Walt Disney Company.* In 2005, Disney's total corporate revenues were $31.9 billion. Disney owns ABC and ABC News, and in 2005, its media network revenues totaled $13.2 billion. In 2005, Disney owned, through ABC, ten television stations and seventy-two radio stations, plus TV network and cable operations, including ESPN, the Disney Channel, Toon Disney, and SOAPnet. In 2005, Disney had joint ventures with A&E Television Networks, Lifetime Entertainment, the History Channel, and E! Networks. Disney distributes films under various studio titles, including Walt Disney Pictures, Miramax Films, and Touchstone Pictures. (In 2006, Disney acquired Pixar, an animated film studio, for $7.4 billion.) The firm also distributes DVDs through Buena Vista Home Entertainment. Disney publications include *ESPN, FamilyFun, Disney Adventures,* and *Wondertime* magazines and Hyperion books. The Disney-owned Buena Vista Music Group includes Walt Disney Records, Buena Vista Records, Hollywood Records, and Lyric Street Records. Disney also owns several parks and resorts in the United States, Europe, and Asia.
- *CBS Corporation.* In 2005, CBS's total corporate revenues were $14.5 billion. The company owns CBS News, and in 2005, its TV network, syndication, cable, and radio revenues totaled $11.4 billion. CBS owns 39 television stations and operates 179 radio stations through CBS Radio. The firm also owns or jointly operates the CW Network (starting in 2006 with Warner Brothers), United Paramount Network (UPN, ended operations in 2006), CSTV Networks (college sports, acquired in 2006), CBS Paramount Television, King World Productions (which produces syndicated programming, such as *Entertainment Tonight, The Dr. Phil Show, Wheel of Fortune, Jeopardy!,* and *The Oprah Winfrey Show*), and Showtime Networks, Inc. Other CBS media holdings include outdoor advertising displays (CBS Outdoor), publishing (Simon and Schuster, Pocket Books, Scribner, Free

Press), and Internet operations (CBS.com, CBSNews.com, CBSSportsLine.com, and CSTV.com). (In 2005, CBS owned the theme park company Paramount Parks, but CBS sold this unit in 2006 to Cedar Fair, LP).

- *The News Corporation.* In 2005, NC's total corporate revenues were $23.9 billion. NC owns Fox Entertainment Group and Fox News, and in 2005, its TV network, cable, and satellite television revenues totaled $10.3 billion. The News Corporation, primarily through the Fox Entertainment Group, operates eight major business segments in the United States: (1) filmed entertainment (Twentieth Century Fox and Fox Searchlight Pictures—films such as *I, Robot* and *Star Wars*); (2) television (25 TV stations owned by Fox, 171 affiliated TV stations, plus programming operations); (3) cable network programming (U.S. cable holdings include the Fox News Channel, National Geographic Channel, Fox Sports Networks, FX Network, SPEED Channel, TV Guide Channel, and Fox Reality); (4) direct broadcast satellite television (mainly in Italy); (5) magazines and inserts (*TV Guide, Weekly Standard*); (6) newspapers (*New York Post*); (7) book publishing (HarperCollins, William Morrow); and (8) other (digital technology and services for digital pay-television platform operators).

Corporate interlocks linking the boards of directors of the largest media firms to nonmedia companies illustrate how the web of superclass owners and employers cuts across the top levels of corporate America. In the 1990s, the six largest electronic media firms at that time (Time Warner, Disney, Viacom, NC, CBS, GE) had eighty-one directors on their boards. This group held "104 additional directorships on the boards of Fortune 1000 corporations."[24] The top eleven electronic- and print-media firms in the 1990s had "thirty-six *direct* [corporate] links, meaning two people who served on different media firm boards of directors and also served on the same board for another Fortune 1000 corporation."[25] In the 2000s, the pattern of substantial director interlocks linking large media and nonmedia firms continued. In 2004, the corporate boards of the five giant electronic media firms listed earlier, plus the five largest newspaper corporations—New York Times Co., Washington Post Co., Tribune Co. (*Chicago Tribune/L.A. Times*), Gannett (*USA Today*), and Knight-Ridder—included 118 directors who "sit on 288 different U.S. and international corporate boards."[26] The substantial number of media-nonmedia interlocks underscore the reality that "the media in the United States effectively represent the interests of corporate America."[27]

The complex and extensive web of media and nonmedia corporate interlocks illustrates how the parent firms of the major U.S. TV news networks and most of the other large media firms outside of the current five corporate giants are integrated into a tightly woven, superclass-based corporate structure. Through interlocks and joint ventures, the media segment of this corporate structure is largely owned or controlled by the same twenty thousand officers and directors of the one thousand largest firms that also supervise and control the shadow political industry.[28] This means that the mainstream electronic and print media are almost exclusively composed of large corporate firms whose policies, personnel, and reporting practices reflect superclass and corporate interests.[29]

Many of the fortunes of the wealthiest Americans are directly tied to media holdings. About 17 percent of the *Forbes* list of the richest four hundred Americans "derived their wealth from media, entertainment, or software. Exactly 20 percent of the fifty largest family fortunes were derived therefrom."[30] But this outcome should not be surprising since "the truth about the news industry has always been that rich businessmen (and a few rich women) own it."[31] And although news media ownership today more often takes a corporate rather than patriarchal form, the top news media CEOs are structurally bound to policies that advance privileged-class interests.[32] Today, the combined influence of superclass-based ownership and credentialed-class management practices, where the news media are concerned, have produced a kind of "corporate ministry of information." As one media critic put it, "It is normal for all large businesses to make serious efforts to influence the news, to avoid embarrassing publicity, and to maximize sympathetic public opinion and government policies. Now they own most of the news media that they wish to influence."[33]

Corporate interlocks that tie media firms' news operations with superclass interests of political control and profits lead to interesting contradictions. As a cultural ideal, news is supposedly delivered by "objective" media sources free from biases. In practice, as we have glimpsed, and as we will see in more detail later, this is never the case. The stakes are too high. For superclass members and their credentialed-class allies to maintain their positions of wealth, power, and privilege, the working class must be persuaded that the economic and political status quo and the institutions that comprise and sustain them are legitimate. This means the news media must provide those who are not members of the privileged class with ideas, information, and interpretations that support a superclass worldview, while ignoring or discrediting alternative views. Thus, news and editorial content trend heavily in the direction of reports and interpretations of events that legitimate the status quo, thereby protecting the interests of superclass members at the top of the class structure.

Of course, the existence of dominant, pro-superclass media reporting trends does not mean oppositional trends, views, or interpretations are totally absent from the media. They do exist, mainly as fragmented and minority positions, but our focus here is on superclass dominance of the mainstream mass media. The following sections explore three major control processes that operate through the information industry. The mainstream ideology, opinion-shaping, and spin-control processes function in ways that not only promote superclass domination of economic and political thinking in the United States but also help conceal the operation and effects of both the shadow political and information industries.

THE MAINSTREAM IDEOLOGY PROCESS

The ideology process consists of the numerous methods through which members of the power elite attempt to shape the beliefs, attitudes and opinions of the underlying population.

—G. William Domhoff, *The Powers That Be*, 1979

The mainstream ideology process is the most general of the three control practices operating as part of the information industry. But before we discuss this process, the term *ideology* needs a bit of clarification. This concept may seem like a remote, abstract reference. In fact, ideology is quite simple. It refers to idea systems that organize our thinking on various subjects. If we think sex is pleasurable—or disgusting—or that sports are fun—or boring— it is because of a complex set of ideas we have learned and accepted that surround those topics and color our experiences with them. Our sex and sports ideologies (i.e., "idea systems") include assumptions and conclusions about these subjects, as well as selected "facts" (gleaned from personal experiences or conveyed to us by credible sources) that "prove" our views are right and those held by others are wrong.

In the economic and political arenas, ideologies exist that have the same basic features as our sex and sports idea systems. Political-economy ideologies consist of assumptions about how power and wealth are (or should be) organized and distributed, along with selected "facts" that "prove" that the views people hold on these topics are "correct." Political-economy ideologies are most often referred to as ranging from "left" to "center" (or middle of the road) to "right." These labels can take on many meanings, but leftist ideologies are basically grounded in the view that democratic government can and should serve as an agent promoting political, economic, and social justice for all citizens. By contrast, ideologies on the right today tend to publicly portray "big government" as an enemy "of the people." However, rightist views typically endorse government subsidies to businesses and favor powerful, government-funded and -controlled police, military, and security agencies. Right-wing views also tend to see nothing wrong with the development of powerful *private* concentrations of wealth and power—as in the case of large corporations.

Whether we know it or not, most Americans have little experience with leftist ideologies but lots of experience with centrist and rightist ideologies. This situation reflects the ongoing socialization of the working class to economic and political ideas and views that promote and reinforce superclass economic and political interests. Such training occurs through several social institutions, including schools and the mass media, with the latter serving, in part, as a major conduit for the ideology process.

The *mainstream ideology process* refers to the powerful, indirect influence that the superclass has, especially through the mass media, upon the political-economy ideological views held by most Americans, including those in the new working class. It refers to the numerous ways that superclass-supported, pro-corporate, free market, individual-choice, "government is bad" (or at best inefficient) ideas get woven into and subtly dominate the content of mass media–disseminated news and commentary. As a result of this process, public debates and discussions on political and economic issues and policies tend to reflect superclass ideological views, preferences, and interests.

Credible evidence exists to support our view that the superclass shares a rather uniform political-economy ideology that in turn dominates public thought via the mainstream ideology process. We also believe that the operation of the process whereby superclass ideological views dominate news and information content delivered to working-class members via the mass media–based information industry can be illustrated by an examination of four key topics. These are (1) the corporate media-management structure, (2) the influence of corporate interests and advertising on media content, (3) the deep structural ideological foundation of the media, and (4) classroom penetration by media-produced materials.

Superclass Political-Economy Ideology

The mainstream ideology process is grounded in superclass leaders' ownership of, and control over, the mainstream media and their shared economic and political ideas, which comprise a dominant "ideological umbrella" spanning a short, neoliberal-centrist-conservative spectrum.[34] Of course, it would be an oversimplification to argue that all superclass members share the same political-economy ideology. But the apparent consensus among superclass leaders favoring domestic austerity policies in the United States, Europe, and elsewhere in the world, as well as corporate-mediated international trade, suggests widespread superclass support for national and international "neoliberal" economic and political policies. Such policies are based on "[free trade], privatization, deregulation, openness to direct foreign investment . . . fiscal discipline, lower taxes, and smaller government."[35] Differences in superclass leaders' ideological views appear to be matters of nuance, emphasis, and degree across the dominant ideological umbrella rather than fundamental differences in values and policy directions.[36] Thus, the core values underlying the superclass neoliberal ideological spectrum emphasize free enterprise, competition, equal opportunity, individualism, and minimal government involvement in business activities.[37] These values and principles reinforce what is claimed by privileged-class leaders to be a superior (compared to the alternatives) and preferred (for all citizens) political and economic status quo.

With the information industry owned and controlled by the same core of superclass leaders who direct the shadow political industry, it is hardly surprising that the political-economy ideological preferences of this group cover a short spectrum. Research on this topic reveals that mass media CEOs are typically economic conservatives interested in profits and markets and that they use the media to promote corporate values consistent with their interests.[38] As one researcher put it, "Media moguls—from Rupert Murdoch . . . to the [NBC] executives of General Electric—may not exactly be 'movement' conservatives. But neither are they 'liberals.'"[39]

A study of CEOs who headed parent firms controlling the major TV networks characterized their political views as conservative. Moreover, three of the four at the time of the study—Jack Welch (GE/NBC), Michael Jordan (CBS), and Rupert Murdoch (News Corporation/Fox)—were described as taking actions aimed at influencing news and commentary content in their media divisions in support of conservative political causes or neoliberal-conservative corporate economic policies (e.g., aggressive downsizing and opposition to government regulation). Michael Eisner (Disney/ABC), characterized as a Democratic Party centrist, was described as holding views that were not much different from those of the first three.[40]

The Corporate Media-Management Structure

Although conservative superclass corporate leaders control enormous media resources, as a group they are too few in number to supervise the details necessary for the translation of their shared ideological views into routine media policies and content. Dependable corporate media managers who hold compatible views are recruited by superclass-dominated corporate boards to handle those tasks. These upper-tier, credentialed-class professionals operate under a supervision and reward structure that ensures pro-corporation content standards are met—along with high profits and bonuses for superclass owners and upper-level media management.[41] The CEOs that oversee large firms with large media divisions are handsomely compensated. For 2005, the average total compensation (salary, bonuses, and stock options) received by the CEOs at the five firms profiled earlier was approximately $23.3 million.[42] Looking only at newspapers, the CEOs at the seven largest publicly held newspaper companies averaged $3.7 million in total compensation for 2005.[43] Media firms may find it easier than some industries to justify high salaries for top executives since profit margins, at least for publicly held newspaper companies, are routinely at or near the 20 percent range.[44] This level is about double the profitability of the average Fortune 500 company.[45]

Unfortunately, lower-level media staffers seldom benefit from the high profits; nor do they share in the largess found among top management and the elite reporting staff. Despite the fact that profit margins in the 50 to 60 percent range are routine for "well-run" television stations in top markets and that profit margins of 20 percent are common for large newspaper chains, media companies continue to cut jobs for reporters and news support personnel.[46] In 2005, newspapers cut about fifteen hundred professional staffers (adding to about two thousand jobs lost in the first half of the decade); employment cuts also occurred in 2005 for network television reporters and support staff (adding to the 35 percent workforce reduction in this area since 1985); at least three hundred professional writers and support staff lost jobs with magazines in 2005 (with hundreds more jobs to be cut in the future); professional and support staff jobs were cut in radio newsrooms in 2005, and more cuts were expected in the future.[47] Media managers claim layoffs and job reductions are necessary due to declining ad revenues. But media critics are skeptical, arguing, "The more proximate and problematic cause . . . is media companies' insistence on ever-higher profits."[48]

Job cuts at the bottom notwithstanding, top corporate media managers extend the superclass ideological "food chain" downward. They recruit and richly reward their immediate subordinates and top media professionals such as network TV news anchors, producers, reporters, writers, and commentators for performing three important tasks: (1) structuring media content that will, for the most part, reflect superclass ideological views and principles, (2) attracting the largest possible audience (with the right demographics, usually young, affluent adults), and (3) not offending corporate advertisers. The third issue is not inconsequential because most media profits come from advertising revenues. In 2005, U.S. corporations spent an estimated $276 billion on advertising with $138 billion of that amount spent on newspaper, television, and radio ads.[49] If all forms of corporate marketing are considered, the total amount spent on advertising could easily exceed $1 trillion.[50]

Corporate Interests, Advertising, and Media Content

Because the news divisions of media firms have emerged as major profit generators in recent years, media managers, producers, and reporters are under increasing pressure to produce media content that conforms to pro-corporate views. For members of this group, the result is a collection of news media policies, practices, traditions, and personal experiences that favor bland, noninvestigative news reporting and toothless commentary. This style of news frequently lapses into corporate cheerleading, ensuring that media ad revenues are not interrupted by negative news stories or controversial, critical commentary concerning high-spending corporate advertising clients.[51]

Soft news-reporting practices are shaped sometimes by covert links between corporate interlocks and media reporting practices and sometimes by direct corporate pressure on the media. Both types of influence result in corporate censorship of the news—in one form or another. The covert influence source is illustrated by an *Extra!* (a media-watch publication) reporter's observation concerning the power of subtle internal corporate pressures on news reporting: "Most people who work for large corporations understand without being told that there are things you should and should not do."[52] As an example, consider the experience of a producer at *20/20* (an ABC TV news program, owned by Disney) who was considering doing a report on executive compensation, a controversial topic because of huge pay packages awarded to corporate executives (as noted in chapter 2). "Two people familiar with the deliberations say the idea was dropped because no one wanted to draw attention to the extraordinarily rich pay package of Disney's chairman [at that time], Michael Eisner."[53]

Direct corporate pressure to change or kill news stories is also placed on media firms, but obviously the most successful attempts are those the public never hears about. One extraordinary case illustrating media managers' efforts to kill a news story that became a matter of public record began in 1997 and continued through the mid-2000s. It involves television reporters Jane Akre and Steve Wilson, Fox TV station WTVT in Tampa, Florida, and an investigative news series. The report Akre and Wilson helped prepare focused on Posilac, a drug based on the genetically engineered recombinant bovine growth hormone (rBGH) and sold by the Monsanto Corporation. Questions were raised about how the drug was tested for safety, possible negative health effects of the drug on cows, and possible health hazards people might face by consuming milk from cows injected with the drug (which increases milk production by up to 30 percent).[54]

As a result of legal pressures brought by Monsanto against Fox News, the investigative series was never broadcast. An attorney representing Monsanto in a February 21, 1997, letter to Fox News CEO Roger Ailes warned that "enormous damage can be done by the reckless presentation of unsupported speculation as fact." The letter was forwarded to the WTVT station and promoted a series of internal discussions and reviews of the series. The reporters stood by their story, but the station management decided not to run it. As the station manager told the reporters, "We paid three billion dollars for these television stations. We'll tell you what the news is."[55]

The reporters said Fox News tried to buy their silence, offering them a settlement "which amounted to nearly $200,000."[56] But in return they would have to sign a gag order "promising never to discuss the rBGH story, Monsanto's involvement, and how Fox responded." They refused and were fired in December 1997. Both reporters sued, "charging that they were fired because they refused to put inaccurate information on the air and threatened to report WTVT to the federal communications commission."[57] In August 2000, a six-person Florida jury agreed with the charges brought by the reporters and "awarded $425,000 in damages to Akre."[58] Fox appealed, and on February 14, 2003, the Florida Second District Court of Appeals "overturned Jane Akre's jury verdict."[59] "After the Appellate Court ruling, Fox sued Akre and Wilson for $2,000,000 in legal costs. In August 2004, the court ruled that Akre and Wilson 'filed their 1998 lawsuit against WTVT-Channel 13 in good faith.'" Thus, while the pair did not have to pay $2 million, "they ended up paying, in settlement, approximately 10 percent of Fox's costs."[60] In January 2005, Akre and Wilson filed a petition with the Federal Communications Commission (FCC) "to deny Fox WTVT in Tampa a license for renewal." The couple says they are "prepared to go as far as they can in an effort to prevent broadcasters from airing slanted coverage on public airways."[61]

Perhaps not surprisingly, the Akre and Wilson lawsuit and trial received very little media coverage. Using their website, the reporters "had to resort to covering their own trial for lack of coverage not only by the mainstream media, but by the liberal/progressive alternative media as well."[62] When Wilson and Akre prepared their original story, it included comments from Dr. Samuel Epstein at the University of Illinois School of Public Health concerning the possible human health risks posed by the use of rBGH. Dr. Epstein also suggested a possible explanation for the dearth of media coverage of the lawsuit and trial in a quote that was included in the reporters' version of the rBGH story. "We are living in the greatest democracy in the world in many ways, but in other ways we are living in a corporate dictatorship in which big government and big industry decide what information the consumer can and should have."[63]

The extent to which the Akre and Wilson story was ignored by the mainstream media was highlighted by the inclusion of their ongoing dispute with Fox in the publication *Censored 2005* as "censored story" number eleven (of the top twenty-five "censored stories") with the heading "The Media Can Legally Lie."[64] The case was followed up by a report in *Censored 2006: The Top 25 Censored Stories*, which included an update of events related to the story and a website address for readers interested in following new developments in the case.[65] This case and others, such as the widely reported "mad cow" lawsuit brought against TV talk show host Oprah Winfrey, illustrate that corporate efforts to directly influence (or silence) news media content are both real and powerful. Oprah's case was somewhat different from the Akre and Wilson episode because she was sued for civil damages by the National Cattlemen's Beef Association (NCBA). The NCBA claimed that Howard Lyman, a guest on Oprah's TV show, made comments "disparaging" beef (while discussing "mad cow disease") that were in violation of a Texas "food disparagement" statute, but a 1998 Texas jury disagreed and ruled in favor of Oprah.[66]

Although these cases illustrate direct corporate actions aimed at shaping media content, such efforts are likely to be far less important than more routine business-media connections. A more common route of corporate influence over media content occurs through the informal clout businesses have as a result of their massive expenditures for mass media advertising. Some sense of the extent of this clout is evident in surveys of reporters and media executives. "In survey after survey, journalists report that they feel outside—or inside—pressure to avoid, slant or promote certain stories that might affect . . . powerful interests."[67] As an example, a 2004 survey of media professionals found about one-third of respondents rated "pressure from advertisers trying to shape coverage" (33 percent) and "outside control of editorial policy" (29 percent) as major problems facing the media industry.[68] Earlier studies produced similar findings. A Pew Research Center–*Columbia Journalism Review* survey found 37 percent of three hundred journalists and news executives reported they avoided stories that might damage advertisers' interests.[69] Another survey of 241 members of the group Investigative Reporters and Editors working at commercial television stations stated, "Nearly three-quarters of the respondents reported that advertisers had 'tried to influence the content' of news at their stations." In this survey, a majority of respondents also reported that advertisers had tried to kill stories. In addition, 40 percent said their stations had caved in to advertiser pressures, 43 percent said they had not, and 59 percent said there was pressure from within their stations "*not* to produce stories that advertisers might find objectionable."[70]

In the print media, the *Wall Street Journal* has reported that large corporate advertisers demand to know magazine content in advance to ensure that their ads do not appear in publications with "offensive content." As an illustration, "Colgate-Palmolive Co. sends its agencies guidelines forbidding them from running ads in magazine issues with 'offensive' sexual content or material the company 'considers antisocial or in bad taste.' Michael Samet, media director at Colgate's lead agency, Young & Rubicam Advertising, says the agency has a 'protocol' . . . to make sure every magazine carrying Colgate's ads honors its rules."[71]

According to the *Journal*, the practice of corporate advertisers' demanding control over magazine content is widespread and involves large firms and entire industries. Such practices may be relevant to *Time* magazine's coverage of Wal-Mart and the giant retailer's influence over news content. Wal-Mart not only places ads in *Time* but also sells the magazine (and many others) in its stores. By some estimates, Wal-Mart stores account for 15 percent of all single-copy magazine sales.[72] Perhaps these factors help explain why "Wal-Mart Nation," a high-profile *Time* article (June 27, 2005) focusing on Wal-Mart's Chinese retail operations, was infused with "a cheerleader theme." And also why the article allowed Wal-Mart spokespersons to "trump" critics who voiced concerns over the company's business practices.[73] In terms of news *selection*, in 2002, Neal Travis, a *New York Post* columnist, cited widespread rumors that "*Time* magazine's original choice for its 2001 person-of-the-year cover was Osama bin Laden—until Wal-Mart intervened." Wal-Mart management did not deny the pressure. A company spokesperson is quoted as having said, "If Osama bin Laden had been on the cover of that magazine, we would not have liked it and would have evaluated how our customers feel before selling it."[74]

Industrywide involvement by advertisers insisting on control over media content is further evidenced by the long-standing policy of tobacco and alcohol advertisers, who demand advance warnings from publications about any articles dealing with people who abuse or who have been harmed by their products. As the *Wall Street Journal* noted, "Big advertisers have always tried to influence the contents of magazines, and every other medium." Such practices are not new, not illegal, and not even unethical: "The American Society of Magazine Editors . . . [does not have] any policy to prevent magazines from giving advertisers advance warnings about stories."[75]

Deep Structure

Conscious corporate efforts influencing media content to ensure a favorable advertising climate are paralleled by a deeper and more pervasive penetration of media organizations by superclass and corporate ideological views and values. *Deep structure* refers to the institutionalization of superclass-based political-economy views and values in the training and reward structures of, and working conditions experienced by, most mass media professionals. In part, this concept is similar to what media critic Ben Bagdikian has termed "internalized bias," the unstated and taken-for-granted understanding that journalists working for mainstream media develop concerning what constitutes "acceptable" (to corporate interests) reporting topics, practices, and news content.[76]

Deep structure acts as a kind of hidden context. It is the vehicle through which superclass-favored values and beliefs are woven into the organizational hierarchies, management policies, print and programming decisions, and daily reporting practices of the mainstream media. And these are the firms that generate most of the electronic and printed news and commentary in the United States. Like a transparent fishbowl shaping and bounding the water world of fish, deep structure imposes constraints and patterns on media policies and practices that are nearly invisible—unless its configurations are consciously perceived.

The deep structure of superclass ideological influence in the electronic media is reflected in many ways, but it is especially evident in how resources are granted or withheld in programming decisions. Corporate-media managers routinely select, showcase, and lavishly support conservative, "free market" corporate cheerleaders. Commercial media examples include John Stossel (ABC TV's *20/20* correspondent), Wolf Blitzer (CNN), Bill O'Reilly (Fox News Channel), and Rush Limbaugh (Premier Radio Networks).[77] Examples on Public Broadcasting Service (PBS) television include Paul Kangas and Susie Gharib (cohosts of *Nightly Business Report*) and John McLaughlin (host of *The McLaughlin Group*, sponsored by GE).[78] By contrast, the same media managers closely scrutinize and often quickly ax the few corporate critics or progressive commentators that typically find short-lived mass media exposure.

Examples of popular progressive reporters and commentators fired, forced to quit, or with shows cancelled because of their views are infrequent, in part because the deep structure filtering process prevents people with such views from accessing highly visible media positions. Also, when such events do occur, media managers routinely deny that such firings are related to the views of those who lose their jobs. One example occurred in 2003 when Phil Donahue's MSNBC television talk show was cancelled, apparently because of his opposition to the U.S. war in Iraq and his progressive political views. "According to an internal NBC memo . . . the Donahue show could be: 'a home for the liberal anti-war agenda at the same time our competitors are waving the flag at every opportunity.'"[79] Earlier, filmmaker Michael Moore had recurring difficulties in getting and keeping his sometimes corporate-biting television programs on the air. His first show, *TV Nation*, ran briefly in the summer of 1994 on NBC but was quickly dropped by the network. It was picked up in 1995 by the Fox Network, only to be quickly dropped again.[80] His second show, *The Awful Truth*, financed by the British Broadcasting Company, aired in the United States on the Bravo satellite/cable channel in 1999 and 2000 but did not return. Coincidence? Or cause and effect? Despite his absence from television, Moore continues to write best-selling books and produce award-winning documentary films.

Bill Moyers's experience at PBS provides a "post hoc" example of how progressive views can lead to television "censorship"—after the fact. Moyers retired in December 2004 as host of the PBS program *Now with Bill Moyers* and then discovered that the chair of the Corporation for Public Broadcasting (CPB) had hired a contractor in 2004 for $10,000 "to monitor *Now* and report on its supposed political bias."[81] After Moyers retired and learned of the monitoring and of other efforts by the CPB chair and board of directors to manipulate PBS's content and programming so as to move the network in an even more conservative and partisan direction, he publicly denounced these actions. Moyers wrote to the CPB chair, "suggesting that the pair debate the

Copyright © Tom Tomorrow. Reprinted with permission.

network's future on a PBS program of [the director's] choice and called for the release of the *Now* monitoring."[82]

Other examples of apparently politically motivated firings of media figures include the 2000 axing of popular and progressive radio talk show hosts Pat Thurston (KSRO, Santa Rosa, California) and Mike Malloy (WLS, Chicago, Illinois). Both shows had high ratings in their respective markets but were axed by corporate management anyway. A report on the firings pointed out that "Thurston didn't shy away from criticizing powerful business interests" and that Malloy tackled "issues involving the environment, foreign policy, and corporate irresponsibility that other hosts rarely touch." However, in both cases, station managers deny that the reporters' progressive views had anything to do with the decisions to fire them.[83] Five years earlier, a similar story occurred as popular corporate critic Jim Hightower had his program, *Hightower Radio,* dropped by ABC (in 1995). Company officials denied that the decision was related to the critical content of his show.[84]

Radio and television shows that are sometimes critical of corporate power clearly have problems simply staying on the air. This fact illustrates that the combination of corporate sponsorship and informal censorship leads to a very narrow range of neoliberal-centrist-conservative, pro-business news, information, and commentary disseminated by virtually all mass media outlets.[85] Such a reality is in sharp contrast to the frequently repeated charge (most often by conservative pundits) that a "liberal bias" exists in mass media news reporting.[86]

Classroom Penetration

The information industry disseminates superclass ideological views not only to the public but also to schools. Classroom programs and educational discounts made available to schools and colleges by the major newsmagazines *(Time, Newsweek, U.S. News and World Report)* ensure that superclass-compatible views and interpretations of national and world events reach high school– and college-age groups in the guise of "educational materials." Where schools are concerned, the information industry frequently works hand in glove with the public relations industry (examined in more detail in the section on spin control). Together, these industries create and promote "educational materials" for the U.S. Chamber of Commerce, the National Association of Manufacturers, and other corporate-sponsored groups that disseminate free, pro-corporate teaching materials to teachers and professors.

The National Council on Economic Education (NCEE) serves as a centralized source of materials and training in support of superclass efforts to shape students' views on economic issues. Founded in 1949 by members of the Committee for Economic Development, the NCEE is governed by a ten-member executive committee and a twenty-one-member board of directors. Many members of both groups also serve as senior corporate officials in many of the largest U.S. firms (e.g., IBM, General Mills, Citigroup). The NCEE is primarily funded by government grants and by donations and grants from large corporations and corporate foundations. The organization has produced an Economics America Schools Program that is provided to students through a network of state councils and university training centers. The NCEE claims that each year its network trains 120,000 teachers serving 8 million students and helps provide economic education programs to over 2,600 school districts involving 40 percent of U.S. students.[87] The scope of business involvement in schools was underscored by a study in *Business Week* magazine, which concluded, "Corporations are flooding schools with teaching aids—and propaganda."[88]

Media critic Ben Bagdikian has pointed out that

> free classroom materials are produced by 64 percent of the 500 largest American industrial corporations, 90 percent of industrial trade associations, and 90 percent of utility companies. . . . The publication *Media Decisions* estimated that as much as $3 billion in corporate money goes into all methods of promoting the corporation as hero and into "explanations of the capitalistic system," including massive use of corporate books and teaching materials in the schools, almost all tax deductible.[89]

These information and public relations industry products are always represented as educational aids and tools. The content is never described for what it is: mainstream-ideology corporate propaganda promoting the interests of the superclass.

Mainstream Ideology Results

The results of an information industry dominated by superclass ownership, political-economy ideological values, pro-corporate managers, and co-opted journalistic professionals are threefold. First, the superclass-approved "pluralistic" model of political power is promoted at several levels and in a variety of forms through the major media firms that make up the information industry. Second, political-economy views that differ from superclass views—and the groups that promote them—are ignored, marginalized, or demonized by the information industry. Third, working-class members are encouraged to embrace superclass values and views as their own and to accept the economic and political status quo as the most desirable institutional arrangement.

Pluralism Promoted

The extensive promotion of a "pluralism model" of politics and government by the information industry is evident in the ideas and imagery used by nearly all mass media where political reporting is concerned. This model rests on an interest-group interpretation of politics in America. A wide range of interest groups is claimed to exist, but the model argues that no one group is dominant in the political process. Such a view of the nature of politics in America is a constant refrain in media reports and commentary throughout the information industry and effectively neutralizes or excludes alternative perspectives on the nature of U.S. politics and political power.[90]

Media accounts of corporate PAC money and political influence, as well as of the recent proliferation of "527 committees" (discussed in chapter 4), with partisan links typically reflect, at an implicit level, pluralist interpretations. Political reporters typically point out that a wide array of "special-interest" PACs and 527 committees exists and then go on to explain that this situation actually promotes democracy. Such a reporting focus reinforces the view that American politics consists of competing, interest-based "veto groups" that check and balance one another's power. From this viewpoint, politics and public policies are seen as a kaleidoscopic swirl of pluralistic confusion with a multitude of PACs, 527 committees, and individual donors competing for political influence in a kind of rotating king-of-the-hill game of governance. According to pluralist imagery, corporate PACs are simply one of many PAC types, and corporate-funded 527 committees represent only one of many 527 "types." These campaign-funding vehicles are typically presented in media reports as fragmented interest groups more often competing than cooperating with one another for narrow gains in the political process. This comforting view reinforces the notion that the U.S. political system ensures no single interest group can corrupt or capture the democratic process.

Corporate PAC donations and the activities of well-funded 527 committees receive extensive media coverage as potential sources of political influence, but reporters typically look only at links between specific PACs, 527 committees, and specific candidates. The idea is to detect evidence connecting the policy-interest "fingerprints" of specific contributors to PACs and 527 committees with the actions of specific elected officials. When such connections are found, they are used by reporters as evidence that the media is an effective watchdog providing the public with tough investigative reporting.

Of course, the problem with "pluralist-based" reporting on corporate money as a source of political influence, whether channeled through PACs or 527 committees, is that the focus on divided interest-group power, rather than upon unified superclass power, in effect calls attention to the trees while ignoring the forest. Pluralist-based reporting leads viewers and readers to the conclusion that no single group dominates the political process—and thereby disguises the nature of superclass political power and the operation of the shadow political industry.

Marginalization of Alternatives

In addition to promoting pluralist-based reporting, the mainstream ideology process also encourages media marginalization and demonization of economic and political views or groups disfavored by the superclass. For example, mass media reports on unions are rarely framed in favorable or positive terms.[91] Also, trade union political contributions or PACs are routinely subjected to media attacks as efforts by "union bosses" to manipulate and control the political process.[92] In fact, virtually all organizations, ideas, and public policies or programs promoting working-class interests are often subject to negative mass media reporting.[93] The negation of alternative worldviews is a necessary part of superclass efforts to control the terms of economic and political discourse in the United States. The reality of conflicting class interests means that the experiences, policy priorities, and legislative preferences of the working class are not the same as those of the superclass (or their credentialed-class allies). The consequences for the superclass of allowing the working class to translate its shared interests and experiences into legitimate political discussion, debate, and coherent policy alternatives without the benefit of "ideological coaching" from the information industry would be to risk the growth of class consciousness and class politics. The mainstream ideology process is part of superclass efforts to prevent these prospects from becoming reality.

Embracing Superclass Values?

Superclass ideology legitimates centrist-conservative politics, predatory corporate business practices, and the existing class system, including the wide array of advantages and privileges it provides for the superclass and its credentialed-class allies, combined with extensive inequalities for the working class. As a result of our exposure to the mainstream ideology process, most of us tend to take the way the world is organized politically and economically—including the whole catalog of extensive class inequities—for granted. We assume that it is sort of natural and that there is not much we can do about it, so we tend to accept it, perhaps with some grousing and complaining, and go on. In fact, what this attitude reflects is our familiarity with only one ideological perspective: the superclass view. This is the case because it is the one that is subtly and powerfully woven into much of what we see, hear, and read in mass media–provided news and commentary via the mainstream ideology process.

Unfortunately for superclass leaders, their political-economy ideological foundations are problematic because the public principles they espouse are often at odds with the routine business practices pursued by the large firms they control. For example, superclass leaders claim to favor the ideals of free enterprise, competition, and equal opportunity. But in practice, the large firms, owned largely by the superclass, clearly prefer to dominate markets and maximize profits through monopolistic or oligopolistic practices that exclude the existence of competitive free enterprise or equal opportunity. Also, although corporate executives pay lip service to individualism, they clearly prefer a labor force tightly regimented by unchallenged corporate rule and a consuming public manipulated and dominated by mass advertising. Finally, whereas large firms oppose government regulation of business, as well as government policies that would expand the "social wage" (i.e., eco-nomic programs that would increase the income and economic security of working-class Americans), they typically support the existence and expan-sion of government programs that channel tax dollars into business revenues and profits. As we will see later in this chapter, reducing the tensions be-tween publicly promoted superclass ideological values and contradictory corporate practices is a major concern of the information industry—often pursued via the opinion-shaping and spin-control processes.

THE OPINION-SHAPING PROCESS

The media elite are the watchdogs of acceptable ideological messages, pa-rameters of news content, and general use of media resources,

—Peter Phillips, *Censored 2005*

The mainstream ideology process morphs seamlessly into the opinion-shaping process. The two processes overlap in many ways, but the key difference is that whereas the former promotes general neoliberal-centrist-conservative ideological values and principles, the latter involves their detailed infusion into the specifics of news programming, content, and commentary. The opinion-shaping process is most evident through the information industry's consistently favorable treat-ment, through images, reports, and interpretations, of superclass-dominated ideas, organizations, and policies. Two widespread media practices help create and reinforce public opinion favorable to superclass interests: deck stacking and selective reporting.

Deck Stacking

Deck stacking refers to the overwhelming preponderance of pro-superclass and pro-corporate media managers, editors, commentators, and reporters within the information industry. One way for superclass media owners and their credentialed-class top-level media managers to subtly achieve this re-sult is through staffing and pay practices that distance upper-tier media pro-fessionals from average workers' experiences and pay levels and link them more closely to the interests (and views) of elite owners and managers. In fact, as average workers today struggle with declining real wages and as the labor force becomes increasingly diverse, recent studies reveal that main-stream media professionals in major markets remain a relatively uniform and well-paid group of mainly white males from middle- and upper-middle-class backgrounds.[94] A survey of 444 journalists based in Washington, D.C., listed in the *News Media Yellow Book* found that 52 percent of the 141 re-spondents reported annual household incomes of more than $100,000, and 14 percent reported incomes of more than $200,000 per year.[95] (Pay levels for media professionals in smaller markets are lower. In 2004, median salaries for local TV staff were $73,000 for news directors, $55,500 for news anchors, and $40,000 for sports anchors.[96])

At the highest reaches of the media hierarchy are elite professionals earning millions, who can be counted on to express views consistent with their super-class owner-employer bosses. In the mid- and latter 2000s, examples of multi-million-dollar annual incomes for media stars included network TV news anchors Brian Williams (NBC, $4 million), Charles Gibson (ABC, $7–10 million), and Katie Couric (CBS, $15 million). TV commentators and "infotainment" personalities with multi-million-dollar annual incomes included Anderson Cooper ($2 million, CNN), Larry King ($7 million, CNN), Dr. Phil McGraw ($45 million, syndicated), Bill O'Reilly ($9 million, Fox), Diane Sawyer ($13 million, ABC), and Oprah Winfrey ($225 million, syndicated; in 2006 Oprah was listed by *Forbes* as having a net worth of $1.4 billion). On radio, Rush Limbaugh's contract reportedly pays him $30 million per year (Premier Radio Network) and octogenarian Paul Harvey is reportedly paid $10 million annually (ABC radio). Even the hosts of TV's premier parodies of news shows (discussed in chapter 7) are well paid: Jon Stewart ($1.5 million, *The Daily Show*) and Stephen Colbert ($1 million, *The Colbert Report*—both on Comedy Central, owned by Viacom).[97]

The uniform staffing of information-industry management and reporting personnel leads to an ideological filtering and opinion-shaping system generating news content and commentary that consistently parallels and reflects, but virtually never challenges, superclass ideological views. This situation begins with built-in structural biases grounded in corporate ownership of the media, leading to owners' hiring and rewarding of managers and editors who reflect pro-superclass and pro-corporate values and views. Acting as gatekeepers, these groups in turn hire and reward reporters who share their views—or who are willing to self-censor their work to conform with the ideological boundaries imposed by the corporate structure and enforced by editorial oversight.[98]

Informal social events promoted by top media management linking editors and reporters with superclass leaders in congenial settings help reinforce a shared worldview and promote cordial media-business ties. For example, in the 1990s, *Time* magazine spent $3 million to "fly dozens of corporate chiefs around the world for nine days . . . [escorted] by *Time*'s top managers and editors." The firms represented included Lockheed Martin, General Motors, Rockwell, Philip Morris, and Mitsubishi, and the executives met with heads of state from India, Hong Kong, Vietnam, Russia, and Cuba. Commenting on the event, the media magazine *Extra!* asked, "How eager will *Time*'s . . . reporters be to scrutinize the firms their bosses have wined and dined across the globe?"[99]

Poll results regarding media professionals' views on labor and their ideological orientations illustrate the nature and extent of deck stacking in the press. A *Los Angeles Times* poll found 54 percent of editors side with business in labor disputes, and only 7 percent side with labor. A survey sponsored by the United Automobile Workers (UAW) union of the one hundred largest daily newspapers found that 60 percent opposed union positions on minimum-wage increases, trade regulations, and plant-closing laws.[100] A Brookings Institution study of Washington, D.C., journalists found that 58 percent identified themselves as either conservative or middle of the road.[101] A survey of Washington-area journalists found that 66 percent characterized their political orientation as center or right on social issues, while on economic issues 83 percent characterized their political orientation as center or right.[102]

Deck stacking extends across all media formats and is especially evident in the lopsided spectrum of viewpoints presented by television news programming and by nearly all nationally syndicated electronic and print commentators. In the mid-2000s, all of the leading political-opinion talk shows on national commercial or public television had centrist or conservative hosts and moderators: *Crossfire, Face the Nation, Meet the Press, Hannity & Colmes, Nightline, The McLaughlin Group, This Week, The O'Reilly Factor,* and *Tavis Smiley.*[103] The situation whereby conservative points of view are presented on TV news shows far more often than "liberal" or "progressive" perspectives extends to the guests interviewed on TV news programs. This lack of balance was documented by an extensive recent study of nearly seven thousand guests appearing on the major Sunday morning news talk shows broadcast by ABC, CBS, and NBC over an eight-year period (1997 to 2005). The study concluded these programs "are dominated by conservative voices from newsmakers to commentators."[104]

Findings from an earlier eighteen-month study of four Sunday morning television talk shows (*Meet the Press, The McLaughlin Group, Face the Nation, This Week*) paralleled the conclusions of the 2006 study noted above. In addition, the earlier study illustrated how deck stacking in television "news" programming extends to the topics discussed (or not discussed). As the study pointed out, the four programs examined *supposedly* encourage national dialogue on major current events and policy issues. And while these shows do "help set the agenda for debate in Washington," the study found that they consistently failed to address important issues related to corporate power. Less than 4 percent of the show's discussion topics over the eighteen-month study period focused on corporate power issues such as "the environment, corporate crime, labor, mergers, consumer rights, corporate welfare, national health care, free trade agreements, redlining, blockbusting, multinational capital flight, tort reform, renewable energy, [and] the commercialization of children." The study also found, like the 2006 study cited above, that "an overwhelming majority of invited guests on the shows are lawmakers, government officials, and politicians—a skew that tends to reinforce narrow parameters of discussion and exclude issues of corporate power."[105]

Research on news programs, including ABC's *Nightline,* CNN's *Crossfire,* Fox's *Hannity & Colmes,* and C-SPAN's *Washington Journal,* yielded findings similar to those cited above from the Sunday morning news talk show studies.[106] Regarding public television news, a six-month study of guests interviewed on the PBS *NewsHour* program in 2005 to 2006 found "elite" sources representing primarily conservative points of view dominated the guest list of this "public" TV news program. The study reported that "current and former government officials . . . account[ed] for 50 percent of total guests. Journalists amounted to 10 percent, with academics at 8 percent, corporate guests at 5 percent and think tank experts account[ed] for 3 percent. . . . Public interest . . . sources . . . representing labor, environmental groups and consumer rights organizations—combined for less than 1 percent of the *NewsHour* guest list."[107] The media watchdog group FAIR pointed out long ago that the results of studies such as those cited above, which document consistent conservative biases in TV news media programming, are predictable: "True advocates for the left—people who actually push for progressive social change and identify with left-of-center activists—are almost invisible on TV."[108]

Syndicated columnists writing for the print media reflect a pattern of centrist-conservative thought similar to television news and commentary programming. Two surveys of the most widely distributed syndicated newspaper political columnists document a pattern of dominance by conservative and centrist writers, such as James Dobson, Cal Thomas, Robert Novak, David Broder, and George Will.[109] This reality has even been acknowledged by the conservative American Enterprise Institute: "Despite the image of a media dominated by liberals, the reality is much different. The most widely syndicated columnists are conservatives."[110]

Selective Reporting

Selective reporting refers to unstated, but routine, news-reporting policies and practices that produce a preponderance of flattering (virtue-exaggerating) news media coverage of superclass-favored and superclass-sponsored issues, organizations, activities, policies, or people and ignore or play down the merits or significance of topics that threaten superclass interests. Selective reporting is especially evident in news media treatment of business and labor issues.

Business Good, Unions Bad

Selective reporting begins with much greater chunks of media time and space devoted to covering business topics as against labor and union issues. A study of national news television broadcasts found that business and economic reporting receives double the amount of time devoted to workers' issues. Moreover, workers are virtually never interviewed or portrayed as "experts," and no worker has ever been selected as "Person of the Week" by *ABC World News Tonight*—although many corporate executives are often chosen for this feature.[111] As noted in chapter 2, no labor leaders have appeared on NBC's

Chris Matthews Show since its debut in 2002, and only a handful appeared on Matthews's MSNBC *Hardball* show over fifteen months in 2004 and 2005.[112] One study of local television news broadcasts found that stations devote fewer than 2 percent of news time to labor issues.[113] In addition to imbalanced television news coverage, there are also many specialty business television programs (e.g., *Wall Street Week, The Nightly Business Report*) and mass-circulation national business publications (e.g., *Wall Street Journal, Business Week, Forbes*) that have no parallels among worker or labor union audiences.

The largely positive media portrayal of business interests, corporate actions, and company executives, including the corporation-as-hero theme, is another feature of selective reporting. This tendency stands in sharp contrast to complaints by some corporate officials that the media often treat businesses harshly. However, the evidence overwhelmingly supports the conclusion that "the standard media—mainstream newspapers, magazines, and broadcasters— have always been reliable promoters of the corporate ethic."[114] This is illustrated by a survey of CEOs from the one thousand largest industries in the United States, which revealed that two-thirds believe media treatment of their companies is good or excellent, and only 6 percent feel it is poor.[115]

When the mainstream media do present what appear to be negative accounts of corporate actions, a closer look at such stories typically reveals a different

truth: "When news shows like *60 Minutes* or *20/20* do segments on 'big business versus the little people,' they usually define the problem in terms of the greed of one group of executives or the excesses of a single company. They never seriously address the nature of capitalism and the structural factors that often lead companies to harm the 'little people.'"[116]

In contrast with how the media treat corporations, when unions are the subject of media reporting, they are most often depicted in negative terms: as outdated, confrontational, out of touch with global economic realities, selfish, and corruption riddled.[117] A UAW study identified six negative myths about unions repeatedly cited in the mass media, including these especially damning notions: "Unions have been slowly strangling American business. Workers and unions demand the moon and make consumers pay for it. Unions can't do anything to reverse the falling fortunes of workers. Unions might have once been valuable, but now have too much power and need to be weakened or eliminated."[118] Despite the reality that these myths are easily refuted by accurate information, the study found such information is seldom reported in the mainstream media.

A university study entitled "Media Portrayals of Organized Labor" also reported a pattern of negative media depictions of unions. This study found unions were frequently portrayed by reporters according to eight negative stereotypes that paralleled the myths identified by the UAW study.[119] The findings from this study and others cited above are not surprising because, as recent researchers have shown, mainstream media coverage of unions, their leaders, and their activities is overwhelmingly hostile and negative.[120] Media critic Ben Bagdikian's observations regarding corporate power and media reporting on unions echo the findings of most research in this area: "The result of the overwhelming power of relatively narrow corporate ideologies has been the creation of widely established political and economic illusions in the United States. . . . [One is] that labor-union-induced wages are a damaging drag on national productivity and thus on the economy. [It is] false but [it has] been perpetuated by corporate-controlled media for decades."[121] (The lessons here? Unions are bad! Silence criticism!)

The Social Security "Crisis"

Selective reporting also applies to specific issues and results in one-sided media presentations that attempt to sway public opinion in the direction of superclass interests and public policies that would serve those interests. Illustrating this practice were reports by many mainstream media outlets in the early and mid-2000s describing the Social Security system as headed for a "major crisis" because of the program's alleged "impending insolvency."[122] As we documented in chapter 4, the 2005 superclass-driven campaign led by President George W. Bush to privatize Social Security failed (at least for the time being). Our purpose here is not to revisit that struggle but to illustrate how mainstream media coverage of the Social Security program and the president's campaign to "reform" it provides an instructive example of selective reporting in support of superclass interests.

While misleading media reports regarding the solvency of the Social Security program are not new, such reports became especially notable in the early and mid-2000s. The story began in 2001 when President Bush's Commission to Strengthen Social Security issued a preliminary report essentially claiming that the Social Security trust fund was useless and that the system, unless "reformed," was doomed. Shortly thereafter, *Newsweek* published a ringing endorsement of the commission's view in a full-page essay by financial reporter Allan Sloan.[123] Later that same year, as the economy slid into recession, the *Wall Street Journal* and the *New York Times* published editorials and op-ed pieces arguing in favor of using funds reserved for Social Security to stimulate an economic recovery. Both pieces essentially argued that Social Security was already bankrupt and that economic growth was the only sure way to sustain the program.[124] The logic of these assessments suggested that only the "free market" could "save" Social Security, and the unstated implication was clear: privatization would be the most effective salvation.

The "Social Security is in crisis" and "Social Security will soon go bankrupt" themes were repeated by mainstream media outlets in news reports and editorials both prior to and during President Bush's 2005 campaign to "reform" the program. In late 2004, these themes were prominently featured in both print and electronic media outlets, including the *New York Times*, *USA Today*, the *Washington Post*, *Time*, NPR, and CNN.[125] In early 2005, ABC's *Good Morning America* "examined the future retirement of a married couple in their 40s." ABC's Claire Shipman observed, "everyone agrees . . . the Social Security system as it exists now won't be able to afford . . . [the couple's retirement] payments."[126]

In the spring of 2005, Bush conducted a "60 day, 35 state tour to spread fear over the financial solvency of Social Security and promote his plan to allow workers to divert nearly a third of the 12.4 percent Social Security payroll tax into private investment accounts."[127] During this campaign, mainstream media outlets typically reported the president's claim that the system would go "bankrupt in 2042" as a matter of fact. The president's portrayal of Social Security as facing a "crisis" and about to go "bankrupt" did not evoke substantive challenges from most mainstream media reporters and pundits. Instead, the president's views were largely accepted by most major media writers, such as David Brooks (*New York Times*) and Robert Samuelson (*Newsweek*). These pundits and others typically confined their comments on the president's plan and on the program generally to "technical" proposals that would supposedly help ensure Social Security's solvency. Examples included suggestions on changing the formula for indexing benefits, raising the eligibility age, and lowering benefits to wealthy people.[128]

The evidence that the mainstream media engaged in selective reporting that favored superclass interests in the mid-2000s national debate on Social Security "reform" is, we believe, powerful and persuasive. In sharp contrast to the selective-reporting practices of the mainstream media, media organizations associated with the alternative power networks published numerous investigative reports, articles, and editorials in the early and mid-2000s calling attention to the class-based interests, resources, and ideological motivations of groups and political figures promoting Social Security privatization schemes. These alternative media outlets documented how superclass-controlled organizations were behind the campaign to privatize Social Security and undermine public confidence in it.[129] There is no doubt that the alternative media played an important role in promoting authentic public understanding of the president's efforts to "reform" Social Security. But the limited resources of, and small audiences for, these media made it difficult for their factual reports and analyses of class-based interests to counter mainstream media selective reporting grounded in superclass-generated propaganda.

Think Tanks (Again!)

Selective reporting on a wide range of topics is reinforced through extensive media reliance on information derived from superclass-funded "official sources," such as think tanks. A mid-2000s study of media references to major think tanks according to their ideological orientations found an overwhelming reliance on conservative and centrist organizations. Using a Nexis database search of major newspapers and radio and TV transcripts for 2005, the study found a total of 27,229 media citations to think tank sources. There were 10,937 references (40 percent) to conservative or right-leaning think tanks, such as the Heritage Foundation, and 12,719 references (47 percent) to centrist organizations, such as the Brookings Institution. By contrast, the study found only 3,573 references (13 percent) to progressive think tanks such as the Economic Policy Institute (730 references).[130]

Given extensive superclass funding of, and media firm links to, conservative-centrist think tanks, the study results should not be surprising. For example, the Heritage Foundation, the conservative think tank most widely cited in 2005 by the U.S. media (2,734 citations), received contributions for its operating revenues of $35 million in 2005.[131] These contributions all came from conservative sources, including individuals ($23.5 million), foundations ($9.5 million), and corporations ($2.1 million). The forty-five largest individual and foundation supporters donated $13.7 million in amounts ranging from $100,000 to $1 million and included ultraconservative sources, such as Richard M. Scaife, the Margaret Thatcher Foundation, and the Sarah Scaife Foundation. Heritage's board of trustees included Steve Forbes (*Forbes* magazine), Richard M. Scaife, and Holland Coors (Coors beer).[132] The Heritage officers and senior employees are well paid to promote conservative views. For example, in 2004, total compensation for CEO Edwin J. Feulner Jr. was $746,285; total income for the organization's ten vice presidents ranged from a high of $450,000 to a low of $219,000; five senior staff members earned an average of $122,000.[133]

THE SPIN-CONTROL PROCESS

The role of public relations is to so muddle the public sphere as to take the risk out of democracy for the wealthy and corporations.

—Robert W. McChesney, *Monthly Review*, November 2000

The *spin-control process* refers to a wide array of propaganda-driven media practices. It involves media owners, managers, reporters, pundits, and commercial and political advertisers using the information industry as a platform for disseminating news, commentary, images, and advertising with a pro-superclass and pro-corporate slant. The objectives of spin control include ideological justifications of the economic and political status quo and the commercial marketing of products, services, and corporate images, as well as media-based marketing of political candidates, public officials, and public policies. Spin control involves a symbiotic linkage between the information industry and the public relations industry, a $10 billion corporate enterprise based on the twin goals of manipulation and deception. Using the information industry as a platform, the public relations industry provides a wide array of services—mainly to superclass, corporate, and political clients—ranging from conventional press releases to commercial and political advertising campaigns to "the hiring of spies, the suppression of free speech, and even the manufacture of 'grass roots' movements."[134] "Surveys show that PR accounts for anywhere from 40 to 70 percent of what appears as news."[135]

The spin-control process operates at two levels. The first involves interpretation: it consists of information-industry-channeled news reporting and commentary that is "shaded"—through media professionals' choices of value-laden terms, images, references, context, and illustrations—in directions that reflect positively on superclass-favored ideas, policies, organizations, and interests and negatively on topics disfavored by elites. The second level involves propaganda, deception, and calculated manipulation. It consists of all forms of advertising and public relations strategies and tactics aimed at manipulating target populations' opinions, attitudes, tastes, and behaviors (mainly those of the working class) on behalf of goals established most often by superclass-controlled corporate and political clients.

Spin control is a complex process with many facets extending beyond the scope of this book. The purpose of this section is simply to highlight, through illustrative examples, how each spin-control level furthers superclass interests, often in ways that conceal the nature and extent of these interests and of superclass power as well.

Spin Control: Interpretation

As noted earlier in this chapter, tensions between superclass ideological assertions that the U.S. economic and political systems are the best in the world and routine corporate practices producing a variety of negative economic and political consequences for the working class are problematic for elites. Efforts to reduce or reconcile these tensions are a routine focus of the spin-control process. Mainstream media reporters and pundits (as well as privileged-class government officials and corporate leaders) typically address these tensions with reports and commentary that "spin" U.S. economic, political, and social problems through interpretations that deflect attention from the class-based structured inequalities that underlie many such problems.

In the world of spin control, problematic societal conditions are typically interpreted as highly complex, difficult to fully comprehend, and challenging to resolve. These qualities stem in part from the complicated causal factors that are typically thought to generate the problems. Of course, the "causes" of problematic societal conditions are never identified as class inequalities. Instead, they are more often interpreted as stemming from multiple sources, such as individual-level qualities (e.g., low levels of intelligence, psychological problems, or dysfunctional cultural qualities), subcultural pathologies, governmental meddling, and temporary, unavoidable, but good-for-everyone-in-the-long-term consequences of large-scale "natural laws." These latter forces often include the wonderful and mysterious "free market" or the equally magical "global economy." Two important effects of spin control regarding societal problems are (1) the public is distracted from the problematic effects of superclass domination and control of the media and indeed of most other institutions in the society, and (2) "solutions" to societal problems that would involve substantial redistributions of class-based resources from the privileged class to the new working class are unlikely to be articulated, considered, or implemented. A detailed example of spin control in the media concerning class inequalities is included in the box reading at the end of this chapter, "Class Issues in the Media: Spinning Inequality."

Demonizing Critics

Switching to a negative spin-control mode is routine in the information industry when it comes to individuals and groups viewed as threats to superclass interests or as critics of the superclass power elite that controls the U.S. government and economy. One example from the mid- and latter 2000s was the nearly universal demonization of Venezuelan president Hugo Chávez by the U.S. mainstream media. Elected president in 1998, Chávez initiated a series of reforms that U.S. progressives have described as "a close replica of Franklin Roosevelt's New Deal."[136] He has cultivated close ties with Fidel Castro in Cuba and denounced the U.S.-supported neoliberal "free market" policies of the International Monetary Fund in Latin America. As a result of his "antisu-perclass" policies, the Bush administration has been very hostile to the Chávez government and supported a military coup against it in 2002 (which failed); in 2005, then U.S. secretary of defense Donald Rumsfeld "compared [Chávez] to Hitler," and U.S. televangelist (and Bush supporter) Pat Robertson "publicly called for the assassination of Chávez."[137]

While "the editors of several major newspapers were quick to denounce" Robertson's threat, there is little doubt that the mainstream media's demo-nization of Chávez "contributed to the heated political climate in which Robertson made his threat."[138] The U.S. mainstream media have not only echoed U.S. government hostility to Chávez but have actively demonized the Chávez regime. This is illustrated by a study of "the opinion pages of the top 25 circulation newspapers in the United States during the first six months of 2005 . . . [which] found that 95 percent of the nearly 100 press commentaries that examined Venezuelan politics expressed clear hostility to the country's democratically elected president."[139]

Despite the fact that Venezuelan polls in the mid-2000s gave Chávez ap-proval ratings of over 70 percent and despite his "government's success in bringing poor and working class Venezuelans into the political process," the U.S. media labeled Chávez a "tyrant" and a "strongman." The *Wall Street Jour-nal* claimed he had "presided over the collapse of democracy in Venezuela."[140] The *Journal's* editorial board suggested *Parade* magazine should include Chávez on its annual list of "the world's worst dictators."[141] U.S. media de-monization of Chávez intensified following his September 2006 speech to the United Nations, where he suggested president Bush was "the devil." After his speech, the *Wall Street Journal* described Chávez as an "aspiring dictator" and as "the kook from Caracas."[142] The *New York Times* labeled Chávez a "buffoon" but also warned he was part of "today's most infectious geopolitical disease: petro-authoritarianism."[143] Media demonization of Chávez continued after his reelection in December 2006 (by 62 percent of the vote) to a third term as president of Venezuela.[144] Responding to pundits' claims that Chávez was a "threat to American interests" in the region, Steve Rendall, a critic of media bias, noted that by "'American interests,' such journalists don't mean what's good for Americans; they mean what's good for American elites."[145]

Spin Control: Propaganda

The public relations industry is the major force driving explicit, calculated spin control through the use of advertising, propaganda of all sorts, and newer techniques, such as the production and placement of difficult-to-spot "fake news" in conventional news outlets and "grassroots" movements to support any given client's interests. The industry is led by large firms, such as Burson-Marsteller, Golin/Harris, Hill & Knowlton, and Ketchum PR. In 2005, the in-dustry employed about 168,000 PR professionals (46,000 PR managers and

122,000 PR specialists), which was nearly double the 85,000 U.S. news reporters employed that year.[146]

As we noted earlier, the impact of PR on news content in the mainstream media is staggering in that it "accounts for anywhere from 40 to 70 percent of what appears as news."[147] Propaganda-based spin control comes in many forms, but three are especially important to promoting and concealing superclass and corporate interests and power: corporate image advertising, "fake news," and "Astroturf" campaigns.

Corporate Image Advertising

Annual expenditures on all methods, including advertising, to promote free market ideology and the image of corporations as "heroes" are estimated at $3 billion.[148] Ads attesting to the altruism and benevolent good works of corporations, such as Dow, DuPont, Ford, General Motors, Mobil Oil, and Phillips, are routinely published in national magazines and aired on network television. Meanwhile, "on so-called 'public TV,' a dozen big corporate polluters—including BASF, Goodyear and Mobil—polish their images by underwriting nature shows."[149] The head of a large advertising agency described the purpose of corporate advertising thus: "It presents the corporation as hero, a responsible citizen, a force for good, presenting information on the work the company is doing in community relations, assisting the less fortunate, minimizing pollution, controlling drugs, ameliorating poverty."[150]

The point of corporate advertising is to create favorable public opinion regarding corporate ideas, motives, and actions. This helps maintain the legitimacy of corporations—and by extension helps protect not only their business interests but also the economic and political interests and power of superclass corporate owners.

Fake News

Fake news refers to reports presented in mainstream media news outlets as legitimate news stories or as commentary on news issues without disclosure that the reports were paid for (either their production or their placement in the media or both) by clients with interests that are served by the reports. Fake news reports presented as authentic news are designed to advance the interests of the client who pays for them. Most clients are corporations, but others include wealthy individuals (often political candidates), government agencies, and nongovernmental organizations. Fake news clients sometimes pay a PR firm to both produce fake news reports and place them in news media outlets. Sometimes clients or client-hired PR firms ensure the placement of fake news in mainstream media news outlets by paying reporters, pundits, or news outlets to incorporate the fake news into legitimate news reporting or commentary. For example, the NewsUSA PR firm offers game show–like prizes, such as refrigerators and gas grills, to newspaper and radio editors for using the audio news releases, newspaper copy, and radio scripts the firm prepares for paying corporate clients and associations.[151] In recent years, fake news has become an increasingly "common and overlooked [tool] of 'perception management'" by clients who want to maximize their influence on public opinion or consumer preferences.[152] Fake news is a perfect means of achieving these goals because the message is delivered as authentic news and thus avoids the credibility problems that may be associated with paid advertising or conventional press releases that identify the source.

Fake news is often prepared for clients by PR firms in the form of a video news release (VNR). VNRs "paid for by corporations, government agencies, and non-governmental organizations are commonly presented as legitimate news segments on local newscasts throughout the United States." These simulated news stories are "designed to be indistinguishable from traditional TV news and are often aired without the original producers and sponsors being identified, and sometimes without any local editing." A recent survey by DS Simon Productions (a major VNR producer) reported that "88 percent of TV stations use VNRs from medical, pharmaceutical and biotech corporations in their newscasts." Doug Simon, head of DS Simon, claimed that at least 90 percent of the VNRs produced by his firm were aired without disclosure.[153] A Florida company known as WJMK produces VNRs that have aired as "news breaks" on public television stations across the United States. These segments "profile healthcare companies and their products" and have been broadcast under the title "The American Medical Review." WJMK officials claimed that thirty million households see each segment, but "the videos do not mention that the companies paid WJMK to produce them."[154]

Federal agencies have funded VNRs in recent years to promote Bush administration policies. Examples include three presidential cabinet departments. The U.S. Department of Education paid Ketchum PR $700,000 for VNRs reporting favorably on the Bush-backed No Child Left Behind law; the U.S. Department of Health and Human Services paid Ketchum PR to create a VNR promoting the Bush administration's Medicare reform bill; the U.S. Department of Agriculture (USDA) paid for internally produced VNRs and audio news releases to endorse international trade policies favored by the Bush administration and to promote USDA "accomplishments."[155] In addition to the use of VNRs, federal agencies also funded favorable fake news through "pundit payola." "Conservative commentators Armstrong Williams, Maggie Gallagher, and Michael McManus were outed for taking money under the table to endorse Bush Administration policies." Williams was "paid $240,000 by Ketchum as a subcontractor on a Department of Education contract to promote No Child Left Behind."[156]

The increasing use of fake news to support elite interests is a major concern not only because it violates traditional journalistic ideals regarding the nature of news (as objective and balanced) and commentary (as an open expression of views with full disclosure of interests), but also because it compromises the ability of ordinary citizens to be fully informed by the media and for democracy to function in a meaningful fashion.[157] In the mid-2000s, FCC Commissioner Jonathan Adelstein warned that "the increasing commercialization of media is one of media consolidation's 'most pernicious symptoms.'" Two prominent examples he cited were forms of fake news: "video news releases masquerading as news" and "thinly disguised payola."[158]

Astroturf Campaigns

Astroturf campaigns involve the use of paid participants in "industry-generated 'citizens' groups who can be relied upon to lobby government and speak eloquently to [the] media."[159] These increasingly sophisticated, pseudograssroots (i.e., "Astroturf"), corporate-sponsored public relations offensives have become a billion-dollar PR subspecialty.[160] Such campaigns further ensure favorable media coverage of superclass-linked corporate interests and enhance the political potency of these interests, especially via federal and state lobbying efforts by corporations and their trade associations. Astroturf campaigns are effective "perception-management" tools routinely utilized to advance superclass-driven corporate agendas. Corporate managers have found that Astroturf campaigns organized by the public relations industry can be very useful in generating positive news media coverage, public opinion, and favorable treatment by policy makers and the courts.

The most successful examples of Astroturf campaigns, from a corporate perspective, are not publicly known because they are the ones whose true nature and purposes were never discovered or publicly revealed. However, examples that have come to light illustrate how such campaigns serve corporate interests via the spin-control propaganda process.

Some publicly known illustrations of Astroturf campaigns have involved "smokers' rights" groups. For example, in the 1990s, Burson-Marsteller (the PR firm mentioned in chapter 4) helped create (with funding from Philip Morris) a "grassroots" group known as the National Smokers Alliance to promote smokers' rights.[161] The alliance was one of many artificial grassroots groups created by U.S. tobacco firms in the 1990s to help protect their economic interests in what is now an $86 billion industry.[162] But the tobacco industry is hardly alone in its use of Astroturf campaigns to generate favorable media coverage or more effective lobbying.

In the late 1990s and early 2000s, Burson-Marsteller, the PR firm for the chemical giant Monsanto, was involved in paying for a "pro-genetic modification demonstration at a recent Food and Drug Administration hearing." The PR firm reportedly gave "some of the 100 participants cash . . . free food, and transportation." Once the story broke, "even Monsanto admitted that the practice of paying people to demonstrate was 'abhorrent.'" In reporting the story, the *New York Times* ran the headline "Monsanto Campaign Tries to Gain Support for

Gene-Altered Food." *Extra!* described this innocuous wording as a "prime example of the 'please don't read this story genre.'" The magazine also noted, "Is it a surprise to learn that in addition to representing Monsanto, Burson-Marsteller is the PR agency for the *New York Times?*"[163]

More recently, the Pharmaceutical Research and Manufacturers Association (PhRMA) representing forty-eight drug companies "funded several pro-industry Astroturf organizations to promote its interests, including the United Seniors Association and Citizens for Better Medicare."[164] Public Citizen published a report showing how "the drug industry used a phony seniors group called United Seniors Association to push its legislative agenda in Congress."[165] The PhRMA-sponsored Astroturf campaign in support of the Bush-backed Medicare prescription-drug bill paid off (aided by $141 million spent by the drug industry for lobbying in 2003, plus millions more in campaign contributions).[166] Congress passed, and the president signed, the Medicare drug bill in early 2003—with no cost-control provisions. It will cost taxpayers about $400 billion over the next ten years as the federal government pays drug companies this amount for drugs used by Medicare-eligible seniors.[167] The fact that the drug benefit could bankrupt the Medicare system over time, as it is currently funded, may be no accident. Some writers have suggested that this was one of the hidden reasons why President Bush and his Republican and Democratic congressional supporters enacted the law.[168] Regardless of whether this view is true or not, in the near term, drug company profits will soar.

The examples cited above represent only the tip of a giant corporate iceberg involving phony "grassroots" campaigns. The public relations industry's expanding use of these campaigns on behalf of corporate clients is well documented in books, scholarly articles, alternative media reports, and websites.[169] Astroturf campaigns traffic in calculated deception but translate into favorable media coverage, political influence, and economic gains for corporate clients, public relations firms, and their superclass owners.

The net effects of such campaigns extend beyond any single-corporation or industry gains. Astroturf campaigns can be (and are) used on behalf of entire clusters of firms and industries to promote classwide policy outcomes favorable to superclass interests. The fact that such campaigns strike at the heart of representative democracy is irrelevant to corporate clients. Superclass Astroturf campaign clients understand that it is possible to combine the sentiments of National Football League coach Vince Lombardi's well-known cliché and singer-songwriter Randy Newman's song title into a single line: "It's Winning and Money That Matters in the U.S.A."

The many forms of spin control discussed in this section and the examples cited illustrate some of the many ways the public relations industry "spins" much of what Americans read, see, and hear in the media in pro-superclass and pro-corporate terms. This section also underscores the point that most spin-control methods and practices are provided mainly to wealthy corporate clients in order to further their economic and political interests—and those of their superclass owners. Finally, this section should remind us that there is a lamentable dearth of "counterspin" agents and practices working on behalf of working-class interests and power.

THE INFORMATION INDUSTRY: CONCLUSIONS

> Our press has . . . disappeared into "the media"—a mammoth antidemocratic oligopoly that is far more responsive to its owners, big shareholders and good buddies in the government than it is to the rest of us, the people of this country.
>
> —Mark Crispin Miller, *Nation*, July 3, 2006

The mainstream ideology, opinion-shaping, and spin-control processes are driven not by a superclass conspiracy but rather by superclass media ownership and a shared ideology that views the economic and political status quo as the best possible world, in accordance with common classwide interests and routine business practices. These factors thread superclass preferences and ideological biases into the fabric of virtually all news reporting, commentary, and advertising generated by the information industry. The industry consistently tilts reporting and commentary on events, institutions, personalities, and policies relevant to superclass interests in directions consistent with those interests. Of course, the three processes operating through the information industry may not always lead to a uniform, superclass-blessed "corporate ministry of information party line" on all issues and topics. But they clearly produce a lopsided presentation of ideologically infused news and commentary that trends in the direction of privileged-class interests on most issues, most of the time. Empirical support for this conclusion is provided by a recent study on inequality and the media, which found that "higher inequality is associated with lower media freedom [and] this effect is stronger in democratic regimes."[170] The study suggests that "in democracies where wealth tilts toward the top, the wealthy have a vested interest in 'capturing' the media and limiting the range of policy options that media grant time and attention."[171]

Root, Root, Root for the Home Team?

Media-based "ideological coaching" may not always lead the working class to share the views and policy preferences of superclass-sponsored opinion shapers. However, such efforts *appear* to predispose public opinion among working-class members in those directions—at least on some critical class-based issues, such as legitimating the accumulation of private wealth and the importance of reducing the federal deficit. For example, even as the United States was emerging from the Great Depression in 1939, a Roper poll found only a minority, 24 percent, agreeing that there should be a law limiting the amount of money a person could earn in a year. By 1992, with economic inequality accelerating, that number had shrunk to a tiny 9 percent.[172] A 2005 *New York Times* poll found that despite growing economic polarization, 75 percent of Americans surveyed thought "the chances of moving up to a higher class are the same as or greater than 30 years ago."[173] The same poll found 76 percent of Americans opposed the federal estate tax, and 50 percent favored the total elimination of federal inheritance taxes.[174] Such findings suggest that large numbers of Americans continue to accept the legitimacy of the current distribution of income and wealth in the United States, a view that favors superclass interests.

On the second issue, many U.S. progressives view the political movement to "balance" the federal budget (especially through a proposed "balanced-budget" amendment to the U.S. Constitution) as a superclass-driven smoke screen for dismantling more social programs.[175] But unlike progressives, sizable numbers of Americans appear to be convinced of the need for the government to "balance its checkbook"—just like average folks. In the mid-1990s, a Gallup poll reported 82 percent of Americans said "significant" deficit reduction should be the top or a high priority for Congress.[176] A 2003 poll found two-thirds of Americans favored a constitutional amendment to require a balanced federal budget.[177] And in 2006, 55 percent of Americans surveyed rated reducing the federal budget deficit as a "top priority."[178] These poll findings and those cited earlier concerning the distribution of income and wealth *appear* to illustrate superclass successes in shaping public opinion on critical economic issues.

A further effect of the control processes operating via the information industry relates to the political awareness of, and choices made by, the working class. By restricting the expression of alternative perspectives, superclass-based media control leads to confusion among working-class members over how the shadow political industry is both driven by and serves superclass resources and interests. It also leads to circumscribed, sterile politics and fatalistic or de facto support among many workers for the economic and political status quo. The lopsided ideological spectrum and stunted political debate presented in the media "leaves most citizens without a coherent view of politics . . . [and] a population unable to select alternative patterns of power sustains the status quo."[179]

The Persistence of Resistance?

The preceding section suggests working-class members frequently share superclass-favored views, but other evidence indicates that significant divisions also exist on some issues. The divergent nature of privileged-class and working-class experiences, interests, and views is evident in results from recent surveys. A 2005 poll conducted by the Pew Research Center compared Americans' views on the condition of the U.S. economy by household income levels. The findings revealed that middle- and lower-income Americans were far more concerned with the condition of the economy than were those with higher incomes. For example, just 38 percent of respondents with household incomes between $50,000 and $75,000 agreed with the statement "the economy is in excellent or good shape." Only 25 percent of respondents with household incomes under $50,000 agreed with the statement, but 45 percent of those with incomes over $75,000 agreed.[180] Another poll found that 47 percent of wealthy Americans (annual incomes at least $200,000) viewed the economic conditions in 2005 as "excellent" or "good," and 52 percent of wealthy investors expected their personal net worth would grow in the next year.[181] An earlier poll that compared average Americans with those of wealthy donors who contributed $5,000 or more to federal political candidates in the 1990s found that while average Americans were concerned with growing economic insecurity and corporate power, elite donors were not. For example, 83 percent of average Americans agreed (almost three-fifths strongly agreed) that "average working families have less economic security today, because corporations have become too greedy and care more about their profits than about being fair and loyal to their employees." By contrast, most large donors disagreed with the statement.[182]

Some recent polls have found that substantial numbers of Americans hold views that are inconsistent with or even hostile to superclass interests and power. The 2005 Pew survey found 45 percent of Americans had an unfavorable opinion of business corporations (65 percent had an unfavorable view of oil companies), and 45 percent said they had a favorable view (which was 20 points lower than in 2001). In that same survey, 53 percent of Americans said corporations make too much profit (39 percent thought corporate profits were fair and reasonable), and 77 percent said too much power is concentrated in the hands of a few large companies.[183] An earlier Preamble Center poll found 70 percent of the respondents believed corporate greed, not the global economy, is behind corporate downsizing. In this same survey, 46 percent saw corporate greed as the biggest obstacle to middle-class living standards, compared with 28 percent who saw government waste and inefficiency as the main problem. Also, 76 percent supported "living-wage laws," and 82 percent favored congressional action for "setting standards for responsible corporate behavior" and lowering taxes on companies that comply.[184]

A 2001 Pew Research Center poll found 44 percent of Americans agree with the view that the United States is now a "have/have-not society." The proportion agreeing with this view was up substantially from 26 percent in 1988 and 39 percent in 1999.[185] In an apparent confirmation of these findings, a 2003 Princeton Survey Research Associates poll found 68 percent of Americans agreed with the statement: "Today it's really true that the rich get richer while the poor get poorer."[186] A 2003 Gallup poll found 64 percent of Americans agreed that money and wealth in the United States "should be more evenly distributed among a larger percentage of the people."[187] In 2006, a survey of

U.S. workers reported, "More than two-thirds of American workers (68%) believed that if more working people joined together in unions, things could be better for working people."[188] A December 2006 Bloomberg/*Los Angeles Times* poll found that nearly three-quarters of Americans "now consider economic inequality a major national issue."[189] As 2006 ended, "polls show populism (a.k.a., challenging corporate economic power) is the 'center' position for the voting public, even though it may not be the 'center' position in a K-Street-owned Washington, D.C."[190]

The results of polls such as those cited above illustrate that despite the superclass biases inherent in the information industry, working-class members are not totally passive vessels filled with superclass-generated information and propaganda. Instead, these poll results provide evidence of resistance among nonelites to the massive dissemination through the information industry of information and commentary that preponderantly supports the status quo. It is apparent that increasing experiences with and knowledge about class-based inequalities among the nonprivileged is fostering a growing awareness of and concerns about the nature and extent of superclass interests, motives, and power in the economic and political arenas.

The Stealth Industries

Despite the size, power, and record of success in promoting superclass interests, most features of the information industry, including details concerning superclass funding and control of its operations, are seldom reported by the mainstream media.[191] The scant media and public attention paid to superclass control of this industry, as well as its control of the shadow political industry, reveals their stealthy qualities: they're there, but they do not register on mainstream media "radar screens" or generate much public attention. Why not? We believe the answer has three parts.

First, these industries are cloaked in the same powerful political force field that drives the class taboo: the mass media's avoidance of reporting on class issues, based in and funded by the superclass and its corporate domain, especially the absence of serious inquiries into the organizational foundations of class inequities.[192] Second, the information and shadow industries consist of numerous legitimate organizations with extensive resources and payrolls. Their links to major corporations, the mainstream media, and the national government make them a routine part of society—a nonstory by media standards. Third, when either industry does become the focus of media reports or books, the "pluralist special-interest group" model typically organizes and drives these accounts.[193] Viewers and readers are left with the impression that both industries consist of a diverse collection of competing organizations and sectors. No mention is made of the existence or importance of the superclass to funding, organizing, and coordinating the activities of these industries.

These factors help ensure that for each industry, the superclass-based political control structures and processes, as well as the class consequences of their actions, are largely shielded from media reporting and public attention. The result is the "stunt" Gore Vidal described in the opening of chapter 4: superclass political dominance vanishes behind the unreported, widespread, business-as-usual routines and legitimacy accorded to most features of the information and shadow political industries. In effect, the organizational foundations of the class empire and the results of its activities are hidden—in plain sight.

CLASS ISSUES IN THE MEDIA: SPINNING INEQUALITY

Earlier in this chapter, we identified the spin-control process as a collection of media practices that, among other things, help provide ideological justifications for the economic and political status quo. The interpretation level of spin control was described as including presentations of problematic societal conditions by mainstream media reports as complex, challenging, and difficult to resolve. Interpreting (or "framing") social problems in these ways, in our view, helps obfuscate the significance of superclass-driven power and resource inequalities to many social problems and also helps ensure that possible "solutions" to such problems will not include redistributive policies that would shift resources from the superclass to the working class.

An interesting and instructive example of how the interpretive dimension of the spin-control process operates in the U.S. media regarding class inequalities occurred in the mid-2000s. As we noted in chapter 2, the *New York Times* published a high-profile series of reports on various aspects of U.S. social-class inequalities in 2005. The *Times* series was both preceded and followed by similar reports in three other major U.S. newspapers (*Los Angeles Times, Wall Street Journal, Washington Post*) and in a major news journal (*Economist*).[1] All five of these major media sources documented growing income inequality in the United States over the last twenty-five years and reported that "social mobility" of young adults from lower- and middle-income families to higher-income ranks appeared to have stalled or even declined in recent years compared to the experiences of their parents' generation. While calling attention to the gloomy growing inequality trend could have set the stage for an examination of class power inequalities and a pointed critique of the increasingly rigid U.S. class structure, none of the reports took such an approach. Instead, the authors of the articles applied spin-control interpretations to the topic. The media "spin" presented the growing inequality trend as a complex and challenging issue but also suggested it was manageable—via individual efforts and modest public policy reforms.

While the interpretation of growing inequality as a complex and challenging issue appeared in some form in at least one or more articles included in the series of reports published by the five publications, some authors were more explicit than others. Regarding complexity, the second article in the *Economist* series expressed the view that growing inequality is a complex issue in part because it "is rooted in fundamental changes in the economy."[2] Similar interpretations were presented in the lead article in the *New York Times* series, the first article in the *Wall Street Journal* series, the second

(continued)

CLASS ISSUES IN THE MEDIA: SPINNING INEQUALITY (*continued*)

article in the *Washington Post* series, and in the first article in the *Los Angeles Times* series. The lead article in the *New York Times* series explicitly echoed the complexity interpretation offered by the *Economist* as the authors noted that "the hidden divisions of class" have been deepened by "globalization and technological change."[3]

The interpretation of the growing inequalities trend as a challenging issue was presented in each of the five series. At various points in each series, articles called attention to how this trend was inconsistent with the American ideals of equality of opportunity and mobility based on merit.[4] Also, to a greater or lesser extent, each series suggested at some point that the challenge of growing inequalities was a manageable issue that could be meaningfully addressed through a combination of individual efforts and modest public policy reforms.

The *New York Times* and the *Washington Post* published explicit interpretations regarding how the growing inequalities trend could be managed.[5] The "solutions" presented by these papers illustrate how the spin-control interpretation approach attempts to calm, defuse, and depoliticize the potential social dynamite of growing class inequalities with modest policy reforms. The *New York Times* published an editorial late in its class series endorsing a number of social policies, including stronger affirmative action programs to help qualified low-income students get into colleges, more antipoverty and early education programs, and tax cuts targeting "the middle class and below." The editorial concluded, "The goal should be a truly merit-based society where class finally fades from importance."[6] The second *Post* article offered a number of specific (and modest) policy suggestions claimed to help reduce rising inequality. These included federal tax law changes that would shift more of the tax burden onto the wealthy without "imposing high marginal rates," modest steps to "soften the rules of [global] competition . . . rebalance the power relationship between labor and capital," require shareholders to approve CEO compensation packages, increase the minimum wage and index it to inflation, and require all companies "to pay half the cost of catastrophic health insurance for their workers."[7]

The spin-control interpretations offered by each of the five publications concealed more than they revealed about the U.S. class structure. The articles in each series interpreted the growing class-inequalities trend in terms that ensured the contentious issue of class power inequalities in the political and economic arenas would not be examined and that the superclass-driven war against the working class would not be discussed. The interpretive spin taken in each series regarding how inequalities could be reduced or managed ensured that only those working-class grievances that could be resolved through individual efforts and modest public policy reforms would be considered and endorsed.

NOTES

1. A listing of the five sources that published analyses of class inequalities in the mid-2000s can be found in chapter 2, note 11.

2. "Middle of the Class," *Economist* (July 16, 2005): 13.

3. Janny Scott and David Leonhardt, "Class in America: Shadowy Lines That Still Divide," *New York Times*, May 15, 2005, 18.

4. See, for example, Scott and Leonhardt, "Class in America," 16–17.
5. The *New York Times* editors and publishers like to think of the paper as *the* authoritative source on news matters. This attitude was evident in the introduction to the *New York Times* book version of the class series. The author acknowledged that the class articles published by other newspapers were well done, but insisted that the *Times* series took "the discussion of class in our country to a new level" (*Class Matters*, xviii).
6. "Class and the American Dream," *New York Times*, May 30, 2005, A14.
7. Steven Pearlstein, "Solving Inequality Won't Take Class Warfare," *Washington Post*, March 15, 2006, D1.

NOTES

1. Peter Phillips and Project Censored, *Censored 2001: 25th Anniversary Edition* (New York: Seven Stories Press, 2001), 38.

2. Quotes are from Peter Phillips and Project Censored, eds., *Censored 2006: The Top 25 Censored Stories* (New York: Seven Stories Press, 2005), 15; the top 2005 story is from Peter Phillips and Project Censored, *Censored 2005* (New York: Seven Stories Press, 2004), 40.

3. Peter Hart and Julie Hollar, "Fear and Favor 2004: How Power Shapes the News," *Extra!* (March–April 2005): 24–29; Peter Hart and Steve Rendall, "Meet the Myth Makers," *Extra!* (July–August 1998): 26–27.

4. Joan Claybrook, "Corporate Accountability," Special anniversary edition, *Public Citizen News* 21(1) (2001): 20–21, 29.

5. Timothy D. Schellhardt, "Are Layoffs Moral? One Firm's Answer: You Ask, We'll Sue," *Wall Street Journal*, August 1, 1996. Also see Robert A. Sirico, "The Capitalist Ethic: True Morality," *Forbes* (December 2, 1996): 85; "Soundbites," *Extra!* (September–October 1996): 5.

6. California Anti-SLAPP Project, "What Are SLAPPs?" on the Internet at http://www.casp/net/intro/html (visited December 22, 2006).

7. Editorial, "$30 Million Can Make Media Shy of Truth," *National Catholic Reporter*, April 24, 1998, 1; one positive sign is that twenty-five states have now passed anti-SLAPP laws, and ten other states have, or are considering, anti-SLAPP bills. California Anti-SLAPP Project, "Other States: Statues and Cases," on the Internet at http://www.casp/net/intro/html (visited December 22, 2006).

8. Robert W. McChesney, *Rich Media, Poor Democracy* (Chicago: University of Illinois Press, 1999), 16–29. Also see Ben Bagdikian, *The New Media Monopoly* (Boston: Beacon Press, 2004), 27–54; Jim Naureckas, "From the Top: What Are the Politics of the Network Bosses?" *Extra!* (July–August 1998): 21–22; Bridget Thornton, Britt Walters, and Lori Rouse, "Corporate Media Is Corporate America," in Peter Phillips and Project Censored, eds., *Censored 2006: The Top 25 Censored Stories* (New York: Seven Stories Press, 2005), 245–62.

9. Pat Aufderheide, "Too Much Media," *In These Times* (May 9, 2005): 28; Mark C. Miller, "Free the Media," *Nation* (June 3, 1996): 9–15; "The National Entertainment State, Special Issue," *Nation* (July 3, 2006): 13–30.

10. Michael Dolny, "Think Tank Survey: Right, Center Think Tanks Still Most Quoted," *Extra!* (May–June 2005): 28–29; Michael Dolny, "Think Tank Survey: Study Finds First Drop in Think Tank Cites," *Extra!* (May–June 2006): 24–25.

11. David Croteau, "Challenging the 'Liberal Media' Claim," *Extra!* (July–August 1998): 9.

12. Bagdikian, *The New Media Monopoly*, 236.

13. Robert W. McChesney, "The Global Media Giants," *Extra!* (November–December 1997): 11.

14. Linda Foley, "Media Reform from the Inside Out: The Newspaper Guild-CWA," in *The Future of Media: Resistance and Reform in the 21st Century*, ed. Robert McChesney, Russell Newman, and Ben

Scott (New York: Seven Stories Press, 2005), 43; U.S. Department of Commerce, *Statistical Abstract of the United States: 2004–2005* (Washington, DC: U.S. Government Printing Office, 2004), 254.

15. Marc Cooper, "Reclaiming the First Amendment: Legal, Factual, and Analytic Support for Limits on Media Ownership," in McChesney, Newman, and Scott, *The Future of Media,* 169; Evan Thomas and Gregory L. Vistica, "Fallout from a Media Fiasco," *Newsweek* (July 20, 1998): 25.

16. John W. Wright, ed., *The New York Times 2006 Almanac* (New York: Penguin, 2005), 392.

17. Phillips and Project Censored, *Censored 2001,* 37.

18. "Fortune 1000 Ranked within Industries," *Fortune* (April 17, 2006): F61.

19. The McClatchy Company, "McClatchy Announces Agreement to Sell Five Knight-Ridder Papers" (press release, June 7, 2006), 2, on the Internet at http://www.mcclatchy.com/176/story/1607.html (visited November 26, 2006).

20. U.S. Securities and Exchange Commission, "Form 10-K, CBS Corporation: For Fiscal Year Ended December 31, 2005," Washington, D.C., I-4 through I-17.

21. News Corporation, "Australian Federal Court Approves News Corporation Reincorporation to United States" (press release, November 3, 2004), 1.

22. Since our focus in this chapter is on the information industry, we limit our attention to the five companies listed because their major media holdings include national electronic news operations. Our listing does not include other large firms with substantial U.S. media holdings, such as Viacom (now largely a U.S. cable TV and movie company since it spun off of CBS Corp. in 2005), Gannett (and similar companies owning large numbers of U.S. newspapers), and Bertelsmann (a German media firm). It should be noted that despite the Viacom-CBS split, both firms are still effectively controlled by Viacom founder Sumner Redstone. See Johnnie L. Roberts, "A Mogul in Full," *Newsweek* (April 24, 2006): 43–44.

23. The summary profiles presented for each of the five media firms, including the revenue figures, are based on information included in various corporate publications produced by each firm. These include 2005 annual reports, 2005 U.S. Securities and Exchange Commission Form 10-K reports, and additional documents found on the five corporate websites available on the Internet. See the bibliography for complete citations for each company website.

24. McChesney, *Rich Media, Poor Democracy,* 29.

25. McChesney, *Rich Media, Poor Democracy,* 29.

26. Thornton, Walters, and Rouse, "Corporate Media Is Corporate America," 245.

27. Peter Phillips, "Self Censorship and the Homogeneity of the Media Elite," in *Censored 1998,* ed. Peter Phillips (New York: Seven Stories Press, 1998), 152.

28. Matt Carlson, "Boardroom Brothers," *Extra!* (September–October 2001): 18–19. Also see Stephanie Dyer, "Lifestyles of the Media Rich and Oligopolistic," in Phillips and Project Censored, *Censored 2005,* 189–97.

29. Bagdikian, *The New Media Monopoly,* 6–9, 15–17.

30. McChesney, *Rich Media, Poor Democracy,* 29.

31. Robert Parry, "The Right-Wing Media Machine," *Extra!* (March–April 1995): 7.

32. Naureckas, "From the Top," 21–22. Also see Bagdikian, *The New Media Monopoly,* 50–54; Jim Naureckas, "Where's the Power: Newsroom or Boardroom?" *Extra!* (July–August 1998): 23.

33. Ben H. Bagdikian, *The Media Monopoly* (Boston: Beacon Press, 1997), 26.

34. Bagdikian, *The New Media Monopoly,* 15, 51, 122; Janine Jackson, "Let Them Eat Baguettes," *Extra!* (March–April 1996): 14–15.

35. William K. Tabb, "After Neoliberalism?" *Monthly Review* (June 2003): 27. In the mid–twentieth century, Austrian economist and Nobel Prize winner Friedrich August von Hayek (the intellectual godfather of contemporary "free market supply-side economics") applied the term *liberal* to followers of free market economics (a meaning nearly the opposite of "liberal" in U.S. political-economy thought today). In the contemporary period, what Hayek labeled as "liberal" economic thought came to be characterized as "neoliberal." See Christian Parenti, "Winning the War of Ideas," *In These Times* (November 17, 2003): 18–21. The importance of neoliberalism to U.S. ruling-class elites as a political-economy ideology is suggested by author David Harvey. He "argues that ruling elites in the United States [have] promoted neoliberalism—or free market

fundamentalism—as 'a project to achieve the restoration of class power' which was threatened economically and politically in the late '60s and early '70s." Quote in David Moberg, "Throw Books at Them," *In These Times* (December 19, 2005): 37.

36. G. William Domhoff, *Who Rules America? Power, Politics and Social Change* (New York: McGraw-Hill, 2006), 78–79, 106.

37. Domhoff, *Who Rules America?* 112, 157.

38. Bagdikian, *The Media Monopoly*, 6.

39. Parry, "The Right-Wing Media Machine," 7.

40. Naureckas, "From the Top," 21–22.

41. Bagdikian, *The New Media Monopoly*, 106; Robert McChesney and John Bellamy Foster, "'Left Wing' Media?" *Monthly Review* (June 2003): 10, 14–15.

42. Average CEO pay is based on the authors' analysis of data reported in corporate reports.

43. Average pay for CEOs at the seven largest publicly held newspaper companies (indexed in the 2006 Fortune 1000 listing) is based on the authors' analysis of data reported in corporate reports. The seven firms were Gannett, Tribune, Washington Post, New York Times, Knight-Ridder, E. W. Scripps, and Dow Jones. The highest-paid CEO was Craig A. Dubow (Gannet, $9.6 million); the lowest paid was Donald E. Graham (Washington Post, $800,000).

44. Journalism.org, "Newspapers," State of the News Media 2006, 25, on the Internet at http://www.stateofthenewsmedia.org/2006/printable_newspapers (visited May 20, 2006).

45. Janine Jackson, "Wall Street's Gain Is Journalism's Loss," *Extra!* (September–October 2001): 20.

46. Bagdikian, *The New Media Monopoly*, 8.

47. Journalism.org, State of the News Media 2006: "Newspapers," 1, 42; "Network Television," 51–52; "Magazines," 26; "Radio," 34–35; Keith J. Kelly, "Time Looks to Trim $100 Million," *New York Times*, December 28, 2005, 32.

48. Jackson, "Wall Street's Gain Is Journalism's Loss," 20.

49. U.S. Department of Commerce, *Statistical Abstract of the United States: 2007* (Washington, DC: U.S. Government Printing Office, 2006), 785.

50. Eyal Press, "Spin Cities," *Nation* (November 18, 1996): 30.

51. Peter Hart and Janine Jackson, "Media Lick the Hand That Feeds Them," *Extra!* (November–December 2005): 21–23; Julie Hollar, Janine Jackson, and Hilary Goldstein, "Outside (and Inside) Influence on the News: Fear and Favor 2005," *Extra!* (March–April 2006): 15–20.

52. Jim Naureckas, "Corporate Censorship Matters: The Case of NBC," *Extra!* (November–December 1995): 13.

53. Janine Jackson and Peter Hart, "Fear and Favor 2000: How Power Shapes the News," *Extra!* (May–June 2001): 21.

54. Sheldon Rampton and John Stauber, "This Report Brought to You by Monsanto," *Progressive* (July 1998): 22–25.

55. Jane Akre, "We Report, They Decide: Fox TV Censors Series on Milk Hazards," *National News Reporter* (June 1998): 13.

56. Rampton and Stauber, "This Report Brought to You by Monsanto," 24.

57. Jim Gordon, "Mystery Milk, Journalistic Debate," *Extra!* (January–February 2001): 29.

58. A. V. Krebs, "Court Upholds Award in Suppressed TV Report," *Progressive Populist* (January 1–15, 2001): 7.

59. Karen Charman, "News You Can't Trust," *Extra!* (July–August 2003): 6.

60. Liane Casten, "Florida Appeals Court Orders Akre-Wilson Must Pay Trial Costs for $24.3 Billion Fox Television: Couple Warns Journalists of Danger to Free Speech, Whistle Blower Protection," in *Censored 2006: The Top 25 Censored Stories*, ed. Peter Phillips and Project Censored (New York: Seven Stories Press, 2005), 165.

61. Casten, "Florida Appeals Court Orders Akre-Wilson Must Pay Trial Costs," 165. See the Akre and Wilson website on the Internet at http://www.foxBGHsuit.com.

62. Krebs, "Court Upholds Award in Suppressed TV Report," 7.

63. Gordon, "Mystery Milk, Journalistic Debate," 30.

64. Liane Casten, "Court Ruled That Media Can Legally Lie," in Phillips and Project Censored, *Censored 2005*, 73–75.

65. Casten, "Florida Appeals Court Orders Akre-Wilson Must Pay Trial Costs," 165.

66. Sheldon Rampton and John Stauber, "Oprah's Free—Are We?" *Extra!* (May–June 1998): 11–12. Also see Ralph Nader, "Product Libel," *Public Citizen News* (May–June 1998): 4.

67. Hollar, Jackson, and Goldstein, "Fear and Favor 2005," 15.

68. Lauer Research, Inc., "Media Professionals and Their Industry" (survey prepared for Department for Professional Employees, AFL-CIO, July 20, 2004), 8.

69. The Pew Research Center for the People and the Press, "Journalists Avoiding the News, Self Censorship: How Often and Why?" on the Internet at http://www.people-press.org/jour00 rpt.htm (visited June 8, 2001).

70. Lawrence Soley, "The Power of the Press Has a Price," *Extra!* (July–August 1997): 11–13.

71. Bruce G. Knecht, "Hard Copy: Magazine Advertisers Demand Prior Notice of 'Offensive' Articles," *Wall Street Journal*, April 30, 1997, A1.

72. Peter Hart, "Superstore Censorship," *Extra!* (November–December 2005): 22.

73. Hart, "Superstore Censorship," 22.

74. Hart, "Superstore Censorship," 22.

75. Knecht, "Hard Copy," A1.

76. Bagdikian, *The Media Monopoly*, 218. Also see Andrew Jay Schwartzman, Cheryl A. Leanza, and Harold Feld, "The Legal Case for Diversity in Broadcast Ownership," in *The Future of Media: Resistance and Reform in the 21st Century*, ed. Robert McChesney, Russell Newman, and Ben Scott (New York: Seven Stories Press, 2005), 159; Norman Solomon, "The Media Oligarchy: Undermining Journalism, Obstructing Democracy," in *Censored 2001*, ed. Peter Phillips and Project Censored (New York: Seven Stories Press, 2001), 277–90; Lawrence Soley, "Corporate Censorship and the Limits of Free Speech," *Extra!* (March–April 1999): 19–21.

77. Rachel Coen, "The Stossel Treatment," *Extra!* (March–April 2003): 15–17; Peter Hart, "'We Do Not Speculate Here,'" *Extra!* (July–August 2005): 30; Peter Hart, "Bill O'Reilly, Media Critic," *Extra!* (November–December 2003): 6; Peter Hart and Janine Jackson, "Stossel's 'Stupid' Schools," *Extra!* (May–June 2006): 6–9; Steve Rendall, "An Aggressive Conservative vs. a 'Liberal to be Determined,'" *Extra!* (November–December 2003): 19–23; Steve Rendall and Anna Kosseff, "I'm Not a Leftist, but I Play One on TV," *Extra!* (September–October 2004): 17–23.

78. Peter Hart and Steve Rendall, "A 'Right-Wing Coup' against PBS's Mythical Bias," *Extra!Update* (June 2005): 1.

79. "Dissent Unwelcome in Wartime," *Extra!* (May–June 2004): 24.

80. Chris Lehmann, "Michael and Me," *In These Times* (October 14, 1996): 39–40.

81. John Nichols, "Moyers Fights Back," *Nation* (June 6, 2005): 8.

82. Nichols, "Moyers Fights Back," 8.

83. Kimberly Pohlman, "Solid Ratings Don't Protect Progressive Radio Voices," *Extra!* (July–August 2000): 22.

84. Edward S. Herman, "The Media Mega-Mergers," *Dollars and Sense* (May–June 1996): 8–13. Also see "Action Alert," *Extra!* (December 1995): 4.

85. Hollar, Jackson, and Goldstein, "Fear and Favor 2005," 15–20. Also see Steve Rendall, "Balancing 'Liberal' Media?" *Extra!* (January–February 2005): 26.

86. Robert W. McChesney, *The Problem of the Media* (New York: Monthly Review Press, 2004), 98–117; Robert W. McChesney and John Bellamy Foster, "'Left-Wing' Media?" *Monthly Review* (June 2003): 1–16; Parry, "The Right-Wing Media Machine," 6–19.

87. National Council on Economic Education, "About NCEE," 2006; additional information about the organization was taken from the NCEE website on the Internet at http://www.ncee.net/about/board.php (visited November 26, 2006). Also see Domhoff, *Who Rules America?* 111–12; Mark Maier, "High School Economics: Corporate Sponsorship and Pro-Market Bias," *Dollars and Sense* (May–June 2002): 13–15, 24–25.

88. Pat Wechsler, "This Lesson Is Brought to You By," *Business Week* (June 30, 1997): 68–69.

89. Bagdikian, *The New Media Monopoly*, 167.

90. Domhoff, *Who Rules America?* 201–204.

91. Larry Gabriel, "Beware of the Man behind the Screen," *UAW Solidarity* (May–June 2006): 20–21; Terry Thurman, "Political Action Is a Year-Round Process" (Region 3 Moving Forward insert), *UAW Solidarity* (November 2001): 1–2.

92. For examples, see Hart and Jackson, "Stossel's 'Stupid' Schools," 8–9; George Melloan, "Whatever Happened to the Labor Movement?" *Wall Street Journal*, September 4, 2001, A23. Also see Janine Jackson, "Major Player or Big Bully?" *Extra!* (January–February 1997): 9–10; "Don't Let Them Fool You!" *AFSCME Public Employee* (March–April 1998): 6–11.

93. Amy Gluckman, "Workers Better Off without Unions?" *Dollars and Sense* (September–October 2005): 5; Croteau, "Challenging the 'Liberal Media' Claim," 4–9; Gail Dines, "Capitalism's Pitchmen," *Dollars and Sense* (May 1992): 18–20.

94. Julie Hollar, "Opinion Omission: Women Hard to Find on Op-ed Pages, TV Panels," *Extra!* (May–June, 2005): 17–22; Jennifer L. Pozner, "Power Shortage for Media Women," *Extra!* (July–August 2001): 8–9. Also see "The Whitening Newsroom," *Extra!Update* (June 2001): 2; Jessica Wakeman and Julie Hollar, "Stand by Your Man," *Extra!* (May–June 2005): 23–24.

95. Croteau, "Challenging the 'Liberal Media' Claim," 8.

96. Journalism.org, "Local TV," State of the News Media 2006, 35.

97. Incomes were compiled from various sources, including Charlie Amter, "Comedy Central Keeps Colbert," *E! Online*, November 2, 2005, on the Internet at http://www.eonline.com (visited July 12, 2006); "The O'Reilly Factory," *Business Week Online*, March 8, 2004, on the Internet at http://www.businessweek.com (visited June 18, 2006); Diane Clehane, Rob LaFranco, and Cathy Piedmont, "Hey, Big Spenders," *TV Guide* (July 18–24, 2004): 22–29; Lea Goldman and Kiri Blakeley (eds.), "The Celebrity 100," *Forbes* (July 3, 2006): 117–61; Josh Grossberg, "Colbert's Book Report," *E! Online*, March 21, 2006; Josh Grossberg, "Stewart Keeps Up 'Daily' Regimen," *E! Online*, March 19, 2004; "Salary Guide," *New York Magazine* (September 26, 2005); Marc Peyser and Johnnie L. Roberts, "The Katie Factor," *Newsweek* (April 17, 2006): 37–42.

98. George Seldes, "Is the Entire Press Corrupt?" *Extra!* (November–December 1994): 26–27.

99. "CEOs Play Reporter," *Extra!Update* (February 1996): 2.

100. David Elsila, Michael Funke, and Sam Kirkland, "Blaming the Victim: The Propaganda War against Workers," *UAW Solidarity* (April 1992): 11–17.

101. Martin A. Lee and Norman Solomon, "Does the News Media Have a Liberal Bias?" in *Taking Sides*, ed. Kurt Finsterbusch and George McKenna (Guilford, CT: Duskin, 1996), 28.

102. Croteau, "Challenging the 'Liberal Media' Claim," 4.

103. Peter Hart, "From the Left, I'm—Nonexistent," *Extra!* (September–October 2003): 15; Peter Hart, "'We Do Not Speculate Here,'" *Extra!* (July–August 2005): 30; Rendall, "An Aggressive Conservative vs. a 'Liberal to be Determined,'" 19–23; Rendall and Kosseff, "I'm Not a Leftist, but I Play One on TV," 17–23; Steve Rendall and Peter Hart, "Time to Unplug the CPB," *Extra!* (September–October 2005): 18–21.

104. Media Matters for America, "If It's Sunday, It's Conservative," February 14, 2006, 1, on the Internet at http://www.essentialaction.org (visited November 26, 2006).

105. George Farah and Justin Elga, "Sunday Morning Political Talk Shows Ignore Corporate Power Issues," Essential Information, on the Internet at http://www.essentialaction.org/spotlight/report/index.html (visited November 26, 2006). Also see George Farah and Justin Elga, "What's Not Talked about on Sunday Morning?" *Extra!* (September–October 2001): 14–17.

106. Dines, "Capitalism's Pitchmen," 20; Steve Rendall, "Failing at Its 'No. 1 Goal,'" *Extra!* (November–December 2005): 28–30; Steve Rendall and Eric Klotz, "*Hannity & Colmes* Fails 'Fair and Balanced' Test," *Extra!* (November–December 2003): 21.

107. Steve Rendall and Julie Hollar, "Are You on the *NewsHour*'s Guestlist?" *Extra!* (September–October 2006): 20.

108. "From the Left: More than a Figure of Speech?" *Extra!Update* (February 1996): 1.

109. Steve Rendall, "Nation's Top Columnists Still Lean Right," *Extra!* (January–February 2000): 11–12; Steve Rendall, "The Hypocrisy of George Will," *Extra!* (September–October 2003): 14–16.

110. Elsila, Funke, and Kirkland, "Blaming the Victim," 12.

111. Jonathan Tasini, "Lost in the Margins: Labor and the Media," *Extra!* (Summer 1990): 2–6.

112. Peter Hart, "Why Is Labor Off TV?" *Extra!Update* (August 2005): 3.

113. Jennifer Gonnerman, "Media Watch," *In These Times* (December 25, 1995): 9.

114. Bagdikian, *The Media Monopoly*, 52.

115. Bagdikian, *The Media Monopoly*, 57.

116. Dines, "Capitalism's Pitchmen," 18.

117. Janine Jackson, "Moribund Militants: Corporate Media on (Re)Organized Labor," *Extra!* (January–February 1996): 6–7.

118. "Media Myths and Facts," *UAW Solidarity* (April 1992): 17.

119. Jonathan Tasini, "Media Stereotypes about Unions," *Extra!* (Summer 1990): 4.

120. Joshua L. Carreiro, "Newspaper Coverage of the U.S. Labor Movement: The Case of Anti-Union Firings," *Labor Studies Journal* 30(3) (2005): 1–20; Christopher R. Martin, *Framed: Labor and the Corporate Media* (Ithaca, NY: Cornell University Press, 2004).

121. Bagdikian, *The Media Monopoly*, 44.

122. Seth Ackerman, "Selling the Social Security Scare," *Extra!* (January–February 2005): 6.

123. Allan Sloan, "A Lot of Trust, but No Funds," *Newsweek* (July 30, 2001): 34.

124. William Safire, "Jimmy That 'Lockbox,'" *New York Times*, September 10, 2001, A29; "Yes, We Have No Bananas," *Wall Street Journal*, September 4, 2001, A22.

125. Ackerman, "Selling the Social Security Scare," 6. Dates of reports for each source are as follows: *New York Times* (November 28, 2004), *USA Today* (November 14, 2004), the *Washington Post* (November 5, 2004), *Time* (November 22, 2004), *NPR (Weekend Edition*, December 4, 2004), and *CNN* (Kathleen Hayes, November 4, 2004).

126. "Everyone Agrees," *Extra!Update* (February 2005): 2.

127. Doug Orr, "Social Security Q&A," *Dollars and Sense* (May–June 2005): 15.

128. Orr, "Social Security Q&A," 17, 19.

129. See, for example, Ackerman, "Selling the Social Security Scare," 6; "A Promise between Generations," *UAW Solidarity* (March–April 2005): 17–25; Dean Baker, "Cutting Our Benefits," *In These Times* (January 3, 2005): 22–23; Editors, "The Great Fear: Stagnation and the War on Social Security," *Monthly Review* (April 2005): 1–11; AFL-CIO, "Front Groups for the Attack on Social Security," 2006, on the Internet at http://www.aflcio/issues/retirementsecurity (visited May 28, 2006); Jim Hightower and Phillip Frazer, "Naming the Names behind the Grab for Social Security," *Lowdown* (April 2005): 1–8; Orr, "Social Security Q&A," 15–20; Doug Orr, "Social Security Isn't Broken," *Dollars and Sense* (November–December 2004): 14–16.

130. Dolny, "Think Tank Survey: Study Finds First Drop in Think Tank Cites."

131. Heritage Foundation, *2005 Annual Report*, Washington, D.C., 26.

132. Heritage Foundation, *2005 Annual Report*, 2, 27, 29.

133. U.S. Department of the Treasury, Internal Revenue Service, "Return of Organization Exempt from Income Tax—Form 990, The Heritage Foundation," 23-7327730 (Washington, D.C., 2004), Schedule A, Statement 18.

134. Press, "Spin Cities," 32.

135. Robert W. McChesney, "Journalism, Democracy, and Class Struggle," *Monthly Review* (November 2000): 7.

136. Greg Palast, "Progressive Interview with Hugo Chávez," *Progressive* (July 2006): 36.

137. Larry Lack, "Is Chávez Hitler or Father Christmas? Venezuela's Handout to Uncle Sam's Shivering Poor," *CounterPunch* (February 2006): 1; Justin Delacour, "The Op-ed Assassination of Hugo Chávez," *Extra!* (November–December 2005): 24.

138. Delacour, "The Op-ed Assassination of Hugo Chávez."

139. Delacour, "The Op-ed Assassination of Hugo Chávez."

140. Delacour, "The Op-ed Assassination of Hugo Chávez."

141. "Dictators on Parade," *Wall Street Journal*, February 15, 2005, A18.

142. Mary Anastasia O'Grady, "Americas: In Chávez's Crosshairs," *Wall Street Journal*, September 22, 2006, A11.

143. Thomas L. Friedman, "Fill 'Er Up with Dictators," *New York Times*, September 27, 2006, A25.

144. Chesa Boudin, "Letter from Venezuela: The Land of Chavismo," *Nation* (December 4, 2006): 18–21; Steve Ellner, "Chávez Consolidates Power," *In These Times*, January 2007, 26–27; Juan Forero, "Venezuela's Chávez Wins Decisive Victory: Leftist President Given Another Six Years to Consolidate His 'Bolivarian Revolution,'" *Washington Post*, December 4, 2006, A14; Simon Romero, "Chávez Wins Easily in Venezuela," *New York Times*, December 4, 2006, A10; Steve Rendall, "The Repeatedly Re-Elected Autocrat," *Extra!* (November–December 2006): 23–25.

145. Steve Rendall, "Imperial Mythology," *Extra!* (November–December 2006): 22.

146. Employment estimates for the U.S. PR industry and for U.S. reporters are based on analyses and extrapolations conducted by Dr. David W. Wright, Wichita State University, using data reported in the *Current Population Survey*, March 2005, for occupational codes that correspond to PR managers (60), PR specialists (2,820), and news reporters (2,810). The authors are grateful for Dr. Wright's assistance in developing these estimates.

147. McChesney, "Journalism, Democracy, and Class Struggle," 7.

148. Bagdikian, *The New Media Monopoly*, 167.

149. Jeff Cohen and Norman Solomon, *Adventures in MediaLand* (Monroe, ME: Common Courage Press, 1993), 45. Also see McChesney, *Rich Media, Poor Democracy*, 252.

150. Bagdikian, *The Media Monopoly*, 58.

151. Janine Jackson, "Prepackaged News: Straight from the Source, No Journalism Required," *Extra!* (March–April 2006): 17.

152. Laura Miller, "Pulling Back the Curtain: The Best of PR Watch," in *Censored 2006: The Top 25 Censored Stories*, ed. Peter Phillips and Project Censored (New York: Seven Stories Press, 2005), 281.

153. Miller, "Pulling Back the Curtain," 284.

154. Peter Hart and Julie Hollar, "Fear and Favor 2003," *Extra!* (May–June 2004): 21–22.

155. Miller, "Pulling Back the Curtain," 282.

156. Miller, "Pulling Back the Curtain," 283.

157. Diane Farsetta and Daniel Price, "Fake TV News: Widespread and Undisclosed," Center for Media and Democracy, Madison, Wisconsin, April 6, 2006, on the Internet at http://www.prwatch.org (visited November 23, 2006).

158. Miller, "Pulling Back the Curtain," 284.

159. Laura Flanders, "Is It Real . . . Or Is It Astroturf?" *Extra!* (July–August 1996): 6.

160. Sharon Beder, "Public Relations' Role in Manufacturing Artificial Grass Roots Coalitions," *Public Relations Quarterly* 43 (1998): 21–30.

161. Ken Silverstein, "Manufactured News," *Extra!* (January–February 1997): 23–24.

162. U.S. Department of Commerce, *Statistical Abstract of the United States: 2006* (Washington, DC: U.S. Government Printing Office, 2005), 658.

163. "Don't Read This Soundbite," *Extra!* (January–February 2000): 5.

164. Laura Miller, "The Best of PR Watch: Spins of the Year," in Phillips and Project Censored, *Censored 2005*, 245.

165. "Advocates Pressed Government, Business to Improve Drug, Food, Worker Protections," *Public Citizen News, 2002 Annual Report* (March–April 2003): 2.

166. Valerie Collins, "To Pass Medicare Drug Bill, Big Pharma Does the K Street Shuffle," *Public Citizen News* (July–August 2004): 5.

167. Frank Clemente, "New Medicare Law Benefits Industry More Than Seniors," *Public Citizen News* (January–February 2004): 1, 8–9.

168. Dean Baker, "Don't Follow the Money," *Extra!* (September–October 2003): 6–7; Trudy Lieberman, "Part D from Outer Space," *Nation* (January 30, 2006): 18–20.

169. Sharon Beder, *The Corporate Assault on Environmentalism* (White River Junction, VT: Chelsea Green Publishing, 1998). Also see Beder, "Public Relations' Role in Manufacturing Artificial Grass Roots Coalitions"; John Stauber and Sheldon Rampton, *Toxic Sludge Is Good for You: Lies, Damn Lies, and the Public Relations Industry* (Monroe, ME: Common Courage Press, 1996); Shawn Zeller, "Thriving in a Crisis," *National Journal* (October 14, 2000): 3262, on the Internet at http://www.prwatch.org or search the Internet using "Astroturf."

170. Maria Petrova, "Inequality and Media Capture" (Working Paper Series, Social Science Research Network, Harvard University, February 6, 2006), 1, on the Internet at http://www.papers.ssrn.com (visited December 28, 2006).

171. Sam Pizzigati, "Most Original Research on the Consequences of Inequality," *Too Much* (December 18, 2006): 4. Quote from Pizzigati, summarizing Petrova's findings.

172. Todd Gitlin, "Unum versus Pluribus," *Nation* (May 6, 1996): 32.

173. Scott and Leonhardt, "Class in America: Shadowy Lines That Still Divide," 16.

174. New York Times, *Class Matters* (New York: Times Books, 2005), 245–46.

175. "Balance This," *In These Times* (May 13, 1996): 4–5.

176. Michael Golay and Carl Rollyson, *Where America Stands, 1996* (New York: Wiley, 1996), 16.

177. National Taxpayers Union, "Democrat Voters Now Strongest Supporters of Balanced Budget Constitutional Amendment, Poll Finds" (press release, April 3, 2003), on the Internet at http://www.ntu.org/main/press_release (visited July 30, 2006).

178. Carroll Doherty, "Do Deficits Matter Anymore?" Pew Research Center, March 14, 2006, 1, on the Internet at http://pewresearch.org/obdeck (visited July 12, 2006).

179. Bagdikian, *The Media Monopoly*, 206.

180. Pew Research Center, "Economy Now Seen through Partisan Prism," January 24, 2006, 2, on the Internet at http://people-press.org/reports (visited July 2, 2006).

181. Luxury Institute, "Economic Attitudes and Indices," *Wealth Report* (January 15, 2006): 2.

182. Robert L. Borosage and Ruy Teixeira, "The Politics of Money," *Nation* (October 21, 1996): 21–22.

183. Pew Research Center, "Public Sours on Government and Business," October 25, 2005, 3; Pew Research Center, "Politics and Values in a 51%–48% Nation," January 24, 2005, 5–6; both surveys are on the Internet at http://people-press.org/reports (visited July 2, 2006).

184. "In Fact," *Nation* (August 26–September 2, 1996): 5.

185. The Pew Research Center for the People and the Press, "Economic Inequality Rising, Boom Bypasses Poor," on the Internet at http://www.people-press.org/june01mor.htm (visited August 12, 2001).

186. Leslie McCall and Julian Brash, "What Do Americans Think about Inequality?" *Demos: A Network for Ideas and Action*, May 2004, 6, on the Internet at http://www.demos-usa.org (visited July 12, 2006).

187. McCall and Brash, "What Do Americans Think About Inequality?" 10.

188. Change to Win, "The American Dream Survey 2006," August 28, 2006, 9, on the Internet at http://www.changetowin.org/features/the-american-dream-survey.html (visited October 18, 2006).

189. Sam Pizzigati, "Best Legislative Reason to Feel Slightly Optimistic about 2007," *Too Much* (December 18, 2006): 6.

190. David Sirota, "Embracing Populism," *In These Times* (December 2006): 4.

191. Michael Dolny, "What's in a Label?" *Extra!* (July–August 1998): 9–10; McChesney, *Rich Media, Poor Democracy*, 63–77; McChesney, "Journalism, Democracy, and Class Struggle"; Mark Lloyd, "Lessons for Realistic Radicals in the Information Age," in *The Future of Media*, 73–95; Parry, "Right-Wing Media Machine," 6–10.

192. McChesney, "Journalism, Democracy, and Class Struggle," 1–15. Also see Solomon, "The Media Oligarchy: Undermining Journalism, Obstructing Democracy," 277–90; and Domhoff, *Who Rules America?* 1–13.

193. Martin N. Marger, *Social Inequality* (Boston: McGraw-Hill, 2002), 247–53, 354–56. Also see Dines, "Capitalism's Pitchmen," 18–20, and Phillips, "Fat City," 49–56.

6

Educating for Privilege: Dreaming, Streaming, and Creaming

> The educational system is an integral element of the reproduction of the prevailing class structure of society.
>
> —Samuel Bowles and Herbert Gintis,
> *Schooling in Capitalist America*, 1976

> *Schooling in Capitalist America* was correct: The extent of intergenerational economic status transmission is considerable. In the United States, knowing the income or wealth of someone's parents is about as informative about the person's own economic status as is knowing the person's years of schooling attained or score on a standardized cognitive test.
>
> —Samuel Bowels and Herbert Gintis,
> *Schooling in Capitalist America Revisited*, 2002

Nick Caradona and Arnie Seebol were an unlikely pair to become good friends in high school. They were from different parts of the city and from widely different ethnic and religious traditions—one was Italian and a nominal Catholic, the other, from a Jewish family with practicing parents and recalcitrant kids. Nick's and Arnie's paths would never have crossed if they had not both passed a citywide exam to get into an "elite" science-oriented high school. Most of the kids in the high school were college bound, but the idea of college had never occurred to Nick or Arnie, or to their parents for that matter.

Nick's and Arnie's parents had a tough time making ends meet because of their unstable, low-income jobs. Only one of the four parents claimed a high school diploma. Nick's parents were separated. When Nick was five years old, his father went to Washington, D.C., to look for work; he drove a cab in D.C. for the rest of his working years, but he never returned to his family. Nick's mother worked as a domestic until he was twelve years old and then took a job

251

as a clerk in a laundry. Arnie's father drove a truck for the *New York Daily News*, and his mother did "home work" for shops in the garment district. Nick and Arnie were both urged by their junior high teachers to take the exam for admission to the select high school, and after being admitted, they both enrolled.

At first, the bond between Nick and Arnie was based on the extremity of their shared differences, focusing on the "dirty secrets" of their elders and their ethnic cultures, namely, the disparaging terms and put-downs they had heard used against members of the in-group and the out-group. Arnie taught Nick the fine points of distinction between a *putz* and a *schmuck*. Nick also learned to smack himself in the head and exclaim *goyisha kopf* whenever he did something stupid. Arnie told him that Jews would use this routine whenever they did something foolish, exclaiming with the phrase that they were acting like Gentiles. It reminded Nick of his grandfather's frequent practice of referring to someone as an American in broken English ("you must be 'Merican"), pronounced in such a way that it sounded very much like *merde de cane*, which Italians would understand literally as "shit of the dog." It was an unschooled double entendre, which Nick taught Arnie to use against other kids in school.

Arnie and Nick soon discovered other bonds. They both liked baseball (Nick, a Yankee fan, Arnie, a Dodger fan), and both had a flair for "hustling," as they were always short of money. They took bets in school from other students, who would choose three baseball players whom they expected would get a total of six hits in that day's ball games. The odds on each bet were three to one. Thus, a kid would bet a nickel that his three favorite players would get a total of six hits that day. If the three players scored the six hits, the bettor won fifteen cents; if not, Nick and Arnie won the nickel. The odds were always with the "bookmaker" as long as there were a sufficient number of bettors. Many kids had favorite ball players who rarely got more than one hit a game, but they bet on them nonetheless. Nick and Arnie would also "pitch pennies" and play cards during the lunch hour. Their high school was huge (five thousand students), so there was always plenty of "action" for Nick and Arnie.

Late in their senior year, Nick started to have problems, academically and otherwise. He went "on the hook" too many times and faked letters of excuse from his mother. In the midst of these problems, he quit high school a month before the end of term, failing to take any final exams. He went to work as a "runner" for a bookmaker and was soon "promoted" to a "writer" in a betting room where men assembled to talk about horse racing and to make bets on races at a number of tracks in New York, New Jersey, and the New England area. Offtrack betting was illegal, but it was carried out openly with the paid-for cooperation of local police.

Arnie graduated on schedule and went to work for his uncle in his dry cleaning store. Arnie would learn all about the business, and he hoped one day to own his own store or several stores.

The preceding vignette calls attention to how the intersection of students' social-class backgrounds and educational opportunities for upward mobility can sometimes be both serendipitous and problematic. Nick and Arnie were kids who showed some talent in elementary school. Their teachers had a "dream" that they were worthy of moving into an educational tracking system that gave talented kids a chance to "make it" in the opportunity contest—meaning a chance to go to college. But Nick and Arnie themselves did not have the dream, and they never gave any thought to the track that could lead to a college education and beyond. It was partly because the cost of college-going was beyond the means of Nick's and Arnie's parents. But it also required Nick and Arnie to forgo the income they would earn from working and the claim to adult status that comes with the end of schooling. Many of Nick and Arnie's classmates were middle class and college bound from years of anticipatory socialization. They were "hothouse" kids who had been cultivated for years in an environment of controlled feeding and sunlight. They did not yearn for the freedom of adult status, for their sense of self was fused with the wishes held for them by their parent cultivators.

Nick and Arnie were working-class kids from low-income, working-class families, and their parents were working too hard to be involved in the school activities of their children. The opportunity provided by their admission to an elite high school does not exist in a vacuum. In Nick and Arnie's case, it existed within the working-class culture that was their everyday reality. Thus, if all the poor kids in East St. Louis were suddenly enrolled in a school with good teachers, facilities, and programs, it would be great for the kids, but only so much could be expected to follow from an enriched educational experience. The kids would still be poor, as would their parents and friends. Their educational system and experience would be contained within a context, a class structure that shapes events that extend far beyond the classroom.

The American Dream of equality of opportunity is contradicted daily in primary and secondary schools throughout the country. A substantial body of research indicates that when students come to the "starting line" in first grade, they do not come as equals. They are advantaged and disadvantaged by their class situation, their race or ethnicity, and their gender; all of this shapes school experiences and educational outcomes.[1]

AMERICAN EDUCATION SYSTEM

> A fundamental premise of the so-called "American Dream" is that the postponement of personal gratification, especially in the pursuit of educational goals, will result in social rewards attached to a prestigious occupational position. . . . In the end, the American Dream is a barrier in public education.
>
> —Adalberto Aguirre Jr. and David V. Baker,
> *Structured Inequality in the United States*, 2000

In effect, if not by design, the American education system functions primarily to transmit advantage and disadvantage across generations. This assertion flies in the face of a powerful and dominant ideology that permeates all levels of society, namely, that education is the great equalizer. Education is what brought Abe Lincoln from a log cabin to the highest office in the land. Education is what gave millions of poor, but aspiring, immigrants in the United States the chance to be whatever they were willing to work for. This is the ideology of the American Dream. The dream is so powerful that parents will compete vigorously to control local schools so that their programs, teachers, and curriculum will serve the interests of their children. Middle-class parents, in particular, work very hard to see that their child gets the teachers with the reputation for being the best math, or science, or literature teacher. In order to improve their child's chances of getting into an elite college, they are also very supportive of efforts to add advanced-placement courses from a local college into the curriculum. In the dream, education is the passport to a future that exceeds (if you are poor) or matches (if you are privileged) the economic situation of your parents.

For the dream to become a reality, schools have to be organized to meet the aspirations of the dreamers. In schools in which all the kids are from professional families, only one kind of education is needed—a college-preparatory program. But when the kids in school come from diverse economic backgrounds, a system must be devised to provide not only the best education to the college-bound children from professional families and to some of the poor kids—who, based on probabilities alone, would be able to compete with the college bound—but also a quality educational experience for those who are not heading to college. The idea behind this system is that the educational experience should be designed to meet the "needs of the child."[2] The system is called *tracking*.

Tracking seems to be a very progressive idea, permitting teachers "to tailor instruction to the ability level of their students. A good fit between a student's ability and the level of instruction is believed to maximize the effectiveness and efficiency of the instructional process."[3] Does it not make sense to identify students who are headed to college, white-collar employment, or mechanical trades and provide them with the particular knowledge and skills that will be most useful—vocational and shop courses for the young men and women going to work in factories, keyboarding and word processing for those who will be clerks and secretaries in corporate bureaucracies, and literature, languages, mathematics, and the sciences for those headed toward colleges and universities? The problem with this theory of tracking is that students' vocations need to be identified fairly early in their young lives to make use of this system. Of course, this is no easy task, but the ideology of the American Dream states that with the help of "objective" testing, student's strengths can be identified and tracked to make the best use of their abilities. Unfortunately, even though well intentioned, tracking can lead to a "dumbing down" curriculum and lowered expectations for those students who don't appear to be college material.

Tracking may have made some sense in the 1950s and 1960s, when the non-college-bound could get good blue-collar jobs in the auto, steel, and rubber industries, and schools were responsible for providing basic numeracy and literacy for skilled and semiskilled workers. It may also have been needed when schools were heterogeneous in terms of the economic backgrounds of their students. If a school had the children of professionals, white-collar clerks, and unskilled workers, tracking was necessary to meet the needs of the students who were college-bound or heading into the labor market. But today, many schools are much more homogeneous in terms of the backgrounds of students and their educational plans. Children from the corporate and managerial classes are generally either in private schools or in suburban schools limited to members of their social class. Virtually all of these students are college bound, so what would be the point of tracking? At the other end of the class-structure spectrum, we have poor rural schools or inner-city schools filled with children from the bottom one-third to one-half of the economic system. The closest thing you might have to tracking in these schools is the effort of dedicated teachers to reach out and identify those with the greatest potential and to groom them for college, hoping that they might have a chance to attend.

These homogeneous schools, which today largely serve the children of the affluent and privileged class, are involved in *streaming*, not tracking. *Tracking* is a competitive metaphor, implying a contest among entrants in a race where all the "runners" have an equal chance to win. *Streaming* is a noncompetitive metaphor, implying that participants are "carried along" to their destination without any substantial competition with their peers. If you go to the right private schools or the better suburban schools, college attendance is the assumed outcome for all involved.

An excellent example of the streaming metaphor is revealed in the following remarks made by the dean of the Harvard Law School when greeting a new class of students at the orientation session:

> The fact is that you are not competing with each other. Your life at the school and your life as a lawyer will be happier and more satisfying if you recognize that your goal is to become the best possible lawyer so that you can serve your clients and society with maximum skills. Although you will experience frustrations from time to time, I think that rather than the *Paper Chase* you will see the school as much closer to the image involved in a letter we received some years ago from a Japanese lawyer who had just been admitted: "Dear Sir: I have just seen the movie *Love Story* with Ryan O'Neal and Ali McGraw and I am looking forward to a very romantic time at the Harvard Law School."[4]

Compare this "laid-back" welcoming speech with the prototypical competitive welcome offered by the dean or professor at a less "prestigious" program: "Look at the person on your right and the person on your left. At the end of the first year, only one of you will still be in the program." Those in the privileged classes attempt to create an elementary and high school educational structure that is characterized by streaming so that their children are "guaranteed" good grades, high test scores, an enriched curriculum, extracurricular activities, and advising that will get them admitted to the country's most elite schools. Privileged-class parents also frequently supplement the school's programs by providing their children with special prep classes for taking the college Scholastic Aptitude Test (SAT). Such prep classes may cost close to $1,000, but as parents know, "It isn't a matter of just getting into college, but of making it into UC-Berkeley or UCLA or MIT."[5]

Children from privileged-class backgrounds have parents with the time, energy, and money to shape experiences outside of school that provide the social and cultural capital needed for continued academic success. One study compared the summer experiences of fourth-grade students from professional families and from lower to working-class backgrounds. Consider the following descriptions of summer activities from two students from professional families.

> Top 10 Things I Did This Summer: (1) I went to Italy; (2) I read a lot; (3) I went bike riding and did much better at it; (4) I had play dates; (5) There was a book club meeting at my house; (6) I got a new piano teacher, and my piano playing really got better; (7) I went on-line more often and improved my typing; (8) I made candy dots and gingerbread cookies; (9) I was involved in a C. U. [California University] research project; (10) I got my school supplies early, and I am looking forward to getting back to school.

> We had sleep-away camp for two weeks—that was so great. Then Vacation Bible School for a week. Then I think we had a free week. This week they had Boy Scout Camp and swimming lessons—next week just swimming lessons. Then, after that grandparents come, they have Science Adventure Camp for a week. Then we all go to Hawaii for two weeks.[6]

In discussing these how-I-spent-my-summer stories, the authors note, "None of the working-class or poor children in our study had summers that were this full of organized and varied activities." And, more importantly, they report finding little evidence that these social-class differences in summer experiences stemmed from parents' values and preferences. The differences could be traced to time, energy, and money. In short, parents from privileged backgrounds have the resources to shape the in-class and out-of-class experiences of their children, and they do so while supporting the myth of the dream and extolling the virtues of equality of opportunity as the hallmark of American society.

THE POWER OF THE DREAM

> If kids go to college because high school jobs are so terrible, they may wind up with these jobs anyway. We won't slow our rising inequality just by jamming more and more kids into college.
>
> —Thomas Geoghagen, *New York Times*, 1997

The myth of the American Dream is a powerful force in American life, and it is based on two distinct beliefs: first, that everyone can aspire to levels of success that exceed their starting points in life because where a person starts life is an accident that can be remedied and, second, that there is equality of opportunity to reach one's goals and that the game has a set of rules that are fair and capable of producing the desired success goals.

The dream can be a source of inspiration for the young and a source of hope for parents who push their children to better themselves. It also serves to legitimate the great inequality in society in wealth, power, and privilege. It leads to the belief that those who receive high rewards are deserving because they have contributed more in terms of effort and hard work. The dream is a comfort to the privileged and a heavy burden for the less fortunate.

The dream is so pervasive in our culture, so embedded in our family rituals and significant celebrations, that we often follow its logic without examination. It is a kind of cultural reflex leading us to continually search for evidence of the dream in action and to urge it on others as a guide for living. Consider the following obituary, which the writer, with little or no evidence, chooses to frame within the myth of the dream. The headline reads, "B. Gerald Cantor, Philanthropist and Owner of Rodin Collection, Is Dead at 79."

This headline, in half-inch type, is accompanied by an almost full-page story reporting the achievements of the deceased. The story begins,

> B. Gerald Cantor, who started out as a boy selling hot dogs at Yankee Stadium, became a wealthy financier and philanthropist, amassed the world's most comprehensive collection of Rodin sculpture in private hands, and gave much of it away to dozens of cultural institutions, died on Wednesday in Los Angeles after a long illness. . . .
>
> Mr. Cantor, who was raised in modest circumstances in the Bronx, and his wife Iris, who grew up three blocks from the Brooklyn Museum, came to be widely known in New York for their generosity to the Metropolitan Museum of Art, the Brooklyn Museum, and to medical institutions in the city. . . .
>
> Before he was 15, Bernie Cantor became a vendor at Yankee Stadium. "I only worked during Sunday double headers," he recalled, because "you could sell more things" in the delay between the two games. . . .
>
> He graduated from DeWitt Clinton High School and went on to study law and finance at New York University from 1935 to 1937. He originally planned to become a lawyer, but he changed his mind when he spotted a lawyer friend who had had to take a job working with a pickax on a construction project of the Works Project Administration.[7]

This fifty-five paragraph story about a well-known philanthropist manages to create, for the casual reader, the clear impression in its opening sentence and in the first few paragraphs that we are dealing with yet another personification of the "rags-to-riches" American Dream.[8] Poor boy works hard—selling hot dogs, no less, at Yankee Stadium (a double dose of the dream being played out in the playground of dreams)—achieves phenomenal success, and gives all his money back to the "people" (actually to museums, hospitals, and at least a half-dozen universities).

But before we can make sense of Cantor's life, we need to know what it means to be raised in "modest circumstances." We also need to know how these modest circumstances carried him to New York University during the height of the Depression. The point of these questions is neither to ignore Cantor's achievements nor to diminish his generosity. The point is to show the ease with which the cultural-production industry of newspapers, TV, films, and so forth creates the powerful myth of the American Dream. Even this straightforward story of one person's life and achievements was "torqued" to feed into the myth. The story not only pumps up the dream, but it also legitimates the wealth of multimillionaires by first saying they "did it themselves, with hard work and dedication," and by then dwelling on how many millions they "gave back."

It is precisely because of such obituaries, *Forrest Gump*–genre films, and other rags-to-riches cultural products that most Americans appear to accept the myth of the American Dream. Figure 6.1 reports the results of a national survey in which Americans were asked to rate the importance of various factors in "getting ahead in life." Almost nine out of ten Americans report that a good education and hard work are the keys to "getting ahead," whereas only six out of ten say the same about natural ability. In contrast, only two out of ten surveyed say that being from a wealthy family and having political connections are very important. The other factors involving social capital (knowing the right people or having well-educated parents) are considered very important by four out of ten Americans.

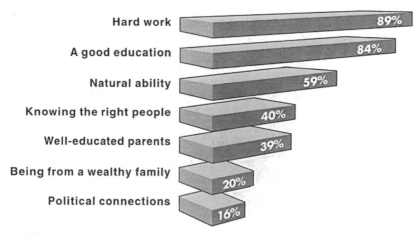

Figure 6.1.   Factors of Success

Note: Figures given are percentages of respondents who rated various factors as very important in "getting ahead in life."

Source: Davis and Smith, 1989.

Americans put their faith in education and hard work as the keys to success. In answering the survey questions, respondents did not have to make a choice between a wealthy family and a good education. They could have chosen both as being very important. The power of the American Dream is not only that it defines the paths to success (education and hard work); it also defines what is not related. The dream cannot tolerate a simultaneous belief in the value of education, which makes great sense in a credentialing society, and the advantage that comes from wealth. The myth creates facts that do not exist (you can be whatever you want to be) and denies facts that do exist (the chances for a poor child to rise to the privileged class are very slim).

The power of the dream among minorities is revealed by findings of a recent study of low-income African American high school students. Students were asked to provide a personal perspective on the importance of their race, class, or gender in limiting or enhancing opportunities for upward mobility ("What can prevent students from doing well in school?" "What is the best way of getting ahead in American society?"). Almost all students accept the "dominant narrative" of how one makes it in America: "When they were asked the best way of getting ahead in American society, without hesitation they discussed the importance of hard work, individual effort, and education."[9] However, they also provided alternative narratives of how race, class, or gender can limit an individual's efforts to improve his or her life chances.

The dream is manufactured in the popular culture, and the main vehicle for achieving it is the school system. Equality of opportunity for all, regardless of accidents of birth, is the official ideology of American education. Education is the great equalizer, providing skills and knowledge, attitudes and values. The dream was not always located in the school system. The Horatio Alger success stories popular around the turn of the century describe the poor boy who "makes it" because of his virtues of thrift, honesty, and hard work.[10] The path to success traveled not through the classroom but through the workplace, where the street urchin turned stock boy came to the attention of the boss because of his virtues. The secular myth of Horatio Alger was consistent with the times in that preparation for the world of work involved acquiring skills and training in the workplace. Even the so-called knowledge-based professions of law, medicine, and the ministry were open to entry through apprenticeship preparation.

At the beginning of the twentieth century, about 72 percent of the U.S. population aged five to seventeen years was attending public elementary and secondary schools. In 1960 the figure was 82 percent, in the mid-1990s it reached 92 percent, and in 2000 it was 95 percent—nearly all elementary-age children are now registered in school. More telling is the fact that in 1900, 6.4 percent of seventeen-year-olds graduated from high school; that figure rose to 68 percent in 1960 and to 71 percent in 1995. At the highest end of the educational process, in 1900 about 29,000 Americans received college degrees (bachelors, masters, doctors, and first professional degree); this figure climbed to 485,600 in 1960 and to 1.706 million in 1999 and 2000.[11]

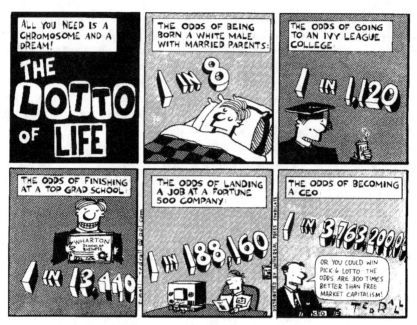

This virtual explosion in America's enrollment at different levels in the educational system probably does not owe simply to the love of learning. Increasingly, in the twentieth century, especially after World War II, good jobs have been linked to educational credentials. First, it was the high school diploma, then the bachelor's degree, and finally the specialized professional degree. Some analysts believe that the strong connection between education and jobs is the result of major technological advances that have changed the skill requirements of jobs. As the proportion of jobs requiring high levels of skill have increased, there has been increased reliance on the formal educational system to provide the required knowledge and skills. However, it is also possible that the increase in educational requirements for jobs is a way that privileged groups protect their access to those jobs that provide the greatest rewards.[12]

As more people enrolled in elementary schools, the high school diploma became the credential for many jobs that were formerly held by people with an eighth-grade education. Then, as enrollments in high school increased, the bachelor's degree became necessary for many jobs formerly held by people with a high school diploma. And so it goes. With expansion of higher education and 1.7 million graduates a year from four-year schools, the new credential derives from *where* you get your bachelor's degree. The privileged classes that control the major corporations and universities keep moving the goalpost whenever too many of the nonprivileged class start to get access to the valued educational credential.

Once schools became established as the place where people's futures were determined, their programs, activities, and curricula took on a larger significance. Schools became the models of a "small society" where the things that were learned formally and informally were relevant for the larger society. Schooling is carried out on a very rigid schedule, starting and ending at a predetermined time. Weekends are free, and there is an established schedule of vacations. Tardiness and absences must be explained, and if they are excessive, they will be punished. The school has established authority figures who must be followed without question. The Pledge of Allegiance and acceptance of God and country all serve to reaffirm the legitimacy of the established order. The daily activities and classes are built around respect for rules, self-discipline, grades, and performance according to externally imposed standards.

Within this "small society" framework, there is variation among schools, usually reflecting the class composition of its students. Schools for the privileged typically provide students with more opportunities for creativity, autonomy, and self-directed activities, whereas schools for the nonprivileged are more concerned with discipline, obedience, and job-related skills. Pressure for these different emphases often comes from parents. Parents who know their children are going to college emphasize enrichment in the arts, music, and cultural activities; those who know their children are headed for jobs emphasize the need for job-related activities.

In addition to the social and technical skills learned at school, students are also prepared for their futures as citizens of a political and economic system. Does schooling have a "liberating" effect on students, calling upon them to question the political-economic order and to play an active role in promoting change or reform? Or does schooling lead students to accept things as they are, believing that they are living in the best of all possible worlds? A number of studies of the schooling experience indicate that schooling has a conservative effect on students and that there are important class differences in this experience.[13]

Students in elementary and high school are encouraged to think about themselves as members of society primarily in courses on government and civic education. A content analysis of civics textbooks in "working-class" and "middle-class" schools indicates that students learn very different things about their government and economy and about their responsibilities as citizens. Moreover, interviews with school administrators, teachers, Parent-Teacher Association officials, and leaders of community civic groups indicate that they have very different views of how the political process should be presented in the school's civic-education program. The main findings from this research follow:

1. Civics textbooks in the working-class school (compared with those in lower-middle- and upper-middle-class schools) are particularly bland, containing more descriptive material about the political process and less

attention to power, influence, and intergroup conflict. Textbooks in the upper-middle-class school give the most attention to the use of power as the main ingredient in resolving political struggles.

2. Parents in the upper-middle-class school endorse the inclusion of "realistic" political themes in the civics programs. These parents view politics "as a process involving the resources of politicians and power, and the conflict-alleviating goal of politics." These views tend to reinforce the content found in the upper-middle-class civics textbooks. Parents from the lower-middle- and working-class communities tend to ignore or avoid "realistic" themes, thereby reinforcing the bland content found in civic textbooks in their schools.

3. Measures of the political attitudes of students taken before and after they had taken civic-education classes indicate that only the attitudes of upper-middle-class students change in the direction of supporting greater awareness of power and conflict in the political process. Students from lower-middle- and working-class schools show little change, suggesting that in their schools and communities "politics is treated and learned as a formal, mechanistic set of governmental institutions with emphasis on its harmonious and legitimate nature, rather than as a vehicle for group struggle and change."[14]

These findings indicate that students at these three socioeconomic levels are being socialized to play different roles in the political system, and this is done in a way that legitimates the existing system of economic and political inequality. Children from working-class and lower-middle-class communities are being prepared to continue the low levels of political participation exhibited by their elders. Moreover, they are prepared for a passive role in the political process because they have been taught that the institutions of government work for the benefit of all citizens. Students from the privileged upper-middle-class community are clearly being prepared to participate in and influence the political agenda. The privileged are made aware of the role of power, influence, and conflict in public affairs, whereas the nonprivileged are encouraged to work together in harmony.

Other research on the effects of schooling indicates that students' early socialization leads them to develop positive and trusting orientations toward the symbols and institutions of political authority.[15] Moreover, schools transmit the idea that government is the main center of power in society, thereby neglecting the role of large corporations and the conflict that exists among competing political and economic interests.[16] This shaping of students' attitudes toward the economic and political order tends to bring them into conformity with the dominant ideology that serves the interests of the privileged class. The longer students are in school, the greater is their exposure to the dominant ideology. In a study of elementary and secondary students from urban schools in the southwestern United States, two-thirds of third graders supported government intervention in the economy through assistance for those out of work and for the poor. The same level of support was found among sixth graders, but less than one-third of the ninth and twelfth graders supported an active role for government. Student attitudes toward private ownership of major industries became increasingly positive across the four grade levels, with 16 percent of third graders being positive compared to 63 percent of twelfth graders. Finally, attitudes toward trade unionism became increasingly negative as they progressed across grade levels. Third graders were least negative toward unionism (17 percent) and twelfth graders were most negative (59 percent).[17]

There may be naiveté and poorly formed attitudes among students (especially third graders), but it is clear from this research that the ideology that benefits the privileged gains greater strength in the minds of students as they move from third to sixth to ninth to twelfth grade. Students do not necessarily start school supporting the ideas of private property, government restraint, or antiunionism, but that is clearly where most of them wind up at high school graduation. Schools function to affirm the legitimacy of the dominant political and economic order and perpetuate the myth of equality of opportunity. In so doing, they serve the interests of the privileged class.

TRACKING AND STREAMING

> The objective of primary and secondary education, as enunciated by the legislators, educators, and community leaders who control it, is to propagate a devotion to the dominant values of the American system.
>
> —Michael Parenti, *Power and the Powerless*, 1978

One of the main concerns of the privileged class is to protect their advantage and to transmit it to their children. In a society where educational credentials are used by the privileged to justify their rewards, it is critical that the rules of the game are designed to give advantage to the children of the privileged class. Of course, others can also play by these rules if they choose, but it may be comparable to poker players who try to draw to an inside straight—a risky bet.

Tracking and streaming are two ways in which the rules of the game are used to give advantage to children of the privileged class. In order to understand how these strategies work, it is important to remind ourselves how precollege public education is financed in the United States. Funds for public education are drawn primarily from local property taxes (state and federal governments also provide funds). The amount of money raised through property taxes depends on the tax rate applied to the assessed value of homes and businesses. Communities with newer and more expensive homes and a strong business community will be able to generate more tax revenue for use in paying salaries of teachers and providing educational resources for students. While affluent families may pay higher property taxes in total dollars, they often pay a lower tax rate than that of poorer communities because the aggregate value of their homes and businesses is larger and a lower tax rate will still generate more to-tal dollars. An additional advantage enjoyed by affluent home owners is the fact that property taxes and mortgage interest are deductible from federal in-come tax, thereby giving the privileged classes a larger indirect subsidy for the education of their children than that received in poorer communities.

Evidence from recent research on the effects of school expenditures indi-cates that higher per-pupil expenditures for instruction are associated with higher levels of student achievement.[18] Higher student achievement comes from smaller class size and a higher ratio of teachers to students. The more money a school can spend on instruction, the more teachers it can hire and the more money it has to pay experienced teachers. The presence of more teachers and better-paid teachers also improves the social environment of the school as lighter workloads both improve teacher morale and enable teachers to get to know students better. This research also reports the interesting find-ing that some types of school spending are a "dead end" for student achieve-ment: capital outlays for building improvements and school-level administra-tion had no impact on student achievement. Spending additional money on more and better teachers is the way to improve education, but such money is often not available in poor school districts.

In heterogeneous school districts, where children of the privileged and non-privileged may be in the same school, there is a single pool of money to fund that school. That money is used to get the best teachers, the most up-to-date books, the best laboratory equipment, films, computers, and other educa-tional resources. In order to give an advantage to the privileged children, it is necessary for the school to develop programs that allocate the best teachers, the most computers, and the best resources to programs that are most likely to be taken by the privileged class. The money is not given to the children of the privileged class but to programs in which they are more likely to enroll. Thus, tracking is invented—a system that allocates resources to programs that are tied to distinct outcomes—a college preparation or a vocational preparation. Tracking is a form of inequality within schools.

In some heterogeneous school districts, children of the privileged and non-privileged may not be in the same school but in different schools in the same school district. In theory, each school in the district should receive the same per-pupil expenditure because the tax money was obtained to support all the schools in that district. Most past research on school funding has compared per-pupil expenditures across school districts, and to no one's surprise, the school districts with affluent families had the highest per-pupil expenditures, and the poorer districts had lower expenditures. Recently, several enterprising researchers obtained data on spending among schools *within* the same school district.[19] They studied spending and student achievement across eighty-nine elementary schools in the same district. Instead of each school having the same per-pupil expenditure for their district, "total per-student spending among elementary schools within the district ranged from $3,045 to $8,165" (p. 20). They also found that inequality in spending appears to reflect the class composition of schools—schools with the highest proportion of poor students.

Students were allocated fewer local tax dollars to spend on instruction and operations that promote a learning environment. Finally, students in schools that received more tax dollars to spend on instruction and operations exhibit higher levels of academic achievement, as measured by performance on state proficiency tests in reading, writing, math, science, and citizenship.

The above-noted inequalities in school spending across schools within the same school district go beyond the already well-known inequalities across school districts. They point to the existence of the powerful and hidden effects of class on how economic resources are distributed to schools. Why two schools in the *same* school district should receive significantly different levels of per-pupil funding can only be understood by examining how school officials, local political leaders, and more affluent parents shape the school budget process in a class-biased manner.

In homogeneous school districts, where almost all the children are from the privileged classes or almost all are from the lower classes, there is no need for tracking. In the rich schools, almost all of the children are headed for college, but in poor schools, maybe one or two out of ten children will go to college. When the percentage attending college in poor schools exceeds one in ten, it is usually because of special circumstances like a local state college or a community college that enables poor students to work or live at home while attending school. However, rich schools have more money to spend on schooling because of the higher value of assessed property in their school districts. With more money, these schools hire better teachers, purchase better equipment, provide more extracurricular activities and better guidance and counseling, and thereby provide a better all-around education. In poor schools with less money to spend, the quality of education suffers in all areas of the schooling experience. Streaming is a form of inequality between schools.

Tracking, despite its official noble intentions, is a process that segregates students by ability groupings, curriculum choices, race, and socioeconomic status. It is a process that separates winners from losers in the contest for good jobs and high income, and it has been used in primary and secondary education to provide different and unequal education for those believed to be college bound and those believed to be heading directly to the labor market. In the early 1970s, about 85 percent of public schools used a system of tracking, and in 1995, two-thirds of high schools were moderately tracked, and 60 percent of elementary schools practiced some form of whole-class ability grouping.[20] Some tracking programs provide maximum separation as students remain in the same track for all their courses, and some provide minimum separation with all students taking at least some courses together. Placing students in tracks based upon beliefs about their futures can be a powerful self-fulfilling prophecy. Track placement is directly and indirectly related to the class and racial background of students. The direct effects are a result of the expectations that teachers and administrators have of children from higher-class backgrounds.[21] The indirect effect occurs because less-privileged children may express less interest in college, receive less parental and peer encouragement to go to college, and lack the achievement scores to be selected for placement in the college track. There is substantial agreement among analysts of tracking, based on strong research evidence, that tracking has negative consequences for low-income and nonwhite students.

However, there are sharply different views on whether tracking should be retained or eliminated.[22] Some see it as a way of providing opportunities for students who might otherwise be ignored; others see it as a way of reproducing social inequality. Although many factors influence how schools choose students for track placement, there is substantial evidence that class and racial background are important.[23] This choice, however, is crucial to a student's future in terms of academic achievement, high school graduation, and college attendance.[24]

Inequality between schools (i.e., streaming) is revealed most sharply in the differences between school districts in the amount of money they spend to educate their students. Per-pupil expenditures are the best single indicator used to compare schools on the quality of their teachers, programs, and facilities. The national average of per-pupil expenditures was $6,584 in the 1999–2000 school year, with some states spending as much as $8,904 per student (Connecticut) and some as little as $3,969 (Utah). Within states, comparisons between rich and poor school districts (based on land values and family income) provide the most revealing evidence of class-based inequality. Urban school districts in larger cities spend far less money than suburban districts. Per-pupil expenditures in 1988 and 1989 in the Chicago area ranged from a high of $9,371 in the suburbs to $5,265 in the inner city. In Camden, New Jersey, suburban spending was $7,725 per pupil, compared with $3,538 in the city. A comparison of six districts in the New York City area revealed a high of $15,084 in the suburbs and a low of $7,299 in the central city. In 1989 and 1990, the wealthiest school district in New York spent $19,238 per pupil, while the poorest district spent $3,127.[25] National data for 1994 indicate that urban school districts spent $4,500 per pupil, compared with $5,066 in nonurban districts. The spending gap between urban and nonurban districts in major cities like New York was about $4,300 per student. Rural areas, which in general are predominantly white, spend far less money on schooling than either the urban or suburban school districts.[26] Wealthy suburban schools that spend nearly twice as much per pupil are able to have better teachers, better facilities, smaller classes, and a variety of enriching activities and programs. Such advantages will never find their way into inner-city schools as long as school funding is based on property taxes.[27] The most important consequence of tracking and streaming is the effect on college enrollment. Students who are in vocational tracks or in high schools composed primarily of students from low-income families are at a great disadvantage. Their educational aspirations are reduced because they receive little encouragement from peers and parents in their social milieu. Even students with high academic achievement and potential are less likely to think about college as a goal.[28] In contrast, students whose friends are the children of doctors, lawyers, and other professionals are likely to receive sustained social encouragement from parents, friends, and teachers to view college attendance as a "natural destination" in their educational careers.

Ample research evidence indicates that even students with high academic achievement and high measured intelligence are not likely to enter college if they are from lower economic groups. One study reports that 91 percent of students with high intelligence and high-social-class backgrounds attend college, compared to 40 percent of students with high intelligence but low-social-class backgrounds.[29] The combination of money to pay for college and the encouragement of peers and parents results in 84 percent of all students from higher-class backgrounds attending college, compared with only 21 percent of all students from lower-class backgrounds.

The advantages of going to college include better chances for higher-prestige jobs and higher incomes. In 1979, a male college graduate received almost 50 percent more income than a high school graduate. In 2003, the advantage of the college graduate increased to 85 percent more income. The U.S. Department of Education National Center for Education Statistics reports that in 2003 the median income of those with a high school diploma was $31,456, while those with a college degree earned $51,084.[30] In short, access to high positions and high income are more closely related to educational credentials today than was the case several decades ago.

Evidence from the past thirty years indicating how education is linked to better jobs and higher earnings has led many to jump on the education bandwagon and to propose more and better education as the solution to many of society's problems. Workers displaced by new technology or plant closings are told that they must improve their skills to find work in the high-tech economy. Young men and women from the poorest groups are encouraged to get a high school degree and to think about going to college, even if only a community college. Politicians love to talk about legislation to increase financial aid to students. In 1999, President Bill Clinton proposed a $1,500 tax credit for college to help pay for the first two years of college. He also proposed a $5,000 tax deduction for college education or job training.[31] The education bill proposed by President George W. Bush in 2001 also contains a number of tuition-related tax credits.

It is hard to argue with the call for more education, for it has certainly worked for those members of the privileged class who have converted their credentialed skills into high-paying positions in business, finance, and the professions. In 1975, about 40 percent of the young men and women from the richest one-quarter of the population earned college degrees. This was about seven times greater than the 6 percent of high schoolers from the poorest one-quarter who went to college. By 1994, eight out of ten sons and daughters from the richest quarter of the population earned a college degree, doubling the rate from twenty years earlier. In contrast, college attendance for the poor increased to a meager 8 percent from the 6 percent of twenty years earlier.[32]

Clearly, the privileged class got the message about the changing global economy in the mid-1970s and the increased importance of credentialed skills in that economy. The privileged class has, in recent years, sent almost all its children to college, as did many families of better-paid blue-collar workers and middle-income groups. But they did not all go to the same type of college, they did not major in the same fields, and they did not enjoy the same rewards in later years.

PRINCETON VERSUS PODUNK: GETTING "CREAMED"?

It is often asserted that new technologies will equalize learning opportunities for the rich and poor. It is devoutly to be wished for, but I doubt it will happen.

—Neil Postman, *Nation*, October 9, 1995

Up to this point, we have demonstrated the strong influence schooling has on the reproduction of class inequality. Contrary to the beliefs contained in the American Dream, education is not the means for providing equality of opportunity to all Americans regardless of their social position at birth. Schooling serves to reproduce inequality through the power of the myth of the American Dream and through the effects of tracking and streaming as the way to deny equal access to the means for upward mobility. We now continue our analysis of schooling by examining the question of who goes to college and where they go.

As noted earlier in this chapter, rates of college attendance have increased dramatically in the past sixty years. In 1940, 216,000 degrees were awarded by American colleges and universities. By 2002 and 2003, some 2.5 million degrees were being awarded by accredited institutions offering degrees at the associate (662,000), baccalaureate (1.311 million), master's and professional (492,000), and doctoral levels (43,300). A total of 16.4 million students were enrolled in 4,070 higher education institutions in 2003, and the number is projected to increase to 18.2 million by 2013. These institutions consist of 2,343 four-year colleges and universities, and 1,727 two-year institutions.[33] The expansion in college enrollments has had the effect of introducing greater diversity into the college environment.

It is probably safe to assume that in the era of small enrollments, the college population was composed of persons with similar social and economic backgrounds. Only the sons and daughters of the most privileged classes attended college. But what are we to say about a time when fifteen million young people are in college? Although they do not represent all of those persons from lower economic backgrounds who would go to college but cannot afford to, it must surely contain some of them. Perhaps what we have is a modified form of the American Dream, where at least some persons from the nonprivileged classes do get access to equality of opportunity. Perhaps.

The main argument of this section is that although the expansion of enrollments at the college level has resulted in larger proportions of nonprivileged youth attending colleges and universities, there has been at the same time movement toward a more rigidly class-based system of inequality within the framework of higher education. This more subtle and less visible form of inequality is reflected in the schools that privileged and nonprivileged students attend and in the areas in which they choose to specialize. Students from homes with modest finances may be more likely to select two-year or four-year

Copyright © Lloyd Dangle. Reprinted with permission.

programs with immediate employment opportunities, rather than advanced degree or professional degree programs. In addition to class-based choices of academic majors, there is some evidence that female and nonwhite students also make career choices that result in lower incomes.[34]

The consequences of class-, race-, and gender-based systems of inequality within higher education are as serious in terms of wasted human resources as the class- or race-based systems of tracking and streaming in high school that determine who goes to college. Let us begin with the approximately four thousand institutions of higher education that are available to serve the needs of America's aspiring youth. Approximately 42 percent of those institutions are two-year colleges that students typically attend either because they lack the academic credentials to be admitted to a four-year institution or because they lack the money to pay for tuition, room, and board. Some enrollees at two-year colleges are nontraditional students who are already employed and are trying to improve their credentials and career opportunities.

The remaining 58 percent, the twenty-three hundred four-year institutions, are also highly differentiated. About two hundred of these institutions are the larger and more prestigious research universities that award almost all the professional and advanced degrees in the United States. These institutions graduate the doctors, lawyers, engineers, scientists, economists, and managers that populate the privileged class. These two-hundred "top" universities can be further subdivided into the Ivy League (Brown, Columbia, Cornell, Dartmouth, Harvard, Pennsylvania, Princeton, and Yale), the top twenty private universities (e.g., Chicago, Stanford, Columbia, Duke), the top twenty state universities (e.g., California-Berkeley, North Carolina, Pennsylvania, UCLA, Texas), the so-called Big Ten (Illinois, Indiana, Iowa, Michigan, Michigan State, Minnesota, Northwestern, Ohio State, Penn State, Purdue, and Wisconsin), and other state universities. And then there are the small "elite" liberal arts colleges that provide high-quality education and strong social ties (the basis of social capital) and have very high tuition (Amherst, Bates, Bowdoin, Clark, Colby, Franklin and Marshall, Hamilton, Haverford, Hobart, Oberlin, Reed, William Smith, Swarthmore, and Tufts, among others).

The point of this little exercise (aside from the fact that we have probably misclassified many schools) is to indicate that higher education is highly differentiated, with a small number of schools that are very selective about their admissions and consistently rated by many sources as among the elite colleges and universities. The difference between the elite and nonelite schools gets greater each day as already-rich colleges continue to get richer through fund-raising programs aimed at their wealthy alumni.[35] The number of elite schools in the United States that confer great advantages on their graduates probably numbers about thirty, or less than 1 percent of all the colleges and universities in the country. The competition to get into elite schools is brutal, and students with wealthy parents are better prepared for the competition.[36] It is no accident that students at elite schools, like Harvard, are from families with a median annual income of $150,000. If you are admitted to one of these thirty elite schools, after graduation the odds are dramatically increased that you will also be admitted to one of the elite graduate or professional schools if you apply. And when schooling is completed, the graduates of elite schools will assume high-level positions in the major institutions of American society and join the privileged class. Students admitted to the "elite 1 percent" are getting "creamed," which is the positive meaning of this term used at the beginning of this section. Those who rise to the top in this system will enjoy the "good life" with all of its material and psychological benefits.

Students who are enrolled at the 1,388 community colleges and at most of the 2,100 nonelite schools are getting creamed in the negative meaning of the term—that is, they are getting "clobbered." Most of these students are caught between a rock and a hard place. They choose to go to college because it is their only hope for getting a decent job. The absence of good jobs for people with only a high school diploma drives most into college. Their parents cannot really afford to cover the costs of college, and so students work and take out loans in the hope that all the debt and sacrifice will pay off in the end. They forgo income for four years and incur debt, yet when they graduate, all they may find is a job paying $10 to $15 an hour, or $21,000 to $31,000 a year. The median starting salary for 2004 college graduates varied widely, from liberal arts majors ($30,212) to chemical-engineering majors ($52,539). In between this range were nursing ($38,920), business ($38,254), and computer science ($49,036). Clearly, graduates with technical-professional degrees receive higher starting salaries, but as many as 40 percent of graduates reported that the job they held did not require a college degree (only 17 percent of engineering graduates said this, but about 50 percent of graduates in the humanities and social sciences said a college degree was not required for their current job).[37] To be sure, at the twenty-one hundred nonelite schools, there is a small minority of graduates who do better. They are usually graduates in engineering or business or those with teaching certificates who have the skill capital and credentials to command better incomes. But they will not be joining the privileged class.

This two-tiered system of schooling for privilege is summarized in figure 6.2. In the top panel of the figure is the secondary school system that was described in the section on tracking and streaming. The children of the wealthiest members of the privileged class enter the stream in the elite prep schools that prepare students primarily for Harvard, Princeton, and Yale. The remaining children of the privileged class are being educated in the resource-rich suburban high schools that are homogeneous in terms of the economic class of their students and are well funded from their property taxes. These students from the privileged class compete among themselves for admission to a small number (about fifty) of elite universities and liberal arts colleges. They are elite because they are well endowed by financial contributions from wealthy alumni and because their admissions procedures are highly selective (i.e., they

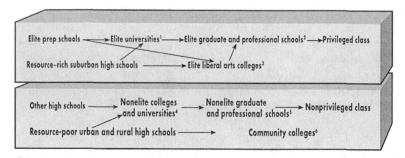

Figure 6.2.   Two-Tiered System of Schooling for Privilege

Notes:

[1]Elite universities: Approximately 20, including Harvard, Yale, Princeton, Chicago, Stanford, Northwestern, California-Berkeley, Michigan, Wisconsin, UCLA, North Carolina, Columbia, Duke, Pennsylvania.

[2]Elite graduate and professional schools: Approximately 15, including Harvard, California-Berkeley, Yale, Chicago, Wisconsin-Madison, Michigan, Columbia, Stanford, Princeton, Cornell, Illinois-Urbana, Pennsylvania.

[3]Elite liberal arts colleges: Approximately 30, including Amherst, Bates, Bowdoin, Brown, Bryn Mawr, Reed, Swarthmore, Tufts, Colgate, Smith, Wellesley, Williams, Oberlin, Hamilton, Franklin and Marshall, Wesleyan of Connecticut, Barnard, Brandeis, Mount Holyoke, Haverford, Hobart, Skidmore, Union.

[4]Nonelite colleges and universities: There are approximately 2,100 schools in this group.

[5]Nonelite graduate and professional schools: There are approximately 200 schools in this group.

[6]Community colleges: There are 1,388 schools in this group.

get applications from many more students than they can ever admit). Some of the graduates of these elite schools go on to the elite schools of law, medicine, business, and engineering, and most of the rest go into entry-level positions in America's major corporations.

The lower panel of figure 6.2 indicates where most students are located. In 2000, 2.8 million students graduated from high school; of that number, about 294,000 graduated from private schools. Enrollments in the fifty elite colleges and universities make up a small fraction of the millions enrolled in higher education, with the overwhelming proportion of students enrolled in the 2,300 nonelite colleges and universities and the 1,727 community colleges. A very small percentage of these students "escape" their nonprivileged paths and are admitted to elite schools, usually owing to their academic achievements and their performance on the SATs that are used with all applications for college.[38] A study of Harvard's admission process indicates that the school does attempt to admit a small number of "working-class" students and "students of color" who have academic merit based on scores on the SAT and other achievement tests.[39] This possibility of "moving up" describes the small amount of creaming from the bottom tier of figure 6.2 into the schooling streams of the privileged class.

The interesting thing about this two-tiered system of schooling for privilege is that the way it works has not changed very much in the past forty years. Graduates of the elite colleges and universities have always obtained better jobs (in terms of prestige, opportunities, and income) than graduates of the nonelite schools, and this is true independent of merit. The prestige of the degree-granting institution has an effect on postcollege jobs and incomes over and above the ability of its individual graduates.

In the 1950s, research compared the incomes of graduates from Ivy League schools, prestigious "technical" schools (e.g., Cal Tech, Carnegie, MIT), elite private colleges, the Big Ten, other Midwestern colleges, and other Eastern colleges. The findings indicated that the median incomes of male graduates are directly related to the prestige ranking of the schools, and this pattern was found across different fields of study. The following summary from the researchers is important for its historic value, given that this was a period before higher education became as differentiated by prestige as it is today.

> Although we have noted that good grades may at least sometimes lead to good incomes, it develops that even the poorest students from the Ivy League share in the general prosperity—and do better than the best students from other schools. Of the Ivy Leaguers who just got by—the C and D students—42 percent had reached the [highest income] level. Of the A students from the Big Ten, only 37 percent had hit that mark, and only 23 percent of the A students from "all other Midwest" colleges. Even the great financial disadvantage of a general education, rather than a specific one, does not seem to hold back the Ivy Leaguers. Of the Ivy League humanities majors, 46 percent had reached the [highest income] bracket, and of the social scientists 50 percent. But even among the Big Ten's engineering graduates, with their highly specific training and all the advantages that go with it, only 23 percent had reached the [highest income] level. [At the time of this study, the "highest income" was about three times the median income for all U.S. men. A comparable "highest income" figure in 2001 would be $118,000.]
>
> What all this amounts to is that the differences in earning power between graduates of rich and famous schools and those from small, obscure schools are so great that they override everything else. Earning power rises steadily with each increase in wealth and prestige of the school. At the extremes, the Ivy League graduates do best of all financially—even when they make poor grades and take a general rather than specific course, both of which are ordinarily handicaps—while the graduates of the smallest schools do not get up to the averages even when they make fine grades and take the type of specific courses that ordinarily produce the biggest incomes.[40]

The pattern of advantage for graduates of elite schools that was observed more than forty years ago is still in operation today. Students from privileged-class backgrounds are more likely to enroll in the most prestigious schools, and they choose programs of study that have the greatest potential for high income.[41] In fact, the effects of privilege on who goes where to college may be greater today than they were forty years ago. Sons and daughters of the privileged class go to better high schools (if not private schools) and are provided with an educational experience that is geared to satisfy entrance requirements at the most selective elite colleges. And as if that is not enough, privileged-class families have the money to help their children prepare for college entrance exams.

The effects of class background on college-going is enduring, as evidenced by the fact that students from families with parents having high levels of education are more likely to obtain advanced education beyond the baccalaureate degree. Among students who obtained a baccalaureate degree, those who entered professional programs (MD, JD) and doctoral programs were more likely to come from families that had higher levels of parental education.[42]

The final barrier for even the brightest working-class high school graduate is the cost of attending an elite college. How can a family earning the median family income of $48,816 a year (2000) afford to pay $30,000 a year for tuition, room, and board? Lacking funds, such students go to state colleges with lower costs, and they obtain financial aid and work to cover expenses. Choosing a major is often driven by practical considerations, such as the need to get a job after graduation. This can lead to vocationally oriented programs such as education, nursing, and technology degree programs, which assure jobs after the baccalaureate degree but allow limited opportunities for achieving high income or for accumulating wealth.

Findings such as those just reported indicate a clear lack of correspondence between the expectations derived from the American Dream and the actual experiences of college graduates. Ability and merit are important for a person's success after college, but where one goes to school is also important.

In the 1960s, there was growing interest in the science-based professions, such as engineering, as an example of a profession open to talented people, regardless of their social and economic origins. In the professions of medicine and law, it is possible that a graduate's family background could influence postcollege success by providing the money to start a practice or the social contacts for attracting wealthy clients. But engineers work in large corporations where their scientific and technical expertise is often thought by many to determine their movement up the corporate ladder. One might assume that an engineer's social and economic background should have less significance for his or her success than might be the case in medicine or law.

Once again, contrary to the myth of equality of opportunity and the belief that engineering is a career open to talent, engineering graduates from higher social origins (based on their father's occupation) were more likely to hold engineering positions that provided greater prestige, power, and income.[43] This finding was based on a study of the graduates from a single university of moderate prestige, not part of the elite schools. When the research was expanded to a national sample of engineering graduates, it was found that engineers with upper social origins earned more money and held more responsible positions than engineers from lower social origins. Moreover, this class difference was found to be true even among engineers who had the highest grades in college and had attended the most selective engineering schools.[44] Thus, even when working-class high school graduates are creamed (i.e., are recruited to elite universities), their final rewards of income and position may not put them in the privileged class.

The American Dream puts great emphasis on a college education as the one true path to upward mobility (along with hard work, of course). Traveling down the "yellow brick road" paved with academic tracks, good grades, and high SAT scores should result in a college degree and entrance into the Emerald City. However, one of the details missing from the official version of the American Dream is that it is not just a college degree that gets you into the privileged class, but one from an elite school. Another detail missing from the American Dream is that it fails to prepare working-class or black students, who are often first-generation college entrants, with a glimpse of the nonacademic obstacles and pressures they will face in college. The dream seems to assume that poor, but talented, adolescents are all prepared to be college students because they are upwardly mobile achievers waiting for a break to come their way (a version of the Horatio Alger stories). It is further assumed that they have the "right stuff" (the values and aspirations) instilled by parents who value education, like-minded college-oriented peers, and teachers who have worked hard to help them with their dream of attending college. In short, the poor but talented black and white students who "make it" have made *socialized choices* to attend college. These choices reveal a temporal sequence whereby the values and aspirations for college come first, and mobility opportunities follow. However, it is also possible that some low-income students wind up in college because of *situational choices* that are unplanned and do not reflect any real preparation for college life. Let us consider this possibility by returning to the story of Nick Caradona, whom we met at the beginning of this chapter.

When we left Nick, he had dropped out of high school and was working as a runner and writer for a "bookmaker." He did this work for several years and aspired to start his own "handbook" as soon as he accumulated enough money and found a good spot (the right neighborhood/ethnic niche). Unfortunately, the Korean War intervened, and Nick was drafted into the Marines. After two years of service, he returned to his old neighborhood with two goals—to buy a car with money he had accumulated in the military, and to take advantage of all his GI benefits while avoiding going to work. After he bought a car, the next thing he did was go to the Veterans Administration (VA) and sign up for the 20/20 Club—collect $20 a week for twenty weeks while allegedly looking for a job ($20 then was equal to $125 today). Nick collected $20 for twenty weeks and returned to the VA to see what was next. The clerk advised that since he didn't graduate from high school, he should consider getting his high school diploma in a night school program. While enrolled, he would get $90 a month. So Nick went to night school, took an English course and a history course, and received a high school diploma. Back to the VA with the "what's next" question.

This time the VA clerk said, "Why not go to college?" The idea had never crossed Nick's mind. The clerk told Nick that his weak academic record would prevent him from getting into a "good" college and suggested that he apply for admission to one of the state teacher's colleges. The most attractive part of this idea to Nick was that he would continue to get $90 per month while going to school. A no-brainer for Nick!

Nick enrolled in the teacher's college and found it to be a very alien environment. He checked into a motel for his very first night at the college, in preparation for the next day's orientation for freshmen. That night he took some records with him to the student union in search of a record player. On the way, he bought a bottle of wine to drink while he was listening to his favorite records (he was into sax players, and he had selections from Benny Carter, Vido Musso, and Coleman Hawkins, among others). Nick set up his records and wine and settled into an easy chair to sip and listen. It didn't take long before he was told, politely, that he would have to leave because alcohol was not permitted on campus. Nick was astounded. You could drink at age eighteen in the state, but you couldn't drink on campus.

Remaining at college was a struggle for Nick, not academically but socially. But for a fortuitous event, Nick would probably not have lasted beyond the first semester. During his first month at school, he ran into a neighborhood buddy he hadn't seen since before the war. Tony Lembo was a neighborhood kid who had played softball with Nick when they were about fifteen. Tony's father had a hot dog pushcart that he set up every day near the subway. Tony had been in the army in Korea, and he was using his benefits to become a physical education teacher. Tony and Nick decided to room together, and soon they met several other ex-GIs and formed a drinking and card-playing circle that sustained them while facing the ambiance of academe.

Nick was following the American Dream, but not quite according to the script linked to the conventional version of the dream. Nick never quite became a part of the college scene but sustained and protected himself by hanging out with other working-class guys who found themselves in the same place, facing similar problems of adjustment. Nick's situation was similar to that facing many working-class African Americans and Hispanics who are the first in their families to attend college. People of color who attend predominantly white colleges face significant hurdles in trying to become a part of academic life.[45] Hopefully, their lives will be better because of having attended college. But using the college degree to get into the Emerald City is another matter!

THE FUTURE: CONTINUING INEQUALITY AND CORPORATIONS IN THE CLASSROOM

Corporations and their foundations have become sacred cows to university administrators. Few professors are willing to jeopardize their standing in universities by publishing research articles critical of these donors.

—Lawrence C. Soley, *Leasing the Ivory Tower,* 1995

The main argument of this chapter is that the American educational system operates in a way that reproduces the existing structures of inequality in the larger society, especially those grounded in class and racial distinction. It achieves this end, first of all, by promoting an ideology that proclaims schooling to be the great equalizer and the main avenue for upward mobility. Second, inequality is perpetuated through a multitiered system of education made up of elite schools, average schools, and weak schools in terms of academic quality. The different quality of these schools is directly linked to class and racial categories of their students. The quality of the educational experience in primary and secondary schools helps to determine a student's chances for attending college.

The inequalities in primary and secondary schools linked to students' social-class membership and/or their racial/ethnic identities are likely to be reinforced and extended in the years ahead. A recent study by Harvard University's Civil Rights Project reports an increasing trend toward segregation in kindergarten through twelfth grade, especially in Northern states like New York, Michigan, Illinois, and California.[46] The study found that 70 percent of black children attended predominantly minority schools in 1998 and 1999, an increase from 66 percent in 1991 and 1992 and from 63 percent in 1980 and 1981. Similar patterns of segregation are reported for Latino students. The study also reports that the pattern of segregated schools closely matches the pattern of high-poverty schools. This is a situation where class- and race-based segregation are used to relegate millions of children to a second-class education.

Projections of demographic trends suggest that primary and secondary schools will have increasing proportions of students of color in highly segregated settings. This should result in increased demands from parents for improvements in the quality of education provided for their children. Privileged-class parents may respond by moving their children from public to private educational settings. This would be consistent with trends that we described as "class secession" in chapter 2, namely, the expansion of private, class-segregated communities and the erosion of privileged-class support for public institutions. Working-class parents may also be attracted to opportunities to move their children out of failing schools into so-called charter schools or other alternatives that appear to offer some benefits as conventional public school budgets decline.

Concern about public education has been part of the basis for some innovations that are currently on the public agenda, namely, the voucher system and the charter school. The voucher system provides families each school year with a voucher ($2,000 to $4,000) that can be used to enroll their children in nonreligious, private schools. There have been attempts to extend the use of vouchers to religious schools, but such efforts have been blocked by lawsuits. Charter schools enable groups of parents, teachers, and community members to propose a new way of providing education for their children. For example, they might wish to emphasize self-paced learning, cross-disciplinary education, or traditional back-to-basics programs. Such groups apply for a charter from the local school board or state board of education to create the new school, and if approved, they receive public funding on a per-pupil basis similar to funding for public schools.

Vouchers and charter schools are attractive ideas because they appear to empower parents who have become frustrated with the public school system's failure to educate their children. Many parents in low-income inner cities have come to view these new ideas as the only way to provide their children with a better education. Unfortunately, only a fraction of inner-city families will be able to take advantage of vouchers or charter schools. Charter schools are not obligated to take all students who apply, and the ability to use a voucher may be dependent on the availability of transportation and other resources to get children to schools outside of their neighborhoods. The main impact of vouchers and charter schools will be to siphon money away from public schools, leaving those left behind with even poorer facilities. The more affluent will take advantage of vouchers to move to private schools, leading to greater segregation in schools.

Students from resource-rich schools receive the kind of preparation that enables them to compete for admission to elite colleges and universities. Students from resource-poor schools are more likely to drop out or to terminate their education with the high school diploma. Those who do go to college attend community colleges and a wide variety of average to good state colleges and universities.

Based on everything we know today about the U.S. economy and the actions of corporations (as discussed in chapter 3), the educational inequalities just described will not only continue; in all likelihood, they will get worse. Students from families in the bottom of the double-diamond class structure will find it increasingly difficult to pay the costs of attending college. Moreover, it is likely to become increasingly apparent that large numbers of college graduates will be unable to find any but the lowest-level jobs available in the service sector. Such a trend will highlight the growing reality that there is a significant mismatch between the kinds of jobs that most colleges prepare most students to enter and the kinds of jobs that are actually available to most non-privileged-class college graduates.

In addition to continuing inequality in schooling, we expect greater involvement of private-sector corporations in the educational system at all levels. At the primary and secondary levels, there will be continuing interest in alternative ways of "delivering" education to the young. The current antiunion, antibureaucracy, antigovernment climate will stimulate proposals to "privatize" education. Edison Schools, Inc., a private-sector firm, enrolls over fifty thousand students in over one hundred schools that they run on a for-profit basis. The privatization movement will probably grow because of the ideology of school choice and a potential multi-billion-dollar market.[47] The CEOs from Fortune 500 firms have become involved in school-reform efforts at the state and national levels.[48] Since these business leaders are used to thinking in terms of the "bottom line," productivity, and efficiency, their involvement gives one pause as to the kind of educational "reforms" that may appear on the nation's agenda. In addition to "for-profit" private schools, we should expect great attention to new educational technology that will reduce the need for teachers and increase dependence on telecommunications-based instruction.

Corporations have already recognized the potential for advertising commercial products to the millions of school children who are today's consumers, as well as consumers of the future.[49] Classroom films, television, and weekly papers are owned by large corporations, and the products developed for schoolroom use are accompanied by corporate logos and advertising material.[50] Many of the proposals to bring corporate expertise and technology into the classroom are based on the assertion that the telecommunications revolution increasingly is available to, and will equally benefit, rich and poor alike. Schooling will therefore be able to deliver on its promise as the "equalizer" as all students will have access to the same educational resources, the same information, and the same master teachers on the information superhighway. Once again, a technological fix appears ready to solve the problem of class inequality. Such promises are reminiscent of the claims made by the educational system that embraced Nick and Arnie, whom we met at the beginning of this chapter. These youngsters were brought by a progressive program into the best schools in the city and exposed to other talented kids who were college bound. But the imagined equalizing force of this experience did not "take." The boys lived in another world outside of the school that superseded and blunted the best intentions of a progressive educational model a generation ago. Like Nick and Arnie, the life experiences of class inequality today will not disappear simply because educational opportunities are extended to working-class kids through the information superhighway.

Finally, we need to consider corporate penetration of higher education.[51] Private firms are no strangers to higher education. Corporate CEOs are prominent as trustees of most major universities but especially the elite schools. Such representation helps to encourage corporate-university relations that result in corporate funding of research and a variety of university programs. In return, corporations get access to the latest knowledge that can be converted into patents on products and processes that benefit the corporations providing the funding. Often, corporations that provide funds for research by faculty or graduate students are able to obtain agreements guaranteeing that the results of the funded research will remain secret for an agreed-upon period of time. The doctoral dissertation in biomedical engineering or pharmacology of a student whose research has had corporate funding can be kept from public disclosure until such time as the corporation that funded the research can realize its expected benefits. Students and professors may not be able to publish the results of such research until given permission to do so by the corporation. This practice of secret or confidential research may have started during the cold war era when the Department of Defense funded research involving national security interests. Today, the private corporations can prevent publication because of private financial interests.

Many faculty at major research universities are active participants in corporate-university relations. Those whose work may have commercial possibilities are actively pursued by corporations with substantial research grants or consulting fees. Some faculty are able to double their incomes through their consulting agreements, especially in several fields in engineering, science, and the business schools. Those faculty with a more entrepreneurial bent often start their own firms in a research park near the university while retaining their academic positions and salaries.

Faculty at large research universities may receive e-mail messages from their research offices with titles such as "Leveraging Your Research by Starting a Business." This "call-out" to faculty, staff, and students is an attempt to stimulate interest in starting a business by offering information on university guidelines for faculty-owned businesses and discussions of where to find capital. These cyberspace messages are supplemented with hard-copy slick brochures with announcements like the following:

> The climate for starting technology based businesses has never been better. Owing to steady or dwindling budgets, coupled with increasing demand of and competition for funds, government support for university research projects is harder to secure. University research programs are seeking alternative funding sources, such as funneling research ideas with commercial potential into start-up businesses. The bottom line: becoming an entrepreneur is not only "in" but is encouraged.[52]

University administrators and boards of trustees generally sidestep evidence of active corporate pursuit of faculty. Universities usually have regulations stipulating that faculty may be involved in "outside activities" for one or more days per week or month, depending on the university. There is no stipulation as to how much they may earn as consultants and no requirement that the university must be reimbursed for the time taken away from university responsibilities. Universities encourage these relationships in part because administrators hope to increase the flow of dollars from the private sector into the university's budget. Also, as noted in chapter 1, university administrators themselves are often actively involved in corporate roles.

In recent years, there has been a decline in federal money coming to universities for their research programs. This money often comes with agreements to cover overhead costs that allow universities to support other activities. In addition to the decline of federal dollars, many public universities have not been able to obtain more state funds or raise tuition. The search for new sources of funding has led many research universities into efforts to link university research to commercial activities like research parks, expanded corporate-university ventures that promise patents, or promising state legislatures that university programs can contribute to economic growth. A major source of new money has been the private sector, which has been only too willing to help—but at a price. The price might be confidential research (as noted earlier). Private sector funding might give the corporation the right to select researchers for projects and define the research topics to be pursued. It might even give corporations a voice on matters of promotions and tenure of faculty who work on corporate projects.

And it is also possible that corporate penetration of academe will have a chilling effect on those faculty members whose inclinations or disciplines tend to raise questions about the role of corporations in American society. Consideration by faculty of sensitive issues, such government regulation of market capitalism, the impact of unrestrained technology on the environment and our communities, and the political power of corporations in a democracy, may be muted by a strong corporate presence within the university. Just as downsizing and plant closings serve to depress wages and discourage unionization, corporate penetration of academe could serve to create a climate of "corporate correctness" that will dominate the minds of students and faculty alike.

CLASS ISSUES IN THE MEDIA: EDUCATION AND WHAT DO POLITICIANS OFFER?

One of the things that we learned in this chapter is that students' social-class position affects their lives in two ways. First, it affects them as members of families who have different economic and social resources. Families with limited resources of time, energy, money, and social connections are less able to get involved with the academic lives of their children and less able to provide the enriching experiences that help to contribute to academic success. Such families often cannot think of college as a realistic option for their children, for that would require an annual expenditure that far exceeds their means. Even state universities with modest tuitions for in-state students have a total cost of at least $15,000 for tuition, room and board, books, and other expenses. Children in families with limited resources are also more likely to think about employment opportunities rather than college-attendance opportunities.

The second way that social class affects students is through the quality of schools that they attend. Students from low-income families tend to live in low-income areas that are unable to provide the level of tax-based funding that can provide the same high-quality schools and teachers that are found in schools supported by the taxes of higher-income families. This is the double-whammy of social-class effects—a cumulative disadvantage that first limits or restricts students' experiences and aspirations, and then provides them with an educational experience that does little to reverse the disadvantage that they bring with them to the schoolhouse.

There have been a number of public policy efforts to make the American Dream of equality of educational opportunity a reality. Let us consider a number of the proposals that have been designed to reduce the double-whammy of how social class produces a cumulative disadvantage for students from low-income families.

(*continued*)

Vouchers and Charter Schools. First are proposals that are based on a recognition that some schools, especially those serving low-income students, are doing a poor job of preparing their students for jobs or higher education. In this section, we discuss the voucher system and charter schools as two relatively new initiatives proposed by political and education leaders. Both initiatives are based on the belief that the way to improve elementary and secondary education is to change from the traditional approach of public education to a market model of education that expands the type of schools that students may attend with public funding. Under the traditional approach, parents and their children obtain educational services through a system of public taxes on all citizens. These taxes are used to pay for the things that are needed to deliver education, such as a curriculum of instruction in basic areas (e.g., science, mathematics, social studies, the arts), teachers with certified training to deliver the curriculum to students, and the support services and facilities needed to make the system work. Under this arrangement, parents and students get little choice in the schools that they attend. Parents or students who are not pleased with the educational services they receive must either find ways to improve their schools, or they must spend additional money to send their children to another school that they believe has a better curriculum or better teachers.

Under the market model, parents and students are viewed as consumers of education, and schools are providers of educational services. Parents, as consumers, receive from the state each year a voucher worth $2,500 or $3,500, which they may use to buy one year of a third grade or a fifth grade education for their son or daughter. They can "spend" this voucher in any public or private school that they choose, and one can assume that they will try to spend their voucher in a school that will deliver the best education for their children. Thus, the voucher system would empower parents and students and would presumably put pressure on schools to improve their educational services in order to attract more parent-consumers. Under this market model, bad schools would attract few vouchers and would either have to improve or go out of business, and good schools would attract vouchers and would be motivated to maintain their high-quality education. Charter schools are a special case of the voucher system whereby fifty or a hundred families may, in effect, pool their vouchers to start their own school and use state-provided funds to hire teachers, create a curriculum, and deliver educational services within state-approved guidelines.

The nation's oldest voucher system was created by the Wisconsin legislature in 1990 and has enrolled most students in Milwaukee. The city of Cleveland, Ohio, has joined Milwaukee in offering vouchers to low-income students. There has been a long-standing battle between proponents and opponents of vouchers and charter schools, and the main issues have centered on costs, equal access, constitutional questions, and performance.

Costs. Will low-income parents be able to use a voucher of between $3,000 and $4,000 to get a child into a private school? Critics of the voucher system like to point out that many private schools charge an annual tuition in excess of $5,000 a year, often as high as $8,000 to $10,000 a year. Will the low-income parent be left with a voucher that is meaningless because she can't pay the cost of private tuition? National data on the costs of private school tuition are lacking, but one study by the Cato Institute (which supports vouchers) surveyed tuition costs at private schools in Atlanta, Indianapolis, San Francisco, and Jersey City.[53] They report that the average cost of private school tuition in these four cities is $3,116, compared to the average tax-funded tuition cost in public schools of $6,857. The tuition numbers indicate that there were many options for low-income families with $3,000 to spend on tuition. However, this study tells us nothing about the quality of education in these "affordable" private schools. Parents spending their vouchers on affordable private schools could very well be jumping out of the frying pan and into the fire when it comes to quality. Moreover, the four cities selected for study in this project are not exactly a random sample of most cities. The tuition costs in Atlanta, Indianapolis, San Francisco, and Jersey City tell us nothing about such costs in New York or Chicago.

Equal Access. Even if a family could buy a better education with their $3,000 voucher, not all families may be able to take advantage of the opportunity. Sending your child to a different school outside of your neighborhood district will entail transportation costs. Not all low-income families have the financial resources to pay for transportation or the additional time that may be needed to transport a student to and from school over a longer distance. Let's face it, neighborhood schools are popular in America because they are conveniently located near students' homes, and they provide families with a sense of security with their children being close by. It is likely that middle-income and upper-income families will be most likely to use vouchers to move their students into private schools. These more affluent families will likely have one or two cars, and the parents will have the type of jobs that provide greater flexibility to blend their work schedules with their child's school schedule. Finally, there is no guarantee that a private school will accept students who apply. Supporters of public education point out that public schools must admit all students, regardless of their learning disabilities or record school performance. Students with questionable academic records, learning disabilities, or behavior problems may not have it easy finding a private school that will admit them.

Constitutional Question? A big unresolved issue is whether public tax money can be converted to vouchers that parents may use to pay for tuition in a private religious school. Many religious schools integrate religion throughout their curricula, and as arms of religious orders, they integrate religious values and doctrine in their curricula, indoctrinating students on such controversial issues as abortion and creationism. They may select employees as well as students on the basis of religion or values, thereby resulting in public money being used to support discrimination. One can expect that using tax-based vouchers to pay for tuition in private religious schools would be challenged as a violation of the U.S. Constitution's Establishment Clause prohibiting the funding of religious institutions.

Performance. After all other questions are answered, what remains is whether private school education paid for with vouchers or through charter schools makes any difference in the academic preparation of students. Private schools and charter schools do not operate in the same state regulatory environment as do public schools. Proponents of private and charter schools say that's a plus and is the main reason why they can deliver a higher-quality education, free of bureaucratic regulations and the influence of teachers' unions. The jury is still out on how voucher students perform

(*continued*)

compared to public school students, or how students in charter schools perform compared to those in public schools. Are there differences in graduation rates, language skills, math scores? The results are mixed and lack definitive answers because the studies are flawed by their samples and by the lack of strict comparability between the groups. We do not know if the test score results of private/charter/voucher students and public school students are the result of curriculum differences, teacher differences, class size, pupil-teacher ratios, or the self-selection of students with different abilities into each school.[54]

No Child Left Behind

The No Child Left Behind (NCLB) Act of 2001 was based on President George W. Bush's proposal to reform the Elementary and Secondary Education Act (ESEA) of 1965, the largest source of K–12 spending by the federal government on education. The Bush initiative was based on the premise that the existing ESEA legislation had led to hundreds of specialized education programs and the expenditure of billions of tax dollars, with little evidence that the academic achievement gap between rich and poor, Anglo and minority, had been reduced. In fact, the gap was wide and growing. The NCLB act proposed to introduce results-oriented reforms and to link academic progress to federal funding for states and schools.

The key feature of NCLB required states receiving Title I money from the federal government to ensure that all student groups met high standards. States must do so by developing measurable goals focused on basic skills and having annual assessments in math and reading in grades three to eight. Low-performing schools that failed to make adequate yearly progress after three years faced the possibility of loss of funding. One of the more important features of NCLB was that the annual test results would be provided to the public, and they would be reported in "disaggregated form," that is, by race, gender, English proficiency, disability, and socioeconomic status. Public availability of this information would enable parents, students, teachers, and administrators to confront the realities of low-performing schools and students and thereby encourage development of more effective programs of instruction and assessment.

The problems with NCLB are those associated with any test- or results-oriented effort to improve the quality of education. Teachers and students can become focused on the tests, while the curriculum can become so tightly linked to annual testing that it ignores the unique features of schools and students and can discourage innovation in trying to deal with special situations. There are also problems concerning the tests themselves and how to ensure that they are comparable from year to year.

Access to Higher Education

The third major effort at the federal level to keep alive the American Dream of equal opportunity is to make higher education affordable to all students who wish to attend. How can we keep open the doors to higher education when the costs of attending college have been growing faster than the incomes of the average families? One initiative supported by college administrators and lawmakers is federal Pell Grants, which range from $400 to $4,050 per academic year for low-income students. In 2003 and 2004, Pell Grants were awarded to 5.1 million students, with the average award in the amount of $2,466. Applicants for grants must provide information on family income, home ownership, family assets, number of dependent children, and the number of children in college. This financial and family information is used to calculate an "expected family contribution," which is then subtracted from the cost of college attendance and used as a basis for determining the amount of the Pell Grant. Although students with annual family incomes as high as $45,000 are eligible for grants, over 70 percent of the awards are to families with incomes below $20,000. However, despite the generosity of the Pell Grants based on financial need, the average Pell Grant covered about 23 percent of total costs at an average four-year public college or university, including tuition, fees, room and board, books, and related school expenses.[55]

Other proposals to defray the costs of higher education have involved tuition tax credits. During the 2004 presidential campaign, candidate John F. Kerry proposed to help poor students by allowing families paying college tuition to deduct up to $4,000 per year from their taxes. If families paid less than $4,000 per year in taxes, they would receive a check from the Internal Revenue Service for the difference between their tax bill and the $4,000 tax credit. While this proposal would certainly reduce college costs for tuition-paying families, it would primarily benefit families who were already sending children to college regardless of family income. So, while upper-income families would benefit from receiving a tax credit, the proposal might not increase the number of low-income students who attend college. In fact, some have argued that low-income families' not sending their children to college is due only partly to financial circumstances and mainly to poor academic preparation in high school.

In 2000, there were about 4 million people who were 18 years old. Of those, 30% dropped out of high school, leaving about 2.8 million who graduated with regular diplomas. Of the 2.8 million kids, only about half took the minimal academic coursework—math, English, science and so on—that almost all colleges require for admission. And of the 1.4 million who passed that hurdle, about 100,000 still couldn't read English at even a bare-minimum level. That leaves only about 1.3 million kids, a mere 32% of the 18-year-old population, who were minimally qualified to apply to college. According to the U.S. Department of Education there were 1,341,000 incoming freshmen at four-year colleges that year. That's almost exactly the number of college-ready graduates in 2000.[56]

This bleak assessment of the academic qualifications of high school graduates underscores the complexity of the problem facing those who wish to increase the number of students going to college from low-income families. Making college affordable for low-income families is essential, but equal in importance to financial need is adequate academic preparation—which takes us back to the cumulative disadvantage of social class for young people from the working class. There will be no realization of the American Dream of equality of educational opportunity until our educational leaders and lawmakers create policies that will (1) improve the quality of education in low-income areas and (2) provide full funding for the costs of college-going for low-income students.

NOTES

1. Roslyn Arlin Mickelson, "The Attitude-Achievement Paradox among Black Adolescents," *Sociology of Education* 63 (1990): 44–61; Patricia A. Adler, Steven J. Kless, and Peter Adler, "Socialization to Gender Roles: Popularity among Elementary School Boys and Girls," *Sociology of Education* 65 (1992): 169–87; Karl S. Alexander, Doris R. Entwisle, and Carrie S. Horsey, "From First Grade Forward: Early Foundations of High School Dropout," *Sociology of Education* 70 (1997): 87–107; Vincent J. Roscigno and James W. Ainsworth-Darnell, "Race, Cultural Capital, and Educational Resources: Persistent Inequalities and Achievement Returns," *Sociology of Education* 72 (1999): 158–78; Samuel R. Lucas and Aaron D. Good, "Race, Class, and Tournament Track Mobility," *Sociology of Education* 74 (2001): 139–56.

2. Michael B. Katz, *The Irony of Early School Reform* (Cambridge, MA: Harvard University Press, 1968).

3. Maureen T. Hallinan, "Tracking: From Theory to Practice," *Sociology of Education* 67 (April 1994): 79.

4. Robert Granfield and Thomas Koenig, "Pathways into Elite Law Firms: Professional Stratification and Social Networks," in *Research in Politics and Society*, vol. 4, *The Political Consequences of Social Networks*, ed. Gwen Moore and J. Allen Whitt (Greenwich, CT: JAI Press, 1992), 325–51.

5. Brian Doherty, "Those Who Can't, Test," *Mother Jones* (November–December 1998): 71.

6. Tiffani Chin and Meredith Phillips, "Social Reproduction and Child-Rearing Practices: Social Class, Children's Agency, and the Summer Camp Activity Gap," *Sociology of Education* 77 (July 2004): 185–210.

7. Eric Pace, "B. Gerald Cantor, Philanthropist and Owner of Rodin Collection, Is Dead at 79," *New York Times*, July 6, 1996.

8. The *Chicago Tribune* published a much abbreviated eight-paragraph story about Cantor obtained from the *New York Times* News Service. The *Tribune* story started with the same lead sentence used in the fifty-five paragraph *Times* story, revealing the extraordinary appeal of the rags-to-riches story, even when it may not be true in its substance.

9. Carla O'Connor, "Race, Class, and Gender in America: Narratives of Opportunity among Low-Income African American Youths," *Sociology of Education* 72 (1999): 137–57.

10. Richard Wohl, "The 'Rags to Riches Story': An Episode of Secular Idealism," in *Class, Status, and Power*, ed. Reinhard Bendix and Seymour M. Lipset (New York: Free Press, 1966), 501–26.

11. U.S. Department of Education, National Center for Educational Statistics, *Digest of Educational Statistics*, ed. Thomas D. Snyder, Charlene M. Hoffman, and Clair M. Geddes, NCES 2001-034 (Washington, DC: Government Printing Office, 2000).

12. For a discussion of these two different views of why educational requirements for many jobs have increased, see Randall Collins, *The Credential Society* (New York: Academic Press, 1979), and Randall Collins, "Functional and Conflict Theories of Educational Stratification," *American Sociological Review* 36 (1971): 1002–19.

13. Edgar Litt, "Civic Education, Community Norms, and Political Indoctrination," *American Sociological Review* 28 (February 1963): 69–75.

14. Litt, "Civic Education, Community Norms, and Political Indoctrination," 72, 73.

15. Dean Jaros, *Socialization to Politics* (New York: Praeger, 1973); Edward S. Greenberg, *Political Socialization* (New York: Atherton, 1970).

16. Alan Wolfe, *The Seamy Side of Democracy* (New York: David McKay, 1973); Ira Katznelson and Mark Kesselman, *The Politics of Power* (New York: Harcourt Brace Jovanovich, 1975).

17. Scott Cummings and Del Taebel, "The Economic Socialization of Children: A Neo-Marxist Analysis," *Social Problems* 26 (December 1978): 198–210.

18. Harold Wenglinsky, "How Money Matters: The Effect of School District Spending on Academic Achievement," *Sociology of Education* 70 (July 1997): 221–37.

19. Dennis J. Condron and Vincent J. Roscigno, "Disparities within: Unequal Spending and Achievement in an Urban School District," *Sociology of Education* 76 (January 2003): 18–36.

20. Christopher Jencks et al., *Inequality: Reassessment of the Effect of Family and Schooling in America* (New York: Harper and Row, 1972); *Education Week,* May 3, 1995, available on the Internet at www.edweek.org.

21. Robert Rosenthal and Lenore Jacobson, *Pygmalion in the Classroom* (New York: Holt, Rinehart and Winston, 1968).

22. Hallinan, "Tracking: From Theory to Practice," and Jennie Oakes, "More Than Misapplied Technology: A Normative and Political Response to Hallinan on Tracking," *Sociology of Education* 67 (1994): 79–91.

23. Sally Kilgore, "The Organizational Context of Tracking in Schools," *American Sociological Review* 56 (1991): 189–203.

24. Karl Alexander, Martha Cook, and Edward McDill, "Curriculum Tracking and Educational Stratification," *American Sociological Review* 43 (1982): 47–66.

25. Jonathan Kozol, *Savage Inequalities* (New York: Harper, 1991); Ron Renchler, *Financial Equity in Schools,* ERIC Digest No. 76 (Eugene, OR: ERIC Clearinghouse in Educational Management, 1994); U.S. Department of Education, *Digest of Educational Statistics, 2000* (Washington, DC: U.S. Government Printing Office, 2001).

26. Noreen Connell, "Underfunded Schools: Why Money Matters," *Dollars and Sense* (March–April 1998): 14–17, 39.

27. Connell, "Underfunded Schools," 14–17, 39.

28. William A. Sewell, A. O. Haller, and G. W. Ohlandorf, "The Educational and Early Occupational Status Attainment Process," *American Sociological Review* 35 (1970): 1014–27.

29. William A. Sewell and Vimal Shah, "Parents' Education and Children's Educational Aspirations and Achievements," *American Sociological Review* 33 (1968): 191–209.

30. Robert Kominski and Rebecca Sutterlin, *What's It Worth? Educational Background and Economic Status,* U.S. Bureau of the Census, Household Economic Studies, P70–32 (Washington, DC: U.S. Government Printing Office, 1992); U.S. Bureau of the Census, 2000; National Center for Educational Statistics (www.nces.ed.gov).

31. Thomas Geoghegan, "Overeducated and Underpaid," *New York Times,* June 3, 1997.

32. Thomas Mortenson of the National Council of Educational Opportunity Associations, Washington, DC, reported in Karen W. Arenson, "Cuts in Tuition Assistance Put College beyond Reach of Poorest Students," *New York Times,* January 27, 1997; Richard Kahlenberg, ed., *America's Untapped Resource: Low-Income Students in Higher Education* (New York: Century Foundation, 2003).

33. U.S. Department of Education, *Digest of Educational Statistics, 2000;* National Center for Educational Statistics, on the Internet at http://nces.ed.gov//programs/digest/d03/tables/dt249.asp.

34. Jerry A. Jacobs, "Gender and Academic Specialties: Trends among Recipients of College Degrees in the 1980s," *Sociology of Education* 68 (1995): 81–98.

35. "Rich College, Poor College," *Business Week* (December 20, 2004): 88–90.

36. "Ever Higher Society, Ever Harder to Ascend," *Economist* (December 29, 2004).

37. U.S. Department of Education, National Center for Education Statistics, *The Condition of Education 1996,* ed. Thomas Smith, NCES 96–304 (Washington, DC: U.S. Government Printing Office, 1996); Deshundra Jefferson, "Most Lucrative College Degrees," *Money Magazine* (September 21, 2004).

38. James Hearn, "Academic and Nonacademic Influences on the College Destinations of 1980 High School Graduates," *Sociology of Education* 64 (July 1991): 158–71.

39. David Karen, "Toward a Political-Organizational Model of Gatekeeping: The Case of Elite Colleges," *Sociology of Education* 63 (1990): 227–40.

40. Ernest Haveman and Patricia Salter West, *They Went to College* (New York: Harcourt, Brace, 1952), 180.

41. Scott Davies and Neil Guppy, "Fields of Study, College Selectivity, and Student Inequalities in Higher Education," *Social Forces* 75 (1997): 1417–38; David Karen, "Changes in Access to Higher Education in the United States: 1980–1992," *Sociology of Education* 75 (July 2002): 191–210.

42. Ann L. Mullen, Kimberly A. Goyette, and Joseph A. Soares, "Who Goes to Graduate School? Social and Educational Correlates of Educational Continuation after College," *Sociology of Education* 76 (April 2003): 143–69.

43. Robert Perrucci, "The Significance of Intra-Occupational Mobility," *American Sociological Review* 26 (1961): 874–83.

44. Carolyn C. Perrucci and Robert Perrucci, "Social Origins, Educational Contexts, and Career Mobility," *American Sociological Review* 35 (1970): 451–63.

45. Robert Perrucci et al., "The Two Faces of Racialized Space in a Predominantly White University," *International Journal of Contemporary Sociology* 37 (2000): 230–44.

46. Diana J. Schemo, "U.S. Schools Turn More Segregated," *New York Times,* July 20, 2001, A12.

47. Peter Schrag, "Edison's Red Ink Schoolhouse," *Nation* (June 25, 2001): 20–24.

48. Douglas D. Noble, "Schools as 'Instructional Delivery Systems,'" *In These Times* (November 30, 1992): 28–29.

49. Marianne Manilov, "Channel One, Joe Camel, Potato Chips, and ABC," *EXTRA!* (July–August, 1966): 18–19.

50. Luke Mines, "Globalization in the Classroom," *Nation* (June 1, 1998): 22–24; William Hoynes, "News for a Captive Audience: An Analysis of Channel One," *Extra!* (May–June 1997): 11–17.

51. For an expanded discussion, see Lawrence C. Soley, *Leasing the Ivory Tower: The Corporate Takeover of Academia* (Boston: South End Press, 1996).

52. Purdue Research Foundation, *Home for High-Tech Business* (W. Lafayette, IN: Purdue Research Park, 1998).

53. David Boaz and R. Morris Barrett, "What Would a School Voucher Buy? The Real Cost of Private Schools" (Briefing Paper No. 25, Cato Institute, March 26, 1996).

54. Sam Dillon, "Collapse of 60 Charter Schools Leaves Californians Scrambling," *New York Times,* September 17, 2004; Sewell Chan, "Study Bolsters Case for Tuition Vouchers," *Washington Post,* September 29, 2004, A12; Diana Jean Schemo, "A Second Report Shows Charter School Students Not Performing as Well as Other Students," *New York Times,* December 16, 2004.

55. Visit www.collegeboard.com; www.acenet.edu.

56. Jay P. Greene and Greg Forster, "Kerry's College Plan Fails Poor Kids," *Los Angeles Times,* August 18, 2004, B13.

7

The Pacification of Everyday Life

The strongest is never strong enough to be master, unless he transforms his strength into right, and obedience into duty.

—Jean-Jacques Rousseau, *The Social Contract*, 1782

In the mid-2000s, national surveys found high levels of public interest and belief in paranormal phenomena, including psychics, ghosts, UFOs, and space aliens. These findings confirmed what earlier polls had shown, viz, since 1990 there has been a steady increase in public fascination with such topics.[1] American popular culture reflected and reinforced these beliefs as media firms increased paranormal and science-fiction-oriented television programs, movies, video games, and Internet websites. Three TV networks featured paranormal-themed, prime-time hit shows in the mid- and latter 2000s (ABC's *Lost*, CBS's *Ghost Whisperer*, NBC's *Medium*), and ABC broadcast a major UFO special report.[2] Cable TV programs such as Sci-Fi's *Ghost Hunters*, WB's *Supernatural*, Court TV's *Psychic Detectives*, and frequent cable specials on UFO sightings and crashes, alien abductions, Bigfoot monsters, and haunted houses also fed growing public interest in paranormal and space alien phenomena. Recent hit movies resonated with the Zoroaster-zoned zeitgeist as indicated by the popularity of trailers, ticket sales, and follow-up video rentals for films such as *Lady in the Water*, *The Lord of the Rings* (the trilogy), *Harry Potter* (all episodes), *A Scanner Darkly*, *Star Wars* (the last three episodes), and *War of the Worlds*. As the first decade of the new century was closing, the culture industry continued to produce, at warp speed, a steady stream of media offerings that both filled and magnified public interest in a wide range of paranormal and science fiction phenomena.

American fascination with paranormal phenomena and space aliens is not a new trend in popular culture. Many earlier films, TV series, books, and magazines have plowed this same ground. But as the window of the new century opens wider, the intensity of public interest in such topics appears to be reaching higher and more sustained levels than in the past. Of course, this cultural trend does not erase public unease over growing economic inequalities and insecurities. And it has not fully displaced popular enthusiasm for optimistic sentimentalism in films like *Forrest Gump* or for public fascination with romantic tragedies like the *Titanic*. But it does underscore the culture industry's tendency to channel mass entertainment in directions that distract public attention from class-based issues. It reminds us that the culture industry is more about distraction and pacification than it is about inspiration or instruction— especially where class inequalities are concerned. But sometimes even the culture industry can surprise us.

From the perspective of social-class analysis, one of the more interesting sci-fi movies dates not from today but from two decades ago. *They Live!* was a 1988 John Carpenter film that explicitly linked extraterrestrial aliens with social-class inequalities and superclass dominance. The movie portrayed creepy reptilian aliens, who mingle with the general population in human form, as evildoers who establish a secret alliance with an elite group of ruling-class humans. In league together, these two groups dominate the nonelite human population through hedonistic consumerism, subliminal mass media–based manipulation and thought control, and, as needed, coercive force.

The secrets of this dark alliance are revealed to the audience through an unemployed laborer who accidentally finds a special pair of sunglasses produced by a growing human resistance movement. Wearing these "shades," the actor walks the streets of an ordinary community, but he views the people and events from a totally new perspective. The audience sees through the eyes of the actor and his special sunglasses. We see aliens who have assumed human forms and the "real" text of disguised messages embedded in mass media content reinforcing alien and ruling-class control of nonelite humans: submit, conform, consume, inform, reproduce, and above all, do not question authority!

They Live! was not a huge box-office success. It barely made a blip on the radar screen of popular culture and quickly dropped from sight. Its theme of an alliance between aliens and the human ruling class was not repeated in the story lines of popular science-fiction films or TV programs in the mid- or late 2000s. Certainly, the film could be critiqued on many grounds, including its tendency to reinforce a conspiratorial view of rich and powerful elites dominating nonelites. Despite its weaknesses, the unusual (by movie standards) class-based features of the film help call attention to how the routine and seemingly "invisible" practices of mainstream social institutions perpetuate privileged-class dominance and at the same time legitimate and reproduce social-class inequalities, especially at the level of everyday life. *They Live!* illustrates that the culture industry sometimes produces films with class themes woven into story lines that call attention to and help illuminate the nature of the process that is the central focus of this chapter—the pacification of everyday life.

PACIFICATION: THE HOMETOWN FILES

The issue holding us back today . . . is the idea that what you do won't make a difference. The elite powers tell us the world is too complicated. They spend a lot of energy fostering despair.

—Bernadine Dohrn, *In These Times*, 2006

Pacification refers to the transformation of potentially disruptive social situations or restive populations into serenity: passive, peaceful, and calm, as dramatically illustrated in *They Live!* In the context of conflicting class interests, pacification also implies the manipulation and control of subordinate classes by dominant classes (but not necessarily in a conspiratorial sense). By linking pacification with everyday life, the title of this chapter is meant to call attention to how the class-related consciousness of average people going about their day-to-day routines is shaped.

In this chapter we consider how the power and advantages of the privileged class are exercised, reinforced, and legitimated at the level of everyday life. To bring this complex process down to earth, we focus first on two case studies, involving community development and drug education. These cases link national trends with local activities and illustrate how privileged-class-dominated organizations promote control of consciousness, ideological domination, and the legitimation of class inequalities among the nonprivileged class. These cases also illustrate how privileged-class power and ideas are embedded in taken-for-granted institutional routines and practices through which the pacification of everyday life occurs. Following the two case studies, we examine the relationship between politics and pacification as illustrated by recent congressional consideration and passage of lobbying and ethics reform legislation and by our view of problems we see associated with the popular "what's the matter with Kansas?" line of political analysis. We then shift our attention to the culture industry. Following up on themes introduced in the opening of this chapter, we consider how this industry, especially through television programming and the movies directed at hometown consumers, reinforces the pacification process.

Our first case study considers the story of how Japanese automobile assembly plants came to be located in several Midwestern communities. It calls attention to the way the privileged class creates local crises, demands local sacrifices, legitimates these sacrifices, and benefits from "solutions" to the problems it creates. It shows how citizens' awareness of local class-related issues is shaped by the interests of the privileged class (often called "community leaders") through local media in the form of local decisions on taxes, bond issues, and financial incentives for business. Average citizens are typically provided by community newspapers with only one way to think about important local decisions—unless they happen to belong to groups with alternative points of view (e.g., taxpayer associations, labor unions, environmental groups).

The second case focuses on the Drug Abuse Resistance Education (DARE) program as a form of symbolic politics. The DARE story calls attention to how, despite its record of ineffectiveness in preventing youth drug use, this school-based drug-prevention program, which came out of the "War on Drugs," has expanded into a cultural and political force serving the economic, political, and ideological interests of the privileged class. We show how DARE grew and how it boosts the careers of its supporters, serves the public relations and political interests of corporate sponsors, and encourages unquestioned acceptance of privileged-class-controlled authority structures. In each instance, our focus is on showing how DARE contributes to public distraction from class issues and to the legitimation of class inequalities.

The two concluding sections of the chapter illustrate how the pacification and legitimation processes introduced in the case studies operate at the level of everyday life in the national political and cultural arenas. The "Politics and Pacification" section considers how the class-based structure of the U.S. Congress has influenced its deliberations and actions on lobbying reform in ways that protect privileged class interests while *appearing* to address public concerns with influence-peddling by lobbyists. In the "Culture Industry and Pacification" section, we focus on the electronic-media dimension of the culture industry, especially television and the movies, to illustrate how this industry helps to distract attention away from class issues and legitimate the new class society. We document the massive size, scope, and largely class-free content of the electronic-media arm of the culture industry to show how it effectively dominates public consciousness and discourages critical thought and reflection. Using this informational and conceptual framework, we illustrate how the routine operation of the industry marginalizes class issues, distracts public attention from class inequalities, and generally contributes to the pacification of everyday life.

GROW OR DIE: THE PRIVILEGED-CLASS THREAT TO SMALL-TOWN AMERICA

A move by a major corporation can have a devastating impact on a local growth coalition. . . . The net result is often a "race to the bottom" as [rival] cities offer tax breaks, less environmental regulation, and other benefits to corporations in order to tempt them to relocate.

—G. William Domhoff, *Who Rules America?* 2002

As we have seen, the privileged class has been very successful in keeping the largest shares of income and wealth for itself. We have also seen that this outcome does not come easy—or cheap. It requires the constant care and feeding of the shadow political and information industries by the superclass. Moreover, shaping and delivering politics and policies favorable to privileged-class interests does not stop at the national level. It continues in states, cities, and towns throughout the United States.

We have to recall that the privileged class consists of some twenty million families, and they do not all live in New York, Washington, D.C., or Los Angeles. Although members of the superclass are more likely to live in exclusive, urban, gated enclaves, the more numerous credentialed class of highly paid professionals is scattered across the country in small communities with names not usually associated with wealth and power. Consider, for example, obscure small towns like Marysville, Ohio; Smyrna, Tennessee; Lafayette, Indiana; Normal, Illinois; Flat Rock, Michigan; and Georgetown, Kentucky. With populations ranging from sixty-five hundred to eighty-five thousand, these small towns shared the experience in the 1980s of becoming the "hometown" of a large Japanese automobile assembly plant. Each city and state was the "winner" in a multistate competition to attract foreign investment. The story behind these winners reveals how the privileged class in America creates crises and then benefits from solutions to the problems they create.

Picture a small town with about twenty thousand to thirty thousand people. The city has a couple of large companies employing about a thousand workers each, a dozen midsize firms, each with two hundred or so employees, and hundreds of small retail and service businesses in the downtown area and on the outer edges of town. One day, out of the blue, one of the large companies announces that it plans to shut down and move to another location. The company "spin" is often that the plant is rather old, and based on a cost-benefit analysis, it would cost too much to upgrade its production line and improve other parts of its support system.

The mayor of the city immediately begins talks with corporate executives about what it would take to make them reconsider. The union representing the workers starts to talk with management about a new contract with wage concessions, productivity-linked benefits, and greater flexibility concerning plant work rules. The threat of eliminating a thousand jobs in a small community sends ripples of anxiety throughout the community. The loss of one thousand workers, each earning, on average, $30,000 annually, would take a lot of buying power out of the community. And the loss of payroll taxes and property taxes on plant and equipment would significantly reduce the city's revenue. The plant and its employees also have traditionally made sizable annual contributions to the United Way and to local churches, to say nothing of volunteer work performed by workers and their families in a variety of community organizations.

Before the city can begin to digest this unanticipated crisis, the local business community starts to pressure the mayor and the city and county councils to spend more money on community-development activities. Maybe they need to hire a development professional and print some special brochures outlining the attractive qualities the town has for new corporations. Of course, all this will cost money, at a time when revenue is declining. To make matters worse, some of the other businesses start to remind the city and county about their own increased costs of doing business. Several would like to expand and employ more people but question the wisdom of such a move at this time. Perhaps, they suggest, a waiver of taxes on new expansion might be helpful. The city has given tax abatements before, but doing so now would mean fewer dollars for schools, fire and police protection, city services, and, of course, the new push for a professional community-development office.

Some of what is described in this story about a hypothetical small town sounds a bit like extortion, blackmail, and bribery, although these activities are not called by those terms in political and business circles. And it is not just a hypothetical story. This story line reflects the basic outline of what has happened—and is still happening—in hundreds of small communities across the United States over the past thirty years.

From the mid-1970s through the mid-2000s, millions of high-wage jobs in the manufacturing industries were lost as a result of waves of plant closings in the auto, steel, rubber, electronics, and textile industries. As we saw in chapter 3, corporate executives closed thousands of U.S. plants and moved their operations to lower-wage foreign production centers. The waves of plant closings and resulting high levels of unemployment had devastating effects on many states and communities faced with the sudden loss of revenue from payroll taxes and corporate property taxes. These losses were magnified by increased demands for public services to assist the unemployed, as well as development expenditures aimed at trying to strengthen local economies. The intersection of structural change in the U.S. economy, plant closings, and increased unemployment resulted in heavy pressure on national and state governments to cut spending. As the federal government tried to save money by cutting assistance programs to states, state and local problems were compounded even further.

Rust Belt states like Michigan, Illinois, and Ohio were hard hit by plant closings involving major corporations and were drawn into "regional wars" of competition for new businesses.[3] And how do communities attract new industries? The short answer is by providing attractive "incentives." In 1991, the fifty states gave $16 billion to businesses to relocate plants in their states. By the mid-2000s, such expenditures were estimated at $50 billion annually.[4] Sometimes the money would lure a corporation to close a plant in one state and move to another state, as in the case of Mack Truck, which moved its production plant from Pennsylvania to Winnsboro, South Carolina, in the late 1980s.[5] And sometimes the money was used to attract foreign corporations to come to the United States.

State "incentive packages" for large, foreign industrial firms typically highlight a powerful "language hook": FREE! (translation: taxpayer subsidized). The list of freebies often begins with land and also usually includes site preparation (roads, water, sewer lines), worker training, and property tax waivers, with the total incentive-package value often reaching $200 million or more. In 1985, the state of Kentucky gave Toyota $12.5 million for land, $20 million to prepare the land for construction, $47 million for road improvements, $65 million for worker training, and $5.2 million to meet the special educational needs of Japanese managers' children. These breaks were all part of the incentive package to attract the firm to Kentucky. When the cost of bond interest payments is added to the "up-front" incentives, the total cost to Kentucky taxpayers reaches $350 million.[6] And the beat goes on. When Toyota decided to expand its production to include more light trucks, Indiana landed the new truck plant in 1996 by providing an incentive package of $75 million.[7] In mid-2006, Honda executives announced Indiana would be the site of a new $550 million auto assembly plant scheduled to open in 2008 or 2009 with two thousand workers. The cost of the incentive package to Indiana taxpayers for the Honda plant was reported to be $141.5 million (future subsidies not included).[8]

Other nations have also gotten in on the incentive-package action. In the 1990s, two German firms, BMW and Mercedes, announced plans to open assembly plants in the United States. When the dust from the state bidding wars settled, South Carolina landed the BMW plant (opened in 1994 in Spartanburg), and Alabama was awarded the Mercedes plant (opened in 1997 in Vance). South Carolina taxpayers kicked in $150 million in direct and indirect subsidies to BMW, and Alabama taxpayers provided Mercedes with a $250 million incentive package.[9] In the mid-2000s, two South Korean auto firms located new assembly plants in Southern U.S. states. A $1.1 billion Hyundai plant was opened near Montgomery, Alabama, in 2005 with the help of a $250 million incentive package, and in 2006, Kia announced plans to build a $1.2 billion plant near West Point, Georgia, aided by incentives totaling $410 million.[10]

Of course, the purpose of the incentives is to attract a company that will bring new jobs to the state and stimulate fading local economies. But the cost in incentives represents an increasingly high price tag for economic growth. In the 1980s, the incentive packages amounted to $50,000 for each job in the Japanese transplants and continued to climb in the 1990s to $79,000 per direct job at the BMW plant and then to a staggering "sticker shock" level of $167,000 per direct job at the Mercedes plant.[11] The cost of incentives for each direct job created in the three Asian transplants noted above varied from $71,000 at Honda-Indiana, to $125,000 at Hyundai-Alabama, to $141,000 at Kia-Georgia.[12] It is important to remember that the incentives states provide to transplants are typically covered by increased state taxes—most often levied on non-privileged-class members—in the form of more sales, property, and income taxes.

The Privileged Class Comes Calling: Pacification in the Heartland

Narrowing our focus to just the decade of the 1980s, we find the states of Michigan, Tennessee, Ohio, Illinois, Kentucky, and Indiana chipping in a total of more than one billion "incentive-package" dollars to land Japanese auto assembly plants. Honda built a plant in Ohio, Nissan located in Tennessee, Mazda went to Michigan, Mitsubishi set up shop in Illinois, Toyota chose Kentucky, and Indiana got Subaru-Isuzu. For the one thousand to two thousand workers who would get jobs in the new plants, the money for the incentives would be seen as well spent. And it would certainly be seen as a good idea by the business community that benefits from growth, especially the banks, lawyers, and realtors who would facilitate the new growth-related business transactions. But most residents in the cities and counties where the plants were located (probably 90 percent) would not join in the benefits. Instead, they got to pay higher taxes to cover the multi-million-dollar incentive packages. They also "won" increased traffic congestion, higher housing costs (for rental units and new homes), and more municipal spending to cover school costs for children who would accompany their parents to the jobs created by the "growth boom."

Obviously, there are economic benefits associated with growth, but benefits for whom? The costs are real, both in terms of dollars in taxes and in the more intangible "quality-of-life" changes that occur when a town grows quickly. But perhaps more important is the fact that nobody asked people in the towns whether or not they thought it was a "good deal" to spend more than $50,000 of taxpayers' money for each new job that would be created. No one asked local citizens if they would prefer to spend the tax money in different ways, such as helping local small businesses expand in the city or providing new educational and recreational facilities for existing families. There were no public referendums on the question of growth or of growth at what cost. The deals were made between the managers of incoming corporations and state and local members of the privileged class (political, business, and professional leaders), and the deals were then sold to the people in the affected communities.

The privileged class typically develops economic projects that it wants and that will serve its interests and then presents the projects to the nonprivileged class as if they will serve the general good. This happens all the time at the national level. It is often so transparent that virtually anyone can recognize how privileged-class interests drive such deals and also generate a "common-good" justification incorporated into the media "spin" on stories about these deals.

A high-profile historical case that occurred a decade ago was the 1997 "balanced-budget agreement" negotiated by then president Bill Clinton and Republican congressional leaders. As part of the deal, both sides agreed to changes in federal tax laws that would reduce the tax on capital gains. This meant that investors would pay lower taxes on the "paper-profit" gains they made when stocks, bonds, commercial real estate, and other investments went up in value compared with what they paid for them. The cut in the capital gains tax primarily benefited members of the privileged class, who are the principal owners of most investments affected by the tax changes. But the justification presented by politicians who supported the tax cut, and the one reported almost without critical examination in the media, was that people who get to keep more of their capital gains will invest or spend the money in ways that stimulate the economy. And when the economy grows, there is a need for more workers to produce the goods and services being purchased by the new dollars available to the privileged from the capital gains tax cut.[13] In short, the capital gains deal was justified by a recycled version of "trickle-down" economic theory, a familiar fairy tale left over from the Reagan era. For average Americans, it was "déjà vu all over again," but the privileged-class-controlled media treated the deal like a great creative leap forward for the good of all mankind.[14] In the mid-2000s, it was "déjà vu continued" as President George W. Bush's tax cuts (on high incomes, capital gains, and stock dividends) received the same kind of "great news! lower taxes on the rich grow the economy" media treatment, despite contrary views held by a majority of average income taxpayers as revealed in national surveys.[15]

A similar story line is used at the local level. The taxpayer-provided incentives for the industry transplants are presented as spending packages that will benefit all residents of the communities. That is the "spin" at the heart of the transplant stories, and it is used to justify the millions of dollars in incentives given to foreign corporations. This story is told locally by the electronic and print media. Local newspapers are especially important in telling this story because they are institutions with long-standing reputations of journalistic objectivity and civic responsibility. Although local newspapers are known to have political biases (to be conservative or liberal, to support Republicans or Democrats), they are often seen as having broad community interests in mind when reporting on issues such as new community-financed construction of schools, libraries, roads, and recreational facilities. These kinds of projects spend public money raised through taxes, and when newspapers examine the pros and cons of public projects, their stories are framed in such a way that the newspaper is presented as seeking outcomes consistent with the community's best interests.

But we must recall that newspapers are, first and foremost, businesses. They are expected to make profits for their owners and stockholders, just like any other business. Some money may be made by expanding circulation, but the sale of advertising space is the engine that drives newspaper profits. Thus, newspapers in the transplant cities have a vested (but typically hidden and unacknowledged) interest in growth, which they share with bankers, realtors, attorneys, construction firms, and the Chamber of Commerce. So, when newspapers in the cities competing for transplants tell the story about incentives and transplant benefits for communities, it is a story spun by card-carrying members of the privileged class.

Local Spin: All the News That's Fit to Print?

We examined newspaper stories written in conjunction with the process of locating Japanese transplant firms in three Midwestern communities by three different hometown newspapers, one in each community where the transplants would be located. The period of coverage for each newspaper was thirteen months, beginning with the first newspaper story that mentioned the possibility of a Japanese auto plant moving to the city or state. The purpose of the analysis was to see how local newspapers dealt with the complex task of assessing the potential costs and benefits of competing for and having new, large manufacturing firms come to their communities. Each of these projects had the potential to produce opposition from a variety of community groups, such as environmentalists, organized labor, and concerned taxpayers, who might have viewed the plant as imposing unreasonable tax increases to cover the costs of the incentives and services to the plant and their employees and families. Given the potential for public controversy and community conflict, we were interested in how the local newspapers presented the story and shaped community thinking on this issue. Because local newspapers are dominated by privileged-class interests, we wondered if the content of news stories about the coming of the transplants might objectively reflect community tensions and divisions related to this story or, on the contrary, would be more of the same of what we often saw at the national level: corporate and privileged-class propaganda masquerading as news. That is, would local news accounts reflect a pro-growth spin aimed at soothing potentially disruptive local fears and concerns and defusing potential opposition? In short, we wanted to see if local newspaper coverage of the transplant story might represent an example of the pacification of everyday life—cooling out the locals while protecting the interests of the privileged class.

The three newspapers and time periods analyzed were the *Lafayette Journal and Courier* (Indiana, December 1986–September 1987), the *Murfreesboro Daily News Journal* (Tennessee, September 1980–September 1981), and the *Lexington Herald Leader* (Kentucky, December 1985–December 1986). In all, four hundred ninety transplant stories were written by the three newspapers in the time periods we examined. All stories were read and analyzed to answer the question, who speaks on the transplants? We ask this question because newspapers make choices about the people and organizations that will be asked to express their opinions about the transplants, incentive money, and what it will mean for the community.

In the 490 stories from the three newspapers, 1,769 persons were named, and their points of view about the transplants presented. A single event could be written up under the headline "Auto Plant Dredges Up Ill Will" or "Auto Plant: A Plan Comes Together." These stories would incorporate the views of different persons to create an impression of divided opinion, conflict, harmony, and agreement or a mixture of costs and benefits to the community. The journalists creating these stories often knew in advance the point of view of the people they interviewed for the story. When they interviewed the city's mayor or a representative of a community-development agency, they could expect a favorable attitude toward the transplant because these community leaders had been involved in developing the package of incentives to attract the new business. On the other hand, when interviewing a labor official, they were likely to get a more critical view of the transplants because of the strong antiunion bias of the Japanese.

When we examined who the 1,769 persons were who spoke through the news stories, we found that 36 percent were from business and industry (corporate executives, representatives of the Chamber of Commerce, attorneys), and 50 percent were local or state elected officials (mayors, state representatives, congressional representatives) or officials of state or local government agencies. Only 13 percent of the 1,769 interviewees were outside of the business-political sectors, such as labor leaders, educators, and social welfare services. This meant that almost nine out of ten opinions on the transplants expressed in news stories came from persons who would be expected to be pro-business or pro-growth or to have pro-transplant interests. In effect, representatives from the privileged class did most of the talking in the newspaper stories. This outcome hardly reflects an effort by newspapers to provide balanced information and analysis to their readers.

When we examined the content of the 490 stories on the transplants and the amount of space devoted to positive or negative accounts about the transplants, the evidence indicated a clear preference for a positive "spin" on the transplant projects. The 490 stories made up a total of 19,331 square inches of space in the three newspapers, and only 17 percent of this space was devoted to stories that could be called "negative" or "critical" of some aspect of the transplant projects. The negative stories were largely clustered around four issues. These included (with sample headlines)

1. the high cost of the financial incentives ("Two Join Suit over Toyota Plant Financing")
2. environmental issues ("Toyota Jobs vs. Environmental Impact Debates")
3. citizens' loss of property ("Path to Auto Plants Cuts across Yards")
4. legal challenges to the state's right to give land to a private corporation ("State's Plan to Give Toyota Land May Be Unconstitutional")

The other 83 percent of the total square inches written about the transplants we characterized as variations of three positive themes. These were (also with sample headlines)

1. blatantly positive ("Auto Plant Gets Community Support")
2. passively positive ("Nissan Decision Opens New Era for County")

3. human-interest positive—descriptive stories of the positive effects of the plants for people directly involved in the projects ("Japanese Family Enjoys New Life in Greater Lafayette")

The overall impact of the newspaper coverage of the transplants was unequivocally positive and supportive of the total idea of providing financial incentives to a private corporation. Rather than being objective, neutral providers of balanced information and opinion, the newspapers acted as cheerleaders for economic growth and the transplant projects. Their coverage and biased story lines concerning the transplants were consistent with the profit-oriented, privileged-class interests of the newspaper owners, publishers, and editors.

The overwhelming representation of pro-growth views in local newspapers illustrates the domination of state and local credentialed-class members in framing economic issues with class-based implications and consequences for local communities. In the case of the transplants, the actions of local credentialed-class members had the effect of reinforcing and reproducing at the local level the interests of the national superclass of corporate and political elites. As the transplant cases illustrate, many communities are caught in a corporate squeeze that starts with multinational corporations closing plants and shipping jobs overseas. Faced with fiscal crises brought on by unemployment and declining tax revenues, these communities are forced to compete with other towns and states facing the same squeeze for the "privilege" of handing out hundreds of millions of taxpayer dollars as "incentives" to lure corporations to bring new jobs to their towns.

The New Catch-22: Private Profits, Public Costs

The all-too-familiar scenario of plant closings followed by competition for the transplants illustrates how a new kind of catch-22 is built into the double-diamond class structure. The essence of the catch is this: profits are private, costs are public, and both are largely underwritten by the working class. Because the profits from doing business are private, they flow largely intact back to members of the privileged class—with few dollars skimmed off by ever lower corporate and capital gains tax rates. But the social costs of plant closings, such as increased unemployment, higher welfare costs, more family violence, increased crime, and higher rates of mental and physical illness, as well as the tax-funded costs of financial incentives to attract new businesses, are public. And both kinds of costs are primarily paid for by members of the working class. The routine business practices of corporations controlled by the privileged class create social problems while generating private profits, but the working class pays, in one form or another, most of the costs associated with the corporate system. Most obviously this includes higher taxes for the working class, but it also includes absorbing most of the human costs associated with corporate-generated social problems: the pain of unemployment, the

confusion of disrupted lives, and the frustration of diminished community services. The double diamond leads to a double deal: a winning hand for the privileged class, a raw deal for the working class.

This new catch-22 of the new class society provides useful insights into the contradiction between class benefits and class burdens where corporate practices and public policies are concerned. But as we have seen, newspaper accounts of the coming of the transplants do not acknowledge the existence of such a catch. The win-win vocabulary that dominated much of the local reporting on the transplants helped obscure the existence of conflicting class interests and coaxed local populations into accepting the deals as being in the best interests of all parties concerned. In a sense, the newspapers were an important part of a communitywide, street-level pacification project aimed at winning the "hearts and minds" of the working class in favor of the transplant projects. No conspiracy was necessary. The routine operation of privileged-class-dominated institutions, as the newspaper coverage illustrates, was sufficient to ensure local pacification. This outcome was evidenced by the absence of significant or sustained local opposition to the transplants in the chosen communities.

DARE: BRINGING THE DRUG WAR HOME

What DARE has excelled in is promotion for their program.

—Lloyd Johnson, University of Michigan, *Youth Today*, April 2001

Symbolic politics describes the political strategy of choosing and using safe political issues and public policies on the part of political elites to advance their interests and those of their privileged-class supporters. For political elites, the issues selected and policies promoted are safe (where their interests are concerned) for two reasons. First, symbolic politics involves a focus on issues that are of great concern to the public (or are presented to the public by political elites in ways that promote public concern). Second, this approach is safe because it generates programs that appear to address public concerns or problems—but in ways that do not threaten privileged-class interests and that have wide appeal among the working class. Symbolic politics are typically associated with at least three levels of symbolic action. First, to promote their own political interests, public office holders may "construct threats" to public well-being. This means political leaders, with the help of superclass sponsors and media attention, select social conditions widely perceived as undesirable and transform them, by policy pronouncements and the mobilization of political resources, into high-priority public "threats" requiring public policy intervention. Second, public office holders can invoke a "scapegoating strategy" whereby social conditions publicly viewed as problematic or "constructed threats" are explicitly or implicitly linked with unpopular or stigmatized groups, which encourages public perceptions of these groups as the source of the problems or threats. Third, political leaders can propose programmatic interventions that they claim will ameliorate problematic conditions or "constructed threats" and also reassure voters that public institutions are responding appropriately to these dangers.[16]

While the next few sections illustrate how the three levels of symbolic politics described above apply to DARE and the U.S. drug war, the concept also applies to other "techniques of distraction" used by legislators in the lawmaking process and by candidates in campaigns for public office. As we illustrate in the section following the DARE case, the embrace of the *appearance* of concern with issues of interest to average voters by lawmakers and candidates, combined with actions that protect privileged-class interests and promote their own careers (often with stealth and out of the public eye), represents another important form of symbolic politics.

DARE as Symbolic Politics

While the mid-2000s provided many examples of symbolic politics (e.g., issues and policies concerning terrorism, immigration, gay rights, abortion, predatory pedophiles), we view the so-called War on Drugs as a classic example of this concept in action. Growing out of a high-profile, politically constructed "threat" (the "drug plague"), the drug war has resulted in numerous multifaceted government programs with national and local class-related implications and consequences, such as the Drug Abuse Resistance Education program. DARE represents a safe, programmatic example of symbolic action claiming to address a threat to the public well-being at the community level. Organized and promoted by members of the privileged class, DARE is a powerful, but unadvertised and unnoticed, part of the everyday cultural routines that reinforce privileged-class interests, help legitimate class inequalities, and thus contribute to the pacification of everyday life.

On the surface, it appears that DARE has everything to do with preventing youth drug use and nothing to do with social-class inequalities. But as in the film *They Live!*, peering beneath surface images can open our eyes to a very different reality. What we find beneath DARE's surface is a drug-education program of questionable effectiveness that over the past decade has become an institutionalized cultural and political force serving the economic, political, and ideological interests of the privileged class. Although there is no evidence that DARE was deployed as part of a conscious, privileged-class conspiracy to distract public attention from growing class inequalities and related social problems, there is evidence that the DARE program does help produce this and other outcomes that serve privileged-class interests.

What Is DARE? A Really Brief History and Overview

DARE is a standardized, copyrighted, school-based drug-prevention program that began in Los Angeles in 1983 to 1984 as a joint effort involving the Los Angeles Police Department (LAPD) and the Los Angeles Unified School District. Following former president Ronald Reagan's launching of his antidrug "crusade" in 1986, DARE expanded rapidly. This expansion was facilitated by DARE America, a nonprofit, tax-exempt corporation formed in 1987 to promote and coordinate DARE.[17] By the mid-2000s, DARE was taught in 80 percent of U.S. school districts and in fifty-four countries worldwide.[18]

The DARE core curriculum was originally designed for fifth and sixth graders and consists of seventeen weekly lessons, each approximately forty-five to sixty minutes in length. All DARE classes are taught by uniformed police officers who have undergone eighty hours of specialized training. Classroom activities are scheduled during the regular school day, and the program encourages student involvement in exercises such as "question and answer [sessions], group discussions, and role-play[ing] activities." DARE's "major goal . . . is to prevent substance abuse among school children"; it strives to accomplish this goal by teaching students "the skills for recognizing and resisting social pressures to experiment with tobacco, alcohol, and drugs." The DARE lessons focus on enhancing students' self-esteem, decision-making, coping, assertiveness, and communication skills and "teaching positive alternatives to substance use."[19] In addition to classroom instruction, the program can involve other activities, such as the use of selected high school students as DARE "role models" in the elementary grades, informal officer-student contacts, teacher orientation, parental education, and community presentations.

Although DARE's basic goals and curriculum structure have remained relatively constant since its inception, over the years DARE has also changed in several ways. Between 1992 and 1994, revisions were made in the core curriculum. Materials were added to place "greater emphasis on the prevention of tobacco use . . . normative beliefs, and on violence prevention and conflict resolution." The presentation format was also changed to make the program more interactive. The revised curriculum was phased in during 1993 and 1994 and was fully implemented after January 1, 1995.[20] Despite the makeover, researchers continued to find that DARE had no long-term effects on drug-use rates among youth exposed to it.

Partly in response to research findings that DARE was ineffective in preventing drug use among youth, DARE America executives and critics met at a U.S. Department of Justice–sponsored meeting in 1998 to discuss ways of improving the program. Additional discussions in 1999 and 2000 involved drug-education researchers, DARE administrators, U.S. government officials, and Robert Wood Johnson Foundation (RWJF) representatives (RWJF often funds health-related projects). As a result of these developments, in 2001 DARE America received a $13.7 million RWJF grant to create a substantially revised DARE curriculum.[21] The new curriculum was designed to prevent not only drug use but youth violence as well. It was also designed to be delivered in a ten-lesson format to middle school students and "reinforced with a second program in the ninth grade."[22] The RWJF grant included funding to evaluate the effectiveness of the new program in reducing drug use and violence among the youth who were exposed to the new curriculum compared to a control group that would not receive the program.

The five-year, RWJF-funded evaluation of the new DARE program, headquartered at the University of Akron, was known as the "Adolescent Substance Abuse Prevention Study." It was directed by principal investigator Dr. Zili Sloboda, who pointed out that "the study is not a DARE evaluation. It focuses on evaluating a new, evidence-based prevention program, 'Take Charge of Your Life,' that draws from both the substance abuse prevention and education research literature. In the study, the program is delivered by D.A.R.E. officers to students."[23] In 2006, the study was in its fifth and final year of data collection. At that time, Dr. Sloboda stated the study was "following a cohort of close to 20,000 students who were in the 7th grade in the 2001–2002 school year attending 122 middle schools in school districts in 6 cities (Detroit, Houston, Los Angeles, Newark [NJ], New Orleans, and St. Louis) that were randomly assigned to either a treatment or control condition."[24] Dr. Sloboda said the research team would continue to collect and analyze data throughout 2006 and hoped "to have a report available in the Spring [of 2007]."[25] Based on Dr. Sloboda's description of the new program and information posted on the DARE website that described the *"Take Charge of Your Life* [program as] the new science-based D.A.R.E. prevention program," it is unclear if the new curriculum will at some point include the "DARE" acronym in its title.[26]

Even though the new curriculum materials differ in many respects from the traditional DARE program, we believe the new curriculum shares the same basic ideological foundations upon which the original DARE curriculum was erected. Based on our review of publicly available information, it appears that the new curriculum does not include any major departures from the basic objectives and fundamental assumptions that guided DARE programs in the past.[27] The following paragraphs summarize key ideas and assumptions we view as embedded in both the traditional DARE program and the new curriculum.

In the past, DARE embraced the same "zero-tolerance/no-use/drug-free" orientations that guided national drug policies. DARE programs also implicitly embraced "free-will" and "user-accountability" principles. This means that all forms of drug use are viewed as driven by free-willed, individual choices, and users must be held strictly accountable for their choices. In the past, the DARE program appeared to assume that it provided students with the information and life-skills resources necessary to guide them into making the "right" choices. If after DARE exposure individuals still chose to use illicit drugs, such choices were viewed as free-willed criminal acts to be condemned and punished by the legitimate application of all available legal sanctions. This logic held—and appears to hold today—despite the acknowledgment by DARE's curriculum materials that structural factors such as mass media advertising (like the $21 billion tobacco and alcohol ad budgets[28]) contribute to public demand for drugs.

In the past, DARE made no distinctions between legal and illegal drugs and advocated total abstinence as the only acceptable approach to all types and categories of drugs. The program also made no real distinction between experimental and frequent drug use. An unstated assumption of earlier DARE programs appeared to be that experimental use of any drug by children or adolescents (this included legal—for adults—"gateway drugs," such as tobacco) constituted "drug abuse" or would inevitably lead to problematic drug use. More realistic approaches to drug use, such as "responsible use" or "harm reduction"—as used in drug-education programs in other nations, such as the Netherlands—were excluded from earlier versions of the DARE program and appear to be excluded from the new curriculum as well.

Despite our skepticism, research findings on the "Take Charge of Your Life" curriculum may yet reveal that it achieves its goals: "The program is designed to reduce the use of tobacco, alcohol, illicit drugs, and prevent youth violence."[29] Even so, it is interesting to note that research reported in 2006 highlights positive impacts of the "new" program "on the attitudes, intentions, and beliefs of the students receiving the program."[30] Researchers in the past reported similar short-term results, but studies that followed DARE program graduates over time found no differences in drug-use rates or patterns of use between DARE- and non-DARE-exposed teenagers. The key question for the "new DARE" program (as it was for the old DARE program) is this: does the program produce measurable differences in *drug-use behaviors* (not just attitudes) among adolescents in the years following their exposure to DARE compared to similar groups of adolescents not exposed to DARE? Perhaps another decade and more millions of research dollars will answer that question. Stay tuned!

DARE: Hometown Drug Prevention or Pacification?

In 1987, DARE came to Kokomo, Indiana, a Midwestern auto factory town with a population of forty-five thousand. In fact, Kokomo was the first Indiana city to adopt the DARE program. The process that led DARE to Kokomo began in 1986, when the mayor and chief of police learned about the program while attending a conference—about the same time the War on Drugs transformed the "drug problem" into a hot-button political issue. By late 1986, local political, educational, and law-enforcement leaders had decided to implement DARE in the Kokomo schools.

We were invited by school and police officials to assess DARE's effectiveness in Kokomo. Our efforts began in 1987, and by the mid-1990s, we had completed several short- and long-term studies of the program. Our most comprehensive project was a seven-year study of DARE's long-term effectiveness in preventing or reducing adolescent drug use. Based on a series of comparisons between the 214 high school seniors exposed to the DARE program in the fifth grade and the 331 high school seniors not exposed to DARE, we found no significant differences in the self-reported drug-use rates of the two groups. Moreover, when we talked to seniors from both groups in focus-group interviews, we heard the students saying in their own words what our questionnaire data revealed: DARE was not effective in keeping kids off drugs. Our findings paralleled those of other researchers across the United States and seemed to present us with a contradiction: although DARE was ineffective as a drug-prevention program, throughout the nation it continued growing rapidly in size, scope, and popularity. We had to wonder why.

When we consider DARE's role in the class-based pacification of everyday life, we can see that our research findings and DARE's resilience and popularity are not at all contradictory. Viewed as a political and cultural force serving privileged-class interests, DARE's expansion and popularity make perfect sense. The following sections describe DARE's emergence as a political and cultural force and describe how the program serves the political, material, and ideological interests of the privileged class.

DARE: A Political and Cultural Force

National interest in the "drug problem" among the political leaders of both major parties crystallized in 1986 with President Reagan's televised "War on Drugs" address to the nation and the subsequent passage of the Anti-Drug Abuse Act of 1986. Once set in motion, the drug war remained a popular focus of political and media attention through the 1990s and the 2000s.[31] (However, in terms of national priorities, the drug war was diminished after September 11 by the "War on Terror" and by U.S.-led wars in Afghanistan and Iraq.) In the 1980s and 1990s, the drug war was transformed from a relatively small number of reactive federal policies into a complex and multifaceted political and organizational force.[32] The Anti-Drug Abuse Act of 1988 systematized the drug war under the Bush I, Clinton, and Bush II administrations into a "national drug control strategy" aimed at controlling both the supply of and demand for illicit drugs in the United States.[33] The latter dimension of this strategy included an emphasis on developing "demand-reduction" programs of all types, including drug education. As the drug war generated more public support for antidrug programs, political interest in, and federal funding for, drug-education programs, including DARE, increased substantially throughout the 1980s, 1990s, and early 2000s but declined in the mid- to latter 2000s. Federal funding for youth-targeted antidrug education grew from $230 million in 1988, to $660 million in 1995, to more than $1 billion in 1997.[34] In the early 2000s, the federal government spent about $2 billion per year on drug-prevention education.[35] However, by 2007 annual federal spending on all forms of drug prevention declined to just over $1.4 billion.[36] Despite the decline in prevention spending, total federal drug control spending increased to $12.6 billion in 2007, up $109 million over the amount spent in 2006.[37]

Substantial federal funding for drug education combined with drug-war-driven popular support for such programs led to the emergence and continued existence of direct and indirect "DARE stakeholder" groups. For the most part, these groups consist of privileged-class individuals and organizations with material, political, and ideological interests in DARE's continuation and expansion.[38] Direct stakeholders are those groups and individuals with explicit links to DARE in terms of direct involvement in supporting and implementing the program, such as DARE America officials and program administrators in schools and law-enforcement agencies. By contrast, indirect stakeholders are those groups and individuals only loosely coupled, and only indirectly involved, with DARE, such as political leaders and corporate sponsors who publicly support or contribute to the program. Both groups benefit from the reflected approval, legitimacy, and widespread public support associated with a program linking a popular cause with traditional authority structures, symbolized by the involvement of schools and law-enforcement agencies.

At the national level, DARE emerged as a bipartisan favorite of political leaders in the late 1980s, and strong political support for the program continued into the mid- and latter 2000s. Powerful members of Congress allied with President George H. W. Bush ensured passage of a 1990 amendment to the 1986 Drug-Free Schools and Communities Act (DFSCA) mandating federal funding for DARE. As amended, the DFSCA required that 10 percent of DFSCA "governor's funds" (30 percent of federal funds made available each fiscal year to states for drug-prevention programs) be used to fund programs "such as Project Drug Abuse Resistance Education."[39] DARE was the only drug-education curriculum specifically targeted for federal funding by the DFSCA, which gave the program a tremendous boost. The Safe and Drug-Free Schools and Communities Act (SDFSCA) of 1994 continued to provide federal support for DARE through the U.S. Department of Education into the 2000s. However, a 2003 General Accounting Office report on DARE was unable to determine the exact amount of federal support that the program might have received through SDFSCA grants from the Department of Education.[40]

Over the years, national political support for DARE has included various high-profile events, including presidential and congressional "National DARE Day" proclamations applauding DARE's contributions to the national campaign against drugs.[41] Perhaps even more important has been the willingness of Congress to continue funding DARE in the face of mounting studies showing the program to be ineffective. The 1998 federal budget included language that gave SDFSCA grantees, such as DARE, two years to show their programs were effective in order to continue to receive funding. In that same year, the Department of Justice appropriations "included some unusual language about DARE crafted by the House Appropriations subcommittee on Commerce, Justice, and Judiciary." The committee essentially directed the DARE America administrators to revise the program to make it more effective.[42] Although DARE was not on the list of "exemplary" or "promising" drug-education programs issued by the Department of Education in January 2001, in the mid-2000s, the DARE website suggested DARE had been recognized by the National Institute for Drug Abuse (NIDA) as the only program that satisfied all eight categories of drug-prevention programs in a NIDA-issued research-based guide identifying standards for prevention programs.[43] It appears that successful efforts by DARE officials to win recognition of the legitimacy of the program by federal agencies (such as NIDA), combined with the RWJF grant funding the DARE curriculum revision and the five-year evaluation study, will ensure continued federal funding of DARE for at least the next several years.

These highly visible federal actions represent the tip of an iceberg of links between national, state, and local politicians and the DARE program. Federal resolutions and funding support, along with similar actions at the state and local levels, link political leaders to the program as indirect DARE stakeholders, who boost their own popularity by being identified with the popular program. At the same time, their political support further legitimates the DARE program and enhances its funding prospects, thereby benefiting individuals and organizations directly involved with its operation and expansion.

DARE's direct and indirect stakeholders have collaborated to embed the program within a complex organizational support structure that helps ensure a continuing flow of resources to sustain its survival and growth. An important feature of this structure is DARE America, a nonprofit corporation organized in 1987 as a 501(c)(3) tax-exempt organization to promote and coordinate the DARE program. Information from recent DARE America federal tax returns provides a sense of the organization's financial stake in the drug war, and it illustrates the financial interests of DARE America's top credentialed-class officers in the continuation of the program.

In 2004 (the most recent year available), the federal form 990 tax return for DARE America, Inc., reported total revenues of $210.9 million. This figure included $204 million "in donated services and use of facilities" (mainly for the services of police officers who are typically paid by their departments for DARE work), $919,144 in "direct public support," $2.78 million in "government contributions (grants)," $2.7 million in "licensee royalties," and $317,172 in "other revenue." Since much federal funding is indirectly channeled to DARE programs through the states in the form of grants, the total amount of federal dollars supporting the program is almost certain to be much higher than $2.78 million. "Media estimates . . . have hovered around $650 million for the entire effort, although DARE has said that figure is probably high."[44] Some of DARE's revenues are channeled to its' employees. DARE's 2003 federal 990 form reported detailed information on incomes paid to a small group of DARE stakeholders employed directly by DARE America. (This information was not included in the 2004 tax return.) DARE employees with substantial annual salaries included Executive Director Charles Parson, $102,500; senior board member Glen Levant (former DARE president and former LAPD assistant police chief), $138,000; the top deputy manager, $100,000; a second deputy manager, $91,667; two lower-level deputy managers, $88,000 each; and the controller, $88,000.[45]

DARE America has been a potent organizational advocate for the DARE program. It has aggressively worked to expand the program by pursuing goals that include "the adoption of DARE in all states and communities . . . support [for] a national DARE instructor training program . . . [and] coordinat[ing] national fund-raising for DARE."[46] The organization has also successfully recruited numerous corporate, political, and entertainment elites, such as TV personality Arsenio Hall and singer Ted Nugent, to serve as DARE spokespersons and fund-raisers.[47] The DARE America Board of Directors consists of well-known national business, political, law-enforcement, educational, sports, and entertainment figures. For example, in 2004, the thirty-four-person board included Lee Baca, Rosey Grier, Helen Mars, Diane Disney Miller, and Ari Swiller.[48]

Another dimension of DARE's organizational support structure consists of a network of ties linking DARE programs to various federal, state, and local government agencies. The Bureau of Justice Assistance (BJA), an agency within the U.S. Department of Justice, serves as a major organizational link tying DARE programs to the federal government. This connection dates to 1986, when former LAPD chief Daryl Gates succeeded in arranging a BJA grant of $140,000 to the LAPD "to share [the] unique DARE Program with other communities throughout the United States."[49] Bureau of Justice Assistance involvement with DARE expanded in the late 1980s and led to agency funding of five regional DARE training centers. The BJA also appoints five of the fifteen members who make up the DARE Training Center Policy Advisory Board, which is responsible for overseeing the training of DARE officers. Other federal agencies with ties to DARE include the National Institute of Justice and the National Institute on Drug Abuse, which have funded DARE evaluation research. The U.S. Department of Education also provides some program funding through the DFSCA, and the U.S. Department of Defense has adopted DARE for use in the schools it operates for dependents of U.S. military personnel. Government linkages also extend down to the state and local levels and involve law-enforcement agencies, schools, and community groups.[50]

In addition to extensive public-sector support, there are numerous links tying DARE to corporate sponsors at the national, state, and local levels. DARE America has been especially instrumental in recruiting national corporate sponsors. For example, the DARE website includes a long list of "D.A.R.E. Sponsors and Supporters." The list contains thirty-four large corporate sponsors, including American Honda, AT&T, General Mills, M&M/Mars, Nextel Communications, Penske Automotive, Sam's Club, Target, and Warner Brothers.[51] Corporate support also extends down to the state and local levels and involves hundreds of large and small firms that contribute to the program.[52] In addition to corporate support, DARE receives foundation grants and awards. The DARE website lists twenty foundation supporters, including American Express Philanthropic Program, Brener Family Foundation, Lund Foundation, McKesson Foundation, Milken Family Foundation, K-mart Family Foundation, and Verizon Foundation.[53]

DARE: Stakeholder Interests and Pacification

Although direct and indirect DARE stakeholders have different types and levels of interest in the program, the preceding section suggests that both groups have shared and overlapping concerns in several areas, including economic, political, and ideological interests. Among direct stakeholders, DARE benefits the material interests of credentialed-class members. This is the case because, like many other programs devised to address social problems, DARE is largely administered, supported, and delivered by members of this class. The top DARE America officials represent one obvious example of how credentialed-class members benefit from public and private resources allocated to fund the program. Other examples are credentialed-class members who administer and coordinate DARE through the BJA-funded DARE regional training centers, the Department of Defense, and local school districts. Also, top credentialed-class administrators in all DARE-connected organizations benefit directly from DARE's popular public image. As one local DARE official confided to us, "DARE is a great PR program for the schools and the police." DARE even serves as a career booster for lower-level law-enforcement officers. A police colonel from Washington State testified during congressional hearings that "a lot of DARE officers are being promoted across our state. . . . [We are] continually looking for officers to train other officers . . . because they end up getting promoted."[54]

Indirect DARE stakeholder groups, such as national political leaders and superclass corporate sponsors, have a number of class-based political and ideological interests that are served by DARE's emphasis on individuals, drugs, and authority. These features of DARE help promote privileged-class interests, legitimate class inequalities, and reinforce the pacification of everyday life in several specific ways.

First, DARE promotes the acceptance of individual-level explanations for, and solutions to, social problems. Second, it encourages a continuing public focus on drug-war issues while distracting public attention from social-class inequalities as sources of social problems. Third, DARE reinforces uncritical acceptance of, and deference to, privileged-class-controlled authority and power structures including, at the community level, the schools, the police, and corporate program supporters. Fourth, it assists in the "demonization of drugs" and helps rally public unity against a common enemy. Fifth, DARE helps legitimate a punitive law-enforcement, antidrug model and harsh sanctions that are used to control drug use, as well as other forms of deviance viewed as stemming from free-willed choices or "bad attitudes."

DARE's ideologically loaded lessons promote privileged-class interests because the indoctrination of working-class students, parents, and citizens with these ideas distracts people from class inequalities, defuses class tensions, constrains the development of class consciousness, and reinforces the legitimacy of privileged-class-dominated social control agencies. The latter feature is especially relevant to DARE's social effects because, as one arm of the larger war on drugs, the program helps legitimate that war. For example, at the student level, DARE can be viewed as "a propaganda tool that indoctrinates children in the politics of the Drug War."[55] And at the societal level, DARE helps reinforce the legitimacy of punitive drug laws and high rates of imprisonment for drug offenses.[56] As journalists Ken Silverstein and Alexander Cockburn point out, "Domestically, the 'drug war' has always been used as a pretext for social control. . . . Essentially, the drug war is a war on the poor and dangerous classes, here and elsewhere. How many governments are going to give up on that?"[57]

Although it is a national program, DARE acts as a franchiselike operation bringing the symbolic politics, actions, distractions, and other features of the drug war relevant to privileged-class interests down to the community level. Even most "DARE-less" communities have some variation of drug education in their schools, not to mention high-profile state and local drug laws in place, so the political and cultural dimensions of the drug war have become permanent fixtures in every community. And although DARE has been subject to some criticism on the basis of its costs and effectiveness and as promoting a kind of "Big Brother is watching" mentality, only a few communities have dropped DARE.[58] But for every community that drops out, more have signed on with the program, and by the mid-2000s, according to the DARE website, "1,000 new communities started D.A.R.E. in the last three years."[59]

As noted earlier, we do not view DARE's pacifying effects as the result of some dark superclass conspiracy. Even so, there is little doubt that DARE's individual-level prevention focus and symbolic messages concerning the drug threat, respect for authority, and condemnation of deviance are consistent with privileged-class interests. They are also consistent with the privileged-class-supported, Rush Limbaugh–like, conservative ideology regarding the causes of, and "cures" for, a wide range of social ills in America today. According to many conservative political leaders, pundits, and commentators, most current problematic social conditions, from poverty to joblessness to drug use, are essentially "attitude problems."[60] The routine "cure" prescribed by this group consists of a short "attitude-adjustment" course (sometimes combined with a kick in the pants).[61] DARE represents a neat fit with the conservative model of the causation of social problems. DARE's match with privileged-class interests and conservative ideology illustrates how a program seemingly far removed from the issue of class inequalities is actually not so far removed after all. By helping to keep public attention focused on winning the drug war—and not on a truly explosive issue like starting a "class war"—in hometowns across the United States, DARE contributes to the pacification of everyday life.

POLITICS AND PACIFICATION

How much more will be required before the U.S. public awakes from its political slumber? . . . The right wing [has enacted] revolutionary changes that have remade the entire sociopolitical structure of the United States.

—Michael Perelman, *Monthly Review*, July–August 2006

The American political system was described many years ago by sociologist William Gamson as one characterized by "stable nonrepresentation." This felicitous phrase is simultaneously a testament to the strength of the system and a condemnation of its fundamental flaw. The system is stable because almost all of its elected and appointed political officials and operatives share the same guiding premises about its economic institutions ("free market capitalism") and its political institutions ("representative democracy"), and because they are all members of the same privileged class. Moreover, as noted in chapter 4, their privileged-class standing is not affected by whether they win or lose in their various political struggles over legislation or elections. The "outs" simply move on to work as consultants to corporations or lobbyists for other governments, as part of the "revolving door" government that takes care of both winners and losers in the privileged class. The nonrepresentative nature of the system is connected to the fact that political officials pay careful attention to the interests of powerful and influential corporations, who were not elected by anyone. The backstage influence of the unelected is part of the normal operation of the system, hidden from public view by the high-profile front-stage activities that appear to be serving the interests of most Americans.

To illustrate how this system works as it relates to symbolic politics and pacification, let us briefly consider the "lobbying and ethics reform" legislation crafted by Congress in 2006. This legislation was supposed to crack down on the corrupt lobbying practices and ethical lapses that produced high-profile congressional lobbying scandals in the mid- and latter 2000s. These included the conviction and imprisonment of former congressman Randall "Duke" Cunningham (R-CA), the guilty plea of "superlobbyist" Jack Abramoff to charges of conspiring to bribe public officials, his agreement to "talk to the Feds about as many as a dozen congressmen" who had accepted money from him, and the indictment (on charges of conspiring to violate a Texas political fund-raising law) and resignation of former U.S. House majority leader Tom DeLay (R-TX).[62] As a result of these and other scandals, in early 2006 it seemed that "nearly every member of Congress want[ed] to sign on to reforming (or at least appearing to reform) the corrupt system of influence peddling in our nation's capital."[63] For a short time, meaningful lobbying-reform legislation appeared to be on a fast track to passage as several bills were introduced and debated in both houses of Congress.

The first intended message of congressional consideration of lobbying-reform legislation, as it was presented in the mainstream media, was that both parties were genuinely concerned about clean government and with ending influence-peddling abuses in Congress. The second intended message was that while the two parties differed somewhat in terms of specific reform measures needed, there was widespread bipartisan support in favor of reform, and the public could be assured that both parties would work together to enact meaningful reforms. The existence of an apparent bipartisan congressional consensus favoring reform legislation gave the average citizen the impression that both parties were "on the same page" and would enact meaningful reforms. Almost on cue, the Senate passed a lobbying and ethics reform bill on March 29, 2006, and the House passed a similar bill in early May. Both bills provided the *appearance* of lobbying and ethics reform, but required virtually no substantial changes in the practices that led to the lobbying scandals. As Public

Citizen reported, the "legislation is not only inadequate, it has made a mockery of the entire lobbying reform drive."[64]

What Congress did in mid-2006 was what has often happened in U.S. lawmaking when money, power, and privileged-class interests are on the line; viz, it enacted symbolic reforms that pacified public outrage by providing the *appearance* of reform but which failed to mandate any meaningful changes that would actually infringe upon privileged-class interests. The lobbying-reform bills passed in 2006 did nothing to break the connections between lobbyists, money, and lawmakers. The bills did not prohibit lobbyists from subsidizing trips for members of Congress (or their staff or other federal officials) or from arranging campaign contributions. The "revolving door" whereby public officials leave office to become highly paid lobbyists was not closed. In short, the legislation left the existing privileged-class-dominated influence-peddling structure intact. Under the "reform legislation," privileged-class lobbyists can legally continue to promote both the special interests of their superclass corporate clients and participate in class-wide lobbying (when their superclass clients' shared class interests intersect on specific issues), using the same kinds of financial donations, gifts, and subsidies that led to the lobbying scandals in the first place.[65] Needless to say, high-profile criticism of the illusory lobbying-reform legislation passed by Congress was not the subject of prime-time TV news reporting or biting editorial commentary in major U.S. print media outlets.

The lobbying-reform legislation was about symbolic politics, not the needs of average Americans for clean government, uncorrupted by privileged-class money's buying legislative or regulatory favors. If the flow of privileged-class funds to members of Congress and other federal officials via "back-channel lobbying," campaign funding, and other practices were actually ended, then the economic and political interests of working-class Americans might have a chance to be heard and maybe even supported in Congress. Of course, such reforms were not enacted. Thus, after the lobbying-reform debates ended and the legislation was signed, sealed, and delivered, the interests of working-class Americans remained on "hold," while privileged-class legislative preferences continued to be fast-tracked through Congress.

Understanding the American political system of "stable nonrepresentation" requires greater attention to what is not discussed in Congress. In the case of the "lobbying reform," we should ask why privileged-class members of Congress will not discuss, let alone enact, meaningful controls on the lobbying practices of privileged-class lobbyists. The reason is that most Democrats and Republicans in Congress are largely funded and supported by, and work for, the same collection of privileged-class lobbyists, superclass corporate executives, and wealthy corporations, as we documented in chapter 4. There are some party-line differences in terms of specific sources and the amounts of money involved, but on the whole, lawmakers in both parties depend on privileged-class funding. This is why Democrats were generally unable to use the mid-2000s congressional lobbying and corruption scandals involving Republican office holders to advance their own prospects.[66] "When people ask why this is so and say the Democrats make a pathetic opposition party, they forget the Democrats must appeal to the rich to fund their campaigns too and cannot stray far from serving these interests. . . . Politicians may seek popular support by responding to public outrage, but they do not bite the hands that feed them."[67]

Another revealing inquiry into the interplay of symbolic politics, pacification, and the protection of privileged-class interests was provided by Thomas Frank in his book *What's the Matter with Kansas?* Frank was puzzled by the fact that in recent years, a majority of the working people of Kansas have consistently voted against their economic and class interests and have joined "the great backlash" against liberal policies and politicians. Why do they join forces with conservative politicians and business interests and support the very people and policies that are responsible for the economic policies that hurt workers? The answer is symbolic politics, described by Frank as the "politics of distraction." Frank maintains that many working-class Kansans have been drawn into supporting conservative politicians because they agree with the positions these candidates take on cultural issues like abortion, homosexuality, and school prayer. Ordinary voters are encouraged by conservative candidates to believe that by supporting them, they are opposing the "cultural elites" who are attacking their traditional values. Many workers in Kansas (and elsewhere) are led by conservative political candidates to focus on the politics of *values* when they vote. Meanwhile, the politics of economic issues and of class interests are largely ignored by conservative candidates in political campaigns (except for some false claims of support for the "middle class"). Thus, conservative candidates win elections by emphasizing their support for the moral values held by many voters. But they quietly support privileged-class economic and political interests and vote for public policies that protect those interests at the expense of working-class voters, who elected them on the basis of their stand on moral values. Frank describes the "bait-and-switch" routine of conservatives this way: "The leaders of the backlash may talk Christ, but they walk corporate."[68]

From our perspective, Frank's "pacification analysis" is useful but incomplete. While he focuses on conservative Republicans as "the problem" for Kansans, we think the focus should be on the privileged class, composed of both Republicans and Democrats. We believe one reason that many Kansans waste their political energies on cultural issues is that neither party has presented them with an agenda of pro-working-class economic issues and policies that they can support. In fact, *both* parties often work together to harm working-class economic interests. After all, it was a Democratic president, Bill Clinton, and a bipartisan congressional vote that produced the North American Free Trade Agreement, which is arguably one of the most anti-working-class pieces of legislation passed in the last several years.[69] As long as pro-working-class economic policies are not on the national political agenda and as long as pro-privileged-class politicians can continue to win elections via the politics of distraction, Kansans and many other working-class Americans are likely to continue to be "pacified" by cultural issues. That is, they are likely to continue to focus their class-based frustrations and energies on cultural issues, which they are led by political candidates to believe they can do something about, like getting prayer into schools or introducing "intelligent design" into biology courses in public schools. That said, the importance of both the Iraq war and economic concerns to many voters in the 2006 midterm elections illustrated, to some extent anyway, that there are limits to the effectiveness of the "politics of distraction" to distract and pacify working-class Americans.

The alternative class-power-network actors, described in chapter 2 and revisited in chapter 8, have a very difficult time trying to get *class issues*, as noted in the preceding sections, on the public agenda for discussion. As the lobbying-reform issue illustrates, the executives, editors, and producers who control mainstream media outlets apparently believe that investigative reports on how *privileged-class interests* (not just "special interests") corrupt the political system and the lawmaking process are not sufficiently important or interesting to their readers and viewers. And alternative media outlets that do provide such coverage lack a large national audience. Without a broad-based social movement and visible national leaders focusing public attention on how privileged-class interests and power dominate government at the expense of the well-being and interests of the working class, the political system will continue to churn out symbolic reforms that amount to little more than rearranging the deck chairs on the Titanic.

THE CULTURE INDUSTRY AND PACIFICATION

> The global media system plays [an] explicit role in generating a passive, depoliticized populace that prefers personal consumption to social understanding and activity, a mass more likely to take orders than to make waves.
>
> —Robert W. McChesney, *Rich Media, Poor Democracy*, 1999

The auto transplants, DARE, lobbying reform, and Kansas politics all illustrate how projects or ideas set in motion by and for the privileged class can dominate public awareness about economic and social issues and confine policy debates to a narrow range of options endorsed by privileged-class-controlled organizations. The effects of symbolic politics upon issue framing, agenda setting, and policy making by the privileged class in these areas help deflect public attention from class inequalities and promote acceptance of an unequal, class-biased status quo. These outcomes are also reinforced by the culture industry, which, as the opening of this chapter suggests, disseminates electronic entertainment products that typically have the effect of distracting public attention from class issues rather than calling attention to them.

The culture industry was briefly mentioned in chapter 5 as part of our introduction to one of its major subdivisions, the information industry. As we noted then, the culture industry encompasses far more than the dissemination of information. It is a complex enterprise composed of large multimedia firms that are increasingly interlocked with even larger conglomerate corporations, advertising agencies, and nominally nonprofit groups (such as the Public Broadcasting Service). The heart of this industry consists of large firms that produce and disseminate a wide range of entertainment, information, and advertising products through television, radio, recorded music, movies, books, newspapers, magazines, and the Internet. This industry is too large and complex to be considered in detail here, but that is not our purpose. Rather, our goal here is to present a brief overview of the scope and content of the electronic-media segment of the industry, especially television and films, to provide a sense of how it contributes to the pacification of everyday life.

The massive scope and everyday reach of the electronic media are evident in the huge distribution networks that disseminate culture-industry products, such as TV and radio programming, sporting events, movies, DVDs, videotapes, audio tapes, CDs, video games, and Internet website materials, to thousands of communities and millions of homes and consumers. In the mid-2000s, the culture-industry infrastructure provided numerous links between various media firms and 6,300 hometown movie theaters (with 38,800 screens), 98 percent of households with TVs (an average of 2.4 sets per household), 92 percent of TV households with VCRs or DVPs/DVRs, and 86 percent of TV households with cable or satellite TV service.[70] In the mid-2000s several firms were providing online services to 95 percent of the 71 million U.S. households with personal computers (out of 112.3 million total U.S. households in 2005).[71] Also, in 2007, annual per person U.S. spending on electronic media usage (not including cell phones or print media) was estimated at $782 compared to $447 in 2000.[72] One result of this extensive penetration of communities and homes by media networks has been that Americans are spending more and more time as passive consumers of electronic media products.

Time spent by individuals on noncommercial activities, such as informal socializing or critical reflection and writing, produces no benefits for culture-industry profits. Only time devoted to the consumption of products generated by culture-industry firms (TV programming, movies, software, commercial websites, videogames, etc.) juices market shares, sales, and profits. The industry has an interest in channeling more and more consumer time into its commercial products. And it is succeeding. In 1988, the average American spent 1,751 hours consuming various electronic media products (TV was number 1 at 1,490 hours, followed by recorded music, home videos, and theater movies), with a total of 3,310 hours devoted to all forms of media consumption (including newspapers, magazines, and books).[73] In contrast, by 2008, it was estimated that American media consumption would be 4,059 hours per person, with 3,681 of those hours devoted to electronic media (not counting cell phones). This includes TV (1,931 hours), followed by broadcast and satellite radio (1,120 hours), recorded music (167 hours), consumer Internet (236 hours), home video games (67 hours), home videos (110 hours), and theater movies (14 hours).[74] This means Americans, for a variety of reasons, are devoting more and more discretionary time to media consumption, especially to electronic media consumption.

The Colonization of Consciousness

To the extent that the awareness and limited free time of new-working-class members are dominated by ideas, programs, activities, and events created by the superclass-owned and credentialed-class-managed culture industry, it means that their consciousness is, in a sense, captured, or colonized, by an outside force. This privileged-class-directed "media force" is driven by class interests that are quite different from those of working-class consumers. For us, then, the colonization of consciousness refers to the ongoing invasion by the culture industry, especially through electronic mass media entertainment and advertising content, of ever larger shares of peoples' time, interests, and imagination. This process is driven by many techniques, including the electronic media firms' constant tracking, creating, and linking of popular cultural trends with media content.[75] It also involves the media's use of compelling imagery (in TV programming, movies, advertising, video games, Web search-engine graphics) and its constant barrage of cleverly produced ads emphasizing the prestige and novelty features of mass, niche, and (upscale and downscale) consumer products.[76] While this process results in a number of consequences, including increases in culture-industry profits, from our perspective the reduction in time available to individuals for all other activities outside of media consumption is among the most important. Of particular importance in this regard is how the colonization of consciousness contributes to the marginalization of class-related issues and interests in individuals' everyday thoughts and discussions as more time and "thought space" are devoted to media products.

Although we may live in a "24/7" world (twenty-four hours a day, seven days a week), each of us can claim only about sixteen waking hours a day, or about fifty-eight hundred hours per year. If we subtract the time devoted to work (about 2,000 hours per year), family, and personal obligations and the 3,681 hours spent on electronic media consumption, we find very little time remains each year for non-privileged-class members to read, think, or talk about public issues, including class inequalities. Moreover, given the taboo nature of class in America and the interests of superclass culture-industry owners, we would not expect to find class-based themes, issues, or interests routinely included in the movie and television content "inserted" in consumers' minds as the colonization-of-consciousness process unfolds.

Movies: Class-Free Content?

Class-related issues and themes are rarely presented in movies, as indicated by a content analysis we conducted in the 1990s of large samples of dramas (699), science-fiction films (750), and documentaries (263) drawn from the *1995 Movie/Video Guide*. In this study, we found that only about 5 percent of the films in each category (thirty-five dramas, forty science-fiction films, fifteen documentaries) included story lines or themes that could be interpreted as critiques of elite-class power or as providing sympathetic portrayals of working-class individuals or organizations (e.g., labor unions).[77] Our short list of thirty-five critical dramas that addressed working-class interests and grievances or critiqued elite-class-dominated institutions included "classics" (from the 1940s on), as well as more recent films.

In 2006, we conducted a second content analysis of movies using similar sample sizes of films in each of the same three general categories used in our 1995 study. As was the case with our earlier study, in 2006 we counted the numbers of films in each category that fit the same criteria employed in 1995.[78] The 2006 results essentially replicated the findings from our 1990s analysis, with one slight difference. In 2006, 8.5 percent of the documentaries sampled (19 out of 223) matched our criteria, compared with 5 percent in 1995.[79] While there may be many reasons for the increase, one interesting finding was that seven of the nineteen documentaries were released after 2001 (and thus could not have been sampled or counted in our first study).

There is no question that the mid-2000s witnessed substantial increases in the numbers of documentary films compared to previous years. For example, forty-five documentaries were released in U.S. theaters in the January–July 2004 period, compared to twenty-nine for the same period in 2003 (twenty-eight in 2002), and this trend continued in 2005.[80] While most recent documentaries have not included critiques of class inequalities or exposés of superclass interests or corporate power, some have. In fact, based on the findings from our 2006 movie study and a review of recent documentary films, we believe the 2001–2006 period witnessed the release of more documentaries that focused either directly on various aspects of class inequalities or were critical of concentrated corporate power and, by extension, critical of at least some features of superclass interests and power than was the case in the 1980s or 1990s.

The recent growth in the number of "class-conscious" documentary films produced in the United States may be due to a number of factors, including expanded audience interest in such films and the economics of filmmaking. These films may resonate with audiences in part because of growing public interest in the intensification of U.S. class inequalities, high-profile corporate scandals (e.g., Enron), and growing public distrust of political and economic institutions, as well as of the mainstream media.[81] The growth of such films has also been driven by the stunning commercial success of some recent class-conscious, entertaining documentaries, beginning with Michael Moore's *Roger and Me*. Released in1989, this film was made on a shoestring budget but grossed nearly $7 million in theaters. Moore's 2004 film in the same vein, *Fahrenheit 9/11*, is the top-grossing documentary of all time, earning over $119 million in theater receipts.[82]

As might be expected, the content of recent class-themed documentary films has varied substantially. Some have highlighted the lifestyles, attitudes, and opinions of the wealthy (especially those who inherited wealth). Some have taken viewers on tours of the underclass and sometimes included critiques of class inequalities ranging from implied to explicit. Others have focused on (and sometimes critiqued) the large corporate structures that generate and perpetuate class inequalities. *Selected* examples of recent documentaries that ranged across these varied class-related themes and topics include Mark Achbar's *The Corporation* (2004), Andy Bichlbaum and Mike Bonanno's *The Yes Men* (2003), Alex Gibney's *Enron: The Smartest Guys in the Room* (2005), Robert Greenwald's *Wal-Mart: The High Cost of Low Price Living* (2005), Jamie Johnson's *Born Rich* (2003) and *The One Percent* (2006) (Johnson is an heir to the Johnson & Johnson fortune), Pepi Leistyna's *Class Dismissed: How TV Frames the Working Class* (2006), Michael Moore's *Fahrenheit 9/11* (2004) and *Sicko* (U.S. healthcare, 2007), Chris Paine's *Who Killed the Electric Car?* (2006), and Morgan Spurlock's *Super Size Me* (2004).[83]

Despite the recent increase in class-themed documentaries, most of these films (with one or two exceptions) were not viewed by large audiences, and the critiques of class inequalities and privileged-class power included in some of these films were not evident in big-budget Hollywood movies in the 2000s. For the most part, the findings from both of our studies regarding the class-related content of most recent nondocumentary films paralleled what movie historian Steven J. Ross found in his review of class themes in the movies. With a focus primarily upon silent films, Ross found that a substantial number of films sympathetic to working-class interests were produced in the United States prior to World War I. However, he points out, the advent of talkies led to the demise of such movies. In a brief discussion of the contemporary period, he notes that class-critical films with "labor-capital" themes have virtually disappeared from the American cinema, reinforcing what we found in our studies.[84] The relative absence of class-related themes in U.S. movies has also been noted by film critic Roger Ebert. In an interview, Ebert observed, "Class is often invisible in America in the movies and usually not the subject of the film. . . . We don't have a lot of class-conscious filmmaking."[85]

While pro-working-class themes are relatively rare in Hollywood films, the *Grapes of Wrath* (1940), starring Henry Fonda, was a notable example of class-conscious filmmaking. We believe this high-profile, classic movie was especially important because it helped establish and legitimate a kind of critical, sympathetic movie treatment of class underdogs in the contemporary era. Bringing the Steinbeck novel of the same title to the screen exposed millions of Americans who had not read the book to its heartbreaking portrayal of the Joad family. Tracing the family's experiences as it migrated from the Dust Bowl during the Great Depression, the movie provides a compelling and sympathetic account of how the Joads and people from similar working-class families were brutalized by the American economic and class structures of the 1930s.

Very few high-profile dramas over the past thirty years have followed in the class-critique, sympathy-for-the-class-underdog film tradition and also featured well-known Hollywood stars. Five titles illustrate, as well as virtually exhaust, the list of contemporary films with both qualities.

1. *Norma Rae:* This 1979 film starring Sally Field compassionately portrays the title character's transformation from passive worker to union activist in a Southern textile plant.
2. *Reds:* Warren Beatty and Diane Keaton star in this 1981 film that presents a sympathetic account of American radical journalist Jack Reed's career, including his reporting on the Russian Revolution.
3. *Remains of the Day:* This 1993 film starring Anthony Hopkins powerfully depicts how the British class system of the 1930s stunted and distorted servants, masters, and human relationships.
4. *Bulworth:* Warren Beatty produced and starred in this 1998 "political farce" that, although flawed in many respects, includes scenes that voice powerful critiques of current American class and race inequities.
5. *Erin Brockovich:* Julia Roberts starred in and won an academy award for best actress in director Steven Soderbergh's adaptation of a true story (2000). Brockovich, a poor single mother, lands a job as a legal aide for a small law firm. In a toxic tort case, she wins the trust of working-class families, documents their health problems linked to environmental toxins, and gathers evidence on toxic chemical releases by a large utility firm. In the end, the plaintiffs receive a limited measure of justice in a legal battle pitting working-class interests against those of the privileged class. The film provides a sympathetic view of workers' interests and portrays Brockovich as a kind of working-class hero—albeit one who becomes a millionaire in the end.

Two boxing films in the mid-2000s featured major-league Hollywood stars and depicted working-class characters in sympathetic terms, but in both movies, the main characters essentially sought to use boxing as a means of *escaping* working-class life. In 2004, Clint Eastwood directed *Million Dollar Baby*, the tragic tale of Maggie Fitzgerald, a "hillbilly" waitress determined to escape her "white trash" heritage. Starring Eastwood, Hilary Swank, and Morgan Freeman, the film won four Oscars (and many other awards). While an excellent film, its main focus is on the personal struggles of the characters, not on class inequalities.[86] In 2005, Ron Howard directed *Cinderella Man*, a movie based on the life story of James Braddock, a working-class boxer who first experienced minor successes in the ring, then appeared "washed up," and, finally, against all odds in the 1930s, won the championship fight of his life. Starring Russell Crowe and Renée Zellweger (as Braddock's wife), the film depicts working-class characters and their lives in humane and sympathetic terms. Even so, the film is ultimately about boxing as a vehicle for "upward mobility" for Braddock and his family. Through his successes as a boxer, he and his family are able to escape the insecurities and uncertainties of working-class life.[87]

A smaller number of dramas, though less well known than the films in our listing above and with much less star power, have followed in the class-critique and sympathy-for-the-class-underdog traditions.[88] Two powerful examples include *Matewan* and *The Killing Floor*. The former is a 1987 film directed by John Sayles that sympathetically depicts the union side of the West Virginia "coal wars" of the 1920s. The latter title is a 1993 film that presents a historically informed account of how Chicago meatpacking firms in the early 1900s resisted unionization by exploiting racial and ethnic divisions and related tensions among the workers.

Although more titles could be added to the examples listed (such as Richard Linklater's 2006 *Fast Food Nation*), the entire group of class-critique dramas identified in our studies makes for very short lists. Few movies in the genres we reviewed in 1995 and 2006 provided critiques of elite-class power or sympathetic accounts of the economic, political, and social-class interests of workers or of workers' class-based personal grievances. Dramas easily recognized as reflecting the class-critique, sympathy-for-the-underdog tradition or science fiction films that include explicit critiques of ruling-class power (such as *They Live!*) are infrequently made, narrowly promoted, and seldom viewed by mass audiences. Moreover, they are notable exceptions to the non-class-based, escapist themes and action story lines routinely depicted in most mainstream American films. In fact, we are likely to see even more escapist action movies in the future as global film-going audiences' tastes become more American-like and as the foreign market for U.S. films continues to grow—to the point where U.S. films often generate more revenue overseas than in the domestic market.[89] Moreover, it has been well documented that "violent action fare is the genre that crosses borders most easily and makes the most commercial sense."[90] Hollywood is also likely to produce more horror films both for domestic consumption and foreign export since seven titles in this genre "topped the box office" in the late-2005-mid-2006 period.[91]

As action and horror films, plus those in other escapist genres, become ever more common, class themes are likely to appear even less often in movies than in the past. The film formula of the future seems to be more action equals more distraction. Speaking to the effects of movie content on culture and class consciousness, film historian Ross maintains that "American filmmakers have helped create a culture whose citizens either no longer view class as an important part of their lives or define the middle class so broadly that class no longer seems to matter."[92]

TV and ABC

So what's on TV? For openers, try advertising. A typical prime-time, thirty-minute, TV-network program now includes about nine minutes of advertising.[93] Local programs have even more. American television networks broadcast over six thousand commercials per week, up 50 percent since 1983.[94] Moreover, advertisers increased their spending on all forms of television advertising (broadcast and cable) from $29 billion in 1990 to $70 billion in 2005.[95] This huge increase in TV ad expenditures reflects not only the increase in broadcast time devoted to advertising but also advertisers' faith in the power of TV to sell more stuff (despite advertisers' problems with viewers who record programs and skip commercials, via Tivo, DVRs, and VCRs).

What kinds of programming do the ads support? Or what else besides ads do we find on TV? The really short answer is ABC: Anything but Class. If we set aside TV news as being part of the information industry (chapter 5), we find TV advertising supports a wide range of programming that, for the most part, ignores class issues and trends heavily toward distraction. A tour of *TV Guide's* 2006 daytime and evening listings reveals recurring programming patterns, particularly for network TV. Mornings are devoted mainly to newsmagazine and talk shows. Afternoons bring soap operas and more talk shows. Evening programming is more diverse and includes paranormal-themed series (e.g., *Ghost Whisperer* [CBS], *Medium* [NBC]), "reality-based" crime shows (e.g., *Cops* [FOX], *Forensic Files* [Court TV]), "realitylike" crime shows (e.g., *NCSI* and *CSI* [CBS], *Law and Order* [NBC]), "reality" programs (e.g., *Survivor* [CBS], *American Idol* [FOX]), sporting events, comedy series (e.g., *George Lopez* [ABC], *How I Met Your Mother* [CBS], *My Name Is Earl* and *The Office* [NBC]), Gen-X-Y nighttime soap opera–like shows (e.g., *Desperate Housewives* [ABC], *The O.C.* [FOX]), dramas (e.g., *Grey's Anatomy* [NBC]), more newsmagazine shows, and more talk shows. Cable, satellite, PBS, syndicated programs, and movies add diversity to daily programming, but studies of TV content reveal a striking absence of programs that depict the lives or concerns of working-class Americans or that deal with class-based inequalities in ways that might promote critical reflection among viewers.

One study of four decades of TV entertainment found that of 262 domestic situation comedies, only 11 percent featured blue-collar, clerical, or service workers as heads of households. By contrast, the vast majority of the series, 70.4 percent, portrayed "middle-class" families with incomes and lifestyles that were more affluent than those of most middle-income American families. In fact, in 44.5 percent of the comedy series studied, the head of the household was a professional.[96]

Another study of thirteen TV situation comedies from the 1990s found the issue of social mobility across class lines is sometimes used as a source of comic tension and moral instruction. On the rare occasions when characters in the series studied aspired to or encountered upward mobility, the outcomes reminded viewers that "achieving inter-class mobility is rare, and the rewards of any substantial social movement will likely be bittersweet." The study concluded that TV situation comedies send mixed and paradoxical messages where social mobility is concerned. On one hand, these programs typically reinforce the myth of America as a land of opportunity where hard work and persistence pay off. On the other hand, on the rare occasions when characters actually encounter social mobility, their experiences tend to be portrayed as disruptive and often undesirable.[97] The net result is the subtle reinforcement of existing class divisions, structures, and locations as normal, natural, and preferred—to the disruptive effects of social mobility.

In the mid- and latter 2000s, only three prime-time network TV comedy series occasionally portrayed working-class characters, families, issues, or problems in somewhat sympathetic or positive terms. Two were animated programs that aired on Sunday nights: *The Simpsons* (created by cartoonist Matt Groening), and *King of the Hill* (devised by Beavis and Butthead creators Mike Judge and Greg Daniels, formerly of *The Simpsons*).[98] The third was *My Name Is Earl* (NBC) starring Jason Lee. Our qualified positive view of some portions of these shows is unlikely to be shared by media scholars. For example, author Diana Kendall maintains that where televised U.S. entertainment programs are concerned, "the most popular portrayal of the working class is *caricature framing*, which depicts people in negative ways, such as being dumb, white trash, buffoons, bigots, or slobs." Kendall uses Homer Simpson, the *King of Queens*'s Doug, and comedian Jeff Foxworthy's ridiculing of the "blue-collar lifestyle" to illustrate how working-class characters are routinely portrayed in negative terms by TV entertainment programs.[99]

We view the *Earl* show as an interesting illustration of how the story lines of popular TV comedies can convey mixed messages regarding the merits of working-class characters. On this show (and a few others), working-class characters are sometimes portrayed in sympathetic terms, but at other times, the characters are portrayed in stereotypical terms "as unattractive, crude, and riddled with flaws."[100] We see this kind of ambivalence toward the working-class as reflecting wider privileged-class views of the working class. Such views appear to have been part of the show's origins. As *Earl*'s creator, Greg Garcia, said, "I wanted Earl to be a derelict, but at the same time somebody you love."[101] A reviewer captured the ambivalence the show evokes: "Earl represents the . . . uncouth epitome of white trash . . . [but] he's not treated as an abject failure. In fact, all of the characters on the show are handled with a goofy kind of respect."[102] Perhaps "goofy" is about the only kind of respect that working-class characters can get in network TV programs. As Jason Lee said of his character,

"Earl's a real dude from Anywhere, Small Town, USA. . . . [T]here is nothing fancy about him."[103]

In the mid- and latter 2000s, cable TV's UPN broadcasted *Veronica Mars*, which one reviewer called "the single most compelling exploration of class anxiety and friction on the little or big screen today." Each episode involves adventure, romance, suspense, and soap opera–like qualities. Viewers follow Veronica, a class-conscious teenage "outsider," as she "negotiates the twin perils of high school and her career as a private investigator in her [father's] firm." Veronica was estranged from her former elite friends due to her father's fall from elite grace by losing his position as sheriff because he was too honest. Veronica's mother left town, so she and her private investigator father live and work together. The program is set in the fictional southern California town of Neptune, which is, as Veronica says, a "town without a middle class . . . [where] your parents are either millionaires or your parents work for millionaires."

Veronica is unusual television because "everything that happens in the show is presented and viewed through a class lens." Each episode involves explorations of class- and inequality-related issues, such as cross-class love affairs, cross-class and same-class personal betrayals, and elite-class corporate corruption—all combined with occasional bouts of teen angst. Working-class Veronica displays mixed emotions about her relationship with the "'09ers" (the elite teen clique labeled by their zip code). She is both resentful and wishful where elites are concerned: "I'd be the best rich person," 'Veronica muses.' "I'd be the perfect combination of frivolous and sensible. Money is so wasted on the wealthy." As a reviewer observed, "*Veronica* expresses the deep ambivalence that the working and middle classes feel about the rise of a monstrously flush ruling class in our midst."[104]

In contrast to the occasional sympathetic treatment of working-class concerns by the three comedy series and the explicit exploration of contentious class issues by *Veronica Mars*, TV newsmagazines such as *60 Minutes, Dateline,* and *20/20* almost never report on working-class concerns or elite-class dominance. The only exceptions are infrequent reports that "expose" infrequent "bad apple" businesses guilty of abusing working-class consumers and occasional stories on corrupt corporate executives—often shown in handcuffs in "perp walks"—as if to prove that no one, including rich corporate elites, is above the law in America. The syndicated, tabloid-style TV "newsmagazines" totally avoid issues concerning the working-class or elite-class abuses of power. The mission of these programs (e.g., *Access Hollywood, E!, Entertainment Tonight, Inside Edition,* and *Extra!*) is to traffic in high-energy celebrity profiles and gossip about the stars, especially reports concerning sex, drugs, deviance, and opulent lifestyles. Such titillating stories appear designed to deliberately appeal to nonelite viewers by providing vicarious thrills and voyeuristic gratification.[105] They seem to say, maybe you can't afford it or do it or would never do it yourself, but you can watch glamorous stars own it and do it—Right here! Right now!

The themes of titillation and distraction are also staples of most daytime TV talk shows. The 2006 season saw the following sampling of shows and topics. Jerry Springer interviewed porn stars and hillbillies; Dr. Phil interviewed women who admit to being "bitches" and guests with bipolar disorders; Montel Williams interviewed a "world-renowned psychic" and a woman in love with a serial killer.[106] Other, more "prestigious" daytime TV talk shows have adopted formats that frequently mix celebrity interviews (usually TV, movie, or sports stars or the suddenly famous or infamous promoting their movies, books, or careers) with topical issues that relate to viewers' interests and concerns (e.g., money, diets, personal problems, current events). For example, *The Oprah Winfrey Show* included interviews (e.g., with Bill and Melinda Gates and Kirstie Alley), topical discussions (e.g., child rape, female teachers having sex with boys, living on the minimum wage), and "personal concerns" (e.g., "Does My Butt Look Big?").[107] On *The Ellen DeGeneres Show*, Ellen interviewed members of "The Producers" cast (e.g., Matthew Broderick and Nathan Lane), Vince Vaughn (from the movie *Break Up*), and Liza Minnelli.[108] Meanwhile, on *The View*, Barbara Walters and her cohosts interviewed Shannen Doherty, Mary-Louise Parker, Gene Simmons, Sally Field, Nora Ephron, and Cuba Gooding Jr.[109]

ABC and the Oprahfication of the Mind

In situation comedies, talk shows, newsmagazines, and other programming formats, ABC—Anything but Class—is what's on TV. ABC is an important factor contributing to the colonization of consciousness, and the ABC focus and content of most TV programming, especially talk shows and newsmagazines, contribute to another phenomena involved in the pacification process: the Oprahfication of the mind. This term refers to how the electronic media, especially television "infotainment" (superficial information presented in "information" or "news" formats but whose primary value is as entertainment), contributes to the demise of critical thinking about current and past social, cultural, and political events and issues.[110]

High-profile media stars (e.g., Oprah Winfrey) projected through powerful TV media platforms help establish a pop-culture conceptual framework that blends current events and celebrity and social issues into short, seamless entertainment packages. As a result, working-class TV viewers are encouraged to concentrate on only the most dramatic or high-profile current events or the most glamorous or sensationalized personalities and issues. The September 11, 2001, terrorist attacks on the United States and the devastation caused by Hurricane Katrina in August 2005 both temporarily interrupted TV talk show attention to infotainment themes and story lines. For a while, hosts shifted their focus to heroic, tragic, and touching human stories associated first with the attacks and later with the hurricane. In the case of September 11, themes of horror, heroism, the face of evil (Osama bin Laden), and the quest for justice (or vengeance) were woven into many TV talk show programs—for a time.

In the case of Katrina, TV coverage captured acts of heroism by working-class volunteers, police officers, firefighters, and some storm victims, displays of incompetence and callousness by some privileged-class officials, and even discussions of how the unequal distribution of suffering among New Orleans residents was heavily influenced by the social factors of class and race.

The transient doses of reality-based content that talk show hosts delivered to TV viewers in the autumn of 2001 and late summer of 2005 may well have promoted national unity, encouraged support for victims of both events, and even informed viewers. But in at least one respect, TV coverage of the September 11 attacks and their aftermath was similar to the more typical content of TV programs: it deflected critical attention from any consideration of class-inequality issues. In fact, the wave of talk show programming devoted to the attacks and the aftermath, like the typical fare delivered to these programs, was soon depleted of novel and compelling story lines, shock value, and ratings utility. As the September 11 TV story lines faded, and as TV attention to the poverty and racial inequalities revealed by Katrina waned (as we noted in chapter 2), waiting in the wings were new angles on familiar

Copyright © Tom Tomorrow. Reprinted with permission.

infotainment topics: breathless reports on pop-culture icons (movie stars, Bill Gates, the Kennedys—our royal family—Marilyn Monroe, and Lady Di—forever), breaking stories on British royalty, new serial killers, the latest movie trailers, hot new fashions, and the long-running Wall Street drama. Through such programming, American TV viewers are coached to conceptualize and think about most news and talk show topics at the most immediate, superficial, and individualized level of detail. Any sense of how social-class inequalities or wider historical or cultural contexts may be linked to current themes is lost to Oprahfication.

American TV viewers are also encouraged to think about social, political, and economic issues through a superficial popular culture lens that brings into dazzling focus "SGP" (shock, glamour, and the perverse) topics while blurring the field of vision where serious issues like working-class interests, grievances, or inequalities are concerned. As our review of TV talk show content suggests, the SGP focus of these shows (and many TV newsmagazines) may sometimes be interrupted by serious events—like the September 11 attacks and Hurricane Katrina—but even those are channeled through, and mined by, the insatiable media appetite for novelty. More routinely, the SGP programming profile ranges across predictable topics with shock and novelty value, such as twisted sexual practices, abuse, body piercing, satanic rituals, plastic surgery gone wrong, tattoos, "extreme" anything, racial strife, and gender bending, along with the latest medical, movie, fashion, hairstyle, and other pop-culture trends.

The SGP focus is reinforced by increasingly common "socialization-to-novelty" experiences among TV viewers and consumers of popular culture generally. Mass media advertising often encourages consumers to devalue stability and continuity in products, packaging, entertainment, and lifestyle trends. Much of the content and many of the commercials in the electronic media reinforce the idea that routine is boring and changes, especially fast-paced novel changes, are good. Viewers are encouraged to think that "been there, done that" experiences equal boring repetition and are to be avoided. Consumers are encouraged to pursue and prefer novel products, experiences, and activities because novelty is presented as the source of fulfillment and fun.[111] Preferences for novel products, images, and activities are driven by the mass media's recognition that speed, action, color, change, and novelty juice viewer interests, as well as TV and merchandise-marketing profits.

SGP programming and accelerated socialization-to-novelty experiences are key factors leading to the Oprahfication of the mind. Oprahfication is a kind of truncated and compartmentalized cognitive style that not only erodes people's capacity for critical thinking but also diminishes even the legitimacy of critical thought. Oprahfication reduces (1) the likelihood that people will think of social issues or current events in terms of class analysis (too boring!), (2) people's ability to think in such terms (they have too little practice or experience), and (3) people's ability to understand or appreciate a class-based analysis of problematic social conditions if it is presented to them (too confusing!). Colonization and Oprahfication are major elements in the pacification of everyday life through the culture industry.

PACIFICATION AND PROVOCATION: TWO SIDES OF EVERYDAY LIFE

Question: If men in power and younger women were all it took to fascinate media, wouldn't we see wall-to-wall coverage of the sweatshop industry?

—*Extra!* "Soundbites," September–October 2001

As we have shown, the pacification of everyday life is a pervasive, complex, and powerful process. The illustrations presented in this chapter suggest that it promotes privileged-class interests through a variety of institutionalized routines and practices that, for the most part, legitimate and reproduce existing class inequalities and at the same time distract working-class members from these issues. However, it is also important to recognize that pacification does not proceed as an unopposed process; nor is it a seamless, one-dimensional force without internal contradictions.

As we noted in chapter 2, alternative class-power networks essentially operate in ways that call attention to, challenge, and contest the pacification process. The provocation efforts of these networks typically operate outside the organizations and structures that dominate the pacification process—but not always. Some branches or substructures of mainstream organizations that drive the pacification process sometimes deliberately include people and ideas from the alternative power networks. For example, public (and on occasion commercial) radio and television broadcasters sometimes include members of the alternative power network on some programs, typically as a means of legitimating their image as providers of "open forums" for discussions of public issues. Whatever the motives of gatekeepers controlling privileged-class-dominated organizations, whenever labor leaders, consumer advocates, or elite-power critics (e.g., AFL-CIO President John Sweeney, Noam Chomsky, Michael Moore, Ralph Nader, Gore Vidal) testify at congressional hearings or appear on TV or radio talk shows and newsmagazines, their messages challenging the pacification process are heard and seen by the working class.

Perhaps more important than token mainstream appearances by members of the alternative power network are the effects that occur as a result of internal contradictions arising from institutional imperatives associated with the routine practices of the organizations that drive the pacification process. At the same time that privileged-class-dominated organizations produce pacifying "products," such as the policies, programs, and entertainment described in this chapter, some features of some products also result in paradoxical effects. That is, some products produced in the routine course of the pacification process may highlight or even challenge class inequalities rather than legitimate them. When this occurs, these features of the pacification process may actually contribute to contradictory outcomes, such as increased class tensions and resentment or even heightened class consciousness.

One illustration of how class provocation and pacification can occur at the same time as a result of routine organizational imperatives and practices can be found in the political arena. As we have seen, candidates for office are largely financed by superclass-provided funds. However, candidates must also appeal to working-class voters. The latter reality can sometimes lead even superclass-funded candidates to take public positions on some issues that appear to reinforce working-class interests at the expense of the privileged class. For example, in the chapter 4 box, "Class Issues in the Media: U.S. Elections and the Class Taboo," we noted that in the 2006 midterm elections, many mainstream media pundits encouraged Democratic candidates to run as "centrist unifiers" and to avoid class-based issues. Many Democratic candidates ignored this advice and "ran aggressively on liberal or populist economic issues—against unregulated free trade and the offshoring of American jobs, against special interests, corporate excesses, and social issues." While we do not view this development as evidence that the 2006 elections were an exercise in "class war," many Democratic candidates did invoke populistlike rhetoric in their campaigns and claimed to support populist-style policies on economic issues of interest to working-class voters. The point is that the emergence of populist and even progressive messages in national political campaigns illustrate how the routine operation of a political system that generally reinforces the pacification process has the potential to generate contradictory messages—at least temporarily and episodically.

The electronic media also illustrate how institutional imperatives can produce contradictions in pacification products. Although most media products help to distract public attention from class issues and serve to legitimate class inequalities, mass media firms are fundamentally money-making businesses. Because TV and movie corporations are driven by profit-maximization concerns, they must deliver a constant stream of novel products to attract viewer attention so as to increase sales and profits. In the absence of explicit censorship and in the routine course of producing creative and marketable products, some movies and TV programs are produced that include content critical of class inequalities or privileged-class interests.

As noted earlier, some movies include story lines that portray working-class characters and interests in sympathetic terms. Thus, studios that typically traffic in pacification products do sometimes produce provocative films that call attention to class inequalities. When viewers identify with or share the concerns of the working-class characters portrayed in such films, the stories can resonate powerfully with audiences, help legitimate class grievances, generate large box-office revenues, and even produce critical acclaim. We know movie studios are not in the business of delivering progressive political messages or stimulating class consciousness. However, if movies with such story lines generate strong profits, then they will be delivered—at least from time to time. Two movies from the recent past with big-name stars illustrating this reality include *A Civil Action* (1999, starring John Travolta) and *Erin Brockovich* (2000, starring Julia Roberts). Both films were based on factual events concerning the negative health effects of toxic-waste products released into the environment by seemingly callous corporations. And while both films are flawed and send mixed class messages (e.g., rogue firms are to blame, not the larger economic system; workers need elite-class advocates; class justice is finally rendered), they do help legitimate some working-class grievances and expose some class-based injustices.

It's clear that few movies focus on class inequalities. However, the ones that do often encourage viewers to empathize with exploited working-class underdogs or to be outraged by exposés of elite-class arrogance and power abuses. These themes are included in classic hits like *Grapes of Wrath*; they are also woven into more recent films critical of elites, such as the two just noted, as well as those noted earlier in this chapter, especially many of the recent documentaries cited that are critical of concentrated corporate and elite power. Although we would agree that most movies are far more likely to have pacifying than provocative effects where class issues are concerned, the routine operation of the pacification process still produces some films that inject critical class-based themes and ideas into popular culture.

Like the movies, television is also most closely associated with pacifying effects. However, even routine television products can produce paradoxical outcomes. For example, some TV newsmagazines and talk show forums have reported on topics that do not necessarily serve privileged-class interests, such as Enron-like corporate scandals, soaring CEO pay levels, CEOs' "backdating" of stock options, plant closings, sweatshops, campaign finance reform, congressional lobbying and ethical scandals, gasoline price gouging, capital gains tax cuts for the rich, corporations' eliminating workers' pension plans, and ethical lapses among professionals (e.g., accountants linked to corporate scandals).[112] Such programming has the potential to fuel class tensions and resentment, increase public cynicism about mainstream institutions (especially corporations and government), and even increase class consciousness. Growing awareness of class-divergent interests is, in part, revealed by recent public-opinion polls. In a 2004 Harris poll, 83 percent of Americans agreed that big companies "have too much power in influencing government policy, politicians, and policymakers in Washington."[113] Public mistrust of at least some members of the superclass was apparent in an earlier *Washington Post* poll that found "88 percent of Americans distrust corporate executives."[114] Popular discontent with the engines of superclass wealth was evident in a 2005 Pew poll that found only 45 percent of Americans "have a favorable opinion of business corporations." These results were very different from poll findings in the mid-1980s to the early 2000s, which reported solid majorities of Americans held positive views of corporations.[115]

Sometimes regularly scheduled TV programs include content that heightens some forms of class consciousness among new-working-class viewers. In the mid- and latter 2000s, *The Daily Show*, hosted by Jon Stewart, and *The Colbert Report*, hosted by Stephen Colbert, blended comedy and news into programs that included occasional critiques of class inequalities couched in humor and satire.[116] (Both programs are broadcast on the Comedy Central cable channel owned by Viacom.) *The Colbert Report* includes especially biting humor; it is a parody of right-wing pundit talk-TV with Colbert as an egotistical and closed-minded cheerleader of all things, people, ideas, and symbols associated with contemporary right-wing conservatism. Each *Report* program includes a commentary segment called "The Word." A June 2006 program presented Colbert as outraged by former Senator John Edwards's plan for ending poverty in America by 2020. This led Colbert to a "Word" segment on class warfare. Colbert's discussion was laced with double-edged satire as he criticized Edwards for his plan to undo the accomplishments of the Bush administration in *creating* more poverty and for threatening to make a liar of Jesus Christ who, as Colbert noted, said "the poor will always be with us." All the while, short, on-screen phrases were displayed as satirical counterpoints to Colbert's right-wing rant favoring more poverty and criticizing liberals who want to help the poor. This and similar kinds of segments on both shows were both entertaining and provocative. Perhaps the comedy content of both shows will allow them to continue. But Colbert's show may not survive if he continues to offend powerful political figures and mainstream media reporters as he did when he performed at the annual White House correspondents' dinner on April 29, 2006.[117]

The mid-2000s also witnessed the development of an "emerging progressive media network" that included not only print media publications but numerous electronic media organizations and resources as well. Progressive electronic media provided programming on radio (Air America), television (*Deep Dish TV, Link TV*), and the Internet (online magazines, portals, and blogs).[118] To some extent this emerging network was part of a broader effort by progressive media reformers to challenge the organizational, legal, and cultural foundations of U.S. mainstream media organizations.[119] The importance of this development is that it may provide the means for more widely disseminating progressive ideas and discussions of public policies that favor working-class interests. At the present time, only limited opportunities exist in the mainstream media for the presentation of these kinds of topics.

The short runs of the rare programs broadcast via mainstream TV channels that are openly critical of class inequalities and powerful individuals and corporations reveal the difficulties faced by producers and writers of progressive media products in getting and keeping their work on the air.[120] As might be expected, progressive television programming critical of elite-class interests and sympathetic to working-class concerns is infrequently produced and aired by major TV networks. Even so, as we noted, such TV programming does on occasion get written, produced, and aired, even in a medium where pacification products, themes, and story lines dominate the airwaves. The TV-as-provocation outcome via mainstream TV channels was perhaps best illustrated in the mid- and latter 2000s by the two comedy programs described above. (Only time will tell if these programs will survive over an extended period given their sometimes "critical" content.) The emerging progressive media network may provide a new venue for extending TV-as-provocation outcomes beyond mainstream TV-controlled channels if the television components of the network can be financially sustained over time. This development has the potential to counter at least some features the electronic media embody as agents of pacification.

The parade of examples illustrating the flip side of the pacification process could go on and on, but the point is that there is another side. The everyday, routine functioning of mainstream social institutions like local newspapers, drug-education programs, Congress, movies, and TV programs does, for the most part, serve to distract nonprivileged groups from class issues, defuse class tensions, and legitimate class inequalities. But at the same time, the daily routines and practices of mainstream institutions occasionally can and do subvert the pacification process. On those infrequent occasions, chunks from the dark mass of conflicting interests from beneath the waterline of the class iceberg churn to the surface and produce transient episodes of inconvenience, embarrassment, and even anger for privileged-class members. Fortunately for them, such "provocations" are usually isolated and quickly smoothed over by the powerful and predictable privileged-class-controlled institutional routines that on a daily basis reinforce the pacification of everyday life. However, in the next chapter we consider the prospects for the emergence of sustained challenges to the deeply ingrained legitimating and distracting features of the pacification process and to the powerfully institutionalized and ever widening class inequalities evident today in the twenty-first century.

CLASS ISSUES IN THE MEDIA:
LENO AND LETTERMAN—PUTTING US TO SLEEP

by Dave Lippman

[Authors' note: The following essay, abridged for use here, was prepared by comedian Dave Lippman. While the time period referenced (late 1990s) is somewhat dated in terms of the topics covered by late-night talk show hosts, we think the essay provides

(continued)

interesting commentary on how the humor these hosts routinely employ relates to the issues of privileged-class power and the pacification of everyday life.]

In the electronic hearth known as television—the electronic replacement for the private living room gathering—there appears to be a discussion of social issues taking place. I refer to the comic monologues offered in the late-night variety shows, which purport to deal with social and political current events. The main subjects of this inquiry are Jay Leno, who inherited an older, more mainstream audience from Johnny Carson; David Letterman, with a younger, putatively more cynical audience; Sinbad, who hosted *Vibe*; Keenan Ivory Wayans, who aims at African Americans and urban and culturally "cutting edge" young people generally; Conan O'Brien, who follows Letterman after midnight and has a strong following on college campuses; and Bill Maher, who provides opinionated comedy about topical issues. For a six-week period in November–December 1997, I recorded the monologue jokes of the six late-night comedy show hosts. The jokes were analyzed in terms of setup, or premise—the news item or observation that provokes the joke—and resolution, or punch line. The process or operation that occurs between setup and resolution is often discussed in terms of conversion, deflection, or reduction.

Turning first to the jokes about the president, the data collected shows that 60 percent of the items about the president are converted to sex jokes (12 percent deal with drugs and fat, and 14 percent refer to popular culture or other standard humor techniques). Insight into how and why this takes place can be gleaned from the comments of Letterman's executive producer, Rob Burnett, regarding the Clinton-Lewinsky story: "It's Christmas in January . . . you wait for stuff like this. The show is written from now till June. The last guy who was close to this was Dan Quayle, the greatest friend a comedy writer ever had."[1] The predecessor to this sex scandal—in his mind—was not another sex scandal but what I would call a prolonged study in the stereotype of [Quayle's] incompetence. Both topics involve stereotypes, and both can and do result in a deflection of attention from other more significant political issues. There were, arguably, more important things to critique about Quayle than his IQ; ditto for Clinton and his zipper.

There are some differences among the comics in their Clinton jokes. Letterman sticks to sex and a little bit of fat: he converts 83 percent of the Clinton stories to Clinton sex jokes, topping Leno's 65 percent. O'Brien also leans on the sex angle, while Wayans and Sinbad eschew Clinton references completely. Maher alternates between sex jokes and pop-cultural references. When there are references to political matters related to Clinton (such as the Whitewater real estate deals, travel office abuses, or fund-raising offenses), they are treated as a catch-all category for free-floating disaffection. When a TV host dwells on political corruption, he may be saying that politicians are crooks, which is a safe enough form of cynicism. He is less likely to be saying that there might somewhere, sometime be less corrupt ones, for whom we might have actual hope. Corrupt politician jokes are as cheap as Bill Gates jokes, and about as educational. Personalized political barbs, in addition to distracting attention from important topics, are generally cheap shots at easy targets, as they often were when directed at President Reagan during his many scandals (over two hundred members of the administration were indicted or resigned under suspicion). Generalized antipolitician sentiment reveals nothing about the political framework into which the corruption is integrated.

To the extent that comedy processes meaning in current events and mediates social fears and confusions, it places the audience in a new, more stable position at the end of the joke. For the individual, it is a cheap response, costing little in self-examination and less in subsequent action. But it is socially expensive: "It's a way not to commit to an issue, a way not to stand up for something" says Bill Maher, who ought to know, but often doesn't seem to.[2] It is irony as a shield, rather than irony as a lance that tears open pretension, exposes hypocrisy, reveals structural patterns. It laughs at corruption, but not to destroy it—only to feel superior to it.

George Lipsitz argues that television protects people from confrontation with impossible desires by reframing their frustrations into manageable questions and doling out diluted satisfactions.[3] Thus, the spectacle of electronic hearth monologue is, within its own terms, doubly satisfying since it provides a limited pleasure while simultaneously obscuring and replacing the larger solutions that would involve far more work to achieve. The way out is through reintegration, reconnection with society and history. This requires dealing with the elevation of consumerism over social responsibility, and that is never easy, for consumerism rules, and has its charms. Perhaps it takes a crisis to give people a new perspective on their social lives; regardless, it will take energy, dedication, creativity, and a sense of humor.

POSTSCRIPT

Since this analysis was written, there's been a lot of blood under the bridge. And with the growth of cable and satellite systems and the further splintering of the market into niches have come new comedy programs with different formats, notably *The Daily Show* and its spin-off, *The Colbert Report*. These are decidedly antiadministration shows, the latter in the convoluted disguise of a right-wing pundit show in the mold of Hannity or O'Reilly. Pollsters are now telling us that a certain youth demographic gets its news primarily from *The Daily Show*. This is certainly an improvement; it indicates, despite the relatively small numbers watching the multiplying niches, an antiadministration drift among viewers (allowing for a percentage that are merely cynical as opposed to analytical or, heaven forbid, prone to active citizenship). It is reminiscent of the turn that came when Leno felt safe offering the U.S. Constitution to Iraq because we weren't using it.

It is difficult to decipher the comic philosophy of *The Daily Show*, in particular vis-à-vis the question of point-of-view comedy versus "balance"—the vexed question that bedevils journalism in general. There are litmus moments, such as the massive February 15, 2003, worldwide anti–Iraq war demonstrations. At that moment, the program showed its colors by shooting barbs not at the demonstrators—it would be normal to make fun of the actors in any targeted event—but at the reactions of the government. There are clearly writer guidelines to which we are not privy. Regrettably, the interview portion of the show does not rise to the cutting-edge level of the opening "monologue"; nor do the mock, on-location-broadcast segments. This has an advantage, making it easier to get to bed earlier. Tivo Stephen for breakfast.

(*continued*)

NOTES

1. David Moore, "Three in Four Americans Believe in Paranormal," *Gallup Poll*, June 16, 2005, on the Internet at http://www.poll.gallup.com/content/default.aspx (visited May 2, 2006). Also see "Do You Believe in Ghosts?" *TV Guide* (November 28, 2005): 19; Frank Newport and Maura Strausberg, "Americans' Belief in Psychic and Paranormal Phenomena Is Up over Last Decade," Gallup Poll Analyses, on the Internet at http://www.gallup.com/poll/releases/pr010608. asp (visited September 29, 2001).

2. Mark Coomes, "Ghostly Shows: They're Baaaack," *Indianapolis Star*, October 6, 2006, E5; Kathy Blumenstock, "ABC Puts UFOs on Its Radar Screen," *Indianapolis Star*, February 22, 2005, E7.

3. Robert Goodman, *The Last Entrepreneurs: America's Regional Wars for Jobs and Dollars* (New York: Simon and Schuster, 1979).

4. Greg LeRoy, *The Great American Jobs Scam* (San Francisco, CA: Berrett-Koehler, 2005), 2.

5. Joseph Weber and Blanca Riemer, "These Days Mack Trucks Isn't Built like Mack Trucks," *Business Week* (July 30, 1990): 40–41.

6. For details on incentive packages, see Peter Eisenger, *The Rise of the Entrepreneurial State* (Madison: University of Wisconsin Press, 1988); Milward H. Brinton and Heide H. Newman, "State Incentive Packages and the Industrial Location Decision," *Economic Development Quarterly* 3 (1989): 203–22; Robert Perrucci, *Japanese Auto Transplants in the Heartland* (New York: Aldine de Gruyter, 1994); LeRoy, *The Great American Jobs Scam*, 47–67.

7. James Derk, "We Got It, Toyota!" *Indiana Business Magazine* (January 1996): 9–13.

8. Ted Evanoff, "A Hoosier Welcome," *Indianapolis Star*, June 29, 2006, C1–C2.

9. "The New Transplants," *UAW Research Bulletin* (January–February 1995): 10–11.

10. Brett Clanton, "Hyundai Factory Finds Sweet Home in Alabama," *Detroit News*, May 16, 2005, A1, A18; "Hyundai's Sweet Home in Alabama," *Ward's Auto World*, May 1, 2002, A1; Jacques Couret and Ryan Mahoney, "State and Kia: Georgia Plant Still a Go," *Atlanta Business Chronicle*, May 18, 2006, on the Internet at http://alantabizjournals.com/atlanta/stories/2006/05/15/daily34.html (visited July 2, 2006).

11. "The New Transplants," 10–11.

12. The per-job-cost sources for the Honda, Hyundai, and Kia plants are those cited above in notes 8 and 10.

13. Michelle Cottle, "The Real Class War," *Washington Monthly* (July–August 1997): 12–16.

14. "Unbalanced! Bipartisan Budget Bill Boosts Billionaires," *Labor Party Press* (November 1997): 4–5.

15. Janine Jackson, "Good News! The Rich Get Richer," *Extra!* (March–April 2006): 6–7.

16. Katherine Beckett, "Setting the Public Agenda: 'Street Crime' and Drug Use in American Politics," *Social Problems* 3 (1994): 425–47. Also see *Ageism on the Agenda*, special issue, *Extra!* (March–April 1997).

17. Earl Wysong and David Wright, "A Decade of DARE: Efficacy, Politics, and Drug Education," *Sociological Focus* 28 (1995): 283–311.

18. DARE Media Kit, "D.A.R.E. Fast Facts," April 18, 2005, on the Internet at http://www.dare.com/home/NewsRoom/Story3a70.asp (visited July 2, 2006).

19. U.S. Department of Justice, Bureau of Justice Assistance, *Program Brief: An Introduction to DARE—Drug Abuse Resistance Education*, 2nd ed. (Washington, DC: Bureau of Justice Assistance, 1991), 3–7.

20. Wysong and Wright, "A Decade of DARE," 285.

21. Patrick Boyle, "A DAREing Rescue," *Youth Today* (April 2001): 1, 16–19.

22. "The New D.A.R.E. Program: An Information Kit for Law Enforcement Officers," Carnevale Associates, Washington, D.C., circa 2003, 7.

23. Dr. Zili Sloboda, personal correspondence with the authors, December 7, 2005.

24. Dr. Zili Sloboda, personal correspondence with the authors, March 8, 2006.

25. Dr. Sloboda, personal correspondence with the authors, December 7, 2005.

26. DARE America, "Where Science Meets the Street" (press release, February 2006), on the Internet at http://www.dare-america.com/home/News Room (visited February 14, 2006).

27. DARE America, "Where Science Meets the Street." "The New D.A.R.E. Program," 1–11.

28. The $21 billion figure includes $15.4 billion spent by the tobacco industry marketing tobacco products in 2003 and an estimated $5.4 billion spent by the alcohol industry marketing alcoholic beverages in 2003. *Sources:* Campaign for Tobacco-Free Kids, "A Broken Promise to Our Children," November 30, 2005, on the Internet at http://www.tobaccofreekids.org (visited July 28, 2006); The Center on Alcohol Marketing and Youth at Georgetown University, "Alcohol Advertising and Youth," January 2006, on the Internet at http://www.camy.org/factsheets/index.php? (visited January 1, 2007). Much of the marketing for both kinds of products is directed at youthful audiences. For examples, see Campaign for Tobacco-Free Kids, "A Broken Promise to Our Children." D. H. Jernigan, J. Ostroff, C. S. Ross, T. S. Naimi, and R. D. Brewer, "Youth Exposure to Alcohol Advertising on the Radio," *Morbidity and Mortality Weekly Report* (September 1, 2006): 937–40. U.S. tobacco and alcoholic beverage sales in 2003 were $86.7 billion and $115.9 billion, respectively. *Source:* U.S. Department of Commerce, *Statistical Abstract of the United States: 2006* (Washington, DC: U.S. Government Printing Office, 2005), 658, 680.

29. "The New D.A.R.E. Program," 1.

30. DARE America, "Where Science Meets the Street."

31. For example, see Eric J. Jensen, Jurg Gerber, and Ginna M. Babcock, "The New War on Drugs: Grass Roots Movement or Political Construction?" *Journal of Drug Issues* 21 (1991): 651–67; James D. Orcutt and J. Blake Turner, "Shocking Numbers and Graphic Accounts: Quantified Images of Drug Problems in the Print Media," *Social Problems* 40 (1993): 190–206; Katherine Beckett, Kris Nyrop, Lori Pfingst, and Melissa Bowen, "Drug Use, Drug Possession Arrests, and the Question of Race: Lessons from Seattle," *Social Problems* 52 (2005): 419–41; Mike Males, "Pot Boiler: Why Are Media Enlisting in the Government's Crusade against Marijuana?" *Extra!* (July–August 1997): 20–21; Salim Muwakkil, "Just Vote No, the War on Drugs Loses at the Polls," *In These Times* (December 25, 2000): 25–26; Marc Cooper, "Plan Colombia," *Nation* (March 19, 2001): 11–18; John Nichols, "Drug Warrior Dissent," *Nation* (May 28, 2001): 8; David J. Jefferson, "America's Most Dangerous Drug," *Newsweek* (August 8, 2005): 41–48; Ira Glasser, "Drug Busts=Jim Crow," *Nation* (July 10, 2006): 24–26.

32. Earl Wysong, Richard Aniskiewicz, and David Wright, "Truth and DARE: Tracking Drug Education to Graduation and as Symbolic Politics," *Social Problems* 41 (1994): 448–72.

33. For example, see Office of National Drug Control Policy, *The National Drug Control Strategy* (Washington, DC: National Criminal Justice Reference Service, 1992), 9. Also see Office of National Drug Control Policy, *National Drug Control Strategy: 2001 Annual Report* (Washington, DC: U.S. Government Printing Office, 2001), 1–7.

34. Budget figures are from the Office of National Drug Control Policy (ONDCP), *National Drug Control Strategy* (Washington, DC: National Criminal Justice Reference Service, 1992), 45; *National Drug Control Strategy* (1994), 79, and *National Drug Control Strategy* (1996), 61–62.

35. Jason Cohn, "Drug Education: The Triumph of Bad Science," *Rolling Stone* (May 24, 2001): 41.

36. Office of National Drug Control Policy (ONDCP), *National Drug Control Strategy: FY 2007 Budget Summary* (Washington, DC: The White House, 2006), 7.

37. ONDCP, *National Drug Control Strategy*, 7.

38. Wysong and Wright, "A Decade of DARE," 298.

39. U.S. Code Annotated, 20 U.S.C.A. sect. 3192, Amendment to Public Law 101-647, Cumulative Annual Pocket Part (St. Paul, MN: West Publishing, 1995), 337.

40. General Accounting Office, "Youth Illicit Drug Use Prevention: DARE Long-Term Evaluations and Federal Efforts to Identify Effective Programs," GAO-03-172R, January 16, 2003 (Washington, DC: U.S. Government Printing Office, 2003).

41. The White House, "National D.A.R.E. Day: A Proclamation by the President of the United States" (press release, April 7, 2006), on the Internet at http://www.whitehouse.gov/news/releases/2006/04 (visited July 2, 2006). For examples of congressional "National DARE Day" proclamations, see various issues of the *Congressional Record* that reference the DARE program listed in the bibliography of Robert Perrucci and Earl Wysong, *The New Class Society: Goodbye American Dream?* 2nd ed. (Lanham, MD: Rowman & Littlefield, 2003), 329–30.

42. Boyle, "A DAREing Rescue," 17, 19.

43. Boyle, "A DAREing Rescue," 17, 19. Also see DARE Media Kit, "D.A.R.E. Fast Facts."

44. Boyle, "A DAREing Rescue," 18.

45. U.S. Department of the Treasury, Internal Revenue Service, "Return of Organization Exempt from Income Tax—Form 990, DARE AMERICA," 95-4242541 (Washington, D.C., 2003).

46. U.S. Department of Justice, *Program Brief*, 11.

47. Dennis Cauchon, "Studies Find Drug Program Not Effective," *USA Today*, October 11, 1993, 1–2.

48. U.S. Department of the Treasury, Internal Revenue Service, "Form 990, DARE AMERICA," ['Board of Directors, 12/21/03.']

49. U.S. Congress, Senate Committee on Labor and Human Resources, *Drug Abuse, Prevention, and Treatment*, 100th Cong., 2nd sess. (Washington, DC: U.S. Government Printing Office, 1988), 198.

50. See Everett M. Rogers, "Diffusion and Re-Invention of Project DARE," in *Organizational Aspects of Health Communication Campaigns: What Works?* ed. Thomas E. Backer and Everett M. Rogers (Newbury Park, CA: Sage, 1993), 139–62. Also see U.S. Congress, House Committee on Education and Labor, Subcommittee on Elementary, Secondary, and Vocational Education, *Oversight Hearing on Drug Abuse Education Programs*, 101st Cong., 1st sess., Serial 101–29 (Washington, DC: U.S. Government Printing Office, 1990); D.A.R.E., "Government," "D.A.R.E. Sponsors and Supporters," on the Internet at http://www.dare.com/sponsors_supporters.asp (visited July 1, 2006).

51. D.A.R.E., "Corporations," "D.A.R.E. Sponsors and Supporters," on the Internet at http://www.dare.com/sponsors_supporters.asp (visited July 1, 2006).

52. See, for example, "Salem, Oregon Police Department," *D.A.R.E. News* (June 2006): 3–4.

53. D.A.R.E., "Foundations," "D.A.R.E. Sponsors and Supporters," on the Internet at http://www.dare.com/sponsors_supporters.asp (visited July 1, 2006).

54. U.S. Congress, House Committee, *Oversight Hearing on Drug Abuse Education Programs*, 57.

55. Family Council on Drug Awareness, "Why D.A.R.E. Does Not Work," 1999, on the Internet at http://www.equalrights4all.org/fcda/dare.html (visited April 18, 2005).

56. Paige M. Harrison and Allen J. Beck, "Prisoners in 2004," *Bureau of Justice Statistics Bulletin* (October 2005): 9–10; Paige M. Harrison and Allen J. Beck, "Prisoner and Jail Inmates at Midyear 2005," *Bureau of Justice Statistics Bulletin* (May 2006): 1–12.

57. Ken Silverstein and Alexander Cockburn, "Why the Drug War Works: It's a Money/Class Thing, of Course," *CounterPunch* (June 15–30, 1998): 4–5.

58. Drug Policy Alliance, "'Just Say No' Will Not Keep Our Teens Safe" (press release, April 11, 2005), on the Internet at http://www.drugpolicy.org/news/pressroom (visited May 5, 2005).

59. DARE Media Kit, "D.A.R.E. Fast Facts."

60. Mark Engler, "Hook, Line and Suckers," *In These Times* (October 24, 2005): 32–33, 37; Frances Fox Piven, "Poorhouse Politics," *Progressive* (February 1995): 22–24.

61. Tough, punitive "solutions" to the problem of drug use often promoted by conservatives like Rush Limbaugh may be somewhat modified if the issue becomes personal—as was the case with Limbaugh and his own well-publicized drug problems. Despite Limbaugh's experiences with problematic drug use and rehabilitation, his overall conservative views did not change. See Arian Campo-Flores and Evan Thomas, "Rehabbing Rush," *Newsweek* (May 8, 2006): 27–29.

62. Michael Isikoff, Holly Bailey, Evan Thomas, "A Washington Tidal Wave," *Newsweek* (January 18, 2006): 40–43; Conor Kenny, "Capital Crimes," *In These Times* (August 2006): 20–25; Carol C. Lam, "Congressman Randall 'Duke' Cunningham Pleads Guilty to Receiving Millions in Bribes," Office of the United States Attorney Southern District of California (press release, November 28, 2005); John Nichols, "What DeLay Left Behind," *Nation* (April 24, 2006): 5–8.

63. Craig Holman, "For Real Lobbying Reform, Stop the Flow of Money," *Public Citizen News* (March–April 2006): 1.

64. Craig Holman, "Public Citizen Will Put Pressure on Congress until Real Lobbying, Ethics Reforms Are Enacted," *Public Citizen News* (May–June 2006): 8.

65. Holman, "Public Citizen Will Put Pressure on Congress until Real Lobbying, Ethics Reforms Are Enacted," 8.

66. It should be noted that Democrats *did* benefit politically in the 2006 elections from the "congressional page sex-scandal." The scandal led to the resignation of Representative Mark Foley (R-FL) in late September 2006 and to serious questions regarding "what the GOP leadership knew about Foley—and what Speaker Hastert & Co. did or did not do [about his behavior]." *Source:* Evan Thomas, "A Secret Life," *Newsweek* (October 16, 2006): 28–37.

67. William K. Tabb, "The Power of the Rich," *Monthly Review* (July–August 2006): 9–10.

68. Thomas Frank, *What's the Matter with Kansas? How Conservatives Won the Heart of America* (New York: Metropolitan Books, 2004), 6.

69. Rober Bybee, "NAFTA's Hung Jury," *Extra!* (May–June 2004): 14–15.

70. Motion Picture Association of America (MPAA), "U.S. Entertainment Industry: 2005 MPA Market Statistics," 22–42, on the Internet at http://www.mpaa.org (visited July 5, 2006). Also see U.S. Department of Commerce, *Statistical Abstract of the United States: 2006*, 733, 737, 794.

71. MPA, "U.S. Entertainment Industry," 46.

72. U.S. Department of Commerce, *Statistical Abstract of the United States: 2006*, 736.

73. U.S. Department of Commerce, *Statistical Abstract of the United States: 1996* (Washington, DC: U.S. Government Printing Office, 1995), 572.

74. U.S. Department of Commerce, *Statistical Abstract of the United States: 2006*, 736.

75. Thomas Frank, *The Conquest of Cool: Business Culture, Counterculture, and the Rise of Hip Consumerism* (Chicago: University of Chicago Press, 1997); also see *The Merchants of Cool*, PBS *Frontline* TV documentary, narrated by Douglas Rushkoff, 2001; Robert W. McChesney and John Bellamy Foster, "The Commercial Tidal Wave," *Monthly Review* (March 2003): 1–16.

76. Robert W. McChesney, *The Problem of the Media* (New York: Monthly Review Press, 2004), 145–52; David Leonhardt, "Two-Tier Marketing," *Business Week* (March 17, 1997): 82–90.

77. Earl Wysong, "Class in the Movies," 1996, unpublished paper; Mick Martin and Marsha Porter, *1995 Video Movie Guide* (New York: Ballantine Books, 1994).

78. We were unable to use the 2006 edition of the *DVD and Video Guide* by Martin and Porter as a source for our 2006 study because this publication no longer classifies films by genre categories. The *VideoHound* publication (listed in note 79 below) we used did classify films into genre categories, but these were more specific than the general categories used in our first study. To replicate the categories used in our 1996 study, we combined film titles from several specific categories used by the *VideoHound* source into the three general categories. For example, the drama category (5,180 films), from which we sampled 518 dramas for our 2006 study, was created by combining films from twelve specific drama categories used to classify drama film titles in the *VideoHound* source (e.g., Adventure Drama, Comedy Drama, Historical Drama).

79. Earl Wysong, "Class in the Movies II," unpublished paper, 2006; Jim Craddock, ed., *Video-Hound's Golden Movie Retriever: 2006* (Detroit: Thomson-Gale, 2006). Our documentary category included films listed by the *VideoHound* source as documentaries and docudramas.

80. Mike Snider, "Documentaries Are Playing to Keen Interest," *USA Today*, July 24, 2004, 1D; Claudia Puig, "True Story: Documentaries Are a Growing Business," *USA Today*, February 25, 2005, 4D.

81. The Pew Research Center, "Public Sours on Government and Business," October 25, 2005, 1–2, 4, on the Internet at http://www.people-press.org/reports (visited July 12, 2006); Project for Excellence in Journalism, "Network TV: Public Attitudes," State of the News Media 2006, May 8, 2006, 59–60, on the Internet at http://www.stateofthenewsmedia.org/2006 (visited May 20, 2006).

82. Box Office Mojo, "Documentary, Lifetime Gross/Theaters," July 2006, on the Internet at http://www.boxofficemojo.com/genres/chart/?id=documentary.htm (visited July 12, 2006).

83. Our examples of class and power-themed documentaries were compiled from a variety of sources, including, for example, "About Current Documentaries," July 12, 2006, on the Internet at http://documentaries.about.com/od/recommendations/a/current_doc.htm (visited July 12, 2006); Gwynneth Anderson, "'Who Killed the Electric Car' Tells of Vehicle's Rise and Fall," *Public Citizen News* (July–August 2006): 5; Craddock, *VideoHound's Golden Movie Retriever: 2006*; Mick Martin and Marsha Porter, *DVD and Video Guide 2006* (New York: Ballantine Books, 2006); Lorenzo Nencioli, "Indies Unleashed," *Dollars and Sense* (May–June 2005): 26–29.

84. Steven J. Ross, *Working-Class Hollywood: Silent Film and the Shaping of Class in America* (Princeton, NJ: Princeton University Press, 1998).

85. Matthew Rothschild, "The Progressive Interview: Roger Ebert," *Progressive* (August 2003): 34.

86. Internet Movie Database, Inc., "Million Dollar Baby," 2004, on the Internet at http://www.imdb.com/title/tt0405159 (visited November 20, 2006); Roger Ebert, "Million Dollar Baby" (movie review), January 7, 2005, on the Internet at http://www.rogerebert.suntimes.com (visited November 20, 2006).

87. Internet Movie Database, Inc., "Cinderella Man," 2005, on the Internet at http://www.imdb.com/title/tt0352248 (visited November 20, 2006); Roger Ebert, "Cinderella Man" (movie review), June 2, 2005, on the Internet at http://www.rogerebert.suntimes.com (visited November 20, 2006).

88. For guides to such films, see John E. Bodnar, *Blue-Collar Hollywood: Liberalism, Democracy, and Working People in American Film* (Baltimore: Johns Hopkins Press, 2003); Tom Zaniello, *Working Stiffs, Union Maids, Reds, and Riffraff: An Organized Guide to Films about Labor* (Ithaca, NY: IRL Press, 1996).

89. Robert W. McChesney, *Rich Media, Poor Democracy: Communication Politics in Dubious Times* (Chicago: University of Illinois Press, 1999), 109.

90. McChesney, *Rich Media, Poor Democracy*, 109.

91. Devin Gordon, "Horror Show," *Newsweek* (April 3, 2006): 61.

92. Ross, *Working-Class Hollywood*, 255.

93. McChesney, *The Problem of the Media*, 146.

94. Jerold M. Starr, *Air Wars: The Fight to Reclaim Public Broadcasting* (Boston: Beacon Press, 2000), 16.

95. U.S. Department of Commerce, *Statistical Abstract of the United States: 2007* (Washington, DC: U.S. Government Printing Office, 2006), 785.

96. Richard Butsch, "Class and Gender in Four Decades of Television Situation Comedy: Plus ça Change . . . ," *Critical Studies in Mass Communications* 9 (1992): 387–99.

97. Lewis Freeman, "Social Mobility in Television Comedies," *Critical Studies in Mass Communication* 9 (1992): 400–406, quote from 405.

98. "Returning at Mid-Season," *TV Guide* (May 29–June 4, 2006): 7; "Returning Favorites," *TV Guide* (September 8, 2001): 4; "Springfield Film Festival," *TV Guide* (April 24–30, 2006): 82.

99. Diana Kendall, *Framing Class: Media Representations of Wealth and Poverty in America* (Lanham, MD: Rowman & Littlefield, 2005), 234.

100. David Hiltbrand, "His Name Is 'Earl' and He's the Fool We Love to Love," *Kokomo Tribune*, April 9, 2006, A11 (Knight-Ridder newspapers).

101. Hiltbrand, "His Name Is 'Earl' and He's the Fool We Love to Love," A11.

102. Hiltbrand, "His Name Is 'Earl' and He's the Fool We Love to Love," A11.

103. David A. Keeps, "*My Name Is Earl*'s Jason Lee," *TV Guide* (October 31–November 6, 2005): 24.

104. Christopher Hayes, "Veronica Mars, Class Warrior," *In These Times* (June 2006): 46–47.

105. Kendall, *Framing Class*, 52, 74.

106. Jerry Springer shows were described in *TV Guide* episode listings on the Internet at http://online.tvguide.com; Dr. Phil shows were described on his website at http://www.drphil.com/shows; Montel Williams shows were described on his website at http://www.montelshow.com (all websites visited July 30, 2006).

107. Examples of programs on *The Oprah Winfrey Show* were taken from descriptions on her website, "Show Archive," 2006, at http://www.oprah.com (visited July 30, 2006).

108. Examples of interviews on *The Ellen DeGeneres Show* were taken from listings provided on her website at http://ellen.warnerbros.com (visited July 30, 2006).

109. Examples of interviews on *The View* were taken from listings provided on its website at http://abc.go.com/daytime/theview (visited July 30, 2006).

110. The Oprahfication of the Mind concept was not developed as a personal criticism of or as a personal attack on Oprah Winfrey. We view *The Oprah Winfrey Show* as the highest-profile contemporary example of many TV entertainment programs organized around a news-like format based on the formula "keep it light, keep it bright, keep it moving!" The purpose of Oprah's show and others like it is to attract and entertain large TV audiences with the "right demographics" so as to maximize profits for the firms that produce the programs and those that advertise on them. There is nothing wrong with entertainment (we're for it!), but when shows like Oprah focus on "serious" topics (like class or race), the treatment is necessarily superficial and often includes a touch of glamour. The end result is that viewers are often entertained, but they are also encouraged to feel as if they've been informed, which we believe is rarely the case in any meaningful sense of the term. Oprah's show, and many others, reflect institutional imperatives of the commercial media which, among others, are to generate large profits and produce content that does not in any serious way question, challenge, or threaten the economic, political, and cultural status quo. Oprahfication is an insidious media-induced process whereby viewers are encouraged to believe that by viewing Oprah-like shows they are being informed, when in fact they are simply being entertained, bedazzled, beguiled, and, ultimately, pacified. (For an example, see the chapter 2 box, "Class Issues in the Media: The American Dream.")

111. Ronald Dahl, "Burned Out and Bored," *Newsweek* (December 15, 1997): 18; McChesney and Foster, "The Commercial Tidal Wave," 10.

112. For further information on these and other topics, see various issues of *Too Much*, edited by Sam Pizzigati, especially in 2005, 2006, and 2007. The issue of CEOs and other corporate executives' "backdating" stock options to maximize their returns emerged in the mid-2000s. One study estimated that some eight hundred fifty American CEOs "had their options backdated to make the 'current' price the lowest monthly price of their company shares. This manipulation stuffed, on average, an extra $1.3 to $1.7 million into executive pockets." Sam Pizzigati, "Greed at a Glance: Peacock Party Time," *Too Much* (November 27, 2006): 2.

113. Steve Rendall and Anna Kosseff, "Are Progressive Views Unpopular?" *Extra!* (September–October 2004): 19.

114. David Sirota, "Debunking 'Centrism,'" *Nation* (January 3, 2005): 18.

115. The Pew Research Center, "Public Sours on Government and Business."

116. Jessica Clark, "In Politics, Comedy Is Central," *In These Times* (August 2006): 38–39; Devin Gordon, "Turning Fake News into Real Careers," *Newsweek* (February 13, 2006): 57; Marc Peyser, "Red, White and Funny," *Newsweek* (December 29, 2003–January 5, 2004): 70–77; Marc Peyser, "The Truthiness Teller," *Newsweek* (February 13, 2006): 48–56.

117. Steve Rendall, "That's Not Funny!" *Extra!Update* (June 2006): 1.

118. Jessica Clark and Tracy Van Slyke, "Welcome to the Media Revolution," *In These Times* (July 2006): 26.

119. Jeffrey Chester, *Digital Destiny* (New York: New Press, 2007); Jeffrey Chester, "A Ten-Point Plan for Media Democracy," *Nation* (July 3, 2006): 21; Jessica Clark and Tracy Van Slyke, "Welcome to the Media Revolution," 20–27; Robert W. McChesney, "A Cornerstone of the Media Reform Movement," *Extra!* (January–February 2006): 6–9; Robert W. McChesney, "The Escalating War against Corporate Media," *Monthly Review* (March 2004): 1–29; Robert W. McChesney, Russell Newman, and Ben Scott, eds., *The Future of Media: Resistance and Reform in the 21st Century* (New York: Seven Stories Press, 2005); "The National Entertainment State: Special Issue," *Nation* (July 3, 2006): 13–30.

120. Two examples of programs openly critical at times of corporate and elite-class power were produced by Michael Moore. During the 1994 (NBC) and 1995 (FOX) summer seasons, Moore's *TV Nation* garnered high ratings and won awards while often featuring entertaining reports that were critical of class inequalities and privileged-class interests. The series was canceled, but Moore later returned with another show, *The Awful Truth*. Broadcast on the Bravo cable channel, this program was similar in style and content to *TV Nation*, but it too disappeared after two seasons (1999–2000). See Miranda Spencer, "TV Nation: A Show for 'The Rest of Us,'" *Extra!* (November–December 1995): 24–25.

8

Class in the Twenty-first Century: Consolidation and Resistance

> Uninformed and misinformed; pauperized or over-worked; misled or be-
> trayed by their leaders—financial, industrial, political and ecclesiastical, the
> people are suspicious, weary, and very, very busy, but they are, nonetheless,
> the first, last, and best appeal in all great human cases. . . . And, though each
> individual in the great crowd lacks some virtues, they all together have what
> no individual has, a combination of all the virtues.
>
> —Lincoln Steffens, *Upbuilders*, 1909

The stories of Forrest Gump and Jim Farley in chapter 1 of this volume focus attention on the intersection of social class and the American Dream. One shines
as idealized fiction; the other illustrates the darkest side of reality, where privileged-class interests and power doom the dream to failure. There is no doubt
which story is more popular. Grossing more than $679 million worldwide
since its release in 1994,[1] *Forrest Gump* is the American Dream personified—its
main character is the classic underdog achiever. But there's more. *Forrest Gump*
also represents another important side of the American Dream: a commitment
to the values of family, friends, community, and conscience.[2] The absence of
those qualities in the hard-edged corporate boardrooms dominating the new
class system of Jim Farley's world helped seal his fate. And Farley's economic
free fall was not broken by a resilient social safety net. Despite popular enthusiasm for the sentimental Gump-like values of mutual compassion and shared
sacrifices, these qualities are largely missing in action when it comes to providing meaningful assistance to the Jim Farleys of today's new working class. The
chilling fact is that the downward mobility of Farley and millions like him actually serves the interests (at least in the short run) of those in the privileged
class in the top diamond of the new class society.

Since chapter 1, we have tracked the contours and exposed the dark side of the new class society. From Jim Farley to the global economy and back to the culture industry, we have documented the corrosive effects of this system on the American Dream. And we have also tracked the processes by which privileged-class advantages have been ever more tightly institutionalized and legitimated. Our travels have taken us from *Forrest Gump* to the taboo land of class analysis, where the strange but vaguely familiar forms of icebergs, global sweatshops, invisible empires, stealth industries, classroom tracks, and pacification schemes cast dark shadows on the future.

So, is it possible to transform the emerging new class society that doomed Jim Farley into a more open and equitable structure? Is an American class system possible that accommodates both sides of the dream: opportunities for Gump-like underdog achievement and a shared, institutionally based commitment to the values of mutual respect, support, and community? Is an American society possible where the needs of the many (the new working class) outweigh the power of the few (the privileged class)? Can we have a class structure with a human face? The current economic, political, and cultural landscape does not appear to favor any major transformations of the new class society toward a more equitable system. But lessons from the past, as well as recent stirrings within the alternative power networks, suggest some tantalizing possibilities.

In this final chapter, we consider the prospects for continuity and change in the new class society through—with apologies to Charles Dickens—a kind of *Christmas Carol*-like set of present, past, and future themes. The section titled "Reality Check of the Present" underscores the current imbalances in class power resources and reminds us how and why the structures of institutional capitalism, racism, sexism, and classism reinforce the new class society. In the "Past as Prologue?" section, we revisit the class-based foundations of the American underdog tradition by recalling those historical moments when working-class Americans forged populist movements to contest the power of the privileged class.

In the "Future of Class Inequalities" section of this chapter, we address four future-oriented topics. We begin with a subsection on consolidation that considers how the struggles between the privileged class and the new working class on issues related to investment, consumption, and social and skill capital—resources at the heart of the new class society—are likely to continue to unfold as we move deeper into the twenty-first century. Our assessment is based on the expectation that privileged-class leaders will continue to pursue policies related to these forms of capital that will further consolidate and reinforce privileged-class dominance.

The subsection on resistance consists of selected examples from what we see as current class-reform activist organizations committed to reversing the increasing economic, political, and cultural inequalities of the new class society. Although many groups are part of the alternative power network working for change, our selections are limited to six cases. They were chosen because of their shared concerns with structural reforms that unite economic, political, and cultural strands of change. Also, we see them as strikingly reminiscent of the American populist tradition in terms of their goals and the language and imagery they use in critiquing current class inequalities.

The third subsection, "Beneath the Waterline," focuses on militant resistance. Here we briefly explore the links between growing class inequalities, the expansion of powerful organizations supporting privileged-class interests, and militant forms of resistance to these developments by individuals and groups, including the use of violence. In the fourth subsection, we contrast the "Scrooge scenario" for reform favored by privileged-class leaders with the populist "structural democracy scenario" favored by class-reform activists. As we will see, these scenarios represent very different approaches to reforming class inequities, with the former emphasizing the importance of individual conscience and the latter emphasizing the importance of democratic participation in developing structural changes in the economic, political, and cultural arenas of American society. We close the chapter with a box titled "Class Issues in the Media: A New American Dream?" Here we consider some ideas and reforms that might provide opportunities for the working class to realize a new American Dream.

REALITY CHECK OF THE PRESENT

If class warfare is being waged in America, my class is clearly winning.

—Warren E. Buffett, Chairman's Letter to
Shareholders of Berkshire Hathaway, 2003

In the mid- and latter 2000s, it was clear that superclass "suits" (organizational elites typically sporting expensively tailored business suits) rule. But not in the old, easy-to-spot and deflate autocratic, robber-baron style. As we have seen, more and more, superclass "suits" affect a common touch—dressed-down, casual, and media savvy—with credentialed-class coaching and backup as needed. We're all in this together, we are told. The message in the new class society is that social class (especially privileged-class origin) does not count in the competition for success. Class divisions are passé. Knowledge, high-tech skills, being a team player, and having a positive mental attitude, we are told, are the keys to success today. But are they?

The analysis of class relations in this book suggests that the balance of class power has shifted decidedly to the privileged class. For the past thirty years, starting in the mid-1970s, this class has been able to accumulate ever greater shares of income and wealth at the expense of the new working class. As we have seen, privileged-class dominance has been achieved by attacking workers' jobs and wages and by reducing spending on social programs, thereby requiring working-class members to pay more for their health care, education, housing, and retirement.

The consequences of thirty years of class warfare by the privileged against the new working class are revealed almost daily in the increasing polarization of social and economic conditions between the top 20 percent of society and the bottom 80 percent. Corporate profits for the five hundred largest industrial and service companies totaled $610 billion in 2005, up 18.8 percent compared to 2004. Revenues for the top five hundred firms totaled $9.1 trillion in 2005, a 10.2 percent increase over 2004.[3] The continued growth of both revenues and profits in 2005 among Fortune 500 firms occurred while total U.S. employment in these firms remained essentially flat for the year, and 286 of Fortune 1000 firms reported employment reductions compared to 2004.[4]

While revenues and profits for the largest firms increased and as CEO compensation levels soared in the mid- and latter 2000s, most workers did not share in the prosperity bounty enjoyed by the privileged class. Instead, as we pointed out in earlier chapters, many workers experienced stagnant or declining real wages. The only increases many workers experienced involved longer hours and a faster work pace. Meanwhile, large firms benefited from lower taxes on corporate revenues and less government oversight of environmental pollution and workplace health and safety. These seemingly obvious class inequalities become much less obvious after being filtered through the information industry and other powerful institutionalized forces. The filtering processes disguise privileged-class-biased corporate practices and government policies. And they legitimate the transfer of increasing shares of all capital forms—investment, consumption, skill, and social—to those in the top tier of the new class system at the expense of those in the bottom tier.

The shift of wealth and power to the privileged class has been justified, in part, by the powerful ideology of "free market fundamentalism" applied to the new global economy. This idea system, termed *neoliberalism*, is often cleverly framed in the language, symbols, and imagery associated with personal freedom and liberty.[5] Messages heralding globalized free trade as the path to liberation from the limitations and narrow constraints of the parochial past are continually communicated to national and international audiences, especially through the mass media. These ideas focus public attention on the need for American businesses and workers to accommodate new competitive forces in the global economy (e.g., workers who will work harder for less money and corporations that can invest more because governments tax and regulate them less). And the threat of global competition has been used over and over again to justify the economic changes that have led to the new class society. Superclass and credentialed-class corporate executives, politicians, media moguls, and policy experts have used the free market, global economy mantra in the same way that the specter of international communism was used to justify repressive domestic political policies in the 1950s and 1960s. The geopolitical threat of communism has been transformed into the geo-economic threat of global competition, which has been both created and managed by institutional capitalism.

Institutional Capitalism and Privileged-Class Dominance

The ability of the privileged class to devise, disguise, and legitimate corporate practices and government policies that serve its interests, but are destructive to working-class interests, is reinforced by several structures described earlier in this book. These class-biased structures and outcomes are typically both part of, and also facilitated by, the deeply embedded economic, political, and cultural power of institutional capitalism. This concept refers to the inter-corporate-network model of business described in chapter 2, as opposed to earlier forms of family or managerial capitalism.[6] It involves large, often multinational firms linked by numerous interlocks of directors who serve on several corporate boards at the same time. And it is driven by the impersonal principles of profit maximization, capital accumulation (especially through increases in corporate stock values), and the necessity of access to capital funds (to finance operations, mergers, and expansions). It is an institutionalized force of staggering size and power dominated by and serving privileged-class interests.

Under this system, investment, worker pay, promotion, security, and production policies of interlocked firms are dictated by how such policies can best serve the impersonal principles that drive the system, especially profit maximization. High profits maximize corporate access to capital pools controlled by investment firms and satisfy large individual and institutional shareholders' demands for the highest possible investment returns and for steady increases in the share values of the stock they hold. As the dominant form of business organization in the United States today, institutional capitalism drives the core sector of the economy and creates smaller firms in the periphery to service core needs. The result is a small number of core firms with superclass owners, major stockholders, and elite corporate managers, a relatively small number of highly paid credentialed-class positions, a shrinking number of middle-income blue-collar jobs, and expanding numbers of poorly paid positions in peripheral firms occupied by larger and larger numbers of new-working-class members.

Institutional capitalism was made possible in part by the legal standing accorded to corporations by shifts in laws governing the corporate chartering process and by the landmark 1886 U.S. Supreme Court case of *Santa Clara County v. Southern Pacific Railroad*. In that case, the Court invoked the Fourteenth Amendment and "defined corporations as 'persons' and ruled that California could not tax corporations differently than individuals."[7] The effect of this decision, which was made by the Court without hearing any formal arguments, conferred upon corporations the same legal rights and constitutional guarantees enjoyed by natural persons.[8] The extension of personlike legal rights and protections to corporations, combined with their huge resources (even by 1886 standards), created an enormous power asymmetry between corporations and people in the American legal system and in the society generally. The social dangers posed by expanding corporations' power and their potential to dominate all other social institutions were noted well before the 1886 case—by Abraham Lincoln. In an 1864 letter he warned that "as a result of the war, corporations have been enthroned and an era of corruption in high places will follow . . . until all wealth is aggregated in a few hands and the Republic is destroyed."[9]

One important result of institutional capitalism today is that the basic business practices guiding, and the ideological premises underlying, large U.S. corporations have spread to and infused the routine structures, policies, and practices of nearly all large-scale organizations in the society.[10] This includes government agencies, universities, schools, and even charities and churches. As massive corporations (and other types of large bureaucracies) have emerged (and merged) gradually over time, they have become an integral part of our collective experiences. Because they have such a pervasive physical presence and are often associated with the satisfaction of routine individual and social needs, it is hard to imagine how economic, political, and cultural activities—indeed, even society itself—could exist without large corporations and similarly structured nonbusiness organizations. The huge organizations located in the economy and in the political and cultural arenas have become so much a part of the routine social landscape that they seem as natural as mountains, forests, rivers, and streams.

With multiple financial, personnel, and ideological links to other large organizations (e.g., government bureaucracies, universities, churches), large corporations populate and dominate the national economy, politics, popular culture, local communities, and how most people think about the new class society.[11] One example illustrating the penetration of American culture by ubiquitous corporations and the ideology and imagery associated with them is the increasing application of the business term *bottom line* to a variety of nonbusiness topics and activities. It has become a shorthand metaphor for the core or most critical feature of almost any activity or topic, such as personal health, family life, sex, movies, politics, drug use, and many others.

Institutional capitalism is a powerful and pervasive organizational force field. It dominates the economic, political, and cultural arenas, shapes ideas and perceptions on a wide array of nonbusiness activities, and helps conceal the power of large corporations in creating, maintaining, and legitimating the new class system. But the hegemonic dominance of institutional capitalism in American society is rendered invisible by its saturation of the total social environment.

Many activities of the large organizations that make up, serve, and legitimate institutional capitalism are organized around, and guided by, a wide range of routine business policies and personnel practices that can be described as "institutionalized." This simply means that the typically unquestioned and taken-for-granted assumptions, policies, and practices governing how privileged-class owners and managers attempt to achieve what they believe are optimal organizational outcomes (which serve privileged-class interests) are built into the routine structures and operations of organizations. We view institutionalized practices concerning how stockholders, employees, clients, customers, or students are routinely treated by organizations as reflecting, in part, traditional cultural norms, as well as economic, political, and cultural interests of the privileged class. Thus, from our perspective, institutionalized policies and practices facilitate preferential treatment by resource-rich organizations for members of the privileged class and at the same time reinforce organizationally based forms of discrimination (often subtle) against, and marginalization of, groups not typically found in the privileged class (i.e., people of color, women, and members of the working class). We term the organizationally based practices that generate such outcomes as institutional racism, sexism, and classism.

Institutional Racism, Sexism, and Privileged-Class Dominance

Embedded in the history and culture of the United States are a set of beliefs, practices, and social structures that can be called institutional racism and sexism. Racism and sexism are based on beliefs that link the physical characteristics of a group—African Americans or women—to a set of psychological and behavioral characteristics that are judged to be inferior to those of other groups.[12] This is ideological racism and sexism, which, when combined with the policies and practices of businesses, schools, media, and other organizations, becomes institutional racism and sexism, a principle of social domination by which groups seen as inferior are exploited economically and oppressed socially and physically. This principle of domination is carried out in schools that fail to provide equal preparation for students of color and women to assume leadership roles in their communities and workplaces, it is reflected in the mass media that either exclude oppressed groups or depict them in unrealistic and demeaning ways, and it is revealed in organizational structures that do not provide all their employees with job ladders and opportunities to learn and grow.

The privileged class benefits from institutional racism and sexism in two ways. The first involves direct benefits associated with the ability to discriminate against blacks and women in employment and wages.[13] Privileged-class employers can reduce labor costs by paying lower wages, denying insurance and pension benefits, and using part-time workers. Of course, privileged-class employers do not view their decisions in the area of wages and benefits as being based on ideological racism or sexism. Most would probably deny any prejudicial beliefs regarding blacks or women. Rather, their decisions would be explained on the basis of the educational background and experience that black or women employees bring to their job. As employers who must be in-terested in maximizing productivity and minimizing costs, they will take ad-vantage of available opportunities, regardless of whether doing so results in a segregated workforce or the employment of vulnerable workers.

The indirect benefits to the privileged class can be traced to the more wide-spread and subtle forms of ideological racism or sexism found in the larger population. Although only a small proportion of Americans would endorse blatant racist or sexist statements ("Women are mentally inferior to men"), a much larger proportion are inclined to believe that racism and sexism are things of the past—that blacks should recognize that they won the civil rights revolution, and women should acknowledge that they have "come a long way, baby!" Believing in the existence of major gains for blacks and women, many Americans now feel that continuing to enforce affirmative action policies only serves to give African Americans and women an unfair advantage. The exis-tence of subtle racism and sexism enables privileged-class employers to ex-clude blacks and women from certain jobs because of the opposition to them by coworkers or customers. Employers also use the employment of blacks and women, or the threat of it, as a way to keep downward pressure on wages and to stifle discontent among white male workers.

Ideological racism may give even the poorest working-class whites the psy-chological gains that may come from feeling superior to others, and ideologi-cal sexism may give working-class men validation of their masculinity when they can exclude women from their jobs and exert control in the home. But in-stitutional racism and sexism are about economic and political power. When the privileged-class Democrats and Republicans in Congress and the White House developed their color-coded attack on welfare, they were also attacking the much larger number of poor whites who also receive welfare, but that fact was never discussed. When privileged-class parents join politicians to fight against efforts at the state level to provide equality in per-pupil expenditures for all schools, it is always a color-coded event. That is, it is presented as a way to improve inner-city schools and create equity between whites and blacks, when in fact there are more poor white children in resource-poor schools in rural and urban America. The debates are color-coded to ensure their defeat, but the true battle is about the privileged class's maintaining its economic and political power. As long as the focus stays on race, the welfare mothers and the inner-city kids will be seen as "victims" of racism and poverty but never as ca-sualties in a class-based struggle.

Institutional Classism and Privileged-Class Dominance

Institutional classism is another abstract label for a powerful, but hidden, force field that also helps reinforce and disguise privileged-class interests. At a general level, classism refers to the unspoken, but widely accepted, belief in American society that the values, social behavior, language patterns, and lifestyles of the privileged class are superior to those of the working class or the lower class.[14] Compared with racism, sexism, or even ageism, classism is largely a silent, hidden "ism"—partly because of the taboo nature of class in America. But classism is similar to racism and sexism in terms of its effects. It leads to prejudice toward, stereotyping of, and discrimination against members of the nonprivileged class, especially those in the lower segments of the working class. *White trash, redneck, trailer park lowlife, welfare bum,* and *slacker* are only a few of the many pejorative terms applied to groups clustered in the lower segments of the new class system.[15]

Classism is based on, and justified by, a widely shared belief system sometimes called the ideology of meritocracy.[16] This idea system views class location as a reflection of talent and effort. It encourages the view that privileged-class positions are occupied by people who possess widely valued and admired traits, such as high intelligence, achievement motivation, and altruism. It also encourages viewing members of the new working class (especially those at the lowest levels) as being justly placed in lower ranks because they obviously lack the valued qualities necessary to "succeed" in a merit-based economic system. The ideology of meritocracy helps justify and legitimate class inequalities by making class divisions seem naturally ordained and views those at the top as rare and gifted visionaries. This is obviously what billionaire John D. Rockefeller Sr. had in mind when he said, "I believe the power to make money is a gift of God. . . . Having been endowed with the gift I possess, I believe it is my duty to make money and still more money, and to use the money I make for the good of my fellow man according to the dictates of my conscience."[17]

Like racism and sexism, classism is embedded, or institutionalized, in the routine practices and policies of organizations dominated by privileged-class members, such as corporations, government, the mass media, public schools, the criminal justice system, and universities. As a result, the operations of nearly the entire organizational establishment of the society trend in directions that exclude, disadvantage, or otherwise marginalize people from the lower classes through everyday routine (but largely unrecognized) practices. Institutional classism refers to a form of hegemony whereby privileged-class-based ideas, values, norms, language styles, and social behaviors prevail in organizations dominated by this class. From schools to the workplace to government, the gatekeepers in privileged-class-controlled organizations actively screen out or marginalize working-class-based values, norms, language styles, and behaviors.

Such gatekeeping practices were evident in a recent study illustrating how Harvard law students "afflicted" with the stigma of working-class origins were subtly (but powerfully) encouraged to disguise this fact. In addition to their classroom work, they learned the importance of distancing themselves from the working-class stigma, as well as how to do it. This was necessary to increase their chances of being selected to join elite law firms and thereby maximize their own career opportunities. The acceptance of these students by privileged-class "organizational masters" in elite law firms required them to demonstrate an easy familiarity with elite cultural codes and conform to the cultural standards, social behaviors, style of dress, and patterns of speech of the privileged class.[18]

The hidden power of privileged-class communication styles illustrates yet another dimension of institutional classism. Teachers and professors in public schools and universities, especially those serving students where many already possess advanced levels of social capital, actively discourage working-class students from communicating in the language styles of their class and penalize their grades if they persist. The same pattern extends to hirings and promotions in the workplace, especially for positions above entry-level ranks, and to the conferring of legitimacy to political candidates by the mainstream media. The "elaborated code," encompassing more abstract conceptual references and complex sentences, routinely structures communication (written and spoken) among members of the privileged class.[19] As a kind of "gold standard," it is the only legitimate communication style or mode of expression accepted or rewarded in classrooms, boardrooms, and the formal political and policy-making arenas.

Hidden class-linked advantages or disadvantages associated with privileged-class gatekeeping practices and with the class-based hegemony of the elaborated code as a communication style are seldom noted or explored by social scientists, media commentators, or social pundits. In fact, the details of these phenomena are virtually unknown to the public. The placement of workers in advanced entry-level career positions, as well as the pace of later career advancement, are typically explained in mainstream academic research or in mass media profiles of "successful people" as functions of merit and talent and not as the result of class-biased gatekeeping practices. Similarly, the differential mastery by students of "proper" communication styles and forms (the elaborated code) is typically viewed as an indicator of merit and talent and not as the result of the advantages or disadvantages associated with privileged- versus working-class origins and experiences.

Some features of privileged-class advantages are informally recognized among segments of the population, as in the commonly circulated aphorism (among the working class) concerning the basis of career success: "It's not what you know, but who you know." This statement reflects a kind of cynical realism among members of the working class, but it is obviously overly simplistic and misses the hidden institutional basis of privileged-class advantages.

As tips of the class-inequalities iceberg, privileged-class gatekeeping practices and rewards for mastery of the elaborated code are but two examples of the myriad ways by which class-biased organizational routines, policies, and practices perpetuate privileged-class interests. They are only two of the many covert threads woven into the fabric of institutional classism. Their powerful presence as sifting and sorting instruments helps make the common economic, political, and cultural successes (and rare failures) of privileged-class offspring, as well as the common failures and rare successes of working-class children within privileged-class-controlled organizations, seem to be "fair" and "impartial" outcomes.

Our reality check of the present leads us to conclude that institutional capitalism and the related institutionalized patterns and practices of racism, sexism, and classism are powerful structures that reinforce the new class society in both obvious and subtle ways. Moreover, these structures are themselves embedded in the dominant power networks that span the economic, political, and cultural arenas of social life. As we have seen, the deeply entrenched force field of institutional capitalism generates an unequal hierarchy of class-based positions, rewards, and relationships. At the same time, the class-based inequalities produced by this system are reinforced and replicated by institutional racism, sexism, and classism. The ideology of classism is particularly potent in that it encourages viewing unequal class outcomes as legitimate, natural, and even inevitable or desirable by large numbers of people in all classes. Thus, racism, sexism, and classism as institutionalized structures help to perpetuate and reinforce, while also disguising, a variety of hidden privileged-class advantages and working-class disadvantages.

THE PAST AS PROLOGUE?

> We meet in the midst of a nation brought to the verge of moral, political, and material ruin. Corruption dominates the ballot box, the legislatures, [and] the Congress. . . . The newspapers are subsidized or muzzled. . . . The fruits of the toil of millions are stolen to build up colossal fortunes. . . . From the same prolific womb of governmental injustice we breed two classes—paupers and millionaires.
>
> —Preamble to the 1892 People's Party National Platform, cited in Howard Zinn, *A People's History of the United States*, 1980

How long can the intensifying inequalities between the privileged class and the new working class continue? That's akin to asking, how long can CEO pay keep going up? A typical headline from the mid-2000s announced, "CEO Pay Soars in 2005 as a Select Group Break the $100 Million Mark."[20] It may *appear* as if CEO pay will continue to soar in the future, but economic scholars Emmanuel Saez and Thomas Piketty analyzed the top 1 percent income group (which today includes most CEOs) in the United States over time and found that "the rich have not always been getting richer compared to everyone else." These researchers found the top 1 percent income group experienced "enormous fluctuations over the last century."[21] The point here is that history, including even the history of income shares received by the rich, does not move in a straight line over time. Thus, the answer to the question of how long class inequalities will continue to widen is obvious: not forever and maybe not even for much longer. The historical record of inequalities (and of most human conditions) indicates fluctuations are more common than straight lines.

So, what are the prospects that significant political or social movements will develop to alter the current imbalance of power that exists between the two great opposing classes in the double diamond? To avoid utopian visions or fantasies driven by hopes or dreams more than by reality, we look first to America's past. We focus on those times when the forces for change converged on a single project—to change the structure of society in order to reduce economic and social inequalities. Popular movements for change have gone by many labels, but "American populism" has endured as a common frame of reference describing many movements from the past aimed at reducing material inequalities. The next section considers lessons from the American populist tradition and provides a context for understanding contemporary reform projects aimed at reshaping the new class society.

Breaking the Taboo: The Recent Past

As we pointed out in the chapter 4 box reading, populist appeals have surfaced in past as well as in recent national political campaigns. Candidates make use of populist appeals in various political circumstances. For example, growing economic inequality and uncertainty, especially when these conditions substantially impact the "middle class," may encourage candidates to include populist messages in their campaigns. This appears to have been the case in the 2006 elections as many Democratic candidates who supported policies described as "economic populism" won their races (as we noted in chapter 2 and in the chapter 4 box). Sometimes, in close elections, candidates will invoke populist rhetoric as a means to gain an edge on their rivals. (To some extent, this seems to have been the case with James Webb and Claire McCaskill, 2006 Democratic winners of very close U.S. Senate elections in Virginia and Missouri.) On other occasions, underdog candidates seeking to attract new voters will strike a populist chord to see if, and how, it takes. In the rare instances of a third-party candidate for the presidency, the basis for that candidacy is often a populist appeal to those who have been "left out" of the political system, urging them to "take back their government."

Despite the potential political value of populist appeals to candidates, such appeals may be viewed as "risky" by candidates concerned with appearing to violate the "class taboo." This appears to have been the case in the 2004 presidential election. As we noted in the chapter 4 box reading, populist messages were largely missing from the campaigns conducted by John Kerry and George W. Bush in 2004, despite the fact that the race was very close. However, in the even tighter 2000 presidential campaign, Al Gore, the democratic nominee, made several efforts to reach working-class voters (without calling them working class). In his convention speech, Gore said he was on the side of "working families" and against "powerful forces and powerful interests." This was a kind of veiled populism by a candidate who was not sure how far to push the theme. In contrast, Ralph Nader, the 2000 and 2004 third-party candidate, presented in each election an explicit progressive populist message that stressed "big money" control over both major parties and highlighted their similarities by referring to them as "Demopubs" and "Republicrats."

The 1996 Republican Party primary provided another example of populist rhetoric, but then it was "reactionary populism." Pat Buchanan was a long-shot outsider who desperately wanted to defeat front-runner Senator Bob Dole, long-time member of, and apologist for, the privileged class. Buchanan knew that in order to have any chance to win his party's presidential nomination, he would have to appeal to working-class Americans who might not usually vote in a primary or even in the general election. Perhaps thinking like his old mentor, Richard Nixon, Buchanan must have thought, How can I appeal to this "silent majority"? How can I mobilize them to vote for me and not for Bob Dole? The answer must have come to him as an epiphany: with a laserlike grasp of reality, he took the extraordinary step (for a politician) of telling the truth. His sound bites at times took on an almost Marxist tone of class analysis: "When AT&T lops off 40,000 jobs, the executioner that did it makes $5 million a year and AT&T stock soars." "Mr. Dole put the interests of the big banks—Citibank, Chase Manhattan, Goldman Sachs—ahead of the American People." "The voiceless men and women in this country have no one to represent them in Washington because the hierarchy of both parties really argues on behalf of these trade deals, which are often done for the benefit of corporations who shut their factories and move them overseas."[22] In a New Hampshire primary stump speech, Buchanan made a rambling allusion to earlier times when revolutionary fervor led the masses to attack elites and take what was rightfully theirs: "'You watch the establishment,' he urged supporters. . . . 'All the knights and barons will be riding into the castle and pulling up the drawbridge, because they're coming. All the peasants are coming with pitchforks after them.'"[23]

High-profile, populist-like rhetoric, especially in presidential campaigns, usually sends shock waves through the privileged class and creates a stir in both political parties. We saw evidence of such reactions in the 2004, 2000, and 1996 elections. In 2000, mainstream media pundits and prominent spokespersons of both political parties denounced Gore's convention speech as "class warfare." Even more strident were attacks by the same groups against Nader in 2000 and 2004 that challenged the legitimacy of his candidacy because he insisted on using "class-warfare" rhetoric. In 1996, the same establishment pundits moved quickly to defuse the class content of Buchanan's campaign and dissipate the emerging discussion of corporate profits and greed—without mentioning the superclass or its interests.

As we noted in chapter 2 and in the chapter 5 box reading, the *New York Times*, in its role as premier dominator of the mainstream ideological process, further defused and obfuscated the issues of conflicting class interests and class power inequalities when it published its multipart "Class Matters" series in 2005. Although the *Times* acknowledged some of the human costs associated with growing economic inequalities, the series' basic spin presented class differences as interesting and inequalities as manageable through individual efforts and modest public policy reforms. This effort, and the others like it, effectively kept the class genie in the bottle and ensured that mainstream public discussions of class power inequalities remained verboten.

Breaking the Taboo: Lessons from History

What political candidates like the Democrats who ran on "economic populism" in 2006 or presidential hopefuls from the past like Gore, Nader, and Buchanan do when they weigh in against superclass and corporate power is not new in American history. The wealthy and powerful, in the form of corporate executives, bankers, politicians, and bureaucrats, have often served as high-profile targets of criticism by individuals and groups attempting to mobilize discontented Americans for change. Historical movements condemning elite-class excesses and promoting working-class reforms have often juxtaposed obvious and easily understood class contrasts by using terms such as the *haves* versus the *have-nots,* the *powerful* versus the *powerless,* and the *fat cats* versus the *common man.* Such references have often served as the images and language of American populism. This historical tradition of protest calling for reforms to reduce economic and social inequities has periodically emerged from the class-based grievances of the working-class majority.

Populist rhetoric has been used by numerous labor organizers, social movement leaders, and even, at times, mainstream politicians to shape and mobilize public discontent. In its classic form, populist messages seek to simultaneously elevate the masses and attack the privileged for their undeserved rewards. When the People's Party was formed in 1892, it pulled together debt-ridden small farmers, hundreds of discontented workers' groups, and several minor parties—all of whom were deeply dissatisfied with how the Democrats and Republicans had been running the country. More than a century ago, leaders of the People's Party praised the virtuous small farmers and laborers as the "producers" who created national prosperity that rightfully belonged to all Americans and heaped scorn on the "plutocrats," "parasites," and "moneyed aristocracy" who were said to wallow in idleness, extravagance, and waste. The use of sharply contrasting class-based images was a central feature of the populist message. As a noted historian of this tradition recently observed, "[Populism is] a language whose speakers conceive of ordinary people as a noble assemblage not bounded narrowly by class, view their elite opponents as self-serving, and seek to mobilize the former against the latter."[24]

The populist social movements of the nineteenth century were grounded in a rhetoric and ideology based on economic grievances and a defense of those who worked as small farmers, wage earners, and small-business people. But populist attacks on corporations, monopoly, and plutocrats were not aimed at the overthrow of capitalism. Rather, the populist reform message called for greater recognition of the importance of the common man in the economic, political, and social arenas and for a fair share of the fruits of workers' productive labor to be returned to these producers of wealth. The relatively modest scope of the populist reform agenda is underscored by author Michael Kazin's point that "through populism Americans have been able to protest social and economic inequalities without calling the entire system into question."[25] Kazin also argues that early populist critiques of American society attempted to build new bonds among people by returning to the core beliefs of the new American nation—rule by the people, reward for hard work and diligence, and faith in God.

The early moments of populism experienced through the People's Party at the end of the nineteenth century found expression in the twentieth century in different bases of discontent shared by widely varied groups. Throughout the twentieth century, populist rhetoric and movements have embraced an array of moral crusades. They began early in the century with the prohibitionists' war against alcohol and closed out the century with the religious Right's attacks on the amoral elites, who, it was claimed, were undermining the core values of the majority. Thus, American populism began the century as a left-liberal tradition aimed at attacking economic, political, and social privileges and inequalities but was later transformed and diverted into conservative forms of moral protest aimed primarily at defending the values of the "moral majority." The targets of populist attacks are superficially the same at both ends of the century: entrenched, irresponsible elites. But for early leftist populists, elite targets were symbolized by "fat cat" and "plutocrat" labels, whereas for contemporary rightist populists, evil is represented by "cultural elites" (as in Hollywood, the media, and "San Francisco values") and by governmental elites who administer the growing bureaucratic state.[26]

As history illustrates, the American populist tradition has been both a powerful and an ambivalent instrument for reform. Many real or aspiring leaders have picked up the populist instrument hoping to play a tune powerful enough to stir the sleeping masses into sweeping away corrupt elites. The power of that tradition rests with its roots in the early American experience, stressing the dignity of the common man and a rejection of the "foreign" influences of aristocracy and elitism. This thread of populism can serve as a bond unifying people to act on behalf of the common good while eschewing privilege and unfair advantage. The ambivalence associated with the populist tradition stems from its majoritarian beliefs, reflected in the support for direct participatory democracy. The majoritarian emphasis does not sit well with members of religious or ethnic groups that are numerically small and therefore feel that their interests will be ignored by the usually white and Christian majority. The majoritarian emphasis also does not sit well with "privileged leftists" who support populist ideology but whose education and credentialed-class privileges make them wary of "marching with the people."

The ambivalence of the populist tradition is partly responsible for the liberal Left's movement into identity movements and identity politics while seeking to give coequal standing to the three major oppressions of class, race, and gender—which still excludes environmentalists, gays, the disabled, the aged, and numerous other groups with specific forms of grievances. The challenge facing the new-working-class majority in the United States involves finding ways to invoke the sentiment opposing privileged-class power of the populist tradition in ways that join the current disparate collection of disaffected groups, movements, and parties into a unified political movement. Only through unity can the new working class pool the modest organizational and personal resources its members possess into a substantial collective force for change, as in the aphorism of the hand and power: each finger is only a modest force, but five fingers united transform the hand into a powerful fist.

THE FUTURE OF CLASS INEQUALITIES

The short term victory in capturing virtually all of the growth of wealth and income while shedding tax obligations may seem like cause for jubilation—at least within some circles—but this victory may turn out to be hollow, even for those at the top of the pyramid.

—Michael Perelman, *Monthly Review,* July–August 2006

Having recounted the past, what is the future of the new class society? We believe there is no single future. Rather, there are many possible futures. The future of class inequalities depends upon the extent to which the trends presented in the following three subsections develop and unfold in the twenty-first century. It is likely that the consolidation trend will be powerful and difficult to change. We expect that privileged-class leaders will make every effort to pursue policies concerning investment, consumption, social, and skill capital that will consolidate and reinforce privileged-class dominance.

On the other hand, it is also likely that the current resistance trend to privileged-class policies that are increasing economic, political, and cultural inequities of the new class society will continue and grow. The growth of organized resistance to class inequalities may be one of the most encouraging stories (for the new working class) of the twenty-first century. Some of the groups involved in these struggles echo the American populist tradition in terms of their goals, language, and the images they use in critiquing unfair privileged-class advantages and class inequalities.

If the future does include reforms in the new class system, their substance will be critical to any meaningful changes in class inequities. Possibilities range from superficial and cosmetic to substantial and structural reforms. The final subsection, "The Scrooge Scenario versus the Structural Scenario," considers this issue.

The Future: Consolidation

> The attacks on middle-class jobs are lending new meaning to the phrase "class war." The ladders of upward mobility are being dismantled. America, the land of opportunity, is giving way to ever deepening polarization between rich and poor.
>
> —Paul Craig Roberts, *CounterPunch*, July 2006

One future trend about which we are certain is that of continuity in the areas of class domination and class struggle. As we move deeper into the twenty-first century, we expect the twenty million families making up the privileged class will continue to dominate virtually all of the elite decision-making positions, as well as most of the professional and managerial information-generating and decision-executing positions in the major economic, political, and cultural institutions that make up the dominant power networks.

The domination by privileged-class members of the U.S. institutional infrastructure means that in their personal and public lives, they will continue to make decisions that reflect institutional imperatives favoring an expansion of already concentrated wealth and power. These decisions can be expected to produce corporate and governmental practices and policies that disproportionately benefit privileged-class interests as against those of the working class. Thus, we expect the trend of the past thirty years, whereby ever larger shares of economic, political, and cultural resources have been shifted to the privileged class, to continue in this century. By "continue," we mean that privileged-class leaders will pursue policies aimed at consolidating the gains made by this class over the past thirty years.

When we speak of consolidation, we refer to efforts to strengthen, deepen, and extend actions and policies that are already in place. We do not refer to totally new actions or policies, such as the ongoing attempt by the privileged class to convert the Social Security system into a private insurance scheme. As privileged-class consolidation efforts unfold, the quality of life among members of the new working class can be expected to deteriorate even further. This downward spiral will continue until, and unless, organized mass political and social resistance movements emerge—akin to those of the populist era—that will represent the interests and press the claims of the working class for a redress of its shared economic and political grievances.

The following five subtopics consider how privileged-class-sponsored consolidation policies related to investment, consumption, social, and skill capital are likely to continue unfolding in the twenty-first century. In focusing on the struggles surrounding these forms of capital, we expect that, at least in the short term, privileged-class-controlled organizations in the economic, political, and cultural arenas will actively support policies that will strengthen and extend the advantages, interests, and power of this class at the expense of the new working class. We also expect that these same organizations will engage in activities aimed at concealing and legitimating corporate practices and governmental policies that shift increasing shares of all forms of capital to the privileged class at the expense of the new working class.

Investment Capital: Continued Export of U.S. Jobs

We have already discussed at length the loss of high-wage manufacturing jobs over the past thirty years. American corporations have moved production overseas or built new production facilities overseas in order to find lower-wage workers and governments that are indifferent to the security and safety of workers and protection of the environment. In chapters 3 and 4, we pointed out that the flight of U.S. capital has been greatly enhanced by the 1993 North American Free Trade Agreement (NAFTA), which many political leaders from both major parties claimed would stimulate trade between the United States, Mexico, and Canada. Although both the Democratic Clinton and Republican Bush II administrations argued that it was good for the United States, there is no doubt that NAFTA facilitated the shift of corporate production from the United States to Mexico. For example, economists estimate that during the 1994–2003 period, NAFTA led to the net loss of over nine hundred thousand U.S. jobs to Mexico.[27] More recently, in the 2001–2006 period, "U.S. manufacturing lost 2.9 million jobs, almost 17 percent of the manufacturing work force."[28] Of that number, perhaps as many as four hundred thousand to five hundred thousand jobs were shifted to Mexico; the exact number is difficult to determine.[29]

Despite mounting U.S. job losses to Mexico in the post-NAFTA period, as the 1990s ended, the Clinton administration strongly supported additional "free trade" policies that would cost more U.S. jobs. Some policy efforts failed, such as the Clinton administration's 1997 request for "fast-track authority" from Congress to expand NAFTA. But others were successful, such as President Bill Clinton's support of legislation that granted U.S. approval of permanent normal trade relations (PNTR) with China in 2000 and his support in 2000, reinforced by support from the new Bush administration, for China's subsequent entry into the World Trade Organization (WTO) in 2001.[30] President Bush continued Clinton's policy of vigorous support for trade policies that threaten U.S. jobs. A high-profile example was the Bush administration's strong support of the Central America Free Trade Agreement (CAFTA). As we noted in chapter 4, even though CAFTA was strongly opposed by labor and consumer groups, it was approved by Congress and signed by President Bush in mid-2005. CAFTA, as we noted earlier, extended "the corporate-led globalization model of NAFTA to five Central American countries and the Dominican Republic."[31]

The U.S. granting of PNTR to China, China's admission to the WTO, and the terms of CAFTA provided even more incentives for U.S. firms to shift investment capital from U.S. plants to factories in low-wage nations. Precise tracking of the U.S. "job-loss scorecard" is difficult because information concerning the numbers of U.S. jobs transferred to low-wage nations is often scattered, concealed, or not reported in a uniform fashion to government or corporate organizations that record U.S. job losses.[32] As a result, tracking U.S. job losses typically involves various organizations that collect information from a variety of sources to count, estimate, and project job losses. For example, in 2004, the AFL-CIO charged that as a result of violations of U.S. trade laws, China was responsible for the loss of 727,000 U.S. jobs. The union requested that the Bush administration apply trade sanctions against China under section 301(d) of the Trade Act, but the request was denied.[33] A report commissioned by the U.S.-China Economic and Security Review Committee estimated that in 2004, 99,000 jobs were shifted from the United States to China and 140,000 jobs were shifted from the United States to Mexico (compared to about 85,000 jobs lost to each nation in 2001).[34] While most U.S. jobs lost to Mexico and China through the mid-2000s involved manufacturing work, the report also included

Copyright © Tom Tomorrow. Reprinted with permission.

estimates of future job losses in the U.S. service sector. The report cited U.S. job tracking firms, which estimated that as many as 3.4 million U.S. service jobs will be moved "off shore" by 2015.[35] That figure may be conservative; Princeton economist and former Federal Reserve vice chairman Alan Blinder has estimated that as many as forty-two to fifty-six million U.S. service-sector jobs are susceptible to offshore outsourcing.[36]

While limitations of space prevent a detailed exploration of privileged-class campaigns in support of legislation granting China PNTR with the United States or China's admission to the WTO, behind-the-scenes support by U.S. superclass-sponsored organizations for these policies occurred and facilitated both developments. As an illustration, in the 1999–2000 period, two super-class organizations, the Business Roundtable and the U.S. Chamber of Commerce, plus several major U.S. firms, such as Boeing and Motorola, collectively "spent $113 million on lobbying, political donations, and advertising" to ensure passage of legislation in Congress granting PNTR to China.[37] Also, as we saw in chapter 4, the ultimate superclass organization, the Business Roundtable, was a major force in creating a classwide coalition that helped facilitate congressional approval of CAFTA.

The U.S. political record regarding free trade policies that threaten U.S. workers' jobs illustrates that such policies have been strongly supported by superclass-sponsored organizations and enacted into law under both Democratic and Republican administrations with bipartisan support in the Congress. Recent free trade policies implemented with support from both political parties show how U.S. trade policy is driven by superclass interests that, in turn, are grounded in and legitimated by the structures of institutional capitalism. Of course, as we noted in chapters 3 and 4 and above, the Clinton administration's efforts to extend NAFTA, its support in granting PNTR to China, and the Bush administration's powerful support for CAFTA all provoked stiff resistance from labor-led coalitions that included public interest, community, environmental, and religious groups, as well as other organizations linked to the alternative power networks. But over the last decade, the alternative power networks' record of opposition to free trade agreements has been limited to a small number of largely symbolic victories, such as the 1997 defeat of "fast-track" authority requested by President Clinton.

As the mid-2000s unfolded, it was clear that privileged-class-supported, consolidation-style trade policies were not hampered by the 1997 congressional vote against extending NAFTA. Since that largely symbolic event, privileged-class leaders have, as we noted, won several free trade expansions through legislative victories and organizational negotiations. These free trade agreements, sometimes denoted by a confusing array of acronyms, are likely to continue to be updated with new arrangements and more members. Regional trade agreements, such as NAFTA, CAFTA, the European Union, and the Association of Southeast Asian Nations, combined with international institutions such as the WTO (which enforces eighteen trade agreements, such as the General Agreement on Tariffs and Trade), the International Monetary Fund, and the World Bank all promote privileged-class interests. In each case, these agreements and organizations "are primarily concerned with granting capital the freedom to move from country to country."[38]

We are at present witnessing a major struggle between privileged-class determination to expand neoliberal-based global trade policies and the alternative power network's efforts to protect worker interests and the environment. On one side, we have multinational corporations, financial institutions, and powerful governments that support unregulated free trade; on the other, there are labor organizations, environmentalists, and, increasingly, a number of developing nations stressing the rights of people to regulate the actions of multinational corporations. The growth of international opposition among developing nations to neoliberal free trade agreements and to the international organizations that support and enforce them, such as the WTO, is an interesting development. Currently, the Geneva-based WTO (formed in 1994) has 148 member nations.[39] Each nation has a WTO representative who participates in the formulation of general rules governing trade. Recent efforts by the WTO to develop new trade policies have been stopped by opposition from representatives of developing nations, especially those in Latin America (e.g., Venezuela, Argentina, Bolivia) and Asia (e.g., India and Thailand), concerned with how their nations are treated under WTO rules.[40] The outcome of growing divisions within the WTO on new international trade policies is unclear at this time. Also unclear is how such divisions might affect a key internal WTO body, the Dispute Resolution Committee (DRC), which handles trade disputes between nations. Corporations may currently use the dispute-resolution process overseen by the DRC to bring claims against a country for any of its regulations that limit the freedom of corporations to buy and sell across the globe. The outcome of the growing divisions within the WTO and perhaps within the DRC is uncertain, but these divisions, along with opposition to many WTO policies by numerous citizens' groups, unions, and other nongovernmental organizations in many developed and developing nations, are likely to impact the nature and extent of privileged-class control over the global economy.

Consumption Capital: Continued Inequality in Jobs, Wages, and Taxes

Privileged-class-based political and economic leaders argue that the U.S. economy and workers are doing fine. They point to what is claimed to be tremendous U.S. job growth, even as millions of jobs have been exported and while many firms continue to report job cuts due to corporate downsizing, outsourcing, and offshoring. In the mid-2000s, critics pointed out that the 2.059 million new U.S. jobs created during the 2001–2006 period fell "seven million jobs short of keeping up with population growth, definitely a serious job shortfall."[41] Of the new jobs that were created over the past half-decade, most are at lower wages, with fewer benefits, and with more insecure job tenure compared to the jobs that were lost. Pay reductions in the last five years occurred even for highly educated workers in high-skill fields, such as software and electrical engineering, marketing, and business administration.[42] The overall effect of these trends has been the imposition of intense pressures by employers on workers, resulting in the lowering of workers' real wages and a substantial weakening of workers' rights and bargaining power.[43]

Privileged-class leaders also point to the relatively low unemployment rate in the latter 2000s (high 4 to low 5 percent range) as evidence that overall the economy is strong and that everyone is benefiting as corporate profits grow and inflation remains low. There are many problems with these interrelated claims. But the government's "official" unemployment rate is fatally flawed in two respects. First, it represents a serious underestimate of actual unemployment. The official estimate is based upon a monthly national sample survey of U.S. households, which asks people a series of questions about whether they are currently working or looking for work. Only those who are unemployed, but claim to be actively looking for work, are classified as unemployed. This approach excludes people who are unemployed but who have not looked for work in the past month. These "discouraged workers" have stopped looking for work because their experiences tell them the search is pointless. Also excluded are employed part-time workers who want full-time jobs but cannot find them. To get a more complete picture of unemployment we would need to combine the "official" unemployment rate (about 4.7 percent in the latter 2000s) with the estimated underemployment rate (about 8.4 percent, counting discouraged workers and part-time workers seeking full-time work). Thus, about 13.1 percent of all workers in the civilian labor force today who want full-time work lack full-time jobs, substantially more than "official" unemployment figures suggest.[44]

The emphasis by privileged-class leaders on expanding job opportunities and low unemployment serves to both mask and legitimate class inequalities linked directly to most workers' diminished access to consumption capital (income). The messages sent by credentialed-class professionals who manage and spin economic news to workers whose real wages have been declining for three decades take one of two forms:

1. When the economy is booming (as was claimed in the late 1990s): "If you can't find a good job, it must be your fault!"
2. When the economy is "average" (as was claimed in the latter 2000s): "Savvy workers with the right credentials can easily find good jobs. If you can't, it must be your fault!"

These privileged-class scripted and mainstream-media-disseminated messages concerning aggregate unemployment rates and other economic opportunities overreport the quantity of work available (creating the illusion of low unemployment), while also underreporting on the diminished quality of the jobs held by more and more members of the working class and so-called middle class. Mainstream media reports ignore the reality that increasing numbers of jobs pay less than "living wages," provide few or no benefits, and offer little or no job security.[45]

While the media tend to marginalize the growth of economic inequalities affecting workers, this has not been the case for the rich. In a series of articles in late 2006, the *New York Times* explored the trend of rapidly growing income inequality within the ranks of the superclass. As a result of federal tax law changes and the compensation practices of resource-rich corporations for elite executives, such as CEOs, hedge fund managers, and merger/takeover specialists, the incomes of the superrich have grown far faster than those of the merely rich. To establish baseline figures, one article in the series noted that 2004 U.S. average real household incomes were $940,000 for the top 1 percent, $4.5 million for the top one tenth of 1 percent (0.1), and $20 million for the top one hundredth of 1 percent (0.01). (Average income for the bottom 90 percent of American taxpayers was $28,355.) Between 1990 and 2004, income increased 57 percent for the top 1 percent, 85 percent for the top 0.1 percent, and 112 percent for the top 0.01 percent. (The bottom 90 percent had a 2 percent increase for the same period.) The trend of increasing income inequality within the top 1 percent between the merely rich and the superrich was described in the article as provoking "a new class war."[46]

Other articles in the *Times* series made it clear that the "new class war" within the superclass most often involves jealousy, resentment, and sniping as the merely rich complain about the lack of "fairness" in the distribution of excessive income to the superrich groups.[47] In an editorial, the *Times* suggested that perhaps income inequalities among those in the top levels have become too extreme and also that "the growing gap between the rich and superrich has an impact on those of us who are neither."[48] Perhaps the editorial makes a partially valid point, but the series and the editorial also miss a larger point. Workers *may* be affected if more physicians (for example) decide to shift out of providing primary health care into careers as physician-executives in HMOs. But high-profile media attention to increasing income inequalities among the rich does not serve workers' interests. In fact, media attention to "class war" at the top glamorizes top-end income inequality (Paris Hilton as a camo-clad class warrior?) and distracts attention away from the *real* class war being waged against workers' incomes, benefits, and jobs by large segments of the superclass with the help of many of its less-rich credentialed-class allies.

The trends that matter to workers are not those of greater income inequality at the top but those of lower incomes and less economic security for the working class. These trends are not glamorous, and they are not accidental. They are the direct result of class-war consolidation practices and policies implemented by corporate and government actions throughout the last thirty years that have shifted consumption capital away from working-class wage earners to an increasingly smaller group of privileged-class families. Examples of consolidation policies that would exacerbate current class-based income disparities and extend them into the next century are especially evident in recent governmental policy trends producing reductions in social programs for the working class and lower taxes for the privileged class.

Social Programs and the Declining Social Wage

The privileged class will continue to press for reductions in federal and state spending for programs that constitute the "social wage," which benefits all or many segments of the working class. In industrialized nations, the term *social wage* refers to government policies ensuring minimum levels of citizens' material well-being through "social programs," such as health care, a mandated minimum wage, unemployment insurance, educational assistance, housing subsidies, income and food assistance to the poor, and old-age pensions.[49] Compared with that of other industrialized nations, the U.S. social wage is very modest and lacks health-care guarantees. The major features were put in place in the 1930s; modest expansions occurred mainly in the 1960s with the passage of federal Medicare and Medicaid legislation.[50] However, in recent years, the social wage has come under attack by privileged-class conservatives for allegedly breeding dependency on government and undercutting individual initiative.

Spending reductions have already occurred or are being planned in several areas, including, for example, federal subsidies for education, housing, and welfare assistance. As a result, living costs for members of the working class are going up as real wages continue to fall (especially for the working poor), producing a free fall in the standard of living among the poorest segments of the new working class. This process is especially evident in the "welfare reform experiment." Organized and legitimated by credentialed-class elites acting on behalf of their own and superclass interests, the "reform" legislation capitalized on resentment among some segments of the working class toward entitlement programs serving the poor.

At the federal level, bipartisan congressional support led to the passage of the Personal Responsibility and Work Opportunity Reconciliation Act, which former president Clinton signed into law in 1996. This measure not only sharply reduced benefits to the poor, but it also imposed time restrictions on the number of years people are eligible for assistance and added training requirements that move welfare recipients as quickly as possible into low-wage jobs. Privileged-class pundits claim the act reduced poverty.[51] But various forms of evidence suggest otherwise. The effects of this legislation have included more downward pressures on wage levels (as thousands of new workers were added to the low-wage labor market), increases in the number of discouraged and underemployed workers, and rising levels of human misery as many of the poor have lost minimal levels of support for food, housing, and health care.[52] Ironically, for the higher-wage members of the new working class who supported welfare "reform," as the poor were forced into the labor market, their presence helped drive down wage rates for all workers.[53]

Privileged-class leaders are also at work on two additional major policy efforts that would shift even more income from the working class to the privileged class. The first is the ongoing battle to "privatize" Medicare and shift more of seniors' medical costs to the aged themselves, while creating higher profits for investment and insurance firms. Currently, nearly all U.S. retirees over age sixty-five and the disabled are eligible for Medicare benefits, including Part A (hospital bills covered by the federal government via payroll taxes), Part B (doctor bills covered by monthly premiums that retirees pay), and Part D (prescription drugs covered by retiree premiums and general tax revenues). Superclass-sponsored conservative think tanks (e.g., the Cato Institute) support "Medicare personal accounts," which would shift a portion of workers' Medicare contributions into investment accounts, which would be used to pay medical bills during retirement. The privatizers also favor federal "premium support" at a fixed level for health-insurance policies to be purchased by seniors from private firms.[54] If implemented, these plans would certainly increase the profits of investment and health-insurance firms. They would also reduce seniors' health security and force many older workers to stay in the labor force longer, which would increase the labor supply and thereby drive down average workers' wages (similar to outcomes that occurred after the Welfare "Reform" Act of 1996).

The second effort, which has received cheers from the privileged class, is the initiative to recalculate the consumer price index (CPI), which is used by the federal government and many other governmental bodies and private firms to estimate the rate of inflation. The annual increase in the CPI is used as the basis for calculating (among other things) annual increases in Social Security checks paid to millions of older Americans. For example, if the CPI for 2007 was 3 percent, then a typical retiree receiving a monthly Social Security check of $1,184 for that year would receive $1,219 per month in 2008. Political and corporate elites know that if the annual CPI is "adjusted" downward by only 1 or 2 percent, they can reduce, by billions of dollars, both federal spending on programs like Social Security and wage costs for workers' incomes linked to cost-of-living increases. If the CPI were adjusted downward, the consequences would be class-biased. That is, millions of low-income older Americans would lose benefits, and millions of workers would get smaller raises. But the privileged class would "win" because members of this class would benefit from higher corporate profits; also, reduced federal spending would support the case for further reductions in federal taxes, especially for high-income taxpayers.[55]

Continued Tax Inequalities: Wealth and Income

While the wages of the new working class are constrained, the income and wealth of the privileged class will continue to grow. Salaries of corporate executives, managers, and other members of the credentialed class continued to increase sharply in the mid- and latter 2000s, just as they have over the past three decades. Because the privileged class owns most of the privately held stocks and mutual funds, bonds, and commercial properties in the United States, increasing stock prices during the 1990s helped expand the wealth of this group. In the mid- and latter 2000s, large segments of the privileged class continued to see substantial wealth and income growth, thanks in part to the phasing in of ever higher levels of federal tax cuts for high-income groups as prescribed by the tax law changes enacted in the 2001–2006 period (described in chapter 4 and discussed below) and to gains in the value of professionally managed investment portfolios held by many members of this group.

The trend of increasing concentration of wealth in the hands of the privileged class is likely to continue well past the first decade of the twenty-first century. Ironically, this trend is (and will be) partly fueled by increasing economic insecurity among new-working-class members, including the insecurity of workers' retirement income. As benefit-defined pension plans (funded by corporate contributions) are increasingly replaced by contribution-defined plans (funded by employee's contributions from wages, such as 401(k) plans), new-working-class members are forced into the stock market hoping for higher returns. To the extent that they can afford to buy stocks, their market purchases help prop up stock prices, which disproportionately benefit privileged-class stock owners.[56]

The expansion of privileged-class wealth holdings and income levels that began with tax cuts under the Clinton administration in 1997 received multiple major boosts from the three major, individual, income-tax-reduction laws supported by President Bush and passed by Congress in the 2001–2006 period. As noted in chapter 4, these laws produced, and will continue to produce, multi-billion-dollar windfalls for the privileged class. Tax cuts enacted in the 1990s and 2000s not only expanded income and wealth inequalities over the past decade, but they will extend these growing inequalities at least to 2010 and likely well beyond that date. With these tax policies in place, to speak of merit-based rewards and equality of opportunity as essential features of the American Dream is more than a cruel joke. It approaches the "big lie" dimensions of the most distorted forms of propaganda.

Social and Skill Capital: Closing the Gates of Opportunity

Our distributional model views social and skill capital as critical factors influencing the processes through which varying levels of the other two capital forms are distributed (or redistributed) to individuals and groups. As we noted in chapter 1, social capital includes people's participation in various kinds of social networks, their acquisition of class-legitimating and class-enhancing formal credentials, and their possession of qualities valued and rewarded by various organizations (e.g., specialized talents and skills). Skill capital is closely related to social capital in that both are often linked to formal educational organizations that develop specialized talents, refine economically valued interests and skills, and help establish access to informal social and career networks of opportunities and practicing privileged-class professional mentors.

As the American economy is transformed by corporate strategies to maximize profit and the market value of stocks (through downsizing, outsourcing, offshoring), the availability of "good jobs" has become increasingly problematic. The number of positions linked to high or even moderate levels of consumption capital (income) has always been finite, but in recent years those numbers have stagnated. Neither the death nor retirement of current workers, nor economic expansion, can be counted on to produce more "good job" openings as the economy is transformed.[57] The situation is akin to a sports team in which only a limited number of player positions are available.

Recent research evidence on the rates of intergenerational occupational mobility indicates that in recent decades it has become more difficult for young men from working-class origins to achieve the higher levels of occupation, education, and income. For example, an early study of U.S. social mobility tracking father and son pairs found that less than 30 percent of the most prestigious occupations (the top quintile) were occupied by sons in 1973 whose fathers had held the same rank (when they were the same age some twenty years earlier as their sons were in 1973). This study found substantial percentages of sons whose fathers held low-ranking jobs experienced upward mobility in the occupational structure in their adult lives.[58]

A contrasting 2007 study found that the adult sons and daughters of fathers who occupied the top socioeconomic (SES) quartile (those with the highest educational, income, and occupational credentials) occupied much larger shares of the top SES quartile in 2004 than the 1973 study found for the top group of father-son pairs. The 2007 study found that the sons of fathers in the top SES quartile occupied 51.4 percent of the top SES positions available to sons from all ranks in 2004 and that the daughters of fathers in the top SES quartile occupied 43.9 percent of the top SES positions available to daughters from all ranks in 2004. These findings mean that there is much less "room at the top" for sons and daughters from lower-ranked SES fathers to move up to and occupy in 2004 as compared to 1973 (at least for sons, as the earlier study did not track daughters). The overall finding was that, compared to a generation ago, it is now far more difficult for members of the working class to rise into higher socioeconomic levels.[59]

So, how are the limited numbers of "good jobs" distributed among the large pool of aspirants? We believe social and skill capital play major roles in the distributional process in terms of providing access to these jobs, as well as in explaining why it is fair and right for the holders of these jobs to occupy them. But, as we have shown, the past three decades have witnessed an expansion of policies, programs, and trends that have restricted opportunities for members of the working class to cultivate social capital at individual or collective levels and to accumulate advanced levels of skill capital. For the younger cohorts of the working class, the result has been a dramatic decline in opportunities to access "good jobs" and to acquire the social and skill capital necessary for upward social mobility to professional careers in the privileged class.

Several kinds of corporate practices, government policies, and social trends are consolidating higher levels of social and skill capital in the hands of privileged-class members while decreasing access to these resources by working-class members. Although the list is long, it begins with the attack on public education by conservative privileged-class members and organizations. This group advocates decreased spending for all forms of public education, including college, while also supporting an expansion of school-voucher systems and privatization schemes. These privileged-class-sponsored efforts are key examples of class consolidation policies related to social and skill capital. Already partially in place, these policies are reshaping how schools influence the distribution of social and skill capital resources to students in ways that will further disadvantage working-class children and reinforce the advantages of privileged-class children.

In state legislatures and the U.S. Congress, neoliberal privileged-class leaders are currently calling for cuts in funding for urban school programs because they claim more money will not solve the problems of these schools. Their claim is based on social Darwinist assumptions that view the urban poor as an underclass so disorganized by antisocial values and hedonistic lifestyles that many of its children are beyond educational redemption—no matter how much money is spent on them.[60] Parallel to calls for deep cuts in publicly funded education are policies advocated by superclass-funded think tanks, where marketplace competition for schools is viewed as a "solution" for those segments of the urban poor that might be redeemed by education. These "experts argue that education will only improve when poor children are given vouchers to attend private schools and private groups are allowed to start and run their own schools with unregulated public funds."[61] Such views are often repeated by mainstream media journalists.[62]

Policies that defund public schools restrict working-class students' opportunities to participate in the kinds of social networks that would lead to the cultivation of an expanded circle of social ties and valued individual skills essential for acquiring a "good job" or a shot at upward social mobility. As high-quality educational experiences are made less accessible to working-class students, and as their parents experience declining real incomes, the likelihood is reduced that such students will even aspire to (let alone acquire) the kinds of formal credentials and advanced skills necessary to access the declining pool of "good jobs" and professional careers.

Privileged-class efforts to defund public education also extend to the university level, as reflected in declining levels of state support for public universities, combined with rapidly rising tuition costs. Between 1996 and 2006, state government appropriations for public colleges and universities increased from $44.4 to $66.6 billion.[63] Even so, this increase was below the rate of inflation for services that period.[64] This means that state funding measured in real dollars (adjusted for inflation) fell. During the same period, tuition and fees paid by students at four-year public colleges and universities more than doubled—as a result of large increases in these charges to students and their parents.[65] Looking to the future, the College Board estimated that for a child born in the early 2000s, four years at a public university would cost $100,000; at private institutions, the cost would be $225,000.[66]

The class-based social- and skill-capital implications of the combination of state defunding and increasing costs of college to students and parents are obvious. As state support drops and tuition costs escalate, fewer working-class students will be able to afford to attend college. Children from working-class families will face ever higher financial hurdles if they hope to attend college as costs exceed the annual incomes (and maybe even the net worth) of their parents. Working-class children will find their choices increasingly limited to the cheapest forms of higher education. And these are likely to include more impersonal, technologically driven, narrowly focused, vocational-style programs that are connected to low-paid jobs with limited opportunities.

By contrast, children from the privileged class have few financial barriers to contend with when considering college attendance. Increasingly, only children from privileged-class families will have access to elite colleges and universities with programs taught by professional faculty and linked to job opportunity networks with higher starting salaries and long career ladders. Moreover, increasingly only children from privileged-class families will be able to realistically consider or afford professional degrees beyond the baccalaureate level. These factors (and others) will conspire to limit the chances of young men and women from the new working class to achieve significant, educationally linked opportunities for occupational and social mobility. Such circumstances will dramatically restrict their ability to access the formal credential dimension of both social and skill capital, but children from privileged-class backgrounds will be much less affected.[67]

The decline of working-class access to social and skill capital resources produces less competition among privileged-class members for these resources. This means adult members of the privileged class will be able to reserve easier access to formal skills and a larger share of social capital resources for themselves and their children. These resources can then be used to legitimate a near monopoly by the privileged class on access to, and legitimation of, high levels of consumption and investment capital, which together almost permanently and exclusively cement membership in this class.

The Future: Resistance

> Once I saw the mountains angry, And ranged in battle-front. Against them stood a little man; I laughed and spoke to one near me, 'Will he prevail?' 'Surely,' replied this other; 'His grandfathers beat them many times.'
>
> —Stephen Crane, *The Red Badge of Courage and Other Writings*, 1960

The privileged-class-based consolidation policies and trends outlined in the preceding section are likely to produce increasing inequalities between the top 20 percent of privileged Americans and the remaining majority. Attempts by members of the new working class to increase their capital shares are likely to be kept in check by the continued mobilization of a variety of potent resources held by the privileged class and deployed along several fronts of the new class war. Any alteration in the distribution of capital resources will have to be initiated by reform-minded people, groups, and organizations grounded in the working class and perhaps linked to lessons from the progressive populist traditions of the past.

There is some evidence that workers' negative experiences with the new economy over the last thirty years have resulted in important changes in the attitudes of average Americans that could be the basis for organized resistance to privileged-class policies. As discussed in chapters 1, 2, and 3, the new economy's focus on global production, investment, and trade has brought with it wage constraints, increased job insecurity, and a contingent, disposable work force. It seems reasonable to expect that the decline in real wages for many workers over the past thirty years, combined with increasing fears of job insecurity and economic uncertainty, could lead to diminished confidence among workers in their ability to achieve the American Dream and in the belief that America offers "opportunity for all." It also seems that these same developments could lead to greater working-class consciousness and to larger numbers of workers recognizing the oppositional class interests of the haves and have-nots.

Recent survey findings reported in chapter 2 indicate that there have been shifts in public attitudes towards the American Dream. As we noted, nearly two-thirds of Americans believe the American Dream is harder to achieve today compared to their parents' generation and to ten years ago.[68] A majority of Americans surveyed said this is the case because the "current society favors the rich" and because "wages for workers are too low."[69] The growth of workers' pessimism about achieving the American Dream appears to be paralleled by increasing levels of class consciousness. In a recent study of class awareness and the extent of oppositional attitudes between persons from different social classes, class consciousness was measured by the level of agreement or disagreement with six statements: (1) "Corporations benefit owners and stockholders at the expense of workers and consumers." (2) "Ordinary workers should have a larger role in planning and managing the operations of large corporations." (3) "Society should place limits on salaries of corporate executives." (4) "Big corporations have too much power in American society today." (5) "If given a chance, non-management employees could run things effectively without bosses." (6) "Much of the blame for the loss of good jobs in this country can be placed on the profit motive of large corporations."

Findings from this research indicate that workers who believe their job situations are poor or who have directly experienced layoffs (of themselves or a

The Hand That Will Rule the World—One Big Union. Solidarity, June 30, 1917.

household member) are more likely to answer the questions in a way that reflects high levels of class consciousness. A second finding was that those persons who have traditional working-class jobs are significantly more class conscious on five of the six questions than persons in managerial or upper-white-collar positions.[70] The findings from this study, plus results from recent American Dream surveys and polls showing increased public distrust of corporations and executives (as noted in chapter 7), suggest that the economic, political, and cultural transformations that have led to what we call the "new class society" may be increasing workers' class consciousness and their awareness of oppositional class interests.[71] Americans with such views may be more readily mobilized into collective political action by organizations that are part of the alternative power networks. Examples of such organizations are considered in the next section.

Many of the themes, messages, and images that were part of the populist tradition found expression in the mid- and latter 2000s. But the progressive traditions of the past were not simply revived. They were revised and updated to meet the needs and conditions of a new century through the activities of a wide array of activist groups and organizations that are part of the alternative power networks. To illustrate organizational forces in these networks that are working for progressive economic, political, and cultural reforms, we focus on organizations actively involved in challenging various aspects of growing class inequalities in six areas: (1) organized labor, (2) economic inequalities,

(3) corporate power, (4) third parties, (5) the Living Wage Campaign, and (6) media reform. We view the organizations we examine in these areas as illustrative of numerous groups in the alternative power networks engaged in activities that have the potential to facilitate significant changes in public discourse concerning class inequalities and perhaps to help reverse the growing polarization of the U.S. class structure. The organizations in all six areas reflect shared concerns with advancing working-class interests and democratic ideals. In many ways, these groups are modern heirs to the populist tradition. They can be viewed as representatives of contemporary populist activism committed to deepening class consciousness among the new working class and to actively mobilizing a variety of economic, political, and cultural resources aimed at transforming the structural bases of the new class society and the many inequalities associated with it.

Organized Labor

In 2005, U.S. organized labor split at the national level. Six unions that withdrew from the AFL-CIO, plus one that remained linked to it, formed the new Change to Win (CTW) federation.[72] As a result of the split, the AFL-CIO, which had been the organizational foundation of the American labor movement since 1955, retained about 9 million of the 13.7 million members it had before the split.[73] The AFL-CIO's annual revenues before the split totaled $145 million in 2003.[74] After the split, the organization's annual revenues were estimated to have declined to about $100 million.[75] The CTW membership was estimated at 5.4 million, and its annual revenues were estimated at about $16 million in 2005.[76]

The reasons for the split appear to reflect different leadership styles and priorities in the two organizations.[77] Even so, both organizations appear committed to the goals of serving as advocates for union members' interests in the workplace, supporting the interests of all workers in the political arena, organizing new members, and negotiating and defending pro-worker collective bargaining agreements with employers.[78] The leaders of both organizations also recognize that working together on some projects is necessary to advance workers' interests. This was evident in the 2006 elections when the AFL-CIO and CTW leaders agreed to coordinate their efforts to maximize union support for pro-worker candidates.[79]

The AFL-CIO shifted to a more activist stance after John Sweeney (former Service Employees' International Union officer) was elected president in 1995.[80] Under Sweeney, the federation increased its support for political activities consistent with labor's interests and for political candidates sympathetic to labor. For example, in 2003 the AFL-CIO Executive Council approved the creation of Working America, "a community affiliate of the AFL-CIO." It was created "to provide a vehicle for workers who do not enjoy the benefits of union representation at work to join the AFL-CIO as associate members and participate in the labor movement's policy and electoral strategy on behalf of working families."[81] Working America claimed 1.7 million members at the time of the 2006 midterm elections, and the AFL-CIO leadership said it played "a central role" in helping many Democratic candidates win their races in 2006.

The AFL-CIO reported that more than 205,000 union members volunteered to work on the 2006 elections nationwide. They visited 8.25 million households, made 30 million phone calls, and distributed 14 million leaflets. The combination of the AFI-CIO's aggressive "get-out-the-union-vote" efforts, combined with similar efforts by Working America volunteers, contributed to what the union termed "a victory for working family friendly candidates in [the 2006 elections]." The AFL-CIO claimed about 75 percent of union voters supported union-endorsed candidates in the 2006 U.S. House and Senate races and that nonunion households supported "Democratic House candidates by a two-point margin." Overall, in 2006, "union households accounted for roughly 1 out of every 4 voters."[82]

The CTW federation also played an active role in the 2006 elections. Members of CTW unions "knocked on 2.3 million doors, made 6.9 million phone calls, distributed 5.6 million worksite flyers, and contributed 356,731 volunteer hours to support candidates and initiatives that can make a difference for working people." The CTW leadership said the organization worked with "the entire labor movement and other progressive partners on congressional races in all 50 states." CTW unions also were claimed to have played important roles in helping elect worker-friendly candidates at the national, state, and local levels in Michigan, Pennsylvania, and Ohio.[83]

In addition to union-based political efforts such as those noted above, both the AFL-CIO and the CTW federation have worked to call greater public attention to economic concerns and policy issues relevant to all workers. For example, in the mid- and latter 2000s, both organizations publicized their support for policies that would increase workers' opportunities to realize the American Dream. In 2005, the AFL-CIO Executive Council approved a plan titled "An Economic Agenda for Working Families: Building Union Power, Reclaiming the American Dream." At the same time, the AFL-CIO officers endorsed a set of proposals titled "Winning for Working Families." Both documents outlined specific steps that the AFL-CIO leadership, staff, and local memberships would take to increase the economic, organizational, human, and political resources of the union to counter corporate assaults on workers' lives and living standards.[84]

In 2006, the CTW federation released the results of a poll it had commissioned titled "The American Dream Survey 2006." Using findings from the survey as a springboard, the CTW leadership publicized its agenda and plans for "Restoring the American Dream." For example, the federation launched a campaign for universal health care, endorsed retirement-security guarantees for workers, described new organizing strategies, and promised to work with unions around the world to raise living standards for all workers.[85] The efforts by both AFL-CIO and CTW leaders to support new policies and programs that would increase workers' chances to realize the American Dream are examples of activities by these organizations that transcend the narrow economic interests of union members (and leaders). By framing new union-supported initiatives in terms of widening *all* workers' access to the "American Dream," both organizations spoke to the needs and interests of the entire working class.

To increase the ability of the AFL-CIO and the CTW to more effectively represent workers' interests in the workplace, leaders of both organizations announced plans in the mid-2000s to devote more union resources to organizing new members. CTW federation leaders said it "will devote three-fourths of its . . . $16 million budget to organizing . . . [and] CTW unions claim that collectively they will spend $750 million a year on organizing." The AFL-CIO announced in 2005 that it was increasing its support for organizing new members with a new "$22.5 million Strategic Organizing Fund."[86] In addition to this fund, individual unions that are members of the AFL-CIO will also spend millions more on organizing new workers.

Future outcomes of efforts by both the AFL-CIO and CTW federation to influence political issues and campaigns, promote policies that will benefit all members of the working class, and organize new union members remain to be seen. Union-sponsored reform efforts have been, and will be, opposed by a wide array of privileged-class resources, including many organizations identified in earlier chapters. Stiff opposition is especially likely to come from the little-known anti-union industry of fifteen hundred consultants who now "earn approximately $500 million each year advising corporations on how to keep unions out of their offices and factories."[87] Antiunion forces also maintain an active and high-profile presence in the U.S. mainstream media and on the Internet through funding of the Center for Union Facts (CUF). This organization, headed by Richard Berman, spends $5 million per year on campaigns that include antiunion ads placed in major U.S. newspapers and the operation of a CUF website. "Berman won't say where his money comes from, [but] it's clear that anti-union interests are financing [his efforts]."[88]

Apart from privileged-class challenges, labor-friendly observers are concerned that the AFL-CIO/CTW split will weaken the chances for meaningful pro-worker reforms in the economic, political, and cultural arenas.[89] Skeptics doubt that the leadership in either organization will actively encourage greater democratic participation of union members in crafting federation policies and priorities.[90] But despite concerns and skepticism, organized labor, including the AFL-CIO, the CTW federation, and their affiliated unions, remains the single most important organizational resource within the alternative power networks for promoting the economic, political, and cultural interests of the new working class. And while unions are often presented in the U.S. mainstream media as outdated and increasingly irrelevant in the global economy,[91] a recent survey reported the public holds a generally positive view of unions in the United States and that Americans approve of unions by a 2:1 margin.[92] The resources and public popularity of unions, plus the benefits they have helped provide for millions of workers, suggest they will continue to play important roles in efforts to challenge class inequalities.

Challenging Economic Inequalities

Although unions remain the most resource-rich force pressing for economic and political reforms in the United States, other recently emerged or reenergized organizations have highlighted growing economic inequalities and helped call attention to the structural roots of such inequalities. Two multidimensional, tax-exempt, activist organizations working in this area are the Council on International and Public Affairs, Inc. (CIPA), and United for a Fair Economy, Inc. (UFE). CIPA "was founded in 1954 as a non-profit research, education, and publishing group."[93] It is located in Croton-on-Hudson, New York, and in 2004 reported total revenues of $468,009.[94] CIPA operates Apex Press and supports various activities promoting social and economic justice. UFE was created in 1996 out of the merger of the Share the Wealth Project and the Joint Project on Equality, both of which were founded in 1994. UFE is a "national, independent . . . nonprofit organization. UFE raises awareness that concentrated wealth and power undermine the economy, corrupt democracy, deepen the racial divide, and tear communities apart. We support and help build social movements for greater equality."[95] UFE is located in Boston; it reported total revenues of $2,261,242 in 2005 (which was double its 2002 total revenues of $1,118,377).[96]

CIPA and UFE jointly publish *Too Much*, "America's only newsletter dedicated to exploring excess and inequality in the contemporary United States and throughout the world."[97] It began publication "in 1995 as a print quarterly . . . then became an online weekly [in 2004]. . . . Subscriptions to the weekly *Too Much* newsletter are free. The *Too Much* Web presence features a full archive of back issues."[98] UFE not only serves as a kind of class-consciousness-raising organization but is also involved in "advocacy and political action, community organizing and coalition building, research and media work, [and] arts and culture [projects]." In 2006, a UFE website page, "Economics Education," stated, "Our economic programs reach thousands of people. . . . Our programs pick up where the think tanks and speechmakers leave off."[99] Another UFE website page, "Our Strategies," noted, "We have conducted our flagship workshop, 'The Growing Divide: Economic Inequality and the Roots of Insecurity' for over 70,000 people in religious congregations, unions, community organizations, and business associations. . . . In the past year, we trained over four hundred people to lead the 'Growing Divide' and other UFE curricula. . . . Our project, Responsible Wealth (RW), is a . . . network of over 750 business leaders, investors and other wealthy people [that] works to build a fairer economy through shareholder activism, support for the living wage, and fair taxes."[100]

Although most Americans have probably never heard of CIPA or UFE, both are active supporters of efforts to "build a powerful fair economy movement that can contest the dominant economic policies and propose policies that ensure shared prosperity."[101] UFE is probably better known than CIPA in part because it "was founded as a 'movement support' organization to provide media capacity, face-to-face economic literacy education, and training resources to organizations and individuals who work to address the widening income and asset gap in our country."[102] *Too Much* is an important vehicle for publicizing UFE's attacks on inequality. The newsletter provides summaries of (and electronic links to) studies documenting the growth of economic inequality in the United States and the world, the various dimensions of this phenomena, and the corrosive social and human effects of inequality on the quality (and quantity) of life. *Too Much* also advocates policies that would reduce inequality. One example is its support for a U.S. "maximum wage," often framed in terms of President Franklin Roosevelt's proposal in 1942 for "a 100 percent tax on all individual income over $25,000 a year, the equivalent of about $314,000 today."[103] While this concept may seem ludicrous to many Americans, it is a central issue considered in *Greed and Good*, a book by *Too Much* editor Sam Pizzigati, and as *Too Much* has reported, a modest version of it aimed at limiting CEO pay was introduced in the U.S. House by Representative Martin Sabo (D-MN) as the Income Equity Act of 2005.[104]

The work, messages, and publications of UFE have been the subject of reports by many national media outlets, such as the *New York Times*, the *Nation*, and Jim Hightower's radio talk show (on independent stations). In 2006, the UFE website claimed, "Our capacity to influence public attitudes through talk radio, print media, and television continues to grow. Our work has also appeared on a variety of blogs and online magazines. . . . We have had more than 2,000 media hits in the past two years. The campaign to preserve the estate tax alone yielded 500 major media hits in a three-month period."[105]

Challenging Corporate Power

While various organizations are working to publicize class inequalities, one interesting group working to reform the organizational foundations of the corporate system that promotes privileged-class interests is the Program on Corporations, Law, and Democracy (POCLAD). POCLAD is an ongoing project supported in part by CIPA.[106] Organized in the mid-1990s by labor activists Richard Grossman and Ward Morehouse, POCLAD is not a membership organization or a coalition of groups. It consists of a small group of individuals "from a variety of social change movements" who "work with membership organizations, coalitions, and individuals . . . in the tradition of people's struggles to replace illegitimate and tyrannical institutions with ones that disperse, rather than concentrate, wealth and power."[107] POCLAD is known as the leader of the "corporate charter movement."[108] The purpose of the program is "to embolden citizens and lawmakers to toughen—or rather enforce—state corporate charter laws. These laws . . . give legislatures the power to limit corporations' activities and revoke their right to do business in their state."[109]

POCLAD is actively working to increase public awareness of how corporate power undermines democracy and to mobilize group efforts to challenge and change laws that grant extraordinary powers to corporations. In 1999, POCLAD began publishing a journal titled *By What Authority*. Its three annual issues typically include articles and commentary analyzing the nature and extent of corporate power and exploring ways of strengthening democracy in the face of such power. In 2003, POCLAD's agenda and reform efforts were reinforced by a new book titled *The Elite Consensus: When Corporations Wield the Constitution*, by George Draffan, director of the Public Information Network. Published by Apex Press, the book's foreword was written by POCLAD founders Grossman and Morehouse.[110]

Since CIPA's revenues in the mid-2000s were only in the half-million-dollar-per-year range (as noted above) and since POCLAD is only one of CIPA's projects, it is clear that POCLAD has a limited resource base.[111] Given its limited resources, POCLAD is unlikely to function as more than a class-consciousness-raising force. However, since POCLAD members often act in concert with, and provide resources to, other like-minded reform groups, perhaps that is a reasonable goal. The 2003 book illustrates this activity as Draffan, reflecting POCLAD's perspective, "describes how corporations leverage power through think tanks and business groups to form an undemocratic system of governance over citizens." As "the latest addition to the POCLAD body of publications,"[112] the *Elite Consensus* reinforces and extends the perspective on corporate power presented in the 2001 POCLAD/Apex book *Defying Corporations, Defining Democracy: A Book of History and Strategy*, edited by Dean Ritz. That book urged activists to learn from past struggles and to seize the offensive by:

- Defining corporations as public entities subordinate to public control;
- Banning corporations utterly from elections, lawmaking, charitable giving, and schools;
- Prohibiting corporations from all discussion and debate about public policy;
- Stripping corporations of 14th Amendment "equal protection" and "due process" of law;
- Divesting corporations of 1st Amendment "freedom of speech";
- Denying corporations the privilege of owning other corporations.[113]

The *Elite Consensus* provided more reasons why the actions proposed in the 2001 book are even more necessary today. In addition to the actions proposed above, POCLAD also advocates rewriting corporate law to require a reconfiguring of corporate governance. For example, a typical twenty-person corporate board of directors could be required to include seven directors elected by shareholders, seven directors elected by employees, and six directors "elected by a number of other constituencies—such as consumers, suppliers, bond-holders, and representatives of local communities."[114]

If implemented as policy, POCLAD's reform agenda would significantly constrain corporate power and impact the current ability of corporations to serve as powerful agents of privileged-class interests. POCLAD's ideas might be dismissed as unrealistic idealism, but the group has succeeded in attracting growing public attention to an important structural dimension of class in-equalities. By encouraging the growth of class consciousness and focusing public attention on a critical feature of the dominant economic power net-work, POCLAD adds to the legitimacy of class analysis and helps break the si-lence of the class taboo.

Third-Party Challenges

In 2006, the Federal Election Commission (FEC) listed eighty-six abbrevia-tions used to "identify the party labels that appeared on the various ballots for the . . . 2004 primary and general elections."[115] Two abbreviations referenced Democrats and Republicans, and eighty-four referenced other parties. Those political parties that stand apart from the two major political organizations are often described by scholars and journalists as "minor" or "third" parties.[116] While we could have profiled many third parties in this section, our focus here is limited to the Green Party of the United States.[117] In our view, this organi-zation provides a contemporary example of a progressive minor party grounded in the populist tradition of challenging privileged-class dominance of the two-party system.

The Green Party of the United States is relatively new but has roots that date to the 1980s. The Greens first met in 1984 in St Paul, Minnesota, and adopted "10 Key Values" that are the foundation for all Green Parties in the United States.[118] Early party-building efforts were sometimes conflicted, but in late 1996, state Greens formed the Association of State Green Parties (ASGP). Four years later, the ASGP became the Green Party of the United States, "a federa-tion of state Green Parties."[119] The FEC recognizes the Green Party of the United States "as the official Green Party National Committee."[120] The Green Party of the United States is also "partners with the European Federation of Green Parties and the Federation of Green Parties of the Americas."[121]

The Green Party is focused on increasing its membership, running candi-dates for office, and winning elections. "The mission of the Green Party of the U.S. is to build the Green Party into a viable political alternative in the United States."[122] The Green Party "does not accept money from corporations."[123] In-stead, party support comes mainly from volunteers and "from small contribu-tions from individual citizens."[124] Current policy positions held by the Green Party were most recently summarized in its "Platform 2004." The platform endorsed policies that party members believed would make the U.S. political process more democratic, end the wars in Iraq and Afghanistan, protect equal rights for all people, ensure living wages for workers, guarantee workers' rights to organize unions, provide national health insurance, reform the criminal justice system, end the domestic drug war, restrict corporate power, and protect the environment.[125]

The Green Party gained widespread national attention in 1996 and 2000 when Ralph Nader was the party's nominee for president.[126] Since 2000, Green Party membership has grown substantially, and it has achieved a measure of success at the ballot box, mainly by running candidates for local offices. In 2005, the Green Party reported a total of 304,796 registered members nationwide in twenty states and the District of Columbia.[127] The Green Party documents the activities of its candidates running for public offices with annual "Election Results" summaries. For example, in 2004, the Green Party ran 436 candidates for 74 types of offices in 42 states and won 71 victories. In 2006, it ran 376 candidates for 67 types of offices in 38 states and won 66 victories.[128] In 2006, the Green Party claimed 220 officeholders in various local offices "from Hawaii to Washington, D.C."[129]

In July 2006, the Green Party held its annual meeting in Tucson, Arizona, attended by delegates, candidates, and leaders from thirty-four states. The meeting focused on the party's "'Peace Slate' of 2006 candidates, ballot access efforts, immigration, the Iraq war, and plans for the 2008 presidential election."[130] In late November 2006, the party issued a public "challenge" to the Democrats "to reverse their party's current pro-corporate direction." The Green Party specifically challenged Democrats in Congress to support a "living wage" (not just an increase in the minimum wage), national health insurance, and the rights of citizens to investigate Congress, to repeal the recent federal bankruptcy "reform" law and Taft-Hartley restrictions on workplace organizing, and to renegotiate several international trade agreements, including NAFTA and CAFTA.[131] As a result of the Green Party's large national membership base (by third-party standards), its willingness to participate in controversial causes consistent with its core values, and its support for progressive reforms, the party attracted substantial media attention in 2006. The Green Party is now the largest and best organized minor U.S. political party with obvious links to the progressive populist traditions and principles of the past.[132]

The Green Party is one of many political organizations that have emerged from the growing inequalities spawned by the new class society.[133] The long-term success of this party (as well as other third parties) remains to be seen, and the problems it confronts are many. For example, national polls in the mid-2000s reported the political-party identification of U.S. adults was distributed as 34 percent Democrat, 31 percent Republican, 24 percent independent (not counting those with no preference).[134] This distribution pattern has been relatively stable for the past twenty years.[135] Any third party hoping to accumulate a significant base of popular support would have to dislodge decades-old party identification traditions. Of course, major shifts have occurred in the past (e.g., the rapid growth of the Republican Party in the 1850s and populist parties in the late 1800s and early 1900s) in the context of national economic and political crises. Thus, the growth of progressive third parties could signal an emerging shift in the political landscape as minor parties challenge the growing inequalities of the new class society.

Living Wage Campaign

As we learned in the opening chapters of this book, many Americans work full-time while earning incomes that put them below or near the poverty line. They are the "working poor," with earnings at the federal minimum wage or barely above that level ($5.15 per hour as of early 2007, unchanged since 1997). Growing concern over the large number of working poor in the United States has led to a coalition of groups (e.g., ACORN [Association of Community Organizations for Reform Now], the AFL-CIO, the Working Families Party) working together to energize a national social movement called the Living Wage Campaign.[136] Working at the local level in many communities throughout the country, campaign activists have sought to pass local city or county ordinances requiring private businesses that benefit from public contracts and some large retail chains ("Big Box Stores") to pay their workers a living wage. Under such ordinances, businesses with city or county contracts, those receiving public financial assistance through tax abatements, loans, or tax financing, or retail stores that meet or exceed a certain size (e.g., nine thousand square feet) are required to meet specified wage standards.

The justification for the Living Wage Campaign is straightforward and based on simple fairness, namely, that public tax dollars should not subsidize poverty-wage work. Allowing companies receiving public money to pay poverty-level wages presents taxpayers with a double bill. The first bill is for the cost of the initial subsidy. The second bill is for the food stamps, medical care, subsidized housing, and social services that poverty-wage workers require to sustain themselves and their families. If workers received a living wage, which might be set at $10.00 an hour, plus another $3.00 per hour in benefits, they would be better able to meet family needs without additional public assistance. These were the amounts included in a "Big Box Ordinance" passed by the Chicago City Council on July 25, 2006, but it was vetoed by Mayor Daley.[137] A $10 per hour wage would produce an annual income for a single parent of about $20,000, which was equivalent to the federal poverty line for a family of four in 2006.[138] Living-wage or minimum-wage ordinances enacted around the United States at the local level in 2006 were reported by ACORN to have set wage levels ranging from $6.75 to $14 an hour (or more) depending on local economic conditions.[139]

ACORN, the most active of the organizations involved in living-wage campaigns, is the nation's oldest and largest grassroots organization of low- and moderate-income people. It claims a membership of over two hundred thousand in over ninety cities.[140] In 1998, ACORN "established the Living Wage Resource Center to track the living wage movement and provide materials and strategies to living wage organizers all over the country."[141] "Over the past decade, ACORN chapters . . . have won living-wage or minimum wage ordinances in St. Louis, St. Paul, Minnesota, Boston, Oakland, Denver, Chicago, Cook County, New Orleans, Detroit, New York City, Long Island, Sacramento, and San Francisco."[142] In 2006, ACORN promoted a "National Campaign to Raise the Minimum Wage." Working with "Let Justice Roll" (a coalition of more than eighty labor, religious, and community groups), the campaign was instrumental in facilitating the passage of minimum-wage increases via ballot initiatives in Arizona, Colorado, Missouri, Montana, Nevada, and Ohio.[143] In addition to working on living-wage campaigns, ACORN helps build community-based coalitions providing a power base for low- and moderate-income people, helps to develop leadership skills, and gets out the message that elected public officials will be held accountable.

Media Reform: FAIR

Efforts to reform the media in the United States gained nationwide attention when the first National Conference for Media Reform was held in Madison, Wisconsin, in November 2003. It was attended by nearly two thousand participants, including Federal Communications Commission commissioners, members of Congress, and large numbers of citizens "who sought media that served the public."[144] A second national conference was held in 2005 in St. Louis, Missouri, and a third, in 2007 in Memphis, Tennessee. Like the first, each subsequent conference involved several media-reform organizations, high-profile reformers (e.g., in 2007, Bill Moyers, Jane Fonda, Jesse Jackson, Phil Donahue, Robert McChesney, and Ben Bagdikian), policy makers, and citizens concerned with an increasingly concentrated commercial media system that is unaccountable to the public interest and that seeks only greater profits and fewer government regulations of corporate media operations.[145] These conferences represent highly visible manifestations of what is now a national movement for media reform in the public interest. While this movement includes many organizations and groups, in this section we focus on only one—Fairness and Accuracy in Reporting (FAIR). We view FAIR as worthy of special attention because of its unique history and its concerns with the links between economic and political inequalities, media criticism, and reform. FAIR has been crucial to the development of the contemporary media-reform movement. Also, through its publications and activities, it has helped illustrate how progressive economic and political reforms are necessary preconditions for full participation by all citizens in the democratic process and for meaningful media reforms in support of the public interest.[146]

FAIR was founded in 1986. During the late 1980s and throughout the 1990s, it became an increasingly important force in support of progressive economic, political, and cultural reforms within the mainstream media. In the 2000s, FAIR not only continued to pursue its own goals but also provided active support to the media-reform movement and the efforts of kindred organizations. FAIR's mission and goals are printed inside the cover of each issue of *Extra!* (its bimonthly "flagship" magazine, which has a total paid and/or requested circulation of approximately fifteen thousand copies per issue).[147] "FAIR, the national media watch group, has been offering well-documented criticism of media bias and censorship since 1986. . . . As a progressive group, FAIR believes that structural reform is ultimately needed to break up the dominant media conglomerates, establish independent public broadcasting, and promote strong, nonprofit sources of information."[148]

In addition to publishing *Extra!*, FAIR also publishes *Extra!Update*, a four-page bimonthly newsletter, and it organizes a number of activities in support of its goals of exposing media biases and censorship. These include maintaining a website (www.fair.org), distributing FAIR's radio program, *CounterSpin*, to more than 130 noncommercial stations, and selling products consistent with its goals from the FAIR Store on its website. Compared with major media firms, FAIR is a very small organization. It relies mainly on *Extra!* subscriber revenues and donations to support a ten-person staff and an annual budget of approximately $1 million.[149]

FAIR is one of many organizations active in the contemporary media-reform movement. It is also one of many small organizations that populate the alternative power networks. Despite its small size, we view FAIR as an especially significant media-reform group because it pioneered the application of populist and progressive ideas and traditions to studying and exposing the biases and power of the media. As we noted, since its founding, FAIR has been joined by other progressive organizations working for media reform.[150] But it was FAIR that almost single-handedly established modern progressive media-critique traditions and standards.[151] It developed and continues to apply methods of inquiry that illustrate how mass media content, management, and ownership reflect privileged-class control of the media industry. It documents how privileged-class control of the media helps maintain class divisions and legitimate privileged-class-biased government and corporate policies that reinforce and perpetuate inequalities in the new class society. FAIR's perspective and goals are consistent with many features of the populist tradition, especially its efforts to increase public class consciousness and critique the antidemocratic dangers and consequences of concentrated economic, political, and cultural power in the mass media.

Beneath the Waterline: Militant Resistance?

> Those who make peaceful revolution impossible make violent revolution inevitable.
>
> —John F. Kennedy, March 12, 1962

While the organizations described above differ in terms of specific goals and strategies, they are similar in two respects. First, they are engaged, to a greater or lesser extent, in class-linked resistance to various features of the new class society. Second, they all utilize conventional, peaceful forms of politics, protest, and dissent. As such, they represent contemporary forms of institutionalized class conflict, or class struggle that is carried out mainly within the boundaries of legal forms of organizational and individual resistance, disagreement, and dissent. Sometimes legal forms of resistance are highly stylized and choreographed, as in the case of consumer boycotts, protest marches, or strikes by labor unions. At other times, legal forms of dissent may be reinforced, often in a calculated manner, by minor forms (usually) of deliberate law-breaking, as when dissidents (sometimes including prominent political figures) engage in acts of civil disobedience *in order* to get arrested and thereby call public attention to their grievances and goals. Another feature of these forms of resistance is that they typically take place in conventional political and institutional settings; they also often generate mainstream media reports on the planned or actual resistance.

While conventional forms of resistance to various structural features and consequences of the new class society are widely evident today, militant resistance, such as confrontational illegal behaviors (felonies) or violent acts of defiance, is rare. No organization, leader, or activist located in the alternative power networks seriously interested in reforming the new class society along more egalitarian lines embraces militant resistance as a strategy. Even so, actions have been taken by individuals in the United States that could be interpreted as militant resistance to structural outcomes generated by the new class society. Submerged beneath the waterline of conventional legal terminology, public awareness, and media labels, incidents of violent "domestic terrorism" (a label used by the federal government) could be interpreted as forms of extreme, militant resistance to material manifestations of the new class society. Two prototypes of radical resistance from the 1990s illustrate this view. The first is Timothy McVeigh, who was convicted in 1997 for the 1995 bombing of a federal building in Oklahoma City that killed 168 people. McVeigh was executed for this crime in 2001.[152] The second is Theodore Kaczynski, the so-called Unabomber, who was convicted in 1998 and sentenced to four life terms, plus thirty years, in prison for making homemade bombs that over a seventeen-year period killed three people and wounded twenty-two others.[153]

McVeigh and Kaczynski did not commit their crimes as conscious acts of protest against, or as deliberate responses to, growing class inequalities. However, both men's crimes do appear in part to reflect their anger toward, resentment of, and personal experiences with structural features of an increasingly unequal society that marginalized their aspirations for attaining their view of the American Dream. It is interesting that the two men could not be more different in terms of their backgrounds. McVeigh, a high school graduate who joined the army, served in a combat role in the first Gulf war and returned to civilian life to work in a number of low-level jobs. Kaczynski is a graduate of Harvard University and a former mathematics professor at the University of California, Berkeley. How did these very different paths lead these two men to the same destination, believing that violent, destructive acts were necessary to call attention to the evils of "big government" in McVeigh's case or the "industrial-technological system" in Kaczynski's case?

McVeigh can be viewed as a part of a much larger group of "the dispossessed," a generation of young Americans with low income, no savings, and limited education and job skills. They are also without social capital, or the ties to people with more resources who may be able to help them on a path to a secure future. Their lives are going nowhere, and they have no prospects. But perhaps of equal importance to their lack of resources, they also lack a moral account for their lives that helps to explain their condition. In short, they cannot even view themselves as "victims" because they embrace a belief in individualism and "picking yourself up by your own bootstraps." McVeigh is an example of the American Dream Betrayed, and he used this language in a 1992 letter to the editor of the *Union Sun and Journal* in Lockport, New York: "The 'American Dream' of the middle class has all but disappeared, substituted with people struggling just to get by with next week's groceries. Do we have to shed blood to reform the current system? I hope it doesn't come to that. But it might." McVeigh's hostility toward the government may have started when he failed to qualify for Army Special Forces. But his rightward drift was solidified by the 1992 battle in Idaho between Randy Weaver, a white separatist, and agents of the U.S. Bureau of Alcohol, Firearms, and Tobacco (which resulted in the death of Weaver's wife) and the siege by federal agents of the Branch Davidians in Waco, Texas, that resulted in the deaths of David Koresh and eighty of his followers.[154]

Kaczynski can be viewed as representative of "the disinherited," a generation of educated young Americans from comfortable social and economic backgrounds with bright prospects for their futures. Instead of inheriting a healthy society, as part of their meritocratic birthright, they have been presented with a society that worships economic growth and technological progress while it destroys the environment and the wilderness areas. Drawing upon their knowledge of science, technology, and politics, many young, educated Americans would probably agree with Kaczynski's apocalyptic views: "The industrial-technological system is a disaster for the human race. There is no way of reforming or modifying the system so as to prevent it from depriving people of dignity and autonomy. . . . We therefore advocate revolution against the industrial system. . . . This is not to be a POLITICAL revolution. Its object will be to overthrow not governments but the economic and technological basis of the present society" (from the Unabomber manifesto). Kaczynski is an example of the American Dream Corrupted, leaving a generation of educated Americans with a society that limits personal freedoms and destroys the natural world.

While McVeigh and Kaczynski are perhaps the best-known recent examples of violent resistance to conventional governmental and social institutions, they were not then (or now) alone in their willingness to use violence to resist (or protest) perceived threats to some set of ideals. In recent history, militant and armed resistance to various features of American social institutions first appeared as an urban phenomenon in the 1960s, but it shifted to rural America in the 1990s. America's hinterlands gave birth to the militia movement, whose members were (and are) concerned about the growing power of the federal government; rural areas also served (and still serve) as home to radical environmental activists who take direct action against commercial developments they view as threats to the environment. What happened in rural America to transform it from the idealized and romanticized vision of the independent farmer, steeped in values of family, community, and God?

One thing that has happened is that rural America has become corporatized just like the rest of the country. Throughout much of the twentieth century, government support and tax benefits have gone primarily to corporate farms and multinational agribusinesses like Archer-Daniels-Midland and Cargill Corporation. The pattern of income and wealth inequality that has produced the double-diamond class structure is clearly revealed in the pattern of landownership in the United States. Landownership has the appearance of Central American feudal agriculture—a small number of very large landowners and most small farmers either driven off the land to work on export-driven corporate farms or left with small subsistence plots. In the United States, the wealthiest 5 percent of landowners own 75 percent of the land, while the poorest landowners (75 percent of all landowners) own 3 percent of the land.[155]

In addition to the economic impoverishment of rural American, farm-dependent towns is the cultural and political marginalization of rural life and values. The privileged class in the United States dominates cultural and political life within a bicoastal, urban framework. Rural America is at best ignored and, at worst, the target of ridicule and stereotypes (has anybody seen Comedy Central's *Blue Collar TV*?). The combination of economic impoverishment and economic-cultural marginalization of rural America, seemingly nourished by traditions of rural radicalism and populism, appears to have facilitated both "right-" and "left-wing" forms of militant resistance. On the right, the militia movement appears to represent contemporary expressions of long-standing and often rural-based suspicions of, and hostility toward, the federal government.[156] On the left, the radical environmental movement can be viewed as a modern version of popular (and often rural-based) distrust of, and hostility toward, industrial-technological systems—somewhat akin to the revolutionary 1811 English Luddites.[157]

It is important to note that neither movement emerged to explicitly challenge growing class inequalities. Acts of militant resistance associated with both movements were (and to some extent still are) directed toward structural features that are part of the new class society. But such acts have typically *not* been claimed by perpetrators to represent resistance to, or protests against, growing economic inequalities and class polarization in the United States. Militant resistance on the right typically targets what militia-style radicals view as an increasingly powerful and illegitimate federal government; on the left, such resistance targets what environmental radicals view as especially egregious corporate (or government) exploitation and/or development of what should be protected land or natural resources.

The militia movement, consisting of loosely organized, armed, right-wing, military-style "citizen" militia groups in several U.S. states, emerged in the 1980s, expanded in size in the 1990s, declined in the early 2000s, and appeared to experience new growth in the mid- to latter 2000s. It was (and is) a movement based on traditions of local control, suspicion of the federal government, and right-wing conservative political views, often including fascist-like ideas and symbols. In the 1990s, "at its peak, the movement had hundreds of groups and thousands of members."[158] Since the September 11 terrorist attacks, militia watch groups agree the movement has declined in size, but in the latter 2000s, these groups claimed a "new" militia movement was emerging. Online discussion groups and websites were among the tools watch groups said were facilitating the growth of a new militia movement.[159]

Today, militia groups are typically grouped with, and counted as part of, an array of many kinds of right-wing extremist groups in the United States, which collectively have an estimated membership of about twenty-five thousand.[160] This membership is largely based today in what the Southern Poverty Law Center Intelligence Project says are "more than 700 hate groups around the nation."[161] Militia groups (as well as many other right-wing extremist groups) are said to be energized now by their traditional fear and suspicion of big government, as well as by multiple conspiracy theories. These include the view that the federal government, not foreign terrorists, orchestrated the September 11 attacks to justify the further expansion of government powers.[162] They "view the 'war on terrorism' as a war directed at themselves, not foreign terrorists . . . and consider anti-terrorism measures such as the 'Patriot Act' merely a prelude to mass gun confiscation and martial law."[163]

Actions by radical environmentalist groups against corporate, industrial, or government projects that such groups believe are harmful to the environment have been called "ecotage" and the FBI claims a small number of "domestic terrorist" groups are responsible for such acts. In 2005, John E. Lewis, deputy assistant director of the Counterterrorism Division of the FBI, testified at a U.S. Senate committee hearing: "One of today's most serious domestic terrorist threats come from special interest extremist movements such as the Animal Liberation Front (ALF), the Earth Liberation Front (ELF), and

Stop Huntingdon Animal Cruelty (SHAC)."[164] A 2006 FBI press release summarized the alleged criminal record of environmental extremist groups: "In 2004, the FBI estimated ELF, ALF and related extremist groups had committed more than 1,100 criminal acts since 1976 with damage estimates over $100 million."[165]

The FBI leadership obviously views these groups as serious threats requiring vigorous law-enforcement actions. Five of the eleven fugitives included in the "Wanted by the FBI for Domestic Terrorism" list posted on the FBI's website in 2006 had ties to either ALF or ELF or both groups.[166] Also in 2006, the FBI charged eleven people "with acts of domestic terrorism on behalf of the extremist Earth Liberation Front (ELF) and Animal Liberation Front (ALF) over a five-year period. The 65-count indictment alleges the defendants committed acts of domestic terrorism between 1996 and 2001 in Oregon, Wyoming, Washington, California, and Colorado. Specifically, the indictment includes charges related to arson, conspiracy, use of destructive devices, and destruction of an energy facility"[167]

The potential for militant resistance by militia groups and radical environmentalists in the pre–September 11 period appeared to be serious. At that time, such groups had been operating for many years. This suggests they had been successful in attracting new members and the resources needed to continue their activities. The structural features of the new class society that helped produce McVeigh, Kaczynski, and organized militant resistance on the right and left have not disappeared. But the September 11 terrorist attacks and several subsequent developments—such as wars in Afghanistan and Iraq, media and government encouragement of America-first patriotism, and the federal government's aggressive antiterrorism policies and practices deployed at home and abroad—appear to have muted (at least partially) Americans' interest in, involvement in, and/or support for militant forms of domestic resistance (rural or urban), at least for the moment. The development of substantial militant resistance movements in the United States to conditions, policies, and practices routinely produced as a consequence of the privileged class pursuing its interests at the expense of the working class appears far less likely in a society engaged in an open-ended "war on terror." Even so, individual acts of violent resistance, such as those carried out by McVeigh and Kaczynski, may well recur, as may small group-based violent actions like those spearheaded by ELF and ALF.

The Future: The Scrooge Scenario versus the Structural Scenario

Inequality is the core issue of our time. Over the last 30 years, America has changed from a nation that aimed to share its bounty into one that doesn't even pretend to try.

—Dan Cantor, Executive Director,
Working Families Party–New York, 2006

In the world according to Dickens, reform is a function of conscience. In *A Christmas Carol*, the ghosts of Christmas Past, Present, and Future visit Ebenezer Scrooge. This gets results. Shown the consequences of his selfishness, Scrooge is appropriately appalled and transformed. He reforms his miserly ways, and the community becomes a better place. It is a powerful and comforting morality tale grounded in an unspoken assumption that the selfish pursuit by the rich of their narrow economic interests can be blunted and redirected by consciousness-raising experiences that awaken a latent social conscience.

The "Scrooge scenario" can be seen as a kind of pattern for reform, favored and promoted by privileged-class leaders, that focuses attention on individual renewal and personal commitment. Media accounts of political corruption involving influence peddlers, lobbyists, insiders, and fixers, as well as economic warts such as sweatshops and child labor, are portrayed as bad apples. The system is sound, we are told; we just need to replace rotten apples or force the bad apples to undergo a publicly reported transformation involving admissions of wrongdoing, acceptance of guilt, and repentance—along with promises to go forth and sin no more.

The "structural democracy scenario" places little faith in the Scrooge approach. Class reformers see undemocratic political, economic, and cultural structures controlled by the privileged class and unaccountable to the public as the problem. The populistlike "structural democracy scenario" is favored by many class-reform activists. The primary aim of this view is to revitalize the practice of democratic participation in politics and government and to extend the principles of democratic participation and governance to the corporate structures that currently dominate the political, economic, and cultural arenas of our society and undergird the many inequalities of the new class society.

Although the structural democracy project of resolving class inequalities is highly problematic and uncertain, we believe it can usefully serve as a point of departure for a national dialogue on the closeted, taboo subject of growing class inequalities. An increasingly class-conscious public can provide the economic, political, and human resources necessary to support existing and yet-to-be-established institutions committed to the interests of the new working class and to reforming the new class society.

As we have seen throughout this book, there is a real and pressing need for structural, not Scrooge-like, changes in our highly unequal new class system. The reforms proposed or initiated by organizations cited in this chapter provide some concrete examples of what real structural changes aimed at redressing class inequities might look like. Such reforms on a much wider scale are essential if we are to begin the process of melting the iceberg of inequality before it rips open the current version of the *Titanic* known as the new class society and sends our democratic experiment to a permanent resting spot at the bottom of history.

CLASS ISSUES IN THE MEDIA: A NEW AMERICAN DREAM?

The American Dream, in its fullest sense, includes both materialistic and communitarian dimensions. As we noted in the chapter 2 box reading, the mainstream media frequently report on the dream but nearly always reference its materialistic dimension. Usually this involves "success stories," but some recent media reports have described the growth of U.S. economic inequalities as threatening the ability of many Americans to achieve the materialistic features of the dream. In contrast, the communitarian side of the dream is seldom reported by the media, but it figures prominently in U.S. history and culture. For example, in the 1930s, "President Franklin Delano Roosevelt reinvigorated the dream of moral community, using the government to affirm that in a time of desperate need, Americans would take care of each other."[1] Classic works in American literature, such as *Our Town*, have celebrated the importance of community values, while others, such as the *Great Gatsby*, have warned that individual economic and social success "should not be achieved at any price."[2] Our history and literature suggest it is important for the two dimensions of the dream to be linked and balanced, but explicit consideration of this issue appears to be absent from most media reports on the American Dream today.

The American Dream is often considered by reform-oriented organizations (e.g., the AFL-CIO and CTW) as an ideal that has been betrayed. Such groups maintain that redemption is possible and that access to the dream can be reestablished through progressive reforms so that all Americans have real opportunities to realize it. Although this is an important and laudable goal, it is our view that the great challenge today does not simply involve reestablishing workers' access to the material dimension of the dream. Rather, it is to develop a more complete "new American Dream," capable of uniting the materialistic and moral dimensions of this ideal. Such a new dream, we believe, would include not only reforms aimed at reversing growing inequalities in the new class society but also policies and structures aimed at promoting a unified, inclusive civil society of shared responsibilities and mutual obligations.

Many features that would be part of a new American Dream can be found today in the reform agendas of groups located in the alternative power networks. These groups have developed proposals for new economic, political, and social policies that they believe will lead to a more just society. In some cases, such groups have successfully implemented some features of their agendas through organizations they created and through legislation they helped enact at the local and state levels (e.g., nonprofit health clinics, low-income housing, recycling projects, environmental protection, minimum-wage increases). A problematic feature of many proposals supported by reform-minded groups is that they often require action at the national level, usually through some combination of national social movements, political parties, elected officials, and federal legislation.[3] Although federally mandated change is the most comprehensive way to achieve large-scale progressive reforms, we do not view national social movements supporting such reforms as possessing sufficient political influence to broker deals at this time. We also have little faith that the current two-party system has enough progressive members to enact policies that will, for example, provide national health care to all Americans, redistribute wealth

(continued)

or income via more progressive individual and corporate tax structures, or protect American jobs by repealing "free trade" policies like NAFTA and CAFTA.

While we doubt that comprehensive reforms consistent with a new American Dream can be enacted at the national level today, this does not mean we think nothing meaningful can be done to move us closer to this dream. As we noted above, many groups in the alternative power networks have already implemented progressive reforms at the local and state levels. In the following sections, we focus on a conceptual model that could provide a framework for thinking about how progressive reforms—those already enacted and those proposed—can be more fully implemented and extended to larger segments of the society. We also discuss two real-world progressive reform projects. Our choices were guided by two considerations. First, we think ideas are important in framing how people think about their lives and alternative ways of living. History teaches us that changes in how people think have often been preconditions for social reform. Thus, we begin with a consideration of what is termed a *social economy model* of economic and social organization, which is very different from the *market economy model* now dominant in the United States. Second, we think real-life, human-scale programs with social economy features serve as important illustrations of what is possible under this model. Thus, we briefly discuss two "bottom-up" examples of direct participation by Americans in such programs: (1) employee stock-ownership plans (ESOPs) and (2) the cooperative movement.

ANOTHER WORLD IS POSSIBLE: THE SOCIAL ECONOMY MODEL

When thousands of social activists met at the U.S. Social Forum in Atlanta, Georgia, in June 2007, the theme was "Another World Is Possible."[4] If enacted, the policies that activists who endorse this slogan favor would transform the U.S. market economy into a social economy. Such a model is attractive in part because of many problems associated with the market economy in the United States, as described in various parts of this book. For example, in chapter 7 we described the "incentive wars" that have been played out in many states and cities competing for economic growth. Such "wars" are based on the competitive logic inherent in a market economy, where incentive costs are balanced against hoped-for economic growth. Gains and losses are calculated in monetary terms, and the bottom line is all that matters in a market economy model.

A social economy model provides an attractive alternative perspective as the basis for organizing the economy at national, regional, and local levels and for managing growth because of its emphasis on goals that go beyond economic considerations. It involves looking at societies and communities as places to both work and live. It is driven by policies that balance economic growth with the requirements of people for secure jobs, living wages, good schools, supportive social services, affordable homes, and sustainable natural resources. A social economy includes concerns with developing human resources that can serve the economic, social, human, and ecological needs of nations, regions, and communities and not simply the economic interests of businesses generally or the interests of a particular firm. In differing forms, social economy models are in place today in many European nations.[5] For example, industrialist Helmut Giesecke has noted that in Germany, "We are not operating a marketplace economy, [but rather] a social marketplace economy." In this model, "government, labor, and business work together to reconcile prosperity with social justice."[6]

Creating a U.S. social economy would require collaborative agreements between workers, government, businesses, and communities. Instead of destructive forms of competition and corporate corruption of politics, new organizations at the national, regional, and local levels could be created linking governmental units, unions, workers, companies, and consumers. These bodies could produce policies aimed at fostering cooperation between and among social and economic actors. The overall goal would be to strengthen the economic and social infrastructures of the society. This would improve the job prospects of workers, enhance economic and social stability, and attend to the bottom-line interests of corporations. We think that framing discussions of progressive reforms in terms of a social economy model would provide a useful way to build public understanding of, and wider support for, such reforms at all levels. The model could also be invoked in discussions of reforms already in place at local and state levels to stimulate ideas and policies that might extend such reforms to regional or national arenas.

WORKER OWNERSHIP AND CONTROL

Working Americans need to get a larger share of the value they create for their employers. An arrangement that has the potential to help workers achieve this outcome currently exists in the form of employee stock ownership plans. ESOPs allow companies to provide profit-sharing plans in the form of company stock. In 2006, there were 9,225 ESOPs in the United States, covering 10.1 million employees with ESOP assets valued at about $600 billion.[7] Many current ESOPs are available only to upper-level managers and professionals, but such plans could and should be more broadly based to include all employees. The National Center for Employee Ownership reports that companies with broad employee ownership and extensive worker participation can benefit from increases in worker motivation and productivity.[8] Given the negative trends affecting workers that we have documented in this book, such as declining job security, stagnant wages, and reductions in company contributions to pension and health-care plans, workers and their unions should press employers to offer more extensive alternative economic benefits. ESOPs have the potential to serve as a vehicle for ensuring that an increasing share of corporate economic resources created by the workers is distributed to the workers.

EXPANDING CIVIL SOCIETY: THE COOPERATIVE MOVEMENT

We believe that the cooperative movement provides Americans with opportunities to expand their control in key areas of everyday life. Cooperatives are businesses that are owned and democratically controlled by their members, who use the coop's services

(continued)

or buy its goods. Cooperatives are not motivated by profit but by serving the needs of members for affordable and high-quality goods and services. The National Cooperative Business Association reports the existence of a wide-range of cooperatives in America.[9] We focus here on only housing and food coops because they are areas where Americans spend a large share of their earned income.

The National Association of Housing Cooperatives reports that about 1.2 million families in America at all income levels live in homes operated through cooperative associations.[10] Coop members own a share of the property in which they live, and they participate in its operation. Every month, coop members pay a proportionate share of all expenses, including mortgage payments, property taxes, maintenance, insurance, and utilities. Food coops operate in much the same fashion, but they provide consumer retail goods to their members.

The central idea of coops is democratic control by members, accomplished by volunteer boards of directors elected by the members, and volunteer committees that oversee a variety of operations associated with the coop. Cooperatives provide mutual support for its members and learning opportunities for how to expand control over critical areas of their lives. They are small-scale examples of the social economy model in action. They also embody solidarity economics and solidarity politics, which enable coop members to transcend the controlling structures of mainstream economic and political life. Many people involved in organizing social life based on principles of cooperation and solidarity believe that cooperatives could expand into a national project providing a democratic, social economy alternative to market economy capitalism.

CONCLUSION

We are not the first authors to suggest that egalitarian reforms could be framed in terms of a social economy or conceptualized as the basis for a new American Dream.[11] Even so, we think our distributional model of class analysis provides a new and useful perspective on the kinds of reforms that would necessarily be at the core of a new dream. As we have seen, our model calls attention to how large organizations, dominated by the superclass and managed by the credentialed class, control the distributive order in ways that lead to a highly unequal distribution of generative resources to the privileged class. One major consequence of these arrangements is the creation and continual reinforcement of the "double-diamond" class structure. To move closer to a new American Dream will require, we believe, the development of a social economy with public policies designed to blunt privileged-class-control of the distributive order. Such policies would have to substantially alter the current concentration of organizational power and redistribute large shares of the generative resources now held by the privileged class to workers.

ESOPs, coops, and similar programs illustrate how some features of a social economy can function on a small scale. But the challenge is to create larger-scale structures that will extend the social economy model throughout the society. Many critics will say such a transformation is unrealistic and far too utopian; it cannot be done. Perhaps they are right. But we agree with many reformers who believe it is important to try. This is the case even though we think development of a social economy at the national level is unlikely to be achieved in the short run. The benefits of such a model would be substantial and greatly improve the quality of working Americans' lives in two major respects. First, the *outcomes* of redistribution reforms developed by democratically constructed and controlled policies, programs, and organizations would increase working Americans' access to the material dimension of the dream. Second, the *processes* of constructing and operating democratically based redistributional policies would provide workers with community-based participation in, and influence over, the programs and structures that would govern, manage, and sustain a social democracy. Such experiences and activities would reinforce the moral and communitarian dimension of the dream. The combination of more equitable outcomes and democratic participation in the processes that would drive greater equity could, we believe, serve as the foundation for a new American Dream, which would reinforce, as journalist Richard Todd put it, "the idea that there is an equality based on worth that transcends net worth."[12]

NOTES

1. Charles Derber, *The Wilding of America: Money, Mayhem, and the New American Dream*, 4th ed. (New York: Worth Publishers, 2007), 159.

2. Derber, *The Wilding of America*, 158. F. Scott Fitzgerald, *The Great Gatsby* (New York: Cambridge University Press, 1991); Thornton Wilder, *Our Town: A Play in Three Acts* (New York: Coward-McCann, 1938).

3. For examples, see "An Alternative State of the Union, Special Issue," *Nation*, February 6, 2006; Green Party of the United States, "Platform 2004"; Christopher Hayes, "The New Democratic Populism," *Nation* (December 4, 2006): 11–14; John Nichols, "The 'Seattle Senators,'" *Nation* (December 18, 2006): 8–10; Ethan Miller, "Other Economies Are Possible," *Dollars and Sense* (July–August 2006); "Taming Global Capitalism Anew," *Nation* (April 17, 2006): 18–27.

4. United States Social Forum, "About the USSF," on the Internet at http://www.ussf2007.org/about (visited January 7, 2007).

5. Jeremy Rifkin, "The European Dream," *Utne* (September–October 2004): 75–79.

6. Derber, *The Wilding of America*, 160.

7. National Center for Employee Ownership, "A Statistical Profile of Employee Ownership," July 2006, on the Internet at http://www.nceo.org/library/eo_stat.html (visited July 13, 2006).

8. National Center for Employee Ownership, "Largest Study Yet Shows ESOPs Improve Performance and Employee Benefits."

9. National Cooperative Business Association, "About Cooperatives," March 2005, on the Internet at http://www.ncba.coop/abcoop_stats.cfm (visited December 15, 2006).

10. National Association of Housing Cooperatives, "About NAHC and Housing Co-ops," on the Internet at http://www.coophousing.org/about_nahc.shtml (visited December 15, 2006).

11. Derber, *The Wilding of America*, 158. Also see Center for a New American Dream, "About Us," on the Internet at http://www.newdream.org (visited December 15, 2006); Richard Florida, "The New American Dream," *Washington Monthly* (March 2003): 26–34.

12. Quoted in Sam Pizzigati, *Greed and Good: Understanding and Overcoming the Inequality That Limits Our Lives* (New York: Apex Press, 2004), xxvii.

NOTES

1. Internet Movie Database, Inc., "All-Time Worldwide Boxoffice" and "All-Time USA Boxoffice," on the Internet at http://www.us.imdb.com/boxoffice/alltimegross (visited July 30, 2006). *Forrest Gump* is now (2006) twenty-third among all films ever released in worldwide gross receipts. It is now fifteenth among all U.S. films ever released with U.S. gross receipts of $329 million (2006). By comparison, *Titanic* is the number-one grossing film of all time in the United States ($600 million) and in the world ($1.8 billion).

2. Charles Derber, *The Wilding of America: Money, Mayhem, and the New American Dream*, 4th ed. (New York: Worth Publishers, 2007), 158.

3. Ellen McGirt, "A Banner Year," *Fortune* (April 17, 2006): 193.

4. "Ranked within Industries, The Fortune 1000," *Fortune* (April 17, 2006): F44–F67.

5. David Harvey, *A Brief History of Neoliberalism* (New York: Oxford University Press, 2005); Naomi Klein, "Signs of the Times," *Nation* (October 22, 2001): 15–20.

6. Michael Useem, *The Inner Circle* (New York: Oxford University Press, 1984), 172–200.

7. Joel Bleifuss, "Know Thine Enemy: A Brief History of Corporations," *In These Times* (February 8, 1998): 16–17.

8. Charles Derber, *Corporation Nation* (New York: St. Martin's Press, 1998). Ted Nace, *Gangs of America: The Rise of Corporate Power and the Disabling of Democracy* (San Francisco, CA: Berrett-Koehler, 2003), 105–30.

9. U.S. President Abraham Lincoln, November 21, 1864, letter to Col. William F. Elkins, quoted in Archer H. Shaw, *The Lincoln Encyclopedia* (New York: Macmillan, 1950), 40; also quoted in Emanuel Hertz, *Abraham Lincoln: A New Portrait*, vol. 2 (New York: Horace Liveright, Inc., 1931), 954.

10. Paul J. Dimaggio and Walter W. Powell, "The Iron Cage Revisited: Institutional Isomorphism and Collective Rationality in Organizational Fields," *American Sociological Review* 48 (1983): 147–60.

11. Charles Perrow, "A Society of Organizations," *Theory and Society* 20 (1991): 725–62. Also see Derber, *Corporation Nation*, 172–86.

12. Joe R. Feagin, *Racial and Ethnic Relations* (Englewood Cliffs, NJ: Prentice Hall, 1989).

13. Robert Cherry, "Institutionalized Discrimination," in *Experiencing Race, Class, and Gender in the United States*, ed. Roberta Fiske-Rusciano and Virginia Cyrus, 4th ed. (Boston: McGraw-Hill, 2005); Barbara Reskin and Irene Padavic, *Women and Men at Work* (Thousand Oaks, CA: Pine Forge Press, 1994); Chris Tilly and Charles Tilly, *Work under Capitalism* (Boulder, CO: Westview Press, 1998).

14. Class Action, "What Is Classism?" and "What Do We Mean by 'Class'?" on the Internet at http://www.classism.org/home_definition.html (visited June 12, 2006); Roberta Fiske-Rusciano and Virginia Cyrus, "Experiencing Race, Class, and Gender in the United States," in Fiske-Rusciano and Cyrus, *Experiencing Race, Class, and Gender in the United States* (Boston: McGraw-Hill, 2005), xvii; Gregory Mantsios, "Class in America: Myths and Realities," in *Race, Class, and Gender in the United States*, ed. Paula S. Rothenberg (New York: St. Martin's Press, 1995), 131–43.

15. Chuck Darrow, "The Term 'White Trash' Should Be Tossed Out for Good," *Courier Post*, March 26, 2006, on the Internet at http://courierpostonline.com/apps/pbcs/article? (visited April 10, 2006); Diana Kendall, *Framing Class: Media Representations of Wealth and Poverty in America* (Lanham, MD: Rowman & Littlefield, 2005), 157–60; Matt Wray and Annalee Newitz, eds., *White Trash: Race and Class in America* (New York: Routledge, 1997); "Without 'White Trash' We Couldn't Read Tabloids," *Jossip*, March 28, 2006, on the Internet at http://www.jossip.com/gossip (visited April 10, 2006).

16. Robert Granfield, "Making It by Faking It," *Journal of Contemporary Ethnography* 20 (1991): 331–51.

17. Quoted in Matthew Josephson, *The Robber Barons* (New York: Harcourt, Brace and World, 1934), 325.

18. Robert Granfield and Thomas Koenig, "Pathways into Elite Law Firms: Professional Stratification and Social Networks," in *Research in Politics and Society*, vol. 4, *The Political Consequences of Social Networks*, ed. Gwen Moore and J. Allen Whitt (Greenwich, CT: JAI Press, 1992).

19. Basil Bernstein, *Class, Codes, and Control*, 3 vols. (London: Routledge and Kegan Paul, 1971–1973).

20. Gary Strauss and Barbara Hansen, "CEO Pay Soars as a Select Group Break the $100 Million Mark," *USA Today*, April 11, 2006, on the Internet at http://www.usatoday.com/money/companies/management/2006-04-07-ceo-alpha (visited April 17, 2006).

21. Sam Pizzigati, "The Evolution of Our Plutocracy," *Too Much* (January 23, 2006): 1.

22. Francis X. Clines, "Fueled by Success, Buchanan Revels in Rapid-Fire Oratory," *New York Times*, February 15, 1996; Elizabeth Kolbert and Adam Clymer, "The Politics of Layoff: In Search of a Message," *New York Times*, March 8, 1996.

23. James Bennet, "Patrick J. Buchanan: Harsh Language for Party Leaders," *New York Times*, February 19, 1996.

24. Michael Kazin, *The Populist Persuasion* (New York: Basic Books, 1995), 1.

25. Kazin, *The Populist Persuasion*, 2.

26. Rachel Cohen, "The Stossel Treatment," *Extra!* (March–April 2003): 15–17; Joseph L. Conn and Rob Boston, "Pat Robertson's Media Empire," *Extra!* (March–April 1995): 13–16; Peter Hart, "Give *Us* a Break!: The World According to John Stossel," *Extra!* (March–April 2003): 10–14; Peter Hart and Janine Jackson, "Stossel's 'Stupid' Schools," *Extra!* (May–June 2006): 6–9; Peter Hart and Steve Rendall, "A 'Right-Wing Coup' against PBS's Mythical Bias," *Extra!Update* (June 2005): 1; Robert Parry, "The Right-Wing Media Machine," *Extra!* (March–April 1995): 6–10; Steve Rendall, "An Aggressive Conservative vs. a 'Liberal to Be Determined,'" *Extra!* (November–December 2003): 19–23; Steve Rendall, "Bush-Hating Nation," *Extra!* (May–June 2006): 10–11.

27. Roger Bybee, "NAFTA's Hung Jury," *Extra!* (May–June 2004): 14–15.

28. Paul Craig Roberts, "The New Face of Class Warfare," *CounterPunch* (July 2006): 3.

29. Our estimate of jobs lost to Mexico is based on information in Kate Bronfenbrenner and Stephanie Luce, "The Changing Nature of Corporate Restructuring: The Impact of Production Shifts on Jobs in the U.S., China, and around the Globe" (paper prepared for the U.S.-China Economic and Security Review Commission, October 14, 2004). The authors estimate that U.S. job losses to Mexico totaled 85,000 in 2001 and 140,000 in 2004.

30. *Public Citizen News, 2000 Annual Report*, "Fighting Permanent Normal Trade Relations Status for China," March–April 2001, 7; Public Citizen, "Beyond the 'Blame Game': Why the WTO Doha Round Talks Have Collapsed—and a Path Forward" (press release, Global Trade Watch, July 26, 2006), 2.

31. "Shifting the Trade Debate, CAFTA and Beyond," *Public Citizen News, 2005 Annual Report*, March–April 2006, 7.

32. Bronfenbrenner and Luce, "The Changing Nature of Corporate Restructuring," 3, 7–8.

33. Kent Wong, "Don't Blame China," *Dollars and Sense* (September–October 2005): 10.

34. Bronfenbrenner and Luce, "The Changing Nature of Corporate Restructuring," ii.

35. Bronfenbrenner and Luce, "The Changing Nature of Corporate Restructuring," 5.

36. Roberts, "The New Face of Class Warfare," 2.

37. "Lobbying for China PNTR Cost $113 Million, Report Says," *Public Citizen News* (November–December 2000): 5, 13.

38. Alejandro Reuss, Arthur MacEwan, Phineas Baxandall, and John Miller, "The ABC's of 'Free Trade' Agreements," *Dollars and Sense* (January–February 2001): 24. Also see Lori Wallach, *Public Citizen's Pocket Trade Lawyer: The Alphabet Soup of Globalization* (Washington, DC: Global Trade Watch 1999, updated 2005).

39. Deborah James, "Will the WTO Strike Out in Hong Kong?" *Dollars and Sense* (November–December 2005): 19.

40. Public Citizen, "Beyond the 'Blame Game,'" 5–6.

41. Roberts, "The New Face of Class Warfare," 3.

42. Roberts, "The New Face of Class Warfare," 2.

43. Robert Pollin, *Contours of Descent: U.S. Economic Fractures and the Landscape of Global Austerity* (New York: Verso, 2005), 207; Vicente Navarro, "Production and the Welfare State: The Political Context of Reforms," *International Journal of Health Services* 21 (1991): 585–614.

44. Lawrence Mishel, Jared Bernstein, and Sylvia Allegretto, *The State of Working America, 2006–2007* (Ithaca, NY: IRL Press, 2007), 230. Also see Michael Yates, "Workers Looking for Jobs, Unions Looking for Members," *Monthly Review* (April 2004): 36–48; Dena Libner, "Unequal Recovery," *Dollars and Sense* (May–June 2005): 30–31.

45. Mishel, Bernstein, and Allegretto, *The State of Working America, 2006–2007*, 123–27, 216–17, 226–30. Also see John Schmitt, "How Good Is the Economy at Creating Good Jobs?" (Washington, DC: Center for Economic and Policy Research, October 2005).

46. Eric Konigsberg, "A New Class War: The Haves vs. the Have Mores," *New York Times*, November 19, 2006, 4.1.

47. Louis Uchitelle, "Very Rich Are Leaving the Merely Rich Behind," *New York Times*, November 27, 2006, A1.

48. *New York Times*, "When the Joneses Can't Keep Up," December 1, 2006, A30.

49. Walter Korpi, *The Democratic Class Struggle* (London: Routledge, 1983).

50. Navarro, "Production and the Welfare State: The Political Context of Reforms." Vicente Navarro and John Schmitt, "Economic Efficiency versus Social Equality?" *International Journal of Health Services* 35 (2005): 613–30.

51. Robert J. Samuelson, "One 'Reform' That Worked," *Newsweek* (August 7, 2006): 45.

52. Randy Albelda, "Welfare Reform Ten Years Later," *Dollars and Sense* (January–February 2006): 6–7, 27; Neil deMause, "The Smell of Success," *Extra!* (November–December 2006): 6–7.

53. Fred Magdoff and Harry Magdoff, "Disposable Workers: Today's Reserve Army of Labor," *Monthly Review* (April 2004): 24–25.

54. Jane Bryant Quinn, "Medicare's in Good Health," *Newsweek* (May 24, 2004): 41.

55. Michael Boskin, "Social Security: The Common Sense of Social Security Reform," *Hoover Institution—Hoover Digest*, no. 2 (2005): 1–4; Kim Moody, "America Gets a Virtual Raise," *Labor Notes* (February 1997): 15–16.

56. Mishel, Bernstein, and Allegretto, *The State of Working America, 2006–2007*, 137.

57. Schmitt, "How Good Is the Economy at Creating Good Jobs?"

58. David L. Featherman and Robert M. Hauser, *Opportunity and Change* (New York: Academic Press, 1978), 91.

59. Earl Wysong and David W. Wright, "What's Happening to the American Dream? Sons, Daughters, and Intergenerational Mobility Today" (paper presented at the Midwest Sociological Society Annual Meeting, Chicago, Illinois, April 4–7, 2007).

60. Mike Males, "Wild in Deceit: Why 'Teen Violence' Is Poverty Violence in Disguise," *Extra!* (March–April 1996): 7–9.

61. Noreen Connell, "Underfunded Schools: Why Money Matters," *Dollars and Sense* (March–April 1998): 14. Also see David Stratman, "School Reform and the Attack on Public Education," *Dollars and Sense* (March–April 1998): 7; "Voucher Program Fails to Deliver," *AFT American Teacher* (November 2001): 14; "Cleveland Private School Voucher Program Comes Up Short—Again," *AFT American Teacher* (May–June 2006): 17.

62. Hart and Jackson, "Stossel's 'Stupid' Schools."

63. Center for the Study of Educational Policy, "Table 4: Tax Appropriations for Higher Education, by State, FY96–FY06," *Grapevine* (January 12, 2006), on the Internet at http://www.coe.ilstu.edu/grapevine/table4_06.htm (visited August 8, 2006).

64. U.S. Department of Commerce, *Statistical Abstract of the United States: 2006* (Washington, DC: U.S. Government Printing Office, 2005), 482.

65. U.S. Department of Commerce, *Statistical Abstract of the United States: 2006*, 184.

66. Don Kuehn, "Saving for College with Section 529 Plans," *AFT American Teacher* (September 2001): 19.

67. Danette Gerald and Kati Haycock, "Engines of Inequality: Diminishing Equity in the Nation's Premier Public Universities," 2006, Education Trust, Washington, D.C.; Daniel Golden, *The*

Price of Admission: How America's Ruling Class Buys Its Way into Elite Colleges—and Who Gets Left outside the Gates (New York: Crown Publishers, 2006).

68. Center for a New American Dream, "New American Dream Survey Report," 2004, on the Internet at http://www.newdream.org (visited August 27, 2005).

69. Center for a New American Dream, "New American Dream Survey Report."

70. Michael Wallace and Azamat Junisbai, "Finding Class Consciousness in the New Economy," in *Research in Social Stratification and Mobility*, ed. Kevin T. Leicht, vol. 20 (Oxford, UK: Elsevier, 2004), 385–421.

71. David Sirota, "Embracing Populism," *In These Times* (December 2006): 4.

72. The six CTW unions that withdrew from the AFL-CIO include the Service Employees International Union (SEIU), the International Brotherhood of Teamsters (IBT), the United Food and Commercial Workers Union (UFCW), the Laborers' International Union of North America (LIUNA), UNITE-HERE (formed in 2004 when the Union of Needletrades, Industrial, and Textile Employees [UNITE] merged with the Hotel Employees and Restaurant Employees [HERE]), and the United Brotherhood of Carpenters and Joiners of America (UBC). The seventh union, the United Farm Workers of America (UFW), joined CTW but also retained its affiliation with the AFL-CIO. See Change to Win, "Who We Are," 2006, on the Internet at http://www.changetowin.org/about-us/who-we-are.html (visited October 18, 2006).

73. Aaron Bernstein, "Labor's New Face, New Tactics," *Business Week Online*, September 27, 2005, on the Internet at http://www.businessweek.com (visited July 14, 2006).

74. U.S. Department of the Treasury, Internal Revenue Service, "Return of Organizations Exempt from Income Tax—Form 990, American Federation of Labor and Congress of Industrial Organizations," 53-0228172 (Washington, D.C., 2003).

75. David Moberg, "The Lay of Labor's New Land," *In These Times* (November 21, 2005): 24.

76. Bernstein, "Labor's New Face, New Tactics."

77. JoAnn Wypijewski, "Is This *Really* an 'Insurgency' to Shake Up the Unions?" *CounterPunch* (June 16–30, 2005): 1, 4–5; David Moberg, "Does Andy Stern Talk His Walk?" *In These Times* (January 2007): 30–31.

78. Chris Kutalik, "What Does the AFL-CIO Split Mean?" *Labor Notes* (September 2005): 7, 10.

79. David Moberg, "Laboring toward Election Day," *Nation* (October 30, 2006): 21–24.

80. Janine Jackson, "Moribund Militants: Corporate Media on (Re)Organized Labor," *Extra!* (January–February 1996): 6–7.

81. AFL-CIO Executive Council, "Approving a Permanent Charter for Working America" (press release, August 9, 2006), 1, on the Internet at http://www.aflcio.org/about us (visited October 18, 2006).

82. AFL-CIO, "Union Member Vote Drove Shift in Balance of Power" (press release, November 8, 2006), on the Internet at http://www.aflcio.org/mediacenter (visited November 27, 2006).

83. Change to Win, "Workers in Change to Win Unions Help Bring Pro-Worker Candidates to Victory" (press release, November 8, 2006), on the Internet at http://www.changetowin.org/for-the-media (visited December 2, 2006).

84. AFL-CIO Executive Council, "An Economic Agenda for Working Families: Building Union Power, Reclaiming the American Dream," June 2005, and AFL-CIO Officers, "Winning for Working Families," April 2005. Both documents are on the Internet at http://www.aflcio.org.

85. Change to Win, "The American Dream Survey," August 28, 2006, and Change to Win, "Restoring the American Dream," 2006. Both documents are on the Internet at http://www.changetowin.org/for-the-media (visited October 18, 2006).

86. Moberg, "The Lay of Labor's New Land," 24–25.

87. G. William Domhoff, *Who Rules America? Power and Politics in the Year 2000* (Mountain View, CA: Mayfield, 1998), 304.

88. Larry Gabriel, "Beware of the Man behind the Screen," *UAW Solidarity* (May–June 2006): 20–21.

89. JoAnn Wypijewski, "Is This *Really* an 'Insurgency' to Shake Up the Unions?" Also see David Moberg, "Labor Splits Open," *Nation* (July 11, 2005): 4–6.

90. David Moberg, "All Apart Now," *In These Times* (September 19, 2005): 26–27; JoAnn Wypijewski, "States of Disunion," *Nation* (August 29–September 5, 2005): 6–8.

91. "Very Old Labor," *Wall Street Journal*, July 26, 2005, A24.

92. John Zogby, John Bruce, and Rebecca Wittman, "Nationwide Attitudes on Unions," Zogby International, February 26, 2004, 6.

93. Council on International and Public Affairs/Apex Press, "Home," 2006, on the Internet at http://www.cipa-apex.org (visited August 8, 2006).

94. U.S. Department of the Treasury, Internal Revenue Service, "Return of Organization Exempt from Income Tax—Form 990, Council on International and Public Affairs, Inc.," 13-6162451 (Washington, D.C., 2004), 1.

95. United for a Fair Economy, "About UFE," 2006, on the Internet at http://www.fair economy .org/about/index.html (visited August 7, 2006).

96. United for a Fair Economy, "Annual Report 2005," 4, on the Internet at http://www.fair economy.org/about/annual_report.html (visited September 14, 2006). Revenues for 2002 from U.S. Department of the Treasury, Internal Revenue Service, "Return of Organization Exempt from Income Tax—Form 990, United for a Fair Economy, Inc.," 04-3286118 (Washington, D.C., 2002), 1.

97. Sam Pizzigati, "About *Too Much*," 2006, 1, on the Internet at http://www.cipa-apex.org/too much/AboutTooMuch.html (visited August 8, 2006).

98. Pizzigati, "About *Too Much*," 1.

99. United for a Fair Economy, "About UFE: UFE Economics Education Program," on the Internet at http://www.faireconomy.org/econ/index.html (visited August 7, 2006).

100. United for a Fair Economy, "About UFE: Our Strategies," on the Internet at http://www.faireconomy.org/about/our_strategies.html (visited September 18, 2006).

101. United for a Fair Economy, "About UFE: The Need to Build a Movement," 2, on the Internet at http://www.faireconomy.org/about/index.html (visited August 8, 2006).

102. United for a Fair Economy, "About UFE: What We Believe," 2, on the Internet at http://www.faireconomy.org/about/index.html (visited August 8, 2006).

103. Sam Pizzigati, "A Most Dangerous YOYO" (book review), *Too Much* (June 19, 2006): 4.

104. Sam Pizzigati, *Greed and Good: Understanding and Overcoming the Inequality That Limits Our Lives* (New York: Apex Press, 2004); Sam Pizzigati, "Can We Legislate against Greed?" *Too Much* (July 11, 2005): 1; Martin Olav Sabo, "Income Equity Act of 2005," *Congressional Record* (July 12, 2005): E1469.

105. United for a Fair Economy, "About UFE: Our Strategies."

106. Council on International and Public Affairs/Apex Press, "Home," 2006, 1–2.

107. POCLAD, "Frequently Asked Questions," 2006, 1, on the Internet at http://www.poclad .org/FAQ.cfm (visited July 14, 2006).

108. Craig Cox, "Taming the Corporate Beast," *Utne Reader* (March–April 1998): 60.

109. Joel Bleifuss, "The New Abolitionists," *In These Times* (April 1, 1996): 13.

110. POCLAD, "*Elite Consensus: When Corporations Wield the Constitution*, Describes 'Shadow Corporate Government'" (press release, September 10, 2003), 2, on the Internet at http://www .poclad.org/pressroom.cfm (visited July 14, 2006).

111. U.S. Department of the Treasury, Internal Revenue Service, "Return of Organization Exempt from Income Tax—Form 990, Council on International and Public Affairs, Inc.," 2.

112. POCLAD, "*Elite Consensus*," 2, 5.

113. Apex Press, "New Book Urges Democratic Offensive to Purge Corporations' Constitutional Authority to Govern," September 10, 2001, on the Internet at http://www.poclad.org/news/dcdd.html (visited October 17, 2001).

114. Fred Block, "Toward Real Corporate Responsibility," *In These Times* (May 27, 1996): 27.

115. Federal Election Commission, "Federal Elections 2004: A Guide to Party Labels," on the Internet at http://www.fec.gov/pubrec/fe2004/partylabels.pdf (visited August 13, 2006).

116. For examples of recent studies of third parties, see Micah L. Sifry, *Spoiling for a Fight: Third Party Politics in America* (New York: Routledge, 2002); David Reynolds, *Democracy Unbound* (Boston: South End Press, 1997).

117. In the first and second editions of this book, we profiled the Labor Party and the New Party as examples of third parties. The Labor Party is still active and has about fourteen hundred members in the United States. In 2006, the Labor Party was certified as an official political party by state authorities in South Carolina, and party leaders plan to run candidates for offices in South Carolina in the near future. The New Party ceased to exist in 1998. Many activists formerly involved in it helped found the Working Families Party (WFP) of New York in 1998 and later a similar party in Connecticut. The WFP promotes economic, political, and cultural changes that reflect the populist tradition. While the WFP membership is quite small (1,531 in 2004, up from 337 in 1999), it has helped win the passage of progressive reforms in New York, such as minimum-wage and living-wage laws. In the 2006 elections, the WFP endorsed several candidates in New York and helped several Democrats win their races, including Eliot Spitzer (elected governor) and Hillary Rodham Clinton (reelected to the U.S. Senate). According to Spitzer, "In a few short years, the WFP has gone from a fledgling movement to a major force in state politics." Invoking references to populist traditions of the past, the *Harford Advocate* reported, "Just below the radar, turn-of-the-20th-century labor politics is alive and doing what it does best—organizing. Connecticut's Working Families Party is fighting for issues that date back to the Wobblies with 21st century techniques." (Quotes from Jim Duncan, Bertha Lewis, and Bob Master, state cochairs, *Working Families Party Annual Report 2004*, 4, on the Internet at http://www.working familiesparty.org (visited August 8, 2006).

118. Green Party of the United States, "A Brief History of the Green Party," 3, on the Internet at http://www.gp.org/history.shtml (visited August 11, 2006). The ten values are "Grassroots Democracy, Social Justice and Equal Opportunity, Ecological Wisdom, Non-Violence, Decentralization, Community-Based Economics, Feminism, Respect for Diversity, Personal and Global Responsibility, and Future Focus and Sustainability." *Source:* Green Party of the United States, "Platform 2004," Milwaukee, Wisconsin, June 2004, 5–6.

119. Green Party of the United States, "About Us," 2006, 1, on the Internet at http://www.gp .org/about.shtml (visited August 11, 2006).

120. Green Party of the United States, "About Us," 1.

121. Green Party of the United States, "About Us," 1.

122. Green Party of the United States, "A Brief History of the Green Party," 1.

123. Green Party of the United States, "Basic Facts," 1, on the Internet at http://www.gp.org/ register (visited August 11, 2006).

124. Green Party of the United States, "A Brief History of the Green Party," 1.

125. Green Party of the United States, "Platform 2004."

126. Green Party of the United States, "A Brief History of the Green Party," 1.

127. Green Party of the United States, "Green Party Ballot Status and Voter Registration Totals," on the Internet at http://www.greens.org/stats (visited December 6, 2006).

128. Green Party of the United States, "Election Results, 2004, 2005, 2006," on the Internet at http://www.greens.org/elections (visited December 4, 2006).

129. Green Party of the United States, "A Brief History of the Green Party," 1.

130. Green Party of the United States, "Greens Hold 2006 Annual Meeting in Tucson, Arizona," 1, on the Internet at http://www.gp.org/press/pr (visited August 11, 2006).

131. Green Party of the United States, "Greens Challenge Democrats in Congress on Wages, Health Care, Ethics" (press release, November 27, 2006), 1, on the Internet at http://www.gp.org/press/pr (visited December 4, 2006).

132. "Third Party (United States)," Wikipedia Encyclopedia, 2006, 8, on the Internet at http://www.enwikipedia.org/wiki/Third_party_(United States) (visited September 18, 2006).

133. Recent detailed and historically informed accounts of progressive political challenges to the traditional two-party system are presented in the books cited above in note 116.

134. See, for example, Harris Interactive, "Party Affiliation and Political Philosophy Show Little Change, According to Harris Poll," March 9, 2005, on the Internet at http://www.harrisinterative.com/ harris_poll/index.asp?PID=548 (visited September 16, 2006); The Pew Research Center for the People and the Press, "The 2005 Political Typology: Beyond Red vs. Blue," May 10, 2005, 8, on the Internet at http://www.people-press.org/reports/display (visited August 11, 2005).

135. Harris Interactive, "Party Affiliation and Political Philosophy Show Little Change, According to Harris Poll."

136. Living Wage Resource Center, "ACORN and the Living Wage," 2006; also see "The Living Wage Movement," 2006, 1. Both titles are on the Internet at http://www.livingwage campaign.org (visited September 11, 2006).

137. Stephanie Luce, "Chicago Living Wage Activists Take on 'Big Box' Retailers," *Labor Notes* (September 2006): 1, 14.

138. U.S. Department of Health and Human Services, "The 2006 HHS Poverty Guidelines," 2, on the Internet at http://aspe.hhs.gov/poverty/06poverty.shtml (visited January 25, 2006).

139. Living Wage Resource Center, "Living Wage Successes," 1–2, on the Internet at http://www .livingwagecampaign.org/index.php?id=1958 (visited September 11, 2006).

140. Living Wage Resource Center, "ACORN and the Living Wage."

141. Living Wage Resource Center, "ACORN and the Living Wage," 2.

142. Living Wage Resource Center, "ACORN and the Living Wage," 2.

143. Living Wage Resource Center, "ACORN and the Living Wage," 2. Also see Katrina vanden Heuval and Sam Graham-Felsen, "Morality of the Minimum," *Nation* (January 1, 2007): 5–6.

144. Russell Newman and Ben Scott, "Introduction," in *The Future of Media*, ed., Robert McChesney, Russell Newman, and Ben Scott (New York: Seven Stories Press, 2005), 5.

145. Sandy Brown, "Activism and Optimism: The National Conference for Media Reform 2005 St. Louis," in *Censored 2006: The Top 25 Censored Stories*, ed. Peter Phillips and Project Censored (New York: Seven Stories Press, 2005), 263–64; "National Conference for Media Reform, January 12–14, 2007, Memphis, Tennessee," on the Internet at http://www.freepress.net/conference (visited January 5, 2007).

146. Robert W. McChesney, "A Cornerstone of the Media Reform Movement," *Extra!* (February 2006): 6–9.

147. "Statement of Ownership," *Extra!* (November–December 2006): 26.

148. "What's FAIR?" *Extra!* (July–August 2006): 2.

149. FAIR's activities and size are summarized from various issues of *Extra!* (its bimonthly newsletter), *Extra!Update,* and information from the organization's website. The annual budget amount is from the U.S. Department of the Treasury, Internal Revenue Service, "Return of Organization Exempt from Income Tax—Form 990, Fairness and Accuracy in Reporting, Inc.," 13-3392362 (Washington, D.C., 2003), 1 (most recent year available).

150. For discussions of media-reform groups, see Peter Phillips and Project Censored, eds., *Censored 2006: The Top 25 Censored Stories* (New York: Seven Stories Press, 2006), 263–80; Ben H. Bagdikian, *The New Media Monopoly* (Boston: Beacon Press, 2004), 131–52; McChesney, Newman, and Scott, *The Future of Media*, 352–65.

151. Jacqueline Bacon, "The Language of Extra!" *Extra!* (January–February 2006): 19–22.

152. Jo Thomas, "The Oklahoma City Bombing: The Verdict," *New York Times* (June 14, 1997): A1; Morris Dees and Mark Potok, "The Future of American Terrorism," *New York Times*, June 10, 2001, 15.

153. David Johnston, "Judge Sentences Confessed Bomber to Four Life Terms," *New York Times*, May 5, 1998, A1.

154. Barbara Ehrenreich, "The Making of McVeigh," *Progressive* (July 2001): 14–15.

155. Osha Gray Davidson, *Broken Heartland: The Rise of America's Rural Ghetto* (Iowa City: University of Iowa Press, 1996).

156. Catherine M. Stock, *Rural Radicals: Righteous Rage in the American Grain* (Ithaca, NY: Cornell University Press, 1996).

157. Steven E. Jones, *Against Technology: From the Luddites to Neo-Luddism* (New York: Routledge, 2006); Adrian Randall, *Before the Luddites* (New York: Cambridge University Press, 1991).

158. Anti-Defamation League, "The Quiet Retooling of the Militia Movement," 2004, 1, on the Internet at http://www.adl.org/extremism/Milita/default.asp (visited October 2, 2006).

159. Anti-Defamation League, "The Quiet Retooling of the Militia Movement," 1.; also see Daniel Levitas, *The Terrorist Next Door: The Militia Movement and the Radical Right* (New York: Thomas Dunne Books/St. Martin's Press, 2002).

160. Kris Axtman, "The Terror Threat at Home, Often Overlooked," *Christian Science Monitor,* December 29, 2003, 2.

161. *Intelligence Report,* "Monitoring Hate and Extremist Activity," September 19, 2006, on the Internet at http://www.splcenter.org/intel/intpro.jsp (visited September 25, 2006).

162. Christopher Hayes, "9/11: Roots of Paranoia," *Nation* (December 25, 2006): 11–14.

163. Anti-Defamation League, "The Quiet Retooling of the Militia Movement," 2.

164. U.S. Federal Bureau of Investigation, "Congressional Testimony: Statement of John E. Lewis, Deputy Assistant Director, Counterterrorism Division, Federal Bureau of Investigation before the Senate Committee on Environment and Public Works," May 18, 2005, on the Internet at http://www.fbi.gov/congress/congres05/lewis051805.htm (visited September 25, 2006).

165. U.S. Federal Bureau of Investigation, "Headline Archives: Eco-Terror Indictments, 'Operation Backfire' Nets 11," January 20, 2006, on the Internet at http://www.fbi.gov/page2/jan06/elf012006.htm (visited September 26, 2006).

166. U.S. Federal Bureau of Investigation, "Wanted by the FBI: Domestic Terrorism," 2006, on the Internet at http://www.fbi.gov/wanted/fugitives/dt/fug_dt.htm (visited September 25, 2006).

167. Federal Bureau of Investigation, "Headline Archives."

Bibliography

"About Current Documentaries." July 12, 2006. Available at http://www.documentaries.about.com.

Ackerman, Seth. "The Most Biased Name in News." *Extra!* (July–August 2001): 10–12, 14–18.

———. "Selling the Social Security Scare." *Extra!* (January–February 2005): 6.

"Action Alert." *Extra!* (December 1995): 4.

Adams, Rebecca. "GOP-Business Alliance Yields Swift Reversal of Ergonomics Rule." *Congressional Quarterly Weekly* (March 10, 2001): 535–39.

Adams, James Truslow. *The Epic of America.* Boston: Little, Brown, 1933.

Adler, Jerry. "The Rise of the Overclass." *Newsweek* (July 31, 1995): 33–46.

———. "The Fight against the Flu." *Newsweek* (October 31, 2005): 39–45.

Adler, Patricia, Steven J. Kless, and Peter Adler. "Socialization to Gender Roles: Popularity among Elementary Boys and Girls." *Sociology of Education* 65 (1992): 169–87.

"Advocates Pressed Government, Business to Improve Drug, Food, Worker Protections." *Public Citizen News, 2002 Annual Report* (March–April 2003): 2.

AFL-CIO. "Young Workers without College Degrees Are the 'Forgotten Majority.'" In *High Hopes, Little Trust: A Study of Young Workers and Their Ups and Downs in the New Economy.* Washington, DC: AFL-CIO, 1999.

———. "Frequently Asked Questions." 2001. Available at http://www.aflcio.org.

———. "Front Groups for the Attack on Retirement Security." 2006. Available at http://www.aflcio.org.

———. "Union Member Vote Drove Shift in Balance of Power." Press release, November 8, 2006. Available at http://www.aflcio.org.

AFL-CIO Executive Council. "An Economic Agenda for Working Families: Building Union Power, Reclaiming the American Dream." June 2006. Available at http://www.aflcio.org.

———. "Approving a Permanent Charter for Working America." Press release, August 9, 2006. Available at http://www.aflcio.org.

AFL-CIO Officers. "Winning for Working Families." April 2005. Available at http://www.aflcio.org.

Ageism on the Agenda. Special Issue. *Extra!* (March–April 1997).

Aguirre, Adalberto, Jr., and David V. Baker. *Structured Inequality in the United States.* Upper Saddle River, NJ: Prentice Hall, 2000.

Akre, Jane. "We Report, They Decide: Fox TV Censors Series on Milk Hazards." *National News Reporter* (June 1998): 12–13.

Akre, Jane, and Steve Wilson. "Fox BGH Suit." 2006. Available at http://www.foxbghsuit.com.

Alba, Richard D., and Gwen Moore. "Ethnicity in the American Elite." *American Sociological Review* 47 (1982): 373–83.

Albelda, Randy. "Farewell to Welfare but Not to Poverty." *Dollars and Sense* (November–December 1996): 16–19.

———. "Welfare Reform, Ten Years Later." *Dollars and Sense* (January–February 2006): 6–7.

Alexander, Karl S., Martha Cook, and Edward McDill. "Curriculum Tracking and Educational Stratification." *American Sociological Review* 43 (1982): 47–66.

Alexander, Karl S., Doris R. Entwisle, and Carrie S. Horsey. "From First Grade Forward: Early Foundations of High School Dropout." *Sociology of Education* 70 (1997): 87–107.

Ali, Lorraine. "Sounding Off on Bush." *Newsweek* (May 15, 2006): 13.

Allen, Michael Patrick. "Elite Social Movement Organizations and the State: The Rise of the Conservative Policy-Planning Network." In *Research in Politics and Society*, vol. 4, *The Political Consequences of Social Networks*, ed. Gwen Moore and J. Allen Whitt. Greenwich, CT: JAI Press, 1992.

Alves, Wayne, and Peter Rossi. "Who Should Get What? Fairness Judgments of Distribution of Earnings." *American Journal of Sociology* 84 (1978): 541–64.

Amott, Teresa. "Will the Economy Be Less Stable?" *Dollars and Sense* (November–December 1996): 22–23.

Amter, Charlie. "Comedy Central Keeps Colbert." *E! Online* (November 2, 2005). Available at http://www.eonline.com.

"An Alternative State of the Union, Special Issue." *Nation* (February 6, 2006): 11–27.

"Anatomy of a Victory." *Nation* (December 19, 2005): 3–4.

Anderson, Charles H. *The Political Economy of Social Class*. Englewood Cliffs, NJ: Prentice Hall, 1974.

———. *Toward a New Sociology*. Homewood, IL: Dorsey Press, 1974.

Anderson, Curt. "House Passes $100 Billion Stimulus Measure." *Indianapolis Star*, October 25, 2001.

Anderson, Gwynneth. "'Who Killed the Electric Car' Tells of Vehicle's Rise and Fall." *Public Citizen News* (July–August 2006): 5.

Anderson, Sarah, John Cavanaugh, Chuck Collins, Eric Benjamin, and Sam Pizzigati. "Executive Excess 2006: 13th Annual CEO Compensation Survey." Washington, DC, and Boston: Institute for Policy Studies and United for a Fair Economy, August 30, 2006.

Anderson, Sarah, John Cavanaugh, Scott Klinger, and Liz Stanton. "Executive Excess 2005: 12th Annual CEO Compensation Survey." Washington, DC, and Boston: Institute for Policy Studies and United for a Fair Economy, August 30, 2005.

Andrews, Edmund L. "Foreign-Profit Tax Break Is Outlined." *New York Times*, January 14, 2005.

———. "House Passes a $2.7 Trillion Spending Plan." *New York Times*, May 18, 2006.

Anti-Defamation League. *Armed and Dangerous: Militia Takes Aim at the Federal Government*. Fact Finding Report, 1994.

———. "The Quiet Retooling of the Militia Movement." 2004. Available at http://adl.org.

Apex Press. "New Book Urges Democratic Offensive to Purge Corporations' Constitutional Authority to Govern." 2001. Available at http://www.poclad.org.

"A Promise between Generations." *UAW Solidarity* (March–April 2005): 17–25.

Arenson, Karen W. "Cuts in Tuition Assistance Put College beyond Reach of Poorest Students." *New York Times*, January 27, 1997.

Aronson, Ronald. "The Left Needs More Socialism." *Nation* (April 17, 2006): 28–30.

Aronowitz, Stanley. *The Last Good Job in America*. Lanham, MD: Rowman & Littlefield, 2001.

Aronowitz, Stanley, and William DiFazio. "High Technology and Work Tomorrow." *Annals of the American Academy of Political and Social Science* 544 (March 1996): 52–76.

Associated Press. "Americans Are Wired into New Bills." *Indianapolis Star*, July 7, 2001.

"A Rising Tide?" *Washington Post*, March 12, 2006.

"A Time for American Leadership on Key Global Issues." *New York Times*, February 11, 1998.

Aufderheide, Pat. "Too Much Media." *In These Times* (May 9, 2005): 28.

Aversa, Jeannine. "Upbeat Jobs News Precedes Election." *Indianapolis Star*, November 4, 2006.

Axtman, Kris. "The Terror Threat at Home, Often Overlooked." *Christian Science Monitor*, December 29, 2003.

Bacon, David. "Class Warfare." *Nation* (January 12–19, 2004): 17–20.

Bacon, Jacqueline. "The Language of Extra!" *Extra!* (January–February 2006): 19–22.

Bagdikian, Ben. *The Media Monopoly*. Boston: Beacon Press, 1997.

———. *The New Media Monopoly*. Boston: Beacon Press, 2004.

Baker, Dean. "Generation Excess." *Extra!* (March–April 1996): 12–13.

———. "Free Trade Fables." *Extra!* (January–February 2000): 18.

———. "Don't Follow the Money." *Extra!* (September–October 2003): 6–7.

———. "Cutting Our Benefits." *In These Times* (January 3, 2005): 22–23.

Baker, Peter, and Jim VanderHei. "A Voter Rebuke for Bush, the War and the Right." *Washington Post*, November 8, 2006.

"Balance This." *In These Times* (May 13, 1996): 4–5.

Balkovic, Brian. "High Income Tax Returns for 2003." *The Statistics of Income SOI Bulletin* (Spring 2006): 8–56.

Baran, Jan Witold, and Carol A. Lanham. "Corporations and PACS: More Important Than Ever." *Metropolitan Corporate Counsel* (July 2004): 1–2.

Barlett, Donald L., and James B. Steele. *America: What Went Wrong?* Kansas City, MO: Andrews and McMeel, 1992.

———. *America: Who Really Pays the Taxes?* (New York: Touchstone, 1994), 93–94.

———. "America: Who Stole the Dream?" *Indianapolis Star*, September 22–29, 1996, Business section. Reprinted from the *Philadelphia Inquirer*.

Barnet, Richard J., and John Cavanagh. *Global Dreams: Imperial Corporations and the New World Order*. New York: Simon and Schuster, 1994.

Barnett, Greg. "Curiously, More of Us Believe in Paranormal." *Indianapolis Star*, June 19, 2001.

Barron, James. "Public Lives: Hear the One about Letterman's Producer?" *New York Times*, February 3, 1998.

Bates, Eric. "Campaign Inflation." *Mother Jones* (March–April 2001): 47–48.

Beckett, Katherine. "Setting the Public Agenda: 'Street Crime' and Drug Use in American Politics." *Social Problems* 41 (1994): 425–47.

Beckett, Katherine, Kris Nyrop, Lori Pfingst, and Melissa Bowen. "Drug Use, Drug Possession Arrests, and the Question of Race: Lessons from Seattle." *Social Problems* 52 (2005): 419–41.

Beder, Sharon. *The Corporate Assault on Environmentalism*. White River Junction, VT: Chelsea Green Publishing, 1998.

———. "Public Relations' Role in Manufacturing Artificial Grass Roots Coalitions." *Public Relations Quarterly* 43 (1998): 21–30.

"Benchmarking Data Available by Industry." *Financial Executive* (December 2004): 12.

Bendix, Reinhard, and Frank W. Howton. "Social Mobility and the American Business Elite—II." *British Journal of Sociology* 9 (1958): 1–14.

Bennet, James. "Patrick J. Buchanan: Harsh Language for Party Leaders." *New York Times*, February 19, 1996.

Berman, Ari. "Big $$ for Progressive Politics." *Nation* (October 16, 2006): 18–24.

Berman, Jay M. "Industry Output and Employment Projections to 2014." *Monthly Labor Review* (November 2005): 45–69.

Bernasek, Anna. "'Temporary' Tax Cuts Have a Way of Becoming Permanent." *New York Times*, May 14, 2006.

Bernhardt, Annette, Martuna Morris, Marck S. Handcock, and Marc A. Scott. *Divergent Paths: Economic Mobility in the New American Labor Market* (New York: Russell Sage Foundation, 2001).

Bernstein, Aaron. "Back on the Edge." *Business Week* (April 23, 2001): 42–43.

———. "Labor's New Face, New Tactics." *Business Week Online* (September 27, 2005). Available at http://www.businessweek.com.

Bernstein, Basil. *Class, Codes, and Control*. 3 vols. London: Routledge and Kegan Paul, 1971–1973.

Berstein, Jared. *All Together Now: Common Sense for a Fair Economy.* San Francisco, CA: Berrtt-Koehler, 2006.

Birnbaum, Jeffrey H. *The Lobbyists.* New York: Times Books, 1992.

———. "The Road to Riches Is Called K Street." *Washington Post,* June 22, 2005.

Bivens, Matt. "Harvard's 'Fitting Choice.'" *Nation* (June 25, 2001): 6–7.

BKSH. "Our Perspective." 2006. Available at http://www.bksh.com.

———. "United States—The Company." 2006. Available at http://www.bksh.com.

Blakely, Edward J., and Mary Gail Snyder. *Fortress America: Gated Communities in the United States.* Washington, DC: Brookings Institution Press, 1997.

Blau, Peter M., and Otis D. Duncan. *The American Occupational Structure.* New York: Wiley, 1967.

Bleifuss, Joel. "The Terminators." *In These Times* (March 4, 1996): 12–13.

———. "The New Abolitionists." *In These Times* (April 1, 1996): 12–13.

———. "Warfare or Welfare." *In These Times* (December 9, 1996): 12–14.

———. "Know Thine Enemy: A Brief History of Corporations." *In These Times* (February 8, 1998): 16–17.

———. "R.I.P. FDR?" *In These Times* (February 28, 2005): 3.

———. "Sanders Steps Up." *In These Times* (June 20, 2005): 16–19, 37.

Block, Fred. "Toward Real Corporate Responsibility." *In These Times* (May 27, 1996): 25–27.

Bluestone, Barry, and Bennett Harrison. *The Deindustrialization of America.* New York: Basic Books, 1982.

Blumenstock, Kathy. "ABC Puts UFOs on Its Radar Screen." *Indianapolis Star,* February 22, 2005.

Boaz, David, and R. Morris Barrett. "What Would a School Voucher Buy? The Real Cost of Private Schools." *Cato Institute Briefing Paper No. 25.* (March 26, 1996).

Bodnar, John E. *Blue-Collar Hollywood: Liberalism, Democracy, and Working People in American Film.* Baltimore: Johns Hopkins University Press, 2003.

Booker, Salih, and William Minter. "Global Apartheid." *Nation* (July 9, 2001): 11–17.

Borosage, Robert L. "Scoundrel Time." *Nation* (November 19, 2001): 6–7, 23.

Borosage, Robert L., and Katrina vanden Heuvel. "Progressives: Get Ready to Fight." *Nation* (November 29, 2004): 11–14.

Borosage, Robert L., and Ruy Teixeira. "The Politics of Money." *Nation* (October 21, 1996): 21–22.

Boskin, Michael. "Social Security: The Common Sense of Social Security Reform." *Hoover Institution—Hoover Digest 2* (2005): 1–4.

Boudin, Chesa. "Letter from Venezuela: The Land of Chavismo." *Nation* (December 4, 2006): 18–21.

Bowden, Charles. "Keeper of the Fire." *Mother Jones* (July–August 2003): 68–73.

Bowles, Samuel, and Herbert Gintis. *Schooling in Capitalist America: Educational Reform and the Contradictions of Economic Life.* New York: Basic Books, 1976.

Boyer, Gabriella. "Corporate America Stacks the NAFTA Debate." *Public Citizen* (July–August 1993): 26.

Boyle, Patrick. "A DAREing Rescue." *Youth Today* (April 2001): 1, 16–19.

Box Office Mojo. "Documentary, Lifetime Gross/Theaters." July 2006. Available at http://www.boxofficemojo.com.

Braddock, Douglas. "Occupational Employment Projections to 2008." *Monthly Labor Review* (November 1999): 51–77.

Bradsher, Keith. "The Latest Fashion: Fear-of-Crime Design." *New York Times Week in Review,* July 23, 2000.

———. "For Workers Sent Abroad, a Tax Jolt." *New York Times,* September 2, 2006, B1, B6.

Breslow, Marc. "Death by Devolution." *Dollars and Sense* (January–February 1996): 20–22, 38.

———. "Government of, by, and for the Wealthy." *Dollars and Sense* (July–August 1996): 23–24.

———. "Job Stats: Too Good to Be True." *Dollars and Sense* (September–October 1996): 51.

Breslow, Marc, and Matthew Howard. "The Real Un(der)Employment Rate." *Dollars and Sense* (May–June 1995): 35.

Brinkmeyer, Eliza. "Vote for CAFTA, Pay the Price." *Public Citizen News* (November–December 2005): 1, 12.

——. "Handful of Pro-CAFTA Reps. Have Received $2.8 Million in Corporate Campaign Cash." *Public Citizen News* (May–June 2006): 13.

Brinton, Milward H., and Heide H. Newman. "State Incentive Packages and the Industrial Location Decision." *Economic Development Quarterly* 3 (1989): 203–22.

Broder, David. "Expanded Trade Authority Faces Political Realities." *Indianapolis Star*, November 7, 2001.

Bronfenbrenner, Kate. "Changing to Organize." *Nation* (September 3–10, 2001): 16–20.

Bronfenbrenner, Kate, and Stephanie Luce. "The Changing Nature of Corporate Global Restructuring: The Impact of Production Shifts on Jobs in the U.S., China, and around the Globe." Prepared for the U.S.-China Economic and Security Review Commission. October 14, 2004. Available at http://www.irl.cornell.edu.

Brookings Institution. *Annual Report 2005.* 2005. Available at http://www.brookings.edu/admin/2005annualreport/AnnualReport2005.pdf.

——. "About Brookings." 2006. Available at http://www.brookings.edu.

Brown, Sandy. "Activism and Optimism: The National Conference for Media Reform 2005 St. Louis." In *Censored 2006: The Top 25 Censored Stories,* ed. Peter Phillips and Project Censored. New York: Seven Stories Press, 2005.

Brown, Sharon P., and Lewis B. Siegel. "Mass Layoff Data Indicate Outsourcing and Offshoring of Work." *Monthly Labor Review* (August 2005): 3–10.

Brownfield, Paul. "The Joke's on Who?" *Los Angeles Times,* February 8, 1998.

Buchanan, Patrick J. *The Great Betrayal: How American Sovereignty and Social Justice Are Being Sacrificed to the Gods of the Global Economy.* New York: Little, Brown, 1998.

Buckley, John E., and Robert W. Van Giezen. "Federal Statistics on Healthcare Benefits and Cost Trends: An Overview." *Monthly Labor Review* (November 2004): 43–45.

Buffett, Warren E. "Chairman's Letter to the Shareholders of Berkshire Hathaway, Inc." *Berkshire Hathaway Inc. 2003 Annual Report.*

Burnett, Bob. "Publisher's Notes." *In These Times* (March 19, 2001): i.

Burris, Val. "Elite Policy-Planning Networks in the United States." In *Research in Politics and Society,* vol. 4, *The Political Consequences of Social Networks,* ed. Gwen Moore and J. Allen Whitt. Greenwich, CT: JAI Press, 1992.

——. "The Myth of Old Money Liberalism: The Politics of the *Forbes* 400 Richest Americans." *Social Problems* 47 (2000): 360–78.

——. "The Two Faces of Capital: Corporations and Individual Capitalists as Political Actors." *American Sociological Review* 66 (2001): 361–81.

Burson-Marsteller. "About Us—Family of Companies." 2006. Available at http://www.burson-marsteller.com.

Bush, George W. Yale University Commencement Address, cited in "Dunce Gets Doctorate." *Nation* (June 11, 2001).

"Bush Tax Plan Will Squeeze Medicare, Education." *UAW Solidarity* (July–August 2001): 4–5.

Business Roundtable. "About Us." 2006. Available at http://www.businessroundtable.org.

——. "About Us: Business Roundtable History." Available at http://www.businessroundtable.org.

——. "Business Roundtable Deeply Disappointed by Doha Talks Suspension." July 24, 2006. Available at http://www.businessroundtable.org.

Butsch, Richard. "Class and Gender in Four Decades of Television Situation Comedy: Plus ça Change . . . " *Critical Studies in Mass Communications* 9 (1992): 387–99.

Bybee, Roger. "NAFTA's Hung Jury." *Extra!* (May–June 2004): 14–15.

By What Authority 3(3) (Summer 2001). Available at http://www.poclad.org.

California Anti-SLAPP Project. "What Are SLAPPs?" 2006. Available at http://www.casp/net.

Campaign for Tobacco-Free Kids. "A Broken Promise to Our Children." November 30, 2005. Available at http://www.tobaccofreekids.org.

Campo-Flores, Arian, and Evan Thomas. "Rehabbing Rush." *Newsweek* (May 8, 2006): 27–29.

Canham-Clyne, John. "When Elites Say 'Cut Medicare,' Press Debates 'How Much?'" *Extra!* (January–February 1996): 12–14.

Carlson, Matt. "Boardroom Brothers." *Extra!* (September–October 2001): 18.

Carreiro, Joshua L. "Newspaper Coverage of the U.S. Labor Movement: The Case of Anti-Union Firings." *Labor Studies Journal* 30(3) (2005): 1–20.

Carroll, William K., and Meindert Fennema. "Is There a Transnational Business Community?" *International Journal of Sociology* 17 (September 2002): 393-419.

Casten, Liane. "Court Rules That Media Can Legally Lie." In *Censored 2005*, ed. Peter Phillips. New York: Seven Stories Press, 2004.

———. "Florida Appeals Court Orders Akre-Wilson Must Pay Trial Costs for $24.3 Billion Fox Television: Couple Warns of Danger to Free Speech, Whistle Blower Protection." In *Censored 2006: The Top 25 Censored Stories*, ed. Peter Phillips and Project Censored. New York: Seven Stories Press, 2005.

CBS Corporation. "2006 Annual Meeting of Stockholders and Proxy Statement." April 14, 2006. Available at http://www.sec.gov.

CBS News/*New York Times* poll. "Foreign Trade and the U.S. Economy." January 31, 2006.

Center for a New American Dream. "About Us." Available at http://www.newdream.org.

———. "New American Dream Survey Report." 2004. Available at http://www.newdream.org.

Center for Public Integrity. "527s in 2004 Shatter Previous Records for Political Fundraising." December 16, 2004. Available at http://www.publicintegrity.org.

———. "527 Frequently Asked Questions." 2005. Available at http://www.publicintegrity.org.

———. "State Lobbyists Near the $1 Billion Mark." 2005. Available at http://www.public integrity.org.

Center for Responsive Politics. "Summary." In *Influence, Inc.*, Washington, DC: Center for Responsive Politics, 2000.

———. *Who's Paying for This Election?* Washington, DC: Center for Responsive Politics, 2000.

———. "2000 Election Overview, Stats at a Glance: Congressional Races." 2001. Available at http://www.opensecrets.org.

———. "2000 Presidential Race: Total Raised and Spent." 2001. Available at http://www.opensecrets .org.

———. "The Calm before the Storm: Wall Street and Social Security Reform." 2001. Available at http://www.opensecrets.org.

———. "Federal Campaign Finance Law: Contribution Limits." 2002. Available at http://www .opensecrets.org.

———. "2004 Election Overview: Business-Labor Ideology Split in PAC and Individual Donations to Candidates and Parties." 2005. Available at http://www.opensecrets.org.

———. "2004 Election Overview: Top Individual Contributors." 2005. Available at http://www .opensecrets.org.

———. "2004 Election Overview: Top Zip Codes." 2005. Available at http://www.opensecrets.org.

———. "2004 Presidential Election." 2005. Available at http://www.opensecrets.org.

———. "Campaign Contributions, 2003-2004." 2005. Available at http://www.opensecrets.org.

———. "Campaign Contributions, 2003-2004: Donors." 2005. Available at http://www.open secrets.org.

———. "2006 Election Analysis." 2006. Available at http://www.opensecrets.org.

———. "2006 Election Overview: Business-Labor-Ideology Split in PAC and Individual Donations to Candidates and Parties." 2006. Available at http://www.opensecrets.org.

———. "2006 Election Overview: Donor Demographics." 2006. Available at http://www.open secrets.org.

———. "Nov. 6 Update." 2006. Available at http://www.opensecrets.org.

Center for the Study of Educational Policy. "Table 4: Tax Appropriations for Higher Education, by State, FY96–FY06." *Grapevine* (January 12, 2006). Available at http://www.coe.ilstu.edu.

Center on Alcohol Marketing and Youth at Georgetown University. "Alcohol Advertising and Youth." January 2006. Available at http://www.camy.org.

"CEOs Play Reporter." *Extra!Update* (February 1996): 2.

Chan, Sewell. "Study Bolsters Case for Tuition Vouchers." *Washington Post*, September 29, 2004, A12.

Change to Win. "The American Dream Survey 2006." August 28, 2006. Available at http://www .changetowin.org.

———. "Restoring the American Dream." 2006. Available at http://www.changetowin.org.

———. "Who We Are." 2006. Available at http://www.changetowin.org.

———. "Workers in Change to Win Unions Help Bring Pro-Worker Candidates to Victory." Press release, November 8, 2006. Available at http://www.changetowin.org.

Charman, Karen. "News You Can't Trust." *Extra!* (July–August 2003): 6.

Cherry, Robert. "Institutionalized Discrimination." In *Experiencing Race, Class, and Gender in the United States*, ed. Roberta Fiske-Rusciano and Virginia Cyrus. 4th ed. Boston: McGraw-Hill, 2005.

Chester, Jeffrey. "A Ten-Point Plan for Media Democracy." *Nation* (July 3, 2006): 21.

———. *Digital Destiny*. New York: New Press, 2007.

Chin, Tiffany, and Meredith Phillips. "Social Reproduction and Child-Rearing Practices: Social Class, Children's Agency, and the Summer Camp Activity Gap." *Sociology of Education* 77 (July 2004): 185–210.

Chomsky, Noam. *The Common Good*. New York: Common Courage Press, 2000.

Church, George J. "Are We Better Off?" *Time* (January 29, 1996): 37–40.

Citizens for Tax Justice. "Final Version of Bush Tax Plan Keeps High-End Tax Cuts, Adds to Long-Term Cost." 2001. Available at http://www.inequality.org.

———. "Post-2001 Tax Cuts Offer Little to Most Americans." 2001. Available at http://www.ctj.org.

———. "Phase in Dates for the Bush Tax Cuts, Including 2003 Legislation (Calendar Years)." Press release, April 13, 2004. Available at http://www.ctj.org.

———. "Bush Policies Drive Surge in Corporate Tax Freeloading: 82 Big U.S. Corporations Paid No Tax in One or More Bush Years." Press release, September 22, 2004. Available at http://www.ctj.org.

———. "CBO Projects $8.5 Trillion in Borrowing over Next Decade under Bush Policies, Effects of the Bush Tax Cuts Enacted through 2004 (with Sunsets) by Income Group (Calendar Years)." Press release, January 26, 2006. Available at http://www.ctj.org.

———. "Tax Cuts on Capital Gains and Dividends Doubled Bush Income Tax Cuts for the Wealthiest in 2003." Press release, April 5, 2006. Available at http://www.ctj.org.

Clanton, Brett. "Hyundai Factory Finds Sweet Home in Alabama." *Detroit News*, May 16, 2005.

Clark, Jessica. "In Politics, Comedy Is Central." *In These Times* (August 2006): 38–39.

Clark, Jessica, and Tracy Van Slyke. "Welcome to the Media Revolution." *In These Times* (July 2006): 20–27.

Class Action. "What Do We Mean by 'Class'?" Available at http://www.classism.org.

———. "What Is Classism?" 2005. Available at http://www.classism.org.

"Class and the American Dream." *New York Times*, May 30, 2005.

Clawson, Dan, Alan Neustadtl, and Denise Scott. *Money Talks*. New York: Basic Books, 1992.

Claybrook, Joan. "Why It's Their NAFTA, Not Ours, Not Yours." *Public Citizen* (November–December 1993): 2, 15.

———. "Corporate Accountability." Special anniversary edition, *Public Citizen News* 21 (2001): 20–21, 29.

Clehane, Diane, Rob LaFranco, and Cathy Piedmont. "Hey, Big Spenders." *TV Guide* (July 18–24, 2004): 22–29.

Clemente, Frank. "New Medicare Law Benefits Industry More Than Seniors." *Public Citizen News* (January–February 2004): 1, 8–9.

"Cleveland Private School Voucher Program Comes Up Short—Again." *AFT American Teacher* (May–June 2006): 17.

Clines, Francis X. "Fueled by Success, Buchanan Revels in Rapid-Fire Oratory." *New York Times*, February 15, 1996.

Cockburn, Alexander. "Dems and Dives." *CounterPunch* (March 1–15, 2005): 1–2.

———. "Presidential Elections: Not as Big a Deal as They Say." *CounterPunch* (June 16–30, 2006): 1, 3–6.

Cockburn, Alexander, and Jeffrey St. Clair. "It Really Was a Coup." *CounterPunch* (December 2000): 2.

———. "How Go the Dems?" *CounterPunch* (February 1–15, 2005): 1–2.

———. "Count Your Blessings: NeoCons and NeoLibs Take a Big Hit as Voters Say No to Bush and Free Trade." *CounterPunch* (November 8, 2006). Available at http://www.counterpunch.org.

Coen, Rachel. "Whitewash in Washington." *Extra!* (July–August 2000): 9–12.

———. "The Stossel Treatment." *Extra!* (March–April 2003): 15–17.

Cohen, Adam. "This Time It's Different." *Time* (January 8, 2001): 18–22.

Cohen, Jeff, and Norman Solomon. *Adventures in MediaLand.* Monroe, ME: Common Courage Press, 1993.

Cohn, Jason. "Drug Education: The Triumph of Bad Science." *Rolling Stone* (May 24, 2001): 41–42, 96.

Coleman, Richard D., and Lee Rainwater. *Social Standing in America.* New York: Basic Books, 1978.

Collins, Chuck. "Horatio Alger, Where Are You?" *Dollars and Sense* (January–February 1997): 9.

Collins, Chuck, and Felice Yeskel. *Economic Apartheid in America.* New York: The New Press, 2000.

Collins, Randall. "Functional and Conflict Theories of Educational Stratification." *American Sociological Review* 36 (1971): 1002–19.

———. *The Credential Society.* New York: Academic Press, 1979.

Collins, Sharon M. "The Marginalization of Black Executives." *Social Problems* 36 (1989): 317–31.

Collins, Valerie. "To Pass Medicare Drug Bill, Big Pharma Does the K Street Shuffle." *Public Citizen News* (July–August 2004): 5.

Coomes, Mark. "Ghostly Shows: They're Baaaack." *Indianapolis Star,* October 6, 2006.

Community Associations Institute. "Data on U.S. Community Associations." 2006. Available at http://www.caionline.org.

Condron, Dennis J., and Vincent J. Roscigno. "Disparities within: Unequal Spending and Achievement in an Urban School District." *Sociology of Education* 76 (January 2003): 18–36.

"Confidence in Institutions." *Gallup Poll News Service.* June 8–10, 2001. Available at http://www.gallup.com.

Congressional Budget Office. "Effective Federal Tax Rates under Current Law, 2001 to 2014." August 2004. Available at http://www.cbo.gov.

———. "Historical Effective Tax Rates, 1979 to 2002." March 2005. Available at http://www.cbo.gov.

———. "Historical Effective Tax Rates, 1979 to 2003." December 2005. Available at http://www.cbo.gov.

Congressional Record. May 8, 1997, S4236–38.

———. May 15, 1997, S4588–91.

———. June 26, 1997, S6449–51.

———. June 27, 1997, S6678–79.

Conn, Joseph L., and Rob Boston. "Pat Robertson's Media Empire." *Extra!* (March–April 1995): 13–16.

Connell, Noreen. "Underfunded Schools: Why Money Matters." *Dollars and Sense* (March–April 1998): 14–17, 39.

Conniff, Ruth. "Will Democrats Abandon Social Security?" *Progressive* (March 1999): 19–23.

———. "The Budget Surrender." *Progressive* (June 2001): 12–13.

Connor, Kenny. "Capital Crimes." *In These Times* (August 2006): 20–25.

"Contingent Workers." *Monthly Labor Review* (August 2005): 2.

"The Conundrum of the Glass Ceiling." *Economist* (July 27, 2005): 63–65.

Cooper, Marc. "Labor-Latino Beat in CA." *Nation* (June 29, 1998): 5–6.

———. "Plan Colombia." *Nation* (March 19, 2001): 11–18.

Corn, David. "Rove-r and Out?" *Nation* (July 16, 2001): 5–6.

———. "And Now, Iraq." *Nation* (November 27, 2006): 5.

Costo, Stephanie L. "Trends in Retirement Plan Coverage over the Last Decade." *Monthly Labor Review* (February 2006): 58–64.

Cottle, Michelle. "The Real Class War." *Washington Monthly* (July–August 1997): 12–16.

Council on International and Public Affairs/The Apex Press. "Home." 2006. Available at http://www.cipa-apex.org.

Couret, Jacques, and Ryan Mahoney. "State and Kia: Georgia Plant Still a Go." *Atlanta Business Chronicle* (May 18, 2006). Available at http://www.atlantabizjournals.com.

Cox, Craig. "Taming the Corporate Beast." *Utne Reader* (March–April 1998): 60–61.

Craddock, Jim, ed. *VideoHound's Golden Movie Retriever: 2006*. Detroit, MI: Thomson-Gale, 2005.

Crane, Stephen. *The Red Badge of Courage and Other Writings*, ed. Richard Chase. Cambridge, MA: Riverside Press, 1960.

Crockett, Harry J., Jr. "The Achievement Motive and Differential Occupational Mobility in the United States." *American Sociological Review* 27 (1962): 191–204.

Croteau, David. "Challenging the 'Liberal Media' Claim." *Extra!* (July–August 1998): 4–9.

Crutsinger, Martin. "Fresh Reports Paint Picture of Recession." *Indianapolis Star*, October 26, 2001.

Cummings, Scott, and Del Taebel. "The Economic Socialization of Children: A Neo-Marxist Analysis." *Social Problems* 26 (1978): 198–210.

"Current Labor Statistics: Tables 34 and 35." *Monthly Labor Review* (July 2006): 126–27.

"Current Labor Statistics: Table 25." *Monthly Labor Review* (May 2001): 90.

Dahl, Ronald. "Burned Out and Bored." *Newsweek* (December 15, 1997): 18.

D'Ambrosio, Antonino. "Progressive Interview: Chuck D." *Progressive* (August 2005): 37–41.

Daniels, Arlene Kaplan. *Invisible Careers: Women Civic Leaders from the Volunteer World*. Chicago: University of Chicago Press, 1988.

DARE America. "Where Science Meets the Street." Press release, February 2006. Available at http://www.dare.com.

DARE Media Kit. "D.A.R.E. Fast Facts." April 18, 2005. Available at http://www.dare.com.

DARE. "Sponsors and Supporters: Corporations." 2006. Available at http://www.dare.com.

———. "Sponsors and Supporters: Foundations" 2006. Available at http://www.dare.com.

———. "Sponsors and Supporters: Government." 2006. Available at http://www.dare.com.

Darrow, Chuck. "The Term 'White Trash' Should be Tossed Out for Good." *Courier Post*, March 26, 2006. Available at http://www.courierpostonline.com.

Dash, Eric. "Off to the Races Again, Leaving Many Behind." *New York Times*, April 9, 2006.

Davidson, Osha G. *Broken Heartland: The Rise of America's Rural Ghetto*. Iowa City: University of Iowa Press, 1996.

Davies, Scott, and Neil Guppy. "Fields of Study, College Selectivity, and Student Inequalities in Higher Education." *Social Forces* 75 (1997): 1417–38.

Davis, James A., and Tom W. Smith. *General Social Surveys, 1972–1998*. Storrs, CT: The Roper Center for Public Opinion Research, 1989.

Davis, Mike. "Who Is Killing New Orleans?" *Nation* (April 10, 2006): 12.

Davis, Russ. "AFL-CIO Unveils Program to Revitalize Labor Movement." *Labor Notes* (March 1997): 1, 14.

Dees, Morris, and Mark Potok. "The Future of American Terrorism." *New York Times*, June 10, 2001.

Delacour, Justin. "The Op-ed Assassination of Hugo Chávez." *Extra!* (November–December 2005): 24–27.

deMause, Neil. "A Welfare Success—but the Program Died." *Extra!* (September–October 2000): 23.

———. "Katrina's Vanishing Victims." *Extra!* (July–August 2006): 17–23.

———. "The Smell of Success." *Extra!* (November–December 2006): 6–7.

Derber, Charles. *The Wilding of America*. New York: St. Martin's Press, 1996.

———. *Corporation Nation*. New York: St. Martin's Press, 1998.

———. *The Wilding of America*. 3rd ed. New York: Worth, 2004.

———. *The Wilding of America: Money, Mayhem, and the New American Dream*. 4th ed. New York: Worth, 2007.

Derk, James. "We Got It, Toyota!" *Indiana Business Magazine* (January 1996): 9–13.

Dicken, Peter. "Technology: The 'Great Growling Engine of Change.'" In *The Transformation of Work in the New Economy*, ed. Robert Perrucci and Carolyn Perrucci. Los Angeles, CA: Roxbury, 2007.

"Dictators on Parade." *Wall Street Journal*, February 15, 2005.

Dillon, Sam. "Collapse of 60 Charter Schools Leaves California Scrambling." *New York Times*, September 17, 2004.

Dimaggio, Paul J., and Walter W. Powell. "The Iron Cage Revisited: Institutional Isomorphism and Collective Rationality in Organizational Fields." *American Sociological Review* 48 (1983): 147–60.

Dines, Gail. "Capitalism's Pitchmen." *Dollars and Sense* (May 1992): 18–20.

"Dissent Unwelcome in Wartime." *Extra!* (May–June 2004): 24.

District of Columbia Bar. "Attorney Resources." 2001. Available at http://www.dcbar.org.

———. "2004–2005 Annual Report." Available at http://www.dcbar.org.

Dobbs, Lou. *War on the Middle Class: How the Government, Big Business, and Special Interest Groups Are Waging War on the American Dream and How to Fight Back*. New York: Viking, 2006.

Doherty, Brian. "Those Who Can't, Test." *Mother Jones* (November–December 1998): 68–71.

Doherty, Carroll. "Do Deficits Matter Anymore?" Pew Research Center. March 14, 2006. Available at http://www.pewresearch.org.

Dolan, Kerry A., and Luisa Kroll, eds. "The World's Richest People." *Forbes* (July 9, 2001): 110–24.

Dolny, Michael. "What's in a Label?" *Extra!* (May–June 1998): 9–10.

———. "Right, Center Think Tanks Still Most Quoted." *Extra!* (May–June 2005): 28–29.

———. "Think Tank Survey: Study Finds First Drop in Think Tank Cites." *Extra!* (May–June 2006): 24–25.

Domhoff, G. William. *The Powers That Be*. New York: Vintage Books, 1979.

———. *State Autonomy or Class Dominance?* New York: Aldine De Gruyter, 1996.

———. *Who Rules America? Power and Politics in the Year 2000*. 3rd ed. Mountain View, CA: Mayfield Publishing, 1998.

———. *Who Rules America? Power and Politics*. 4th ed. Boston: McGraw-Hill, 2002.

———. *Who Rules America? Power, Politics, and Social Change*. 5th ed. Boston: McGraw-Hill, 2006.

Donovan, Doug, and Peter Kafka. "Hosts with the Most." *Forbes* (March 19, 2001): 164–66.

"Don't Let Them Fool You." *AFSCME Public Employee* (March–April 1998): 6–16.

"Don't Read This Soundbite." *Extra!* (January–February 2000): 5.

Dooley, David, JoAnn Prause, and Kathleen A. Ham-Rowbottom. "Underemployment and Depression: Longitudinal Relationships." *Journal of Health and Social Behavior* 41 (2000): 421–36.

Dorgan, Byron L. *Take This Job and Ship It*. New York: Thomas Dunne Books, 2006.

Downs, Alan. *Corporate Executions*. New York: AMACOM, 1995.

"Do You Believe in Ghosts?" *TV Guide* (November 28, 2005): 19.

Draut, Tamara. *Strapped: Why America's 20- and 30-Somthings Can't Get Ahead*. New York: Doubleday, 2005.

Dreifus, Claudia. "Interview: Gore Vidal, the Writer as Citizen." *Progressive* (September 1986): 36–39.

Dreiling, Michael C. "The Class Embeddedness of Corporate Political Action: Leadership in Defense of the NAFTA." *Social Problems* 47 (2000): 21–48.

Drinkard, Jim. "Lobbying Costs Hit $100 Million a Month." *Indianapolis Star*, March 7, 1998.

Drug Policy Alliance. "'Just Say No' Will Not Keep Our Teens Safe." Press release, April 11, 2005. Available at http://www.drugpolicy.org.

Drutman, Lee, and Charlie Cray. "The People's Business." *In These Times* (March 14, 2005): 16–19, 28.

DuBoff, Richard B. "Social Security: Hardly Secure at the *New York Times*." *Extra!* (March–April 1997): 10–11.

———. "Globalization and Wages: The Down Escalator." *Dollars and Sense* (September–October 1997): 36–40.

DuBoff, Richard B., and Edward S. Herman. "Mergers, Concentration, and the Erosion of Democracy." *Monthly Review* (May 2001): 14–29.

Dubose, Louis. "Bush's Hitman." *Nation* (March 5, 2001): 11–15.

Dudzic, Mark. "Time to Abandon Illusions about Democrats." *Labor Party Press* (January–February 2005): 8.

———. "The Midterm Elections: A Return to Politics as Usual." *Party Builder* (November 2006): 1. Available at http://www.thelaborparty.org.

Duncan, Jim, Bertha Lewis, and Bob Master. *Working Families Party Annual Report 2004.* Available at http://www.workingfamiliesparty.org.

Duncan, Greg J., and Wei-Jun J. Yeung. "Extent and Consequences of Welfare Dependence among America's Children." *Children and Youth Services Review* 17 (1995): 157–82.

Dunham, Kemba J., and Greg Ip. "Weak Economy Takes Unusually Heavy Toll on White-Collar Jobs." *Wall Street Journal*, November 5, 2001.

Dunham, Richard S. "Privatizing Social Security: Despite the Slump, Support Is Solid." *Business Week* (August 13, 2001): 41.

Durbin, Dee-Ann. "Specter of Delphi Deal Leads to GM Upgrade." *Indianapolis Star*, May 13, 2006.

Dwyer, Paul E. "Salaries of Congress: A List of Payable Rates and Effective Dates, 1789–2006." *CRS Report for Congress* (April 18, 2006): 1.

Dye, Thomas R. "Organizing Power for Policy-Planning: The View from the Brookings Institution." In *Power Elites and Organizations*, ed. G. William Domhoff and Thomas R. Dye. Newbury Park, CA: Sage, 1987.

———. *Who's Running America? The Clinton Years.* 6th ed. Englewood Cliffs, NJ: Prentice Hall, 1995.

———. *Who's Running America? The Bush Restoration.* 7th ed. Upper Saddle River, NJ: Prentice Hall, 2002.

Dyer, Joel. *Harvest of Rage: Why Oklahoma City Is Only the Beginning.* Boulder, CO: Westview Press, 1998.

Dyer, Stephanie. "Lifestyles of the Media Rich and Oligopolistic." In *Censored 2005*, ed. Peter Phillips. New York: Seven Stories Press, 2004.

Ebert, Roger. "Million Dollar Baby: Review." *Chicago Sun Times*, January 7, 2005. Available at http://www.rogerebert.suntimes.com.

———. "Cinderella Man: Review." *Chicago Sun Times*, June 2, 2005. Available at http://www.rogerebert.suntimes.com.

"Economic Focus." *The Economist* (September 2, 2006): 66.

Economic Policy Institute. "Data Zone: Family Income Limits by Quintile, 1947–2004, Share of Aggregate Income by Quintile." 2006. Available at http://www.epinet.org.

Editorial. "$30 Million Can Make Media Shy of Truth." *National Catholic Reporter* (April 24, 1998): 1.

Editors. "The Nader Campaign and the Future of U.S. Left Electoral Politics." *Monthly Review* (February 2001): 1–22.

Edsall, Thomas. "Rich Liberals Vow to Fund Think Tanks; Aim Is to Compete with Conservatives." *Washington Post*, August 7, 2005.

Education Week. May 3, 1995. Available at http://www.edweek.org.

Egan, Timothy. "Economic Squeeze Plaguing Middle-Class Families." *New York Times*, August 28, 2004, A12.

Ehrenreich, Barbara. *Fear of Falling.* New York: Harper, 1989.

———. "When Government Gets Mean: Confessions of a Recovering Statist." *Nation* (November 17, 1997): 11–16.

———. "The Making of McVeigh." *Progressive* (July 2001): 14–15.

———. *Bait and Switch: The (Futile) Pursuit of the American Dream.* New York: Metropolitan, 2005.

"The 89 Percent Liberal Media." *Extra!* (July–August 1998): 10.

Eisenger, Peter. *The Rise of the Entrepreneurial State.* Madison: University of Wisconsin Press, 1988.

Ellner, Steve. "Chávez Consolidates Power." *In These Times* (January 2007): 26–27.

Ellis, Michael. "Ford to Cut 10% of White-Collar Jobs." *Indianapolis Star*, November 22, 2005.

El Nassar, Haya. "Gated Communities More Popular and Not Just for the Rich." *USA Today*, December 16, 2002.

Elsila, David, Michael Funke, and Sam Kirkland. "Blaming the Victim: The Propaganda War against Workers." *UAW Solidarity* (April 1992): 11–17.

Endicott, Evan. "Musical Memento." *In These Times* (July 23, 2001): 26–27.

Engardio, Pete. "The Future of Outsourcing." *Business Week* (January 30, 2006): 50–58.

Engler, Mark. "Hook, Line and Suckers." *In These Times* (October 24, 2005): 32–33, 37.

English, Jane. "Bush Eyes 'Fast Track' Authority." *Public Citizen News* (July–August 2001): 1, 7.

Evanoff, Ted. "Battle for Prosperity." *Indianapolis Star*, November 13, 2005.

———. "A Hoosier Welcome." *Indianapolis Star*, June 29, 2006.

"Ever Higher Society, Ever Harder to Ascend." *Economist* (January 1, 2005).

"Everyone Agrees." *Extra!Update* (February 2005): 2.

"Explosive Job Growth." *Mother Jones* (May–June 2006): 17.

Fackelmann, Kathleen. "Fired Up over Smoking." *USA Today*, May 18, 2005.

Family Council on Drug Awareness. "Why D.A.R.E. Does Not Work." 1999. Available at http://www.equalrights4all.org.

Farah, George, and Justin Elga. "Sunday Morning Political Talk Shows Ignore Corporate Power Issues." 2001. Available at http://www.essentialaction.org.

———. "What's *Not* Talked About on Sunday Morning?" *Extra!* (September–October 2001): 14–17.

Farley, John E. *Sociology*. Englewood Cliffs, NJ: Prentice Hall, 1990.

Farsetta, Diane, and Daniel Price. "Fake TV News: Widespread and Undisclosed." Center for Media and Democracy. April 6, 2006. Available at http://www.prwatch.org.

Faux, Jeff. *The Global Class War: How America's Bipartisan Elite Lost Our Future—and What It Will Take to Win It Back*. New York: Wiley, 2006.

———. "The Party of Davos." *Nation* (February 13, 2006): 18–22.

Feagin, Joe. *Racial and Ethnic Relations*. Englewood Cliffs, NJ: Prentice Hall, 1989.

Featherman, David L., and Robert M. Hauser. *Opportunity and Change*. New York: Academic Press, 1978.

Fedarko, Kevin. "Knobby Fires." *Outside* (June 2001): 24–26.

Federal Election Commission (FEC). All FEC documents cited in all chapters available at http://www.fec.gov.

"Federal Election Commission, Political Party Committees Donating Funds to Certain Tax-Exempt Organizations and Political Organizations." *Federal Register* (March 16, 2005): 12787–90.

"Fighting Permanent Normal Trade Relations Status for China." *Public Citizen News, Annual Report 2000* (March–April 2001): 10–12.

Fineman, Howard. "Move Over, Gray Panthers." *Newsweek* (September 10, 2001): 29.

Fineman, Howard, and Rich Thomas. "Snip! Snip! Snip!" *Newsweek* (February 19, 2001): 18–22.

Fisher, Dana R., Kevin Stanley, David Berman, and Gina Neff. "How Do Organizations Matter? Mobilization and Support for Participants at Five Globalization Protests." *Social Problems* 52 (2005): 102–21.

Fiske-Rusciano, Roberta, and Virginia Cyrus. "Experiencing Race, Class, and Gender in the United States." In *Experiencing Race, Class, and Gender in the United States*, ed. Roberta Fiske-Rusciano and Virginia Cyrus. 4th ed. Boston: McGraw-Hill, 2005.

Fitzgerald, F. Scott. *The Great Gatsby*. New York: Cambridge University Press, 1991.

"The 500 Largest U.S. Corporations." *Fortune* (April 16, 2001): F1–F19.

"The 400 Home Page, Campaign Inflation." *Mother Jones* (2001): 1–5.

Flanders, Laura. "Is It Real . . . or Is It Astroturf?" *Extra!* (July–August 1996): 6.

Florida, Richard. "The New American Dream." *Washington Monthly* (March 2003): 26–34.

Foerstel, Karen. "No Allowance, but Look at the Perks." *Congressional Quarterly Weekly* (March 17, 2001): 576.

Foley, Linda. "Media Reform from the Inside Out: The Newspaper Guild-CWA." In *The Future of Media: Resistance and Reform in the 21st Century*, ed. Robert McChesney, Russell Newman, and Ben Scott. New York: Seven Stories Press, 2005.

Forero, Juan. "Venezuela's Chávez Wins Decisive Victory: Leftist President Given Another Six Years to Consolidate His 'Bolivarian Revolution.'" *Washington Post*, December 4, 2006.

"Fortune 500 Largest U.S. Corporations." *Fortune* (April 17, 2006): F1–F19.

"The Fortune 1000 Ranked within Industries." *Fortune* (April 17, 2006): F44–F47.

Foundation Center. "Aggregate Fiscal Data by Foundation Type, 2003." 2005. Available at http://www.fdncenter.org.

———. "Top 100 U.S. Foundations by Asset Size." 2005. Available at http://www.fdncenter.org.

———. "Top 100 U.S. Foundations by Total Giving." 2005. Available at http://www.fdncenter.org.

Frank, Tom. "Let Them Eat Lifestyle." *Utne Reader* (November–December 1997): 43–47.

Frank, Thomas. *The Conquest of Cool: Business Culture, Counterculture, and the Rise of Hip Consumerism*. Chicago: University of Chicago Press, 1997.

———. *One Market under God*. New York: Doubleday, 2000.

———. *What's the Matter with Kansas? How Conservatives Won the Heart of America*. New York: Metropolitan Books, 2004.

Frank, Ellen. "Reaganomics Redux: What to Expect from a Bush Presidency." *Dollars and Sense* (July–August 2001): 7.

———. "Dear Dr. Dollar." *Dollars and Sense* (January–February 2006): 31.

Free Press. "National Conference for Media Reform, January 12–14, 2007, Memphis, Tennessee." Available at http://www.freepress.net.

Freeman, Lewis. "Social Mobility in Television Comedies." *Critical Studies in Mass Communication* 9 (1992): 400–406.

Friedman, Thomas. "Fill 'Er Up with Dictators." *New York Times*, September 27, 2006.

"From the Left: More than a Figure of Speech?" *Extra!Update* (February 1996): 1.

"Frontlines." *UAW Solidarity* (November 2001): 4–5.

Gabriel, Larry. "Beware of the Man behind the Screen." *UAW Solidarity* (May–June 2006): 20–21.

Gallup, George, and S. F. Rae. *The Pulse of Democracy*. New York: Simon and Schuster, 1940.

Gans, David N. "Physicians: Working Harder and Enjoying It Less." *MGMA Connexion* (November–December 2006): 22-23.

Garfinkle, Norton. *The American Dream vs. the Gospel of Wealth: The Fight for a Productive Middle-Class Economy*. New Haven, CT: Yale University Press, 2006.

Garnett, Stacie. "It's Tough to Be Young Today." *Dollars and Sense* (September–October 1997): 50.

General Accounting Office. "Youth Illicit Drug Use Prevention: DARE Long-Term Evaluations and Federal Efforts to Identify Effective Programs." GAO-03-172R, January 16, 2003. Washington, DC: U.S. Government Printing Office, 2003.

General Electric. *GE 2005 Annual Report*. 2006. Available at http://www.ge.com.

General Motors. "GM North America to Undergo Major Capacity Reduction." Press release, November 21, 2005.

Geoghagen, Thomas. "Overeducated and Underpaid." *New York Times*, June 3, 1997.

Gerald, Danette, and Kati Haycock. "Engines of Inequality: Diminishing Equity in the Nation's Premier Public Universities." Washington, DC: The Education Trust, 2006.

Gettings, John, and David Johnson. "Wonder Women." Infoplease. November 20, 2005. Available at http://www.infoplease.com.

Ghilarducci, Teresa. "The End of Retirement." *Monthly Review* (May 2006): 12–27.

Gilbert, Dennis, and Joseph A. Kahl. *The American Class Structure*. Chicago: Dorsey Press, 1987.

Gitlin, Todd. "Unum versus Pluribus." *Nation* (May 6, 1996): 28–34.

Glasser, Ira. "Drug Busts = Jim Crow." *Nation* (July 10, 2006): 24–26.

Glenn, David. "Adding Brains to Labor's New Political Muscle." *In These Times* (December 14, 1997): 22–25.

Gluckman, Amy. "Workers Better Off without Unions?" *Dollars and Sense* (September–October 2005): 5.

Goetzman, Keith. "Righteous Babe: Interview with Ani DiFranco." *Utne Reader* (July–August 2001): 94–96.

Golay, Michael, and Carl Rollyson. *Where America Stands, 1996*. New York: John Wiley and Sons, 1996.

Golden, Daniel. *The Price of Admission: How America's Ruling Class Buys Its Way into Elite Colleges—and Who Gets Left outside the Gates*. New York: The Crown Publishing Group, 2006.

Goldman, Lea, and Kiri Blakeley, eds. "The Celebrity 100." *Forbes* (July 3, 2006): 117–61.

Gonnerman, Jennifer. "Media Watch." *In These Times* (December 25, 1995): 9.

Goodman, Robert. *The Last Entrepreneurs: America's Regional Wars for Jobs and Dollars*. New York: Simon and Schuster, 1979.

Gordon, David M. *Fat and Mean: The Corporate Squeeze of Working Americans and the Myth of Managerial "Downsizing."* New York: Free Press, 1996.

Gordon, Devin. "Turning Fake News into Real Careers." *Newsweek* (February 13, 2006): 57.

———. "Horror Show." *Newsweek* (April 3, 2006): 60–62.

Gordon, Jim. "Mystery Milk, Journalistic Debate." *Extra!* (January–February 2001): 29–30.

Gosselin, Peter G. "If America Is Richer, Why Are Its Families So Much Less Secure?" *Los Angeles Times*, October 4, 2004.

Granfield, Robert. "Making It by Faking It." *Journal of Contemporary Ethnography* 20 (1991): 331–51.

Granfield, Robert, and Thomas Koenig. "Pathways into Elite Law Firms: Professional Stratification and Social Networks." In *Research in Politics and Society*, vol. 4, *The Political Consequences of Social Networks*, ed. Gwen Moore and J. Allen Whitt. Greenwich, CT: JAI Press, 1992.

Granovetter, Mark. *Getting a Job: A Study of Contacts and Careers*. Cambridge, MA: Harvard University Press, 1974.

"The Great Fear: Stagnation and the War on Social Security." *Monthly Review* (April 2005): 1–11.

Greene, Jay P., and Greg Forster. "Kerry's College Plan Fails Poor Kids." *Los Angeles Times*, August 18, 2004, B13.

Greenberg, Edward S. *Political Socialization*. New York: Atherton, 1970.

Green Party of the United States. "About Us." 2006. Available at http://www.gp.org.

———. "A Brief History of the Green Party." 2006. Available at http://www.gp.org.

———. "Basic Facts." 2006. Available at http://www.gp.org.

———. "Election Results, 2004, 2005, 2006." 2006. Available at http://www.gp.org.

———. "Green Party Ballot Status and Voter Registration Totals ." 2006. Available at http://www.gp.org.

———. "Greens Challenge Democrats in Congress on Wages, Health Care, Ethics." Press release, November 27, 2006. Available at http://www.gp.org.

———. "Greens Hold 2006 Annual Meeting in Tucson, Arizona." 2006. Available at http://www.gp.org.

———. "Platform 2004." 2006. Available at http://www.gp.org.

Greider, William. "Saving the Global Economy." *Nation* (December 15, 1997): 11–16.

———. "Nader and the Politics of Fear." *Nation* (March 12, 2001): 15–18.

———. "Stockman Returneth." *Nation* (April 2, 2001): 4–6.

———. "The Right and U.S. Trade Law: Invalidating the 20th Century." *Nation* (October 15, 2001): 21–29.

———. "Rebels." *Nation* (January 9–16, 2006): 16–18.

———. "Born-Again Rubinomics." *Nation* (July 31–August 7, 2006): 20–23.

———. "Watershed." *Nation* (December 4, 2006): 14–18.

Grossberg, Josh. "Stewart Keeps Up 'Daily ' Regimen." *E! Online* (March 19, 2004). Available at http://www.eonline.com.

———. "Colbert's Book Report." *E! Online* (March 21, 2006). Available at http://www.eonline.com.

Guldin, Bob. "Flawed Bankruptcy Law Rewards Finance Industry, While Families Beset by Health Costs Lose Protection." *Public Citizen News* (May–June 2005): 11.

Gup, Ted. "The *Mother Jones* 400." *Mother Jones* (March–April 1996): 43.

———. "Fakin' It." *Mother Jones* (May–June 1996): 53–54.

Gustafson, Sven. "38,000 at Ford Taking Buyout." *Indianapolis Star*, November 30, 2006.

Gutman, Huck. "Soldiers for Hire." *Monthly Review* (June 2004): 11–18.

Hacker, Jacob B. *The Great Risk Shift: The Assault on American Jobs, Families, Health Care, and Retirement and How You Can Fight Back.* New York: Oxford University Press, 2006.

Hallinan, Maureen T. "Tracking: From Theory to Practice." *Sociology of Education* 67 (1994): 79–85.

Hammer, David. "Pressured, Ohio's Ney Resigns from Congress." *Indianapolis Star,* November 4, 2006.

Hardt, Michael, and Antonio Negri. *Empire.* Cambridge, MA: Harvard University Press, 2000.

Harris Interactive. "Party Affiliation and Political Philosophy Show Little Change According to Harris Poll." March 9, 2005. Available at http://www.harrisinteractive.com.

Harrison, Bennett, and Barry Bluestone. "The Crisis of the American Dream." In *Great Divides,* ed. Thomas A. Shapiro. Mountain View, CA: Mayfield Publishing, 1998.

Harrison, Paige M., and Allen J. Beck. "Prisoners in 2004." *Bureau of Justice Statistics Bulletin* (October 2005): 9–10.

———. "Prisoner and Jail Inmates at Midyear 2005." *Bureau of Justice Statistics Bulletin* (May 2006): 1–12.

Hart, Peter. "Give *Us* a Break! The World According to John Stossel." *Extra!* (March–April 2003): 10–14.

———. "From the Left, I'm Nonexistent." *Extra!* (September–October 2003): 15.

———. "Bill O'Reilly, Media Critic." *Extra!* (November–December 2003): 6.

———. "Move to the Right! Pundits' Advice for Kerry Has a Familiar Ring." *Extra!Update* (June 2004): 1.

———. "We Do Not Speculate Here." *Extra!* (July–August 2005): 30.

———. "Why Is Labor off TV?" *Extra!Update* (August 2005): 3.

———. "Superstore Censorship." *Extra!* (November–December 2005): 22.

Hart, Peter, and Seth Ackerman. "Bill O'Reilly's Sheer O'Reillyness." *Extra!* (July–August 2001): 19–20.

Hart, Peter, and Julie Hollar. "Fear and Favor 2003." *Extra!* (May–June 2004): 21–22.

———. "Fear and Favor 2004: How Power Shapes the News." *Extra!* (March–April 2005): 24–29.

Hart, Peter, and Janine Jackson. "Media Lick the Hand That Feeds Them." *Extra!* (November–December 2005): 21–23.

———. "Stossel's 'Stupid' Schools." *Extra!* (May–June 2006): 6–9.

Hart, Peter, and Steve Rendall. "Meet the Myth Makers." *Extra!* (July–August 1998): 26–27.

———. "A 'Right Wing Coup' against PBS's Mythical Bias." *Extra!Update* (June 2005): 1.

———. "Move Over—Over and Over." *Extra!* (July–August 2006): 12–16.

Hartman, Thom. *Screwed: The Undeclared War against the Middle Class—and What We Can Do about It.* San Francisco, CA: Berrett-Koehler, 2006.

Hartung, William D. "New War, Old Weapons." *Nation* (October 29, 2001): 4–5.

Harvey, David. *A Brief History of Neoliberalism.* New York: Oxford University Press, 2005.

Haveman, Ernest, and Patricia Salter West. *They Went to College.* New York: Harcourt, Brace, 1952.

Hayes, Christopher. "Veronica Mars, Class Warrior." *In These Times* (June 2006): 46–47.

———. "The New Democratic Populism." *Nation* (December 4, 2006): 11–14.

———. "9/11: Roots of Paranoia." *Nation* (December 25, 2006): 11–14.

Hearn, James. "Academic and Nonacademic Influences on the College Destinations of 1980 High School Graduates." *Sociology of Education* 64 (1991): 158–71.

Hecker, Daniel E. "Occupational Employment Projections to 2014." *Monthly Labor Review* (November 2005): 70–81.

Hellander, Ida. "A Review of Data on the Health Care Sector of the United States." *International Journal of Health Services* 31 (2001): 35–53.

———. "A Review of Data on the U.S. Health Sector." *International Journal of Health Services* 36 (2006): 787–802.

Helwig, Ryan T. "Worker Displacement in a Strong Labor Market." *Monthly Labor Review* (June 2001): 13–28.

———. "Worker Displacement in 1999–2000." *Monthly Labor Review* (June 2004): 54–68.

Henriques, Diana B. "Ties That Bind: His Directors, Her Charity." *New York Times,* March 21, 1995.

——. "Putting Corporations in the Dock." *New York Times*, September 14, 2003.

Henson, Kevin D. *Just a Temp*. Philadelphia: Temple University Press, 1996.

Henwood, Doug. "American Dream: It's Not Working." *Christianity and Crisis* (June 8, 1992): 195–97.

——. "TV on Social Security: It's Broke, Fix It." *Extra!* (May–June 1999): 8–12.

Herbert, Bob. "The Mobility Myth." *New York Times*, June 6, 2005.

Heritage Foundation. *2005 Annual Report*. Available at http://www.heritage.org.

Herman, Edward S. "The Media Mega-Mergers." *Dollars and Sense* (May–June 1996): 8–13.

Herman, Tom. "Tax Report." *Wall Street Journal*, October 24, 2001.

Hertz, Emanuel. *Abraham Lincoln: A New Portrait*. Vol. 2. New York: Horace Liveright, Inc., 1931.

Herzenhorn, David. "The Story behind the Generous Gift to Harvard Law School." *New York Times*, April 7, 1995.

Hightower, Jim. "Class War." *Dollars and Sense* (November–December 1997): 7.

Hightower, Jim, and Phillip Frazer. "Social Security Ain't Broke, So Don't Fix It, Tweak It." *Lowdown* (March 2005): 2.

——. "Naming the Names behind the Grab for Social Security." *Lowdown* (April 2005): 1–8.

——. "It Was a 'Throw the Bums Out' and a 'Change America's Direction' Election." *Lowdown* (December 2006): 1–4.

Hill, Catherine. "Privatizing Social Security Is Bad, Particularly for Women." *Dollars and Sense* (November–December 2000): 17–19, 35.

Hiltbrand, David. "His Name Is 'Earl' and He's the Fool We Love to Love." *Kokomo Tribune*, April 9, 2006, A11 (Knight-Ridder newspapers).

Hipple, Steven. "Contingent Work in the late-1990s." *Monthly Labor Review* (March 2001): 3–27.

Hochschild, Arlie, and Anne Machung. "The Second Shift: Working Parents and the Revolution at Home." In *Working in America*, ed. Amy S. Wharton. Mountain View, CA: Mayfield Publishing, 1998.

Hodge, Robert W., Paul M. Siegel, and Peter H. Rossi. "Occupational Prestige in the United States: 1925–1962." In *Class, Status, and Power*, ed. Reinhard Bendix and Seymour M. Lipset. New York: Free Press, 1966.

Hodge, Robert W., and Donald J. Treiman. "Class Identification in the United States." *American Journal of Sociology* 73 (1968): 535–47.

Hodge, Robert W., Donald J. Treiman, and Peter H. Rossi. "A Comparative Study of Occupational Prestige." In *Class, Status, and Power*, ed. Reinhard Bendix and Seymour M. Lipset. New York: Free Press, 1966.

Hodson, Randy, and Teresa A. Sullivan. *The Social Organization of Work*. 2nd ed. Belmont, CA: Wadsworth, 1995.

——. *The Social Organization of Work*. 3rd ed. Belmont, CA: Wadsworth-Thomson, 2002.

Hoffman, Hank. "Time Is Tight." *In These Times* (November 12, 2001): 7–8.

Hojnacki, Marie, and David C. Kimball. "PAC Contributions and Lobbying Contacts in Congressional Committees." *Political Research Quarterly* 54 (March 2000): 161–80.

Hollar, Julie. "Opinion Omission: Women Hard to Find on Op-ed Pages, TV Panels." *Extra!* (May–June 2005): 17–22.

Hollar, Julie, Janine Jackson, and Hilary Goldstein. "Fear and Favor 2005: Outside (and Inside) Influence on the News." *Extra!* (March–April 2006): 15–20.

Holman, Craig. "For Real Lobbying Reform, Stop the Flow of Money." *Public Citizen News* (March–April 2006): 1, 4.

——. "Public Citizen Will Put Pressure on Congress until Real Lobbying, Ethics Reforms Are Enacted." *Public Citizen News* (May–June 2006): 8.

Hoynes, William. "News for a Captive Audience: An Analysis of Channel One." *Extra!* (May–June 1997): 11–17.

——. "The Cost of Survival." *Extra!* (September–October 1999): 11–19.

Huber, Joan, and William H. Form. *Income and Ideology: An Analysis of the American Political Formula*. New York: Free Press, 1973.

Hurst, Charles E. *Social Inequality*. Boston: Allyn and Bacon, 1995.

Husseini, Sam. "Talking about Talk." *Extra!* (May–June 1996): 20.

———. "Checkbook Analysis." *Extra!* (May–June 2000): 23–24.

"Hyundai's Sweet Home in Alabama." *Ward's Auto World*, May 1, 2002.

"In Fact." *Nation* (August 26–September 2, 1996): 5.

"Inside the 500." *Fortune* (April 16, 2001): 232–33.

Internet Movie Database, Inc. "Million Dollar Baby: Review." 2004. Available at http://www .imdb.com.

———. "Cinderella Man: Review." 2005. Available at http://www.imdb.com.

———. "All-Time USA Boxoffice." 2006. Available at http://www.imdb.com.

———. "All-Time Worldwide Boxoffice." 2006. Available at http://www.imdb.com.

Isikoff, Michael. "On Delay's Trail: The E-mail Factor." *Newsweek* (April 10, 2006): 6.

Isikoff, Michael, and Evan Thomas. "Back on the Stand." *Newsweek* (May 8, 2006): 30–31.

Isikoff, Michael, Holly Bailey, and Evan Thomas. "A Washington Tidal Wave." *Newsweek* (January 16, 2006): 40–43.

Jackman, Mary R., and Robert W. Jackman. *Class Awareness in the United States*. Berkeley: University of California Press, 1982.

Jackson, Janine. "Moribund Militants: Corporate Media on (Re)Organized Labor." *Extra!* (January–February 1996): 6–7.

———. "Let Them Eat Baguettes." *Extra!* (March–April 1996): 14–15.

———. "We Feel Your Pain." *Extra!* (May–June 1996): 11–12.

———. "Major Player or Big Bully?" *Extra!* (January–February 1997): 9–10.

———. "Wall Street's Gain Is Journalism's Loss." *Extra!* (September–October 2001): 20–21.

———. "Good News! The Rich Get Richer." *Extra!* (March–April 2006): 6–7.

———. "Prepackaged News: Straight from the Source, No Journalism Required." *Extra!* (March–April 2006): 17.

Jackson, Janine, and Peter Hart. "Fear and Favor 2000: How Power Shapes the News." *Extra!* (May–June 2001): 15–22.

Jacobs, Jerry A. "Gender and Academic Specialties: Trends among Recipients of College Degrees in the 1980s." *Sociology of Education* 68 (1995): 81–98.

James, Deborah. "Will the WTO Strike Out in Hong Kong?" *Dollars and Sense* (November–December 2005): 19–22, 36.

Jaros, Dean. *Socialization to Politics*. New York: Praeger, 1973.

Jefferson, David J. "America's Most Dangerous Drug." *Newsweek* (August 8, 2005): 41–48.

Jefferson, Deshundra. "Most Lucrative College Degrees." *Money Magazine* (September 21, 2004).

Jencks, Christopher, et al. *Inequality: Reassessment of the Effect of Family and Schooling in America*. New York: Harper and Row, 1972.

Jensen, Eric J., Jurg Gerber, and Ginna M. Babcock. "The New War on Drugs: Grass Roots Movement or Political Construction?" *Journal of Drug Issues* 21 (1991): 651–67.

Jernigan, D. H., J. Ostroff, C. S. Ross, T. S. Naimi, and R. D. Brewer. "Youth Exposure to Alcohol Advertising on the Radio." *Morbidity and Mortality Weekly Report* (September 1, 2006): 937–40.

Jezer, Marty. "Soft Money, Hard Choices." *Dollars and Sense* (July–August 1996): 30–34, 42.

———. "The Missing Candidate." *Progressive Populist* (November 1, 2000): 14–15.

Johnson, David S., John M. Rogers, and Lucilla Tan. "A Century of Family Budgets in the United States." *Monthly Labor Review* (May 2001): 28–45.

Johnston, David. "Judge Sentences Confessed Bomber to Four Life Terms." *New York Times*, May 5, 1998.

Johnston, David Cay. *Perfectly Legal: The Covert Campaign to Rig Our Tax System to Benefit the Super Rich—and Cheat Everybody Else*. New York: Portfolio, 2003.

Jones, Steven E. *Against Technology: From the Luddites to Neo-Luddism*. New York: Routledge, 2006.

Josephson, Matthew. *The Robber Barons*. New York: Harcourt, Brace and World, 1934.

Journalism.org. "Local TV." State of the News Media 2006. Available at http://www.stateofthenews media.org/2006/index.asp.

——. "Magazines." State of the News Media 2006. Available at http://www.stateofthenewsmedia .org/2006/index.asp.

——. "Network Television." State of the News Media 2006. Available at http://www.stateofthe newsmedia.org/2006/index.asp.

——. "Newspapers." State of the News Media 2006. Available at http://www.stateofthenews media.org/2006/index.asp.

——. "Radio." State of the News Media 2006. Available at http://www.stateofthenewsmedia.org/ 2006/index.asp.

Judis, John B. "The Most Powerful Lobby." *In These Times* (February 21, 1994): 22–23.

Kadlec, Daniel. "Zap." *Time* (March 26, 2001): 26–31.

Kahlenberg, Richard, ed. *America's Untapped Resource: Low-Income Students in Higher Education.* New York: The Century Foundation, 2003.

Kalet, Hank. "We Need Electoral Reform Now." *Progressive Populist* (August 1–15, 2001): 19.

Karen, David. "Toward a Political-Organizational Model of Gatekeeping: The Case of Elite Colleges." *Sociology of Education* 63 (1990): 227–40.

——. "Changes in Access to Higher Education in the United States: 1980-1992." *Sociology of Education* 75 (July 2002): 191-210.

Katz, Michael B. *The Irony of Early School Reform.* Cambridge, MA: Harvard University Press, 1968.

Katznelson, Ira, and Mark Kesselman. *The Politics of Power.* New York: Harcourt Brace Jovanovich, 1975.

Kazin, Michael. *The Populist Persuasion.* New York: Basic Books, 1995.

Keeps, David A. "*My Name Is Earl*'s Jason Lee." *TV Guide* (October 31–November 6, 2005): 24.

Kelly, Keith J. "*Time* Looks to Trim $100 Million." *New York Times*, December 28, 2005.

Kelman, Ari. "In the Shadow of Disaster." *Nation* (January 6, 2006): 13–15.

Kendall, Diana. *Framing Class: Media Representations of Wealth and Poverty in America.* Lanham, MD: Rowman & Littlefield, 2005.

Kennickell, Arthur B. "Currents and Undercurrents: Changes in the Distribution of Wealth, 1989–2004." U.S. Federal Reserve System. 2006. Available at http://www.federalreserve.gov.

Kenny, Conor. "Capital Crimes." *In These Times* (August 2006): 20–25.

Kentor, Jeffrey, and Yong Suk Jang. "Yes, There Is a (Growing) Transnational Business Community: A Study of Global Interlocking Directorates, 1983–1998." *International Sociology* 19 (September 2004): 355–68.

Kerbo, Harold R. *Social Stratification and Inequality.* 5th ed. Boston: McGraw-Hill, 2003.

——. *Social Stratification and Inequality.* 6th ed. Boston: McGraw-Hill, 2006.

Kerson, Roger. "Buyouts Offer Options to Ford Workers." *UAW Solidarity* (November–December 2006): 6–7.

Kilgore, Sally. "The Organizational Context of Tracking in Schools." *American Sociological Review* 56 (1991): 189–203.

Klein, Naomi. "Signs of the Times." *Nation* (October 22, 2001): 15–20.

——. "Trading on Terrorism." *In These Times* (November 12, 2001): 9.

Kluegel, James K., and Eliot R. Smith. *Beliefs about Inequality: Americans' Views of What Is and What Ought to Be.* New York: Aldine DeGruyter, 1986.

Knecht, G. Bruce. "Hard Copy: Magazine Advertisers Demand Prior Notice of 'Offensive' Articles." *Wall Street Journal*, April 30, 1997.

Knoke, David. *Organized for Action: Commitment in Voluntary Associations.* New Brunswick, NJ: Rutgers University Press, 1981.

Knott, Alex. "Industry of Influence Nets More Than $10 Billion." Center for Public Integrity. 2006. Available at http://www.publicintegrity.org.

Koeber, Charles, and David W. Wright. "W/Age Bias in Worker Displacement: How Industrial Structure Shapes the Job Loss and Earnings Decline of Older American Workers." *Journal of Socio-Economics* 30 (2001): 343–52.

Kohut, Andrew. "Globalization and the Wage Gap." *New York Times*, December 3, 1999.

Kolbert, Elizabeth, and Adam Clymer. "The Politics of Layoff: In Search of a Message." *New York Times*, March 8, 1996.

Kominski, Robert, and Rebecca Sutterlin. *What's It Worth? Educational Background and Economic Status*. U.S. Bureau of the Census, Household Economic Studies P70-32. Washington, DC: U.S. Government Printing Office, 1992.

Konigsberg, "A New Class War: The Haves vs. The Have Mores." *New York Times*, November 19, 2006.

Koretz, Gene. "Downsizing's Painful Effects." *Business Week* (April 13, 1998): 23.

———. "Downsized in a Down Economy." *Business Week* (September 17, 2001): 36.

Kroll, Luisa, and Lea Goldman, eds. "Billionaire Bacchanalia." *Forbes* (March 27, 2006): 111-78.

Korpi, Walter. *The Democratic Class Struggle*. London: Routledge, 1983.

Kozol, Jonathan. *Savage Inequalities: Children in America's Schools*. New York: Harper, 1991.

Krebs, A.V. "Court Upholds Award in Suppressed TV Report." *Progressive Populist* (January 1-15, 2001): 7.

Krugman, Paul. *Mother Jones* (November–December 1996).

Kuehn, Don. "Saving for College with Section 529 Plans." *AFT American Teacher* (September 2001): 19.

Kutalik, Chris. "What Does the ALF-CIO Split Mean?" *Labor Notes* (September 2005): 7, 10.

"Labor Party to Seek Ballot Access in South Carolina." *Labor Party News* (December 2005): 3.

Lack, Larry. "Is Chávez Hitler or Father Christmas? Venezuela's Handout to Uncle Sam's Shivering Poor." *CounterPunch* (February 2006): 1, 8-9.

Ladd, Everett Carll, and Karlyn H. Bowman. "The Nation Says No to Class Warfare." *USA Today*, May 1999, 24-26.

Lam, Carol C. "Congressman Randall 'Duke' Cunningham Pleads Guilty to Receiving Millions in Bribes." Office of the United States Attorney Southern District of California. Press release, November 28, 2005.

Lauer Research, Inc. "Media Professionals and Their Industry." Survey Prepared for Department of Professional Employees, AFL-CIO, July 20, 2004.

Lavelle, Louis. "Special Report: Executive Pay." *Business Week* (April 16, 2001): 76-108.

———. "For Female CEOs, It's Stingy at the Top." *Business Week* (April 23, 2001): 70-71.

Lee, Martin A., and Norman Solomon. "Does the News Media Have a Liberal Bias?" In *Taking Sides*, ed. Kurt Finsterbusch and George McKenna. Guilford, CT: Duskin Publishing Group, 1996.

Lehmann, Chris. "Michael and Me." *In These Times* (October 14, 1996): 39-40.

Leland, John. "Blessed by the Bull." *Newsweek* (April 27, 1998): 51-53.

Leonhardt, David. "Two-Tier Marketing." *Business Week* (March 17, 1997): 82-90.

LeRoy, Greg. *The Great American Jobs Scam*. San Francisco, CA: Berrett-Koehler, 2005.

Levison, Andrew. "Who Lost the Working Class?" *Nation* (May 14, 2001): 25-32.

Levitas, Daniel. *The Terrorist Next Door: The Militia Movement and the Radical Right*. New York: Thomas Dunne Books/St. Martin's Press, 2002.

Levy, Clifford J. "New York Attorney General Remakes Staff by Patronage." *New York Times*, November 10, 1995.

Lewis, Charles. "The Buying of the President." *Dollars and Sense* (July–August 1996): 28, 41.

Libner, Dena. "Unequal Recovery." *Dollars and Sense* (May–June 2005): 30.

Lieberman, Trudy. "Part D from Outer Space." *Nation* (January 30, 2006): 18-20.

Lindsey, Brink. "Job Loss and Trade: A Reality Check." Trade Briefing Paper No. 19. Cato Institute, March 17, 2004.

Lippman, Dave. "Leno and Letterman—Putting Us to Sleep." Unpublished manuscript, 2004.

Lipset, Seymour M., and Reinhard Bendix. *Social Mobility in Industrial Society*. Berkeley: University of California Press, 1959.

Lipsitz, George. "The Meaning of Memory." In *Private Screenings: Television and the Female Consumer*, ed. Lynn Spigel and Denise Mann. Minneapolis: University of Minnesota Press, 1999.

Litt, Edgar. "Civic Education, Community Norms, and Political Indoctrination." *American Sociological Review* 28 (February 1963): 69-75.

"Little Support for Bush's Social Security Agenda." *American Teacher* (September 2005): 17.

Living Wage Resource Center. "ACORN and the Living Wage." 2006. Available at http://www.livingwagecampaign.org.

———. "The Living Wage Movement." 2006. Available at http://www.livingwagecampaign.org.

———. "Living Wage Successes." 2006. Available at http://www.livingwagecampaign.org.

Lloyd, Mark. "Lessons for Realistic Radicals in the Information Age." In *The Future of Media: Resistance and Reform in the 21st Century*, ed. Robert McChesney, Russell Newman, and Ben Scott. New York: Seven Stories Press, 2005.

"Lobbying for China PNTR Cost $113 Million, Report Says." *Public Citizen News* (November–December 2000): 5, 13.

Lohr, Steve. "Offshore Jobs in Technology: Opportunity or a Threat?" *New York Times*, December 22, 2003.

Lohr, Steve. "Debate over Exporting Jobs Raises Questions on Policies. *New York Times*, February 23, 2004.

Lucas, Samuel R., and Aaron D. Good. "Race, Class, and Tournament Track Mobility." *Sociology of Education* 74 (2001): 139–56.

Luce, Stephanie. "Chicago Living Wage Activists Take on 'Big Box' Retailers." *Labor Notes* (September 2006): 1, 14.

Lustig, Jeffrey R. "The Politics of Shutdown." *Journal of Economic Issues* 19 (1985): 123–59.

Luxury Institute. "Economic Attitudes and Indices." *Wealth Report* (January 15, 2006): 2.

Lyman, Rick. "A Partly Cloudy Forecast for Theater Owners." *New York Times*, March 12, 2001.

MacEwan, Arthur. "Ask Dr. Dollar." *Dollars and Sense* (May–June 2001): 41.

Macionis, John J. *Sociology.* Upper Saddle River, NJ: Prentice Hall, 2001.

MacMillan, John. "Class Action in the News" (quoting Felice Yeskel). Class Action: Building Bridges across the Class Divide. April 1, 2006. Available at http://www.classism.org.

Magdoff, Fred, and Harry Magdoff. "Disposable Workers: Today's Reserve Army of Labor." *Monthly Review* (April 2004): 18–35.

Maiba, Hermann. "Grassroots Transnational Social Activism: The Case of Peoples' Global Action." *Sociological Focus* 38 (February 2005): 41–63.

Maier, Mark. "High School Economics: Corporate Sponsorship and Pro-Market Bias." *Dollars and Sense* (May–June 2002): 13–15, 24–25.

Makinson, Larry. *The Big Picture: Money Follows Power Shift on Capitol Hill.* Washington, DC: Center for Responsive Politics, 1997.

———. "Business, Labor, and Ideological Donors." In *Who's Paying for This Election?* Washington, DC: Center for Responsive Politics, 2000.

Males, Mike. "Wild in Deceit: Why 'Teen Violence' Is Poverty Violence in Disguise." *Extra!* (March–April 1996): 7–9.

———. "Pot Boiler: Why Are Media Enlisting in the Government's Crusade against Marijuana?" *Extra!* (July–August 1997): 20–21.

———. "The Myth of the Grade-School Murderer." *Extra!* (May–June 2001): 30.

Malone, Julia. "Campaign the Most Costly: Near $4 Billion." *Indianapolis Star*, November 7, 2004.

Mandel, Michael J. "How the Super-Rich Lucked Out Twice." *Business Week* (May 14, 2001): 52.

Mangan, Katherine S. "A Shortage of Business Professors Leads to 6-Figure Salaries for New Ph.D.'s." *Chronicle of Higher Education* 47 (May 4, 2001): A12–A13.

Manilov, Marianne. "Channel One: Joe Camel, Potato Chips, and ABC." *Extra!* (July–August 1996): 18-19.

Mantsios, Gregory. "Class in America: Myths and Realities." In *Race, Class, and Gender in the United States*, ed. Paula S. Rothenberg. New York: St. Martin's Press, 1995.

———. "Media Magic: Making Class Disappear." In *Race, Class, and Gender in the United States*, ed. Paula S. Rothenberg. New York: St. Martin's Press, 1995.

Marable, Manning. *The Black World Today*, February 22, 2000.

Marger, Martin N. *Social Inequality: Patterns and Processes.* 2nd ed. Boston: McGraw-Hill, 2002.

———. *Social Inequality: Patterns and Processes.* 3rd ed. Boston: McGraw-Hill, 2005.

Marin, Rick, and Yahlin Chang. "The Katie Factor." *Newsweek* (July 6, 1998): 53–58.

Martin, Christopher R. *Framed: Labor and the Corporate Media*. Ithaca, NY: Cornell University Press, 2004.

Martin, Mick, and Marsha Porter. *1995 Video Movie Guide*. New York: Ballantine, 1994.

——. *DVD and Video Guide 2006*. New York: Ballantine, 2006.

Martinez, Theresa A. "Popular Culture as Oppositional Culture: Rap as Resistance." *Sociological Perspectives* 40 (1997): 265–86.

Marshall, Jeffrey, and Ellen M. Heffes. "Recruiter's Study Finds Changes, and Progress." *Financial Executive* (November 2005): 10.

Masci, David. "Senate Rejects Striker Bill; More Action Unlikely." *Congressional Quarterly* (July 16, 1994): 1936.

Maynard, Micheline. "Ford Eliminating up to 30,000 Jobs and 14 Factories." *New York Times*, January 24, 2006.

Maynard, Micheline, and Nick Bunkley. "Ford Offering 75,000 Buyout Packages." *New York Times*, September 16, 2006, B2.

McCall, Leslie, and Julian Brash. "What Do Americans Think about Inequality?" Demos: A Network for Ideas and Action, May 2004. Available at http://www.demos-usa.org.

McChesney, Robert W. "The Global Media Giants." *Extra!* (November–December 1997): 11–18.

——. *Rich Media, Poor Democracy: Communication Politics in Dubious Times*. Chicago: University of Illinois Press, 1999.

——. "Journalism, Democracy, and Class Struggle." *Monthly Review* (November 2000): 1–15.

——. "Global Media, Neoliberalism, and Imperialism." *Monthly Review* (March 2001): 1–19.

——. "The Escalating War against Corporate Media." *Monthly Review* (March 2004): 1–29.

——. *The Problem of the Media*. New York: Monthly Review Press, 2004.

——. "A Cornerstone of the Media Reform Movement." *Extra!* (January–February 2006): 6–9.

McChesney, Robert W., and John Bellamy Foster. "The Commercial Tidal Wave." *Monthly Review* (March 2003): 1–16.

——. "The 'Left-Wing' Media?" *Monthly Review* (June 2003): 1–16.

McChesney, Robert W., Russell Newman, and Ben Scott, eds. *The Future of Media: Resistance and Reform in the 21st Century*. New York: Seven Stories Press, 2005.

McClatchy Company. "McClatchy Announces Agreement to Sell Five Knight-Ridder Papers." Press release, June 7, 2006. Available at http://www.mcclatchy.com.

McDonald's Corporation. "Notice of 2006 Annual Shareholders Meeting and Proxy Statement." April 17, 2006.

McGinn, Daniel, and Keith Naughton, "How Safe Is Your Job?" *Newsweek* (February 5, 2001): 34–43.

McGirt, Ellen. "A Banner Year." *Fortune* (April 17, 2006): 192–96.

McIntyre, Robert S. "Testimony on Corporate Welfare." U.S. House of Representatives, Committee on the Budget. June 30, 1999. Available at http://www.ctj.org.

McKenzie, Evan. *Privatopia*. New Haven, CT: Yale University Press, 1994.

McKinnon, John D., and John Harwood. "Wall Street Ponies Up to Back Bush's Social Security Plan." *Wall Street Journal*, June 12, 2001.

Media Matters for America. "If It's Sunday, It's Conservative." February 14, 2006. Available at http://www.essentialaction.org.

"Media Myths and Facts." *UAW Solidarity* (April 1992): 17.

Melloan, George. "Whatever Happened to the Labor Movement?" *Wall Street Journal*, September 4, 2001.

Meyer, Lisa. "Militia Movement." 2001. Available at http://www.encarta.msn.com.

Mickelson, Roslyn Arlin. "The Attitude-Achievement Paradox among Black Adolescents." *Sociology of Education* 63 (1990): 44–61.

"Middle of the Class." *Economist* (July 15, 2005): 13.

Miller, Ellen, and Randy Kehler. "Mischievous Myths about Money in Politics." *Dollars and Sense* (July–August 1996): 22–23.

Miller, Ethan. "Other Economies Are Possible." *Dollars and Sense* (July–August 2006): 11–15.

Miller, John. "More Wealth for the Wealthy: The Estate Tax Giveaway and What to Do about It." *Dollars and Sense* (November–December 1997): 26–28, 33.

——. "Tax Cuts: Clinton and Congress Feed the Wealthy." *Dollars and Sense* (November–December 1997): 43.

——. "When Is the Economy in a Recession?" *Dollars and Sense* (July–August 2001): 10–11, 32.

——. "Getting Back More Than They Give." *Dollars and Sense* (September–October 2001): 60–62.

Miller, John, and Ramon Castellblanch. "Does Manufacturing Matter?" *Dollars and Sense* (October 1988): 6–8.

Miller, Laura. "The Best of PR Watch: Spins of the Year." In *Censored 2005*, ed. Peter Phillips. New York: Seven Stories Press, 2004.

——. "Pulling Back the Curtain: The Best of PR Watch." In *Censored 2006: The Top 25 Censored Stories*, ed. Peter Phillips and Project Censored. New York: Seven Stories Press, 2005.

Miller, Mark C. "Free the Media." *Nation* (June 3, 1996): 9–15.

Miller, Matthew, and Tatiana Serafin, eds. "The Forbes 400." *Forbes* (October 9, 2006): 294, 296–304.

Miller, Matthew, and Peter Newcomb. "The Forbes 400." *Forbes* (October 10, 2005): 89.

Miller, S. M. "Born on Third Base: The Sources of Wealth of the 1996 *Forbes* 400." United for a Fair Economy (February 1997).

Mines, Luke. "Globalization in the Classroom." *Nation* (June 1, 1998): 22–24.

Mishel, Lawrence, Jared Bernstein, and John Schmitt. *The State of Working America, 2000–2001*. Ithaca, NY: Cornell University Press, 2001.

Mishel, Lawrence, Jared Bernstein, and Sylvia Allegretto. *The State of Working America, 2004/2005*. Ithaca, NY: Cornell University Press, 2005.

——. *The State of Working America, 2006/2007*. Ithaca, NY: IRL Press, 2007.

Moberg, David. "Tear Down the Walls: The Movement Is Becoming More Global." *In These Times* (May 28, 2000): 11-14.

——. "Election Reflection." *In These Times* (December 14, 2004): 23, 37.

——. "Class Consciousness Matters." *In These Times* (July 11, 2005): 28–29.

——. "Labor Splits Open." *Nation* (July 11, 2005): 4–6.

——. "All Apart Now." *In These Times* (September 19, 2005): 26–27.

——. "The Lay of Labor's New Land." *In These Times* (November 21, 2005): 24–25.

——. "Throw Books at Them." *In These Times* (December 19, 2005): 26–27, 37.

——. "Delphi Dodges Union Contract." *In These Times* (June 2006): 30–31.

——. "Laboring toward Election Day." *Nation* (October 30, 2006): 21–24.

——. "Does Andy Stern Talk His Walk?" *In These Times* (January 2007): 30–31.

"Monitoring Hate and Extremist Activity." *Intelligence Report*. September 19, 2006. Available at http://www.splcenter.org.

Monroe, Ann. "Getting Rid of the Gray." *Mother Jones* July–August 1996):29.

Moody, Kim. "America Gets a Virtual Raise." *Labor Notes* (February 1997): 15–16.

——. "NAFTA, WTO, MAI, IMF, FTAA, AGOA . . . Where Does It End?" *Labor Notes* (May 1998): 10, 16.

——. *Workers in a Lean World: Unions in the International Economy*. New York: Verso, 1998.

Moore, David. "Three in Four Americans Believe in Paranormal." Gallup Poll. June 16, 2005. Available at http://www.galluppoll.com.

Moore, James H., Jr. "Project Pension Income: Equity or Disparity?" *Monthly Labor Review* (March 2006): 58–67.

Moore, Stephen. "How to Slash Corporate Welfare." *New York Times*, April 5, 1995.

Moore, Thomas S. *The Disposable Work Force*. New York: Aldine de Gruyter, 1996.

Morehouse, Ward. "New Book Urges Democratic Offensive to Purge Corporations' Constitutional Authority to Govern." 2001. Available at http://www.poclad.org.

Motion Picture Association of America. "U.S. Entertainment Industry: 2005 MPA Market Statistics." 2006. Available at http://www.mpaa.org.

Moyers, Bill. "Which America Will We Be Now?" *Nation* (November 19, 2001): 11–14.

"Mr. Kerry's Choice." *Washington Post*, July 7, 2004.

Mullen, Ann L., Kimberly A. Goyette, and Joseph A. Soares. "Who Goes to Graduate School? Social and Educational Correlates of Educational Continuation after College." *Sociology of Education* 76 (April 2003): 143–69.

Murray, Charles. "The Shape of Things to Come." *National Review* (July 8, 1991): 29–30.

Muwakkil, Salim. "Just Vote No: The War on Drugs Loses at the Polls." *In These Times* (December 25, 2000): 25–26.

Nace, Ted. *Gangs of America: The Rise of Corporate Power and the Disabling of Democracy.* San Francisco, CA: Berrett-Koehler, 2003.

Nader, Ralph. "Product Libel." *Public Citizen News* (May–June 1998): 4.

———. "Testimony on Corporate Welfare." U.S. House of Representatives, Committee on the Budget. June 30, 1999. Available at http://www.nader.org.

National Association of Housing Cooperatives. "About NAHC and Housing Co-ops." Available at http://www.coophousing.org.

National Center for Educational Statistics. 2006. "Welcome to NCES." Available at http://nces.ed.gov.

National Center for Employee Ownership. "A Statistical Profile of Employee Ownership." July 2006. Available at http://www.nceo.org.

———. "Largest Study Yet Shows ESOPs Improve Performance and Employee Benefits." July 2006. Available at http://www.nceo.org.

National Center for Responsive Philanthropy. "$1 Billion for Ideas: Conservative Think Tanks in the 1990s." Press release, March 12, 1999.

National Cooperative Business Association. "About Cooperatives." March 2005. Available at http://www.ncba.coop.

National Council on Economic Education. "About NCEE." 2006. Available at http://www.ncee.net.

"The National Entertainment State, Special Issue." *Nation* (July 3, 2006): 13–30.

National League of Cities. "The American Dream in 2004: A Survey of the American People." 2004. Available at http://www.nlc.org.

National Taxpayers Association. "Democrat Voters Now Strongest Supporters of Balanced Budget Constitutional Amendment, Poll Finds." Press release, April 3, 2003. Available at http://www.ntu.org.

National Trade and Professional Associations of the United States. Washington, DC: Columbia Books, 2006.

Naughton, Keith. "Lock and Download." *Newsweek* (October 22, 2001): 61–62.

Naureckas, Jim. "Corporate Censorship Matters: The Case of NBC." *Extra!* (November–December 1995): 13.

———. "From the Top: What Are the Politics of Network Bosses?" *Extra!* (July–August 1998): 21–22.

———. "Where's the Power: Newsroom or Boardroom?" *Extra!* (July–August 1998): 23.

Navarro, Vicente. "Medical History as Justification Rather Than Explanation: A Critique of Starr's *The Social Transformation of American Medicine.*" *International Journal of Health Services* 14 (1984): 511–28.

———. "Production and the Welfare State: The Political Context of Reforms." *International Journal of Health Services* 21 (1991): 585–614.

Navarro, Vicente, and John Schmitt. "Economic Efficiency versus Social Equality?" *International Journal of Health Services* 35 (2005): 613–30.

Nencioloi, Lorenzo. "Indies Unleashed." *Dollars and Sense* (May–June 2005): 26–29.

Neustadtl, Alan, and Dan Clawson. "Corporate Political Groupings: Does Ideology Unify Business Political Behavior?" *American Sociological Review* 53 (1988): 172–90.

"The New D.A.R.E. Program: An Information Kit for Law Enforcement Officers." Carnevale Associates, Washington, D.C., circa 2003.

Newman, Katherine S. *Falling from Grace: The Experience of Downward Mobility in the American Middle Class*. New York: Free Press, 1988.

———. *Declining Fortunes*. New York: Basic Books, 1993.

Newman, Russell, and Ben Scott. "Introduction." In *The Future of Media: Resistance and Reform in the 21st Century*, ed. Robert McChesney, Russell Newman, and Ben Scott. New York: Seven Stories Press, 2005.

Newport, Frank, and Maura Strausberg. "Americans' Belief in Psychic and Paranormal Phenomena Is up over Last Decade." Gallup Poll. June 8, 2001. Available at http://www.galluppoll.com.

News Corporation. "Australian Federal Court Approves News Corporation Reincorporation to United States." Press release, November 3, 2004. Available at http://www.newscorp.com.

———. *News Corporation 2000 Annual Report*. 2005. Available at http://www.newscorp.com.

"News Watch." *Labor Notes* (November 2006): 4.

"The New Transplants." *UAW Research Bulletin* (January–February 1995): 10–11.

New York Times. *Downsizing of America*. New York: Random House, 1996.

———. *Class Matters*. New York: Times Books, 2005.

New York Times/CBS News Poll. January 20–25, 2006.

Nichols, John. "After Fusion: The New New Party." *In These Times* (March 22, 1998): 18–20.

———. "Behind the DLC Takeover." *Progressive* (October 2000): 28–30.

———. "Drug Warrior Dissent." *Nation* (May 28, 2001): 8.

———. "Moyers Fights Back." *Nation* (June 6, 2005): 8.

———. "Being Like Bernie." *Nation* (August 15–22, 2005): 15–18.

———. "What Delay Left Behind." *Nation* (April 24, 2006): 5–8.

———. "What Can Sherrod Brown Do for the Democrats?" *Nation* (October 2, 2006): 11–14.

———. "The 'Seattle Senators'." *Nation* (December 18, 2006): 8–10.

Nike Corporation. "Notice of Annual Meeting of Stockholders and Proxy Statement." August 12, 2005.

Nitschke, Lori. "Tax Plan Destined for Revision." *Congressional Quarterly Weekly* (February 10, 2001): 318–21.

———. "Coalitions Make a Comeback." *Congressional Quarterly Weekly* (March 3, 2001): 470–74.

———. "Tax-Cut Bipartisanship Down to One Chamber." *Congressional Quarterly Weekly* (March 10, 2001): 529–32.

Nitschke, Lori, and Wendy Boudreau. "Provisions of the Tax Law." *Congressional Quarterly Weekly* (June 9, 2001): 1390–94.

Noble, David F. *Forces of Production: A Social History of Industrial Automation*. New York: Knopf, 1984.

Noble, Douglas D. "Schools as 'Instructional Delivery Systems.'" *In These Times* (November 30, 1992): 28–29.

Nye, Peter. "Lobbying and Gift Reform Shines Sunlight on Influence Peddling." *Public Citizen* (January–February 1996): 1, 3.

Oakes, Jeannie. "More Than Misapplied Technology: A Normative and Political Response to Hallinan on Tracking." *Sociology of Education* 67 (1994): 84–89.

O'Brien, Bill. "Clean Up Campaign Funding." *DallasNews.com*, November 10, 2006. Available at http://www.dallasnews.com.

O'Connor, Carla. "Race, Class, and Gender in America: Narratives of Opportunity among Low-Income African American Youths." *Sociology of Education* 72 (1999): 137–57.

Office of Congressman Dick Armey. "Washington's Lobbying Industry: A Case for Tax Reform—Executive Summary." June 19, 1996.

Office of Management and Budget. *Budget of the United States Government: Fiscal Year 2002*. Washington, DC: U.S. Government Printing Office, 2001.

———. "Appendix: Department of Health and Human Services, 'Administration for Children and Families, TANF.'" *Budget of the United States Government: Fiscal Year 2007*. Washington, DC: U.S. Government Printing Office, 2006.

———. "Analytical Perspectives, Supplemental Materials: 27, Detailed Function Table." *Budget of the United States Government: Fiscal Year 2007*. Washington, DC: U.S. Government Printing Office, 2006.

———. "Historical Tables." *Budget of the United States Government: Fiscal Year 2007*. Washington, DC: U.S. Government Printing Office, 2006.

Office of National Drug Control Policy. *The National Drug Control Strategy*. Washington, DC: National Criminal Justice Reference Service, 1992, 1994, 1996, 1998.

———. *National Drug Control Strategy: 2001 Annual Report*. Washington, DC: U.S. Government Printing Office, 2001.

———. *National Drug Control Strategy: FY 2007 Budget Summary*. Washington, DC: The White House, 2006.

Office of Technology Assessment. *Technology and Structural Unemployment*. Washington, DC: Congress of the United States, 1986.

O'Grady, Mary Anastasia. "America: In Chávez's Crosshairs." *Wall Street Journal*, September 22, 2006.

Oliver, Melvin, Thomas M. Shapiro, and Julie E. Press. "'Them That's Got Shall Get': Inheritance and Achievement in Wealth Accumulation." In *Research in Politics and Society*, ed. Richard E. Ratliffe, Melvin Oliver, and Thomas M. Shapiro. Vol. 15. Greenwich, CT: JAI Press, 1995.

Omicinski, John. "Public in Poll Supports Church, Police, Military." *Indianapolis Star*, June 26, 2001.

"The 100 Largest U.S. Multinationals." *Forbes* (July 17, 1995): 274–76.

"Opposing Harmful Trade Measure for Africa." *Public Citizen News, Annual Report 2000* (March–April 2001): 10–12.

"Opposing the World Trade Organization." *Public Citizen News, Annual Report 2000* (March–April 2001): 10–12.

Oprah Winfrey Show. "What Class Are You? Inside America's Taboo Topic." August 24, 2006. Available at http://www.oprah.com.

———. "Show Archive: August 2006." Available at http://www.oprah.com.

Orcutt, James D., and J. Blake Turner. "Shocking Numbers and Graphic Accounts: Quantified Images of Drug Problems in the Print Media." *Social Problems* 40 (1993): 190–206.

"The O'Reilly Factory." *Business Week Online* (March 8, 2004). Available at http://www.businessweek.com.

Orr, Doug. "Social Security Isn't Broken." *Dollars and Sense* (November–December 2004): 14–16.

———. "Social Security Q&A." *Dollars and Sense* (May–June 2005): 15–20.

Orum, Anthony M., and Roberta S. Cohen. "The Development of Political Orientations among Black and White Children." *American Sociological Review* 38 (1973): 62–74.

Overton, Spencer. "The Donor Class: Campaign Finance, Democracy, and Participation." *University of Pennsylvania Law Review* 153 (2004): 73–118.

Pace, Eric. "B. Gerald Cantor, Philanthropist and Owner of Rodin Collection, Is Dead at 79." *New York Times*, July 6, 1996.

Palast, Greg. "Progressive Interview with Hugo Chávez." *Progressive* (July 2006): 35–39.

Parenti, Christian. "Winning the War of Ideas." *In These Times* (November 17, 2003): 18–21.

Parenti, Michael. *Power and the Powerless*. New York: St. Martin's Press, 1978.

Parks, Daniel J. "Bush May Test Capitol Hill Clout Early with Expedited Tax-Cut Proposal." *Congressional Quarterly Weekly* (January 6, 2001): 41–42.

———. "Under Tight Spending Ceilings, Democrats Lower Their Sights." *Congressional Quarterly Weekly* (June 9, 2001): 1362–64.

Parrish, Geov. "Wrecking Social Security." *Progressive Populist* (March 15, 2005): 13.

Parry, Robert. "The Right-Wing Media Machine." *Extra!* (March–April 1995): 6–10.

———. "Who Buys the Right?" *Nation* (November 18, 1996): 5–6.

Paulin, Geoffrey, and Brian Riordon. "Making It on Their Own: The Baby Boom Meets Generation X." *Monthly Labor Review* (February 1998): 10–21.

Pearlstein, Steven. "Solving Inequality Won't Take Class Warfare." *Washington Post*, March 15, 2006.

Pepper, Margo. "No Corporation Left Behind." *Monthly Review* (November 2006): 39–41.

Perelman, Michael. "Some Economics of Class." *Monthly Review* (July–August 2006): 18–28.

Perine, Keith. "Class Action Lawsuit Measure Advances amid Heavy Lobbying, Concern over State Law." *Congressional Quarterly Weekly* (April 12, 2003): 882.

Perkins, Joseph. "Caught in the News Media's Liberal Bias." *Indianapolis Star*, July 18, 1998.

Perrow, Charles. "A Society of Organizations." *Theory and Society* 20 (1991): 725–62.

Perrucci, Carolyn C., and Robert Perrucci. "Social Origins, Educational Contexts, and Career Mobility." *American Sociological Review* 35 (1970): 451–63.

Perrucci, Carolyn C., Robert Perrucci, Dena B. Targ, and Harry Targ. *Plant Closings: International Context and Social Costs*. Hawthorne, NY: Aldine de Gruyter, 1988.

Perrucci, Robert. "The Significance of Intra-Occupational Mobility." *American Sociological Review* 26 (1961): 874–83.

——. *Japanese Auto Transplants in the Heartland*. New York: Aldine De Gruyter, 1994.

Perrucci, Robert, and Bonnie L. Lewis. "Interorganizational Relations and Community Influence Structure." *Sociological Quarterly* 30 (1989): 205–23.

Perrucci, Robert, and Marc Pilisuk. "Leaders and Ruling Elites: The Interorganizational Basis of Community Power." *American Sociological Review* 35 (1970): 1040–57.

Perrucci, Robert, and Earl Wysong. *The New Class Society*. Lanham, MD: Rowman & Littlefield, 1999.

——. "Organizational Power, Generative Capital, and Class Closure." Paper presented at the Pacific Sociological Association annual meeting, San Francisco, California, March 31, 2001.

——. *The New Class Society: Goodbye American Dream?* 2nd ed. Lanham, MD: Rowman & Littlefield, 2003.

Perrucci, Robert, et al. "The Two Faces of Racialized Space in a Predominantly White University." *International Journal of Contemporary Sociology* 37 (2000): 230–44.

Petrova, Maria. "Inequality and Media Capture." Working Paper Series, Social Science Research Network, Harvard University. February 6, 2006. Available at http://www.papers.ssrn.com.

Pew Research Center. "Economic Inequality Rising, Boom Bypasses Poor." 2001. Available at http://www.people-press.org.

——. "Journalists Avoiding the News, Self Censorship: How Often and Why?" 2001. Available at http://www.people-press.org.

——. "The 2005 Political Typology: Beyond Red vs. Blue." May 10, 2005. Available at http://www.people-press.org.

——. "Public Sours on Government and Business." October 25, 2005. Available at http://www.people-press.org.

——. "Economy Now Seen Through Partisan Prism." January 24, 2006. Available at http://www.people-press.org.

——. "Once Again, the Future Ain't What It Used to Be." 2006. Available at http://www.pewresearch.org.

——. "Politics and Values in a 51%–48% Nation." January 24, 2006. Available at http://www.people-press.org.

Peyser, Marc. "Red, White and Funny." *Newsweek* (December 29, 2003–January 5, 2004): 70–77.

——. "The Truthiness Teller." *Newsweek* (February 13, 2006): 48–56.

Peyser, Marc, and Johnnie L. Roberts. "The Katie Factor." *Newsweek* (April 17, 2006): 37–42.

Phillips, Jim. "What Happens after Seattle?" *Dollars and Sense* (January–February 2000): 15–16, 31–32.

Phillips, Kevin. "Fat City." *Time* (September 26, 1994): 49–56.

Phillips, Peter. "Self Censorship and the Homogeneity of the Media Elite." In *Censored 1998*, ed. Peter Phillips. New York: Seven Stories Press, 1998.

Phillips Peter, and Project Censored, eds. *Censored 2001: 25th Anniversary Edition*. New York: Seven Stories Press, 2001.

——. *Censored 2005: The Top 25 Censored Stories*. New York: Seven Stories Press, 2004.

——. *Censored 2006: The Top 25 Censored Stories*. New York: Seven Stories Press, 2005.

Pitts, Leonard. "Images of Poor Will Fade Away." *Indianapolis Star*. September 24, 2005.

Piven, Frances Fox. "Poorhouse Politics." *Progressive* (February 1995): 22–24.

Pizzigati, Sam. *Greed and Good: Understanding and Overcoming the Inequality that Limits Our Lives*. New York: Apex Press, 2004.

——. "Can We Legislate Against Greed?" *Too Much* (July 11, 2005): 1.

——. "About *Too Much*." 2006. Available at http://www.cipa-apex.org.

——. "The Evolution of Our Plutocracy." *Too Much* (January 23, 2006): 1.

——. "Stat of the Week: Estate Tax Odds." *Too Much* (June 5, 2006): 4.

——. "A Most Dangerous YOYO." *Too Much* (June 19, 2006): 4.

——. "Campaign 2006: A Glaringly Missing Issue." *Too Much* (November 3, 2006): 3.

——. "The New Congress: Why Deep Pockets Can Relax." *Too Much* (November 13, 2006): 3.

——. "Greed at a Glance: Peacock Party Time." *Too Much* (November 27, 2006): 2.

——. "Best Legislative Reason to Feel Slightly Optimistic about 2007." *Too Much* (December 18, 2006): 6.

——. "Most Original Research on the Consequences of Inequality." *Too Much* (December 18, 2006): 4.

——. "Most Pithy Political Take on Our Current Predicament." *Too Much* (December 18, 2006): 6.

POCLAD. "*The Elite Consensus: When Corporations Wield the Constitution* Describes Shadow Corporate Government." Press release, September 10, 2003. Available at http://www.poclad.org.

——. "Frequently Asked Questions." 2006. Available at http://www.poclad.org.

Pohlman, Kimberly. "Solid Ratings Don't Protect Progressive Radio Voices." *Extra!* (July–August 2000): 22.

Political Money Line. "Money in Politics Databases: Overall Spending for Federal Lobbying." 2005. Available at http://www.fecinfo.com.

——. "2005 Lobbying Reports Covering 1/1/05–6/30/05." 2006. Available at http://www.political moneyline.com.

——. "2005 Lobbying Reports Covering 7/1/05–12/31/05." 2006. Available at http://www.political moneyline.com.

——. "Federal Lobby Directory: Individual Lobbyists." 2006. Available at http://www .fecinfo.com.

Polivka, Anne E. "Contingent and Alternative Work Arrangements, Defined." *Monthly Labor Review* (October 1996): 3–9.

Pollin, Robert. *Contours of Descent: U.S. Economic Fractures and the Landscape of Global Austerity*. New York: Verso, 2005.

Pomery, John. "Running Deficits with the Rest of the World—Part I." *Focus on Economic Issues*. West Lafayette, IN: Purdue Center for Economic Education, Fall 1987.

Postman, Neil. "Virtual Students, Digital Classroom." *Nation* (October 9, 1995): 377–82.

Powell, Lewis F. "Attack on American Free Enterprise System." August 21, 1971. Available at http://www.historyisaweapon.com.

Powers, Richard. "American Dreaming." *New York Times Magazine* (May 7, 2000): 66–67.

Pozner, Jennifer L. "Power Shortage for Media Women." *Extra!* (July–August 2001): 8–9.

Press, Eyal. "Spin Cities." *Nation* (November 18, 1996): 30–33.

"Programs and Achievements/Program Directions." Boston: United for a Fair Economy, 37 Temple Place, ca. 1997.

Project for Excellence in Journalism. "Network TV: Public Attitudes." State of the News Media 2006, May 8, 2006. Available at http://www.stateofthenewsmedia.com/2006/index.asp.

Public Campaign. *Hard Facts on Hard Money*. Washington, DC: Public Campaign, 2001.

Public Citizen. *Unfairness Incorporated: The Corporate Campaign against Consumer Class Actions*. Public Citizen's Congress Watch, June 2003.

——. "Beyond the 'Blame Game': Why the Doha Round of Talks Have Collapsed—and a Path Forward." Global Trade Watch. Press release, July 26, 2006. Available at http://www.citizen.org.

Pugh, Tony. "Massive Immigration Steers Population, Reapportionment." *Indianapolis Star*, December 29, 2000.

Puig, Claudia. "True Stories: Documentaries Are a Growing Business." *USA Today*, February 25, 2005.

Purdue Research Foundation. *Home for High-Tech Business*. West Lafayette, IN: Purdue Research Park, 1998.

Quinn, Jane Bryant. "Tax Cuts: Who Will Get What." *Newsweek* (June 11, 2001): 30.

———. "Private Accounts Won't Work." *Indianapolis Star*, September 17, 2001.

———. "Medicare's in Good Health." *Newsweek* (May 24, 2004): 41.

———. "The Economic Perception Gap." *Newsweek* (November 20, 2006): 59.

Rampton, Sheldon, and John Stauber. "Oprah's Free—Are We?" *Extra!* (May–June 1998): 11–12.

———. "This Report Brought to You by Monsanto." *Progressive* (July 1998): 22–25.

Randall, Adrian. *Before the Luddites*. New York: Cambridge University Press, 1991.

"Ranked within Industries, the Fortune 1000." *Fortune* (April 17, 2006): F44–F67.

Rector, Robert, and Rea S. Hederman Jr. "Two Americas: One Rich, One Poor? Understanding Income Inequality in the United States." *Heritage Foundation Reports* (August 24, 2004).

Reed, Adolf L., Jr. "The 'Public Is Bad; Private Is Better' Scam." *Labor Party News* (October 2005): 1–2.

———. "The Real Divide." *Progressive* (November 2005): 27–32.

Reich, Robert B. *The Next American Frontier*. (New York: Times Books, 1983).

———. "Secession of the Successful." *New York Times Magazine*, January 20, 1991, 16–17, 42–45.

———. *The Work of Nations: Preparing Ourselves for the Twenty-first Century*. New York: Knopf, 1991.

Reinhard, David. "The Democratic Convention: In Search of Two Americas." *The Oregonian*, July 29, 2004, B13.

Renchler, Ron. *Financial Equity in Schools*. ERIC Digest No. 76. Eugene, OR: ERIC Clearinghouse in Educational Management, 1994.

Rendall, Steve. "Nation's Top Columnists Still Lean Right." *Extra!* (January–February 2000): 11–12.

———. "Media See the Poor as Aggressors in 'Class War.'" *Extra!* (January–February 2001): 10.

———. "The Hypocrisy of George Will." *Extra!* (September–October 2003): 14–16.

———. "An Aggressive Conservative vs. a 'Liberal to Be Determined.'" *Extra!* (November–December 2003): 19–23.

———. "Balancing 'Liberal' Media." *Extra!* (January–February 2005): 26.

———. "Failing at Its 'No. 1 Goal.'" *Extra!* (November–December 2005): 28–30.

———. "Bush Hating Nation." *Extra!* (May–June 2006): 10–11.

———. "That's Not Funny!'" *Extra!Update* (June 2006): 1.

———. "Imperial Mythology.'" *Extra!* (November–December 2006): 22.

———. "The Repeatedly Re-Elected Autocrat.'" *Extra!* (November–December 2006): 23–25.

Rendall, Steve, and Peter Hart. "Time to Unplug the CPB." *Extra!* (September–October 2005): 18–21.

Rendall, Steve, and Julie Hollar. "Are You on the *NewsHour*'s Guestlist?" *Extra!* (September–October 2006): 20.

Rendall, Steve, and Eric Klotz. "Hannity and Colmes Fails 'Fair and Balanced' Test." *Extra!* (November–December 2003): 21.

Rendall, Steve, and Anna Kosseff. "Are Progressive Views Unpopular?" *Extra!* (September–October 24, 2004): 19.

———. "I'm Not a Leftist, but I Play One on TV: Progressives Excluded as Right Battles Center." *Extra!* (September–October 2004): 17–23.

Responsible Wealth. "Who We Are." July 7, 2006. Available at http://www.responsible wealth.org.

Reskin, Barbara, and Irene Padavic. *Women and Men at Work*. Thousand Oaks, CA: Pine Forge Press, 1994.

"Returning Favorites." *TV Guide* (September 8, 2001): 4.

"Returning at Mid-Season." *TV Guide* (May 29–June 4, 2006): 7.

"Springfield Film Festival." *TV Guide* (April 24–30, 2006): 82.

Reuss, Alejandro, Arthur MacEwan, Phineas Baxandall, and John Miller. "The ABCs of 'Free-Trade' Agreements." *Dollars and Sense* (January–February 2001): 24.

Reynolds, Alan. "Offshoring Which Jobs?" *Washington Times,* June 6, 2004.

Reynolds, David. *Democracy Unbound.* Boston: South End Press, 1997.

"Rich College, Poor College." *Business Week* (December 20, 2004): 88–90.

"The Rich Get a Good Return on Their Campaign Investments." *Sanders Scoop* (Winter 1998): 1.

Riechmann, Deb. "Clinton Signs Measure to Open China to U.S. Goods." *Indianapolis Star,* October 11, 2000.

Rifkin, Jeremy. "The European Dream." *Utne* (September–October 2004): 75–79.

Roberts, Johnnie L. "A Mogul in Full." *Newsweek* (April 24, 2006): 43–44.

Roberts, Paul Craig. "The New Face of Class Warfare." *CounterPunch* (July 2006): 1–6.

Rogers, David. "U.S. Annual War Spending Grows." *Wall Street Journal,* March 8, 2006.

Rogers, Everett M. "Diffusion and Re-Invention of Project DARE." In *Organizational Aspects of Health Communication Campaigns: What Works?* ed. Thomas E. Backer and Everett M. Rogers. Newbury Park, CA: Sage, 1993.

Romano, Michael. "Bigger Payday for Some Docs." *Modern Healthcare,* July 17, 2006.

Romero, Simon. "Chávez Wins Easily in Venezuela." *New York Times,* December 4, 2006.

Roscigno, Vincent J., and James W. Ainsworth-Darnell. "Race, Cultural Capital, and Educational Resources: Persistent Inequalities and Achievement Returns." *Sociology of Education* 72 (1999): 158–78.

Rosenthal, Robert, and Lenore Jacobson. *Pygmalion in the Classroom.* New York: Holt, Rinehart and Winston, 1968.

Ross, Andrew. "Duct Tape Nation: Land Use, the Fear Factor, and the New Unilateralism." *Harvard Design Magazine* (Spring–Summer 2004): 1–5.

Ross, Steven J. *Working-Class Hollywood: Silent Film and the Shaping of Class in America.* Princeton, NJ: Princeton University Press, 1998.

Rothman, Robert A. *Working: Sociological Perspectives.* 2nd ed. Upper Saddle River, NJ: Prentice Hall, 1998.

——. *Inequality and Stratification: Race, Class, and Gender.* 5th ed. Upper Saddle River, NJ: Pearson–Prentice Hall, 2005.

Rothschild, Matthew. "The Progressive Interview: Roger Ebert." *Progressive* (August 2003): 33–37.

Rousseau, Jean-Jacques. *The Social Contract,* trans. Charles Frankel. New York: Hafner Publishing Co., 1947.

Rubin, Beth A. *Shifts in the Social Contract.* Thousand Oaks, CA: Pine Forge Press, 1996.

Rushkoff, Douglas (narrator). "The Merchants of Cool." PBS *Frontline* TV Documentary, 2001.

Sabo, Martin Olav. "Income Equity Act of 2005." *Congressional Record* (July 12, 2005): E1469.

Safire, William. "Jimmy That 'Lockbox.'" *New York Times,* September 10, 2001.

——. "The Body Politic Will Reject a 'Charisma Transplant.'" *New York Times,* July 7, 2004.

"Salary Guide." *New York Magazine* (September 26, 2005).

"Salem, Oregon Police Department." *D.A.R.E. News* (June 2006): 3–4.

Samuelson, Robert J. "Great Expectations." *Newsweek* (January 8, 1996): 24–33.

——. "Indifferent to Inequality?" *Newsweek* (May 7, 2001): 45.

——. "One 'Reform' That Worked." *Newsweek* (August 7, 2006): 44.

Schaefer, Richard T. *Sociology.* 10th ed. New York: McGraw-Hill, 2007.

Scharf, Adria. "Tax Cut Time Bomb." *Dollars and Sense* (March–April 2004): 39.

Schellhardt, Timothy D. "Are Layoffs Moral? One Firm's Answer: You Ask, We'll Sue." *Wall Street Journal,* August 1, 1996, A12.

Schemo, Diana J. "U.S. Schools Turn More Segregated." *New York Times,* July 20, 2001.

——. "A Second Report Shows Charter School Students Not Performing as Well as Other Students." *New York Times,* December 16, 2004.

Scherer, Michael. "Make Your Taxes Disappear!" *Mother Jones* (March–April 2005): 72–77.

Schlozman, Kay L., and John T. Tierney. *Organized Interests and American Democracy.* New York: Harper and Row, 1986.

Schmitt, John. "How Good Is the Economy at Creating Good Jobs?" Washington, DC: Center for Economic and Policy Research, October 2005.

Schor, Juliet B. "Keeping Up with the Trumps: How the Middle Class Identifies with the Rich." *Washington Monthly* (July–August 1998): 34–37.

Schrag, Peter. "Edison's Red Ink Schoolhouse." *Nation* (June 25, 2001): 20–24.

Schrammel, Kurt. "Comparing the Labor Market Success of Young Adults from Two Generations." *Monthly Labor Review* (February 1998): 3–9.

Schwartz, Felice N. "Management Women and the New Facts of Life." In *Working in America*, ed. Amy S. Wharton. Mountain View, CA: Mayfield Publishing, 1998.

Schwartzman, Andrew Jay, Cheryl A. Leanza, and Harold Feld. "The Legal Case for Diversity in Broadcast Ownership." In *The Future of Media: Resistance and Reform in the 21st Century*, ed. Robert McChesney, Russell Newman, and Ben Scott. New York: Seven Stories Press, 2005.

Scott, Janny, and David Leonhardt. "Class in America: Shadowy Lines That Still Divide." *New York Times*, May 15, 2005, 1, 16–18.

Scott, Robert E. "NAFTA's Hidden Costs." Washington, DC: Economic Policy Institute, May 2001.

Seider, Maynard S. "American Big Business Ideology: A Content Analysis of Executive Speeches." *American Sociological Review* 39 (1974): 802–15.

Seldes, George. "Is the Entire Press Corrupt?" *Extra!* (November–December 1994): 26–27.

"Set to Organize." *Labor Party Press* (January 1999): 1, 4.

Sewell, William A., A. O. Haller, and G. W. Ohlandorf. "The Educational and Early Occupational Status Attainment Process." *American Sociological Review* 35 (1970): 1014–27.

Sewell, William A., and Vimal Shah. "Parents' Education and Children's Educational Aspirations and Achievements." *American Sociological Review* 33 (1968): 191–209.

Shaiken, Harley. *Work Transformed: Automation and Labor in the Computer Age*. New York: Holt, Rinehart and Winston, 1985.

Shane, Scott. "Nader Is Left with Fewer Votes, and Friends, after '04 Race." *New York Times*, November 4, 2004.

Shaw, Archer H. *The Lincoln Encyclopedia*. New York: Macmillan, 1950.

Sherman, Scott. "An Appeal to Reason." *Nation* (March 10, 1997): 15–19.

"Shifting the Trade Debate, CAFTA and Beyond." *Public Citizen News, 2005 Annual Report* (March–April 2006): 7.

Shuldiner, Allan, and Tony Raymond. *Who's in the Lobby? A Profile of Washington's Influence Industry*. Washington, DC: Center for Responsive Politics, 1998.

Sieder, Sam D. *Second Rate Nation: From the American Dream to the American Myth*. Boulder, CO: Paradigm, 2005.

Sifry, Micah L. "How Money in Politics Hurts You." *Dollars and Sense* (July–August 2001): 17–20.

———. *Spoiling for a Fight: Third Party Politics in America*. New York: Routledge, 2002.

Sifry, Micah L., and Nancy Watzman. *Is That a Politician in Your Pocket? Washington on $2 Million a Day*. Hoboken, NJ: John Wiley and Sons, 2004.

Silverstein, Ken. "Manufactured News." *Extra!* (January–February 1997): 23–24.

Silverstein, Ken, and Alexander Cockburn. "Why the Drug War Works: It's a Money/Class Thing, of Course." *CounterPunch* (June 15–30, 1998): 4–5.

Simmons, Robert G., and Morris Rosenberg. "Functions of Children's Perceptions of the Stratification System." *American Sociological Review* 36 (1971): 235–49.

Sirico, Robert A. "The Capitalist Ethic: True Morality." *Forbes* (December 2, 1996): 85.

Sirota, David. "Debunking 'Centrism'." *Nation* (January 3, 2005): 18–19.

———. "A Primary Concern: Free Trade Could Be Key for Democrats in '08." *In These Times* (April 2006): 28–29.

———. "Embracing Populism." *In These Times* (December 2006): 4.

———. *Hostile Takeover: How Big Money and Corruption Conquered Our Government—and How We Can Take It Back*. New York: Crown Publishers, 2006.

Skala, Nicholas, and Ida Hellander. "A Review of Data on the U.S. Health Sector." *International Journal of Health Services* 36 (2006): 157–76.

Sklar, Holly. "CEO Ponzi Scheme." 2001. Available at http://www.inequality.org.

Sklar, Leslie. *The Transnational Capitalist Class.* Oxford: Blackwell, 2001.

Sloan, Allan. "A Lot of Trust, but No Funds." *Newsweek* (July 30, 2001): 34.

Sloboda, Zili. Personal correspondence with the authors. December 7, 2005.

———. Personal correspondence with the authors. March 8, 2006.

Smith, Jeremy. "Intellectual Snobs versus Political Slobs." *Dollars and Sense* (May–June 1998): 38–39.

Smith, Wesley J. "Nobody's Nader." *Mother Jones* (July–August 1996): 61–63.

Smith-Said, Stephan. "Why Neil Young Is Wrong." *Progressive* (July 2006): 32–33.

Snider, Mike. "Documentaries Are Playing to Keen Interest." *USA Today*, July 24, 2004.

Snow, Tony. "What the Class Warriors Don't Get about $1.6 Trillion." *Lafayette Courier Journal*, February 10, 2001.

Social Security Administration. "Maximum Taxable Earnings." 2006. Available at http://www.ssa.gov.

"Social Security Heist." *Nation* (July 9, 2001): 3.

Soley, Lawrence C. *Leasing the Ivory Tower: The Corporate Takeover of Academia.* Boston: South End Press, 1996.

———. "The Power of the Press Has a Price." *Extra!* (July–August 1997): 11–13.

———. "Corporate Censorship and the Limits of Free Speech." *Extra!* (March–April 1999): 19–21.

Solomon, Norman. "Media Moguls on Board." *Extra!* (January–February 1998): 19–22.

———. "The Media Oligarchy: Undermining Journalism, Obstructing Democracy." In *Censored 2001*, ed. Peter Phillips and Project Censored. New York: Seven Stories Press, 2001.

———. "Media Fire Shots across Edwards' Bow." *Extra!Update* (August 2004): 1.

Solowey, Fred J. "Selling Social Insecurity." *Extra!* (March–April 1998): 22–23.

"Soundbites." *Extra!* (May–June 1996): 5.

Source Watch. "Lobbying." 2006. Available at http://www.sourcewatch.org.

Spencer, Miranda. "TV Nation: A Show for 'The Rest of Us.'" *Extra!* (November–December 1995): 24–25.

"Spokane Just Says No to DARE Program." *Kokomo Tribune*, October 6, 1996.

Starr, Jerold M. *Air Wars: The Fight to Reclaim Public Broadcasting.* Boston: Beacon Press, 2000.

"Statement of Ownership." *Extra!* (November–December 2006): 26.

Stauber, John, and Sheldon Rampton. *Toxic Sludge Is Good for You: Lies, Damn Lies, and the Public Relations Industry.* Monroe, ME: Common Courage Press, 1996.

———. "Watching the Watchdogs: How Corporate PR Keeps Tabs on Reporters." *Extra!* (May–June 1996): 22.

Steffens, Lincoln. *Upbuilders.* Seattle: University of Washington Press, 1968 (originally published in 1909).

Stelzer, Irwin M. "Death and Taxes: The House Votes to Eliminate the Inheritance Tax." *Weekly Standard*, May 9, 2005.

Stendler, Cecelia Burns. *Children of Brasstown: Their Awareness of the Symbols of Social Class.* Urbana: University of Illinois Press, 1949.

Stern, Seth. "Republicans Win on Class Action." *Congressional Quarterly Weekly* (February 21, 2005): 460.

———. "2005 Legislative Summary: Class Action Lawsuits." *Congressional Quarterly Weekly* (January 2, 2006): 46.

Stevenson, Richard W. "U.S. to Report to Congress NAFTA Benefits Are Modest." *New York Times*, July 11, 1997.

Stillman, Don. "The Devastating Impact of Plant Relocations." *Working Papers* (July–August 1978): 42–53.

Stock, Katherine M. *Rural Radicals: Righteous Rage in the American Grain.* Ithaca, NY: Cornell University Press, 1996.

Stohl, Michael, and Harry R. Targ. *Global Political Economy in the 1980s.* Cambridge, MA: Schenkman, 1982.

Stratman, David. "School Reform and the Attack on Public Education." *Dollars and Sense* (March–April 1998): 7.

Strauss, Gary, and Barbara Hansen. "CEO Pay Soars in 2005 as a Select Group Break the $100 Million Mark." *USA Today*, April 11, 2006.

Street, Paul. "The Personal and the Structural in New Orleans: Media Lessons from Katrina." *Dollars and Sense* (November–December 2005): 10–11.

Strobel, Frederick R., and Wallace C. Peterson. *The Coming Class War and How to Avoid It*. Armonk, NY: M. E. Sharpe, 1999.

Strope, Leigh. "Job Cuts Hit 21-Year High." *Indianapolis Star*, November 3, 2001.

Tabb, William K. "After Neoliberalism?" *Monthly Review* (June 2003): 25–33.

———. "The Power of the Rich." *Monthly Review* (July–August 2006): 6–17.

"Taming Global Capitalism Anew." *Nation* (April 17, 2006): 18–27.

Tasini, Jonathan. "Lost in the Margins: Labor and the Media." *Extra!* (Summer 1990): 2–6.

———. "Media Stereotypes about Unions." *Extra!* (Summer 1990): 4.

Tate, Greg. "The Color of Money." *Nation* (February 23, 2006): 23–26.

"Tax Cut Madness." *Nation* (June 4, 2001): 3–4.

Ten Eyck, Tiffany. "As Auto Workers Meet, Concessions Continue and Union Remains Silent." *Labor Notes* (July 2006): 1, 14.

———. "Rank and File Auto Workers Reflect on Past Actions, Plan for Future." *Labor Notes* (December 2006): 6–7.

"Third Party (United States)." Wikipedia. 2006. Available at http://www.enwikipedia.org.

Thomas, Evan. "The Lost City: After Katrina." *Newsweek* (September 12, 2005): 43–52.

Thomas, Evan, and Gregory L. Vistica, "Fallout from a Media Fiasco." *Newsweek* (July 20, 1998): 24–26.

Thomas, Jo. "The Oklahoma City Bombing: The Verdict." *New York Times*, June 14, 1997.

Thompson, Hunter S. *Generation of Swine*. New York: Vintage Books, 1988.

Thomson, Allison. "Industry Output and Employment Projections to 2008." *Monthly Labor Review* (November 1999): 33–50.

Thornton, Bridget, Britt Walters, and Lori Rouse. "Corporate Media Is Corporate America." In *Censored 2006: The Top 25 Censored Stories*, ed. Peter Phillips and Project Censored. New York: Seven Stories Press, 2005.

Thurman, Terry. "Political Action Is a Year-Round Process." (Region 3 Moving Forward insert). *UAW Solidarity* (November 2001): 1–2.

Tilly, Chris. *Half a Job: Bad and Good Part-Time Jobs in a Changing Labor Market*. Philadelphia: Temple University Press, 1996.

———. "Next Steps for the Living Wage Movement." *Dollars and Sense* (September–October 2001): 36–39, 48.

Time Warner. *Time Warner 2005 Annual Report*. 2006. Available at http://www.timewarner.com.

———. "Notice of Annual Meeting of Stockholders and Proxy Statement." April 4, 2006. Available at http://www.timewarner.com.

Tilly, Chris, and Charles Tilly. *Work under Capitalism*. Boulder, CO: Westview Press, 1998.

Tisserand, Michael. "The Katrina Factor." *Nation* (January 1, 2007): 18–19.

Tobiasen, Linda G., ed. *The Foundation Grants Index, 1996*. New York: Foundation Center, 1995.

Thomas, Evan. "A Secret Life." *Newsweek* (October 18, 2006): 28–37.

Tomaskovic-Devey, Donald. *Gender and Racial Inequality at Work*. Ithaca, NY: IRL Press, 1993.

Toner, Robin. "Optimistic, Democrats Debate the Party's Vision." *New York Times*, May 9, 2006.

"The Top Paid CEOs." *Forbes* (May 18, 1998): 224–99.

Tudor, Jeannette F. "The Development of Class Awareness in Children." *Social Forces* 49 (1971): 470–76.

Turman, Katherine. "Interview: Chris Martin." *Mother Jones* (January–February 2004): 78–79.

"2005: Year in Review." *Labor Party News* (January 2006): 3.

"2006 Survey of Law Firm Economics." *CareerJournal.com*. Available at http://www.careerjournal.com.

Uchitelle, Louis. "U.S. Corporations Expanding Abroad at a Quicker Pace." *New York Times*, July 25, 1998.

——. "Blacks Lose Better Jobs Faster as Middle-Class Work Drops." *New York Times*, July 12, 2003.

——. "Surge in Jobs Mostly Bypasses the Factory Floor." *New York Times*, May 11, 2004.

——. *The Disposable American: Layoffs and Their Consequences*. New York: Knopf, 2006.

——. "Here Come the Economic Populists." *New York Times*, November 26, 2006.

——. "Very Rich Are Leaving the Merely Rich Behind." *New York Times*, November 27, 2006.

Uchitelle, Louis, and N. R. Kleinfield. "On Battlefield of Business, Millions of Casualties." *New York Times*, March 3, 1996.

"Unbalanced! Bipartisan Budget Bill Boosts Billionaires." *Labor Party Press* (November 1997): 4–5.

"Unions Join Protests over the Next Step in Free Trade, the FTAA." *Labor Notes* (January 2004): 8–9.

United for a Fair Economy. "Annual Report 2005." 2005. Available at http://www.faireconomy.org.

——. "Wealthy Say, 'No, Thanks' to Tax Cuts." Press release, April 6, 2005. Available at http://www.faireconomy.org.

——. "Victory on Estate Tax." July 6, 2005. Available at http://www.faireconomy.org.

——. "About UFE." 2006. Available at http://www.faireconomy.org.

——. "Ten Super-Wealthy Anti-Estate Tax Families Listed on Forbes 400." Press release, September 27, 2006. Available at http://www.faireconomy.org.

U.S. Bureau of the Census. "Current Housing Reports, Series H150/03." *American Housing Survey for the United States*. Washington, DC: U.S. Government Printing Office, 2004.

——. "Income Inequality (Middle Class)—Narrative." 2005. Available at http://www.census.gov.

U.S. Citizenship and Immigration Services. "H-1B Frequently Asked Questions." Available at http://www.uscis.gov/graphics/howdoi/h1b.htm.

U.S. Code Annotated. 20 U.S.C.A. sect. 3192. Amendment to Public Law 101-647. Cumulative Annual Pocket Part. St. Paul, MN: West Publishing, 1995.

U.S. Congress, House Committee on the Budget. *Unnecessary Business Subsidies*. 106th Cong., 1st sess. Serial 106-5. Washington, DC: U.S. Government Printing Office, 1999.

U.S. Congress, House Committee on Education and Labor, Subcommittee on Elementary, Secondary, and Vocational Education. *Oversight Hearing on Drug Abuse Education Programs*. 101st Cong., 1st sess. Serial 101-129. Washington, DC: U.S. Government Printing Office, 1990.

U.S. Congress, House Committee on Ways and Means. *Comprehensive Tax Reform*. 99th Cong., 1st sess. Serial 99-41. Washington, DC: U.S. Government Printing Office, 1985.

——. *Impact, Effectiveness, and Fairness of the Tax Reform Act of 1986*. 101st Cong., 2nd sess. Serial 101-92. Washington, DC: U.S. Government Printing Office, 1990.

——. "428 Major Companies and Organizations Support the American Jobs Creation Act." Press release, July 8, 2004.

U.S. Congress, Senate Committee on Labor and Human Resources. *Drug Abuse, Prevention, and Treatment*. 100th Cong., 2nd sess. Washington, DC: U.S. Government Printing Office, 1988.

U.S. Commerce Department, U.S. Bureau of the Census, Foreign Trade Division. Washington, DC: U.S. Government Printing Office, 2000.

U.S. Commerce Department, Foreign Trade Division, Washington, DC: U.S. Government Printing Office, 2005.

U.S. Department of Commerce, *Statistical Abstract of the United States: 1996*. Washington, DC: U.S. Government Printing Office, 1995.

——. *Statistical Abstract of the United States: 2000*. Washington, DC: U.S. Government Printing Office, 2000.

——. *Statistical Abstract of the United States: 2006*. Washington, DC: U.S. Government Printing Office, 2005.

——. *Statistical Abstract of the United States: 2007*. Washington, DC: U.S. Government Printing Office, 2006.

U.S. Department of Education, National Center for Educational Statistics. *The Condition of Education, 1996*, ed. Thomas Smith. NCES 96-304. Washington, DC: U.S. Government Printing Office, 1996.

———. *Digest of Educational Statistics*, 2000. National Center for Educational Statistics. Available at http://www.nces.ed.gov

———. *Digest of Educational Statistics*, ed. Thomas D. Snyder, Charlene M. Hoffman, and Clair M. Geddes. NCES 2001-034. Washington, DC: U.S. Government Printing Office, 2001.

U.S. Department of Health and Human Services. "The 2006 HHS Poverty Guidelines." Available at http://aspe.hhs.gov.

U.S. Department of Justice, Bureau of Justice Assistance. *Program Brief: An Introduction to DARE—Drug Abuse Resistance Education*. 2nd ed. Washington, DC: Bureau of Justice Assistance, 1991.

U.S. Department of Labor, Bureau of Labor Statistics. "Union Members in 2006." Press release, January 25, 2007.

———. *Occupational Projections and Training Data, 2006–2007 Edition*. Washington, DC, February 2006.

U.S. Department of the Treasury, Internal Revenue Service. "2002 Returns of Active Corporations," "The Statistics of Income Tax Stats—Corporation Data by Sector or Industry," Internal Revenue Service. Available at http://www.irs.gov/taxstats/bustaxstats/article/0,,id=131744,00.html#_activecorps.

———. "Return of Organization Exempt from Income Tax: Form 990: United for a Fair Economy, Inc." 04-3286118. Washington, DC, 2002.

———. "Section 527 Political Organizations Revised Tax Filing Requirements." Press release, November 2002.

———. "Return of Organization Exempt from Income Tax: Form 990: American Federation of Labor and Congress of Industrial Organizations." 53-0228172. Washington, DC, 2003.

———. "Return of Organization Exempt from Income Tax: Form 990: DARE America." 95-4242541. Washington, DC, 1995, 1996, 2003.

———. "Return of Organization Exempt from Income Tax: Form 990: Fairness and Accuracy in Reporting, Inc." 13-3392362. Washington, DC, 2003.

———. "IRS Acts to Enforce Reporting and Disclosure by Section 527 Political Groups." Press release, August 19, 2004.

———. "Return of Organization Exempt from Income Tax: Form 990: Council on International and Public Affairs, Inc." 13-6162451. Washington, DC, 2004.

———. "Return of Organization Exempt from Income Tax: Form 990: The Business Roundtable." 23-7236607. Washington, DC, 2005.

———. "Return of Organization Exempt from Income Tax: Form 990: The Heritage Foundation." 23-7327730. Washington, DC, 2005.

———. "Individual Income Tax Returns, Preliminary Data, 2004." *The Statistics of Income SOI Bulletin*. Washington, DC: U.S. Government Printing Office, Winter 2005–2006.

———. "Filing Requirements for Section 527 Organizations." 2006. Available at http://www.irs.gov.

U.S. Federal Bureau of Investigation. "Congressional Testimony: Statement of John E. Lewis, Deputy Assistant Director, Counterterrorism Division, Federal Bureau of Investigation before the Senate Committee on Environment and Public Works." May 18, 2005. Available at http://www.fbi.gov.

———. "Headline Archives: Eco-Terror Indictments, 'Operation Backfire' Nets 11." January 20, 2006. Available at http://www.fbi.gov.

———. "Wanted by the FBI: Domestic Terrorism." 2006. Available at http://www.fbi.gov.

U.S. Labor Education in the Americas Project. "A Union Activist's Guide to CAFTA." *Labor Notes* (June 2005): 8–9.

U.S. Securities and Exchange Commission. "Form 10-K, CBS Corporation: For Fiscal Year Ended December 31, 2005." Washington, DC

———. "Form 10-K, General Electric Company: For Fiscal Year Ended December 31, 2005." Washington, DC

———. "Form 10-K, Viacom Inc.: For Fiscal Year Ended December 31, 2005." Washington, DC

United States Social Forum. "About the USSF." 2007. Available at http://www.ussf2007.org.

Useem, Michael. *The Inner Circle*. New York: Oxford University Press, 1984.

vanden Heuval, Katrina, and Sam Graham-Felsen. "Morality of the Minimum." *Nation* (January 1, 2007): 5–6.

Vanderpool, Tim. "Secession of the Successful." *Utne Reader* (November–December, 1995): 32–34.

Vanneman, Reeve, and Lynn Weber Cannon. *The American Perception of Class.* Philadelphia: Temple University Press, 1987.

"Very Old Labor." *Wall Street Journal,* July 26, 2005.

Viacom Incorporated. "2006 Annual Meeting of Stockholders and Proxy Statement." April 14, 2006. Available at http://www.sec.gov.

Vidal, Gore. "The End of History." *Nation* (September 30, 1996): 11–18.

"Voucher Program Fails to Deliver." *AFT American Teacher* (November 2001): 14.

Wakeman, Jessica, and Julie Hollar. "Stand by Your Man." *Extra!* (May–June 2005): 23–24.

Wall, Suzanne. "Union Candidates Use a 'Bottom-Up' Approach to Winning Political Power." *Labor Notes* (April 1998): 3.

Wallace, Michael, and Azamat Junisbai. "Finding Class Consciousness in the New Economy." In *Research in Social Stratification and Mobility,* ed. Kevin T. Leicht. Vol. 20. Oxford, UK: Elsevier, 2004.

Wallach, Lori. "Corporate Protectionism." *Public Citizen: Special Anniversary Issue* 21(1) (2001): 10–11, 27.

———. *Public Citizen's Pocket Trade Lawyer: The Alphabet Soup of Globalization.* Washington, DC: Global Trade Watch, 1999, updated 2005.

"Wall Street Leads Top Campaign Contributors on *Mother Jones* 400." *Mother Jones.* 2001. Available at http://www.motherjones.com.

Walsh, Mary Williams. "More Companies Ending Promises for Retirement." *New York Times,* January 9, 2006.

Walt Disney Company. "2006 Annual Meeting of Shareholders and Proxy Statement." January 11, 2006. Available at http://corporate.disney.go.com.

Ward, Kevin. "Militia Movement and the Internet." 2001. Available at http://www.rutgers.edu.

Washington, Laura S. "Debunking the '60s with Ayers and Dohrn." *In These Times* (September 2006): 17.

Watson, Noshua. "Inside the 500." *Fortune* (April 16, 2001): 232–33.

Webb, Jim. "American Workers Have a Chance to Be Heard." *Wall Street Journal,* November 15, 2006.

Weber, Joseph, and Blanca Riemer. "These Days Mack Trucks Isn't Built Like Mack Trucks." *Business Week* (July 30, 1990): 40–41.

Wechsler, Pat. "This Lesson Is Brought to You By." *Business Week* (June 30, 1997): 68–69.

Weissman, Steve. "Discharge Petition May Force Hastert's Hand." *Public Citizen News* (September–October 2001): 6.

Weller, Christian. "The Commission Straw Man: Social Security Well Prepared for Retirement of Baby Boomers in 2016." *Economic Policy Institute,* Issue Brief 159, July 19, 2001.

Wells, Susan J. "Looking for Trouble." *HR Magazine* (January 2001): 38–42.

Wenglinsky, Harold. "How Money Matters: The Effect of School District Spending on Academic Achievement." *Sociology of Education* 70 (July 1997): 221–37.

Wessel, David. "As Rich-Poor Gap Widens in the U.S., Class Mobility Stalls." *Wall Street Journal,* May 13, 2005.

Whalen, Charles J., Paul Magnusson, and Geri Smith. "NAFTA's Scorecard: So Far, So Good." *Business Week* (July 9, 2001): 54–56.

"What's FAIR?" *Extra!* (July–August 2006): 2.

"When the Joneses Can't Keep Up." *New York Times,* December 1, 2006.

White House. "National D.A.R.E. Day: A Proclamation by the President of the United States." Press release, April 7, 2006. Available at http://www.whitehouse.gov.

———. "Fact Sheet—Extending the President's Tax Relief: A Victory for American Taxpayers." Press release, May 17, 2006. Available at http://www.whitehouse.gov.

——. "Fact Sheet: The President Signs Emergency Funding Bill." Press release, June 15, 2006. Available at http://www.whitehouse.gov.

"The Whitening Newsroom." *Extra!Update* (June 2001): 2.

Wiedenbaum, Murray L. *Business, Government, and the Public.* Englewood Cliffs, NJ: Prentice Hall, 1977.

Wilder, Thornton. *Our Town: A Play in Three Acts.* New York: Coward-McCann, 1938.

Willis, Derek. "Debating McCain-Feingold." *Congressional Quarterly Weekly* (March 10, 2001): 524–27.

Wise, Timothy A. "World Trade Talks Collapse." *Dollars and Sense* (September–October 2006): 44–45.

"Without 'White Trash' We Couldn't Read Tabloids." *Jossip.* March 28, 2006. Available at http://www.jossip.com.

Wohl, R. Richard. "The 'Rags to Riches Story': An Episode of Secular Idealism." In *Class, Status, and Power,* ed. Reinhard Bendix and Seymour M. Lipset. New York: Free Press, 1966.

Wolfe, Alan. *The Seamy Side of Democracy.* New York: David McKay, 1973.

Wolfe, Charles, and Kip Lornell. *The Life and Legend of Leadbelly.* New York: HarperCollins, 1992.

Wolff, Edward N. *Top Heavy: The Increasing Inequality of Wealth in America and What Can Be Done about It.* New York: Twentieth Century Fund, 1996.

——. "Changes in Household Wealth in the 1980s and 1990s in the U.S." Working Paper No. 407, Levy Economics Institute and New York University, May 2004.

Wollman, James, and James McBride. "Medicare Part D Gets an 'F'." *Dollars and Sense* (January–February 2006): 29–30.

Wong, Kent. "Don't Blame China." *Dollars and Sense* (September–October 2005): 10–11, 36.

"Working to Tell the Untold Story." *Too Much* (Winter 2000): 8.

Wray, Matt, and Annalee Newitz, eds. *White Trash: Race and Class in America.* New York: Routledge, 1997.

Wright, David. "Changes in Hourly Earnings and Weekly Earnings, 1947–2005." *Work Series* (Wichita State University), November 2006, A19–A20.

Wright, Erik O. *Classes.* London: Verso, 1985.

——. *Interrogating Inequality.* London: Verso, 1994.

Wright, John W., ed. *The New York Times Almanac, 2006.* New York: Penguin, 2005.

Wu Dunn, Sheryl. "When Lifetime Jobs Die Prematurely." *New York Times,* June 12, 1996.

World Wide Packets. "Annual Report and Accounts 2005." 2006. Available at http://www.wwp.com.

Wypijewski, JoAnn. "Is This *Really* an 'Insurgency' to Shake Up the Unions?" *CounterPunch* (June 16–30, 2005): 1, 4–5.

——. "States of Disunion." *Nation* (August 29–September 5, 2005): 6–8.

Wysong, Earl. "Class in the Movies." *High Risk and High Stakes: Health Professionals, Politics, and Policy.* Westport, CT: Greenwood Press, 1992.

——. Unpublished paper, 1996.

——. "Class in the Movies II." Unpublished paper, 2006.

Wysong, Earl, Richard Aniskiewicz, and David Wright. "Truth *and* DARE: Tracking Drug Education to Graduation and as Symbolic Politics." *Social Problems* 41 (1994): 448–72.

Wysong, Earl, Robert Perrucci, and David Wright. "A New Approach to Class Analysis: The Distributional Model, Social Closure, and Class Polarization." Paper presented at the 2002 meetings of the American Sociological Association, Chicago, Illinois.

Wysong, Earl, and David Wright. "A Decade of DARE: Efficacy, Politics, and Drug Education." *Sociological Focus* 28 (1995): 283–311.

——. "Is Social Mobility a Social Problem? Recent Intergenerational Mobility Trends, the American Dream, and the Media." Paper presented at the 2006 meetings of the North Central Sociological Association, Indianapolis, Indiana.

——. "What's Happening to the American Dream? Sons, Daughters, and Intergenerational Mobility Today." Paper presented at the Midwest Sociological Society Annual Meeting, Chicago, Illinois, April 4–7, 2007.

Yang, Catherine. "Chairman Bernanke Goes up the Hill." *Business Week Online* (February 16, 2006). Available at http://www.businessweek.com.

Yardley, Jim. "Well-Off but Still Pressed, Doctor Could Use Tax Cut." *New York Times*, April 7, 2001.

Yates, Michael. "Workers Looking for Jobs, Unions Looking for Members." *Monthly Review* (April 2004): 36–48.

Yule, Robert. "Super-Wealthy Families Try to Repeal Estate Tax." *Public Citizen News* (May–June 2006): 1, 11.

Yeoman, Barry. "Subsidies at Sea." *Mother Jones* (May–June 2001): 72–77, 112–13.

"Yes, We Have No Bananas." *Wall Street Journal*, September 4, 2001.

Zaniello, Tom. *Working Stiffs, Union Maids, Reds, and Riffraff: An Organized Guide to Films about Labor.* Ithaca, NY: IRL Press, 1996.

Zeller, Shawn. "Thriving in a Crisis." *National Journal* (October 14, 2000): 3262.

Zernike, Kate. "Antidrug Program Says It Will Adopt a New Strategy." *New York Times*, February 15, 2001.

Zinn, Howard. *A People's History of the United States.* New York: Harper Colophon Books, 1980.

Zogby, John, John Bruce, and Rebecca Wittman. "Nationwide Attitudes on Unions." Zogby International, February 26, 2004.

Zweig, Michael, ed. *What's Class Got to Do with It?* Ithaca, NY: IRL Press, 2004.

Zweigenhaft, Richard L. "Making Rags out of Riches." *Extra!* (January–February 2004): 27–28.

Zweigenhaft, Richard L., and G. William Domhoff. *Diversity in the Power Elite: Have Women and Minorities Reached the Top?* New Haven, CT: Yale University Press, 1998.

Index

About the Authors

Robert Perrucci is professor of sociology at Purdue University in West Lafayette, Indiana. He is past president of the Society for the Study of Social Problems and has served as associate editor of the American Sociological Review and as editor of the American Sociologist, Social Problems, and Contemporary Sociology. His teaching and research interests have focused on work and organizations, and inequality and political economy. Books that reflect his core interests include *Networks of Power: Organizational Actors at the National, Corporate and Community Levels*; *Plant Closings: International Context and Social Costs*; and *Japanese Auto Plants in the Heartland: Corporatism and Community*. His most recent publication in 2007 is an edited collection of readings with Carolyn Cummings Perrucci, *The Transformation of Work in the New Economy*.

Earl Wysong is professor of sociology at Indiana University, Kokomo. His commitment to critical sociology, strengthening working-class institutions, and social equity has caused him much personal and professional grief. But he is too dumb to cure and too smart to worry about it. His current research interests include class analysis, intergenerational mobility, the American Dream, organizations, and worker access to family-friendly workplace benefits. Although his speed-lashed prose and high-energy style have frequently been muted by mainstream editors and reviewers, he has still managed to publish several memorable articles, book chapters, reviews, and assorted rants. He is the author of *High Risk and High Stakes: Health Professionals, Policy, and Politics*. Angry but hopeful, his social expedition continues. He is grateful to his coauthor for sharing the ride.